# Unleash the power of
# CorelDRAW

## Skill Sessions

If you need to learn about a specific feature of CorelDRAW, go right to that skill session. In it, you'll learn the ins and outs of that topic—why you would want to use it, how to use it, and a few examples. The skill sessions are broken up into a series of workshops that cover everything from the basics to more advanced topics. Here's a list of the workshops you'll find:

Basic Skills Workshop

Manipulation Workshop

Effects Workshop

Text Workshop

Bitmap Workshop

Output Workshop

Advanced Topics Workshop

## The Color Pages

*CorelDRAW! 6 Unleashed* contains two eight-page, full color inserts filled with original art created in CorelDRAW and its companion software pieces. Browse through these sections to get a better idea of the artistic power that you can obtain from CorelDRAW.

## Projects Workshops

The best way to learn CorelDRAW is to tackle real-world projects. This section gives you the opportunity to follow along as the authors use CorelDRAW to design and create useful examples.

## What's on the CD-ROM

You'll find a treasure chest full of software on the CD-ROM included with this book. Here's a sample of the types of software you'll find:

- Supporting files for projects and skill sessions in the book
- Hundreds of unique, professional graphics and photos from leading graphics and photo suppliers
- Award-winning CorelDRAW images
- Sample plug-in filters for Corel PHOTO-PAINT
- Listings of Corel-related, third-party resources
- Evaluation versions of commercial software
- Shareware and freeware utilities
- Internet and CompuServe connection software

For more information about the CD-ROM, see Appendix D.

# CorelDRAW! Unleashed ™

Foster D. Coburn III
Carlos F. Gonzalez
Pete McCormick

**SAMS**
PUBLISHING

201 West 103rd Street
Indianapolis, Indiana 46290

# Copyright © 1996 by Sams Publishing

FIRST EDITION

International Standard Book Number: 0-672-30754-5

Library of Congress Catalog Card Number: 95-70100

99  98  97      4  3  2

Interpretation of the printing code: the rightmost double-digit number is the year of the book's printing; the rightmost single-digit, the number of the book's printing. For example, a printing code of 96-1 shows that the first printing of the book occurred in 1996.

*Composed in FC Serifa Roman and MCPdigital by Macmillan Computer Publishing*

*Printed in the United States of America*

| | |
|---|---|
| **Publisher and President** | *Richard K. Swadley* |
| **Acquisitions Manager** | *Greg Weigand* |
| **Development Manager** | *Dean Miller* |
| **Managing Editor** | *Cindy Morrow* |
| **Marketing Manager** | *Gregg Bushyeager* |

**Acquisitions Editor**
*Christopher Denny*

**Development Editor**
*Kelly Murdock*

**Software Development Specialist**
*Wayne Blankenbeckler*

**Production Editors**
*Mary Inderstrodt*
*Bart Reed*

**Copy Editors**
*Kim Hannel*
*Chuck Hutchinson, Elaine Sands, Tonya Simpson, Heather Stith*

**Technical Reviewers**
*Giuseppe DeBellis, John Faunce, Michael Moss*

**Editorial Coordinator**
*Bill Whitmer*

**Technical Edit Coordinator**
*Lynette Quinn*

**Formatter**
*Frank Sinclair*

**Editorial Assistants**
*Sharon Cox, Andi Richter, Rhonda Tinch-Mize*

**Cover Designer**
*Tim Amrhein*

**Cover Art**
*Robert Travers*

**Book Designer**
*Alyssa Yesh*

**Production Team Supervisor**
*Brad Chinn*

**Production**
*Bront Davis, Ayanna Lacey Kevin Laseau, Tim Griffin Nancy Price, Andrew Stone Susan Van Ness, Mark Walche, Terrie Deemer, Michael Brummitt, Mike Henery, Paula Lowell, Carol Bowers, Charlotte Clapp, Colleen Williams*

# Overview

V

# Contents

## Part IX   Graphics Toolkit Workshop   711

### Skill Session 76   Introduction to PHOTO-PAINT    713

# Contents

]

# Introduction

The delay of Windows 95 gave us a way to miss the summer, as we were busy documenting the latest from Corel. This book was particularly troublesome because we were constantly working with new versions of CorelDRAW and Windows 95. We were definitely writing about a moving target this time.

We consider this book a living project because fully documenting a program as complex as CorelDRAW is impossible. There is always one more gem you find just after you thought you knew it all. There are usually several different ways to accomplish the same effect (especially in CorelDRAW 6). None of them are wrong, none are right. Each user prefers the method that is easiest and most productive for him or her. Rather than showing you how to create a complex drawing, we have described how to create all the building blocks for that drawing. Once you understand how to use the effects, you can put your own creative talents to work. If you find something we missed or a new way to create an effect, feel free to let us know about it. Our goal is to produce the best book possible, and your input will help us achieve that goal.

There are many people who must be thanked for helping us to get this project finished. Most important are our wives, friends, and families, who knew they could always find us in front of the computer at any time of the day or night. Their patience has been most appreciated.

"Doctor" Dickson took some fantastic photographs of several of us to include in the book. We certainly can't compare to many of his models, but he still did a great job.

The folks at Corel have been extremely helpful in getting this book out the door. Kelly Greig had the insufferable task of dealing with the beta team to get Corel's product out on time while still putting out her own "product." We all hope she is enjoying her well-deserved time with her family. Christel Mack was always working behind the scenes to assist Kelly in keeping us all stocked with CDs, which was one heck of a task. Bill Cullen, as always, was there with answers and assistance whenever we got stuck. Kim Connerty seemed to always be working day and night, logging the bugs that were reported. She was ably assisted by John Senez, Ross Norrie, and many whom that we haven't mentioned. Rus Miller put even more great stuff in the print engine and missed his summer of hog riding. Lucian Mustatea has brought PHOTO-PAINT a long way in the past two releases, and we are really enjoying the new capabilities. Mike Bellefeuille has been extremely helpful in working with us as authors, user group leaders, seminar leaders, and who knows what else. Mike Daschuk is finally off the road, so we won't cross paths quite as often (at least until he starts showing off CorelCAD). One of these days we all need to stop and relax for a couple days. Thanks for all your help, eh?

All of the folks on the CompuServe forums have been a tremendous help in providing wit, wisdom, and ideas for this book. Thanks to all of you, and I'm sure we'll type again soon.

We've met several thousand of you in our travels. Hearing about how each of you use the product helps us to provide you with the best information we can. Thank you for giving us the ideas. We hope to see you all soon.

Last and most important, we thank you, the reader, for purchasing our book. If we have turned on the light of understanding, inspiration, and creativity, we have done our job.

# Skill Session: Basic Skills Workshop

# 1

# Installing CorelDRAW 6

Read the Readme file. Every new program tells you to read its Readme file. In this case, it's extremely important for you to read this file because of last-minute changes Corel made prior to shipping the product.

Before you begin the installation process, you should take a look at what is on each of the four CorelDRAW 6 CD-ROMS. The contents of each CD are summarized here:

>   CD1: Program files, CorelDRAW templates, fonts, symbols, patterns and fills, 3D models, thesaurus, hyphenation, proofreader, and dictionary
>
>   CD2: Video clips, sound files, actors and props, charts, CorelMAP, Corel MOTION 3D library, and slide backgrounds
>
>   CD3: Photos, bitmaps, PAINT tutorial files, and floating objects
>
>   CD4: Clip art, clip art, and more clip art

Knowing what is on each CD is important for two reasons: to know generally where to find a particular video clip or photo you are looking for and to understand the implications of running CorelDRAW 6 from the CD. Although running CorelDRAW from the CD might sound like a good idea to save disk space, doing so prevents you from accessing many of the other files available on the other CDs, especially clip art.

# Corel *TIP!*

If you choose to run CorelDRAW from the CD, not only will it run much more slowly, but you will be unable to access many of the valuable files, including the clip art located on CD4.

Whether you are installing for the first time or adding additional products or fonts, insert Disc 1 and choose Setup. (See Figure 1.1.)

*Figure 1.1.*
*Initial install options.*

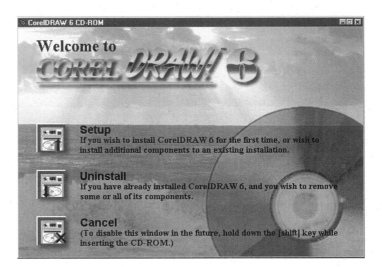

# Corel *TIP!*

After your initial install, if you want to insert this CD without the Setup menu appearing automatically, press the Shift key while inserting the CD and hold it down until the drive light goes off on your CD-ROM. This way, you can gain access to the files contained on the CD without going through the install process.

Next, you are prompted to close any other existing programs that you may have running. (See Figure 1.2.) Although you are not required to exit other programs, doing so certainly is a good idea. If you are unsure whether any other programs are running, press Alt+Tab to check. If other programs are running, using this shortcut switches between them and enables you to close them.

*Figure 1.2.*
*Setup warning to close*
*other programs.*

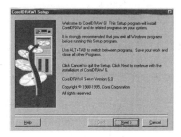

After closing any open programs and returning to the dialog box shown in Figure 1.2, click Next. The next dialog box asks for user information. Enter the information as appropriate. A second screen asks you to verify the previously entered information. After you complete this process, CorelDRAW 6 generates your product serial number.

# Corel *NOTE!*

Write down this serial number on the title page of your user manual and use it to fill out the product registration card or run Corel's Registration Wizard program.

Before you choose an installation method (see Figure 1.3), you should examine what is installed in each method. If disk space is an issue, use Table 1.1 as a guide. Keep in mind that these values are only approximates. If you have either a Syquest or Bernoulli tape drive, consider installing CorelDRAW on that drive. This way, you can save lots of hard drive space, and the program will run almost as fast.

*Figure 1.3.*
*Setup Options dialog box.*

**Table 1.1. Drive space required for various installation methods.**

| Installation Method | Approximate Drive Space Required |
|---|---|
| Full Installation | 170 MB |
| Custom Installation | 130–160 MB |
| Minimum Installation | 130 MB |
| CD-ROM Installation | 30 MB |

Also, you can create a smaller installation profile by using the Custom option if you are very selective.

The full installation includes everything except the bar code utility. Keep in mind that this installation does not include all the 1032 TrueType fonts. By default, only 12 are installed. To install the Adobe Type 1 fonts, you must use Adobe Type Manager in a separate installation process.

Products included in the full installation or available in the custom installation include the following:

>     CorelDRAW
>     Corel PHOTO-PAINT
>     Corel PRESENTS
>     Corel DREAM 3D
>     Corel MOTION 3D
>     CorelDEPTH
>     Corel MULTIMEDIA MANAGER
>     Corel OCR-TRACE
>     Corel FONT MASTER
>     Corel CAPTURE
>     Utilities
>     Import/Export Filters
>     TrueType Fonts

Scanners are also available if you use the custom installation.

## Full Installation

If you have to count free disk space on your computer's disk drives using your finger on the screen to count every three decimal places and you lose count, then this option is for you.

After you select Full Installation, select Next to move to the next dialog box. Tell the installation program where to install the programs and where to place temporary files while the program is running in the Choose Destination Location and

Temp Drive Selection dialog boxes, making sure enough space is available on that drive. The next dialog box (Program Folder Selection) enables you to approve the default program group (folder) Corel Graphics or to create a new one for the Corel products. All of the above are personal preferences.

One final dialog box appears, enabling you to verify that you have sufficient space for the install. The installation program then takes over.

## Custom Installation

For most users, I recommend installing only the elements you think you will use. If you will never look at the tutorials, don't install them. If you don't know what one of the new products does, either jump ahead in this book and check it out, or simply install each product as it is needed. Using this approach, you also can uninstall products that you won't use again or find out that you will never probably use.

After you choose custom installation and specify an installation directory, the Select Programs and Accessories dialog box appears. (See Figure 1.4.)

*Figure 1.4.*
*The Select Programs and*
*Accessories dialog box.*

Within the Programs and Accessories list box are all products available for installation. If the check box is checked and not shaded, all options for that particular product will be installed. If the check box is shaded, then only some of the options have been selected for installation.

If you are certain you do not want to install a particular program, uncheck its check box. For those programs that you want to install, highlight each one and refer to the Module Description area on the upper-right side of the dialog box. This area gives you a brief description of the program and tells you how many of the options will be installed. To customize them, click the Details button. Examples of this are shown in Figures 1.4 and 1.5. Select Details about the Symbols.

In Figure 1.5, the Symbols option is highlighted. In the Item Description section, notice that by default only 6 of 58 symbols will be installed. Change this number by first clicking the Details button.

Figure 1.5.
The Programs Options
dialog box.

Alter the Individual Symbol Selection dialog box, shown in Figure 1.6, to install either all the symbols, some of the symbols, or none of the symbols. Click the Continue button to continue.

Figure 1.6.
The Individual Symbol
Selection dialog box.

# Corel*NOTE!*

> During almost any stage of the installation process, you can quit by clicking the Exit button. A second dialog box then appears, asking you to confirm your desire to exit.
>
> Be careful not to select the Exit button (like in Figure 1.6) thinking you are exiting the option detail selection process.

After you customize all the Options for a particular program, click the Continue button. You then return to the Select Programs and Accessories dialog box, enabling you to continue the installation selection process.

Go through each of the programs, selecting the programs and options you want to install. Then, click the Next button. (If you change your mind, you can normally click the Back button to go back to the previous dialog box.) The Temp Path Selection dialog box then appears, asking you to specify drives and directories in which Corel can place its temporary files.

Continuing to the next dialog box, you can change the default program group (Corel Graphics) for all the Corel programs. The final dialog box reconfirms how much disk space the install will use and how much space is available. The Installation Wizard then begins the installation process.

## Minimum Installation

If the installation of Windows 95 left you room only for a small grocery list on your computer, then minimum installation is your only option. You should upgrade or add additional hard disk space soon, however. (You are missing out on some fantastic products for which you paid good money. Buy additional disk space; it's worth the cost.)

After you choose the minimum installation option, the resultant dialog box prompts you for an installation directory. Next, you arrive at the Select Programs and Accessories dialog box. (See Figure 1.7.) Your only customization choices concern Import/Export Filters and TrueType Fonts.

*Figure 1.7.*
*Select Programs and*
*Accessories dialog box.*

Unless the defaults don't include an import/export filter that you need, I recommend not changing any of the options. Click Next to proceed to the Temp Path Selection dialog box. Here you can specify which drives and directories you want Corel programs to use while running.

In the following dialog boxes, you can change the default program group for Corel programs. A final dialog box then appears, confirming how much drive space the installation will take and how much is available. Clicking Next finalizes the installation process. Then the Installation Wizard takes over.

## CD-ROM Installation

The CD-ROM installation method is not recommended. Not only is it very slow, but also you will be unable to use many of the more valuable features of the product. (See the tip earlier in this chapter.) In some cases, however, such as with a laptop having a very small or full hard disk and an external CD-ROM drive, this method might be your only choice for a quick demonstration or presentation.

After you choose the CD-ROM installation option, the resultant dialog box prompts you for an installation path. After you enter this information, the Select Programs and Accessories dialog box appears.

This dialog box looks almost identical to the one that appears if you are doing a custom installation. Follow the same general procedures that are outlined in the section on custom installation. Note one very important difference, however: the program sizes are very small. Only the executables are transferred to the hard disk. Any optional files remain on the CD. (See Figure 1.8.)

*Figure 1.8.*
*The Programs Options*
*dialog box.*

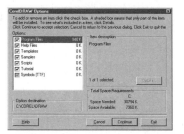

Proceed through the next two dialog boxes choosing drives and directories for Corel's temporary files and the program group in which to place the applications. One final dialog box confirms the amount of disk space that will be consumed and the amount of disk space available. From this point on, the Installation Wizard takes over.

**2**

# Getting Started in CorelDRAW

To launch CorelDRAW, click the Start button at the bottom of the Windows 95 main screen, choose Programs from the menu, and then click Corel Graphics from the Programs menu. When the Corel Applications menu appears, click the CorelDRAW 6 entry.

When you launch CorelDRAW, the main CorelDRAW screen appears. Figure 2.1 shows the CorelDRAW screen and all the elements that make up the screen.

The following is a brief description of each of the elements that make up the default CorelDRAW screen, beginning at the top of the screen:

> Title bar—The title bar, located at the very top of the screen, tells you the name of the file that is currently open.
>
> Menu bar—The menu bar displays the names of the primary menus, beginning with the File menu on the left. (See Skill Session 3, "Using Menus and Dialog Boxes," for a thorough description of the menus.)

Ribbon bar—The ribbon bar, located directly beneath the menu bar, contains various buttons that function as shortcuts to certain commands. (See Skill Session 3 for more information.)

Rulers—Beneath the ribbon bar is the horizontal ruler. The vertical ruler displays on the left side of the screen next to the toolbox.

If you drag the alignment aid icon, located in the top-left corner where the rulers intersect, you can change the zero points of the rulers. By default, the zero points line up with the page dimensions of the page size you select. (For more information on the rulers, see Skill Session 4, "Customizing and Setting Preferences.")

Toolbox—The toolbox, located on the left side of the screen, provides the tools for drawing and filling objects. Table 2.1 lists the tools provided, beginning at the top. (For a complete description of each of these tools, see Skill Sessions 6 through 16.)

Figure 2.1.
The CorelDRAW initial screen.

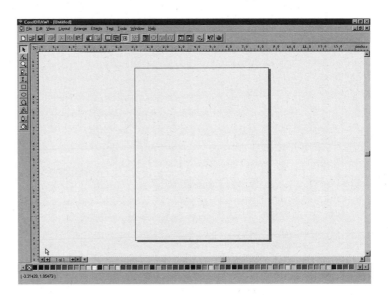

**Table 2.1. The tools in the toolbox.**

| Icon | Tool | Function |
| --- | --- | --- |
| | Pick | Selecting and transforming objects |
| | Shape | Node-editing and shaping objects |
| | Zoom | Changing the viewing window |

| Icon | Tool | Function |
|------|------|----------|
| | Pencil | Drawing lines, curves, and PowerLines |
| | Dimensions | Drawing Dimension, call-out, and connector lines |
| | Rectangle | Drawing rectangles and squares |
| | Ellipse | Drawing ellipses and circles |
| | Polygon | Drawing polygons, spirals, and graph paper |
| | Text | Adding Artistic and Paragraph text |
| | Outline | Setting outline attributes |
| | Fill | Setting fill attributes |

If you hold the cursor over a particular tool, a tooltip message will pop up to remind you of the tool's function.

## Color Palette

Use the color palette, located at the bottom of the screen, to select solid fill and outline colors for objects. The default palette is Custom. (See Skill Session 67, "Color Models and Color Palettes.")

## Status Line

The status line, located at the bottom of the screen, is blank until you select an object. The status line is a very important element of the CorelDRAW screen, because it can provide information about every object in your drawing.

Figure 2.2 shows two rectangles: The rectangle on the left has an outline only with no fill, and the rectangle on the right has a color fill with no outline. The first rectangle is selected. Notice the boxes located at the far right of the status line. These boxes tell you what outline and fill attributes are applied to the selected object. In this case, the fill box on the far right has an × in the center, which means the selected object does not have a color fill. The outline box shows the color of the outline, and the width of the outline is displayed to the left of the box. Notice that the center of the status line also displays the rectangle's width, height, and center point relative to the rulers.

Figure 2.2.
*The rectangle on the left is selected.*

Pick
Shape
Zoom
Pencil
Dimension
Rectangle
Ellipse
Polygon
Text
Outline
Fill

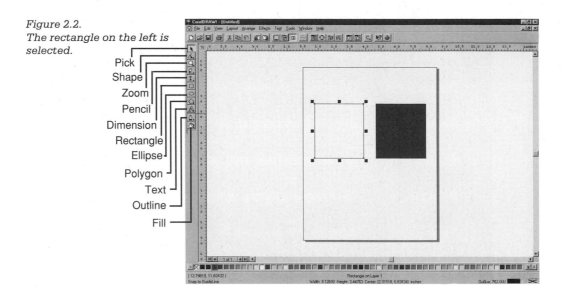

Figure 2.3 shows the same two rectangles; however, this time the second rectangle selected. The status line now shows the fill color in the box on the right and the word None next to the outline box, indicating the object has no outline.

Figure 2.3.
*The rectangle on the right is selected.*

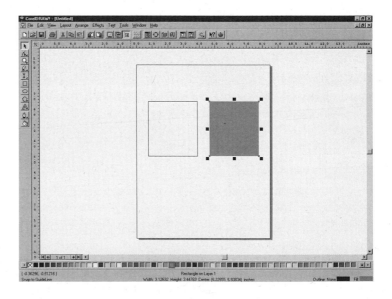

Figure 2.4 shows the second rectangle rotated. The status line will indicate the angle of rotations as you rotate the object but will not show the degree of rotation after it's been rotated.

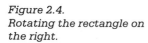

*Figure 2.4.*
*Rotating the rectangle on*
*the right.*

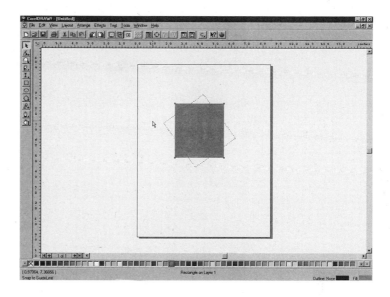

## Printable Page

The *printable page* is the area defined by the page border. The page border can be turned on or off in the Page Setup dialog box, which is accessed through the Layout menu. If you turn off the page border, your drawing will still print, but only within the page dimensions defined in the width and height Parameter boxes in the Page Setup dialog box.

## Window Border

By dragging the window border, you can resize the CorelDRAW window. This is useful if you're running more than one Windows program at a time.

## Page Counter

The page counter, located at the bottom-left corner of the screen, displays the page number you're working on if your project consists of multiple pages. (See Skill Session 69, "Page Setup.")

## Scroll Bars

The scroll bars enable you to move the image view you're working on up or down and left or right. This feature comes in handy when you're zoomed in on an image.

## Basic Mouse Techniques

Using a mouse or pen in CorelDRAW is mandatory when you're creating objects in your projects. Certain functions can be done with the keyboard; these are described in the next section, "Basic Keyboard Techniques."

A standard two-button mouse has left (primary) and right (secondary) buttons. The left and right buttons can be reversed by changing the settings in the Windows Control Panel. The left button is used for most of the functions, such as selecting menus, drawing, and so on. The right button is used extensively in CorelDRAW 6 for tasks such as accessing property dialog boxes. You can also assign a special function command to the secondary mouse button by selecting a function from the Right Mouse Button–Action Parameter box. This Parameter box is found in the Options dialog box in the Advanced section. The Options dialog box is accessed through the Tools menu. For example, you might want to assign Edit Text to the right mouse button if you are using a lot of text in your projects.

The mouse can be used for everything except typing text in dialog boxes. You can use the mouse to draw, scroll up or down in Parameter boxes, change a number value, select colors from the color palette, and so on.

## Basic Keyboard Techniques

In CorelDRAW, the keyboard is used primarily to type text on the screen and names and numbers in dialog and parameter boxes. Many users may take exception to this statement. These are the users who prefer to use the many shortcut key commands available in CorelDRAW. (See the Command References.)

## Corel*NOTE!*

There are so many shortcut key commands that the average user will learn only a few special ones for his or her working style. For example, here are a few of my favorite keyboard shortcuts:

- ■ Press the spacebar to toggle between the last two tools used in the toolbox.
- ■ Use the Tab key to select objects on the screen.
- ■ Use Ctrl+Q to convert text to curves.
- ■ And of course, use the popular Delete key to remove objects.

## Exiting CorelDRAW

To exit the CorelDRAW program, select Exit from the File menu, or press Alt+F4 if you want to use the shortcut method.

If you've forgotten to save your work, a message appears that asks you if you want to save it. If you select Yes, a Save AS dialog box appears that lets you name your file (if you haven't already done so). If the file has a name, it is saved when you choose Yes. If you choose No, CorelDRAW exits, and any changes you have made to a new or existing file are lost.

# 3

# Using Menus and Dialog Boxes

CorelDRAW contains nine separate pull-down menus plus the Help menu. The Window menu was not present in the previous version (version 5) but has since been added to give the same look and feel as other Windows 95 applications. In addition, the Special menu in version 5 has become the Tools menu in version 6.

When you choose any of the menu headings (which include File, Edit, View, Layout, Arrange, Effects, Text, Tools, Window, and Help), a pull-down list of commands appears. You can select each command either by clicking the command or using the keyboard.

To use the keyboard technique, press the underlined letter in the command when the menu is activated. This method is a variation of the shortcut key technique. The full shortcut method involves activating the command without using any of the menus. For example, press Alt, press L, and then press P to access the Page Setup dialog box from the Layout menu. To learn all the shortcut keys, refer to the Command Reference section at the end of the book.

You can also choose various dialog box options using either the mouse or the keyboard. Choosing with the mouse is usually just a matter of clicking an item in a list or scrolling down a list box to locate an item to click. If the option is executable, you can speed things up by double-clicking the option instead of taking the extra step of clicking OK. For example, you can open a file by double-clicking on its filename in the Open dialog box, which you access using the File menu.

# Corel*NOTE!*

In Windows 95, you no longer can maneuver around in dialog boxes from the keyboard by using the Tab key. Quick-keys are still available, however. Quick-keys are single key sequences used for common tasks, enabling you to bypass the normal menu system. An example is Ctrl+P to print.

## Menu Bar

As previously noted, the CorelDRAW's menu bar is broken down into nine pull-down menus, not including Help. In this section, you look at each of these menus.

Figures 3.1 through 3.20 show the menus as they appear when they're selected. The default settings are shown in these figures. For more information on how to customize the menu bar, see Skill Session 4, "Customizing and Setting Preferences."

*Figure 3.1.*
*The File menu.*

*Figure 3.2.*
*The Edit menu.*

*Figure 3.3.*
*The View menu and its*
*Color Palette submenu.*

*Figure 3.4.*
*The View menu and its*
*Bitmaps submenu.*

*Figure 3.5.*
*The View menu and its*
*Color Correction submenu.*

*Figure 3.6.*
*The View menu and its*
*Properties submenu.*

*Figure 3.7.*
*The Layout menu.*

*Figure 3.8.*
*The Arrange menu and its*
*Transform submenu.*

*Figure 3.9.*
*The Arrange menu and its*
*Order submenu.*

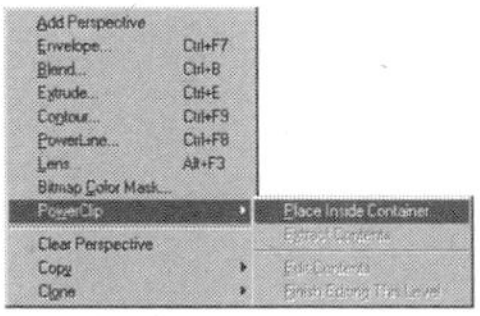

*Figure 3.10.*
*The Effects menu and its*
*PowerClip submenu.*

*Figure 3.11.*
*The Effects menu and its*
*Copy submenu.*

*Figure 3.12.*
*The Effects menu and its*
*Clone submenu.*

*Figure 3.13.*
*The Text menu and its*
*Proofreading submenu.*

*Figure 3.14.*
*The Tools menu and its*
*Roll-Up Groups submenu.*

*Figure 3.15.*
*The Tools menu and its*
*Color Manager submenu.*

*Figure 3.16.*
*The Tools menu and its*
*Dimensions submenu.*

*Figure 3.17.*
*The Tools menu and its*
*Create submenu.*

*Figure 3.18.*
*The Tools menu and its*
*Scripts submenu.*

*Figure 3.19.*
*The Windows menu.*

*Figure 3.20.*
*The Help menu.*

# Toolbar

The toolbar, which is now fully customizable in CorelDRAW 6, is displayed just below the menu bar. It contains several shortcut icons for performing functions in CorelDRAW. If you place the mouse pointer over an icon, a yellow label (called a tooltip) appears telling you what action the icon performs. More detailed information appears on the status line (by default at the bottom of your screen).

For more information on how to customize the toolbar, see Skill Session 4.

Table 3.1 lists the shortcut icons, in the order they appear from left to right, and the functions they perform.

**Table 3.1. Toolbar icons.**

| Icon | Function |
|------|----------|
| New | Creates a new drawing. |
| Open | Opens an existing drawing. |
| Save | Saves the current file; if it hasn't been saved before, the Save As dialog box appears. |
| Print | Displays the Print dialog box, enabling you to change printer options or to print to a file. |
| Cut | Deletes the selected objects from the screen and places them on the Windows Clipboard. |
| Copy | Copies the selected objects to the Windows Clipboard. The original remains on-screen. |
| Paste | Places all objects that reside on the Windows Clipboard on the CorelDRAW screen. |
| Import | Opens the Import dialog box, which enables you to import other objects into your CorelDRAW drawing. |
| Export | Opens the Export dialog box, which enables you to export all or part of your drawing from CorelDRAW to a different file format. |
| Full-Screen Preview | Shows a full-screen preview of your image. Press Esc to return to the CorelDRAW screen. |
| Wireframe | Toggles between preview and wireframe mode. Any object fills are not displayed. |
| Snap To Guidelines | Toggles the Snap To Guidelines feature on and off. |
| Group/Ungroup | Groups/Ungroups two or more selected objects. |
| Align and Distribute Roll-Up | Opens the Align and Distribute roll-up. |
| Convert To Curves | Converts the selected object to a curve object. |

| Icon | Function |
|------|----------|
| To Front | Moves the selected object or group of objects in front of all other objects on the screen. |
| To Back | Moves the selected object or group of objects behind all other objects on the screen. |
| Transform Roll-Up | Opens the Transform roll-up. |
| Symbols Roll-Up | Opens the Symbols roll-up. |
| Application Launcher | Launches other installed Corel applications. |
| Context Help | Produces a cursor with a question mark to enable you to click other menu screen items for specific help on a particular item. |
| Tutor Notes | Provides access to help for many of the basic tools and functions. |

## Changing Dialog Box Settings Using the Keyboard

Figure 3.21 shows the Tools Options dialog box. The keystroke combination to open this dialog box is Alt+T+P. You can also access this dialog box from the Tools menu.

*Figure 3.21.*
*The Tools Options*
*dialog box.*

For the most part, using a mouse in Windows 3.1 was optional. You could use the Tab key to navigate among available choices. Windows 95 is entirely different. Navigating with the Tab key is no longer possible in dialog boxes; you must use a mouse. This is not to say that quick-keys aren't available. In many cases, they are still your best choice for quickly accomplishing certain tasks.

In the Tools Options dialog box, for example, pressing Tab enables you to switch only between the first tab (in this case, General) and the standard Windows 95 buttons at the bottom of the dialog box. These standard buttons are the OK, Cancel, and Help buttons.

To access the first scrolling menu that enables you to change the horizontal spacing of duplicates and clones, two choices are available. The first and most obvious choice is to simply click the up or down arrow of the chosen box. The second alternative is to use the quick-key, which in this case is the Alt key combined with the H key. These quick-keys are not case sensitive.

In the case of the pull-down menu (currently displaying inches in Figure 3.21) adjacent to the Horizontal scrolling menu just mentioned, the only way to alter it is by using a mouse. You can select or deselect check boxes, such as the Automatically center new PowerClip contents check box shown near the bottom of Figure 3.21, using either method.

## The Windows Control Menu

You access the Windows Control menu (see Figure 3.22) by clicking the Corel balloon icon in the top-left corner of the screen, above the File menu on the title bar. In Windows 3.1, the Control menu was the (-) icon that appeared in the upper-left corner on every Microsoft Windows window.

*Figure 3.22.*
*The Windows Control*
*menu.*

To access the Control menu using the keyboard, hold down the Alt key and press the spacebar.

# Corel*NOTE!*

In Windows 95, the Switch-To feature is no longer available on the Control menu because Windows 95 has its own task bar located at the bottom screen. This task bar represents the Windows 3.1 equivalent of minimizing a window into an icon. In addition, any running programs that are not minimized also are shown.

# Corel *TIP!*

If you are running an application such as CorelDRAW full-screen and the Windows 95 task bar is not visible at the bottom of the screen, you can access it by pressing the Alt key and the Esc key.

## The Magic of the Right Mouse Click

One of the most talked-about features of Windows 95 is the ability to right-click an object either as a shortcut or to obtain additional information. CorelDRAW 6 takes advantage of this handy feature almost everywhere. Figure 3.23 shows the default menu from right-clicking an empty page.

*Figure 3.23.*
*The default right-click*
*menu.*

Now take a look at what you can find by right-clicking a complex object—in this case, some banana clip art. Figure 3.24 shows the clip art's properties, found beneath the Properties menu at the very bottom of the menu.

*Figure 3.24.*
*An object's Properties*
*menu.*

## Getting Help

You can find help within CorelDRAW either by using the traditional Windows Help menu from the main menu bar or by using the context-sensitive Help tool (second button from the right on the toolbar). You also can find context-sensitive help under the Help menu; it is the second menu item labeled What's This?.

First, look at the traditional Windows help method. Choose Help from the main menu bar and then choose Help Topics. The Help Topics dialog box appears. A shortcut key, F1, is also available to open this dialog box. If you're like most users, you'll find that using the Find tab is the most efficient way to find the help you are looking for. See Figure 3.25.

*Figure 3.25.*
*The Help Topics Find tab.*

Type a word or phrase in the first input box of the Find tab. In the second list box, you can narrow down your search if necessary. In the third list box, you can go directly to the appropriate help topic if found by simply double-clicking it.

Using the context-sensitive help, What's This?, is even simpler to use. Simply click its icon (second from the right) and then click a button, roll-up, or various other objects on the desktop, and it will automatically bring up the appropriate help.

## Windows 95's Windows

With the disappearance of Windows 3.1's Control menu—the gray (-) box always in the upper left corner—came the three gray buttons in the upper right corner of every Windows 95 window. Because the use of these buttons is straightforward, little explanation is necessary.

The leftmost button simply minimizes the window to the task bar at the bottom of the screen. The rightmost button closes the window. The middle button either maximizes the window to full-screen (if only one window is shown on the button) or reduces the screen to its original size before it was maximized (if two windows are shown cascaded).

As a final note concerning manipulating windows within CorelDRAW, you can move them and resize them just as you did in Windows 3.1. To move a window, just left-click the title bar and drag it to wherever you want to place the window. To resize a window, simply place the mouse pointer at the edge of the screen and wait for the double-sided arrows to appear. Click the left mouse button and resize the window as you would in Windows 3.1.

**4**

# Customizing and Setting Preferences

Until CorelDRAW 6, the user interface was basically static. You could move the status bar from the bottom of the screen to the top, you could place roll-ups anywhere on the screen, and you could change the settings of the right and left mouse clicks in several different ways. You could not change much else.

Well, things have changed. A better question to ask now is "What can't be customized?" For the most part, the only thing that you can't change is the primary toolbar, located on the upper-left side of the screen.

To start, take a look at those things that are already on the desktop which can be rearranged. Later in this chapter, you will examine how to make additions to the default desktop, customize pull-down menus and roll-ups, and then set general preferences.

## Status Bar

The key to customizing the status bar is the right click. This is true for all the objects you will examine in this chapter.

By right-clicking the status bar (by default located at the bottom of the screen), the Status Bar Properties menu shown in Figure 4.1 is revealed.

*Figure 4.1.*
*The Status Bar Properties*
*menu from the status bar.*

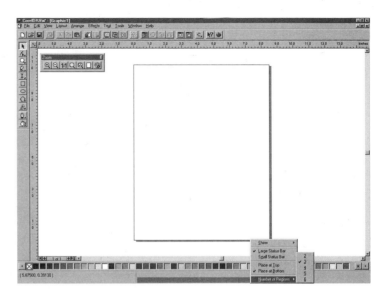

Start with the last menu item, Number of Regions. By default, the status bar is broken down into three regions, but up to six regions can be displayed (if you would like to add additional information to the status bar or display it a different way). Each region contains two cells, one on top of the other. The defaults are shown in Table 4.1.

**Table 4.1. The default regions for a large status bar with six regions.**

| Mouse Coordinates | Object Information | Large Color Swatch | None | None | None |
|---|---|---|---|---|---|
| Snap Constraints | Object Details | Large Color Swatch | None | None | None |

To change any of the regions, simply right-click the region and then choose one of the nine items from the Show flyout menu.

The other four menu items obtained by right-clicking on the status bar are self-explanatory, enabling you to place the status bar at either the top or bottom of the screen and select either a large or small status bar. If you select a small status bar, only one cell is available per region.

# Corel*NOTE!*

You can place the status bar only at the top or bottom of the desktop by dragging it with the mouse. You cannot place it on the sides.

## Toolbar

By right-clicking in the area bordering the toolbar buttons (at the top of the desktop) or toolbox (on the left side of the desktop), the menu shown in Figure 4.2 is displayed.

*Figure 4.2.*
*The Toolbars Properties menu can be selected from either the toolbar or toolbox.*

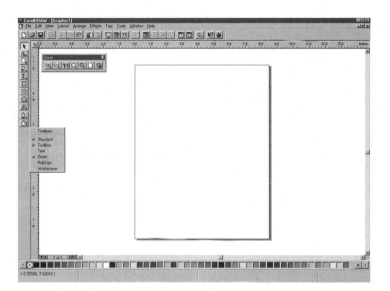

By default, the Standard toolbar (displayed horizontally at the top of the desktop) is displayed, along with the toolbox (displayed vertically along the left side) and Zoom toolbar (free-floating). Figure 4.3 shows all the toolbars displayed.

The Workspace toolbar is an excellent choice for permanent placement on your desktop. Within this one toolbar, you have almost complete control of your desktop. It includes all the features of the menu shown in Figure 4.2 with the additional control of the rulers, the color palette, and the status bar.

Now you're ready to create your own toolbar. Right-click the area between the buttons on the toolbar as you did before to open the menu shown in Figure 4.2. Then choose the top menu item, Toolbars. The Toolbars dialog box appears, as shown in Figure 4.4.

*Figure 4.3.*
*The default desktop with*
*the addition of the Text*
*toolbar, the Roll-Ups*
*toolbar, and the*
*Workspace toolbar.*

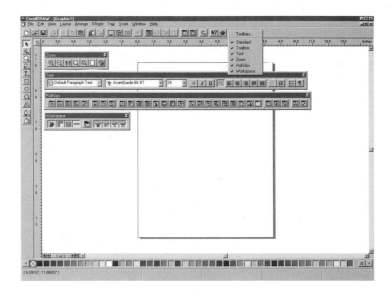

*Figure 4.4.*
*The Toolbars dialog box.*

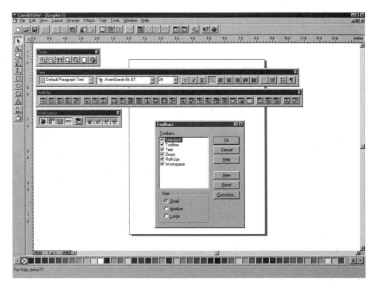

# Corel *TIP!*

If you are using a monitor resolution of 1024×768 or greater, change the button size to
Medium or Large in the Toolbars dialog box. This way, you'll find that the toolbar is much
easier to see and work with. Changing the button size is not recommended for monitor
resolutions below SVGA because the buttons won't fit on the screen and would occupy
too much of the desktop.

Two features of the Toolbars dialog box are the New and Reset buttons. Click the New button to create a new toolbar. Give it a name such as Custom or My Toolbar if you are struggling in the creativity department; then click Customize. A sugarcube size object then appears on the screen. You can place buttons on this object by using the Customize dialog box shown in Figure 4.5.

*Figure 4.5.*
*The Customize dialog box.*

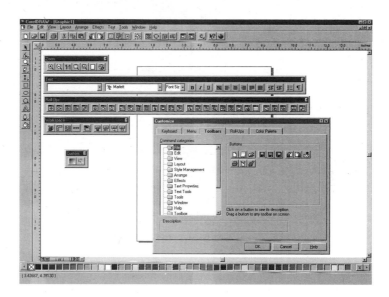

At this point, you are free to scroll through the menus in the Command categories from File to Apply Styles, adding as many buttons as you like to your custom toolbar. To add a button, simply drag it onto your custom toolbar. To remove it, drag it back.

You probably realize now that toolbars are not the only thing that you can customize using this Customize dialog box. Before you proceed, place the toolbar that you just created in a convenient place along with the others. Figure 4.6 shows the desktop before toolbar placement.

Figure 4.7 shows the desktop after toolbar placement. The Workspace and custom (the one just created) toolbar are placed at the top left of the desktop. The Text and Roll-Ups toolbars are placed beneath the Standard toolbar at the top of the desktop. The Zoom toolbar is placed on the left side of the desktop.

The Customize dialog box is also accessible via the Main menu; you simply choose Tools and then Customize.

*Figure 4.6.*
*The desktop prior to*
*toolbar placement.*

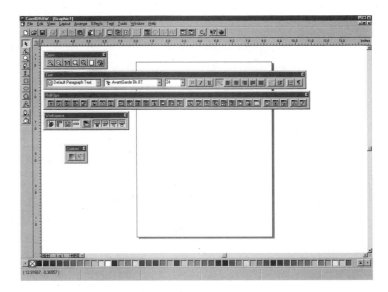

*Figure 4.7.*
*The desktop after toolbar*
*placement.*

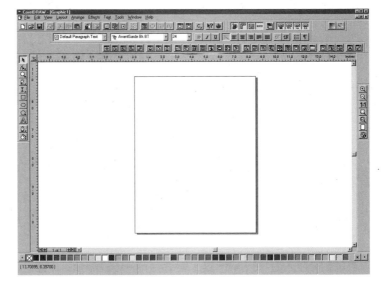

## Keyboard

The first tab of the Customize dialog box is Keyboard (see Figure 4.8). On this tab, you can add, edit, or delete shortcut keys. The default settings are saved in the file DEFAULT.ACL, which is located in the DRAW folder in the INSTALLATION directory.

*Figure 4.8.*
*The Keyboard tab of the*
*Customize dialog box.*

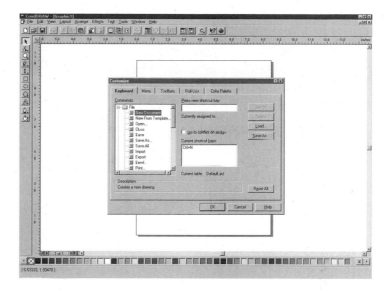

# Corel *TIP!*

If you are one of several users who use CorelDRAW on a particular machine, you may want to create your own shortcut key file via the Tools | Customize | Keyboard menu.

Within the scrollable Commands list box are 19 folders. Folders with pluses next to them may be exploded; those with minuses may be rolled up. Nine of these folders are menus from the main menu bar (see Figure 4.8), ten come from other places including various dialog boxes and roll-ups. Some of them already have shortcuts assigned to them; many do not. Go ahead and add your own shortcuts.

## Menus

Apparently nothing is sacred when it comes to customization. Not only can you add menu items to the main menu, but you also can rearrange the existing menu and even change the order of menu items in each of the nine main menu items.

If you would like to see the File menu on the right side of the menu system, you are in luck. To move this menu, highlight &File in the Menu list on the right side of the Menu tab in the Customize dialog box (see Figure 4.9). Then click the Move Down button until this menu is at the bottom of the list. Items at the bottom of the list appear on the right side of the menu.

*Figure 4.9.*
*The Menu tab of the*
*Customize dialog box.*

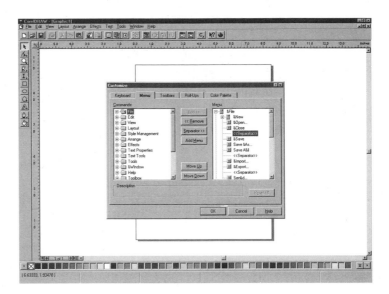

Your next question probably is "What is this & thing?" It is the shortcut key. Notice that in the case of File, the & appears before the F; thus, F is underlined on the main menu bar. In the case of Effects, the & appears before the c; thus, c is the shortcut key. You must press the Ctrl or Alt key when the pressing the shortcut key.

Once again, if you're not happy with the way Corel put together the menu structure, fix it! Separators are also available; you can insert or delete them in any of the menus.

## Roll-Ups

Although you may not choose to customize the previously mentioned areas, roll-ups are probably one area that most users will want to change. This fact is especially true if you just can't get used to the new roll-up groups. Keep in mind that you can also ungroup them on the desktop and they will stay ungrouped until you regroup them again.

As in the other list boxes, the plus signs indicate that you can explode the roll-up group to display the roll-ups within the group. (See Figure 4.10.) Minus signs indicate that the parent may be rolled up.

The icon next to each item indicates with an arrow facing either to the right or to the left that the roll-up will either be right-aligned or left-aligned. You can move these roll-ups to either side using either of the Move buttons.

*Figure 4.10.*
*The Roll-Ups tab of the*
*Customize dialog box.*

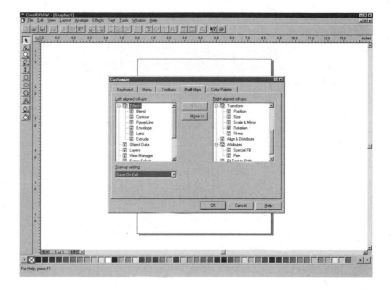

## Color Palette

The final tab on the Customize dialog box is the Color Palette. Its two purposes are to change the settings of the Color Well (the color bar by default at the bottom of the desktop) and to change the function of the second mouse button. (See Figure 4.11.)

*Figure 4.11.*
*The Color Palette tab of*
*the Customize dialog box.*

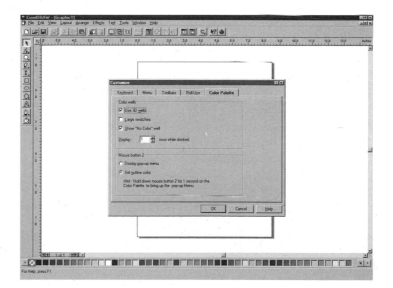

The first check box in the Color Wells section is just personal preference. This box is checked by default and adds a 3D effect to the color swatches. The second check box simply makes the color swatches larger. The third check box toggles the No Color Well, which is the white box on the left side of the Color Well with a black × in it. This well extracts any fill from an object.

The last two items in the Color Palette tab—Display pop-up menu and Set outline color—determine the function of the second mouse button (normally the right mouse button).

The second is the default; you probably shouldn't change this option because, if you hold down the mouse button for two seconds, you can get the first choice, the pop-up menu. A short click still sets the outline color.

## Rulers

By double-clicking either of the rulers, you can access the Grid & Ruler Setup or the Guidelines Setup (see Skill Session 19, "Grid and Ruler Setup," and 20, "Guidelines," for additional information). In the Grid & Ruler Setup, you can customize what unit of measure the ruler is in and also set the origin. If you change the unit of measure in the top section, the unit of measure also changes in the origin section below.

The most important feature here, however, is the Edit Scale button. Many of the standard scales are present, but you also can set a custom scale.

You can make similar modifications in the Guidelines Setup.

The funny-looking symbol at the intersection of the rulers in the upper-left corner (known in Corel help files as "the gray box where the rulers meet" or "the area where the rulers meet") has one interesting feature. Press and hold Ctrl+Shift and drag this "thing" out on to the desktop. Essentially, you can place this origin anywhere on the desktop. This marker indicates the 0,0 origin of the page.

## Options

Tools | Preferences has been changed in CorelDRAW 6 to Tools | Options. The Options dialog box is divided into three sections, arranged like files; they are General, Display, and Advanced. At the top of the dialog box, you see a tab for each section. Click the appropriate tab to view a section. (See Figure 4.12.)

*Figure 4.12.*
*The Options dialog box*
*with General selected.*

## General Options

The General options of the Options dialog box are settings that control various functions that aren't specific to a particular category. Each option is described briefly in the following sections.

### Place Duplicates and Clones

Use the Place duplicates and clones option to determine how far away the duplicated or cloned object will be placed from the original. If you enter a positive value, such as 0.50 inch, in both the Horizontal and Vertical boxes, the duplicate or clone copy will be offset half an inch above and half an inch to the right of the original. In addition to inches, you can use millimeters, picas, and points.

### Nudge

The Nudge function affects the arrow keys on your keyboard. The value you put in the Nudge parameters box is the distance the selected object or objects and the curved node or nodes will move when you press an arrow key.

When you press and release the up-arrow key, for example, the object moves upward by the distance you set in the Nudge parameters box. When you press and hold an arrow key, the object moves in that direction until you release the key. The object or curved node always moves in the direction of the arrow key being pressed.

### Constrain Angle

When you hold down the Ctrl key while performing the following functions, the degree of angle is constrained by the number you put in the Constrain angle parameters box:

- Skewing and rotating objects
- Adjusting control points and handles when drawing curves in Bezier mode
- Drawing straight lines in freehand mode
- Changing the angles in the fountain fill previews

### Miter Limit

The Miter limit option determines the lower limit for creating miter joints at the corners of objects. If you draw an object with angles below the limit entered in the parameters box, the joints will be beveled. This option eliminates the problem of corner joints extending far beyond the actual corners at small angles.

### Undo Levels

The number you enter in the Undo levels parameters box sets the number of times you can reverse (undo) an action or operation using the Undo command in the Edit menu. This setting also applies to the Redo command in the Edit menu. This setting no longer has a maximum number to which you can set it.

# Corel *NOTE!*

The higher the number you set for Undo levels, the more memory is required by your system. Your system has to keep everything you did during a session in memory, up to the number of undos you set. If you set Undo levels to 99, for example, your system's memory would have to store the last 99 actions you did in memory. Storing this many actions can greatly slow down the system and even cause you to run out of memory. The default setting for Undo levels is 4.

## Display Options

The Display options of the Options dialog box are settings that control various options related to previewing and displaying objects. (See Figure 4.13.) Each option is described briefly in the following sections.

*Figure 4.13.*
*The Options dialog box*
*with Display selected.*

## Preview Fountain Steps

The value you set for Preview fountain steps determines the number of bands used in fountain fills that display on-screen. The number you set also affects how your drawings will appear when they're exported in the following formats:

- Illustrator (AI, EPS)
- Computer Graphics Metafile (CGM)
- MAC PICT (PCT)
- Windows Metafile (WFM)
- All bitmap formats (PCX, TIF, and so on)

The default is 50 steps; in most cases, this number is adequate. The maximum is 256.

# Corel*NOTE!*

You can override the settings you entered in Options by changing them in the Fountain Fill Dialog box at the time you create a fountain fill. You can also override this setting in the Print Options dialog box for selected objects.

## Preview Colors

The Preview colors section of the Display tab is fairly straightforward. If you're using a 256-color graphics card, choose 256-color dithering for the best screen display. If you have a standard VGA card, the setting should be Windows dithering. If you have a full 24-bit card, it will default to Windows dithering and give you a proper 16-million-color display.

## Full-Screen Preview

The Optimized 256-color palette option of the Full-screen preview section is self-explanatory, but it may or may not give you a better display, depending on your particular graphics card. It will generally produce a better display with most graphics cards if you're using Windows dithering.

## Interruptible Refresh

When you enable Interruptible refresh, you can stop the redrawing of complex drawings by clicking anywhere on the screen or pressing any key. This capability can be useful when you want to isolate a particular object or select a different tool or menu without having to wait for the screen to redraw.

Here's one thing to be careful about when you use Interruptible refresh: Even if you can't see an object on-screen, you can still select it. All the objects are there, even if they haven't been redrawn. Having all objects available but not visible can lead to problems when you have complex drawings with lots of objects. If you stop the redraw to select an object just after it has been redrawn, you may find that when you try to select it, a different object is selected. This happens because all objects are drawn from back to front. You can lessen this problem if you use wireframe mode instead of preview mode.

### Manual Refresh

When you enable Manual refresh, you can redraw the screen by clicking the scroll bar buttons.

### Use 3D Wells for Color Palettes

The Use 3D wells for color palettes option has no impact on anything but the color palette at the bottom of the desktop. It simply adds a 3D effect to the palette.

### Auto-Panning

When you click Auto-panning, you turn on the Auto-panning feature. This feature enables you to drag an object beyond the visible portion of your screen's working area. When you drag an object outside the working area, the screen scrolls so that you can still see your object. To disable this feature, click the check box again.

### Show Snap Location Marks

With Snap to Grid (right-click the ruler to turn it on or off) turned on and the Show snap location marks option checked, a small blue rectangle will appear showing you where an object will be placed if it were to snap to the grid.

### Show Tooltips

This feature toggles on and off the yellow pop-up help labels that identify tools and buttons when you place the pointer over one of them.

## Advanced Options

The Advanced options of the Options dialog box are a mixture of various backup options, file options, and various unrelated features. (See Figure 4.14.) Each option is described briefly in the following sections.

Figure 4.14.
*The Options dialog box
with Advanced selected.*

### Select Directory

Click Select Directory and, in the resulting dialog box, select the directory where
you want your Auto-backups to reside. You might want to create a custom directory for these files.

### Make Backup on Save

When you enable the Make backup on save option, a separate backup file with the
extension .BAK is created when you save your files. Enabling this option is very
useful for ensuring that the original file isn't accidentally overwritten or corrupted.
To open the file in CorelDRAW, you must change the .BAK extension to .CDR.

### Auto-Backup Minutes

Auto-backup creates a special backup file every few minutes while you're working
on a file. The number of minutes between each backup is determined by the
number you type in the parameters box.

This backup file is not to be confused with the one created by the Make backup on
save method. The Auto-backup file is created in case of a system failure while
you're working in CorelDRAW. If you have a system failure, you can retrieve the
lost file at the point where it was last backed up. The backup file is given the
extension .ABK instead of .CDR. To retrieve the file, open the directory where the
backup file resides (see the next section) and change the extension from .ABK to
.CDR. You then can open the file you lost due to the system failure.

### Interruptible Saving

By checking the Interruptible saving box, you can interrupt the saving of a file to
disk. This capability may not sound like much unless the file you are saving is very
large. I know of no reason not to check this box.

## Optimize for Storage/Speed

Like many things in life, you can't have it both ways; you can optimize either storage or speed, not both. Either CorelDRAW saves its file using compression, which saves space but takes longer to load, or it doesn't and the file makes itself at home on large portions of your shrinking disk.

## PopUp Menu Customization

This PopUp Menu Customization section enables you to set the top menu item when you right-click the desktop. Setting it to something like 2x Zoom or Edit Text can be a real time-saver.

## Gamut Alarm Color

Gamut alarm color is the color that will be displayed when colors are out of gamut. Pick one that you don't use very often.

## Enable Multitasking

My recommendation is not to enable multitasking as it tends to cause unexpected crashes.

# Skill Session: Text Options

**5**

# Roll-Ups

CorelDRAW provides menus, dialog boxes, keyboard shortcuts, and icons to activate specific functions. Another way CorelDRAW enables specific functions is through roll-ups. *Roll-ups* are mini-windows that contain various options. They are called roll-ups because they act like a window shade and can be "rolled up" to show just the title bar.

Roll-ups can remain on your screen and can be moved to any location you want so that its functions are always available, or you can have it close after a single use (like a dialog box). If you like having several roll-ups available, you can arrange them in a cascading list to conserve screen space. (See Figure 5.1.)

Figure 5.1.
*The Tools menu with Roll-Up Groups highlighted and the Roll-Up Groups flyout menu.*

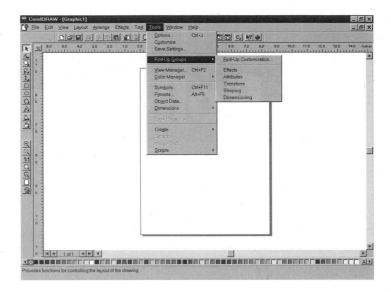

## Roll-Up Functions

To close a roll-up, right-click it and choose Close, Close All, or Auto Close from the menu. To move a roll-up, point to the window's title bar, hold the left mouse button down, and drag the roll-up to a new location.

To arrange the active roll-up, right-click it and choose Arrange, and the roll-up will position itself. To arrange more than one roll-up, choose Arrange All. This repositions all roll-ups to the top corners of the drawing window.

When you want to roll the window up or down, use one of the following three methods: click the arrow in the top-right corner of the window, right-click the roll-up and select Roll-up or Down from the menu, or double-click the roll-up's title bar.

To receive help on roll-ups, right-click the title bar of an open roll-up and select Help from the menu. You can also get help by pressing Shift+F1 and clicking the roll-up.

The Roll-Up Customization command allows you to alter the positioning and grouping of the roll-ups. Select one of the available options to apply to your roll-ups.

If you want to modify the alignment of any roll-up, select Customize from the Tools menu. The Roll-Ups tab is automatically selected. Choose the roll-up you want to modify and press Move. Changing a roll-up's alignment causes it to appear on the other side of the window.

If you want to change the original roll-up configuration, select Customize from the Tools menu. The Roll-Ups tab is automatically selected. Press the arrow below the Start-up setting section and choose a start-up option.

If you would like to give a roll-up group a different name, select Customize from the Tools menu. The Roll-Ups tab is automatically selected. Choose the roll-up group you want to rename, press the name tag of the roll-up group, and then type in a new name.

When using roll-ups, you can order them for easier access. Use the Roll-Up Customization command to group roll-ups together. This allows you to create a single roll-up window that provides access to the commands of various roll-ups. (See Figure 5.2.)

Figure 5.2.
The Roll-Ups tab in the
Customize dialog box.

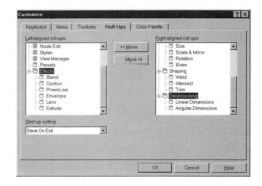

## Tool Pull-Down Menu Default Roll-Ups

Besides finding roll-ups in the toolbox and with their respective menus, they can all be accessed from the Tools menu. Select Tools, then Roll-Up Groups, and a flyout menu is displayed with six commands:

**Roll-Up Customization**   This command opens the Customize dialog box and displays the Roll-Ups section.

**Effects**   This command opens the Effects Roll-Up Group in blend mode.

**Transform**   This command opens the Transform Roll-Up Group in skew mode.

**Dimensioning**   This command opens the Dimensioning Roll-Up Group in angular mode.

**Shaping**   This command opens the Shaping Roll-Up Group in trim mode.

**Attributes**   This command opens the Attributes Roll-Up Group in pen mode.

The modes in which the roll-up groups open up are the default settings. When you change from one mode to another and close a roll-up in the new mode, it will default to that mode next time you use it. (See Figure 5.3.)

*Figure 5.3.*
*The default roll-up groups.*

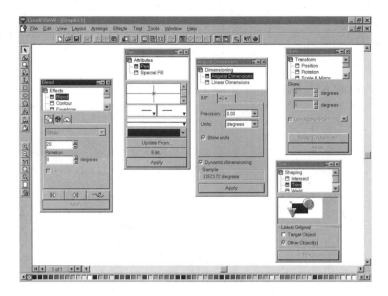

## Creating Roll-Up Groups

Use this procedure when you want to create a roll-up group. Bring up the roll-ups you want to group. Hold down the Ctrl key and select the desired roll-up. The cursor's icon changes. Next, drag the selected roll-up onto another roll-up. Keep adding roll-ups until your group is complete. You can also rename the roll-up to suit your needs. (See Figure 5.4.)

*Figure 5.4.*
*A new roll-up group*
*created from the Layers*
*Manager and the Align &*
*Distribute roll-ups.*

# Removing Roll-Ups from Groups

To remove a roll-up from a group, select its icon and pull it out of the group window. Roll-up groups maintain drag-and-drop support; therefore, you can instantly group or ungroup roll-ups while you continue with your project. (See Figure 5.5.)

*Figure 5.5.*
*Removing a roll-up from its*
*group.*

The following is an alphabetical list of roll-ups and their location in this book. See Table 5.1.

**Table 5.1. Where to find more information on roll-ups.**

| Name of Roll-Up | Where to Find Information |
| --- | --- |
| Bitmap Color Mask roll-up | Skill Sessions 45–47 |
| Blend roll-up | Skill Session 30 |
| Contour roll-up | Skill Session 32 |
| Dimension roll-up | Skill Session 10 |
| Envelope roll-up | Skill Session 29 |
| Extrude roll-up | Skill Session 31 |
| Fill roll-up | Skill Session 16 |
| Fit Text To Path roll-up | Skill Session 40 |
| Layers roll-up | Skill Session 21 |
| Lens roll-up | Skill Session 34 |
| Node Edit roll-up | Skill Session 7 |
| Object Data roll-up | Skill Session 59 |
| Pencil Tool roll-up | Skill Session 9 |
| PowerLine roll-up | Skill Session 33 |
| Presets roll-up | Project 61 |
| Styles roll-up | Skill Session 58 |
| Symbols roll-up | Command Reference 62 |
| Transform roll-up | Skill Session 26 |

# 6

# The Pick Tool

The Pick tool is the first and most versatile tool in CorelDRAW's toolbox. Choose the Pick tool by pressing the spacebar (except when in text-editing mode) or clicking on the Pick tool icon in the toolbox.

## Pick Tool Properties Menu

Each of the tools in the toolbox has a Tools Properties menu. To access this menu, click the tool with your right mouse button and choose Properties from the menu that appears. For the Pick tool, you will see the dialog box shown in Figure 6.1.

Selecting the crosshair cursor option changes your normal arrow cursor into crosshairs that extend the full length and width of the drawing area, as shown in Figure 6.2. When you go outside of the drawing area, the cursor returns to the normal arrow.

The Treat all objects as filled option allows you to select unfilled objects as if they were filled. This can be helpful as it is sometimes difficult to select their outline quickly.

The Draw objects when moving option, if selected, redraws your objects before you finish moving them when you stop your movement for the amount of time specified in the Delay to draw when moving parameters box. An example of this is shown in Figure 6.3.

Figure 6.1.
The Pick Tool Properties
dialog box.

Figure 6.2.
The Crosshair cursor.

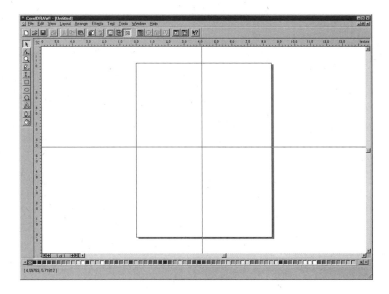

Figure 6.3.
An object that is redrawn
while in the process of
being moved.

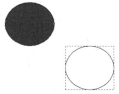

## Selecting Objects

The Pick tool is primarily used for selecting objects. The easiest way to select an object is to click its outline once with the Pick tool.

# Corel *NOTE!*

When you're in preview mode, you can also select filled objects by clicking anywhere inside the object. Unfilled objects may be selected in the same fashion if you check the Treat all objects as filled option in the Pick Tool Properties dialog box.

There's a set of eight squares surrounding the object's perimeter. These squares are called the *object handles*. An example is shown in Figure 6.4. Notice that the status line changes to show that an object has been selected. The default status line indicates what type of object is currently selected, where it is located, the fill color, the outline width, and the outline color. If you would like to have more information displayed, then you can modify the status line. This process is described in Skill Session 4, "Customizing and Setting Preferences."

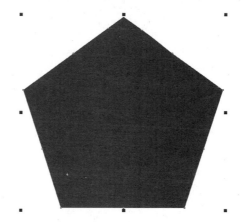

*Figure 6.4.
Object handles surround-
ing a selected polygon.*

To select multiple objects, hold down the Shift key while you click the objects. When you select multiple objects, the status line indicates how many objects are selected and the object handles surround the perimeter of all objects selected, as shown in Figure 6.5. To deselect an object, click it a second time while holding down the Shift key.

*Figure 6.5.
Object handles surround-
ing several selected
objects.*

Another way to select multiple objects (or even a single object) is by marquee-selection. Using the Pick tool, hold down the left mouse button to draw a box around all objects you want to include in the selection group. As you draw the box, a dotted blue line is shown on-screen. (See Figure 6.6.) If you select more objects than you want, use the Shift key in conjunction with the Pick tool to deselect any objects.

## Corel *TIP!*

Hold down the Alt key while marquee-selecting and you will select the objects inside the marquee box as well as the objects intersected by the marquee box.

## Corel *TIP!*

Double-click the Pick tool to select all the objects in a drawing.

*Figure 6.6.*
*Marquee-selection using*
*the Pick tool.*

## Corel *NOTE!*

Using marquee-selection is a great way to select objects that might be hidden behind other objects.

In earlier versions of CorelDRAW, once an object was grouped with other objects, it was impossible to work with that object unless the group was first ungrouped. CorelDRAW 6 enables you to select objects within groups by holding down the Ctrl key and clicking the object. The status line then indicates that a child object has been selected, and the object handles are round instead of square. (See Figure 6.7.)

# Corel *TIP!*

Objects in nested groups can be selected by continuing to click while holding down the Ctrl key until the desired object is selected.

This method works with groups and extrude groups, but not with blend groups or contour groups. These groups must first be separated for this new method to work.

The Tab key can be extremely useful for finding objects. Each time you press the Tab key, the current selection moves forward one object in the drawing. Press Shift+Tab to move backward one object. To deselect all objects, press the Esc key or click a blank part of the drawing window.

*Figure 6.7.*
*Selecting an object within*
*a group.*

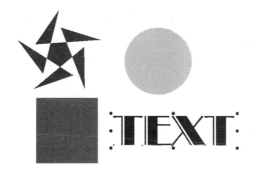

## Manipulating Objects

Once you have selected an object or objects, you can use the Pick tool to manipulate them. Probably the most important usage of the Pick tool is to move objects into different positions. Select the objects, click them with the Pick tool, and then drag them to the desired position. The objects jump to the grid, guidelines, or other objects, depending on what you specified in the Layout Snap To options. For more accurate positioning, it is usually best to place a guideline exactly where you want the object to go, or to use the Transform roll-up. (See Skill Session 26, "Transform.") Press the + key or click the right mouse button to make a copy of the selected object(s). Another way to quickly duplicate an object is to press Ctrl+D (for duplicate). This places an identical object in front of the original object, offset by the amount you specified in Preferences.

# Corel*NOTE!*

Clicking the right mouse button does not produce duplicates on pressure-sensitive digitizing tablets, because the right mouse button is used to lock the pressure level when the left button is also depressed.

If moving the object by dragging it isn't accurate enough, the arrow keys can come in quite handy. Use the ↑, ↓, ←, and → keys to move the object in the indicated direction by the amount that's set as the nudge factor in the Preferences dialog box. The default setting is .1 inch, but you might want to set this to .01 inch for smaller nudges.

## Distorting Objects

You can distort an image while it's selected by manipulating the object handles. As the Pick tool moves over an object handle, it changes to a crosshair cursor, as shown in Figure 6.8. The object can be distorted simply by clicking and dragging it with the crosshair cursor until it's the desired size and shape. The object can be scaled both horizontally and vertically with the corner handles, whereas the top, bottom, and side handles allow changes in only one direction. Several examples of these changes are shown in Figure 6.9.

Figure 6.8.
Grabbing an object handle
with the crosshair cursor.

Hold down the Ctrl key while stretching and scaling to constrain movement to increments of 100 percent. This constraint is also a great way to horizontally or vertically mirror an object—drag a center handle across the object in the direction that the object is to be mirrored. Hold down the Shift key to stretch and scale from the center point out; hold down the Shift and Ctrl keys to invoke both constraints at once. Figure 6.10 contains examples of each type of constraint.

Figure 6.9.
Sizing and shaping an
object with the Pick tool.

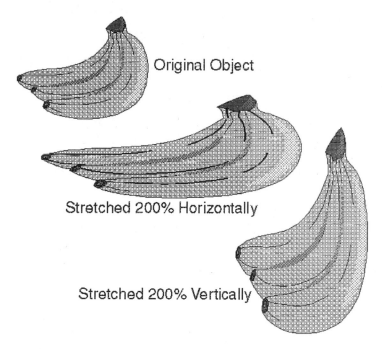

Original Object

Stretched 200% Horizontally

Stretched 200% Vertically

Figure 6.10.
Stretching and scaling
with constraints.

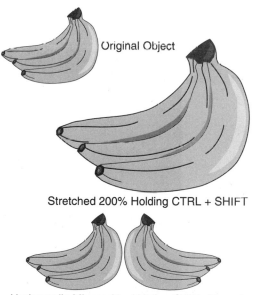

Original Object

Stretched 200% Holding CTRL + SHIFT

Horizontally Mirrored by Holding CTRL, Dragging
Across Object, and Hitting Right Mouse Button

## Rotating and Skewing Objects

Click a second time on an object to bring up the rotate and skew handles. The four corner handles change to arced, double-headed arrows, and the center handles change to double-headed arrows, as shown in Figure 6.11. At the center of the object, there is a circle surrounding a point (this is referred to as the thumbtack), which represents the center of rotation. You can move the thumbtack freely by clicking it and dragging it to the location you want. If you hold down the constrain key (the Ctrl key), the thumbtack will snap to any of the eight handles or to the center of the object.

*Figure 6.11.*
*The rotate and skew*
*handles.*

Drag a corner handle to rotate the selected object freely around the center of rotation. Hold down the Ctrl key while rotating to constrain the rotation to the amount set in Preferences. This amount defaults to 15 degrees. While the object rotates, a dotted outline represents where the object will redraw when you release the mouse button. The status line always displays the amount of rotation that has been applied. An example is shown in Figure 6.12.

Click the center handle of a selected object to skew the object in one of the directions that the two arrows point. The Ctrl key also constrains the skewing angle to what is set in Preferences. The status line displays the amount of skew that has been applied, and a dotted outline represents the new shape. Figure 6.13 provides an example of skewing.

*Figure 6.12.*
*Rotating an object.*

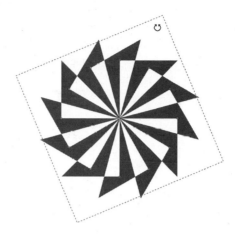

*Figure 6.13.*
*Skewing an object.*

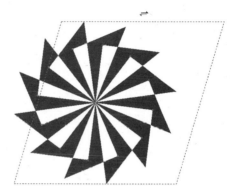

## Right Mouse Button Object Properties Menu

The Pick tool can also be used to pop up the Right Mouse Button Object Properties menu. (See Figure 6.14.) Click any object with the right mouse button to get an extensive menu of functions that pertain to that particular object. These options are different depending on the object; therefore, what you see might be radically different from the options shown in Figure 6.14. This functionality is discussed throughout the book as it pertains to the type of object being explained.

Figure 6.14.
The Right Mouse Button
Object Properties menu.

**7**

# The Shape Tool

The Shape tool is the most useful tool in CorelDRAW because of the many things it does. It acts with each type of object differently, and when used in conjunction with the Ctrl and Shift keys, it can do even more.

## Node Edit Tool Properties

The Node Edit Tool Properties dialog box is accessed by clicking with your right mouse button on the Shape tool and choosing Properties from the menu. The menu shown in Figure 7.1 appears.

Figure 7.1.
*The Node Edit Tool*
*Properties menu.*

The Auto-reduce option is the amount of standard deviation from the line allowed for nodes to be removed. If the node is outside of the standard deviation, then it is not removed. In other words, the higher the number specified in this parameters box, the more nodes are removed. But, by removing more nodes, the shape of the curve might be altered more than you like.

## Selecting Nodes

To choose the Shape tool, click its icon (the second one down on the toolbox) once or press F10. Your cursor will change to ▸ . Next, select the object you want to modify, just as you would do with the Pick tool. Notice that each of the object's nodes has changed into an enlarged square point. (See Figure 7.2.) The status line reports how many nodes exist on the selected path.

Figure 7.2.
*Selecting an object with*
*the Shape tool.*

To highlight the individual nodes, click them with the Shape tool. A highlighted node is hollow if it belongs to a linear segment and is filled if it belongs to a Bézier curve segment. For nodes on a Bézier curve, the status line indicates whether the node is a cusp, smooth, or symmetrical node; also, up to two Bézier control points protrude from each node. Figure 7.3 shows linear, cusp, smooth, and symmetrical nodes and their associated Bézier control handles.

The first node of a curve is larger than the rest because it doesn't have an associated line segment. Each node after the first is associated with the line segment preceding the node. When a segment is selected, you see a round marker at the point you clicked. (See Figure 7.4.) You can add a node at this marker or just drag it directly to shape the curve.

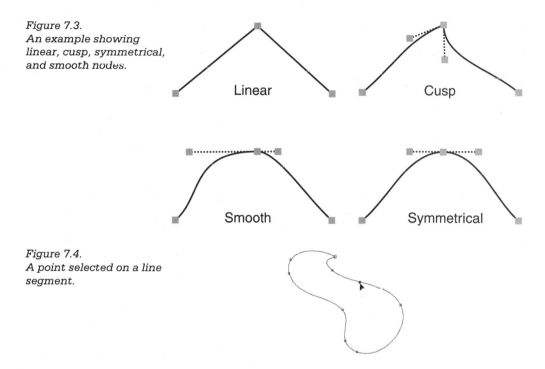

*Figure 7.3.*
*An example showing*
*linear, cusp, symmetrical,*
*and smooth nodes.*

Linear

Cusp

Smooth

Symmetrical

*Figure 7.4.*
*A point selected on a line*
*segment.*

# Corel *TIP!*

The Home key takes you to the first node of a curve, and the End key takes you to the last node. These nodes are the same for a closed curve. Shift+Home toggles the selection of the first node, and Shift+End toggles the selection of the last node. Shift+Home selects the first subpath, and Shift+End selects the last subpath. Ctrl+Shift+Home toggles the selection of the first subpath, and Ctrl+Shift+End toggles the selection of the last subpath.

# Corel *NOTE!*

There are times when a Bèzier control handle is hidden by the node itself. In order to adjust that handle, deselect all nodes, hold down the Shift key, and then drag the Bèzier control handle.

To select multiple nodes, hold down the Shift key and click the nodes to be selected. Click a previously selected node to deselect it. To marquee-select multiple nodes, drag an imaginary rectangle around all the nodes you want to select. The status line reports the current number of nodes selected; therefore, you should always check it to make sure you've selected the appropriate number.

To see how nodes work, follow these steps:

1. Choose the Rectangle tool and draw a rectangle that fills most of the page, similar to the one shown in Figure 7.5.
2. Convert it to curves by choosing Convert To Curves from the Arrange menu, or by pressing Ctrl+Q.
3. The status line should now read "Curve on Layer 1, Number of Nodes: 4."
4. Click each of the four nodes and watch the status line. The node in the corner where the rectangle originated will say "First Node of a Closed Curve," while the other nodes will say "Selected Node: Line Cusp."

*Figure 7.5.*
*A simple example to help*
*you understand nodes.*

## The Node Edit Roll-Up

To bring up the Node Edit roll-up, double-click any selected node or the Shape tool itself, or press Ctrl+F10. Figure 7.6 shows the Node Edit roll-up.

*Figure 7.6.*
*The Node Edit roll-up.*

# Corel *TIP!*

You can also access the functionality of the Node Edit roll-up by right-clicking a node with the Shape tool. An example of the pop-up menu is shown in Figure 7.7.

*Figure 7.7.*
*The Node Edit pop-up*
*menu.*

Not all of the functions in this Node Edit roll-up are currently active. Click the Add (+) button or press the plus (+) key on your keyboard to add a node to the rectangle from the example in Figure 7.5. Click the Delete (-) button or press the minus (-) key on your keyboard to change the rectangle to a triangle. Press the Break key to break the curve at the currently selected node. Examples of all three are shown in Figure 7.8.

*Figure 7.8.*
*Using Add, Delete, and*
*Break.*

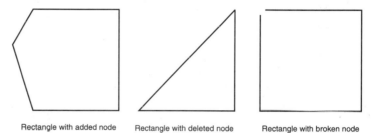

Rectangle with added node     Rectangle with deleted node     Rectangle with broken node

# Corel*NOTE!*

You can nudge nodes by using the ↑, ↓, ←, and → keys, just as you can nudge whole objects when they are selected with the Pick tool.

In this example, the Auto-Reduce button has no effect because there's no way to reduce the number of nodes that make up the rectangle. The To Curve button changes the currently selected segment to a curve (rather than a straight line) and causes Bézier control handles to appear, as shown in Figure 7.9. The Bézier control handles have been moved slightly so they're visible in the figure. They would normally sit right on the line.

Notice that the node type is Cusp. This means that the Bézier handle can be moved toward and away from the node. It can also be rotated around the node without affecting the line on the other side of the node. When a node is a cusp, the Smooth button is available. Choosing Smooth will automatically move the Bézier handle so that it's collinear to the adjoining straight segment. You can move the handle back and forth along that line segment, but you cannot rotate it because it must stay in line with the line segment on the other side of the node. (See Figure 7.10.)

*FIgure 7.9*
*Changing a segment from*
*a line to a curve.*

*Figure 7.10.*
*Using Smooth.*

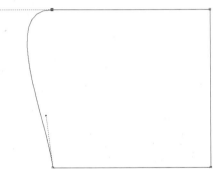

Select all of the nodes on the rectangle by dragging a marquee box around all four nodes. Click the To Curve button, and all of the line segments become curves instead of lines. Each of the nodes is still a cusp, but when you click just one node and select Smooth, the Bézier handles align with one another. Moving the handles in and out has no effect on the opposite handle, but rotating one handle also rotates the opposite handle. Now click the Symmetrical button to change that same node to a symmetrical node and then try the same procedure. Moving one Bézier handle has the same effect on the opposite Bézier handle, no matter if you move it in and out or rotate it.

Repeat the preceding process, but this time start with an ellipse. Be sure to convert the ellipse to curves; otherwise, the Shape tool creates a totally different effect (see the section, "Shaping Rectangles and Ellipses," later in this skill session). Notice that different parts of the Node Edit roll-up are highlighted, and that each of the nodes begins as a symmetrical node instead of a cusp node.

Draw another circle, but this time use the Pencil tool. Figure 7.11 shows a circle drawn with the Pencil tool. Notice that the edges are very rough and the status bar indicates 25 nodes. This is mainly due to the difficulty of drawing precisely with a mouse, and partly due to the fact that, for demonstration purposes, freehand curve tracking is set to 1, which produces a large number of nodes.

Figure 7.11.
*A circle drawn with the
Freehand tool.*

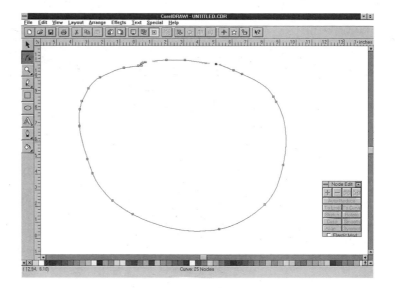

Select all the nodes on the hand-drawn circle by marquee-selecting them. Double-click a node if the Node Edit roll-up is not already active. Click the Auto-Reduce button; many of the extraneous nodes should go away without affecting the shape of the circle. By adjusting Curves Auto-Reduce in the Preferences dialog box, you can change the distance between deleted nodes. Figure 7.12 shows the same circle after Auto-Reduce has been used. Notice that there are now seven nodes instead of 25.

Figure 7.12.
*Using Auto-Reduce to
reduce the number of
nodes.*

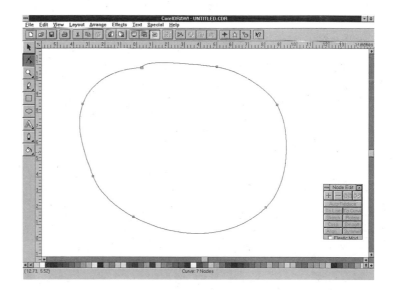

# Corel *NOTE!*

The Auto-Reduce button is not active unless the Shape tool is selected.

## Adding and Deleting Nodes

To add a node, double-click where you want the new node to go and click the Add (+) button in the Node Edit roll-up.

# Corel *TIP!*

Here's another way to add nodes. Select an existing node and click the Add button. A node is added exactly halfway between the selected node and the next node on the path. To determine which segment is considered to be the highlighted segment (and thus the one where the new node will be added), press Shift+Ctrl. The selected node moves to the next node on the path. Tab back to the previously selected node and then press Add.

# Corel *NOTE!*

Node ordering seems to be the reverse of object ordering, in that Shift+Tab goes to the next node and Tab goes to the previous node. The previous node is not necessarily in any particular direction from the current node. The node ordering is dependent on the direction in which the object was drawn and can seem to make no sense whatsoever.

If you select more than one node, a new node appears in the middle of each node's segment. A great example of this is making an octagon from a circle. (See Figure 7.13.) Here is how to do it:

1. Create a circle using the Ellipse tool. Hold down the Ctrl key to constrain it to a perfect circle.
2. Convert the circle to curves by using Arrange | Convert To Curves.
3. Switch to the Shape tool and select all the nodes by marquee-selection.
4. Double-click one of the nodes, and the Node Edit roll-up appears (if it hasn't already).
5. Click the Add button. The circle now contains eight equidistant nodes.
6. Again, select all the nodes. Click the To Line button in the Node Edit roll-up. The object should be a perfect octagon.
7. Rotate the resultant octagon 22.5 degrees to straighten it.

Earlier in this Skill Session, you saw that the Auto-Reduce function is a way to delete nodes. Another way is to select the nodes to be deleted and either click the Delete (-) button or press the Delete key. This gives you control over which nodes are deleted. The best way is to delete most of the nodes with the Auto-Reduce function and then selectively delete other extraneous nodes with the Delete function.

*Figure 7.13.*
*Converting a circle to an octagon by adding nodes. This can also be easily created with the Polygon tool.*

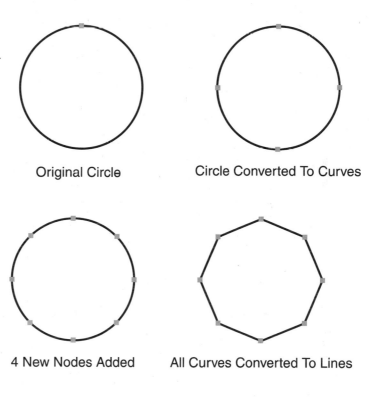

Original Circle          Circle Converted To Curves

4 New Nodes Added          All Curves Converted To Lines

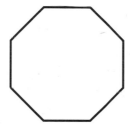

Final Octagon After Rotation

## Shaping Curves

The Shape tool's most beneficial feature is that it gives you the ability to shape curves until you create just the right effect. You can do this in two different ways:

- ◼ By physically moving nodes to different locations.
- ◼ By adjusting the Bézier handles to alter the curvature entering and leaving that node.

Figure 7.14 shows an object before its nodes are adjusted and two examples of what it might look like after its nodes are adjusted.

*Figure 7.14.*
*Before and after examples*
*of shaping curves.*

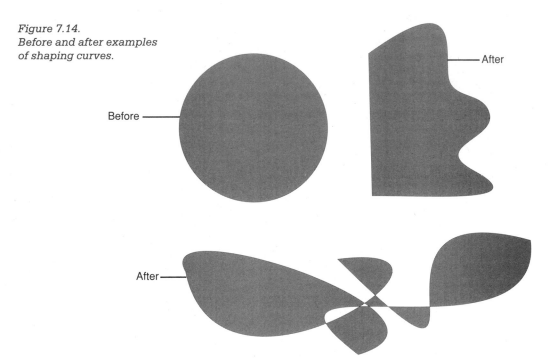

You can move nodes individually or in groups. In the same way a dining room table can be expanded by putting in extra leaves, an object can be stretched by choosing all the nodes on one end and pulling them away from the other end. This method doesn't distort curves the way that stretching the whole object does. Figure 7.15 shows the same object stretched using these two different methods. Note that when you use the Ctrl key while moving nodes, you constrain movement either horizontally or vertically.

CorelDRAW 6 provides the extra benefit of elasticity. When you check the box labeled Elastic Mode and stretch an object, all nodes selected do not necessarily move a uniform distance and angle. They move a relative distance. Figure 7.16 shows the same stretch as the examples in Figure 7.15, but this time using Elastic Mode.

*Figure 7.15.*
*The same object,*
*stretched with both*
*the Pick tool and the*
*Shape tool.*

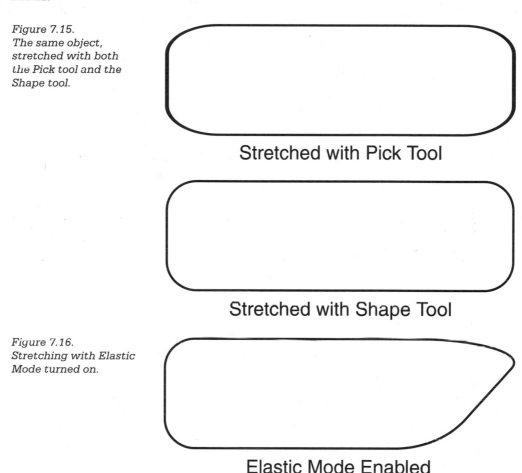

Stretched with Pick Tool

Stretched with Shape Tool

*Figure 7.16.*
*Stretching with Elastic*
*Mode turned on.*

Elastic Mode Enabled

You can align nodes by selecting two nodes and clicking the Align button in the Curve roll-up. Figure 7.17 shows the Node Align dialog box that appears when you click the Align button.

You have three options in this dialog box: Align Horizontal, Align Vertical, and Align Control Points. Choose Align Horizontal to align the nodes on a horizontal path from the first node chosen; choose Align Vertical to align the nodes on a vertical path from the first node chosen; or choose both Align Horizontal and Align Vertical to place the second selected node on top of the first node (the line between them may stick out). Choose Align Horizontal, Align Vertical, and Align Control Points to align the Bézier control handles with the first node selected.

Figure 7.17.
The Node Align
dialog box.

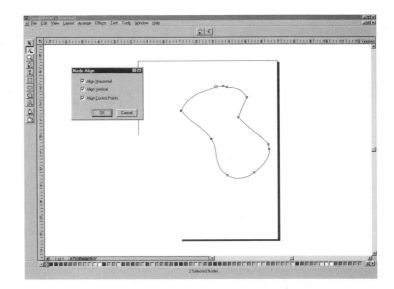

You can create other interesting effects by stretching a group of nodes. Figure 7.18 shows a word that has been converted to curves, and below that is the same word distorted with the node-stretching technique. This is a great way to make a logo more interesting.

Figure 7.18.
Distorting text by stretching groups of nodes.

## Stretching and Rotating Nodes

The Node Edit roll-up also provides a way to stretch and rotate individual nodes. The best way to explain this is to show a brief example. Follow these steps:

1. Draw a circle with the Ellipse tool, making sure to hold down the Ctrl key until after you let go of the mouse.
2. Convert the circle to curves using Arrange | Convert to Curves or CTRL+Q.
3. Select all of the nodes and click the Add (+) button in the Node Edit roll-up. You now have eight nodes.
4. Deselect all of the nodes and then reselect every other node so that you now have only four nodes selected.
5. Click the Stretch button and move the handles inward while holding down the Shift key.
6. Now click the Rotate button and rotate the handles 45 degrees.

Figures 7.19, 7.20 and 7.21 show the ellipse with eight nodes, the shape of the ellipse after stretching it, and finally the shape of the ellipse after rotating it.

*Figure 7.19.*
*An ellipse with eight*
*nodes (before it is*
*stretched and rotated).*

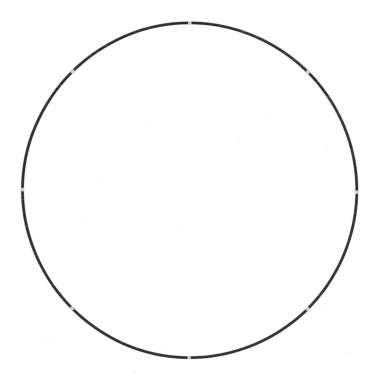

Figure 7.20.
The ellipse after stretching four nodes.

Figure 7.21.
The ellipse after stretching and rotating the four
nodes.

## Adding Line Segments

Line segments can be added to close a shape by clicking the button in the Node Edit roll-up. Figure 7.22 shows a curve before and after adding a line segment.

*Figure 7.22.*
*A curve before and after*
*adding a line segment.*

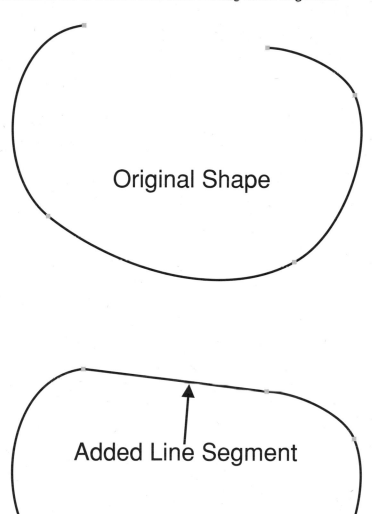

Original Shape

Added Line Segment

## Shaping Rectangles and Ellipses

When you use the Shape tool with rectangles and ellipses, you can produce drastically different results than you can with those same objects after they've been converted to curves. In all previous examples, you were told that these objects must first be converted to curves. In this section, the objects are modified first.

Create a rectangle by dragging out an area with the Rectangle tool. Switch to the Shape tool and click the node in the upper-left corner. Drag this node to the right and notice that the corners of the rectangle are now rounded. The status bar shows the corner radius of each corner. Note that this radius is distorted (as indicated in the status line) if the original rectangle is transformed in any way. To avoid this, the rectangle must be completely redrawn in the desired shape. Figure 7.23 shows four examples: a rectangle, the rectangle after its corners have been rounded, the rectangle stretched before its corners were rounded, and a rectangle that was redrawn to the same size as the stretched one and then had its corners rounded.

# Corel *TIP!*

By right-clicking the rectangle and choosing Properties from the menu, you can enter a numerical value for the roundness of the corners.

Depending on where you move the node, using the Shape tool on an ellipse can create either arcs or wedges. Each ellipse has just one node. It's found at the top for ellipses drawn from the top down and at the bottom for ellipses drawn from the bottom up.

Draw an ellipse with the Ellipse tool and then switch to the Shape tool. Select the ellipse with the Shape tool and then click on its node. Drag the node around the outside of the ellipse to change it into an arc. Drag the node around the inside of the ellipse to change it into the shape of a pie with a wedge cut out of it. Hold down the Ctrl key while dragging the node in order to constrain the node to angles that are multiples of the constrain angle set in Preferences. Figure 7.24 shows an ellipse before any changes have been made, the same ellipse changed into an arc, and the ellipse changed into a pie shape. The status bar indicates the angle of the arc or pie measured from the 3 o'clock position. The status bar also indicates "distorted" for a noncircular ellipse.

*Figure 7.23.*
*The effects of stretching*
*and rounding a rectangle*
*with the Shape tool.*

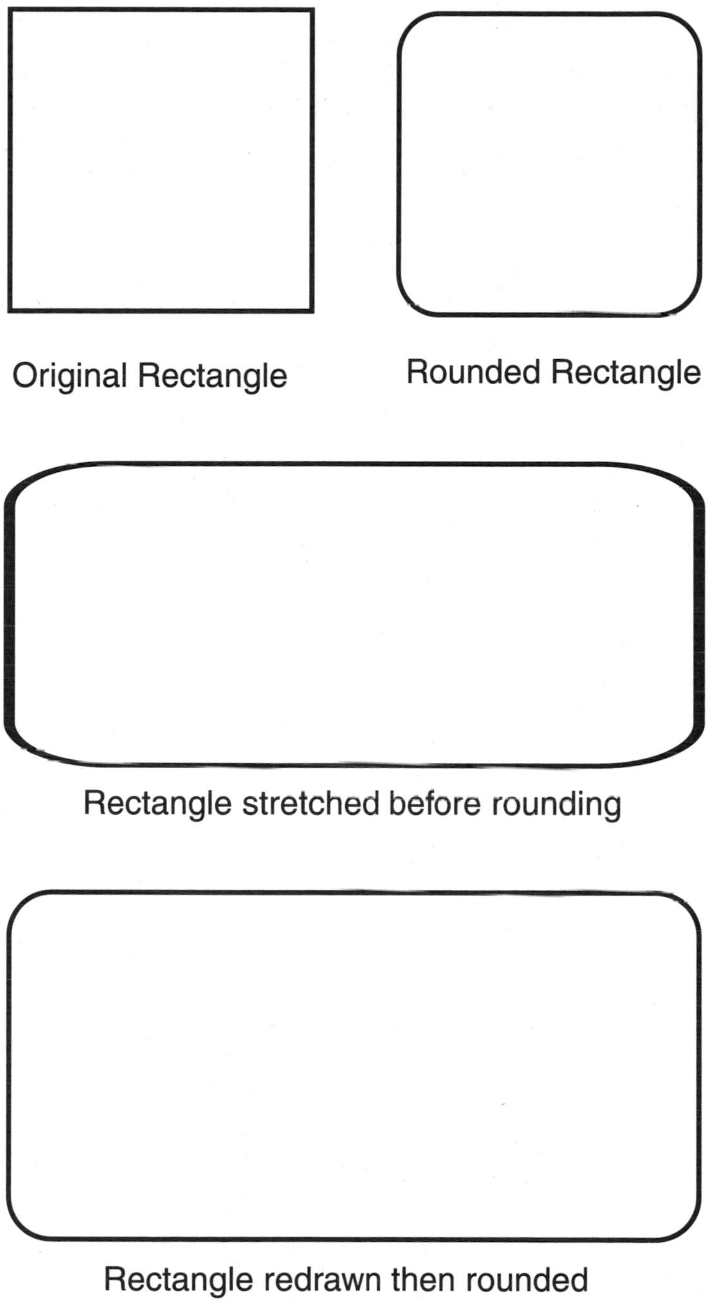

Original Rectangle     Rounded Rectangle

Rectangle stretched before rounding

Rectangle redrawn then rounded

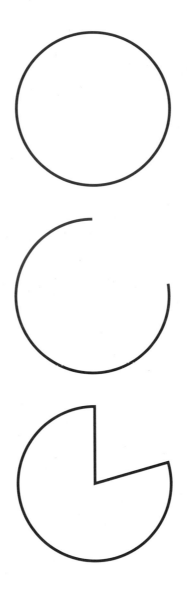

*Figure 7.24.*
*Using the Shape tool on an*
*ellipse to create an arc and*
*a wedge.*

# Corel *TIP!*

By right-clicking an ellipse and choosing Properties from the menu, you can type in values for the angles as well as specify whether you want a pie or arc shape.

## Shaping Polygons, Spirals, and Grids

Shaping polygons and stars can provide some incredible effects. These objects can have multiple sets of nodes depending on the complexity chosen when creating the object. (See Skill Session 13, "Polygon, Star, Spiral, and Grid Tools.") When one node of each set is moved, all other nodes in the set move similarly.

Let's start with a five-pointed star. Here are the steps to follow:

1. Select one of the inner nodes and pull it even with the outer nodes.
2. Pull the node in a counterclockwise rotation while keeping it even with the outer nodes.
3. Fill the object.

You should see something similar to the object shown in Figure 7.25.

*Figure 7.25.*
*The shape created from moving and rotating a node in a five-pointed star.*

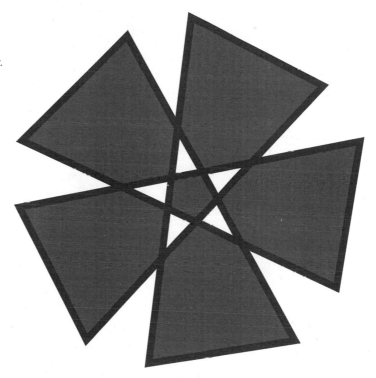

Now that you've tried modifying a simple polygon, try creating some shapes with more points and then modifying them in many different ways. Figure 7.26 shows several examples of objects created in this fashion.

Spirals have nodes at 90-degree increments. Therefore, there are four nodes for each complete rotation. Each of these nodes is a symmetrical node. Moving any one node has no effect on the other nodes; therefore, there are few special effects that can be created by editing these nodes. One interesting thing to do is to select all the nodes and convert all the curves to lines. Figure 7.27 shows the spiral before and after converting the curves to lines.

*Figure 7.26.*
*Shapes created by node-editing polygons.*

*Figure 7.27.*
*A spiral before and after converting the curves to lines.*

Original Spiral          Converted to Lines

Grids are nothing more than a group of objects (rectangles); therefore, they have no nodes. Each of the individual objects can be node-edited by clicking any one of them while holding down the Ctrl key. However, nothing can be done to the grid as a whole.

## Shaping Envelopes

The process of shaping envelopes (see Skill Session 29, "Enveloping") is similar to that of shaping other polygonal objects. You can move nodes by clicking and dragging them (like nodes in any other object). For any of the first three envelope types (line, single curve, and double curve), the Ctrl and Shift keys constrain the node you're moving:

- Hold down the Ctrl key to move both the selected node and its opposite node in the same direction.
- Hold down the Shift key to move the selected node in one direction and its opposite node in the opposite direction, both the same distance from their starting points.
- Hold down both the Ctrl and Shift keys to move either all four center nodes or all four corner nodes the same amount in opposite directions.

Figure 7.28 shows rectangles that have been modified with node movement, with the Ctrl key and node movement, with the Shift key and node movement, and with the Ctrl+Shift key combination and node movement.

*Figure 7.28.*
*Using the Ctrl and Shift keys to constrain node movement when shaping envelopes.*

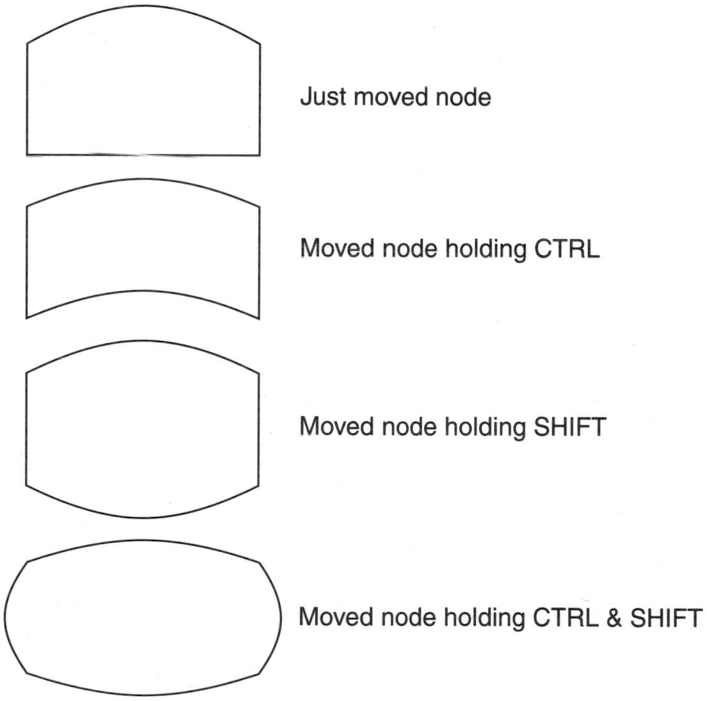

Just moved node

Moved node holding CTRL

Moved node holding SHIFT

Moved node holding CTRL & SHIFT

## Cropping Bitmaps

You can use the Shape tool to crop a bitmap. This should be done carefully because a cropped bitmap takes up the same amount of space on disk as an uncropped one. Sometimes the best method is to just rescan the bitmap until it's the correct size for the space.

When a bitmap is selected with the Shape tool, it has a node at each corner. These nodes can be selected and moved just as if the bitmap were a rectangle that had been converted to curves. Nodes can be added, reshaped, and modified just as any other nodes; therefore, you can create any shape you desire out of a bitmap. In a way, this is a way to manually PowerClip a bitmap.

Figure 7.29 shows a bitmap before and after it has been cropped. Usually, it is better to crop a bitmap when importing. This is discussed in Skill Session 46, "Cropping and Hiding Bitmaps."

*Figure 7.29.*
*Freda's ear gets cropped*
*out of the picture.*

Before     After

## Manually Kerning Text

You can kern text manually with the Shape tool. Enter a word of text and switch to the Shape tool. Select the object, and nodes will appear to the left of each character in the string. These nodes can be dragged in any direction, and the character will follow. To select more than one character, hold down the Shift key and click additional nodes, or draw a marquee box around all desired nodes.

It's usually a good idea to hold down the Ctrl key while you drag character nodes, because it constrains all movement to the baseline. Another option is to use the Text | Align to Baseline command after you kern the text, because this removes any vertical shifts that occur. The Ctrl key constraint applies even to text that has been fitted to a path.

You can also adjust text spacing by using the Shape tool in conjunction with →
and ↓. Click and move → to adjust the spacing between characters; hold down the

Ctrl key to adjust the spacing between words. Use ↓ to adjust the line spacing for Artistic text. Used in conjunction with the Shift key, the line spacing adjustment applies to Paragraph text. Ctrl+↓ adjusts the space between paragraphs.

## Editing Character Attributes

When a character's node is selected, the character's attributes can be changed as if they were a separate object. Click a color in the color palette with the primary mouse button to change the character's color. Use the secondary mouse button to change the character's outline color. Double-click the node to bring up the Character Attribute dialog box. (See Skill Session 37, "Changing Text Attributes.")

## The Knife Tool

The Knife tool provides a quick way to cut objects apart. Everywhere you click a line with the Knife tool, the line apart will be cut apart. Right-click the Knife tool and the Tool Properties dialog box appears, as shown in Figure 7.30.

*Figure 7.30.*
*The Knife Tool Properties*
*dialog box.*

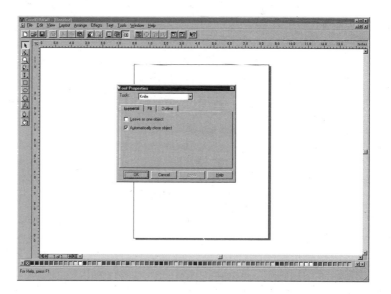

The Leave as one object option leaves objects combined rather than automatically breaking them apart when checked. The Automatically close object option draws a line segment connecting the "knifed" nodes; therefore, you get a closed shape when this option is checked.

With a straight line, one click will divide the line into two separate objects. On an ellipse, two separate clicks will divide the ellipse into two arcs.

# The Eraser tool

The Eraser tool allows you to erase part of a closed object. As you click and drag your cursor over a filled object, an area around your cursor will be erased. Right click the Eraser tool and the Tool Properties dialog box appears, as shown in Figure 7.31.

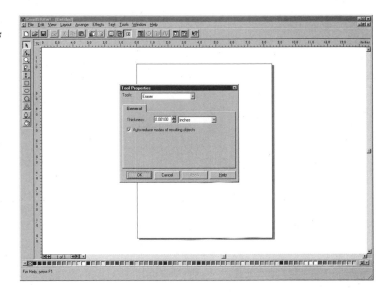

Figure 7.31.
*The Eraser Tool Properties dialog box.*

The Thickness control sets the size of the area erased by the tool. By checking the Auto-reduce nodes of resulting objects option, the number of nodes surrounding the erased area will be minimized. Without checking this option, you will typically receive a large number of nodes.

Basically, CorelDRAW is using the technology in the contour feature to contour the line you are drawing and then to trim that shape from the original object. Because all of this is done on-the-fly, it is somewhat invisible. Figure 7.32 shows an ellipse before and after a "bite" is erased from it.

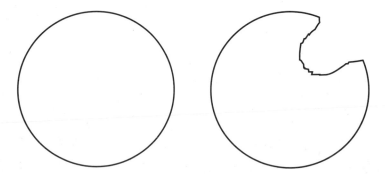

Figure 7.32.
*An ellipse before and after a portion of it is erased.*

# 8

# The Zoom Tool

When you use the Zoom tool in conjunction with the scroll bars, you can look at a drawing from almost any view imaginable. You can zoom many ways—the Zoom tool actually has six different variants. You can zoom in as tight as the screen width (approximately .0035 inches), and you can zoom out to show as much width as 165 feet. (These numbers are approximate and might vary slightly from system to system.)

## Zoom Tool Properties

Right-click the Zoom icon to get the Zoom Tool Properties dialog box shown in Figure 8.1. Here you will find several ways to customize the functionality of the Zoom tools.

The right mouse button can be used in two different ways when the Zoom tool is selected. It can be used to perform the function specified in the Tools Options Advanced dialog box, or it can be used to zoom out, which is the default function.

By checking the Use traditional zoom flyout check box, the flyout in the toolbox will behave as in previous versions of CorelDRAW. Because the functionality of the Zoom tools has changed dramatically, users of previous versions might find this method more comfortable to work with.

Figure 8.1.
The Zoom Tool Properties
dialog box.

The Edit Resolution button brings up the screen shown in Figure 8.2. The default values for our system were set to 1022 horizontal and 1040 vertical. But by changing them to 816 horizontal and 876 vertical, the on-screen rulers measure exactly 1 inch in both directions. By making this adjustment, the Zoom Actual Size command will be accurate.

Figure 8.2.
The Edit Resolution
dialog box.

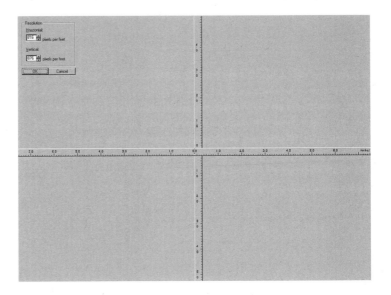

## Zoom Tools

The Zoom tools have changed quite a bit from previous versions of CorelDRAW. Many of the tools are not part of the flyout in the toolbox anymore. The toolbox only gives access to the Zoom In tool and the Panning tool, as shown in Figure 8.3. The other Zoom tools can be accessed through the Zoom toolbar shown in Figure 8.4, which can be placed on any edge of the screen or can be free-floating. Skill Session 4, "Customizing and Setting Preferences," describes this functionality.

Other ways to access the Zoom tools are through the View Manager (this is described later in this skill session) or by selecting the Zoom tool in the toolbox and then right-clicking; you will then be presented with a menu of zoom options from which to choose. (This is also described later in this skill session.)

*Figure 8.3.*
*The Zoom tool flyout.*

*Figure 8.4.*
*The Zoom toolbar.*

## Zoom In

Using the Zoom In tool is similar to doing marquee-selection with the Pick tool. When you click the Zoom tool, the first button on the flyout is the Zoom In tool. Click this tool or use the F2 keyboard shortcut; the cursor changes to a magnifying glass. Drag a marquee rectangle around the area to be zoomed, and the screen is redrawn showing just the marquee-selected area. Figure 8.5 shows a screen before being zoomed. Figure 8.6 shows the marquee rectangle being drawn around the objects. Figure 8.7 shows the screen after the zoom. This tool appears on both the Zoom flyout and the Zoom toolbar.

*Figure 8.5.*
*An unzoomed view.*

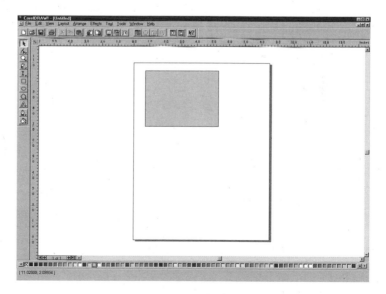

Figure 8.6.
*Marquee-selecting the area on which to zoom in.*

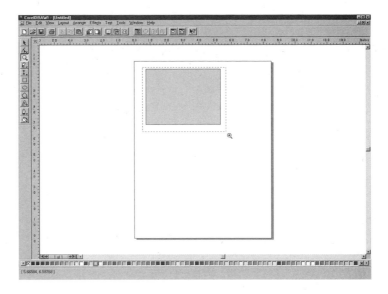

Figure 8.7.
*The zoomed view.*

# Zoom Out

The Zoom Out tool returns the screen to the view displayed before the last Zoom In. To use Zoom Out, select the Zoom tool from the flyout and then right-click in the drawing window and choose Zoom Out. You can also choose the icon from the Zoom toolbar. The keyboard shortcut is F3. If you've just used one of the other Zoom tools, this tool zooms the display out to show twice the area that was previously showing.

## Zoom Actual Size

Zoom Actual Size (1:1) attempts to zoom so that the objects on-screen are exactly the size shown in the status bar. To use Zoom Actual Size, select the Zoom tool from the flyout, right-click in the drawing window, and then choose Zoom 1:1. You can also choose the icon from the Zoom toolbar. CorelDRAW does this by attempting to guess the resolution (in dots per inch) of the display on which it's being run. You can't count on this, but you are able to change the resolution to more closely match your display. To do this, use the Zoom Tool Properties dialog box discussed earlier in this skill session. Figure 8.8 shows the object from Figure 8.5 after Zoom Actual Size has been chosen.

*Figure 8.8.*
*Using Zoom Actual Size.*

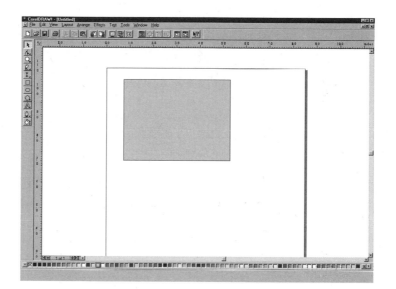

## Zoom To Selection

Zoom To Selection zooms to show all the objects that are currently selected at the largest size possible. To use Zoom To Selection, select the Zoom tool from the flyout, right-click in the drawing window, and then choose Zoom To Selection. You can also choose the icon from the Zoom toolbar. The keyboard shortcut is Shift+F2. This can also be done rather easily by using the marquee tool, but it takes one less step to accomplish the task with the keyboard shortcut. Notice in Figure 8.9 how the screen is zoomed to just outside the selection handles.

*Figure 8.9.*
*Using Zoom To Selection.*

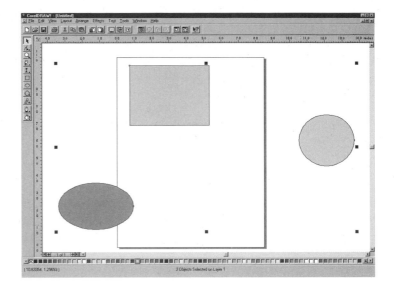

## Zoom To Fit

Zoom To Fit zooms to show all the objects in the drawing. To use Zoom To Fit, select the Zoom tool from the flyout, right-click in the drawing window, and then choose Zoom To Fit. You can also choose the icon from the Zoom toolbar. The keyboard shortcut is F4. This can produce the same effect as the Zoom In tool when there are just several small objects to be enlarged. It can also be very handy for finding objects that have disappeared from view, either because the screen is zoomed in very tight or the objects are off the page. The Zoom To Fit tool doesn't necessarily zoom in or zoom out; it always changes the view to fit all the objects on one screen. Figure 8.10 shows the effect of the Zoom To Fit tool when there are several objects outside the defined page.

## Zoom To Page

Zoom To Page zooms so that the defined page fills the whole screen. To use Zoom To Page, select the Zoom tool from the flyout, right-click in the drawing window, and then choose Zoom To Page. You can also choose the icon from the Zoom toolbar. The keyboard shortcut is Shift+F4. Again, it doesn't zoom to any exact size, but rather the page size as defined by Page Setup. If you display the page frame, you'll find this concept a little easier to understand. Figure 8.11 shows a screen with a couple of objects displayed in the middle of a page. After you choose Zoom To Page, the screen looks like Figure 8.12.

*Figure 8.10.*
*Using Zoom To Fit.*

*Figure 8.11.*
*Before Zoom To Page.*

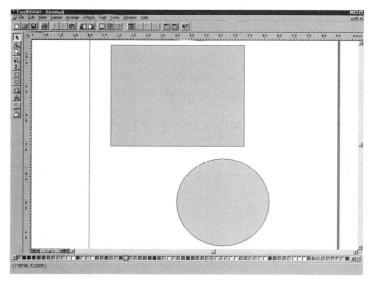

Figure 8.12.
*After Zoom To Page.*

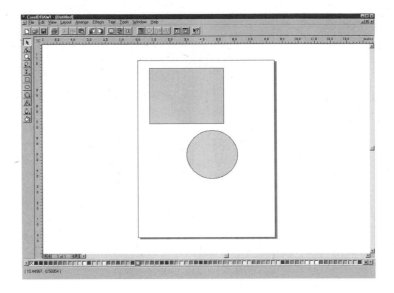

## Panning

The Panning tool allows you to manual pan the screen to a desired location. You first select the Pan icon from the Zoom flyout. Drag the cursor in the direction you wish to pan. The cursor will leave a temporary path behind it so that you see which direction your screen will pan. Once you release the mouse button, the screen redraws in its new position. Figure 8.12 shows the screen before panning. Figure 8.13 shows the Pan icon being dragged down most of the length of the page, and Figure 8.14 shows the screen after panning.

Figure 8.13.
*Dragging the Pan icon in the direction you wish to pan.*

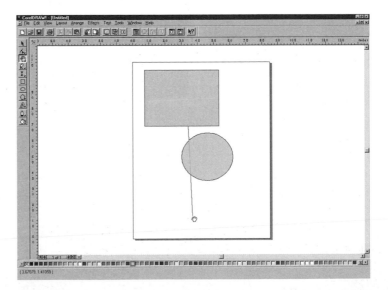

Figure 8.14.
*The screen view after panning.*

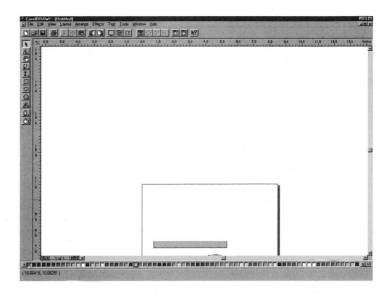

## View Manager

The View Manager gives you a way to save various views of a document so that you can easily switch between them. This is different than having multiple windows of the same document open. To open the View Manager, choose View Manager from the Tools menu or double-click the Zoom tool. An example of the View Manager is shown in Figure 8.15.

Figure 8.15.
*The View Manager.*

When you've found a view that you would like to save for future reference, simply choose New from the View Manager flyout menu, and a new view will be listed. Use the Rename command in the flyout to give the new view a name other than the default. As you can see in Figure 8.15, three views (each with custom names) have been created. By selecting Switch To View or double-clicking the view name, you are able to switch to the selected view.

## Right Mouse Button Zoom Options

One of the most flexible ways to zoom is by selecting the Zoom tool in the toolbox and then right-clicking an object. A menu will appear that is similar to the one shown in Figure 8.16. This lists each of the Zoom tools as well as some predefined zoom levels on the Zoom flyout menu. Select the zoom you want, and your screen is updated. Note that if you choose Zoom In, you still need to marquee the area you want zoomed.

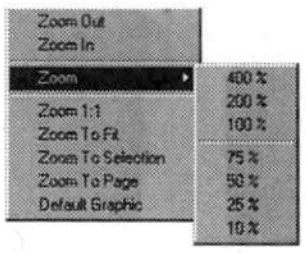

*Figure 8.16.*
*Right mouse button zoom*
*options.*

# 9

# The Pencil Tool

The Pencil tool is actually two different types of pencils. The flyout menu that contains these tools appears when you press and hold down the left mouse button while selecting the Pencil tool, as shown in Figure 9.1. You can then select either of the tools by dragging the cursor to the desired tool and releasing the mouse button.

*Figure 9.1.
The Pencil tool flyout
menu.*

# Pencil Tool Properties

Right-click the Pencil tool and select Properties from the menu to get the Pencil Tool Properties dialog box shown in Figure 9.2. The General tab contains five settings for customizing the behavior of the Pencil tools.

*Figure 9.2.
The Pencil Tool Properties
dialog box.*

## Freehand Tracking

The number you enter in the Freehand Tracking parameters box determines how closely CorelDRAW tracks your freehand drawing when it calculates the Bézier nodes used in the object you draw. The lower the number you enter, the greater the number of nodes CorelDRAW will create, because CorelDRAW tries to recreate your freehand line as close as it can to your intended shape. Using a higher number causes the shape to be drawn more loosely, and therefore with fewer nodes. The minimum setting is 1, the maximum setting is 10, and the default setting is 5.

## Autotrace Tracking

Setting the Autotrace Tracking parameters box follows the same logic as setting the Freehand Tracking parameters box, but Autotrace Tracking applies to autotracing bitmaps.

## Corner Threshold

The number you enter in the Corner Threshold parameters box determines whether smooth nodes or cusps are used when you're drawing freehand or autotracing. The minimum setting is 1 and the maximum setting is 10. The lower the number, the more cusp nodes used; the higher the number, the more smooth nodes used. The default setting is 5.

## Straight Line Threshold

Setting the Straight Line Threshold parameters box follows the same logic as setting the Corner Threshold parameters box. When you're drawing a straight line with the freehand tool, the smaller the number in the parameters box, the more curve nodes used to represent the line. The larger the number in the parameters box, the more straight lines nodes used to represent the line.

## Auto-Join

The setting in the Auto-Join parameters box determines how close a line's beginning node must be to its end node before you can join the two nodes, and thus creating a closed object. An example of this is drawing a freehand circle. Use the Pencil tool to draw a circle. When you reach the beginning point of the circle, you want the last node to join with the first node to form a closed object—the circle. If the last node doesn't join with the first node, you'll have an open path. An open path can't be filled with a color, and therefore your circle will only be the outline of a circle.

The lower the number you enter in the Auto-Join parameters box, the more precise you need to be when you move the last node close to the beginning node. A higher number enables you to be less precise.

# Freehand Curves

The first tool on the flyout is the Freehand Pencil tool (keyboard shortcut, F5). When this tool is selected, the status bar says "Drawing in Freehand Mode on Layer X" and the cursor appears. By holding down the left mouse button and dragging the mouse in various directions, you create a line that follows the path of the mouse. As soon as you release the mouse button, the line ends. The number of nodes on the new line is related to the accuracy specified in the General section of the Pencil Tool Properties dialog box, the length of the line, and the number of directional changes. When using the Freehand Pencil tool, you normally get more nodes than you need. Therefore, it is a good idea to use the Shape tool to clean up the curves you've drawn. This is described in Skill Session 7, "The Shape Tool." Figure 9.3 shows a line drawn with the Pencil tool in freehand mode.

*Figure 9.3.*
*A line drawn with the*
*Pencil tool in freehand*
*mode.*

You can draw straight lines by left-clicking the starting point of a line and then left-clicking the endpoint of the line. If you hold down the Ctrl key while drawing a straight line, you will constrain it to a multiple of the angle that's set in Tools | Options | General tab's Constrain Angle option. Figure 9.4 shows two straight lines, one of which is constrained with the Ctrl key so that it is at a 45-degree angle.

*Figure 9.4.*
*A straight line and a*
*constrained straight line.*

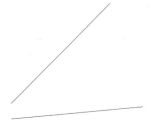

The Freehand Pencil tool can also be used to autotrace bitmaps. If a bitmap is selected when the Freehand Pencil tool is chosen, the Freehand Pencil tool is used as an autotrace tool and the status line reads something similar to "Autotracing on Layer 1." The trace created is very crude, and you normally will be better off tracing it using another method. For more information about using this and other methods for autotracing bitmaps, see Skill Session 47, "Manual Tracing Versus Autotracing."

# Corel *TIP!*

If you hold down the Shift key while drawing a line, you can retrace over the line and erase what you have previously drawn.

The second tool on the flyout is the Bézier tool. Bézier mode enables you to create lines by connecting dots. This method gives you complete control over where each node is placed, and therefore the lines tend to be less complex and more accurate. If you have never used the Bézier tool, it might be difficult to get the hang of it. Click the left mouse button at each place you want a node to appear. If you want to shape the curve while placing the nodes, hold down the left mouse button and Bézier handles will appear. As long as you continue to hold down the mouse button, you can make adjustments to the handles by dragging them in any direction. Figure 9.5 shows a curve being created with the Bézier tool.

*Figure 9.5.*
*Creating a curve with the*
*Bézier tool.*

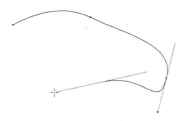

Another way to use the Bézier tool is to just click everywhere you want a node. All the lines will be straight, so your objects will appear boxy. After drawing the lines, you can then use the Shape tool to edit the lines to get the shape you want. Figure 9.6 shows an original shape drawn with the Bézier tool and then the modified version after using the Shape tool.

The Bézier tool is very helpful when you are manually tracing a bitmap. Just make sure that the bitmap isn't selected when you select the Bézier tool. Otherwise, the Bézier tool will automatically try to trace the object as described with the Free-hand Pencil tool.

*Figure 9.6.*
*Creating shapes with the*
*Bézier tool.*

# 10

# The Dimension Tool

The Dimension tool gives you four tools for drawing dimension lines, which are special lines that contain a measurement value as text. You'll also find tools for drawing callouts and for connecting objects.

## Dimension Tool Properties

The Dimension Tool Properties dialog box is accessed by selecting the Dimension tool, right-clicking it, and then choosing Properties from the drop-down menu. The Dimension Tool Properties dialog box is shown in Figure 10.1.

Figure 10.1.
The Dimension Tool
Properties dialog box.

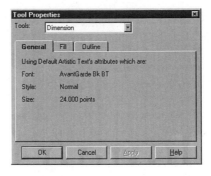

## Dimension Lines

Dimension lines enable you to assign various types of measurements to objects. This comes in handy when you're working with CAD-like drawings that need to show the sizes of objects. There are four types of dimension lines, which are used for drawing horizontal, vertical, diagonal, and angular lines. If you use the wrong type of dimension line to draw a line, you'll get a dimension of zero. For example, if you use the Horizontal Dimension tool to draw a vertical line, the value will read zero because there's no horizontal dimension. Diagonal dimension lines drawn with the Diagonal Dimension tool can be constrained to the constrain angle with the Ctrl key. The main differences between dimension lines and regular lines are that there are tick marks to indicate the endpoints of the dimension line, and the measurement of the line itself appears in the middle of the line. Figure 10.2 shows a sample drawing with each of the four types of dimension lines.

Figure 10.2.
A sample drawing with
corresponding dimension
lines.

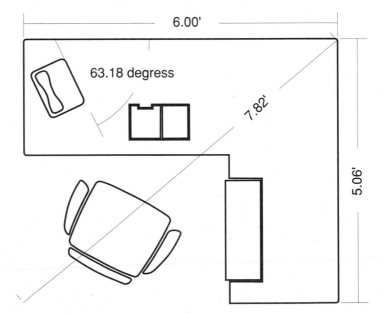

Creating horizontal, vertical, and diagonal dimension lines is a three-click process. First, click where the line begins. Next, click where the line ends. And finally, click in the middle of the line where the text is to appear. To measure an object accurately, use the Snap To Objects command in the Layout menu. This causes the dimension line to snap to the nodes of the object being measured. The dimension measurement can be scaled to many popular measuring systems using the Layout Grid and Ruler Setup, Edit Scale dialog box. For more information on choosing the dimension format, see Skill Session 19, "Grid and Ruler Setup." The text is displayed according to the rules set in the Linear Dimensions roll-up, which is shown in Figures 10.3 and 10.4. The shortcut key for the Linear Dimensions roll-up is Alt+F2.

*Figure 10.3.*
*The Linear Dimensions*
*roll-up—Units.*

*Figure 10.4.*
*The Linear Dimensions*
*roll-up—Text.*

The Units portion of the roll-up enables you to choose which style of numbers you want to use. You can choose from Decimal, Fractional, U.S. Engineering, and U.S. Architectural. You can also specify the number of decimal places and the units being measured. The Show Units check box controls whether or not the text for the units are included in the dimension line. The Dynamic Dimensioning check box, at the bottom of the roll-up, allows the dimension measurement to change when the object is resized when checked.

The Text portion of the roll-up (click the second tab) enables you to add a prefix or suffix (or both) to the text part of the dimension lines. It also has five buttons you can use to specify how the text is positioned. The text can appear above, below, or in line with the dimension line. You can also choose whether the text is rotated with the line or is always horizontal.

Dimension-line text can be formatted just like any other text. Select the text by clicking it. The status bar indicates that Control text is selected. Once it has been selected, it can be edited just like any other Artistic text. If you click and drag the text to another location, the lines will adjust to meet with the text.

The dimension line can be linked to an object if you have Snap To Objects enabled while you draw the line. As you're drawing, you'll see little blue rectangles appear when you snap to a point. You can't establish this link after you draw the line. The snap point for the dimension line can be the end of a line, a corner of a rectangle, a node on a multi-segment line, the center of a bounding box, or the midpoint of a rectangle side. The dimension is updated any time the object is moved, scaled, or rotated as well as any time changes are made to the snap point.

# Corel*CAUTION!*

The link between an object and an associated dimension line can be broken by using the Arrange | Separate command. If a snap point is deleted from an object, the associated dimension line is also deleted. Some operations such as adding perspective, applying an envelope, and applying an extrusion, cannot be performed on objects that have associated dimension lines.

Angular dimension lines work slightly differently than the other dimension lines. They require four clicks. The first click is in the center of the angle; the next click is one end of the angle; the third click is the other end of the angle, and the last click is where the text will appear. Angular dimension lines also have a different roll-up, as shown in Figures 10.5 and 10.6. The options on the Angular Dimensions roll-up work identically to the Linear Dimensions roll-up described previously.

*Figure 10.5.*
*The Angular Dimensions*
*roll-up—Units.*

*Figure 10.6.*
*The Angular Dimensions*
*roll-up—Text.*

## Callouts

Callouts are created with the Callout tool, the fourth button in the Dimension flyout. This tool links a line and associated text to an object. If the point to which the callout is connected is moved, the callout moves with it.

To create a callout, make sure that Snap To Objects is selected. Click once where the callout should start (the object being pointed to), click a second time where you want an elbow, and click a third time where you want to place the text. If you don't want to have an elbow in the line, just double-click as the second step. After the last click, you can type in the desired text. Figure 10.7 shows a callout with an elbow in the line. Once you have drawn the line, you can move any of the three points (beginning, elbow, and end) with the Shape tool.

*Figure 10.7.*
*An example of a callout.*

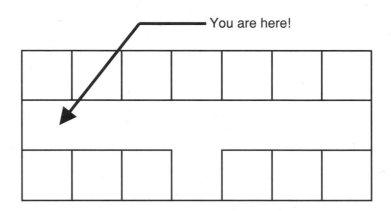

## Connector Line Tool Properties

The Connector Line Tool Properties dialog box is accessed by right-clicking the Connector Line icon and choosing Properties from the menu. (See Figure 10.8.)

*Figure 10.8.*
*The Connector Line Tool*
*Properties dialog box.*

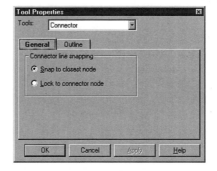

There are two options to choose from for connector line snapping. The first is "Snap to closest node." This means that the line will be connected to an object but will move its endpoint to the closest node, producing the shortest path between two connected objects. If you choose "Lock to connector node," then the line will stay connected to the same node at all times. Examples of each of these types of connector nodes is shown in Figure 10.9.

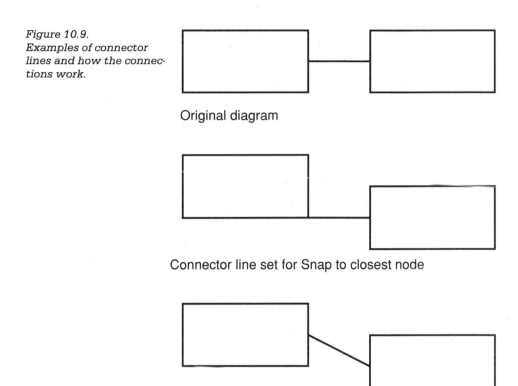

Figure 10.9.
*Examples of connector lines and how the connections work.*

Original diagram

Connector line set for Snap to closest node

Connector line set for Lock to connector node

## Connector Lines

Connector lines are used to link a line dynamically between two objects. If Snap To Objects is turned off, then the lines will behave as standard straight lines. But with Snap To Objects turned on, the lines will attach themselves to objects. A blue square appears on the object when the line snaps after you let go of the mouse button. When the control objects are moved, the lines automatically move with them.

# 11

# The Rectangle Tool

The Rectangle tool is used to create rectangles, squares, rounded rectangles, and rounded squares. When you use it with the Ctrl key and the Shift key, you can create many different effects.

## Rectangle Tool Properties

Right-click the Rectangle tool icon and choose Properties from the menu to get the Rectangle Tool Properties dialog box, as shown in Figure 11.1. This dialog box allows you to adjust the Corner Roundness setting for any rectangle drawn. If the setting is 0, perfectly square corners are drawn. If the setting is 100 (the maximum), ellipses are drawn. The number in the setting is a percentage of the width that will be rounded.

*Figure 11.1.*
*The Rectangle Tool*
*Properties dialog box.*

## Rectangles

Use the Rectangle tool in its standard configuration to draw rectangles of any size and shape. Hold down the left mouse button, drag the cursor from one corner of the rectangle to the opposite corner, and then release the mouse button. The status line indicates the height, width, and center location of the rectangle. Figure 11.2 shows a rectangle.

*Figure 11.2.*
*Drawing a rectangle with*
*an origin where the*
*guidelines meet.*

Although you can create squares by using the standard Rectangle tool and watching the status line closely, it is much easier to hold down the Ctrl key along with the left mouse button while dragging out the appropriate square. Be sure to release the mouse button before the Ctrl key. If you release the Ctrl key first, the Rectangle tool creates a standard rectangle instead. Figure 11.3 shows a square.

You can use the Rectangle tool in conjunction with the Shift key to produce yet another set of effects. The Shift key causes the rectangle or square to be drawn from the center out (rather than from corner to corner). Try this by drawing a rectangle while holding down the Shift key and dragging the cursor in any direction. Note that the rectangle's center is exactly where the cursor was when the mouse button was first pressed, and the vertical and horizontal movements are symmetrical on each side of the center point. Figures 11.4 and 11.5 were drawn in the same manner as Figures 11.2 and 11.3, except that the Shift key was held down.

*Figure 11.3.*
*Drawing a square with an*
*origin where the guide-*
*lines meet by using the*
*Ctrl key.*

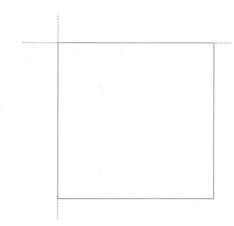

*Figure 11.4.*
*Drawing a rectangle with*
*a center where the*
*guidelines meet.*

*Figure 11.5.*
*Drawing a square with a*
*center where the guide-*
*lines meet by using the*
*Shift key.*

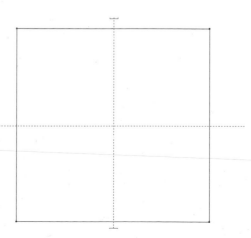

You can create rounded rectangles and squares by using the Shape tool in conjunction with a pre-existing rectangle or square. This is covered in depth in Skill Session 7, "The Shape Tool." Figure 11.6 shows examples of these shapes.

*Figure 11.6.*
*Drawing a square and a*
*rectangle with rounded*
*corners.*

## Exact Sizing and Placement

The Transform roll-up enables you to precisely size and place the object after you have drawn it. Unfortunately, there's no way to specify the size of an object before it's drawn. You might want to carefully monitor the status bar as the object is being drawn because it will indicate the size and placement of the object. Guidelines can also be very useful for placing and sizing objects. See Skill Session 26, "Transform," for more information on the Transform roll-up and Skill Session 20, "Guidelines," for more information on guidelines.

# 12

# The Ellipse Tool

You use the Ellipse tool to create ellipses, circles, arcs, and wedges. With a little of your ingenuity, the Ellipse tool is also very useful for creating many free-form shapes.

## Ellipse Tool Properties

Right-click the Ellipse tool and choose Properties from the menu to get the Ellipse Tool Properties dialog box, as shown in Figure 12.1. Here you can enter values for the angles of ellipses, pies, and arcs.

If you select the Ellipse option button, the angles remain at zero. If either of the angles are changed, they automatically return to zero the next time the dialog box is opened. If you select either the Pie or Arc option button, you can enter any angle between 0 and 360 degrees. The 0 and 360 degree points are at 3 o'clock; the 90 degree point is at six o'clock; the 180 degree point is at 9 o'clock, and the 270 degree point is at 12 o'clock. You can also select whether the line runs clockwise or counterclockwise between the two angles.

As an example, if you were to enter 90 and 180 for the starting and ending angles respectively, an arc or pie could cover either 90 degrees or 270 degrees, depending on whether you select clockwise or counterclockwise.

*Figure 12.1.*
*The Ellipse Tool Properties*
*dialog box.*

## Ellipses

To draw an ellipse, click the Ellipse tool, hold down the left mouse button, and drag from one corner of the ellipse to the opposite corner. While you hold the mouse button down, the status bar indicates the height, width, starting point, current point, and center location of the ellipse. After you release the mouse button, the status bar shows the height, width, and center location only. Figure 12.2 shows an ellipse being drawn, and Figure 12.3 shows the ellipse after the mouse button has been released. Notice the changes in the status bar.

*Figure 12.2.*
*The status bar while an*
*ellipse is being drawn.*

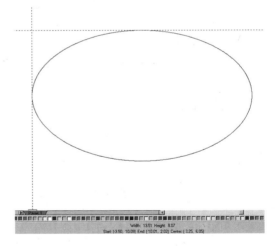

## Corel *NOTE!*

> Ellipses, circles, arcs, and wedges are all surrounded by an imaginary rectangle that is tangent to each of the extreme points.

Just as with the Rectangle tool, you can constrain theEllipse tool to fully symmetrical objects (that is, circles) by holding down the Ctrl key. Remember not to release the Ctrl key until after you release the mouse button, otherwise the object might revert to an ellipse. Figure 12.4 shows a circle.

*Figure 12.3.*
*The completed ellipse.*
*Notice that the status bar*
*has changed.*

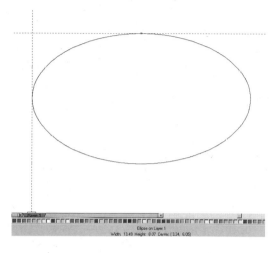

*Figure 12.4.*
*Drawing a circle with an*
*origin where the guide-*
*lines meet.*

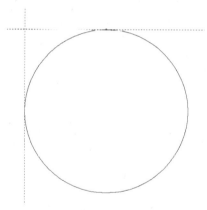

You can use the Shift key to draw ellipses and circles from the center out, rather than from corner to corner. In order to do this, hold down the Shift key while dragging the cursor from the center point outward in any direction. All movement in either the horizontal or vertical direction is mirrored on the other side of the center point. Release the mouse button and then release the Shift key. For a circle, hold down both the Ctrl key and the Shift key while dragging outward from the center point. Figure 12.5 shows an ellipse drawn with the same starting and end points as the one in Figure 12.3, and Figure 12.6 shows a circle drawn with the same starting and end points as the one in Figure 12.4. Notice the differences between drawing these objects with the Shift key and drawing them without it.

You can create arcs and wedges from circles and ellipses by using the Shape tool. First draw the appropriate shape with the Ellipse tool. Then, switch to the Shape tool and adjust the node to make either an arc or a wedge. See Skill Session 7, "The Shape Tool," for more information about how to create these shapes. Also note that this can be done in the Object Properties dialog box, which is available by right-clicking the object and choosing Properties from the menu. Figure 12.7 shows an example of each.

*Figure 12.5.*
*Drawing an ellipse with a*
*center where the guide-*
*lines meet by using the*
*Shift key.*

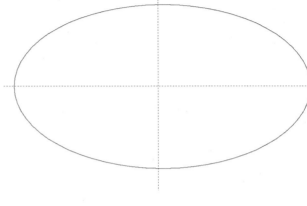

*Figure 12.6.*
*Drawing a circle with a*
*center where the guide-*
*lines meet by using the*
*Ctrl and Shift keys.*

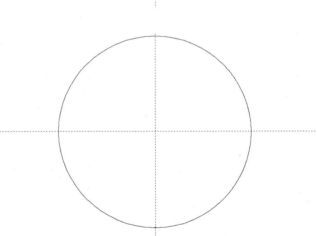

You can also use the Ellipse tool to create objects of a more free-form nature. This tool creates objects that are much smoother than those drawn freehand with the Pencil tool. First, draw an ellipse that's approximately the size and shape of your desired object. Then, convert the ellipse to curves (Ctrl+Q) and switch to the Shape tool. Use the Shape tool to add and place nodes until the object is the correct size and shape. See Project 3, "Drawing with Ellipses," for an example of how to do this.

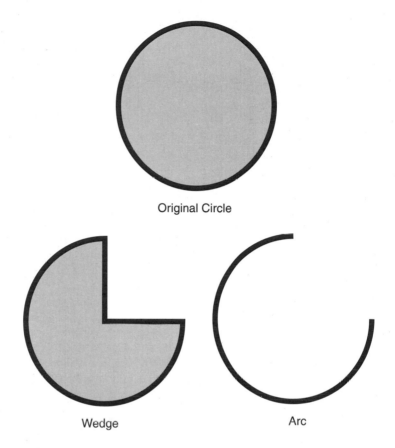

*Figure 12.7.*
*A pie wedge and an arc*
*created from a circle.*

Original Circle

Wedge

Arc

## Exact Sizing and Placement

It is sometimes very important to know the exact radius and center of a circle. Because CorelDRAW doesn't provide this capability directly, you must perform some tricks to achieve the same results. The best way to do this is with a good set of guidelines and a well-defined grid. The most accurate way to draw circles is from the center out, with the center point either at the intersection of two guide-lines or at a well-spaced grid point. Place a guideline at the correct radius, and—voila!—a perfectly sized and placed circle. Ellipses are much more difficult, because there's no real way to know where the foci are located and what the radii are. If the circle or ellipse is drawn but not correctly located, use the Transform roll-up to put the object at the proper position. This is described in Skill Session 26, "Transform."

# 13

# Polygon, Star, Spiral, and Grid Tools

The Polygon, Star, Spiral, and Grid tools are new to CorelDRAW 6. They provide a easy way to create shapes that previously have been very difficult to create.

To access the flyout for these new tools, click and hold down the Polygon tool icon in the toolbox. From the flyout, choose the tool you want to use. Figure 13.1 shows the Polygon flyout.

*Figure 13.1.*
*The Polygon, Spiral,*
*and Grid flyout.*

## Polygon Tool

The Polygon tool not only allows you to draw polygons, but it also allows you to draw stars. Before you can draw a polygon or star, right-click the Polygon tool. A small menu will appear. Choose Properties from the menu to bring up the Tool Properties dialog box. The dialog box lets you choose between drawing a polygon, a star, or a polygon as a star. Figure 13.2 shows the Tool Properties dialog box with all its options.

*Figure 13.2.*
*The Tool Properties*
*dialog box.*

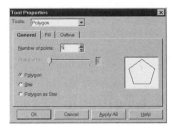

## The Basic Polygon Tool

Let's begin with the basic Polygon tool. By definition, a *polygon* is a closed plane figure bounded by three or more line segments. When you open the Tool Properties dialog box, you can choose the number of points to assign to the polygon. The default is five points. Think of points as the number of sides to the polygon. You can change the number of points by entering the number in the Number of Points parameters box.

You could enter the number three in the parameters box and draw a triangle polygon. Practice drawing polygons using different point settings. The actual method for drawing polygons is to click and drag just as you do when drawing rectangles and ellipses. Holding down the Ctrl key will constrain the polygon to equal sides.

After you have drawn a polygon, you can change its basic shape dramatically by node editing it. This is done differently than the method used for normal shapes. You can only move one node or two adjacent nodes (on the same line) at a time with the Shape tool. While this may seem to be a limitation—it isn't, as the skill session will show.

Figure 13.3 shows many variations on the basic polygon. An explanation of the methods used to create the different polygons is described in the following list:

| Row | Description of the Shape |
| --- | --- |
| 1 | A basic 5-sided polygon. |
| | A 10-sided polygon. |
| | A 15-sided polygon. |
| | A 25-sided polygon (notice the number of nodes on this polygon). |
| 2 | A basic 5-sided polygon that has been changed by dragging one node toward the center using the Shape tool. |
| | A 10-sided polygon changed by dragging one node toward the center using the Shape tool. |

A 15-sided polygon changed by dragging one node toward the center using the Shape tool.

A 25-sided polygon changed by dragging one node toward the center using the Shape tool.

3    A basic 5-sided polygon that has been changed by dragging one node toward the center using the Shape tool with a rotating motion.

A 10-sided polygon that has been changed by dragging one node toward the center using the Shape tool with a rotating motion.

A 15-sided polygon that has been changed by dragging one node toward the center using the Shape tool with a rotating motion.

A 25-sided polygon that has been changed by dragging one node toward the center using the Shape tool with a rotating motion.

*Figure 13.3.*
*Basic polygons and*
*their variations.*

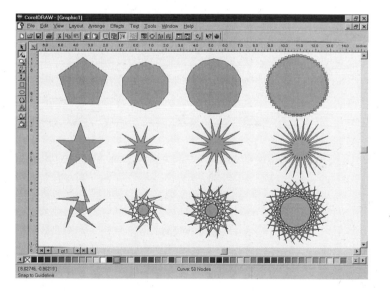

## The Polygon as Star Tool

Checking the Polygon as Star option in the Tool Properties dialog box lets you draw star-shaped polygons. The Sharpness slider control setting determines the shape of the star—it is activated when you choose the Polygon as Star option. The amount of sharpness you apply controls the shape of the star. The number of points assigned to the star also affects the appearance of the star shape.

Figure 13.4 shows the Tool Properties dialog box with Polygon as Star checked and the Sharpness control set to 75. The preview box shows the effect the sharpness control has on the basic five point polygon shape.

*Figure 13.4.*
*The Tool Properties dialog*
*box with Polygon as Star*
*checked and Sharpness*
*set to 75.*

Just as you discovered using the basic polygon, the many variations on the shape you create is determined by the number of points and the direction you drag when node editing. Using the Sharpness control adds even more variation to the shapes you can create.

Figure 13.5 shows some of these variations, which are described in the following list:

| Row | Description of the Shape |
| --- | --- |
| 1 | A 5-point polygon star with Sharpness set to 75. |
|  | A 10-point polygon star with Sharpness set to 25. |
|  | A 25-point polygon star with Sharpness set to 50. |
| 2 | A 5-point polygon star with Sharpness set to 75. It was node-edited by dragging a single node outward with a rotating motion. |
|  | A 10-point polygon star with Sharpness set to 25. It was node-edited by dragging a single node outward with a rotating motion. |
|  | A 25-point polygon star with Sharpness set to 50. It was node-edited by dragging a single node outward with a rotating motion. |
| 3 | A 5-point polygon star with Sharpness set to 75. It was node-edited by dragging a single node inward with a rotating motion. |
|  | A 10-point polygon star with Sharpness set to 25. It was node-edited by dragging a single node inward with a rotating motion. |
|  | A 25-point polygon star with Sharpness set to 50. It was node-edited by dragging a single node inward with a rotating motion. |

*Figure 13.5.*
*Various shapes created with the Polygon as Star tool.*

## The Star Tool

Checking the Star option in the Tool Properties dialog box lets you draw star-shaped objects. The minimum setting for the number of points is 5, and the maximum is 500. The Sharpness slider control setting is not available until the number of points is seven or higher. The number of degrees of sharpness increases as the number of points increases. Star shapes can be node-edited the same as polygons. The difference between *Polygon as Star* and *Star* is that a *Polygon as Star* is a solid object and a *Star* has a hollow center.

To draw a star, check the Star option in the Tool Properties dialog box. Enter the desired number of points and adjust the sharpness slider. The preview window will display the effect for your settings. Figure 13.6 shows six different star shapes, and each shape is described in the following list:

| Row | Description of the Shape |
| --- | --- |
| 1 | A basic 5-point star. |
|  | A 10-point star with Sharpness set to 3. |
|  | A 25-point star with sharpness set to 5. |
| 2 | A 5-point star node-edited by dragging two adjacent nodes diagonally down and to the left. In order to see which nodes were used, refer to the arrows that point to the nodes on the basic 5-point star (the first figure). |

*continues*

| Row | Description of the Shape |
|-----|--------------------------|
|     | A 10-point star with Sharpness set to 3. It was node-edited by dragging a single node upward with a rotating motion. |
|     | A 25-point star with Sharpness set to 3. It was node-edited by dragging a single node outward with a 180 degree rotation. |

*Figure 13.6.*
*Various shapes created*
*with the Star tool.*

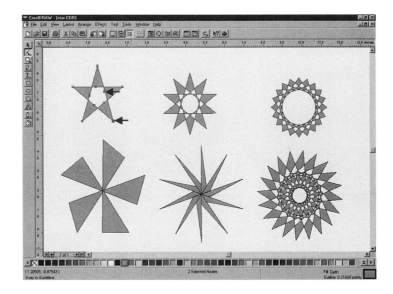

## The Spiral Tool

The Spiral tool lets you draw spirals, which in previous versions of CorelDRAW were next to impossible to draw. Click the Polygon tool flyout to access the Spiral tool. Next, right-click the Spiral icon and select Properties from the menu to bring up the Tool Properties dialog box.

# Corel*NOTE!*

When the dialog box first appears, it might not display the Spiral tool settings. If it doesn't, scroll the Tool parameters box to find the Spiral tool.

The Tool Properties menu shows only a Number of Revolutions parameters box, which is defaulted to 4. No other settings are available. Simply type in the number of revolutions you want and click the OK button. Click and drag the cursor just as you would when drawing an ellipse. Figure 13.7 shows several spirals drawn on-screen. The image on the far right is two spirals blended together. The double cone effect in the blend was achieved by horizontally mirroring the top spiral. This method changes the mapping of the nodes, thereby creating the effect.

*Figure 13.7.*
*Various spirals and*
*a blended spiral.*

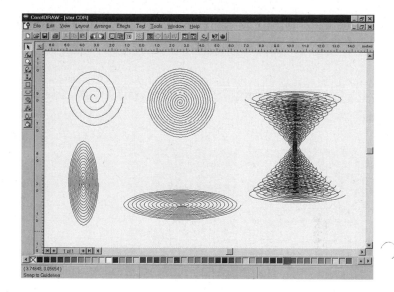

Figure 13.8 shows a spiral with a calligraphic effect applied to the outlines (see Skill Session 15, "The Outline Tool"). To make the effect look like a coiled ribbon, the last node on the outside of the spiral was moved in against the nearest outside node. The two center nodes were deleted, and the last center node was moved against the nearest inside bottom node.

*Figure 13.8.*
*A spiral with a calligraphic*
*outline applied.*

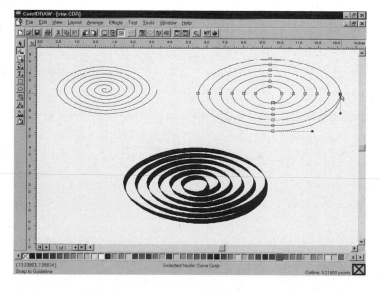

# The Grid Tool

The Grid tool allows you to draw grids of various sizes. You can determine the number of cells a grid can contain in both width or height. When a grid is drawn, it is made up of individual rectangles, which are automatically grouped together as a group of objects. Select the Grid tool from the Polygon tool flyout. Right-click the Grid tool and select Properties from the menu. The Tools Properties dialog box will appear. (See Figure 13.9.) If Grid is not shown in the Tools parameters box, then scroll until you find it. Enter the number of cells for both width and height in the parameters boxes and click the OK button. Draw the grid by dragging the cursor the same way you would if you were drawing a rectangle.

*Figure 13.9.*
*The Tools Properties*
*dialog box with Grid*
*selected.*

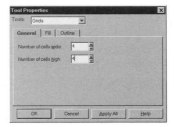

Figure 13.10 shows various grids, each with a different number of cells. Figure 13.11 shows two different effects applied to a grid. The grid on the left is a basic grid. The center object shows the grid after it has been ungrouped and all the individual rectangles combined into one single curve object. This single curve object was then extruded using the Extrude roll-up. The object on the right was ungrouped and combined just like the center object, but prior to extruding two additional, smaller rectangles were used to trim the sides of the combined rectangles. (See Skill Session 24, "Weld, Intersection, and Trim.") After the trimming was done, the resultant shape was extruded.

*Figure 13.10.*
*Three grids drawn with*
*the Grid tool.*

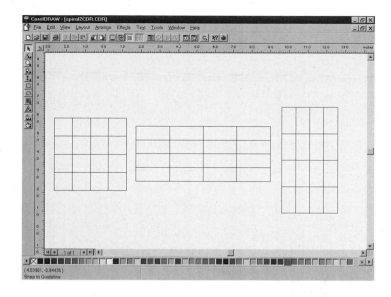

*Figure 13.11.*
*An extruded grid after*
*being ungrouped and*
*combined.*

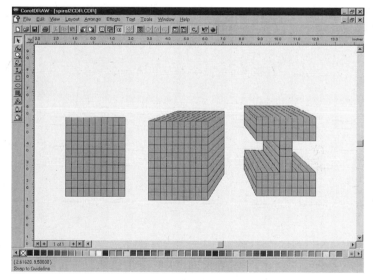

# 14

# The Text Tool

The Text tool, like some of the other tools, is actually two tools in one: one tool for adding Artistic text, and the other for Paragraph text. Both tools are found on the Text tool flyout menu, as shown in Figure 14.1.

## Text Tool Properties

Each of the Text tools has its own Properties dialog box. To access the dialog boxes shown in Figures 14.2 and 14.3, right-click the tool icon and choose Properties from the menu.

In the Tool Properties dialog box you can change many of the attributes of the text. These attributes will be described later in this skill session. By clicking the Apply button, you can assign the settings you've made as the default text for the selected tool. The warning box shown in Figure 14.4 appears so that you don't accidentally change the default.

Figure 14.1.
The Text tool flyout menu.

Figure 14.2.
The Artistic Text Tool
Properties dialog box.

Figure 14.3.
The Paragraph Text Tool
Properties dialog box.

Figure 14.4.
Text Attributes warning
dialog box.

## Artistic Text

An Artistic text string can be no longer than 32,000 characters. This limit is no longer reduced to 250 characters if the text is to be transformed or when you're using a more complex font. To add Artistic text to a drawing, choose the Text tool (or press F8) and then click the cursor on the page where the new text string should begin. Once you've placed the cursor, just type the desired text right on the page. Once the text has been entered, it can be edited in one of two ways: You can click your cursor within the text and then edit on the page or you can use the Edit Text dialog box. You bring up the Edit Text dialog box by choosing Edit Text from the Text pull-down menu or by pressing Ctrl+Shift+T. Figure 14.5 shows the Edit Text dialog box.

The Edit Text dialog box enables you to edit the text in a WYSIWYG format because it uses the current font. If you want to make changes to other attributes, such as font, style, point size, justification, and spacing, they can be accessed by selecting the Character button at the bottom of the dialog box or by simply using the buttons along the top of the dialog box. Note that any changes made will occur only on highlighted text. The Character Attributes dialog box can be used to change many different attributes of the text. (See Figure 14.6.) You might find it much easier to change text attributes by using the Text toolbar. Skill Session 37, "Changing Text Attributes," explains how to access this new toolbar.

*Figure 14.5.*
*The Edit Text dialog box.*

*Figure 14.6.*
*The Font tab of the*
*Character Attributes*
*dialog box.*

The Character Attributes dialog box can also be brought up directly by pressing Ctrl+T. The point size for fonts can range from a minuscule .001 points to a humongous 3000 points. Existing styles are shown in the Style drop-down box, but some TrueType weights aren't accessible by their exact names, because CorelDRAW sees them only as Normal and Bold. Note that this doesn't affect any of the fonts that come packaged with CorelDRAW.

The next three fields can be used to place underlines, overlines, and strikeouts. These all give you the option of using single or double lines, and they can apply to individual words or to entire passages. The Placement field enables you to change to subscript or superscript. The Effect field enables you to change text to either small caps or all caps.

On the Alignment Tab (shown in Figure 14.7), the Spacing section enables you to change character, word, and line spacing. This section is exactly the same for Paragraph text. Alignment can be left, right, center, fully justified, force justified, or none at all (which is essentially left justified). For more information on the many things you can accomplish with this dialog box, see Skill Session 37.

Figure 14.7.
*The Alignment tab of the*
*Character Attributes*
*dialog box.*

The Text toolbar provides access to many of the same attributes found in the Edit Text dialog box. Figure 14.8 shows the Text toolbar.

Figure 14.8.
*The Text toolbar.*

# Paragraph Text

The Paragraph Text tool is on the right side of the text flyout menu. It should be used for blocks of text that span multiple paragraphs or when no effects will be applied to the text. Each paragraph is limited to 32,000 characters, and no more than 32,000 paragraphs can be contained in a frame. You can also have up to 32,000 linked frames. Therefore, you will run out of memory long before you reach these limits. The text can be typed directly into a frame you create by dragging out an appropriately sized rectangle with the primary mouse button, or the text can be imported into a file by using the File | Import command.

When you import text using the File | Import command, pages are added to accommodate all the text contained in the file.

Text can also be entered in the Edit Text dialog box described earlier. This dialog box is exactly the same for both types of text.

The Text toolbar can also be used with Paragraph text. The main difference between the Text toolbar for Paragraph text and the one for Artistic text is that more options are available for Paragraph text—such as Columns, Bullets, and Indenting. The many options available in the Paragraph dialog box and the Columns dialog box are covered in depth in Skill Session 38, "Paragraph Text Attributes."

# 15

# The Outline Tool

The Outline tool is as important to understand as the Fill tool (see Skill Session 16) because outlines are often applied to new objects you create. The Outline tool also determines the look of straight and curved lines that aren't outlines of objects but rather lines you have drawn. You might think of it as a tool that determines certain attributes of lines that are also used as outlines. The reason for this approach is that you're dealing not only with outline widths and colors, but also with dashed lines and lines with arrowheads. These lines don't outline an object, but rather are objects in and of themselves.

## Setting Outline Defaults for Graphic Objects

### Corel *NOTE!*

The most common mistake users make is to accidentally change the outline default settings. When this happens, quite often the object or text will appear as a big blob on the screen or worse yet, it won't appear at all. What the user did was to select a very wide outline when no objects were selected on the page. If your default outline widths or color change accidentally, follow the steps below to reset the defaults.

Follow these steps to set the default outline width and color for graphic objects. Text and Paragraph text defaults should be set separately, because you normally wouldn't want outlines on text.

1. Make sure no objects are selected before you set defaults.
2. Click the Outline tool in the toolbox. This brings up the flyout menu.
3. Click the Outline tool icon in the flyout menu. (See Figure 15.1.)

*Figure 15.1.*
*The Outline tool*
*flyout menu.*

When you click this icon with nothing selected, an Outline Pen dialog box appears with a message telling you that nothing is selected and asking you to choose the types of objects to which the default will apply. (See Figure 15.2.)

*Figure 15.2.*
*The default Outline Pen*
*dialog box.*

4. Select Graphic; leave the Artistic Text and Paragraph Text boxes blank.
5. Click OK. A larger Outline Pen dialog box appears. (See Figure 15.3.)

*Figure 15.3.*
*The Outline Pen dialog*
*box for setting graphic*
*defaults.*

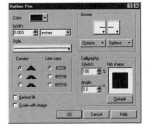

# Corel *TIP!*

The Outline Pen dialog box presents several options. You're setting the default settings, so remember that the settings you choose will apply to every object you draw. Another way to access this dialog box is to select an object before you click on the Outline Pen icon. When you use this method, you change the settings only for the individual object you selected.

6. The first thing you should do is set the default color. Click the Color button and a color palette appears. (See Figure 15.4.) Choose the color for all your outlines. You can access custom colors by clicking on the Others button at the bottom of the color palette.

*Figure 15.4.
Setting the default
outline color.*

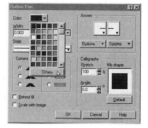

7. The next step is to set the default outline width. You have the following choices of units of measure: inches, millimeters, picas, and points. Select the units of measure and enter a value in the parameters box.

# Corel *NOTE!*

Normally, the only settings you would set as defaults are the outline width and color. All the other settings in the Outline Pen dialog box are used for specific attributes you want to assign to a specific object's outline.

# Corel *TIP!*

A good outline setting to use is 1 point. Because the default outline width is primarily used for screen viewing only, you'll change an individual object's outline width separately depending on what you're designing.

8. Click OK after you have selected the color and the width. You have just set your outline defaults for graphic objects.

## Setting Outline Defaults for Text

Most users prefer not to have an outline when they enter text or import paragraph text. This is because if the defaults are set too wide the outlines cover the text and all you see is a black blob. If the outline color defaults to white, there's a chance you won't even be able to see the text. Figure 15.5 illustrates these possibilities.

*Figure 15.5.*
*Using outlines with text*
*might cause problems.*

Follow these steps to set the outline default to no outline:

1. Click the Outline tool in the toolbox to display the flyout and then click the X icon, the first icon on the bottom row of the flyout menu. (Refer to Figure 15.1.)
2. The small Outline Pen dialog box appears. Select both Artistic Text and Paragraph Text. Do not select Graphic.
3. Click OK.

Your text will not have an outline when it's typed on the page or imported.

## Corel*NOTE!*

If you try to set the default outline width to 0 in the Outline Pen dialog box instead of clicking the × in the flyout, you get an Invalid Width error message telling you that the width must be between 0.1 and 288.0 points. If your settings are in inches, the error message tells you that the width must be between .001 and 4.0 inches.

## Optional Settings for Outlines

The Outline Pen dialog box provides you with many settings to apply to outlines. To change outline settings, first select the object you want to change. Click the pen tool in the toolbox and then click the pen icon in the flyout menu. This brings up the Outline Pen dialog box again. Remember, the changes you make here will affect only the object selected. The various settings are described in the following sections.

# Corel*TIP!*

If you know you're going to use outline settings other than the defaults for an entire project, you might want to make these settings the defaults. But be sure to reset these changes when you're through with the project.

## Corners

There are three corner attributes:

- ■ Square corners. This is the most often used option because it provides a look that fits most shapes.
- ■ Rounded corners.
- ■ Beveled corners.

Figure 15.6 shows each option applied to a rectangle.

*Figure 15.6.*
*The three styles of*
*corners, from left to right:*
*square, rounded, and*
*beveled.*

## Line Caps

There are three Line Caps settings. Line caps determine how far the end of a line extends beyond the termination point of the line. Figure 15.7 shows each option applied to a straight line.

*Figure 15.7.*
*Three styles of line caps.*

## Behind Fill

You should check Behind Fill if you'll be using an outline on certain types of fonts. The reason for this is that normally an outline is drawn after the object is drawn, so it's placed on top of the object. When you check the Behind Fill box, the outline is drawn before the object. The benefit of this is that the original design of the text is not altered by the outline. If you use a very stylized font, all the original attributes are still there. Figure 15.8 illustrates the use of behind fill on text.

*Figure 15.8.*
*Text without behind fill*
*(left) versus text with*
*behind fill (right).*

When you use behind fill, make the outline width twice as wide as you want the finished outline to be because the text will cover half of the outline when it's drawn on top of it. Notice that in Figure 15.8, even though the outline of the behind-filled letter on the right is twice that of the letter on the left with the outline on top, the behind-filled letter looks better.

## Scale With Image

The Scale With Image feature scales the size of the outline when you resize an object using any of the corner selection handles. If this box is not checked, the size of an object's outline remains the same when the object is resized. Figure 15.10 shows the effect of using Scale With Image. Notice the small rectangle within the larger one on the left. It was reduced in size, using a corner selection handle, without Scale With Image, so the outline stayed the same. The smaller rectangle on the right used Scale With Image, and its outline scaled proportionately smaller.

## Corel*NOTE!*

It is important to understand that if you resize an object using one of the middle selection handles, the Scale With Image feature will scale only two sides of the object. Therefore, you need to be careful when resizing objects with the Scale With Image enabled. You might not see the difference on screen, but it will be very apparent when it is printed.

*Figure 15.09.*
*Resizing an object with*
*Scale With Image enabled*
*and disabled using corner*
*selection handles.*

## Arrowheads

Adding arrowheads to the ends of single lines can be very useful in your designs. The dialog box offers left and right selection boxes that are labeled Arrows. The left box is for selecting an arrowhead at the start of a line, and the right box is for the end of a line. Click the appropriate box to bring up a menu of arrowhead designs. (See Figure 15.10.)

*Figure 15.10.*
*Choosing an arrowhead.*

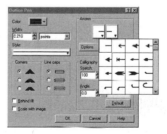

Below each selection box is an Options button. When you click one of these, a pull-down menu with four options appears. (See Figure 15.11.) The first option is None. This option is a quick way to remove an arrowhead from a line. The second option is Swap. This option comes in very handy when you accidentally put an arrowhead on the wrong end of the line. When you click Swap, the arrowhead switches to the other end of the line.

*Figure 15.11.*
*The Options pull-down*
*menu.*

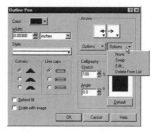

The Third option is Edit. This option brings up the Arrowhead Editor dialog box (see Figure 15.12), which enables you to change the size of the arrowhead. You can also create a mirror image of the arrowhead by clicking the Reflect buttons.

*Figure 15.12.*
*The Arrowhead Editor*
*dialog box.*

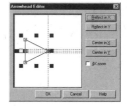

# Corel*NOTE!*

To create your own custom arrowheads, choose the Create Arrow command from the Special menu.

The fourth option is Delete From List. When you select this option, a message box asks you to verify that you want to delete the arrowhead currently displayed in the selection box. This way, if you click this option by mistake, you're given the chance to say No to deleting the arrowhead.

## Style

The Style option box is a narrow horizontal box with a solid line running through it. Click this box and a pull-down menu appears with an assortment of dotted and dashed lines. (See Figure 15.13.) If you want to change back to a solid line, select the solid line at the very top of the dialog box.

Figure 15.13.
The Style option box and
drop-down menu.

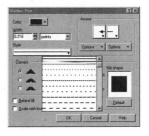

## Calligraphy

The Calligraphy settings enable you to change the rectangular shape and angle of
a line. When you change the nib shape from its default setting, Square, you can
add calligraphic effects to outlines. Figure 15.14 illustrates the use of these effects.
The objects on the left were given normal outlines. The objects on the right used a
Stretch setting of 10 and an Angle setting of 45.

Figure 15.14.
Adding calligraphic effects
to objects.

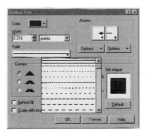

The Stretch parameter box enables you to scroll or type a new number below 100.
You will notice that the square is shortened as the number is reduced.

The Angle parameter box enables you to scroll or type a number to change the
angle of the rectangle or default square. Figure 15.16 shows the Stretch and Angle
parameter boxes. Next to the preview window, notice the change in the shape of
the line with Stretch set to 10 and Angle set to –40.

Figure 15.15.
The Outline Pen dialog
box showing the Stretch
and Angle parameter
boxes.

The best way to get the effect you want is to try different settings until you achieve the desired result.

## The Color Roll-Up

Access the Color roll-up by clicking the second icon from the left at the top of the Outline Pen flyout. It is one way to choose a color for outlines. The Color roll-up is shown in its default display in Figure 15.16. The default display is the RGB color model. Click the down arrow next to the parameter box showing RGB to select different color models or palettes. The Color roll-up accessed from the Outline Pen flyout is identical to the Color roll-up accessed from the Fill tool flyout. We will discuss this roll-up further in Skill Session 16. Frankly, it is easier to change colors using the Pen roll-up described below.

*Figure 15.16.*
*The Color roll-up in the*
*default display.*

# Corel*NOTE!*

The roll-up is part of a roll-up group containing the Pen, Color, and Special Fill. If you click any of these listings, the roll-up will redisplay showing the listing selected. When you click Pen, the Pen roll-up described below appears. When you select Special Fill, the roll-up will display the various fill options. Unfortunately you can't use the Special Fill options on outlines because outlines can't be filled. Only objects can be filled.

## The Pen Roll-Up

The Pen roll-up gives you quick access to outline attributes if you need to change them. To access the roll-up, click the third icon from the left at the top of the Outline tool flyout menu.

Figure 15.17.
The Pen roll-up.

## Line Width

The top window of the roll-up is the Line Width setting. It defaults to a hairline width. Use the scroll arrows next to the line width preview window to change the line width. A visual representation of the line width will display. Scrolling all the way down causes the box to display a large X in the window; this represents No Outline.

## Arrowheads

Just below the Line Width window are the Arrowhead settings. They function just as they do in the main Outline Pen dialog box. The left button is for adding an arrowhead to the beginning of a line, and the right one is for the end of a line. If you need to swap ends or edit the arrowhead, click the Edit button in the roll-up.

## Styles

The narrow horizontal box below the arrowheads is for changing outline styles. It functions the same as it does in the main Outline Pen dialog box. Click this box and a roll-up menu appears with a choice of line styles. At the very top of this menu is the default, a solid line.

## Color

The next choice you have is the outline color. To choose a color, click the solid black box just above the Update From button. A color palette appears. (See Figure 15.18.) Click the Others button at the bottom of the palette to access the Select Color dialog box. The Select Color dialog box enables you to choose custom colors as well as custom palettes. (See Figure 15.19.)

Figure 15.18.
The Pen roll-up with the
color palette rolled down.

Figure 15.19.
The Select Color
dialog box.

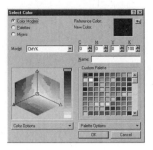

## Update From

Use the Update From button to copy one object's outline attributes to another object. Select the object you want to modify and click the Update From button. An arrow appears on-screen in place of the normal cursor. Use this arrow to click the object from which you want to copy outline attributes. (See Figure 15.20.) Your first object will now take on the outline attributes of the target object.

Figure 15.20.
Copying the outline
attributes from one object
to another.

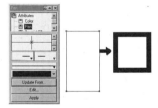

## Edit

The Edit button can be used at any time to edit the object's outline. Click this button to bring up the main Outline Pen dialog box.

## Apply

The Apply button is the most important button of all. You can make all the changes you want, but none of them will take effect until you click Apply.

# Corel*NOTE!*

Now that you have learned more than you will ever what to know about the Outline tool settings, there is one more dialog box added in CorelDRAW 6 that may save you more time than most of the previous options described. The dialog box is called the Object Properties dialog box. If you right-click an object, the Object Properties menu appears. Click Properties at the bottom of the menu to bring up the Object Properties dialog box. (See Figure 15.21.)

Click the Outline tab in the Object Properties dialog box to reveal the outline property settings. Many of the basic settings can be changed in this dialog box. If you need further outline editing, click the Edit button to bring up the main Outline Pen dialog box.

*Figure 15.21.*
*The Object Properties*
*dialog box with the*
*Outline tab selected.*

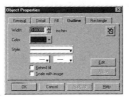

# 16

# The Fill Tool

The Fill tool is a very important tool in terms of learning CorelDRAW. The various options it offers and how you use them determine how your finished project will look. Making the right choices in selecting the colors, gradient fills, textures, and patterns can make the difference between a mediocre project and a superb one. You can create the perfect design and layout and use the perfect font, but if the color and texture schemes are poor, the result is a disaster. CorelDRAW 6 includes several fill features that can make anyone a graphic artist.

The Fill tool provides access to the Uniform Fill dialog box. It is here that you can choose from several color models and palettes. Choosing the correct one for your projects when it's time to print is very important. There are really two basic color choices: Spot and Process color fills. Skill Session 67, "Color Models and Color Palettes," provides the basics to guide you in making the correct choice of models and palettes.

## Setting the Default Color

Setting up a default color is essential so that each time you start a new project your text and objects will be filled with the same color.

To change the default color, first make sure you have no objects selected on-screen. Click the Fill tool, located at the bottom of the toolbar. A flyout appears, as shown in Figure 16.1. Now click the color wheel icon.

*Figure 16.1.*
*The Fill tool flyout.*

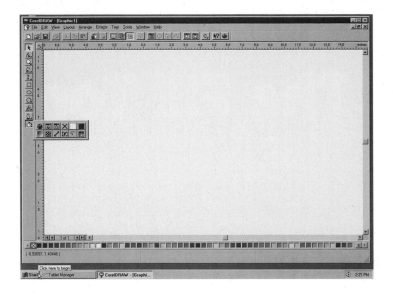

When you click the color wheel icon with nothing selected, a small Uniform Fill dialog box appears with the following message: `Changing fill properties when nothing is selected will modify the attributes used by tools when creating new objects. Click on the boxes below to choose which tools will receive new default settings.` Most of the time, you'll want text to have a fill color, so click on the Artistic text and Paragraph text check boxes. If you want objects other than text to have a fill, you should check the Graphics check box as well. (Many users prefer to have only an outline appear when they draw objects, so they don't check the Graphics check box.) Click the OK button. A larger Uniform Fill dialog box appears (see figure 16.2). The current default color is shown in a preview window at the top right of the dialog box. The preview window is divided in two sections. The upper section is the current color and is referred to as the reference color. The lower section displays the new color. To change to a new color, you can either click with your left mouse button on your color of choice in the palette at the bottom right of the dialog box, or you can choose a custom color from the CMYK color model at the lower left of the dialog box. Before you can choose a custom color, you have to click on a color in the palette.

When you have selected your default color, click the OK button in the Uniform Fill dialog box.

If you want to change to a completely different color, color model, or palette before you choose a default color, click either Palettes or Mixers at the top left of the uniform dialog box. After you have selected a color, click the OK button in the Uniform Fill dialog box.

Figure 16.2.
The Uniform Fill
dialog box.

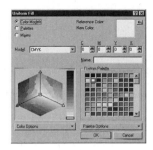

# Corel*NOTE!*

The palette and color you chose are now your defaults. This means that whenever you draw an object or type text for the first time, the object or text will be filled with this color.

## Uniform Fill

The Uniform Fill dialog box offers a choice between color models, color palettes, and color mixers for filling objects with solid colors. The default display is the CMYK color model and the custom palette. Refer to Skill Session 67 for a description of all the color models and palettes and how they can be used.

To fill an object with a solid color, select the object and click the color wheel icon in the Fill tool flyout menu. The fill color of the selected object is displayed in the preview window at the upper right of the dialog box (If you select an object with no fill, the preview window will display the default color.) The preview window is divided in two sections. The top section is the current color and is referred to as the reference color. The bottom section displays the new color. You can change the CMYK values of the selected color by typing or scrolling the parameters boxes located below the preview window if you've chosen the default CMYK color model and the custom palette. You can also click anywhere in the 3D color model to select a color. Before you can choose a custom color, you have to click on a color in the custom palette. The preview window shows the changes made and the reference color (the one you started with). After you make changes, click the OK button. The changes are reflected in the selected object.

You can assign a name to your custom color and add it to the default palette by typing a name in the Name box and then clicking the OK button.

The Palette Options button displays a flyout from which you can rename a color, delete a color, open a new palette, open a different palette, save a palette after you have added custom colors, and rename a palette by choosing Save As. Figure 16.3 shows the Uniform dialog box with the Palette Options flyout displayed.

Figure 16.3.
*Changing a color in the*
*Uniform Fill dialog box.*

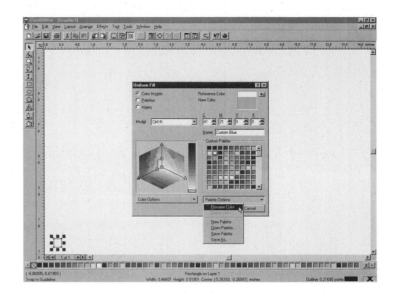

## Mixers

A new option in CorelDRAW 6 is the capability to choose custom colors from either a color blend or a mixing area. Click the Mixers option in the upper-left corner of the Uniform Fill dialog box. You can choose either Color Blend or Mixing Area from the Mode parameters box. Each option is described in the following sections.

## Color Blend Mode

When you choose the Color Blend option (see Figure 16.4), a grid of blended colors, comprising the combination of the four colored squares shown at each corner of the grid, is displayed. The color grid allows you to blend different colors to create custom colors. To change the combination of blended colors, click one or all of the corner squares and choose a new color from the drop-down color palette. After you have chosen a new color, click the Auto-Blend button, and the grid redraws using the new color or colors.

If you click the Color Options button (located below the Auto-Blend button), a drop-down list appears, offering several options. The options are described in the following list:

   **Add Color to Palette**   This option lets you add your custom color to the custom palette at the lower right of the Uniform Fill dialog box.

   **Add All Grid Colors** to Palette   This option could be helpful if you need very subtle changes in colors.

**Swap Color**   This option lets you switch between the color you select from the color blend grid and the last color you selected from the grid.

**Grid Size**   This option lets you choose the size of the grid from a drop-down list. The grid sizes range from 3×3 to 25×25. The larger the grid size, the more color choices you have.

**Color Model**   This option lets you choose between CMYK, RGB, and HSB color models.

*Figure 16.4.*
*The color blend mode*
*display and its options.*

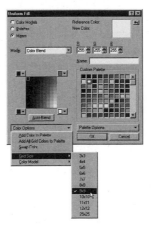

## Mixing Area

When you choose Mixing Area from the Mode parameters box, a mixing area window appears, as shown in Figure 16.5. To use the mixing area, click the eye dropper icon and select a color from the colored circles. Choose the Paintbrush tool, located next to the eye dropper icon, and use it to paint in the mixing area. When you see a color you have created within the mixing area and you want to use it as a fill, select the eye dropper icon again and click on that color. It replaces the current color in the color preview window.

# Corel*NOTE!*

Just below the mixing area is the Blend parameters box. When you select the Paintbrush tool, this parameters box becomes active. The default is 50 percent, but a more realistic setting is in the 90 percent range. The higher the setting, the more the blending effect will be achieved.

You can save the mixture of colors you have painted in the mixing area along with several other options by clicking the Color Options button, located below the mixing area. The various options are described in the following list:

**Add Color to Palette**   This option lets you add your custom color to the custom palette at the lower right of the Uniform Fill dialog box.

**Swap Color**   This option lets you switch between the color you select from the mixing area and the last color you selected from the mixing area.

**Brush Size**   This option lets you choose between small, medium, and large brush sizes.

**Brush Type**   This option lets you choose between a hard, medium, or soft brush when you're mixing.

**Color Model**   This option lets you choose between CMYK, RGB, and HSB color models.

**Load Bitmap**   This option allows you to load a new mixing area. When you select this option, you will be presented with a choice of two mixing areas: pnt_roll.BMP and pntarea.BMP. These bitmaps are located in the Custom folder of the CorelDRAW folder. The default is pntarea.BMP. Choosing pnt_roll.BMP gives you a more blended mixing area to start with.

# Corel*NOTE!*

You can create custom mixing areas in Corel PHOTO-PAINT. Make the new file size 173×68 pixels so it will fit correctly in the mixing area window. Save your new file in the Coreldrw/Custom folder so that it will be readily available. Try using a photo of a person so you can add flesh tone colors to CorelDRAW's palette.

**Save Bitmap**   This option allows you to save a mixing area so that it can be opened again.

**Clear Bitmap**   This option lets you remove all color from the mixing area. This comes in handy when you have used up the mixing area trying to create new colors.

*Figure 16.5.*
*The mixing area*
*and its options.*

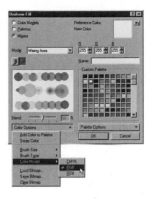

## Custom Fill Tools

Access the Custom Fill tools from the Fill tool, located at the bottom of the toolbox. A flyout appears when you select the icon. The first icon in the top half of the flyout is the color wheel. (See this chapter's "Uniform Fill" section.) The various fill types are shown in Figure 16.6 and are described in the following sections.

*Figure 16.6.*
*The Fill flyout and the*
*name of each icon.*

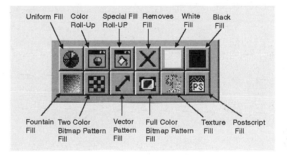

## The Fountain Fill Dialog Box

To access the Fountain Fill dialog box, click the first icon on the left in lower half of the Fill flyout. The default fountain fill is a linear fill, which goes from left to right using the colors black and white. You can produce some interesting effects using the four types of fountain fills as well as changing the appearance of each type by editing them. The various editing options in the Fountain Fill dialog box (see Figure 16.7) are described in the next section.

There are four basic fountain fills: linear, radial, conical, and square. Choose a fountain fill type by clicking the down arrow in the Type parameters box, located at the top left of the dialog box.

*Figure 16.7.*
*The Fountain Fill*
*dialog box.*

## Editing Fountain Fills

You are not restricted to the default settings of the four basic fountain fills. Changing colors, angles, offsets, steps, and edge pad can dramatically change the appearance of the basic fountain fill. The various editing options are described below.

### Changing Colors

To change the colors in a fountain fill, click the From and To buttons in the Color Blend section of the dialog box. When you click either of the buttons, you can choose a new color from the drop-down palette. If you need a color not found in the palette, click Other at the bottom of the drop-down palette. This action brings up another dialog box similar to the Uniform Fill dialog box. From this dialog box you can choose a custom color from the color model. You can even choose a completely new palette or use the mixing areas.

### Changing Angles

If you want to change the angle of the fill (for example, left to right instead of bottom to top), place the cursor in the center of the preview box and drag. A line appears that enables you to rotate the direction of the fill. Hold down the Ctrl key to constrain movement to 15-degree increments. For radial, conical, and square fills, a crosshair replaces your cursor in the preview window. Drag the crosshair to move the center point. With conical and square fills, use the right mouse button or hold down the Shift key when dragging in order to constrain the angle of the fill.

### Changing Offsets

You can manually enter the center offsets of fills in all fills but the linear fill by scrolling or typing the numbers in the Horizontal and Vertical parameters boxes, located beneath the Center Offset section of the dialog box. You can also manually change the angle of all fills but the radial fill in the Angle parameters box, located at the top center of the dialog box.

### Changing Steps

The Steps parameters box shows the number of steps in the fountain fill. The number 20, displayed in Figure 16.7, is the default number and is grayed out. To change the number of steps, click the lock icon (next to the parameters box). This enables you to change the number of fountain stripes you want in the fill. You can choose any number between 2 and 256.

### Edge Pad

The parameters box under the Steps box is called Edge Pad. The number you set in this box determines how long the beginning and ending colors remain a solid color before they start blending with the next color. The higher the number, the longer the color will remain solid.

## Color Blend

In the center of the Fountain Fill dialog box is the Color Blend section. This section contains choices for varying the look of your fountain fills (see Figure 16.8). The various options are described in the following sections. The To and From color buttons were described in the previous section.

### The Mid-Point Slider

The Mid-Point slider, located at the lower left of the dialog box, is available only while using direct fills. Its function is to control the location of the mid-point color in the color blend. For example, using the slider's default (50) and a direct fill from black to white, the center of the blend would be 50 percent gray. If you moved the slider to 25, the 50 percent gray value would shift to the lower quarter of the blend. If you moved the slider to 75, the 50 percent gray value would shift to the upper three quarters of the blend.

Using the Mid-Point slider on a linear fountain fill functions in a similar fashion. Imagine a fill from red to orange. Depending on the rotation selected, it is possible to have the blend travel around the entire color wheel. Using the default of 50 percent, the center of the color blend would be blue. If you move the slider to 25 percent, the color blue would appear near the lower portion of the fountain fill.

### Direction Buttons

The direction buttons are located to the left of the color wheel. The first button is the Direct button. The Direct method is the default setting. The colors that have been used in the To and From palettes blend directly from one color to the next. The color wheel, located next to the direction buttons, will show a straight line from one color to the other, blending the beginning color with the ending color as it passes through the color spectrum. You can modify a direct fountain fill by clicking on either the To or From button and choosing a new color from the drop-down palette.

The second button depicts a counterclockwise rotation. When you select this option, the colors will blend from one to the other in a counterclockwise direction. There will be a elliptical line showing the path around the color spectrum that the blend will travel. If you choose Red to Red, the blend will pass through the entire color spectrum.

The third button depicts a clockwise rotation. Choosing this button is the reverse of choose the counterclockwise button.

*Figure 16.8.*
*The Fountain Fill dialog box, showing a rotated blend selected.*

## Custom Fills

A custom fill enables you to add more colors to the fountain fill. In order to create custom fills, select Custom in the Fountain Fill dialog box. This brings up a display that shows new options. (See Figure 16.9.) The first thing you'll notice is a horizontal color bar that displays the fountain fill going from the first color to the second (from left to right). At the top-left and top-right corners of the color bar are small squares, which represent the starting and ending points of the fill and cannot be moved. When you click one of these squares, its color is displayed in the Current box, located above the color bar. Here is the procedure for adding additional colors to the fountain fill:

1. Double-click the color bar with the left mouse button. A triangular marker is placed at that point.
2. Click on a new color from the color palette (located on the right side of the dialog box).
3. Click and drag the marker to the position on the color bar where you want the color change to take place.
4. Type in a specific value in the Position parameters box for exact positioning.
5. Repeat Steps 1–4 for each additional color.
6. To remove a marker, double-click the marker or press the delete key.

7. To save your custom fountain fill so that you can use it again, give it a name and type this name in the blank Presets parameters box. Once you have given it a name, click the plus (+) button, located next to the Presets parameters box. (See the next section, "Preset Fountain Fills.")

Figure 16.9.
*The Fountain Fill dialog*
*box with Custom selected.*

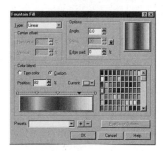

## Preset Fountain Fills

In the lower-left corner of the Fountain Fill dialog box is the Presets parameters box. (See Figure 16.10.) It contains custom fountain fills that can be used just as they are. To use a preset fountain fill, follow these steps:

1. Click the down arrow on the Presets parameters box. Scroll through the list of names until you find the preset you want. Select the preset fill from the list, and the preview window will display it.

2. If this is what you want, click the OK button.

3. If you don't like the colors, choose custom and change them by clicking on the colors' respective markers and changing them to new colors from the color palette.

4. If you want to use this preset again with the new colors you chose, click the plus (+) button, located next to the Presets down arrow.

5. A message appears asking if you want to overwrite the existing preset. If you choose Yes, the preset will be saved with the new colors you selected.

6. If you want to save a preset that you have modified without overwriting the original, type over the preset name with a new name and click the plus (+) button.

7. If you want to delete a preset fountain fill completely, click the minus (-) button.

Custom fills can be applied to linear, radial, conical, and square fills. Figure 16.11 shows some examples of different fountain fills using some of the options described previously.

Figure 16.10.
The Fountain Fill dialog
box with a Preset selected.

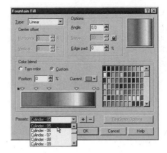

Figure 16.11.
Linear, Radial, Conical,
and Square fills

Figure 16.12.
Linear, Radial, Conical,
and Square fills with
added custom stripes

## Two-Color Bitmap Pattern Fills

The second icon from the left on the bottom of the Fill flyout is the two-color
pattern icon. When you select this icon, theTwo-Color Bitmap Pattern dialog box
appears. The preview window displays the default polka-dot-dot pattern. Click in
the preview window to bring up a menu of patterns from which to choose. The OK

button confirms your selection from the Pattern menu (you can also double-click the selected pattern). At the top of the pattern menu are three buttons: File, OK, and Cancel. Select File to open a pattern from a source other than the default directory. Click the Cancel button to return to the roll-up without selecting anything.

## Coloring Two-Color Bitmap Patterns

Two color Bitmap patterns are black and white bitmap fills. When you change colors, you're changing the black and white pixels to different colors. The color buttons are located at the upper right of the dialog box. The Back button defaults to white and the Front button defaults to black. Click the respective buttons to reveal the color palette and choose a new color for either Back or Front.

## Editing Two-Color Bitmap Pattern Fills

If you want to modify the pattern in any way or create a completely new pattern, click the Create button in the Two-Color Bitmap Pattern dialog box as shown in Figure 16.13. The Two-Color Bitmap Pattern Editor dialog box appears, as shown in Figure 16.14. Two-color bitmap patterns are bitmap patterns; therefore, when you are editing these patterns, you are doing so with a pen as if you were in PHOTO-PAINT.

To modify an existing pattern, select a pen size and click in the grid area with the left mouse button to add additional pixels. To remove pixels, click the pixels with the right mouse button. The pen size is measured in pixels—1×1 is one pixel, 2×2 is a square of four pixels (two across and two down), and 4×4 is a square of 16 pixels, (four across and four down). Once you are satisfied with the pattern, click the OK button. The modified pattern will take the place of the original. You won't be asked to overwrite the existing pattern, so remember that you have permanently changed the pattern until you modify it again.

To create a completely new pattern, select an existing pattern and then a new grid size. Selecting a new grid size will clear the previous pattern. You can then reselect the original grid size with a clean grid. Grid sizes are measured in pixels (just as the pen is measured in pixels). Paint your new pattern using the pen, and when you are satisfied, click the OK button. Your new pattern will appear at the bottom of the Pattern menu.

# Corel *NOTE!*

Use the entire screen grid when you make a pattern. This ensures that the pattern size matches the bitmap size you selected.

Figure 16.13.
The Two-Color Bitmap
Pattern dialog box.

Figure 16.14.
The Two-Color Bitmap
Pattern Editor dialog box.

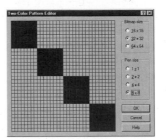

## Tiling Patterns

To tile your pattern, select the Tiling button at the lower left of the Two-Color
Bitmap Pattern dialog box. (See Figure 16.15.) *Tiling a pattern* means putting more
than one complete image of the pattern within the object you're filling. If the
object you're filling is larger than the size of the tile, it will tile automatically. You
can control the size of the tile by selecting one of the default settings—Small,
Medium, and Large—or you can choose a custom size by entering the size in the
Tile Size parameters boxes. You can also control the first tile offset by a percent of
the tile width for both the *x* and *y* offset. You can choose between rows or columns and set the percent of tile side offset.

Figure 16.15.
The Two-Color Bitmap
Pattern dialog box
expanded for tiling.

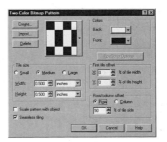

## Vector Patterns

The Vector pattern icon is a double arrow. It is the third icon from the left on the
bottom of the Fill flyout. When you select the Vector pattern icon, the Vector
Pattern dialog box appears.

A Vector pattern is a vector image, and therefore is not unlike a basic CDR file.
Patterns are originally made as a CDR file and saved with a .PAT extension by

using the Create Pattern command in the Special Menu. (See Skill Session 62, "Creating Custom Arrowheads, Patterns, and Symbols.")

Click in the preview window to view the Vector patterns available. Click the Load button in the Vector Pattern dialog box (see Figure 16.16) to select a pattern by name. Use the Import button to access patterns you may have stored in folders other than the default folders. Vector patterns can be tiled the same as two-color patterns.

Figure 16.16.
The Vector Pattern dialog
box after you click in the
preview window.

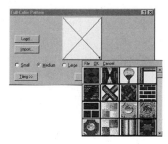

## Changing Colors in Vector Patterns

You cannot change a Vector pattern's colors from the dialog box as you can with two-color Bitmap patterns. You must follow these steps to open a pattern file prior to editing it:

1. Open the pattern you want to edit by using the Open command in the File menu.
2. Choose Pattern file *.Pat in the List Files of Type scroll box.
3. Using the folders list in the Open dialog box, change to the folder where the pattern files are located. The default is Coreldrw\Custom.
4. Select the pattern by name from the list.
5. Click the OK button.

The pattern you choose opens like a normal CDR file. You can now change the color scheme just as you would a CDR image. The pattern opens on-screen as a group, so you need to ungroup the objects in the pattern before you make changes. Do not resize the original pattern unless you have a specific reason for doing so. After you have made your changes, select Save from the File menu. This method permanently changes the default pattern's colors. If you want to keep the colors in the default pattern, choose Save As from the File menu and assign a new name to your edited image. The next time you look for your new pattern, it will appear at the bottom of the pattern display in the Full Color dialog box.

# Corel*NOTE!*

You are not limited to using vector objects as full-color pattern fills. You can use full-color bitmap images as well. (See Skill Session 62.)

## Texture Fills

# Corel*NOTE!*

Texture fills are bitmap images used to fill objects in CorelDraw. There are over 100 default texture fills available in the Texture Fill dialog box. Each of these hundred-odd textures can be modified to look completely different from the default texture. The number of variations that can be assigned to each texture could amount to over a million. We have found that very few CorelDRAW users are taking advantage of these incredible fills. The complaint we hear most is that texture fills are jagged when printed. The jagged appearance is caused by not setting the resolution and tile settings high enough. (Read the section "Texture Options" to learn how to get good results.)

The texture icon is the next-to-last icon at the bottom of the Fill flyout. When it's selected, the Texture Fill dialog box appears. (See Figure 16.17.) At the top left of the dialog box is the Texture Library parameters box. There are three libraries from which to choose: the default styles library and two samples libraries. The styles library contains original texture styles, while the samples libraries contain variations of the original styles. Click the down arrow to choose a new texture library.

Directly below the Texture Library box is a list box containing the names of the individual textures within each library. To select a texture, scroll the list box. When you click a name, a preview of the texture is displayed in the preview window. When you're satisfied with the texture, click the OK button.

*Figure 16.17.*
*The Texture Fill*
*dialog box.*

## Editing Textures

The Texture Fill dialog box contains a number of parameter selection boxes that enable you to make changes to various attributes of the selected texture. Each texture contains one common parameters box called Texture #. This box shows the identification number of the displayed texture. You can scroll or type any number from 1 to 32,768. Each time you change the texture number, the look of the texture will change to some degree. To see the effect of the changes made in the parameters boxes, you must click the Preview button.

## Texture Parameter Variations

Let's review the other editing variations available by changing the numbers in the parameters boxes. The texture Rock-Swirled-Eroded 2C, located in the styles library, has been used for this example. Different textures can show different parameters.

The following parameters are explained using the texture Rock-Swirled-Eroded 2C.

**Softness**   A higher number softens the edges of the object. A lower number sharpens the object and makes the edges more defined.

**Density**   A higher number increases the number or closeness of the components in the object.

**Grain**   A higher number increases the color intensity.

**Rainbow Grain**   The higher the number, the more color values are used to create a rainbow color effect.

**Brightness**   The higher thenumber, the brighter the image. This is great for shading objects.

**1st Mineral**   Clicking the color button brings up a color palette from which you can choose a new color. If you select More from the bottom of the palette, it brings up the Select Color dialog box. (This is the same as the Uniform Fill dialog box.) From this dialog box you can change palettes and so on.

**2nd Mineral**   Making changes here is the same as in 1st Mineral.

**Light Intensity**   The higher the number, the less color is visible.

**Eastern Light**   A higher number will increase the three-dimensional effect as it simulates directional lighting.

**Northern Light**   Making changes here is the same as in Eastern Light.

**Light**   Determines the color of light illuminating the object. Click the color button to choose a new color from the color palette.

When you first look at the dialog box, notice the small lock icons next to each parameters box. By default, all but Texture # are in the locked position. The reason they default to the locked mode is that when you click the Preview button (located beneath the preview window) without making any changes in the parameters boxes, the texture number will change in a random order. This is very useful when you want to see other variations of a texture without manually typing in a new number every time. Simply keep clicking the Preview button and the numbers will change. If you click any of the lock icons, you will unlock them. The next time you click in the preview window without making any changes, all the unlocked icons and their respective settings will randomly change along with the texture number. A reverse variation on this method might be to lock the texture number and unlock all the other parameters. This would keep the texture number the same but would randomly change all the other parameters.

## Saving, Deleting, and Importing Texture Fills

When you edit a particular texture and want to save it for future use, click the plus (+) button next to the texture library name. This will bring up the Save Texture As dialog box, which allows you to give your new texture a name and save it in either one of the samples libraries (or you can overwrite the library name to create a custom library of your own). Figure 16.18 shows the Save texture dialog box. To delete a texture, simply select the texture and click the minus (-) button next to the library name.

# Corel*NOTE!*

You cannot save an edited texture in the styles library. When you delete any custom textures, palettes, custom colors, or patterns, they are permanently deleted from the disk.

*Figure 16.18.*
*The Save Texture*
*As dialog box.*

## Texture Options

The Options button, located beneath the Help button, brings up the Texture Options dialog box. (See Figure 16.19.) This dialog box allows you to set the resolution and maximum tile size of the texture fill. The settings you make here are the keys to texture fills without the jaggies.

*Figure 16.19.*
*The Texture Options*
*dialog box.*

The two options available in the Texture Options dialog box are described below.

**Resolution**    The default setting is 120 DPI. Change the number for the resolution to twice the line screen of your final output device. (Refer to Skill Session 70, "Scanning," to get a better understanding of resolution and line screens.)

**Maximum Tile**    This setting is as important as Resolution. The number you use is based on the size of the object your filling. Use the following formula: LDO (longest dimension of object) × LPI (lines per inch) = tile size. When you have determined the tile size, choose the next higher setting from the drop-down list box.

Suppose you are outputting an image measuring 3×5 inches at 133 line screen. Using the formula, the correct number to type in the Resolution parameters box would be 266 (133 × 2). Still using the same formula, you would multiply 5 (the longest dimension of the object) by 266 (the resolution). This gives you the number 1330. The next higher setting in the Maximum Tile parameters drop-down list box is 2049.

Figure 16.20 shows several custom texture fills that were made from the default textures.

*Figure 16.20.*
*Samples of various custom*
*texture fills.*

## PostScript Texture

PostScript texture is the last icon (identified by the letters PS) in the Fill tool flyout menu. When you select this icon, the PostScript Texture dialog box (see Figure 16.21) appears. It contains a menu listing texture names and a preview window that can display the texture selected. The preview window, by default, shows the name of the texture you selected. If you click the Preview Fill button, the texture will display. (See Figure 16.22.) The lower-left portion of the dialog box is the Parameters section. Various settings are offered, depending on which texture is selected. Click the Refresh button in the dialog box to preview the texture after making changes in the Parameters section. When you fill an object with a PostScript fill, it will not display on the CorelDRAW screen or in full-screen preview mode because of the excessive redraw time required. Objects filled with PostScript textures instead display a series of PSs.

*Figure 16.21.*
*The PostScript Texture*
*dialog box.*

*Figure 16.22.*
*The PostScript Texture*
*dialog box with the*
*Preview Fill option*
*enabled.*

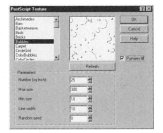

# Corel*NOTE!*

PostScript fills in the past required a PostScript printer. They can now be printed on any CorelDRAW-supported printer. CorelDRAW 6 converts the PostScript fills to bitmaps for use in non-PostScript printers.

Figure 16.23 shows a few of the default PostScript fills.

*Figure 16.23.*
*Sample default PostScript*
*fills.*

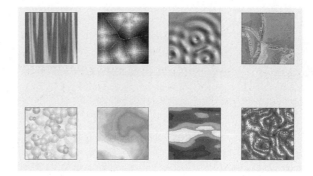

## The Special Fill Roll-Up

The Special Fill roll-up (see Figure 16.24) gives you on-screen access to all of the fills (except for Solid and Postscript fills) that are found in the Fill flyout. Click the Special Fill Roll-Up icon (the third icon on the top in the Fill flyout menu) to display the Special Fill roll-up. Many users find that they can work faster in CorelDRAW when they use the Special Fill roll-up to choose fills.

*Figure 16.24.*
*The Special Fill roll-up*
*with the default palette*
*displayed.*

The advantage of using the Special Fill roll-up instead of opening the various dialog boxes to apply fills is negated if you need to use more than basic fills. Suppose you want to apply a fountain fill using an edge pad or a custom color. This requires you to click the Edit button in the Fill roll-up to access the Fountain Fill dialog box so the changes can be made. For simple fills requiring no custom settings, the Special Fill roll-up works well. An important thing to remember when using the Special Fill roll-up is that after making any changes to an object's fill, you must click the Apply button before the changes take effect.

# Corel*NOTE!*

It's important to differentiate the Special Fill roll-up settings from the settings in the
Fountain Fill dialog box. If an object is filled using the Uniform Fill dialog box, its fill does
not appear in the palettes or preview window of the Special Fill roll-up when the object is
selected. Conversely, a fill created using the Special Fill roll-up does not appear in the
Fountain Fill dialog box palettes or preview windows. This is also true regarding the
other special fills on the bottom of the flyout. Choose one method as your primary
method to help eliminate confusion when you work with fills.

## The Color Roll-Up

The Color roll-up is accessed by clicking the second icon from the left at the top of
the Fill flyout. It is used for filling objects with solid colors (just as the Uniform fill
dialog box does). It falls into the same category as the Special Fill roll-up in that
you should choose a primary method for filling objects with solid colors. Either
work with the Uniform Fill dialog box or the Color roll-up. The Color roll-up is
shown in its default display in Figure 16.25. The default display is the RGB color
model. Click the down arrow next to the parameters box showing RGB to select
different color models or palettes. To edit a color model, click the arrow button just
above the parameters box displaying the color model. A flyout will appear with
several options. If you select Palette in this parameters box, you can edit the
selected color by choosing Edit from the flyout. This brings up the Select Color
dialog box. This dialog box is identical in every way to the Uniform Fill dialog box.

*Figure 16.25.*
*The color roll-up*
*displayed in the*
*default configuration.*

# Corel*NOTE!*

Now you have learned more than you will ever what to know about the Fill tool settings. There is one more dialog box that has been added in CorelDRAW 6. This dialog box can save you more time than most of the previous options described. The dialog box is called the Object Properties Dialog box. If you right-click on the object you want to fill, the Object Properties pop-up menu appears. Click on Properties at the bottom of the pop-up menu to bring up the Object Properties dialog box. (See Figure 16.26.)

Click on the fill tab in the Object Properties dialog box to reveal the fill property settings. All of the fill options previously described can be used in this dialog box except Postscript fills. If you need further editing, Click on the Edit button to bring up the appropriate dialog boxes.

Figure 16.26.
The Object Properties
dialog box with the Fill tab
selected.

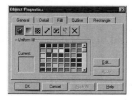

# Skill Session: Manipulation Workshop

# 17

# Aligning and Distributing

To align or distribute objects, use the Align & Distribute roll-up. Select it from the Arrange menu or use the Align/ Distribute icon from the ribbon bar. The roll-up can be used in align mode or distribute mode by selecting the corresponding button.

When a button is pressed, it becomes darker in color than those that are not pressed. To indicate no alignment, make sure the buttons are not pressed. There are two double-headed arrows that can only be used in distribute mode.

## Aligning

You can alignany selected object(s) to the center of the page as well as to the grid. When you align to the grid, CorelDRAW uses the grid setup that you've established using Grid Setup in the Layout menu.

When using the Align & Distribute roll-up to align objects to each other, remember that the objects will be aligned to the last object selected.

You can override this feature only by selecting the Align to Center of Page or Align to Grid options. In Figure 17.1, there are three different objects in different positions on-screen.

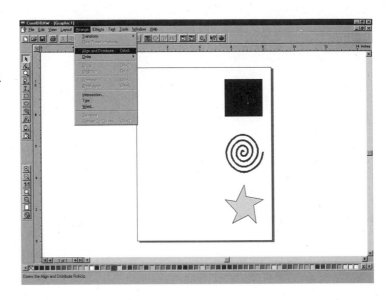

Figure 17.1.
*Three objects on-screen,
and the Arrange menu
with the Align & Distrib-
ute command highlighted.*

To invoke the Align & Distribute roll-up, pull down the Arrange menu and select
Align. The Align dialog box appears. (See Figure 17.2.) You can select various
options for aligning selected objects.

Figure 17.2.
*The Align & Distribute
roll-up with the available
options for aligning.*

Choose the Align to Center of Page option. Note that the Center options in both
the Vertically and Horizontally sections are automatically enabled. Figure 17.3
shows the effect the Align to Center of Page option has on the selected objects.

*Figure 17.3.*
*The three objects aligned*
*to the center of the page.*

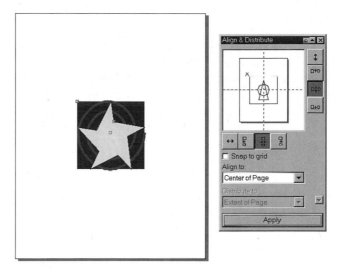

Aligning objects to a grid works the same as aligning objects to the center of the page. The Snap to Grid or Show Grid options in the Layout menu don't have to be enabled for this to work. The grid is set up in 1-inch increments.

In the Align & Distribute roll-up, select Center in both the Vertically and Horizontally sections and check the Align to Grid check box. With these settings, the centers of the objects align to the grid.

# Corel *TIP!*

You must check one of the alignment boxes before the Align to Grid option can be enabled.

Figure 17.4 illustrates the difference between the Align to Grid option and the Align to Center of Page option. Here the centers of the objects have been aligned to the grid (which is set at 1-inch increments and is also being displayed), not to the center of the page.

In Figure 17.5, the three objects are in different positions. To align the top side of the other objects with the top of the square, select the other objects first and then select the square.

Figure 17.4.
*Three objects aligned with*
*the Align to Grid option.*

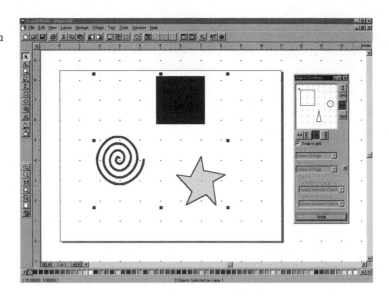

Figure 17.5.
*The Align & Distribute*
*roll-up with Top enabled*
*in the Vertically section,*
*and the three objects*
*before alignment.*

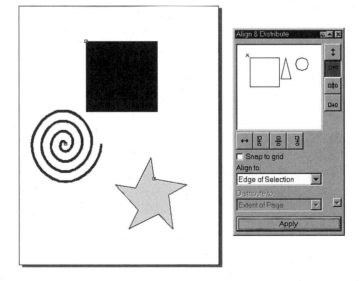

From the Align & Distribute roll-up, select Top in the Vertically section and press
the Apply button. Now the two objects are aligned with the top of the square. (See
Figure 17.6.)

*Figure 17.6.*
*The top side of the other*
*two objects aligned with*
*the top of the square.*

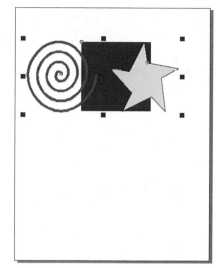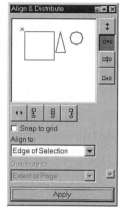

# Corel *NOTE!*

In the Align & Distribute roll-up, you can select one option from the Vertically section and one from the Horizontally section. You cannot select more than one option at the same time from either section.

Notice that two of the objects have been reduced: the spiral and the star. (See Figure 17.7.) This will make it easier for you to see the effects of the alignment options.

Select the spiral and the star. Next, select the square and bring up the Align & Distribute roll-up. In the Vertically section, select Top. In the Horizontally section, select Left. Click the Apply button. Figure 17.8 shows what happens after the options in the dialog box are applied to the three selected objects.

In Figure 17.9, the set of three objects has been duplicated 15 times, and each set has been aligned differently.

# Corel *NOTE!*

You can align more than three objects. Three objects have been used in these examples for the sake of simplicity.

*Figure 17.7.*
*The three objects, with*
*the spiral and the star*
*reduced.*

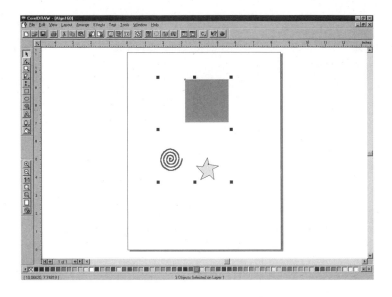

*Figure 17.8.*
*The three objects after*
*alignment.*

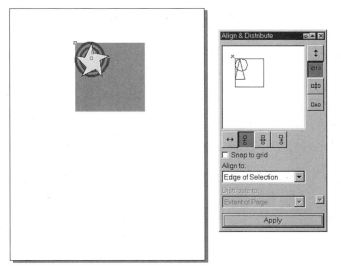

*Figure 17.9.*
*Fifteen sets of three*
*objects, all aligned in*
*various ways.*

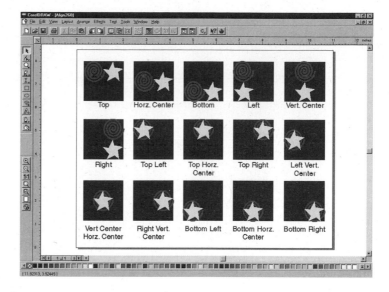

# Distributing

Select the double-headed arrows to activate the distribute option. In conjunction with the align mode, there are quite a few ways to distribute objects: top sides, left sides, center, and so on. Below the Distribute To section is a pull-down menu. From here, choose whether to distribute selected objects to the extent of those selected objects or the extent of your current page.

To the right of the Distribute To section is an arrowhead that points down. Press this arrowhead to expand the Align & Distribute roll-up and show the Options section. The Options section contains two drop-down lists. From here you can select whether to distribute horizontally or vertically by Space between objects, Left edges of objects, Center of objects, or Right edges of objects.

Let's put the Distribute options to use. Select a computer hard drive symbol from the computer category in the Symbols roll-up. Then duplicate and move it six times. Select the seven hard drives and invoke the Align & distribute roll-up.

In the roll-up, select the horizontal distribute double headed arrow from the horizontal section; in the vertical section, select the align to top button. In the Align to: section choose Edge of Page. In the Distribute to: section choose Extent of page. And from the Options section pick Space between objects from the drop down list. (See Figure 17.10.)

*Figure 17.10.*
*Seven computer hard*
*drive symbols before and*
*after distributing horizon-*
*tally.*

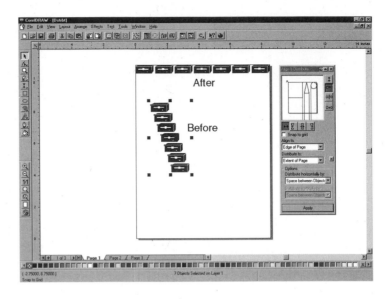

Change the settings in the roll-up to distribute the seven hard drive symbols vertically. Select the vertical distribute double headed arrow from the vertical section; in the horizontal section select the align to right button. In the Align to: section choose Edge of Page. In the Distribute to: section choose Extent of page. From the Options section pick Space between objects from the drop-down list. (See Figure 17.11.)

*Figure 17.11.*
*Seven computer hard*
*drive symbols before and*
*after distributing verti-*
*cally.*

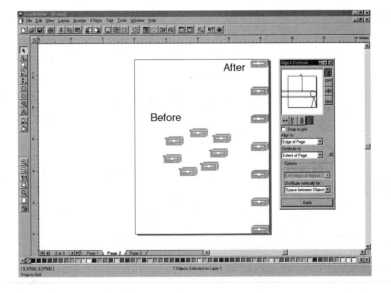

Select a horn symbol from the music category in the Symbols roll-up. Then duplicate and move it six times. Select the seven horns and, in the Align & distribute roll-up, select the horizontal distribute double headed arrow from the horizontal section.

In the Distribute to: section choose Extent of page. From the Options section, pick Space between objects from both of the drop down lists and press the apply button. Then in the vertical section select the double headed arrow from the vertical section and press the apply button. This distributes the horns diagonally. (See Figure 17.12.)

*Figure 17.12.*
*Seven horn symbols before and after distributing diagonally.*

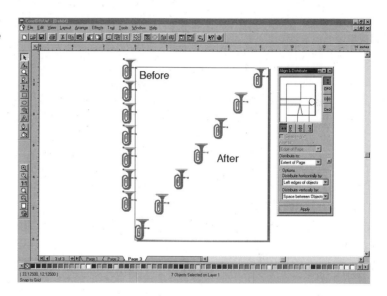

# 18

# Object Ordering

The Order command allows you to select objects or groups of objects and move them to different levels within the drawing. To understand how this command works, you need to remember that each time you draw a new object on the page, that object is in front of all the previously drawn objects or groups of objects. To access the Order command, select Order from the Arrange pull-down menu; a flyout will appear, giving you a choice of the different order options. Figure 18.1 shows the flyout menu.

## Corel*NOTE!*

There is a new way in CorelDRAW 6 to access the Order flyout: With an object or objects selected, right-click one of the objects. This method brings up the Object Properties menu from which you can select the Order command flyout. Some users might find this method a little faster than selecting the Order commands from the Order flyout in the Arrange pull-down menu.

*Figure 18.1.*
*The Order flyout menu,*
*selected from the Arrange*
*pull-down menu.*

The Order flyout menu offers seven choices:

■ Select To Front to move the selected object in front of all other objects. For example, you could use this command to move text previously placed on-screen in front of a new object.

■ Select To Back to move the selected object behind all other objects. For example, suppose that as an afterthought you create a background for an illustration. By creating the background last, you place it in front of everything else. To solve this problem, select the new background and choose To Back from the Order command flyout menu.

Figure 18.2 illustrates the use of To Back in the Order command flyout.

*Figure 18.2.*
*Using the To Back option*
*to position objects.*

# Corel*NOTE!*

If you somehow deselected an object after you sent it to the back, it might be hidden by a larger object. To select the object again, hold down the Shift key and then press the Tab key. Each time you press the Tab key while the Shift key is held down, objects are selected in order from back to front.

■ Select Forward One to move the selected object forward one level at a time.
■ Use Back One to accomplish the opposite of Forward One.

■ Select Reverse Order to reverse the order of two or more objects or groups of objects. Imagine two objects, one in front of the other. Select the two objects either by marquee-selection or by holding down the Shift key while clicking each object. Choose Reverse Order from the Order command flyout menu, and the two objects exchange places. (See Figure 18.3.)

*Figure 18.3.*
*Using the Reverse Order*
*option.*

■ The In Front of option comes in handy when there are many objects on-screen. Suppose you want to move a specific object to a specific place and in a certain sequence. For example, there are 20 objects on-screen and you have created a new object that you want to place just in front of an object that was created earlier in the drawing. The quickest way to do this is to select the new object and then select the In Front of option from the Order flyout menu. A large arrow will appear in place of the cursor. Use this arrow to point to the object that you want your new object to appear in front of. Figure 18.4 illustrates the method—the pear is selected and the arrow points to the peach in the cornucopia. The pear will be placed in front of the peach and behind the grapes and cherry.

*Figure 18.4.*
*Using the Behind option.*

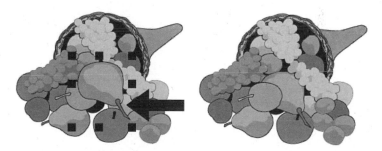

■ The Behind option is the reverse of the In Front of option. It places the selected object behind the "pointed to" object.

At left is an example of the Transparency Lens. The red circle just has a red fill in it, but the green and blue circles both use a transparency lens. Use of the Transparency Lens is explained in more detail in Skill Session 34.

At right is an example of the Brighten Lens. The text "RAINY NIGHTS" had a Brighten Lens of 40% applied to it. The text was converted to curves before printing so that the text would print as a single object thus making the print file considerably smaller. The Brighten Lens is explained in detail in Skill Session 34.

At left is an example of the Invert Lens. The word "INVERT" had the Invert Lens applied to it. Again the text was converted to curves so that the print file would be smaller. The Invert Lens is explained in detail in Skill Session 34.

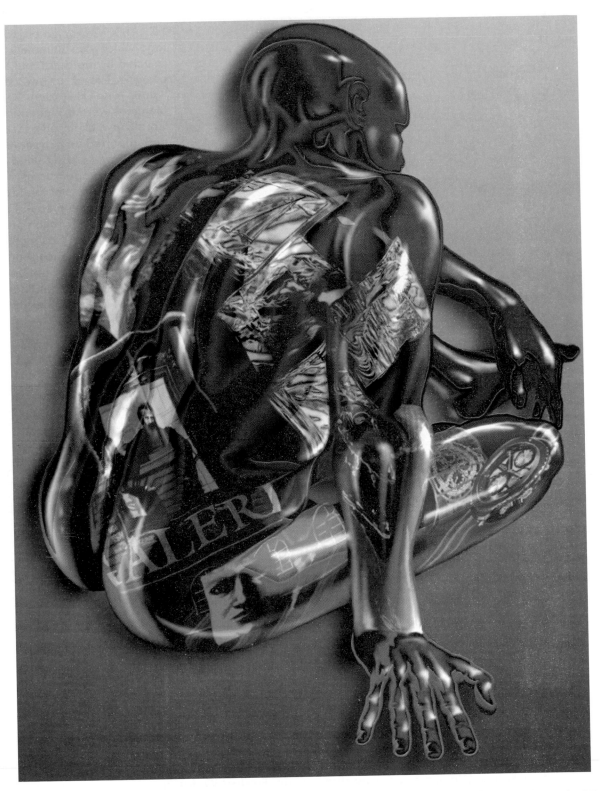

Robert Travers was the winner of the Landscapes, Landmarks, and Abstracts category of Corel's World Design Contest for January 1995 with the image shown above.

# 19

# Grid and Ruler Setup

With Grid and Ruler Setup, you can set a grid to any specification required to complete almost any project. Illustrations that demand exact measurements, such as blueprints or maps, can be created faster when you use Grid and Ruler Setup. To activate the Grid and Ruler Setup dialog box, select Grid and Ruler Setup from the Layout pull-down menu. You can also activate it by double-clicking the rulers with the cursor. (See Figure 19.1.)

The Grid and Ruler Setup dialog box (Figure 19.2) has a Ruler tab and a Grid tab. Press the Ruler tab to see options for changing the horizontal and vertical ruler in the Units section. Here is a list of the available measurement units:

  Inches
  Millimeters
  Picas, points
  Points
  Ciceros, didots
  Didots
  Feet
  Miles
  Centimeters
  Meters
  Kilometers

Figure 19.1.
*The Layout pull-down*
*menu with the Grid and*
*Ruler Setup command*
*highlighted.*

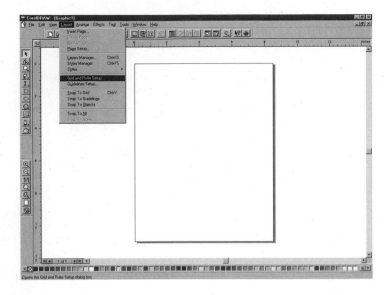

Press the Grid tab to see options for setting the grid frequency and origin, showing the grid, and snapping to the grid.

Figure 19.2.
*The Grid and Ruler Setup*
*dialog box with its*
*available options.*

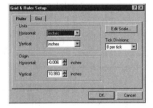

# Corel *NOTE!*

The grid can be displayed on-screen and is represented by a series of dots. To enable this
option, select Grid and Ruler Setup from the Layout pull-down menu. Press the Grid tab
and find the Show Grid option located at the lower-left corner of the Grid and Ruler Setup
dialog box. An × indicates that this option is enabled.

Below the Show Grid option is the Snap To Grid option. This option is helpful
when you know what size you want certain objects to be. For a rectangle that is to
be 2" × 3.5", you can set a grid at 0.5-inch increments. It's easier to fulfill that
specific requirement with the Snap To Grid option enabled than it is to draw the
rectangle freehand.

The Snap To Grid option is also found in the Layout pull-down menu. To enable or disable this option, simply select it from the Layout pull-down menu. Another way to enable or disable the Snap To Grid option is to press Ctrl+Y.

When accuracy counts, setting up the grid and then enabling the Snap To Grid option will decrease drawing time and ensure that the objects are the sizes they need to be. The Snap To Grid option can also assist you with aligning various elements.

Draw a rectangle with the Snap To Grid option off. Then, draw a second rectangle with the Snap To Grid option on. Observe how the second rectangle clings to the grid as you draw. (See Figure 19.3.)

*Figure 19.3.*
*The selected rectangle is drawn with the Snap To Grid option enabled.*

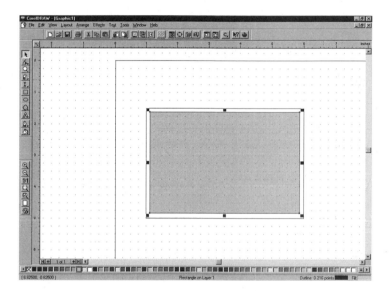

You can also turn the grid on or off by using the Layers manager. (See Skill Session 21, "Layers.") To turn the grid on or off, right-click Grid in the Layers manager; in the Layers Settings dialog box, enable or disable the Visible option. (See Figure 19.4.)

There is yet another method of turning the Snap To Grid option on or off: Pull down the Layout menu and select Snap To Grid. The Snap To Guidelines, Snap To Objects, Snap To All, and Snap To None commands are also available.

When you save your document, the Snap To Grid option settings are saved along with that document. This feature allows you to have the Snap To Grid option enabled in one document and disabled in another document.

*Figure 19.4.*
*The Layers manager and*
*the Grid Settings dialog*
*box for the Grid layer with*
*the Visible option dis-*
*abled.*

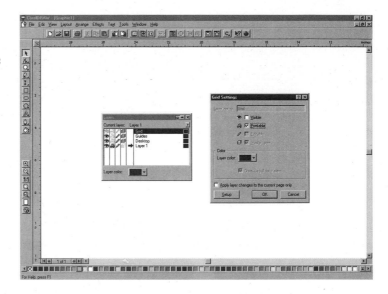

Draw a 2"×1" rectangle with the Snap To Grid option enabled. If you need to draw an object to scale, you can use ratios (for example, a 1:10 ratio can be set, with 10 inches equal to 1 mile) for building schematics or maps. You can use the Drawing Scale command in the Layout pull-down menu.

In the Grid and Ruler Setup dialog box, you change the grid frequency by entering new values in the Horizontal and Vertical sections. Type a value or use the up and down arrows. The measurement system can be changed from inches to millimeters, picas, or points.

# Corel*NOTE!*

When you open a new drawing, it retains the grid and ruler setup information used for the last document. If the Snap To Grid option is enabled in one file, that option will carry over into all subsequent files until you disable it.

In the Frequency section, you can set the amount of occurrence (per unit of measurement) for both the horizontal and vertical grid. You can also change values by retyping them or using the up and down arrows. By using the grid and its options, you can quickly create a grid to your specific measurements. (See Figure 19.5.)

*Figure 19.5.*
*The grid frequency can be*
*changed to different*
*values from the default*
*settings.*

# Measurement Systems

CorelDRAW's ruler displays the currently selected measurement system in use. This information is found on the top-right side of your screen on the horizontal ruler. When you change the measurement system from inches to feet, the rulers display that change. The look and operation of the rulers transform when the Paragraph Text tool is in use. A white zone displays on each ruler and denotes the height and width of the paragraph frame. Use this zone to add indents, tabs, and to carry out assorted word processing–related tasks. Access to formatting choices is available by clicking any of these zones with the right mouse button.

## Using Rulers

If you don't already have your rulers on, pull down the View menu and select the Rulers option. A check mark appears next to the Rulers option when it is enabled. The rulers appear on-screen. (See Figure 19.6.)

*Figure 19.6.*
*The View pull-down menu*
*with the Rulers option*
*enabled and the rulers on-*
*screen.*

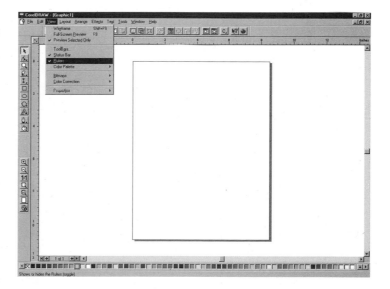

The rulers have several functions you can activate on-screen. Double-click the rulers to invoke the Grid and Ruler Setup dialog box. Click the rulers and drag away from them to place guidelines on the screen. (For more information on guidelines, see Skill Session 20, "Guidelines.")

With the right mouse button, click the rulers in the top-left corner where they meet, and a pop-up box appears with three options. Two of them are shortcuts to the Grid and Rulers Setup and Guidelines Setup options. The other option is the What's This help shortcut. Click the section at the top-left corner of the rulers and pull the crosshairs onto the screen to set the zero points on the rulers. You can use the crosshairs to check the alignment of your objects. (See Figure 19.7.)

## Corel *TIP!*

Double-click the Crosshairs icon to reset the zero points to the default setting.

To move both the vertical and horizontal rulers to your object(s), hold down the Shift key and click the top-left corner of the rulers. With the Shift key held down, move the rulers close to the object. Release the Shift key to set your rulers down. The vertical and horizontal rulers can be moved independently of each other to almost any location on-screen. Hold down the Shift key and select either the horizontal or vertical ruler to move it.

In the Grid & Ruler Setup dialog box, Ruler Unit is where you can select from different units of measurement, such as inches, meters, and centimeters. Ruler Origin indicates where the zero points are set on the rulers.

When you use the Zoom tool, the ruler's hash marks change accordingly. The closer you zoom in on objects in your document, the more accurate the display of your ruler becomes.

## Corel *TIP!*

When you move your rulers to a location on-screen, you can set them back to their original positions by holding down the Shift key and double-clicking where the rulers cross over each other. This also applies to each ruler individually as well.

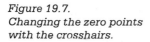
*Figure 19.7.*
*Changing the zero points*
*with the crosshairs.*

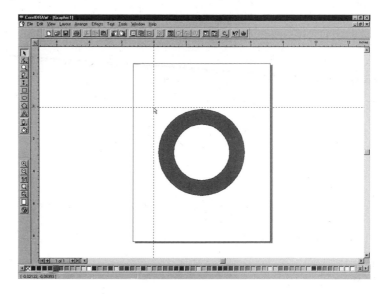

## Drawing Scale

Use the Drawing Scale option to set the World Distance. This option comes in handy with drawings that contain objects that aren't drawn to scale, such as the roads on a map. You can set your measurements in ratios; for example, 1 inch could be equal to 3 miles.

Press the Edit Scale button in the Grid and Ruler dialog box to bring up the Drawing Scale dialog box. Choose a setting from the Typical Scales list or enter new values in the Page Distance and World Distance sections. Change the setting to 1:00 inch = 7.0 feet. (See Figure 19.8.)

*Figure 19.8.*
*The Drawing Scale dialog*
*box with the Set World*
*Distance option enabled.*

Select the 2"×1" rectangle. Notice that the status line now reflects the changes that were made in the Drawing Scale dialog box. The status line now tells you that the rectangle is 14'×7'.

**20**

# Guidelines

You'll find the Guidelines Setup command in the Layout pull-down menu. Use guidelines for aligning objects. On-screen, the guidelines appear as blue dashes. Place as many guidelines as you need in your document. (See Figure 20.1.)

In the Layout pull-down menu, select Snap To Guidelines. With this option enabled, objects will snap to the guidelines. CorelDRAW saves the guidelines with the drawing. The guidelines will not print unless you set that option in the Layers Manager. (For more information on layers, see Skill Session 21, "Layers.")

*Figure 20.1.*
*The Layout pull-down*
*menu with Guidelines*
*Setup highlighted.*

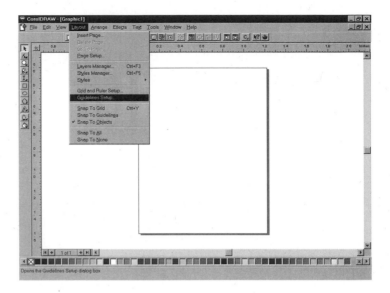

## Setting Guidelines

To set guidelines, click and hold the left mouse button on either the vertical or horizontal ruler and drag away from it. A guideline appears on-screen. Use the rulers to place the guidelines, or call up the Guidelines dialog box and set deliberate positions for the guidelines.

There are three tabs in the Guidelines Setup dialog box. They are Horizontal, Vertical, and Slanted. If one or more guidelines are on your screen, their positions will be in the section below the three tabs in the Guidelines Setup dialog box.

Select the Slanted tab to display information for diagonal guidelines. The Specify pull-down menu lets you choose between Angle and 1 Point, or 2 Points. You can alter the X and Y coordinates of the slanted guideline as well as determine the angle in degrees.

## Changing Guideline Positions

To change the position of a guideline, select it, and with the left mouse button held down, drag the guideline to its new position. To modify the location of the guideline from within the Guideline Setup dialog box, type in a new value and press the

Move button. It uses the measurement system set up by the grid. The Show Guidelines and Snap To Guidelines options are at the lower-left corner of the dialog box; they enable you to display guidelines and snap objects to them, respectively.

You can use any of the arrow keys (left, up, down, or right) to cycle through the available measurement systems. Use the Tab key to cycle through the other options in the Guidelines Setup dialog box. Use the four buttons on the right side of the dialog box to add, move, delete, or clear guidelines from either the horizontal, vertical, or slanted sections, whichever is currently selected in the View section. (See Figure 20.2.)

*Figure 20.2.*
*The Guidelines Setup*
*dialog box.*

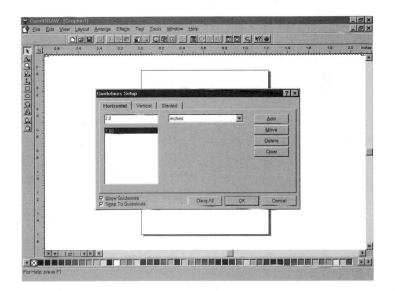

When the Snap To Guidelines option is enabled, objects that are brought near the guidelines seem to stick to the guideline. With Snap To Grid selected, click the vertical ruler and drag the guideline to the 1-inch position. Do the same with the guideline from the horizontal ruler. Then, modify another into a tilted position. (See Figure 20.3.)

*Figure 20.3.*
*Vertical, diagonal, and*
*horizontal guidelines,*
*placed at the 1-inch marks*
*on the rulers.*

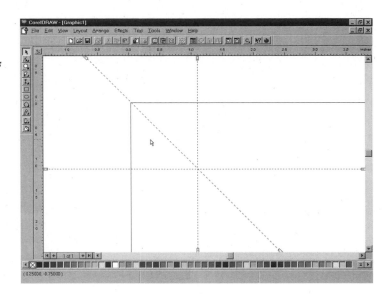

## Slanted Guidelines

The new slanted guidelines can help you draw a shape with odd angles, such as a polygon. Place two horizontal and two vertical guidelines on the screen and position them so they form a rectangular shape. Then place a diagonal guideline so that it crosses over the other four guidelines and forms the shape of a polygon.

Draw a polygon with the Freehand tool by placing a node where the guidelines intersect each other. Ensure the Snap to Guidelines option is enabled. Then move the polygon away from the guideline. See how it seems to stick to the guideline as you move it along. This will help you when you need to align objects to specific areas on your document. You can place a guideline at the required increment on the ruler and move any objects to that position. (See Figure 20.4.)

Guidelines can also be used to help create setups for projects such as company logos, letterhead, statements, business cards, or forms. Place guidelines where you want to position graphic elements and text. (See Figure 20.5.) Use the rulers to help you set up the guidelines.

You can use predetermined requirements to create the document. Use the Guidelines Setup dialog box to add and place the guidelines. (See Figure 20.6.)

*Figure 20.4.*
*The polygon after it has*
*snapped to the guidelines.*

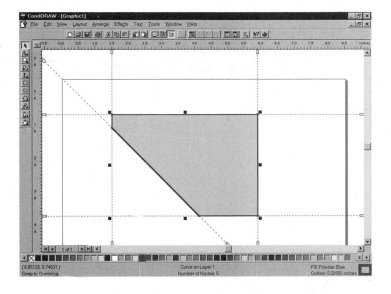

*Figure 20.5.*
*Guidelines positioned*
*where elements are to*
*be placed.*

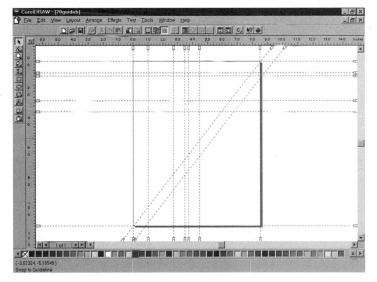

*Figure 20.6.*
*Use the Guidelines Setup*
*dialog box to add and*
*place guidelines at exact*
*positions.*

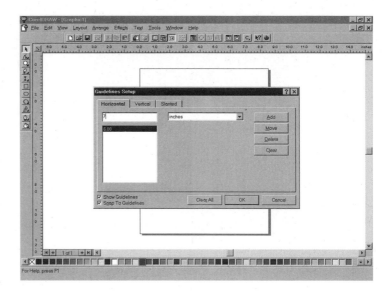

# Guideline Color

In the Layers Manager, the default Layer color is set to blue. Click the color button, and a pull-down menu appears. (See Figure 20.7.) Select a color from the palette or click the Others button to select different color choices. Pull a guideline onto the screen to see the new color displayed or bring up the Guide Settings dialog box and change the color there. After you select a new color, click OK to see the guidelines' color change in the document. All guidelines on this layer will take on the same attributes.

*Figure 20.7.*
*The Layers Manager and*
*the Guides Settings dialog*
*box, with a color selected.*

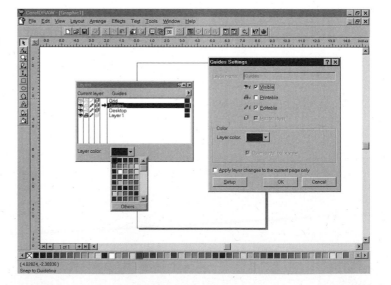

# Corel*NOTE!*

You can print your guidelines. From the Layers manager, bring up the Guides settings dialog box, enable the Printable option and press the OK button. The guidelines will now print along with the rest of your document

## Create Guidelines from Other Objects

Select Guides from the list in the Layers Manager. New objects that are placed or drawn on this layer take on the attributes of a guideline. You can use this feature to create odd-shaped guidelines. Drawings of objects as well as text can be placed on the Guides layer. (See Figure 20.8.)

*Figure 20.8.*
*A polygon (or any other shape) that is drawn on the Guides layer becomes a guide.*

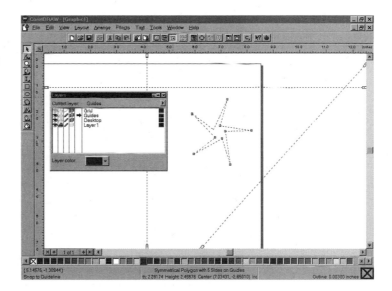

# Corel*NOTE!*

You can import objects onto the Guides layer as well. A vector-based image, such as a CDR or EPS file, appears on-screen as a dashed line. However, an imported bitmap object, such as a CPT or TIF file, shows a dashed line only around that bitmap's bounding box.

## Sample Statement

Use the guidelines to align text and other objects with each other. If you need to fit an illustration or logo into a specific area, use the guidelines to assist you in resizing these elements. (See Figure 20.9.)

*Figure 20.9.*
*Using the guidelines to place and resize various elements.*

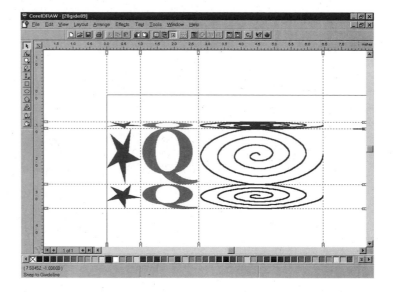

Figure 20.10 is a close-up of a sample form. It is a statement set up by using the guidelines. Elements were created and then positioned according to predetermined specifications.

Figure 20.11 is a full-page view of the statement. Twenty guidelines were used to set up this statement. Once the guidelines are in place, setting the elements up to create the statement is a breeze.

Figure 20.10.
A statement created by
using the guidelines.

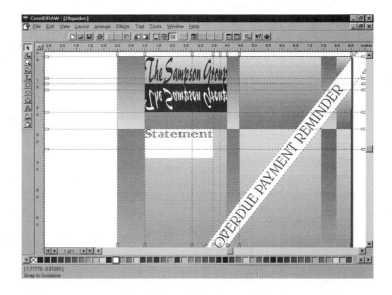

Figure 20.11.
The finished statement.

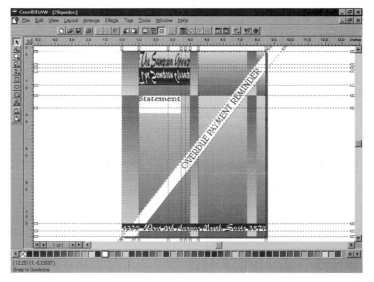

205

# 21

# Layers

Every time you draw an object in CorelDRAW, you create
a new layer on the page. Understanding this basic fact
will help you understand the complex world of working
with layers. The layers described in this skill session are
not the layers you automatically create when you draw
objects on the screen; rather, they are special layers that
can contain certain portions of your drawing. You can
place one object or many objects on these special layers.
This skill session will teach you the purpose of the
Layers Manager and how you can use it to organize
objects in your drawings. Organization can save you time
and prevent accidental changes to your drawings.

## The Layer Manager

Figure 21.1 is a drawing that represents the concept of
layers. The black outlines represent a cross section of a
page containing three separate layers. The three gray
objects in each layer represent three separate objects
drawn on each layer. Every object you draw on the page
is placed above the last object drawn, including text.
This is what is meant when we say you are creating
layers automatically when you draw objects. Each object
can be moved in front of or behind another object by
using the Order command in the Arrange pull-down
menu.

When you create special layers using the Layers Manager, you create a subset of layers that can be stacked in
any order relative to each other. All objects assigned to a
special layer can be moved relative to each other within

that layer. All of these special layers and the objects assigned to them make up the completed drawing. This ability to create special layers containing portions of the drawing provides the organizational flexibility referred to earlier.

*Figure 21.1.*
*A cross section of a page*
*using three layers.*

Layer 1

Layer 2

Layer 3

Using the Layers Manager to create multiple layers can be very confusing and, therefore, counter-productive for many CorelDRAW users. If you take the time to learn how to work in a multiple-layers environment, you could find it very useful. The most important fact to remember is that it's not necessary to use multiple layers for most projects. This author has created hundreds of complex drawings using only a single layer (the default, Layer One) with great success.

The Layers Manager is accessed by clicking on Layers Manager in the Layout pull-down menu. Figure 21.2 shows the Layers dialog box in the default configuration. The dialog box is divided into columns containing different icons. Each column and their icons are described in the following sections.

*Figure 21.2.*
*The Layers dialog box*
*displayed in the default*
*configuration.*

## Column 1

The first column, filled with Eye icons, controls whether a layer is visible or invisible. Click the icons to toggle between the two options. If the icon is grayed out, the layer will be invisible. Making a layer invisible eliminates the sometimes lengthy redraw time of an object. Making a layer invisible occasionally helps if the layer overlaps other objects in your drawing, making them hard to work on.

## Column 2

The printer icons in the second column can be toggled on and off to prevent or allow the printing of certain layers. The printer icons that are grayed out by default can be turned on, allowing you to print the Grid and Guidelines in a drawing. Unless you are printing to a paper size larger than the page size, you wouldn't activate the printer icon for the Desktop layer (because objects on the desktop will not print).

## Column 3

The Pencil icons in the third column are used to lock specific layers. The purpose of locking a layer is to prevent the accidental editing or moving of objects on the locked layer. When objects are on a layer that has been locked, they can not be selected or edited. This can confuse the new user who has not dealt with layers before. If you are unable to select an object, the first thing you should check is whether the object is on a locked layer. A layer is locked if the pencil icon is grayed out.

## Column 4

The icons in the fourth column represent the master layer. The Grid, Guides, and Desktop are on the master layer by default. The master layer is a repeating layer. Any object on a layer that has been assigned to the master layer will appear on every page of a multi-page document. This ability to place an object on a master layer allows you to use a masthead, or any other object that you want to appear on every page, without having to manually place it on each page. To make any layer a master layer, simply click the grayed out Master Layer icon to make it active.

## Column 5

The fifth column contains an arrow pointing to the layer you are working on. If you want to draw an object on any layer other than the one to which the arrow points, you must move the arrow to the desired layer to make it active. This is one of the areas of confusion that we mentioned in the beginning of the skill session. If you decide to create your projects using multiple layers, you must pay constant attention to the active layer. Otherwise, you will end up drawing on layers unintentionally. The status line always shows which layer an object is on when the object is selected.

## Column 6

The sixth column contains the names of all the layers in the drawing or multiple-page project. When you first open the Layers Manager, none of the layer names are highlighted. You must highlight a name by clicking on it before you can access the Settings dialog box. (See the Settings dialog box shown in Figure 21.4.)

To the right of the layer names are colored squares showing the color assigned to that particular layer. You can change the color for each layer by clicking on the Layer Color button at the bottom of the dialog box. You assign a color to a layer so that you can identify layers by color when you view your drawing in wireframe mode.

You can also view a layer in a pseudo-wireframe view while in preview mode by enabling the Override Full Color view box in the Settings dialog box. (See the section "Settings" later in this skill session.)

# The Layers Flyout Menu

The Layers flyout menu is accessed by clicking on the arrow button at the upper right of the Layers Manager dialog box. Figure 21.3 shows the menu when it is accessed. The menu lists various commands that are described later in this chapter.

*Figure 21.3.*
*The Layers flyout menu.*

## Switch to Layer

The Switch to Layer command is somewhat redundant. Its purpose is to move the pointing arrow in the Layers Manager so that the arrow points to the layer that is highlighted. You can accomplish this much faster by simply clicking the arrow and dragging it to the layer you want to work on.

## New

Click the New Layer command to add additional layers.

## Delete

Click the Delete command to delete a layer. If you delete a layer that contains objects on other pages, you get a warning message asking if you really want to delete the layer. If you click the OK button in the warning box all objects on the layer regardless, of the page they are on will be deleted. This is not something to worry about because if you delete a layer, you would normally assume that any objects on that layer would also be deleted. If you don't want certain objects deleted when the layer is deleted, you should move those objects to a different layer before you delete the layer.

## Rename

If you want to rename a layer, first select the layer name in column 6. Then click the Rename command. The Layers name bar will be highlighted, and your cursor will change to text cursor. You can now type a new name for your layer. Using the

Rename command in the Layers flyout menu is not necessary in Windows 95. You can double-click the name and type a new name directly in the Layers name bar.

## Settings

Choose Settings to bring up the Settings dialog box. The settings in this dialog box are used when you want to apply custom settings to layers. The word Settings will be grayed out in the menu if you don't have a layer name selected and highlighted in the Layers Manager. The settings are described and shown in Figure 21.4.

*Figure 21.4.*
*The Settings dialog box.*

The Settings dialog box is used to change the settings for a specific layer. The name of the selected layer is displayed in the Layer name box at the top of the dialog box.

All of the following settings in the dialog box are duplicates of the settings in the Layers Manager dialog box described earlier. These settings are Visible, Printable, Editable, Master Layer, and Layer Color. They are included in the Settings dialog box to enable changes to apply to specific layers only.

The last setting in the dialog box—Apply layer changes to the current page only—is the reason for the duplicate settings. This setting and the Override full color view setting are described below.

## Apply Layer Changes to the Current Page Only

Placing a check mark in this box applies all the settings you have changed in the Settings dialog box to the selected layer on the page you are working on. This special setting would be used only if your document contains multiple pages.

## Override Full Color View

When you put a check mark in the Override Full Color View check box, the object fills are hidden for all the objects on a layer except the outline. You can assign a color to the outline for easy identification of the objects by clicking on the Layer Color button. Using Override Full Color View is another way of hiding an object without making it completely invisible. This method reduces the redraw time of complicated objects while still letting you to see their location on the page.

## Move To

Click the Move To command to move objects in your drawing to a different layer. When you select an object and then click the Move To command, your cursor changes to an arrow. Use the arrow and point to the layer to which you want to move the object.

## Copy To

Click the Copy To command to copy an object to a different layer. When you use this command, the original object remains on its layer and a copy is placed on the new layer.

## Edit Across Layers

This command is checked by default. If you remove the check mark from this command, you can select only objects that are on the active layer.

# Working with Layers

Now that you have learned what the different icons represent and how the different settings work, it's time to put some of them to practice. The first lesson is an exercise in moving layers up and down in the stacking order. The second lesson takes you through the steps required to place a single layer on several pages, while making the layer invisible in one.

## Lesson One—Moving Layers in the Stacking Order

Figure 21.5 shows a hamburger with all the fixings. This example has been used before, but it really is the best and easiest way to describe the way layers work. The actual filename is Hamburgd.CMX located on the CorelDRAW 6 number 4 CD. The clip art file was ungrouped, and the common objects were broken apart before any layering was used.

*Figure 21.5.
An example of moving
layers in the stacking
order.*

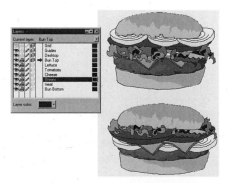

When you look at Figure 21.5, notice that we have given each layer a real name instead of the defaults of layer 1, 2, and so on. You should get in the habit of doing this when you create new layers because it's hard to remember which objects are on numbered layers. In this example, we created six new layers for a total of seven. Each layer was given a name that most closely represented what was to be put on that layer. After this was done, each of the groups of objects making up the parts of the hamburger were moved to their respective layers using the Move command in the Layers flyout. To change the layers name, just double-click it and retype the desired name.

After you have moved all the objects to their respective layers, finishing the hamburger simply becomes a matter of clicking on a layer and moving it to a different position in the stacking order. The layer at the top of the stacking order will be in front of all other layers, and so on down the list. Creating the image is simply a matter of rearranging the layers to get different effects. But if you think this is really very simple, you are thinking wishfully. Although everything we have just described is correct, you must do one more thing before your hamburger will look like those in Figure 21.5. When you move the layers in the stacking order, the layers will not always seem correct in the image. In the case of the hamburger, you will need to select the individual object groups and drag up or down until they seem correct.

## Lesson Two—Hiding Layers

Figure 21.6 is an example of a four-page booklet. A masthead appears on the two left-hand pages, but it doesn't appear on the two right-hand pages. The masthead was placed only once on the first left-hand page. By changing the settings in the Layers and Settings dialog boxes, it was placed again on the second left-hand page without being placed in either of the right-hand pages. Follow the steps below to recreate this effect.

*Figure 21.6.*
*A four-page booklet with*
*the masthead showing on*
*pages one and three.*

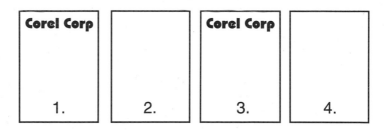

1. Open a new drawing.
2. Add three more pages by clicking the Insert page command in the Layout pull-down menu. You can also add pages by clicking on the + button next to the page counter at the lower left of the screen.

3. Open the Layers Manager by clicking Layers Manager in the Layout menu.

4. Move the pointing arrow in the Layers Manager so that it points to Layer One.

5. Click the Master Layer icon in column 4 next to layer 1 to make it active.

6. Type a word at the top of page one.

7. Click the page two tab in the lower-left corner of the screen to move to page two.

8. Click the layer name (Layer One) to highlight it.

9. Click the arrow at the upper right of the Layers Manager dialog box to bring up the flyout menu and choose Settings from the menu. You must have the layer name highlighted; otherwise, the word *Settings* will be grayed out in the flyout.

10. Remove the check mark from the box next to Eye icon and put a check mark in the box labeled "Apply Layer changes to the current page only."

11. Click the page four tab at the bottom of the screen to move to page four, and repeat steps 8 through 10.

12. Now click each page tab at the bottom of the screen to see that the masthead only appears on pages one and three.

This technique of hiding layers, along with the objects placed on the layers, can be very useful in your projects.

# Corel*NOTE!*

If your projects can benefit from using layers, you should spend some time exploring the various settings and commands until you know them very well. If you will be using layers only occasionally, be very careful and pay attention to which layer you're working on. If you don't, you will become very frustrated.

# 22

# Grouping
# and
# Ungrouping

The Group command, located in the Arrange menu, allows you to select individual objects and group them into a single group of objects so that the group can be treated as one object. Each object within the group retains its original attributes. It is one of the most useful commands you will use in CorelDRAW because it keeps all the elements within an individual drawing from being accidentally moved or altered. It also allows you to move the group as a single entity or apply many of CorelDRAW's effects to the entire group with one command.

To further understand the concept of grouping, visualize how you would draw a computer room. The room consists of tables, chairs, and equipment. Each chair is made up of several objects, as are all the other objects in the room. When you have finished drawing the chair, you should select all the objects that make up the chair and group them together. The next object you draw might be a monitor. When you finish the monitor, select all its objects and group them together. When you are finished with the entire drawing, you should select all the individual groups and group them together into a master group. Figure 22.1 illustrates how grouping objects helps keep your drawings together in separate groups as well as how individual groups can be put into a Master group.

*Figure 22.1.*
*Individual groups,*
*grouped together into a*
*master group.*

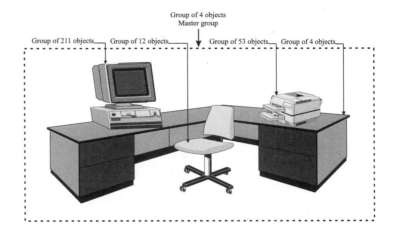

# Corel*NOTE!*

A complicated drawing can become cluttered with individual objects. You should form the habit of creating groups from those objects that share a commonality with each other.

To use the Group command, follow these steps:

1. Select the objects you want to group, either by marquee-selection or by clicking each object with the Pick tool while holding down the Shift key.

2. Click the Arrange menu and select Group.

There are three methods for grouping objects:

1. Click the Group icon on the ribbon bar.

2. Right-click the selected objects to bring up the Object Properties menu. From the Object Properties menu select Group.

3. Use the shortcut key sequence of Ctrl+G.

When you select a group of objects, the status line will show how many objects are in the group. There is a limit of 99 groups within a single or *master group.* There is no limit to the number of objects within a single group.

# Corel*NOTE!*

When you create a master group composed of several objects or groups of objects (or both), the status line, as mentioned before, will show how many objects are in the group. The difference this time is that groups will be counted as single objects. Therefore, when you ungroup a master group, you need to realize that you will still be left with the individual groups that were included in the master group.

A good example of a time when using the Group command is helpful is when working with clip art. Most clip art is made up of many individual objects that have been grouped together into a single group. If the objects were not grouped, it could be possible to accidentally select an object and move it out of place. You would also be prevented from applying an effect to the entire clip art image if the objects were left as single objects. As a group, objects can be moved or manipulated as a single entity. Figure 22.2 shows a clip art image in its original grouped form and after it has had an envelope effect applied to the group.

*Figure 22.2.*
*A clip art group and an*
*envelope effect applied to*
*the group.*

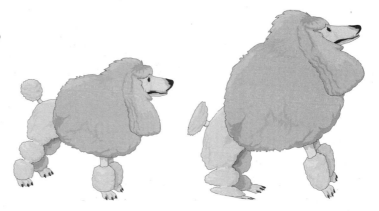

## Editing Objects Within a Group

CorelDRAW 4,5, and 6 allow you to edit individual objects within a group. This feature eliminates the need to ungroup a group of objects to make changes to individual objects.

## Child Objects

The object that is selected from within the group is called a *child object*. The clip art of Sylvester Stallone in Figure 22.3 was modified using the Child selection method. The right eyelid was selected as a child object and stretched down to make the eye appear swollen.

Here is how to edit any object within a group:

1. Hold down the Ctrl key and click the object you want to edit.

   The selected object has eight round handles instead of the customary square handles. (See Figure 22.3.)

2. The status line shows that the object is a child object.

3. Release the Ctrl key. The object remains selected. You can now change the object with many of the features and effects available in CorelDRAW for single objects, such as Move, Rotate, Shape, Size, Fill, and so on.

# Corel*NOTE!*

To delete a child object from within a group, you must select the Shape tool while the child object is selected and then select all the nodes on the object. With all the nodes selected, either press the Delete key or click the Minus icon in the Node Edit roll-up. If the object is not a single curve object, you need to convert that object to a curve using the Convert To Curves command in the Arrange menu before you can delete it.

*Figure 22.3.*
*Modifying a child object*
*within a group.*

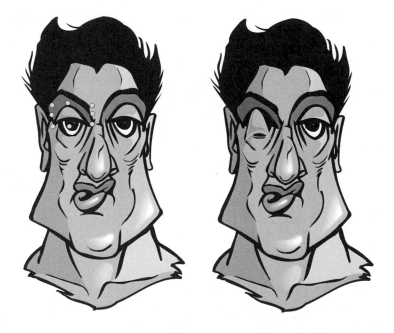

## Ungrouping

To ungroup a group of objects, use one of the following four methods:

1. Click Ungroup in the Arrange menu.
2. Click the Ungroup icon on the ribbon bar.
3. Right-click the group to bring up the Object Properties menu. From the Object Properties menu, select Ungroup.
4. Use the shortcut key sequence of Ctrl+U.

# 23

# Combining, Breaking Apart, and Separating Objects

The Combine command in CorelDRAW has a number of applications. The function of the Combine command is to take two or more objects and make them into a single object. The resultant single object becomes a curve, and it can be manipulated the same way as any other curve. You can even combine objects that are not touching or overlapping.

# Corel*NOTE!*

When you think of objects, remember that a single line is an object the same as rectangles, ellipses, and text.

In the earlier versions of CorelDRAW, the Combine command was used for many different tasks, including combining two objects into one object to form an entirely different shape. The Combine command in later versions has been relegated to only a few uses because of the introduction of the Weld, Trim, and Intersection commands. These new commands make it easier to create shapes that were previously created through the use of the Combine command.

The tasks that the Combine command can still best be used for is creating masks, combining objects to create complex patterns, and joining lines or curve segments.

## Creating Masks

Perhaps the most common use of the Combine command is to create masks. Figure 23.1 shows how combining a rectangle and text can create a transparent hole in the rectangle in the shape of the text. The purpose of a mask is to allow an underlying object to show through the holes in the mask. To create a mask similar to the one shown in Figure 23.1, follow these steps:

1. Import a bitmap image into the page area by selecting Import from the File menu. Choose the drive and folder where you have the bitmap image stored. A good source for bitmap images is Corel's Photo CD. Select the desired file and then click OK.
2. Draw another rectangle large enough to cover the bitmap image. This will become the object with the hole in it.
3. Type some text on the screen and center it on top of the rectangle. Use a bold style font for the best effect.
4. Select the rectangle and the text by marquee-selection or by clicking each object while holding down the Shift key.
5. Click the Arrange menu and select Combine. The rectangle is now your mask with the shape of the text knocked out of it.
6. Drag the mask on top of the bitmap image.
7. With the new mask selected, fill it with any of CorelDRAW's fills or fill it with the background color.

The final image in Figure 23.1 shows the rectangle mask filled with a solid fill and the bitmap image showing through the text. The image at the bottom shows the mask filled with the background color, giving the illusion that the text is filled with a bitmap.

*Figure 23.1.*
*An illustration of the*
*basic masking technique.*

## Creating Effects

The Combine command can also be used to create some unusually complex objects. Figure 16.2 shows how combining twelve overlapping ellipses can create a beautiful pattern. Follow these steps to create a similar pattern:

1. Draw an ellipse using the Ellipse tool.

2. Select the Pick tool and then select the ellipse. Fill the ellipse with a color of your choice and give it a contrasting outline color.

3. Click the ellipse a second time to display the rotation and skew arrows.

4. Click the center of the rotation thumb tack in the center of the ellipse and drag it to the bottom of the ellipse.

5. Select Transform from the Arrange menu and choose Rotate from the flyout. A roll-up will appear with Rotation selected.

6. Type the number 30 in the Angle parameters box and then click Apply To Duplicate.

7. Continue to click Apply To Duplicate until you have 12 ellipses. You can use the shortcut key Ctrl+R after you click Apply To Duplicate the first time. The ellipses will be duplicated each time you use the shortcut key sequence.

8. Marquee-select all twelve ellipses, click the Arrange menu, and then click Combine. That's all there is to it. Pretty, isn't it?

*Figure 23.2.*
*Combining 12 ellipses to*
*create a pattern.*

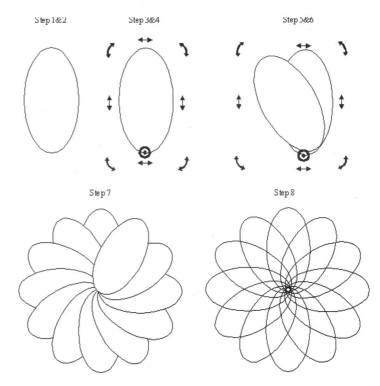

## Combining Objects to Conserve Memory and Redraw Time

You can conserve memory and files sizes as well as speed up screen redraw by using the Combine command.

The types of objects that can be combined to take advantage of this feature must share the same attributes. An example of the type of object that meets this criteria is a grid comprised of 20 vertical lines and 20 horizontal lines. A file saved with all the separate lines making up the grid would be approximately 30 KB. If you marquee-select all the lines and combine them, the file would be reduced to approximately 24 KB. This might sound insignificant, but it represents a 20 percent reduction in file size. The secondary benefit is that the screen redraw time will be much faster.

# Corel*NOTE!*

> Objects that don't share the same attributes will assume the attributes of the last selected object when combined.

## The Break Apart Command

The Break Apart command is located directly beneath the Combine command in the Arrange menu. Its function is the opposite of the Combine command.

Perhaps the best example of a time to use the Break Apart command is when modifying clip art. Many clip-art images are comprised of certain objects that have been combined. In Figure 23.3, the horse on the left is in its original form. If you wanted to change the color of the horse's tail, you might assume that after ungrouping the clip art, you could click the tail and change its color. In this example the tail has been combined with the horse's mane. Therefore, if you change the color of the tail, you would also change the color of the mane. To change just the color of the tail, you need to click the tail and then select the Break Apart command. This action separates the tail from the mane, allowing you to color the tail and mane separately.

*Figure 23.3.*
*Using the Break Apart*
*command to edit clip art.*

## The Separate Command

The function of the Separate command is to separate the different objects that are part of an effect. It is used only on certain effects in CorelDRAW and often precedes the Ungroup command whenever it is used. To access the Separate command, select it from the Arrange menu or from the Object Properties menu. To access it from the Object Properties menu, click the object with the right mouse button.

It's important to know when to use the Separate command. You use it only when you want to edit with the following effects: Blend (including Fit Blends to Path),

Contour, Extrude, PowerLines, Fit Text to Path, Dimension Lines, Connector Lines, and Clones.

When you apply one of the preceding effects to an object, the object could include several different parts that make up the effect. When you want to separate those parts for editing, first use the Separate command. All the effects, except for Cloning, will have a group of objects remaining. For example, when you create a blend, it becomes a blend group. The example at the upper left in Figure 23.4 shows a blend group with the control objects defined.

When you use the Separate command on the blend group, the remaining parts become the two original control objects, which are now normal objects, and the center of the blend, which is now a normal group of objects. The example at the upper right in Figure 23.4 shows a blend after it has been separated. The Control objects are now normal rectangles, and the center portion of the blend is now a group of 10 objects. This group of objects is made up of the number of steps you put in your blend.

To edit the objects within this group, choose the Ungroup command from the Arrange menu. The example at the lower left of Figure 23.4 shows the ungrouped objects moved apart to illustrate the fact that they are indeed ungrouped.

If you want to edit an object within the group without using the ungroup command, you can do so by holding down the Ctrl key and clicking an object within the group. This action will make it a child object. The example at the lower right in Figure 23.4 shows an object selected from within the group using the Control key selected method. You must always separate an effect to have complete editing control over all objects within the effect.

# Corel*NOTE!*

Separating clones is different. To separate all clones at once, you must select them all, either by clicking them separately while holding down the Shift key or by marquee-selecting them. When you select a clone object individually and choose Separate, only that clone object is separated from the other clones. This is handy if you're modifying the original and don't want the changes to affect a particular clone. (See Figure 23.5.)

*Figure 23.4.
Separating and
ungrouping for complete
editing control.*

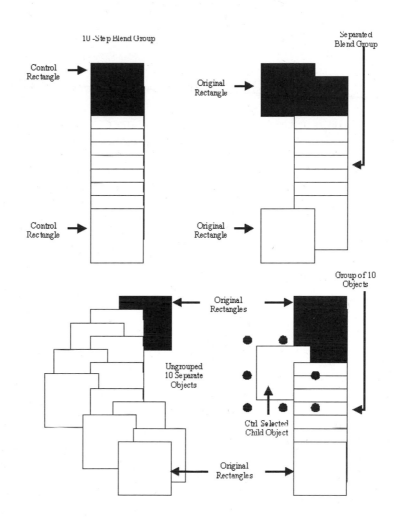

10-Step Blend Group

Control
Rectangle

Control
Rectangle

Separated
Blend Group

Original
Rectangle

Original
Rectangle

Original
Rectangles

Ungrouped
10 Separate
Objects

Original
Rectangles

Group of 10
Objects

Ctrl Selected
Child Object

Original
Rectangles

Figure 23.5.
Separating and modifying clones.

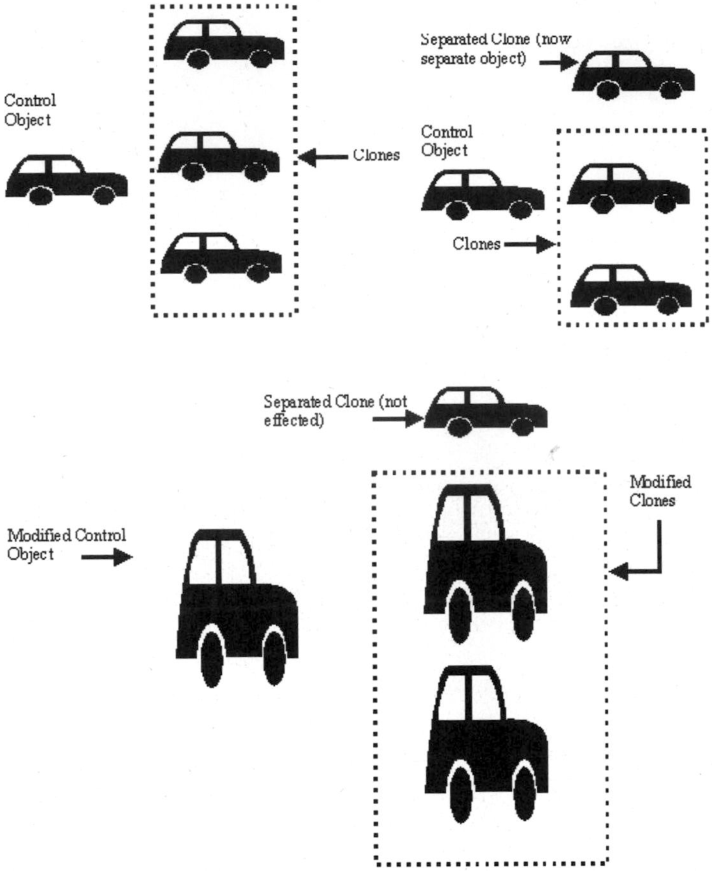

# 24

# Weld, Intersection, and Trim

This entire skill session describes the functionality of the Weld, Intersection, and Trim commands using the roll-ups. Those of you who have become accustomed to using these commands in previous versions of CorelDRAW can customize the Arrange menu so that each of the commands—Weld, Intersection, and Trim—can be used as Quick commands, which is the way they worked previously. To find out how to make these commands function as Quick commands, refer to Skill Session 4, "Customizing and Setting Preferences."

## Corel *NOTE!*

CorelDRAW 6 has added functionality to the Weld, Intersection, and Trim commands through the use of roll-ups.

In the interest of simplicity and clarity, the roll-ups in Figures 24.1, 24.6, and 24.10 showing the individual Weld, Intersection, and Trim roll-ups have been separated from the main group that contain all three roll-ups. To separate the individual roll-ups, click on the name of the command in the roll-up group and drag it out onto the page.

## Weld

The Weld roll-up, accessed by clicking on Weld in the Arrange pull-down menu, enables you to create custom shapes by welding two or more objects together to form a single object.

Welding is an additive process that requires two or more objects to overlap each other before they can be welded. What actually takes place is that the areas that overlap are thrown away and the outside perimeter of the objects welded form one single object. Figure 24.1 shows the Weld roll-up with a before and after example of welding. The first example shows two rectangles that overlap each other to form a cross. The second example shows the results after welding the two rectangles. Notice the intersecting lines of the two rectangles have disappeared and the two rectangles have become a single object.

*Figure 24.1.*
*The Weld roll-up with a*
*before and after example.*

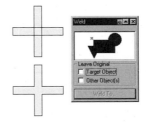

The Weld To button at the bottom of the Weld roll-up is the default method for welding. If you're only welding one object to another, you might want to use this method. In order for the Weld command to work, all objects being welded and must in some way overlap at least one other object. To weld two overlapping objects, select one of the objects (this first object is called the *Other Object,* think of it a *modifying object*) and then click on the Weld To button. A pointing arrow will replace the cursor. Use the arrow to click on the second object. (This object is called the *target object*.) The two objects will be welded together.

When you weld several overlapping objects together at once, you have to first select all the objects except one, and then click on the Weld To button. When the cursor changes to an arrow, use the arrow to click on the remaining object (target object). If you used the preceding method to create the Teddy Bear in Figure 24.2, you would have to select seven of the ellipses and then click on the Weld To button. When the cursor changed to an arrow, click on the remaining ellipse. Unfortunately, this can be somewhat confusing. The good news is that you can customize the way you weld objects using the method that was used in CorelDRAW Versions 4 and 5. (See Skill Session 4.)

The other options in the roll-up provide you the choice of leaving the original of either the target objects or other object(s) after the weld function is executed. Put a checkmark in the appropriate boxes to retain either the original or target objects, or both.

Figure 24.2 uses eight ellipses welded together to create a silhouette of a teddy bear. The eyes, nose, mouth, and buttons were added after the eight ellipses were welded.

*Figure 24.2.*
*Eight ellipses welded together to create a teddy bear.*

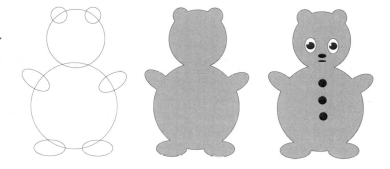

Figure 24.3 illustrates how by welding several rectangles and an ellipse together you can create silhouettes of more complicated objects.

*Figure 24.3.*
*Several objects welded to create a silhouette of a propane torch.*

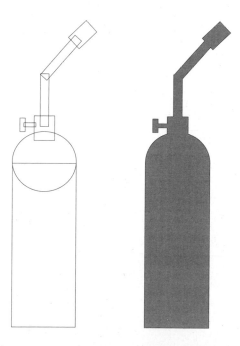

Figure 24.4 shows a gear created with the Weld command and the Extrude effect. Follow the steps below to create your own gear.

1. Draw a rectangle close to that shown in step 1 of Figure 24.4.

2. Use the Shape tool to slightly round the corners of the rectangle.

3. Convert the rectangle to curves using the Convert To Curves command in the Arrange menu.

   Marquee-select the rectangle with the Shape tool. Double-click on one of the nodes with the Shape tool to bring up the Node Edit dialog box. Click on the diagonal straight line icon (middle left) in the Node Edit dialog box. This will produce the bevel effect for the first tooth of your gear. Your rectangle should now look like that shown in Step 3 in Figure 24.4.

4. Select the rectangle again with the Pick tool. Click on the rectangle a second time to display the rotation arrows and center of rotation Thumb Tack. Click and drag on the Thumb Tack to position it at the bottom center of the rectangle.

   Click on the Transform roll-up from Arrange menu and choose Rotation from the flyout. Type the number 30 in the Parameters box in the roll-up and click on Apply to duplicate. Your drawing should look like step number 4 in Figure 24.4.

5. Continue to click on the Apply to Duplicate button until you have duplicated the teeth a full 360 degrees. Refer to step 5 in Figure 24.4 to see if your drawing looks correct at this stage. You should have 12 teeth in your drawing.

6. Select the Ellipse tool, place the crosshair in the center of the rotated teeth, and draw a circle from the center out by holding down the Ctrl and Shift keys while you drag. Draw your circle outward until it looks like Step 6 in Figure 24.4.

7. Now its time to weld. Marquee-select all the teeth by Shift-clicking on each tooth. Click on the Weld To button and use the arrow to click on the circle. Your new object should now look like Step 7 in Figure 24.4.

8. Now it's time to cut a hole in the center of the gear. Draw a circle using the Ellipse tool, using the same method you used in Step 6 above. If you have trouble centering the circle, select the gear and the circle and center the circle using the Align & Distribute command in the Arrange menu. With the circle centered and both objects selected, choose the Combine command in the Arrange menu. This command will cut the hole in the Gear. Check your drawing with Step 8 in Figure 24.4.

9. Now it's time to make your gear look like a gear. Select the Extrude roll-up from the Roll-Ups menu in the View menu. Select the object you created in Step 8 above and click on Apply in the Extrude roll-up. Locate the vanishing

point indicated by an ×, and click and drag it a little to the right and up on the page. Click on Apply again, and your gear is complete.

*Figure 24.4.*
*Several objects welded to create a gear.*

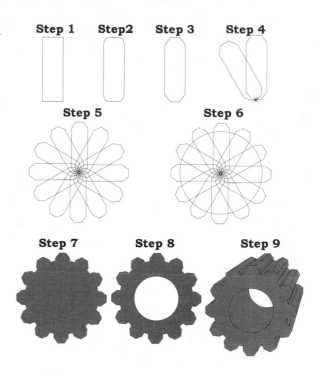

Perhaps one of the most common uses of weld is to create street or road maps. Figure 24.5 shows a sample of a simple street map.

The process to create street maps is easy. Simply draw a rectangle for each street and place them in their appropriate positions, and weld them together. If you have streets that curve, you can convert the rectangle to curves using the Convert to Curves command in the Arrange menu. Then change the shape of the curve using the Shape tool.

*Figure 24.5.*
*Several rectangles welded to create a street map.*

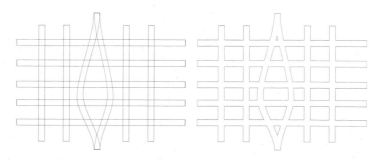

# Intersection

The Intersection command provides an easy way to create some interesting effects. The function of the Intersection command is to create new objects where there are two or more overlapping objects. The shape of the new objects will be in the shape that is common too the overlapping objects. Figure 24.6 shows the Intersection roll-up.

Figure 24.6.
The Intersection roll-up.

The Intersect With button at the bottom of the Intersection roll-up is the default method for welding. If you are intersecting only one object to another, you might want to use this method. To intersect two overlapping objects, select one of the objects. (This first object is called the *other object*.) Then click on the Intersect With button. A pointing arrow will replace the cursor. Use the arrow to click on the second object (called the *target object*). A new object will be created in the shape of the area that is common to the two overlapping original objects.

The other options in the roll-up provide you the choice of leaving the original of either the target or other object (the first object you select) after the intersection function is executed. Put a check mark in the appropriate boxes to retain either the original or target objects, or both. The example in Figure 24.7 retained the original objects.

Figure 24.7 shows three views of two circles overlapping each other. The first view shows the two circles overlapping each other. The center view shows the highlighted new object that was created using the intersect With button. The third view shows the three objects filled with different shades of gray to give the illusion of looking through one circle on to the second circle. If you filled the objects with color you could fill the back one red, the top one blue and the middle intersected object purple. This would give the effect of looking through a blue ball on to a red ball.

Figure 24.7.
Using the Intersection command on two overlapping circles.

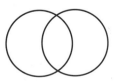 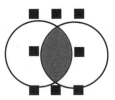 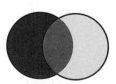

Figure 24.8 shows text that has been cut in half and filled with different fills using the Intersection roll-up. Follow the steps below to create this effect yourself.

*Figure 24.8.*
*Text cut in half using*
*different fills.*

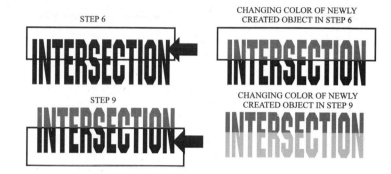

1. Type the word Intersection using a bold typeface.
2. Click on the Arrange menu and select the Intersection roll-up.
3. Put a checkmark in the boxes corresponding to the words Target Object and Other(s)Objects in the Leave original section of the roll-up.
4. Draw a rectangle over the top half of the text. Press the spacebar to select the rectangle.
5. Click the Intersect with button at the bottom of the Intersection roll-up.
6. The cursor will change to an arrow. Use the arrow to click on the text object. The intersection will be performed, and the newly created intersected object will be selected. Change its color by choosing a color from the color palette. The original rectangle and text will still be visible.
7. Select the rectangle you drew in Step 4. Click the top/center selection handle and drag downward across the text so that it covers the bottom half of the text.
8. Remove the checkmarks you put in Step 3 from both the Target Object and Other Object(s) boxes.
9. Click the Intersect with button and use the arrow to point at the bottom half of the original text.
10. The Intersection function will again be applied; this time, because you removed the checkmarks from the Target and Other Object(s) boxes, you will be left with just the top and bottom half intersected objects. Color the newly created bottom half a different color than the top half. That's all there is to it. Try using the rectangle to cover only a third of the text as you intersect to create a tri-colored text object.

Now apply an extrude effect to the two separate parts of the text you just created. Refer to Figure 24.9 as you proceed.

*Figure 24.9.*
*Extruded intersected text.*

STEP 1

STEP 4

X Step 4 vanishing point

Step 5 vanishing point X

STEP 5

STEP 6

STEP 7

STEP 9

1. Select both halves of the intersected text and apply a 1 pt. outline. Color the outline white by clicking on white in the color palette with the right mouse button.

2. Click the Extrude roll-up in the Effects menu. Choose Small Back and VP Locked to Object from the Parameters boxes.

3. Click the top section of text.

4. Click the Apply button in the Extrude roll-up.

5. Click the vanishing point ×, and drag it upwards and to the right until you are satisfied with the amount of extrusion.

6. Click the Apply button again to extrude the text.

7. Click the bottom section of text.

8. Click the Apply button in the Extrude roll-up again.

## Corel*NOTE!*

Notice that the vanishing point stayed the same as the top section ensuring that the perspective is the same for the top and bottom. If your image doesn't look right, you're not seeing things. The problem is that the lower section is on top of the upper section. This occurred because when you first intersected the original text, you started from the top instead of the bottom. I have purposely taken you through these steps because I know in the real world this could happen to you. So how do we fix things? Go to Step 8.

9. Click on the upper section of the extruded text so you have the Extrude group selected. (Check the status line to make sure.)

10. Click on the Arrange menu and select Order from the pull-down menu. From the flyout select To-Front. Your piece is now finished.

## Trim

The Trim command functions similar to a cookie cutter. Like the Weld and Intersection commands, it requires objects to be overlapping in order to work. It is an excellent method to create new shapes quickly that would otherwise be very time-consuming. (See Figure 24.10.)

*Figure 24.10.*
*The trim roll-up.*

CorelDRAW 6 has put this command in the form of a roll-up, just as they have with the Weld and Intersection commands. The Trim button at the bottom of the roll-up functions in the following manner.

Draw two objects and place them so that they overlap each other. Select the object you want to use as the cutting object (the cookie cutter). Click on the Trim button and use the arrow to click on the object you want to cut (the target object). The target object will be trimmed to the new shape.

Refer to Figure 24.11 and draw the five circles. Select all the smaller circles by Shift-clicking on each circle. These circles will be the cutters. Click on the Trim button and use the arrow to click on the large circle. Figure 24.11 shows both examples of using the Trim command.

*Figure 24.11.*
*Using the Trim Selection method to create shapes.*

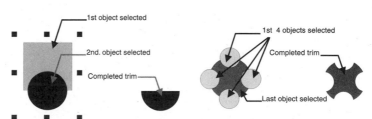

# Corel *NOTE!*

> Don't be confused with the options in the Trim roll-up. Think of the Trim function as a cookie cutter and remember that the first selected object or objects are the cookie cutter and the last object selected is the object that gets cut (trimmed).

Figure 24.12 illustrates the use of trim to create block letters. The use of the word *modifier* is used instead of *other object,* because it best describes what you are doing. The modifiers are the first object or objects selected, and the target object is the object that gets trimmed or cut.

*Figure 24.12.*
*Using the Trim method to*
*create shapes.*

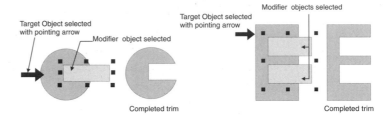

Now that you have seen some examples, practice creating the shape in Figure 24.13 by following the steps here:

1. Draw five circles in a row.

2. Draw a rectangle across the lower half of all five circles. Select the circles either by marquee selection or by clicking on each circle while holding the Shift key. With all five circles selected, click on the Trim button in the Trim roll-up. Use the pointing arrow and click on the rectangle.

3. If your new shape doesn't look like the shape in step 3, ensure that there are no check marks in the Leave Original check boxes.

The trim command can be effective when using simple lines as the cookie cutter. See if you can create the shape in Figure 24.14 by following the steps here:

1. Draw a rectangle on the screen. With the Freehand Pencil tool, draw a curved line completely across the rectangle.

2. With the line selected, click on the Trim button in the Trim roll-up and use the pointing arrow to click on the rectangle. Select the rectangle again and click on the Break Apart command in the Arrange pull-down menu. You can now select the separate parts of the rectangle and move them apart from each other.

*Figure 24.13.*
*Using the Trim method*
*to create scallops.*

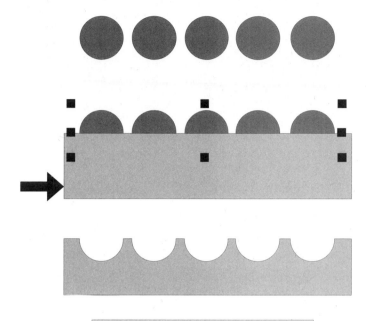

*Figure 24.14.*
*Using the Trim method*
*to cut a rectangle in half.*

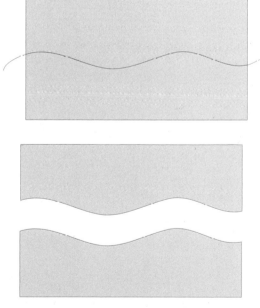

The other options in the roll-up provide you the choice of leaving the original of either the Target or Other Object(s) after the trim function is executed. Put a check mark in the appropriate boxes to retain either the target or other object, or both.

# 25

# Converting to Curves

Most of the objects you draw in CorelDRAW are either ellipses, rectangles, text, or freehand shapes. Many effects can be applied to these objects, but the original object, in most cases, still maintains its identity. For example, if you apply an Extrude effect to a rectangle, it's still a rectangle, even though it's referred to as a Control Rectangle in the status line. If you blend an ellipse into a rectangle, the selected ellipse is shown on the status line as the Control Ellipse and the rectangle is shown as the Control Rectangle. If you apply an Envelope effect to text, the new shape is still text. The point of all this is that although you can change the shape and look of these basic objects with different effects, you can manipulate them in other ways if you convert them to curves. The exceptions to this are objects that have been drawn freehand. Freehand objects are created as curves from the beginning and can be manipulated without being converted to curves again.

# Corel *TIP!*

Unless you're absolutely sure that your printer (or whomever you're sending your files to)
has the same fonts you use in your document, get in the habit of converting all your text
to curves before you send out a CDR file. If the person printing your file doesn't have the
font you use in your document or drawing, the file will be printed using the printer's
default font. If this happens, all the effort that went into choosing that special font will go
up in smoke.

Figure 25.1 illustrates the effect of Convert To Curves on basic objects.

To convert an ellipse or a rectangle to a curves, select the object and choose
Convert To Curves from the Arrange pull-down menu, or right-click the object and
select Convert To Curves from the Object Properties pop-up menu.

A basic ellipse has only one node. When you convert it to curves, it has four nodes.
When you look at Figure 25.1, you see a basic ellipse with a single node. When you
click and drag the node outside the ellipse with the Shape tool, you create an arc.
When you click and drag inside the ellipse, you create a pie shape. When you
convert the ellipse to curves, you can change the shape completely with the four
nodes that are added. The shapes next to the ellipse, arc, and pie shape in Figure
25.1 were created after the ellipse was converted to curves. You can even add
extra nodes to continue manipulating the shape. (See Skill Session 7, "The Shape
Tool.")

A basic rectangle has a node at each corner. If you drag one of the nodes in a
rectangle with the Shape tool before it has been converted to curves, you round
the corners of the rectangle. Figure 25.1 shows a rectangle with the corners
rounded. When you convert it to curves, it still has the same four nodes, but they
affect the shape in a different way. After you convert the rectangle to curves, each
node can be moved independently in order to create a new shape. You can add
extra nodes (as with the ellipse) to create any shape you can imagine.

Converting text to curves can produce some interesting text effects. Figure 25.2
includes a simple illustration of manipulating text after it has been converted to
curves. The bottom nodes of each letter have been pulled down to give the letters
the look of wet paint. Even though there seems to be an unlimited number of fonts
to choose from in CorelDRAW, you can vary the look of each one to be different
from the rest.

*Figure 25.1.*
*Before and after convert-*
*ing an ellipse and a*
*rectangle to curves.*

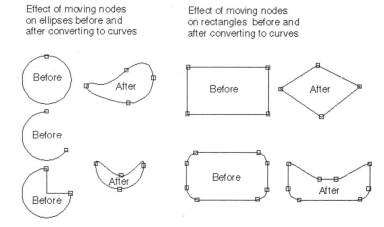

Effect of moving nodes
on ellipses before and
after converting to curves

Effect of moving nodes
on rectangles before and
after converting to curves

*Figure 25.2.*
*Before and after convert-*
*ing text to curves.*

# 26

# Transform

Transforming objects involves five different actions that can be applied to an object or group of objects. The roll-up is comprised of a group of commands, all relating to transforming objects. They enable you to change the position, size, scale, angle of rotation, and skew of selected objects.

To access the Transform roll-up, click Transform Roll-Up in the Arrange pull-down menu. When the flyout menu appears, choose Position. The roll-up first appears as shown in Figure 26.1. Notice that the cursor is pointing to an arrowhead icon. Click this icon to expand the roll-up. The expanded roll-up reveals the absolute coordinates grid.

## Corel *NOTE!*

When you access the roll-up, the Relative Position box should be checked. If it is not, put a check mark in the box. You should get in the habit of putting a check mark in this box, because the most common thing you'll do in CorelDRAW is move objects. If you simply want to move an object two inches to the right, it will work correctly only if the Relative Position box is checked.

When you choose Position from the Transform roll-up, the roll-up opens with Position highlighted. This is the command used to move objects. When it is selected, the roll-up displays the configuration shown in Figures 26.1 and 26.2. The other commands—Rotation, Scale and Mirror, Size, and Skew—are described later in the chapter.

Objects can be moved or placed in relative or absolute positioning. Understanding how to use the two different methods is extremely important. If you don't learn how the two methods differ from each other, you will become very frustrated when placing objects on-screen.

*Figure 26.1.*
*The Transform roll-up as*
*it appears when it is first*
*accessed from the Effects*
*menu.*

*Figure 26.2.*
*The Transform roll-up*
*when it is expanded.*

## Relative Positioning

Relative positioning is probably used more often than absolute positioning, because most users simply want to move an object horizontally or vertically in one direction or the other. Think of relative positioning as moving the object a certain distance relative to the object's current position.

When moving objects using the relative method, do not pay any attention to the circled dot in the absolute coordinates grid. If you somehow move the dot on the grid after you have entered the relative position coordinates in the Horizontal and Vertical parameters boxes, you will have to re-enter the coordinates. The reason for this is that when you move the circled dot on the grid after entering the coordinates, the horizontal and vertical entries automatically change. You will understand this automatic change more fully when you read the section on absolute positioning.

The basics for moving objects using the relative positioning method are very simple. To move an object a specified distance and direction, enter the appropriate numbers in the Horizontal and Vertical parameters boxes in the roll-up. Remember, you're moving an object relative to its current position on the page. Entering a positive number in the Horizontal parameters box moves the object to the right. Entering a positive number in the Vertical parameters box moves the object up on the page. Negative values move the object in the opposite directions.

Follow these steps to move a rectangle 2 inches to the left. Figure 26.3 shows a rectangle that was moved 2 inches to the left as well as the original rectangle, which is left in its original position.

1. Draw a rectangle on the page.
2. Put a check mark in the Relative Position box.
3. Type -2.0 inches in the Horizontal parameters box.
4. Type 0.0 inches in the Vertical parameters box.
5. Click the Apply To Duplicate button.

The Apply To Duplicate button is used so that you can see the results more clearly. Usually you would click the Apply button, because you want to move just the object, not a duplicate of the object.

*Figure 26.3.*
*Moving a rectangle two*
*inches to the left using*
*relative positioning.*

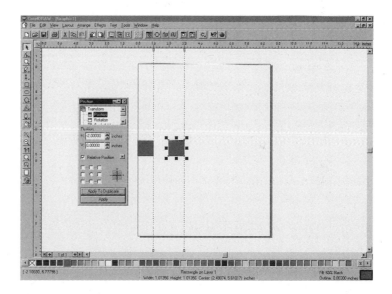

The previous example was easy. In the following example you'll move a rectangle 4 inches to the right and 3 inches down. (See Figure 26.4.)

1. Select the original rectangle.
2. Put a check mark in the Relative Position box.
3. Type 4.0 inches in the Horizontal parameters box.

4. Type -3.0 `inches` in the Vertical parameters box.

5. Click the Apply To Duplicate button.

*Figure 26.4.*
*Using relative positioning*
*to move a square down*
*and to the right.*

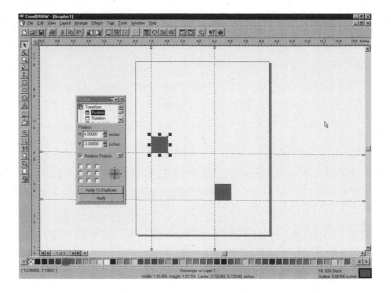

You should now be an expert at moving objects using relative positioning.

Remember, never move the circled dot in the absolute coordinates grid. If you move the circled dot after you enter the coordinates in the parameters boxes, the parameters will change to the position of the circled dot relative to the rulers. What does this mean? It means that you shouldn't pay any attention to where the circled dot is on the coordinates grid when you want to move an object a specified distance in any direction.

## Absolute Positioning

Absolute positioning means you can move an object to an exact position on the page. To move an object using absolute positioning, the Relative Position box should not be checked.

Figure 26.5 shows a rectangle (square) on the screen. There is a circled dot in the center square of the absolute coordinates grid. Notice that the Horizontal and Vertical parameters boxes show the position, relative to the rulers, of the exact center of the square. In this illustration, the coordinates are 5.0 inches horizontal and 3.0 inches vertical. Any time you draw an object on-screen, the exact center is shown in these parameters boxes if the Relative Position box is not checked. Draw a rectangle to verify that this is true.

*Figure 26.5.*
*A square with its center*
*position coordinates*
*shown in the roll-up.*

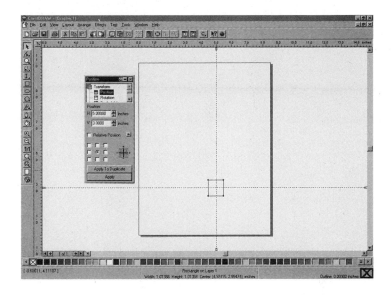

Now, move the object using absolute positioning. Notice in Figure 26.6 that guidelines are placed at 4.0 inches horizontal and 7.0 inches vertical. To move the square so that the exact center is placed where the guidelines intersect, type the new coordinates in the parameters boxes and click the Apply button. Figure 26.6 verifies that the square was moved to the place where you intended to place it.

*Figure 26.6.*
*The same square moved*
*using absolute position-*
*ing.*

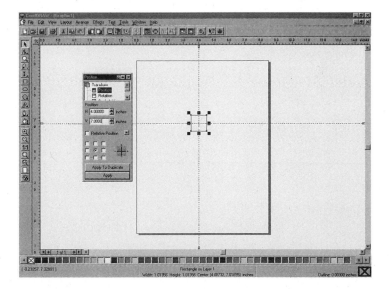

That seemed easy enough. Now, move the same square so that the lower-left corner of the square is positioned at the same coordinates as before—4.0 inches horizontal and 7.0 inches vertical. Click the lower-left box in the coordinates grid. This places a check mark in this new location. Click the Apply button, and the square moves to its new position. (See Figure 26.7.)

*Figure 26.7.*
*A square with its lower-left corner coordinates shown in the roll-up.*

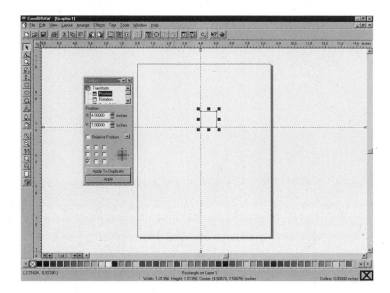

These examples show that where you place the circled dot on the coordinates grid relates directly to how the object will be moved and placed in relation to the rulers and guidelines.

## Rotating

To access the Rotation roll-up, click Rotation in the Transform roll-up. To rotate an object means to rotate the selected object or group of objects around a designated point. This designated point is called the *center of rotation* in the Transform roll-up. It is also referred to as the Center of Rotation thumb tack.

## Relative Rotating

Figure 26.8 shows the Transform roll-up in the expanded configuration, with Rotation selected. Notice the familiar relative coordinates grid. When the roll-up is first accessed, it appears with none of the boxes checked, and the relative coordinates box is also not checked. The default is the exact center, even though the center of the grid does not show a circle dot. CorelDRAW computes the exact center when you select the object. Note that the numbers shown in the Horizontal and Vertical parameters boxes reflect the exact center in relation to the rulers when the object on the left is selected.

Draw a rectangle and then select it. Next, click the rectangle again to display the corner rotation arrows. Notice that the thumb tack is in the exact center of the object.

*Figure 26.8.*
*The Transform roll-up,*
*showing the center of*
*rotation with the object*
*selected.*

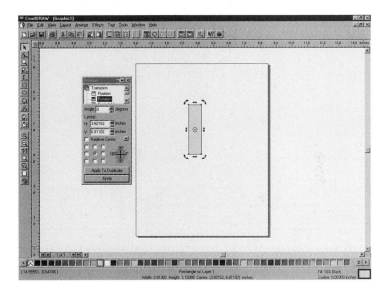

In Figure 26.9, the rectangle is rotated 90 degrees using the default center setting. The degree of rotation is determined by the number you enter in the Angle of Rotation box. If you enter a negative number, the object rotates clockwise; a positive number rotates the object counterclockwise.

In Figure 26.10, the same rectangle is rotated 90 degrees to the left, but this time the center of rotation is moved to the lower-left corner of the rectangle. Notice that a check mark is placed in the lower-left corner of the grid. This example is the key to understanding how to use the relative coordinates grid when rotating objects.

# Corel*NOTE!*

Each outside box in the relative coordinates grid is relative to the outside perimeter of the selected object. For example, if you place a check mark in the upper-left corner of the grid, the center of rotation is the upper-left corner of the object.

*Figure 26.9.*
*The effect of rotating a*
*rectangle 90 degrees using*
*the default center setting.*

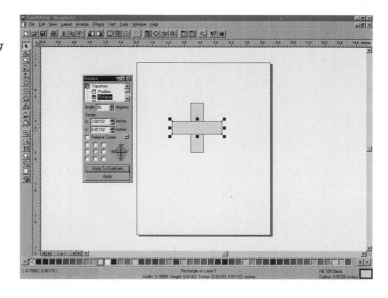

*Figure 26.10.*
*The effect of rotating a*
*rectangle 90 degrees, with*
*the center of rotation*
*moved to the lower left.*

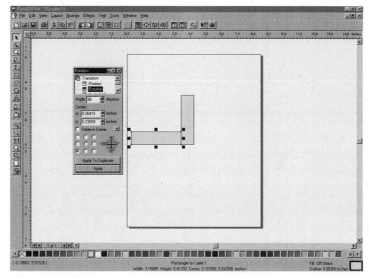

Figure 26.11 shows a rectangle rotated 30 degrees after a check mark has been placed in the right, center box of the grid. Notice that the center of rotation is exactly in the middle of the right side of the rectangle.

*Figure 26.11.*
*A rectangle rotated with*
*the center of rotation*
*located at the right center.*

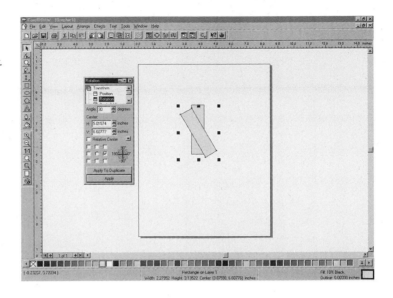

## Absolute Rotating

You can rotate an object from a specified center of rotation by entering the coordinates in the Horizontal and Vertical parameters boxes. Figure 26.12 illustrates a duplicate object rotated with a specified center of rotation. Notice that the center of rotation is set at 6.0 inches horizontal and 6.0 inches vertical. The object is then rotated 30 degrees to the left. The × marks the spot of rotation, and a line is drawn to show the center of the duplicate object.

*Figure 26.12.*
*An object rotated with*
*a specified center of*
*rotation.*

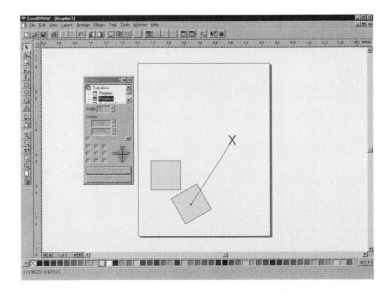

253

# Corel *TIP!*

> You can rotate an object manually by double-clicking the object and dragging one of the corner rotation arrows. To move the center of rotation manually, click the thumb tack and move it to the desired location. This method works best for the user who doesn't require precise measurements.

## Scale and Mirror

When you select Scaling & Mirror in the Transform roll-up, you can scale and mirror objects. You can also scale and mirror an object in one operation by making your changes in the parameters boxes and clicking either the Horizontal or Vertical button before clicking the Apply button. How to scale and mirror objects is covered in the following sections.

## Proportional Scaling

Scaling involves changing the size of an object either horizontally and vertically (or both). The amount of scaling is governed by the numbers you type in the Horizontal and Vertical parameters boxes. Figure 26.13 illustrates six different scaling functions. Each object is increased 200 percent in size, both horizontally and vertically. A check mark is placed in the Proportion box above the grid. Checking the Proportion box allows you to enter a new number in either the Horizontal or Vertical parameters boxes, and the other parameters box will change to the same number. If you remove the check mark from the Proportion box, you can scale an object's horizontal and vertical dimensions by different percentages.

The coordinates grid of nine boxes in the lower-left corner of the Scaling & Mirror roll-up is the key to determining the direction of scale. The checkered squares represent the original object before scaling. The location of the ×s on each original object coincides with the placement of the check mark on the coordinates grid.

*Figure 26.13.*
*Scaling objects using the*
*Transform roll-up.*

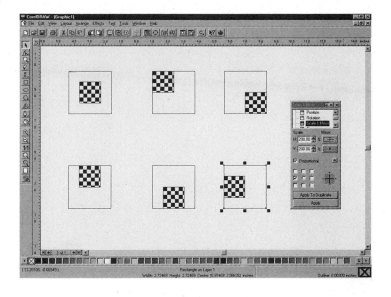

## Mirror

Figure 26.14 illustrates the mirroring process. Next to each scaling parameters box is a mirror button. The buttons show an arrow pointing to the right for the horizontal button and up for the vertical button. This is merely a visual representation of the buttons' functions and does not indicate the direction of the mirroring action. The placement of the check marks in the coordinates grid determine the direction of the mirror. Figure 26.15 shows four objects mirrored 100 percent in four different directions: north, south, east, and west. The original objects have a checkerboard fill. The arrows point to the direction that each object was mirrored. To mirror an object, follow these simple steps:

1. Select the object to mirror.

2. Put a check mark in an outside square of the coordinates grid.

   If you want to mirror the object horizontally and to the left, put a check mark in any of the squares on the left side of the coordinates grid.

   If you want to mirror the object vertically and to the top, put a check mark in any of the squares along the top of the coordinates grid.

3. Click either the Horizontal or Vertical mirror buttons, depending on the type of mirror you want to apply.

4. Click the Apply button.

Figure 26.15 illustrates the same mirror effect as shown in Figure 26.14, except that the scaling on the object on the left was set to 200 percent horizontally and 100 percent vertically and the object on the right had the scaling set to 200 percent vertically and 100 percent horizontally. You can change the percentage of scaling to anything between 1 and 3000. You cannot enter a negative value.

*Figure 26.14.*
*Mirroring objects using*
*the Transform roll-up.*

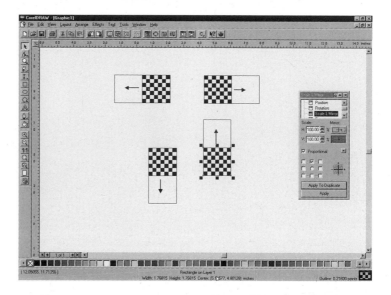

*Figure 26.15.*
*The mirror effect with*
*changes in scaling.*

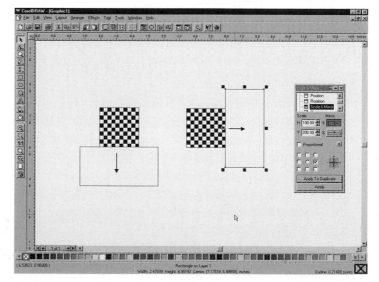

# Size

The Size command is very straightforward. To change the size of a selected object, enter the horizontal and vertical dimensions in the appropriate parameters boxes. Figure 26.16 shows the original object at 5.0 inches horizontal and 5.0 inches vertical. The original object is resized to business card dimensions (3.5 inches horizontal and 2.0 inches vertical).

*Figure 26.16.*
*Resizing an object using*
*the Transform roll-up.*

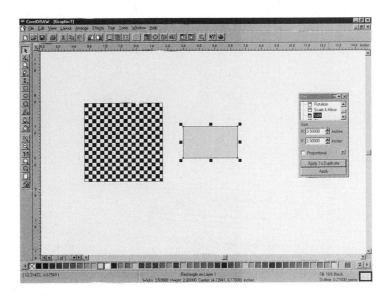

# Skew

The last command in the Transform roll-up is Skew. Skewing objects gets you back to the coordinates grid settings. Put a check mark in the Use Anchor Point box when you want to skew an object from a side rather than the default center setting. Figure 26.17 shows an object horizontally skewed 15 degrees with the anchor point set to the default center. Notice that the skew moved the top of the object to the left. Had –15 degrees been entered, the object would have been skewed to the right.

Figure 26.18 shows the same object horizontally skewed 15 degrees, but the anchor point check mark has been moved to the bottom row in the coordinates grid. The Skew coordinates grid functions the same as the coordinates grid for mirroring. The anchor point is set according to a particular side, not a specific square.

In Figure 26.19, the original object is vertically skewed 15 degrees with the anchor point moved to the right side of the coordinates grid.

*Figure 26.17.*
*A 15-degree, horizontally*
*skewed object with the*
*default anchor point.*

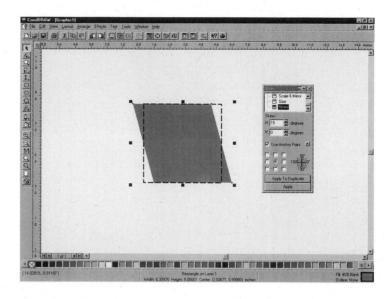

*Figure 26.18.*
*A 15-degree, horizontally*
*skewed object with the*
*anchor point at the*
*bottom left of the coordi-*
*nates grid.*

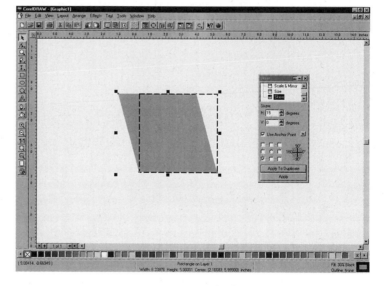

*Figure 26.19.*
*A 15-degree, vertically*
*skewed object with the*
*anchor point moved to the*
*top right of the coordi-*
*nates grid.*

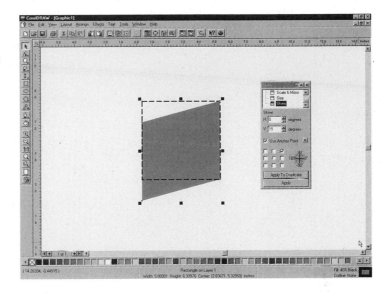

# Apply To Duplicate

The Apply To Duplicate button lets you apply the settings you make in any of these commands to a copy of the selected original object. The original object remains as is—it's not affected by the changes. Apply To Duplicate is used in all the figures shown in this skill session so that you can see the before and after changes.

# 27

# Cloning

The Clone command is found in the Edit and the Effects pull-down menus. Using the Clone command on an object changes it into a master object and creates a duplicate called the cloned object. A clone is a double of an object that takes on the same attributes as the object it is cloned from.

## Clone Command, Edit Pull-Down Menu

Creating a clone is as simple as choosing an object and selecting the Clone command from the Edit pull-down menu. Grouped and ungrouped objects can be cloned.

The Clone command is similar to the Duplicate command, but it performs differently. The distinction is that the object from which you clone becomes the *master object*. The master object is linked with its clones. Change the master object's attributes, and the clones take on the same attributes. Nearly all attributes you specify for the master object will automatically be assigned to the clones. (See Figure 27.1.)

If you change an attribute, such as an outline color, on the cloned object, the clone loses its link to the master object. When you produce a clone from another object, it offsets itself by utilizing the same settings as the Duplicate command.

These settings are located in the Options dialog box. The default settings for placing duplicates and clones is 0.25

inches. For more information on setting preferences, see Skill Session 4, "Customizing and Setting Preferences" and Command Reference 8, "Tools Menu Commands." (See Figure 27.2.)

*Figure 27.1.*
*The Clone command in*
*the Edit pull-down menu.*

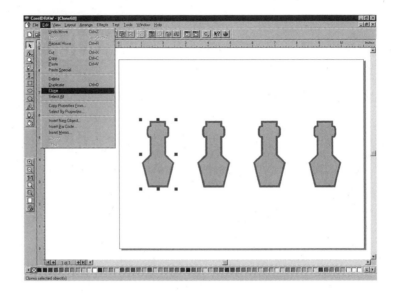

*Figure 27.2.*
*Select Options from the*
*Tools pull-down menu to*
*see the Options dialog*
*box, where the Place*
*Duplicates and Clones*
*section is found.*

If a drawing contains a master object and its clones, you can find out which is which by using the Object menu. Click one of the objects in the group with the right mouse button, and the Object menu appears.

If the object you pick is a master object, a command for selecting its clones appears in the menu. When you have a clone selected, the menu has a command for selecting its master. (See Figure 27.3.)

*Figure 27.3.*
*The clone is selected and*
*the Object menu displays*
*Select Master.*

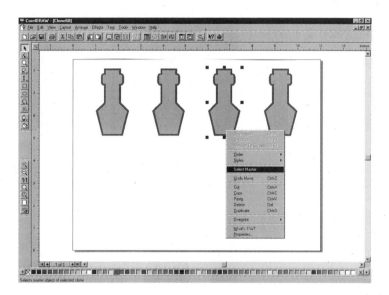

If the master object and cloned objects are grouped, you will not be able to distinguish one from the other. To find out which part of a group of objects is a clone and which part is the master, first select one of the grouped objects with the Ctrl key.

This allows you to select a single or *child* object from the group. Once you have the child object selected, press the right mouse button. The object menu displays whether it is a clone or a master.

If you cut or copy a cloned object to the Clipboard and paste it back into your drawing, the cloned object will revert to a normal object. Attributes applied to its master will no longer affect it. If you cut or copy a clone and its master, when they are pasted back into your drawing, they will retain their master/clone relationship.

# Corel*NOTE!*

> You can use the Clone command to reproduce objects. Most attributes implemented on the original will also be applied to the clones.

## Clone Command, Effects Pull-Down Menu

Select this command and a submenu appears with other commands for cloning another object's effects. The four effects you can clone are Blend, Contour, PowerLine, and Extrude. After you choose this command, a large black arrow appears. Use it to pick out the object from which you want to clone the effect. (See Figure 27.4.)

*Figure 27.4.*
*The Clone command and its flyout submenu, located at the bottom of the Effects pull-down menu.*

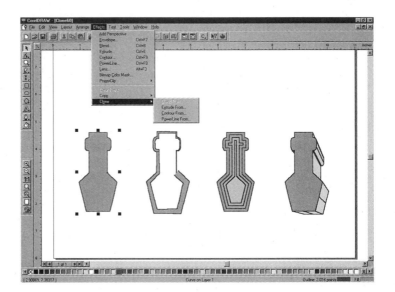

# Corel*NOTE!*

> If you select an object from which you want to clone an effect and it does not have an effect applied to it, the command will be unavailable.

The commands in the Clone submenu are made usable when there is an object in your document that has one of the four effects applied to it. You can have four objects in your document, and each one of them could possess one of the four effects applied to it.

1. Select a normal object. A *normal* object is an object without effects of any kind applied to it.

2. In the Effects pull-down menu, select Clone.

3. In the Clone submenu, select an available effect. The cursor converts to a large black arrow.

4. Click the object that has the effect you want to clone. The normal object is redrawn with the cloned effect applied to it.

Make sure an object (or objects) with the extrude, PowerLine, or contour effects applied to it is in your drawing. When you have one object picked out, the available commands in the Clone submenu include Extrude From, Contour From, and PowerLine From. Blend From will be grayed out. If you have two objects selected, the available commands will be Blend From and PowerLine From. Selecting three objects makes PowerLine From the only available command in the clone submenu.

# Skill Session: Effects Workshop

# 28

# Perspective

The Add Perspective command in the Effects pull-down menu can be used on individual objects and groups of objects to add the illusion of distance and depth to your drawing.

## Corel *NOTE!*

The perspective effect is the only effect that you can't activate through a roll-up.

The illusion of a cactus-lined road heading toward the horizon requires the use of perspective. As the road appears to get farther away, its width narrows and the trees along side it look smaller. The road is created from two rectangles grouped together. They are shown at the top section of Figure 28.1; the bottom section shows the group with perspective applied. (See Figure 28.1.)

*Figure 28.1.*
*The rectangles and stripes*
*before and after using the*
*Add Perspective com-*
*mand.*

WITH OUT PERSPECTIVE

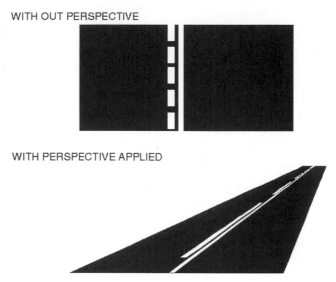

WITH PERSPECTIVE APPLIED

To apply perspective to an object or group of objects, do the following:

1. Select the object or group of objects.
2. Click Add Perspective from the Effects pull-down menu.
3. The Shape tool is automatically selected for you, and a selection box with four handles becomes visible around the object.
4. To create a one-point perspective, pull either vertically or horizontally on the handle(s) to accomplish the desired perspective. Hold down the Ctrl key to suppress your motion according to the settings in the Options dialog box. (If you hold down the Ctrl and Shift keys simultaneously, the opposing handles will move either in the opposite direction or in the same direction.)

   Drag the handle straight across toward the middle of the object, and an × representing the vanishing point appears. Click this × and drag it to alter the perspective even more.
5. To create a two-point perspective, drag the handle(s) toward the middle of the object. Two vanishing-point ×s become visible, permitting you to modify the vanishing points individually.
6. Drag a handle or vanishing point and release the left mouse button. The object is redrawn with the new perspective.

# Corel *TIP!*

Moving the vanishing points too close to the object will cause the object to snap back to its original perspective.

If you use the perspective effect on the trees, they would appear to be lying down. To ensure that the trees follow the same perspective as the road, draw a guideline from the top of the large foreground tree to the horizon.

Position a smaller tree in the background then set the two trees apart from each other. Blend between them to create the illusion of perspective. (This example uses four blend steps. You should use as many steps as you need.) Adjust the trees so they do not exceed the height of the guideline. (See Figure 28.2.)

*Figure 28.2.*
*Adding "blended" cactus*
*in perspective.*

Figure 28.3 illustrates the treatment of perspective on text. Notice how, through the use of perspective, you can indicate shadows receding toward the horizon. This gives the illusion of the text coming toward or going away from the viewer.

Select the arrow from the Symbols roll-up, make two duplicates, and place them apart on the page. Choose the Add Perspective command and select an arrow; then move the nodes to alter the arrows perspective. Different perspectives were applied to the other arrows.

To apply the arrows perspective to the text, select the text, choose the Effects pull-down menu, and select the Copy command. From the Copy command flyout menu, pick Perspective From and the cursor turns into a large black arrow. Use it to select the arrow. The text now has the same perspective as the arrow.

# Corel *NOTE!*

You cannot apply perspective to Paragraph text.

When you add perspective to Artistic text, you can still change its attributes (for example, change the font from Adlib to Diskus). Despite the perspective effect you can also change all or any of the characters in the selected artistic text object at once.

To change a single character or different characters within a word, or a word within a sentence, select the text with perspective applied. Then press Ctrl+Shift+T to bring up the Edit Text dialog box.

With your cursor, marquee-select the character(s) or word you want to change and then click the Character button. The Character Attributes dialog box will appear. Select the desired font and press the OK button. Then press the OK button in the Edit text dialog box to exit and return to the drawing window. (See Figure 28.3.)

*Figure 28.3.*
*Artistic text characters*
*modified within a word*
*and various uses of*
*perspective on text.*

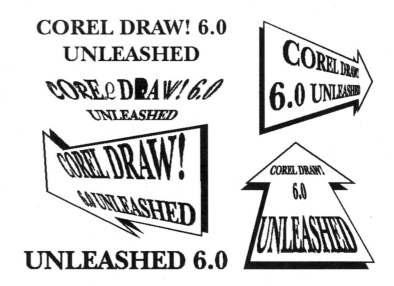

Figure 28.4 illustrates the use of perspective on a black-and-white geometric pattern. This is a very good way to show depth on a floor.

Figure 28.4.
Using perspective on a
pattern fill.

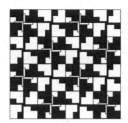

To restore an object's original shape, select Clear Perspective from the Effects pull-down menu or Clear Transformations from the Arrange pull-down menu. If an object has had perspective applied to it two or more times, you must select Clear Perspective just as many times to get back to the original object's shape.

Use theCopy Perspective From command to copy the perspective of one object to another object.

The cursor changes into the Pick tool. Move the tip of the arrow to the object you are copying and click it. The perspective is copied to your selected object. (See Figure 28.5.)

# Corel*NOTE!*

> If you apply an effect to an object that has perspective applied to it, you won't be able to copy that object's perspective.

You can copy perspective to an object with the lens or PowerClip effects applied to it. You can also copy perspective to an object with an Envelope effect as long as the object isn't Paragraph text. However, you cannot add perspective to an object with the blend, extrude, or contour effects applied to them.

To change the perspective on a text object that has the Fit Text to Path command applied to it, use the Ctrl key in combination with right mouse button. Select the text by itself, then add perspective to it.

Figure 28.5.
*Copying perspective from*
*one object to another.*

BILLBOARD WITHOUT
PERSPECTIVE APPLIED.

BILLBOARD WITH PERSPECTIVE
COPIED FROM ROAD.

# 29

# Enveloping

CorelDRAW's envelope effect is a way to reshape objects. "Distort" might be a better description. To access the envelope effect, choose the Envelope roll-up from the Effects pull-down menu. You can apply several kinds of enveloping effects to objects by using the different enveloping modes in the roll-up.

A description of the different components that make up the roll-up follows:

Add New: You must always begin by clicking the Add New button before applying a new envelope to a selected object.

Add Preset: This button applies predefined shapes to a selected object (see "Using Presets" later in this chapter).

Create From: This button enables you to use the shape of another object and apply it to a new object (see "Create From" section).

Mode buttons: These buttons are located just below the Create From button. The mode buttons enable you to choose which style of envelope you want to use. From left to right they are straight line mode, single curve mode, double curve mode, and unconstrained mode.

Mapping modes: The mapping mode parameters box is just below the Mode buttons. The mapping modes consist of Putty (the default mode), Original, Vertical, and Horizontal. Choosing different mapping modes is another way of changing the appearance of the envelope.

Reset Envelope: Click the Reset Envelope button to undo the last change you made to the envelope. To undo all changes, you must use the Clear Envelope command in the Effects menu.

Apply: This button could be the most important of all. If you don't click Apply, none of your enveloping changes will take effect.

You can apply envelopes to any object or group of objects except named effects groups (that is, blend groups, contour groups, and extrude groups) and bitmaps.

## Corel*NOTE!*

CorelDRAW 6 has grouped many of the effects found in the Effects pull-down menu into a single roll-up. When you select Envelope in the Effects pull-down menu, the Envelope roll-up appears as part of a group of effects listed in the list box.

In the interest of simplicity and clarity, the Envelope roll-up shown in this skill session has been separated from its main roll-up group. To separate the individual roll-ups, click the name of the effect in the roll-up group and drag it out onto the page while still holding down the left mouse button. Release the left mouse button and the roll-up will display as a single roll-up.

## Basic Shapes

To create an envelope, select the object you want to envelop, choose an editing mode, and click Add New in the roll-up. A "marching ants" selection box surrounds the object with eight editing nodes, and the Shape tool is selected automatically.

These nodes are not like nodes you are familiar with, unless you choose the unconstrained mode (which is described later in this skill session). The nodes on the straight line, curve, and double curve are constrained to act in a specific way. You can move them in any direction, but the enveloping effect constrains to the mode selected. If you choose the single curve mode and drag a corner node, for example, the line on which the node is attached will be curved. You can move only one node at a time, but you can continue moving nodes until you are satisfied with the shape. Experiment with how the nodes work on a rectangle and then on an ellipse.

When you hold down the Shift key and drag a node, the line on the opposite side of the rectangle will move in the opposite direction. If you hold down the Ctrl key and drag a node, the line on the opposite side of the rectangle will move in the same direction. If you hold down the Shift and Ctrl keys at the same time while dragging a node, the lines on all four sides of the rectangle will move in opposite directions of each other. Figure 29.1 shows how applying the single curve mode to a rectangle while holding down the different keys separately and together affects the shape of the envelope.

*Figure 29.1.*
*Using the Shift and Ctrl*
*keys to produce various*
*effects.*

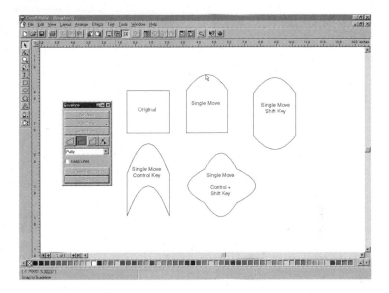

# Corel*NOTE!*

If you use the straight line mode on a rectangle, you don't get straight lines. This happens because a rectangle has only four nodes, and even though the envelope provides eight of its nodes, the lines will still be curved. To solve the problem, you need to convert the rectangle to curves and add four more nodes before applying a straight line mode envelope. Figure 29.2 shows the before and after effect that converting to curves has on a rectangle when using the straight line mode.

When you use the unconstrained mode, the envelope nodes behave like the nodes that are on any curved object. You therefore can change the type of node from smooth to cusp and so on, and you can add nodes. To change the type of node or add nodes, double-click a node to open the Node Edit dialog box. Figure 29.3 shows a few enveloped shapes that you can make using the unconstrained mode. Remember that you can envelop groups of objects, not just single objects. The nodes on the center top and bottom in the image on the far right were converted to cusp nodes.

*Figure 29.2.*
*Enveloping a rectangle*
*with the straight line*
*mode before and after*
*converting to curves.*

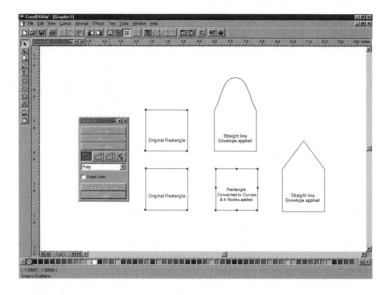

*Figure 29.3.*
*Using the unconstrained*
*mode to create different*
*envelope effects.*

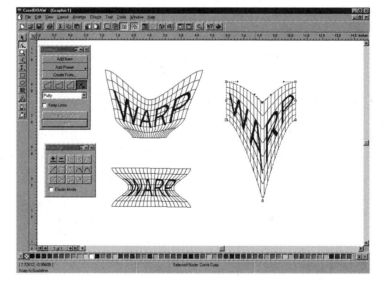

# Using Presets

The Add Preset button enables you to select an object (the *target object*) and apply a preset envelope effect to it. When you select a target object and then click the Add Preset button, a flyout menu appears. Select the shape you want to apply to the target object from the choices in the flyout menu and then click Apply.

Figure 29.4 shows the result of using a Circle Preset on Paragraph text. As you can see, it created more of an ellipse than a circle. It created this shape because the formatting of the text was such that there wasn't enough text to fill the circle.

Unfortunately, using Presets is pretty much a happy accident situation, in that the preset shape rarely changes the target object to what you expect. You are better off using the Create From button in the roll-up when you want to apply a shape of one object to another. The example on the right in Figure 29.4 shows the result of using the Create From method on the same Paragraph text and applying it to a predrawn circle. (See the "Create From" section.)

*Figure 29.4.*
*Using a Preset and the*
*Create From method on*
*Paragraph text.*

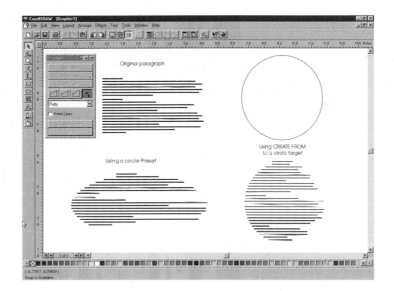

## Create From

The fascinating Create From effect works quite well, especially with text. The function of this effect is to give an object the shape of another object. Figure 29.4 shows a block of Paragraph text being enveloped so that it matches the shape of a circle. Text reshaped with an envelope is still text. This means that you can edit it and change its attributes, but you cannot change attributes of individual characters.

You can use this effect many ways. Follow these steps to create the examples shown in Figures 29.5 and 29.6:

1. Draw a circle using the Ellipse tool and make it the target object.
2. Type BUBBLE in all caps.
3. Click the Create From button and use the arrow to click the circle.
4. Click Apply.

279

*Figure 29.5.*
*The Create From effect,*
*using the putty mapping*
*mode.*

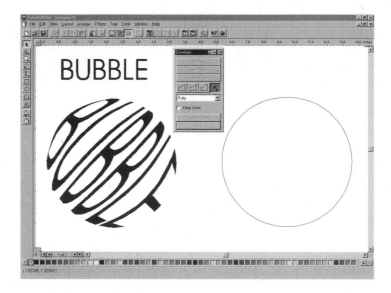

*Figure 29.6.*
*The Create From effect,*
*using the vertical mapping*
*mode.*

That was easy. I bet you expected the word *BUBBLE* to be displayed in a different way. In Figure 29.5, the word is angled down and to the right because the default setting in the Mapping Modes parameters box has been left at Putty. If you scroll in the parameters box until you find Vertical and then click Apply again, you will get the example shown in Figure 29.6.

Follow these steps to create the example shown in Figure 29.7:

1. Draw a grid using the Grid tool. (For this example, use a setting of 7 vertical and 20 horizontal.)

2. Ungroup the grid using the Ungroup command in the Arrange menu. With the grid still selected, click the Combine command in the Arrange menu (to make the grid a single object).

3. Open the Symbols roll-up and select the Airplane from the ZapfDingbats library. Drag the Airplane symbol out onto the page.

4. Select the grid again and click the Create From button. Use the arrow to click the Airplane.

5. Click Apply.

*Figure 29.7.*
*The Create From effect,*
*using a grid mapped to a*
*symbol.*

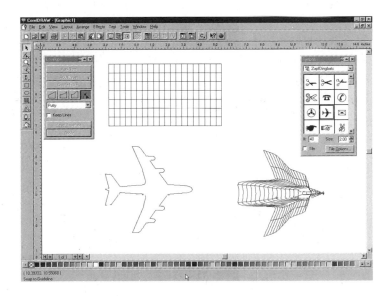

Again, the effect here may not be exactly what you anticipated, but it is interesting.

## Other Ways to Use Envelope

A handy way to use the envelope effect is on Paragraph text, when you want to wrap the text around a graphic. Figure 29.8 shows a block of Paragraph text on the left and the text wrapped around a graphic on the far right. The middle image illustrates the technique you use to accomplish this effect.

*Figure 29.8.*
*Using the Create From*
*effect on Paragraph text*
*to wrap text around a*
*graphic.*

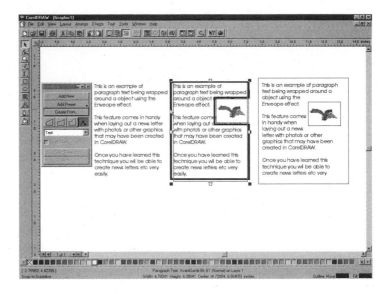

Follow these steps to wrap Paragraph text around a graphic:

1. Import your Paragraph text and graphic image into CorelDRAW.
2. Place the graphic image on top of the text.
3. Click the Pencil tool flyout and choose the Bézier tool.
4. Draw a box around the text block using the Point to Point method, making sure to go around the graphic.
5. Select the text using the Pick tool and click the Create From button in the Envelope roll-up. Use the arrow to click the box you just drew and click Apply.
6. Your text now wraps around the graphic. You can delete the box because it was used only as a pattern in which the text could flow.

The cars in Figure 29.9 are imported from Corel's clip art. An unconstrained envelope effect was applied to the rear of one car and the front of the other. This effect could go over big with body shops or perhaps personal injury lawyers.

Figure 29.9.
*Using an unconstrained
envelope applied to
clip art.*

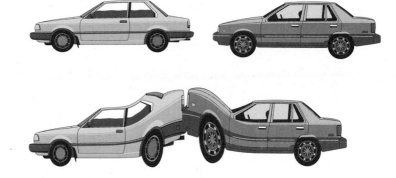

## Copying an Object's Envelope

Copying an envelope from one object to another is not the same as using the
Create From effect. To copy the envelope attributes from one object to another,
follow these steps:

1. Select the object to which you want to copy the envelope attributes.
2. From the Effects menu, choose Copy. A fly-out menu appears.
3. Choose Envelope From. The pointer then changes to an arrow.
4. Use the arrow to click the object that has the envelope attributes you want to
   copy. The selected object now takes on the envelope of the other object.

## Corel*NOTE!*

You cannot copy an enveloped object if it has had another effect applied to it.

# 30

# Blending

CorelDRAW's Blend effect morphs one object to another in a series of intermediate steps. You can blend single objects or groups of objects, and you can force the blend to follow a specific path.

The Blend feature does a great deal more than simply blend one object with another. It's important to understand the separate parts of a blend and the difference between single blends and multiple blends. Blends can also be used in ways that are not commonly associated with the normal artistic use of blending. They can be used to make grids, graphs, or anything that requires evenly spaced objects to illustrate an idea or message. Figure 30.1 shows the Blend roll-up.

*Figure 30.1.*
*The Blend roll-up*
*separated from the*
*Effects roll-up group.*

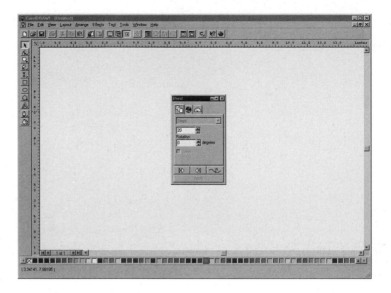

## The Basic Blend

Figure 30.2 illustrates how to achieve a basic blend. Draw two rectangles on the screen, one above the other. Select the two objects, either by marquee-selecting them or by holding down the Shift key while clicking each object. Click the Effects pull-down menu and select the Blend Roll-Up command. In the Blend roll-up, click the first icon, which depicts three cascading objects. This icon enables you to choose the number of steps you want in a blend. In Figure 30.2, five steps are chosen. Next, click the Apply button at the bottom of the dialog box. CorelDRAW creates a five-step blend.

*Figure 30.2.*
*The basic blend.*

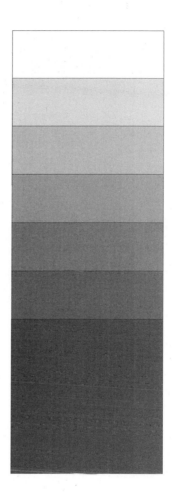

## The Parts of a Blend

If you click the center of the newly created blend, the status line tells you that it is a blend group. A *blend group* is different from a normal CorelDRAW group. If you click the first or last object of the blend group, the status line tells you that it's a control rectangle. If you had drawn circles, the status line would say "Control Ellipse." A blend group is made up of three parts: the two control objects and the group of five objects representing the number of steps you have selected. (See Figure 30.3.)

Figure 30.3.
The three parts
of a blend group.

You can change the direction in which a basic blend moves from beginning to end by clicking one of the control objects and dragging it to a new position. (See Figure 30.4.)

Figure 30.4.
Changing the direction of
a basic blend.

## Editing Basic Blends

There will be times when you'll want to edit a blend group. For example, you might want to change a color or delete one or more objects. To do this, click the blend group and then select the Separate command from the Arrange menu. Once you separate a blend group, it becomes three separate objects. (See Figure 30.5.) The first and last objects return to their original form (rectangle, curve, ellipse, and so on). The middle objects form the third group, which represents the number of steps you originally selected for the blend group. This group of objects is now like any normal CorelDRAW group. You can ungroup it with the Arrange pull-down menu's Ungroup command, or you can select objects within the group by holding down the Ctrl key and clicking the desired object. This method makes the selected object a child object, which you can modify without ungrouping the entire group. (See Skill Session 22, "Grouping and Ungrouping.")

*Figure 30.5.*
*The individual parts*
*of a blend group.*

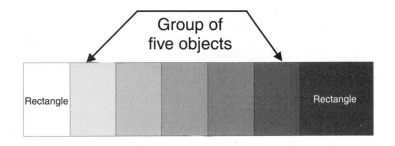

*Figure 30.6.*
*Placing a blend on*
*an ellipse path.*

## Blend Variations—Fitting a Blend to a Path

Making a blend follow a specific path is one of the easier blend variations. The purpose of this is to create various effects that would be difficult to do manually. Figure 30.6 illustrates a series of flowers placed on an ellipse.

To fit a blend to a path, follow these steps:

1. Create a basic blend using two objects. The example in Figure 30.6 uses a flower taken from the Symbols roll-up.

2. Draw an ellipse for your path.

3. Click the Fit to Path icon from the Blend roll-up. (See Figure 30.1.) The icon is a small arrow pointing at a wavy line. It's located in the lower-right corner of the Blend roll-up.

4. A flyout menu appears from which you select New Path.

5. The cursor changes to a wavy arrow. Use the arrow to click the path you created. You must click the line if your ellipse has no fill.

6. Click the Apply button.

7. The blend now follows the new path. The number of steps in your blend will determine how far along the path the blend will travel.

8. If you want the blend to go from the beginning to the end, click the Full Path box in the Blend roll-up. *This box becomes visible only when you're putting a blend on a path.*

9. If using Full Path causes your blend to break apart or stack up, increase or decrease the number of steps in the blend until you get the desired effect. You can create evenly spaced objects along your path by selecting the right amount of steps.

10. If your objects don't align correctly, click the rotation box in the Blend roll-up.

You can fit a blend to the path of any single object, including a curved or straight line. Once the blend is attached to the path, you can change the shape of the path. The blend will automatically follow the new shape. If the path is an ellipse (like the example in Figure 30.6), you could select the ellipse with the Pick tool and stretch the ellipse into a new shape. You could also convert the ellipse to curves and distort the original ellipse using the Shape tool. The blend will follow the new shape. You might have to increase or decrease the number of steps in the blend in order to get the proper spacing.

Fitting blends to the path of a single line provides additional flexibility. Figure 30.7 shows a blend of cars fit onto a curved line. Try duplicating this effect by following these steps:

1. Select a car from the Symbols roll-up and make a duplicate copy by pressing the + key on the keyboard.

2. Blend the two cars using the six-step blend.

3. Draw a wavy line for your path with the Pencil tool.

4. Click the Fit to Path icon from the Blend roll-up. The icon is a small arrow pointing at a wavy line located in the lower-right corner of the Blend roll-up. Select New Path from the flyout. Use the cursor provided to point to the wavy line created in Step 3.

5. Put a check mark in the Full Path box and click the Apply button. Notice that the cars are placed on the path, with the rear wheels touching the path. Unfortunately, this is as good as it gets until you do some editing.

6. To align the cars along the path, you first need to separate the blend from the path. Click a car in the center of the blend and choose Separate from the Arrange menu. Select the same car again and choose Ungroup from the Arrange menu. Each car can now be individually rotated to align it to the path. To rotate the cars for correct alignment, select each car and click until you see the rotation arrows. Click and drag the center of rotation thumb tack to the bottom of the rear tire. Now click and drag one of the rotation arrows until the front wheel touches the line. This might sound complicated, but it isn't once you try it.

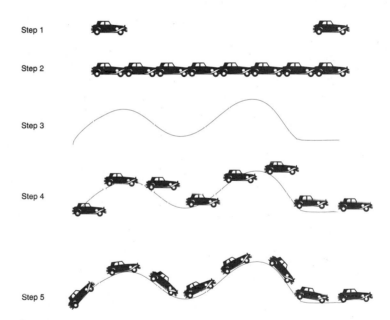

*Figure 30.7.*
*Fitting a blend group*
*to a single path.*

# Corel*NOTE!*

The blend and the path have been linked together. This enables you to click and drag either of the blend's control objects to make the blend travel a specific distance along the path. This is a variation of the Full Path choice you made earlier.

Figure 30.8 illustrates another blend method similar to the morphing effect. Follow these steps to re-create this effect:

1.  Type two different words on the page.

2.  Select both words and create a 20-step blend. Type -90 (degrees) in the Rotation parameters box, put a check mark in the Loop box, and then click the Apply button.

3.  Select the middle of the blend group and choose Separate from the Arrange menu. Select the original text at the top and then right-click it to bring up the Object Properties menu. Choose Order and then from the flyout choose To Front. Moving the original text to the front lets the viewer see both original words.

*Figure 30.8.*
*Morphing two words.*

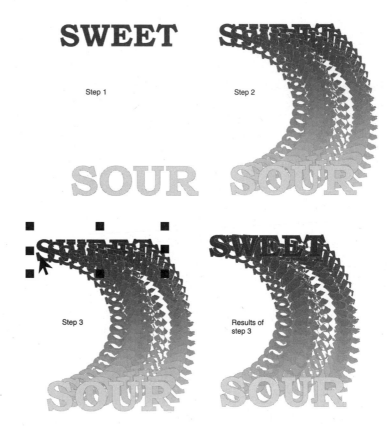

## Neon Effects

To create the look of neon, as shown in Figure 30.9, follow these steps:

1.  Type some text on the screen using your favorite font. A narrow artistic style will usually give you the best results.

2.  Remove the fill from the text and change the outline width to 6 or 8 points.

3. Change the outline color to neon red. This color is in the default palette.

4. Make a duplicate of the text and place it directly on top of the first text. The easy way to do this is to hit the + key on the numeric keyboard.

5. Change the width of the duplicate's outline to 1 point.

6. Change the outline color to white.

7. Marquee-select the two objects and then blend them with a 20-step blend.

You can experiment with different line widths to get different effects.

*Figure 30.9.*
*Creating a neon effect*
*with the Blend feature.*

## Making Grids and Charts

Grids are easy to make with the Blend feature. Refer to Figure 30.10 and follow these steps:

1. Select the Pencil tool, hold down the Ctrl key, and then draw a horizontal line across the top of your page and a second horizontal line across the bottom of the page.

2. Select the two lines and blend by the number of steps you need.

3. To complete the grid, draw a vertical line from the top to the bottom of the page on the left side and another one on the right. Blend these two lines by the number of steps you need.

# Corel *TIP!*

Use the rulers and guidelines to make the corners square.

Bar charts are equally easy to create. Refer to Figure 30.10 and follow these steps:

1.  Create a long rectangle and a short rectangle, and then blend the two together using the number of steps you need.

2.  To make the middle bars different lengths, separate and ungroup the blend and then stretch the bars that need to be changed.

*Figure 30.10.*
*Creating a grid and bar*
*chart with the Blend*
*feature.*

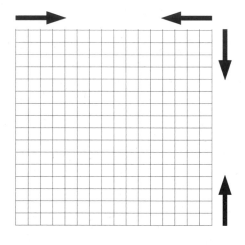

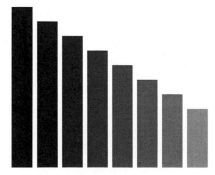

## Soft Shadow Effects

Creating drop shadows is a very common practice when you're working with text. It creates the illusion that the text is above the surface of the paper. Creating a soft drop shadow is a variation on this effect. It can be more pleasing to the eye in certain circumstances. The process of creating the soft drop shadow is almost the same as that for creating the neon effect. Figure 30.11 shows an example of the soft shadow effect. Follow the steps below to create a soft shadow effect:

1. Type some text on the screen using your favorite font.
2. Make a duplicate of the text. The easy way to do this is to press the + key on the numeric keyboard. This puts the duplicate right on top of the original.
3. Select the duplicate and move it below the original text.
4. Remove the fill from the duplicate text and change the outline width to 7 points.
5. Make the outline the same color as the background. Draw a temporary object with a dark fill and place it behind the text so you can see it.
6. Make a duplicate of this shadow text by pressing the + key (just as you did in Step 2).
7. Change the width of the duplicate's outline to 1 point.
8. Change the duplicate's outline color to a darker shade of the background color.
9. Marquee-select the two objects and blend with a 20-step blend. You can experiment with different line widths to get different effects.
10. Now that you've completed the soft shadow, select the original text and right-click to bring up the Object Properties menu. Click the Order command and choose To Front from the flyout. Now you can place the original text on top of the shadow. Group all the objects together and place them at the appropriate spot on the page.

*Figure 30.11.
Creating a soft
shadow effect.*

## Multiple Blends and Rainbow Blends

The Blend command can be used to create many other interesting effects. Figure 30.12 illustrates the process of adding a blend to another blend. Follow these steps to create cascading cards:

1. Import a playing card from Corel's clip art library. Make two duplicates of the card and arrange the cards as shown in Step 1.

2. Select the top-right card and the bottom-right card, and create a 20-step blend. Type 45 in the Rotation parameters box, put a check mark in the Loop check box, and then click the Apply button.

3. Select the bottom control card from the blend, hold down the Shift key, and select the bottom-left card.

4. Use the same setting from Step 2 to apply the second blend.

*Figure 30.12.*
*Adding a blend to a blend.*

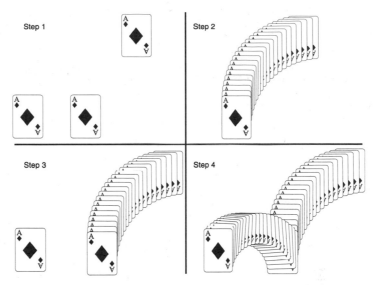

Figure 30.13 shows the Blend roll-up with the color wheel icon selected. You can create rainbow effects in your blends when you use different colors for your control objects. Choose one of the three icons on the left of the large color spectrum wheel to set the direction through which the color blend will travel. For example, if one control object is red and the second control object is blue, when you chose the top icon, the color blend travels directly from the first control object's color, through the color wheel, to the second control object's color. This form of blending creates a blend of muted reds and blues. When you choose the clockwise icon, the blend travels from the first control object's color to the second control object's color in a clockwise direction (through the purples and pinks of the color spectrum). Choosing the counterclockwise icon causes the blend to pass through the yellows and greens. A line will appear on the color wheel showing the direction of the blend when you choose any of the directional icons. This can aid you in making sure your colors are blending in the direction you want.

Figure 30.13.
The Blend roll-up with the
color wheel icon selected.

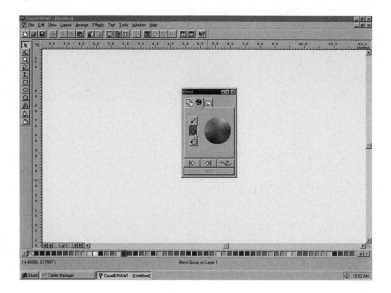

# 31

# Extruding

CorelDRAW's Extrude feature enables you to add three-dimensional effects to objects. To use this feature, choose the Effects pull-down menu and then choose Extrude. The Extrude roll-up appears on-screen as part of a roll-up group. The default configuration shows a preset extrude in the preview window. (Preset extrudes are covered later in this skill session.)

## Corel*NOTE!*

CorelDRAW 6 has grouped many of the effects found in the Effects pull-down menu into a single roll-up. When you click on the word Extrude in the Effects pull-down menu, the Extrude roll-up appears as part of a group of effects listed in the list box.

In the Extrude roll-up, the five tab icons above the preview window enable you to control certain extrude effects. The second icon is the Depth tab; you use it to select the type of extrude. The default configuration of the Extrude roll-up with the Depth tab selected is Small Back. (See Figure 31.1.)

*Figure 31.1.*
*The Extrude roll-up*
*showing Small Back.*

You can select the following extrudetypes by clicking the down arrow in the list box just below the preview window: Small Back, Small Front, Big Back, Big Front, Back Parallel, and Front Parallel.

Two other settings in the roll-up control the look of an extrude. The bottom list box defaults to VP Locked to Object (VP means vanishing point). Later in this skill session, you learn how to choose where the vanishing point locks to.

The last setting you need to be concerned about is the Depth setting. The number you enter in the Depth parameters box determines how deep the extrude will be. The maximum depth is 99. If you set the depth to 99, the extrude will end at the vanishing point.

When you click the small Page icon across from the Depth parameters box, the roll-up changes to a new configuration. (See Figure 31.2.) This configuration enables you to enter absolute coordinates for the vanishing point measured from the Page Origin or the Object Center. If you're creating a perspective drawing, you may want to use this method for defining the vanishing point.

*Figure 31.2.*
*The Extrude roll-up*
*displaying the vanishing*
*point absolute positioning*
*configuration.*

## The Basic Extrude

As an example, start with a basic extrude applied to a rectangle. Draw a rectangle on the page and use the default settings of Small Back and a depth setting of 20. The preview window shows a representation of a rectangle extruded to the back. It does not represent the depth setting you choose.

Click the Edit button in the roll-up to reveal the vanishing point. A small × then appears on the page. Click the vanishing point and drag it upwards and to the right until you see a cube effect. Your cube should look something like the one shown in Figure 31.3. When you like the look of the extrude, click Apply in the roll-up. Your extruded rectangle is then drawn on the page.

*Figure 31.3.*
*The basic extrude.*

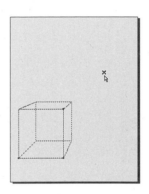

Now select the extruded object and move it to a new location on the page. Notice that the cube hasn't changed its appearance. I edited the newly moved object in Figure 31.4 to show the vanishing point in the same relative position to the cube as it was in its original position. The cube did not change in appearance because I used the default setting of VP Locked to Object. This setting simply means that no matter where the object is moved, the cube is not altered in appearance.

*Figure 31.4.*
*The extrude after being*
*moved to a new location*
*on the page.*

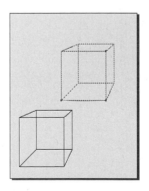

Before you go on to other settings, move your cube back to its original position and change the Depth setting from the default of 20 to 50. Now click Apply. Your cube should now look similar to the one shown in Figure 31.5. Notice that the extrude is lengthened and is getting closer to the vanishing point.

Figure 31.5.
*The extrude with a depth*
*setting of 50.*

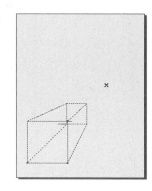

## Variation of the Basic Extrude

To create a variation of the extrude, this time draw a rectangle just as you did before, and choose Small Back and a depth of 20. In the second list box of the Extrude roll-up, scroll down and choose VP Locked to Page. Then click Edit. Move the vanishing point until you get a cube effect just like you did when creating the basic cube in the preceding section. Click Apply to draw the completed cube.

Select the extruded cube and move it to the lower left of the page. Make three duplicates of the cube and place them in each of the remaining corners of the page. (See Figure 31.6.) Notice that when you move the cubes, their vanishing points appear to change. They changed because you chose VP Locked to Page. This means when you move an extruded object around on the page, it is always extruded in the direction of the vanishing point's location. Its location is determined by where you originally placed it when creating your original cube.

Figure 31.6.
*An original and three*
*duplicate extruded*
*rectangles with the*
*vanishing point locked to*
*the page.*

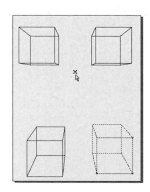

# Manually Controlling Rotated Extrudes

Sometimes you may want to rotate an extruded object to show a different perspective. The Rotate tab icon is the middle icon in the row of tab icons above the preview window in the Extrude roll-up. When you select this icon, the Extrude dialog box changes to the configuration shown in Figure 31.7.

*Figure 31.7.*
*The extrude roll-up with*
*the rotate tab selected*
*and a cube being rotated.*

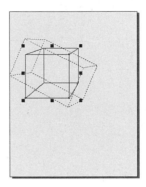

To rotate an extruded object manually, first select the object and place the cursor over the arc ball (the CorelDRAW logo); then click and drag using the hand cursor. The arc ball rotates, displaying the rotation that can be applied to the extruded object. When you're satisfied with the rotation angle, release the mouse button and click Apply.

Try rotating the cube you drew previously. Rotate it to an angle similar to the arc ball shown in Figure 31.7. The size of the cube changes from a cube to a longer box like the one shown in the figure. The cube's changing sizes is a problem if you expected a rotated cube-shaped figure like you started with instead of a long box. I consider this a bug in the program, but others don't.

To make your rotated cube look like a rotated cube instead of a long box, change the Depth setting to one-half of its original setting. Using the cube you created, change the Depth setting from 20 to 10. Your cube should now look more like you expected. Figure 31.8 shows the original cube at the bottom, the cube rotated with the original depth setting of 20 in the middle, and the cube rotated with the depth setting changed to 10 at the top.

Figure 31.8.
The original extruded
rectangle and two rotated
extrudes—one with a
depth of 20 and the other
with a depth of 10.

## Precisely Controlling Rotated Extrudes

If you are not comfortable with manually rotating your extrudes using the arc ball, you can precisely control the three-dimensional rotation of your extrudes by using the Angle, Phi, and Theta controls in the Extrude roll-up. To access these controls, click the Page icon just above the Edit button in the Extrude roll-up.

Figure 31.9 shows the original extruded cube, the manually rotated cube with the depth setting unchanged, and a newly created cube using the following precise settings: Angle 214, Phi 19, and Theta 63.

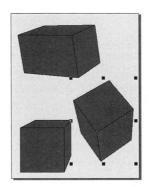

Figure 31.9.
An extrude rectangle
using precise settings.

## Applying Lighting Effects

The Light source tab icon is depicted by a light bulb. Figure 31.10 shows the Extrude roll-up displaying the light source configuration. Use the three light bulb icons alongside the preview window to apply different lighting effects to your objects.

Figure 31.10.
*Five extruded boxes with
different lighting effects
applied.*

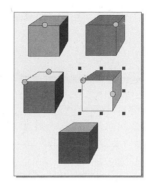

The preview window shows a grid surrounding a shaded ball. Clicking the number 1 icon places a circle with its number in the front right position on the grid. You can move the circle 2 to any point on the grid where lines intersect to control the lighting. You can also adjust the intensity of the light by moving the Intensity slider in the roll-up.

Figure 31.10 also shows four extruded boxes with different lights applied to each. Small circles on each box indicate where the lights are placed on the grid. It becomes obvious that the results from applying these light sources do not accurately shade the boxes. Therefore, I won't spend any more time describing the effect other than to point out that you can do a better job of creating the effect of lighting your extrudes by separating and ungrouping the extrudes, thereby enabling you to manually choose the colors for each side of the box. I used this method to light the box at the bottom of Figure 31.10.

## Filling Extrudes

You can always separate and ungroup an extrude and then separately fill each object that made up the extrude, but you also can fill the extrude in its extruded state. You can fill an extrude in three ways: Use Object Fill, Solid Fill, and Shade. Each type is described in the following sections. To display the fill configuration in the Extrude roll-up, click the Color Wheel icon.

### Use Object Fill

When you select Use Object Fill, the color of the extruded portion will be the same as the original object before it was extruded. If you start with a rectangle filled with red and then extrude the rectangle, for example, the extruded portion will be filled with the same color as the original rectangle. The top extrude in Figure 31.11 was filled using the Use Object Fill method. Notice all three sides are the same color.

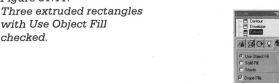

*Figure 31.11.*
*Three extruded rectangles*
*with Use Object Fill*
*checked.*

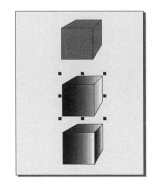

In the Use Object Fill configuration of the Extrude roll-up, you see a check box called Drape Fills. If you check this box, any fill other than a solid fill will fill all three sides of the object in a continuous fashion. For example, the middle extrude in Figure 31.11 was filled with a fountain fill with the Drape Fills box checked. Notice how the fountain fill fills all three sides of the extrude as if it were a single object.

For the extrude at the bottom of the figure, I used the same fountain fill without the Drape Fills box checked. Notice the difference between it and the middle object. In the bottom extrude, the fountain fill was applied to each side separately.

## Solid Fill

When you select the Solid Fill option, the original rectangle can be filled with any of CorelDRAW's many fills, and the extruded portion will be filled with a solid color fill. To choose a solid color fill for the extruded portion, click the down arrow next to the Using color button in the roll-up. Figure 31.12 shows an extruded rectangle with the original rectangle filled with a texture fill and the extruded portion filled with a solid color.

*Figure 31.12.*
*An extruded rectangle*
*with Solid Fill checked.*

## Shade Fill

When you select the Shade Fill option, you can shade the extruded portion using two different colors selected from the From and To color palettes accessed by clicking their respective color buttons. The shading effect is the same as a two-color fountain fill. Figure 31.13 shows an extruded rectangle at the top filled with a solid fill and the bottom extruded rectangle filled using the Shade option. Notice the drop-down color palette accessed by clicking and holding the bottom color button.

*Figure 31.13.*
*An extruded rectangle*
*with a solid fill and one*
*with a shaded fill.*

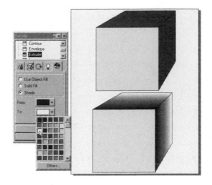

# Corel*NOTE!*

If you change the original rectangle's color from the color palette at the bottom of the CorelDRAW screen after you have applied a shaded fill, the color shown on the From button will change to the new color selected. This causes the shading to go between the color shown on the To button and the color chosen from the palette at the bottom of the CorelDRAW screen. The final result will be a solid color filling the original rectangle and the same color blending to the color shown on the To button in the extruded portion.

## Preset Extrudes

You access preset extrudes by clicking the first tab icon in the Extrude roll-up. These presets are the same ones found in the Presets roll-up under the Tools menu (see Skill Session 61, "Presets"). The advantage of using presets is that the extrude effect, including the fill color, is already defined. All that is necessary to apply the preset effect to a selected object is to select the preset you want to use and click the Apply button.

Figure 31.14 shows the Extrude roll-up in the preset configuration and four presets applied to the word *CorelDRAW*. Notice that the note flyout shows the extrude effects used for the selected preset, including the font used.

*Figure 31.14.*
*The Extrude roll-up in the*
*preset configuration and*
*certain presets applied*
*to text.*

# 32

# Contour

Contour was first introduced in CorelDRAW 5. To access the Contour roll-up, select it from the Effects menu.

## Corel*NOTE!*

The Contour roll-up in Figure 32.1 has been separated from the main roll-up group, which contains the other effects in the Effects menu. This was done for simplicity and clarity.

Contouring is very straightforward. When you add contouring to an object, duplicates of the object arc created, either toward the center of and smaller than the original or away from and larger than the original. To visualize this effect, think of a map with contour lines showing altitude.

## Corel*NOTE!*

You can apply contours only to single objects and Artistic text. This can include two or more objects that have been combined to form a single object. (See Skill Session 23, "Combining, Breaking Apart, and Separating Objects.")

The Contour roll-up, shown in Figure 32.1, gives you three ways to control the look of a contour. The first option is To Center. Click this check box to force the added contour shapes toward the center of the original object. When you click To Center, the Steps parameters box is grayed out, because the To Center option uses the number entered in the Offset parameters box to determine the necessary number of steps needed for equal spacing.

*Figure 32.1.*
*The default Contour*
*roll-up.*

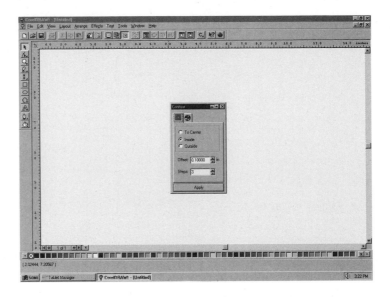

When you click the color wheel icon at the top of the roll-up, the roll-up changes to display a large color wheel. (See Figure 32.2.) In this display mode, you can choose a different fill and outline color from the original object. This new color will blend with the original object's color if more than one offset step is defined. Choose the slanted arrow icon for a normal blend effect. Choose either of the rotation icons for rainbow effects. You have a choice of clockwise or counterclockwise.

# Corel*NOTE!*

Important! When you use the To Center option, the number of new shapes created will become extremely large if the Offset parameters box is set to less than .01 inch. The reason for this is because the To Center option keeps creating new shapes until it reaches the center of the original object.

The Offset parameters box sets the spacing between the shapes that are added in the contouring process. The amount of offset is equal on all sides. (Think of it as the amount of spacing rather than the amount of offset.)

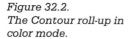

*Figure 32.2.*
*The Contour roll-up in*
*color mode.*

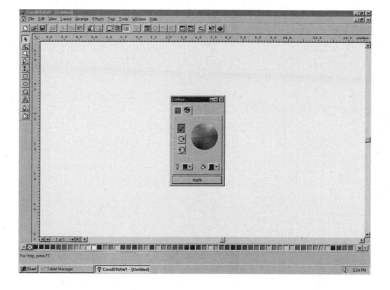

Figure 32.3 illustrates how using the To Center option affects the look of a contour. The left contoured triangle fits into an area 2 inches square. Therefore, it's limited to two steps because the offset is set to 0.3 inches. Remember, the 0.3 inch offset applies to all three sides of the triangle; therefore, you're decreasing the overall size of the first triangle by nine-tenths of an inch. Only two triangles will fit into a space of just over two inches. If the original triangle is enlarged but the offset is left the same, you will see more steps.

The middle contour in Figure 32.3 contains six steps in the triangle, because the offset is reduced to 0.1 inches. The contour on the right has 12 steps in it, with an offset of 0.05 inches.

*Figure 32.3.*
*Contours created with the*
*To Center option.*

The second option, Inside, also forces the added shapes toward the center of the original object. However, unlike the To Center option, the Inside option lets you choose the number of steps you want in the contour. The total number of steps you can use is limited by the size of the original object and the size of the offset. It is possible to use up to 999 steps if the object is large enough and the offset is small enough. The distance between each step is always determined by the number you enter in the Offset parameters box. Using different offset settings changes the appearance of the contour dramatically.

Figure 32.4 illustrates two different contours created with the Inside method. The rectangle on the left fits inside a four-inch square area. Seven steps is chosen, and 0.1 inches is used for the offset. Notice the difference between this contour and the To Center contours in Figure 32.3. The reason for the obvious difference is that the contour in Figure 32.4 has only seven steps designated as well as a small offset; therefore, the center object is larger.

The contour on the right in Figure 32.4 uses the same offset, but with only three steps. Notice that the center of the contour is even larger.

*Figure 32.4.*
*Contours created with the*
*Inside option.*

The third option is Outside. Choosing the Outside option forces the new contour shapes outward, away from the original. You don't have the same limitations you have with the other options when it comes to figuring out how many shapes will fit inside a given area. This is because you're expanding shapes, not contracting them. As with the Inside option, the number of steps is limited to 999. Keep in mind that the number you enter in the Offset parameters box has a great deal to do with the final results. Figure 32.5 illustrates some variations of the Outside option, beginning with a single triangle.

*Figure 32.5.*
*Contours created with the*
*Outside option.*

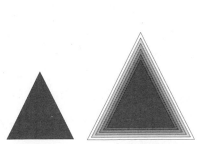
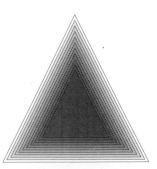

The first contour in Figure 32.5 has an offset of 0.1 and five steps. The second contour has an offset of 0.1 and ten steps.

The other options you have to consider are the outline and fill colors. Clicking either the Outline or Fill button brings down a color palette. Quite often you'll want to use a different color for the outline than the one you use for the fill in order to show more of a contour look. The size of the outline is determined by the default outline setting.

When you create a contour, the original object's color blends with the color selected in the color configuration of the Contour roll-up. This is best illustrated by selecting black from the roll-up's Fill palette and contouring an object already filled with white.

# Corel*NOTE!*

If you blend two triangles together with the Blend effect using the same colors and dimensions for the inside and outside triangles as those for the contours, you won't be able to tell the difference between the blended object and the contoured object. Figure 32.6 illustrates this point. This doesn't mean you can do everything with contours that you can do with blends; Figure 32.6 is one exception. It's used to point out that if you select a contour thinking it's a blend, you can't change it as you could if it were a blend. Always look at the status line to see what kind of object you've selected.

*Figure 32.6.*
*Comparing a contoured*
*object (left) to a blended*
*object (right).*

## Applying Contours to Other Objects

You can apply a contour to almost any single object, as long as the object meets the criteria given at the beginning of this chapter. Figure 32.7 shows a contour applied to a freehand shape.

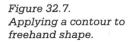

*Figure 32.7.*
*Applying a contour to*
*freehand shape.*

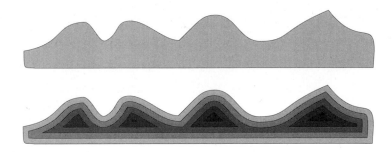

## Editing Contours

Editing contoured objects is similar to most other methods of editing objects that have effects applied to them. First, select the contoured object and then select Separate from the Arrange menu. This separates the contour group from the original object. If you want to further edit the objects that make up the contour group, select the group and then select Ungroup from the Arrange menu. This final ungrouping enables you to change the individual parts of the contour.

## Contouring Text

Contouring text can produce some interesting effects. Figure 32.8 illustrates how fonts can be contoured to change them to bolder or lighter weights when bold and narrow weights aren't available for a particular font in the font list. The first example uses the To Outside method to create a bold-weight version of the font Huxley Vertical BT. The second example uses the To Inside method to create a narrow-weight version of the font Balloon BD BT. In this example, the text on the left is the original font; the text in the center has the contour effect applied to it, and on the right is the contoured portion of the text, which has been separated from the original text.

The contour effect in Figure 32.9 is achieved by applying a one-step, outside contour to the text. After it is separated from the original text, the contoured portion is filled with a vertical fountain fill of black to white; the original text portion is filled with a reverse-direction fountain fill of white to black.

*Figure 32.8.*
*Two different types of contoured text.*

Outside Bold
Inside thinner

*Figure 32.9.*
*Special effect text contouring.*

CONTOUR

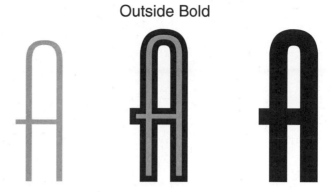

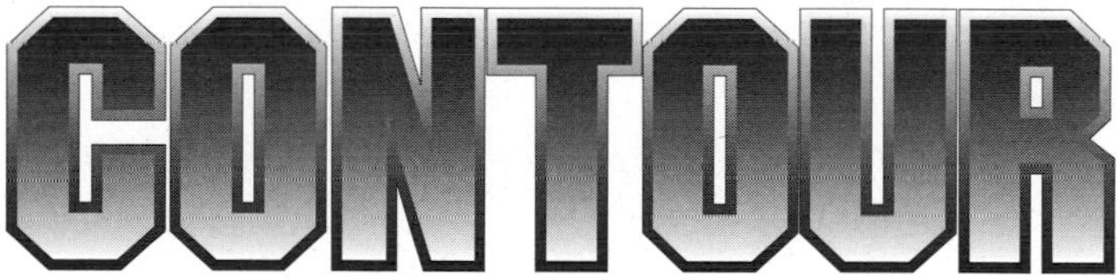

# 33

# PowerLines

PowerLines were first introduced in CorelDRAW 4. Their purpose is to create lines with variable weights to give your illustrations a hand-drawn look (perhaps this feature should be named PowerShapes). Semantics notwithstanding, the PowerLine feature provides a way for those who thought they couldn't draw a straight line to become artists.

At first glance, the previews of the preset shapes offered in the selection list box appear to be fairly boring, and for most users they are. The real power of PowerLines is being able to edit these preset shapes into something you will find exciting and new. However, there is a trade off when using PowerLines—the number of nodes generated in a PowerLine will be very large. The nodes generated from drawing a similar shape using a conventional method would be far less. Figure 33.1 shows the PowerLine roll-up, which is accessed from the Effects menu.

*Figure 33.1.*
*The PowerLine*
*roll-up.*

Figure 33.2 shows the effects certain presets have on a straight line drawn horizontally across the screen with the Pencil tool. The first five lines have the presets Wedge 1, Wedge 3, Wedge 4, Trumpet 4, and Teardrop 1 applied to them. The two bottom shapes are formed with

the presets Nib and Leaky Pen. You can apply a preset to an existing line or create the preset shape as your drawing with the Pencil tool by putting a check mark in the Apply when drawing lines check box.

Beginning with Figure 33.3, you will be taken through the steps required to create a beautiful vase. You will do this with only three basic edits to one of the standard presets.

# Corel *NOTE!*

In order to apply other effects to a PowerLine, you must first separate it with the Separate command from the Arrange menu.

*Figure 33.2.*
*A few basic preset*
*shapes.*

**To begin drawing the vase,** follow these steps:

1. **Open the PowerLine** roll-up from the Effects pull-down menu. Make sure that the Apply when drawing lines check box is not checked.

2. Draw a straight vertical line down the center of the page using the Pencil tool.

3. In the PowerLine roll-up, click the down arrow in the Preset list box.

4. Scroll down to Max Width and enter 2.0 in the parameters box.

5. With your vertical line selected, click the Apply button. Figure 33.3 shows the shape you should have at this point.

6. Click the Shape tool.

7. Double-click the top node of your original line. The Node Edit roll-up will appear on-screen. Click the Edit Width button. The Node Edit roll-up will change its configuration.

8. With the Shape tool still selected, click part way down the center line. This places a small circle on the line. (See Figure 33.4.)

*Figure 33.3.*
*Beginning a PowerLine*
*shape.*

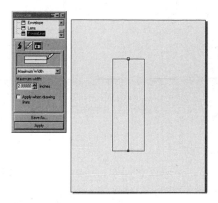

*Figure 33.4.*
*Adding a circle node.*

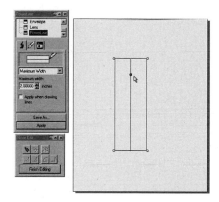

9. Click the + button in the Node Edit roll-up. A new horizontal line appears with pressure edit handles in place of the small circle. (See Figure 33.5.)

*Figure 33.5.*
*The pressure edit line*
*and handles.*

# Corel *NOTE!*

If you do not follow these steps exactly, you will not be able to edit the shape.

10. With the Shape tool still selected, click on one end of the line and drag toward the center line until you reach the desired position. (See Figure 33.6.)

*Figure 33.6.*
*Beginning the shape*
*of the vase.*

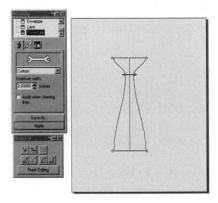

11. Click farther down the center line to add a new circle.
12. Click the + button again. A new set of pressure edit handles appears.
13. Drag one of the handles outward to the desired position. (See Figure 33.7.)

*Figure 33.7.*
*It's looking more*
*like a vase.*

14. Click the center line a short distance from the bottom.
15. Click the + button again and drag one of the handles inward to the desired position. (See Figure 33.8.) Click the Finish Editing button in the Node Edit roll-up.

Figure 33.8.
The finished shape.

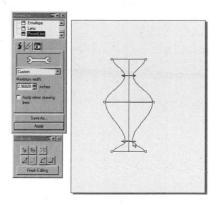

**16.** Select your shape and fill it with a texture fill. In this project, the texture fill Cosmic Minerals was used. (See Figure 33.9.)

Figure 33.9.
The completed vase.

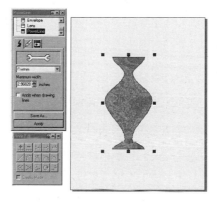

Congratulations—you just created a beautiful vase!

# Corel *NOTE!*

When you create something you like and want to use it again in other projects, you can save it by clicking the Save As button at the bottom of the PowerLine roll-up. A dialog box appears where you can give your shape a name. The next time you want to create your custom shape, it will be available in the Preset list box.

Figure 33.10 shows the original vase and a new one that was drawn with a simple straight line (the same length as the original) with the newly saved Vase preset selected in the Preset selection box.

*Figure 33.10.*
*The original vase and a*
*new vase drawn using the*
*new Vase preset.*

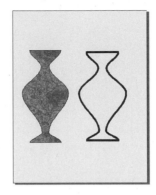

# Corel*NOTE!*

When you use your new shape preset, be sure you enter the same numbers in the Max Width parameters box as you did for the original. If you forget the numbers, simply experiment with a few different settings. If you don't draw the beginning line the same length as the original, the shape will be either squatty or skinny. You can adjust for this by stretching the shape up or down to the proper dimensions with the Pick tool. You cannot stretch horizontally.

Here's how to dissect a PowerLine to see what it contains:

1. First, select the vase shape. The status line tells you that it's a PowerLine on Layer 1.
2. Click the Separate command in the Arrange menu. The status line now tells you the shape is a group of two objects. (See Figure 33.11.) There are actually three objects on-screen (if you include the original line you drew to create the PowerLine).

*Figure 33.11.*
*A separated PowerLine.*

3. Select the Un-Group command in the Arrange menu.
4. Select each object and move them apart. The first object is your new vase.

The second object is the original line. The third object is an outline of the vase. (See Figure 33.12.)

Figure 33.12.
The individual parts
of a PowerLine.

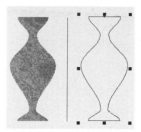

5. Delete the second and third objects.

6. Click the vase with the Shape tool.

7. Marquee-select the entire shape. Notice the number of nodes that make up your vase. The status line indicates 79 nodes. (See Figure 33.13.) Double-click on one of the nodes to bring up the Node Edit roll-up.

Figure 33.13.
A PowerLine with
nodes selected.

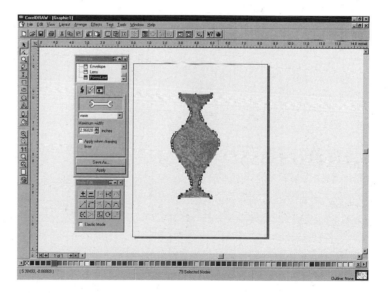

8. Click the Auto-Reduce icon in the Note Edit roll-up. Notice the number of nodes has been reduced to ten. (See Figure 33.14.) The number of nodes that will be removed using the Auto-Reduce method is determined by the settings in the Node Edit Tool Properties dialog box (see Skill Session 7, "The Shape Tool").

*Figure 33.14.*
*Reducing the number*
*of nodes with the*
*Auto-Reduce button.*

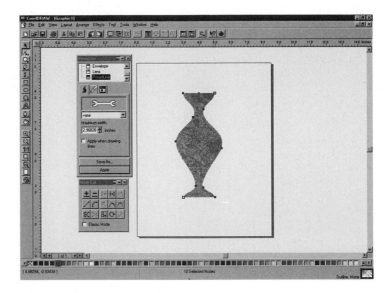

# Corel*NOTE!*

When you're working with PowerLines, remember that the number of nodes created in each object can become very large. For more information on how important it is to use the Auto-Reduce function, refer to the section "Dissecting PowerLines" later in this skill session. Get in the habit of separating and ungrouping your PowerLines, and then use the Auto-Reduce method on each object when you're sure you won't be making any more changes.

If you want to apply any additional effects to your PowerLine shapes, you must first separate the PowerLine.

Figure 33.15 shows our vase filled with a custom radial fountain fill to give it a more three-dimensional look. An ellipse was draw across the top of the vase and filled with a linear fountain fill to add more realism. Finally, a wall and floor were added and a duplicate of the vase was made and filled with a solid gray fill to create a shadow effect.

Figure 33.15.
*Adding effects to give the
appearance of three
dimensions.*

## Other Uses for PowerLines

There are many more effects you can create with PowerLines. For example, you can apply a PowerLine to shapes you have already drawn. This method can produce some painterly effects in your drawings.

The preset you'll use most after you create custom shapes will probably be the Nib preset. Using Nib enables you to draw shapes with a calligraphic style.

PowerLines are something completely different than what you usually find in vector-drawing programs. There are many more effects that can be accomplished with this tool. Experiment and practice using PowerLines—the more you use them the more effects you will discover.

## Dissecting PowerLines

PowerLines can produce some interesting effects, but they can also be a nightmare when you try to print them. This is because of the huge number of nodes they contain beneath the surface. Now we'll take a look at what PowerLines are really made of.

Figure 33.16 shows a horseshoe-shaped line that is made up of five nodes. Apply the Wedge 3 PowerLine to it so that it looks more like a crescent moon, as shown in Figure 33.17.

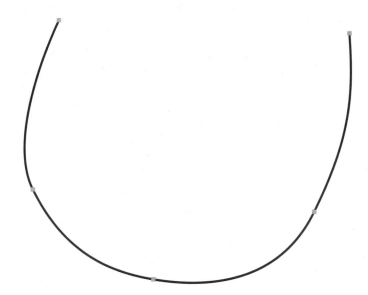

*Figure 33.16.*
*The original line*
*with five nodes.*

When you look at the newly created PowerLine, it seems like just one object. After all, when it's selected, the status line reads "PowerLine on Layer 1." Let's start dissecting.

Select the PowerLine and choose the Arrange | Separate command. Deselect the PowerLine and select it again with the Pick tool. Move the top object away to reveal the object underneath. If you look at the PowerLine now, you'll see two different objects, as shown in Figure 33.18. One is the original line and the other is a group of eight objects. It sure looks like one object, though!

Now ungroup the "group of eight objects" to see what really makes up the PowerLine. In Figure 33.19, I've exploded the eight pieces to make them more visible. Four of the pieces are open paths that cannot be filled, and they're the same shapes as closed paths that can be filled. The only reason they exist is so an outline can be applied to the PowerLine as a whole. Also notice the number of nodes contained in each object. Table 33.1 shows the node count for each object and the total number of nodes for this very simple line. You'll see in the next step that you can reduce this quite a bit without changing the look of the line.

*Figure 33.17.*
*The original line with*
*the Wedge 3 PowerLine*
*applied to it.*

*Figure 33.18.*
*Separating the*
*PowerLine.*

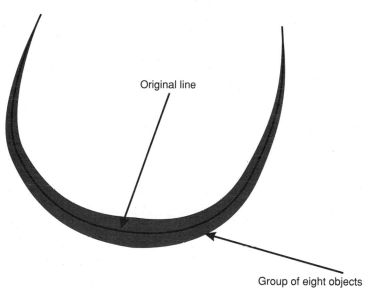

Original line

Group of eight objects

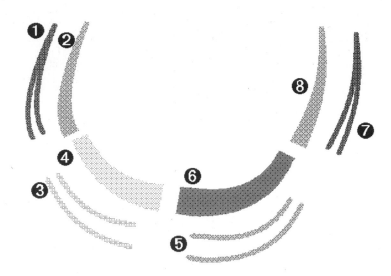

*Figure 33.19.
The eight objects
of the PowerLine.*

**Table 33.1. Node count for the eight objects.**

| | |
|---|---|
| Object 1 | 131 nodes |
| Object 2 | 131 nodes |
| Object 3 | 135 nodes |
| Object 4 | 135 nodes |
| Object 5 | 136 nodes |
| Object 6 | 136 nodes |
| Object 7 | 132 nodes |
| Object 8 | 132 nodes |
| Total | 1068 nodes |

By selecting each of the eight pieces and using the Auto-Reduce icon in the Node Edit roll-up (see Skill Session 7), you can drastically reduce the number of nodes. Figure 33.20 shows the eight pieces after they've been auto-reduced. There's no change in appearance, but the total node count has dropped, as shown in Table 33.2.

**Table 33.2. The node count for the eight objects after they've been auto-reduced.**

| | |
|---|---|
| Object 1 | 6 nodes |
| Object 2 | 6 nodes |
| Object 3 | 4 nodes |
| Object 4 | 6 nodes |

| Object 5 | 5 nodes |
|----------|---------|
| Object 6 | 7 nodes |
| Object 7 | 4 nodes |
| Object 8 | 5 nodes |
| Total | 43 nodes |

*Figure 33.20.*
*The eight objects after*
*auto-reduction.*

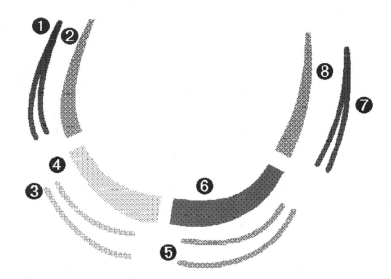

Now the four outlined objects are unnecessary for what you're going to do, so you can delete them. Figure 33.21 shows the result of this. Select all of the objects and use the Weld roll-up to weld them back into one object. Select all of the nodes of this new object, auto-reduce one more time, and you'll get the object shown in Figure 33.22. It has just 9 nodes. That's 1059 nodes fewer than the original bunch.

On the preceding PowerLine, it wasn't too difficult to do the cleanup necessary to get a workable object. This isn't so easy with a pressure PowerLine, as you'll soon see. Figure 33.23 shows a PowerLine drawn with a pressure-sensitive pen on a digitizing tablet. Unfortunately, the pressure lines don't look very nice to begin with.

After separating and ungrouping, you get the unruly mess shown in Figure 33.24. Notice that the control runs down the middle of the PowerLine and contains 72 nodes. The PowerLine itself is made up of 200 individual objects with a total of 11,698 nodes. Not only is this object overly complex for printing, but it will also eat up over 100KB of disk space for one line. A simple weld of all the objects cannot be done, because you will get the error message shown in Figure 33.25. Pressure PowerLines are definitely something to avoid.

*Figure 33.21.*
*The four necessary*
*objects.*

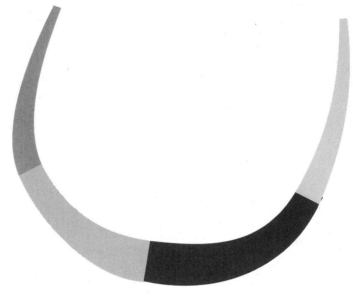

*Figure 33.22.*
*The final shape after*
*welding and auto-*
*reducing.*

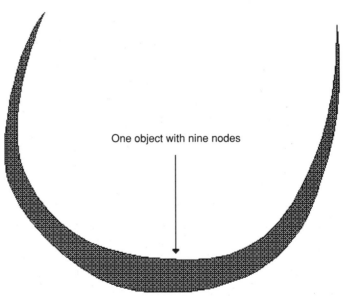

One object with nine nodes

*Figure 33.23.*
*A PowerLine drawn with*
*a pressure-sensitive pen.*

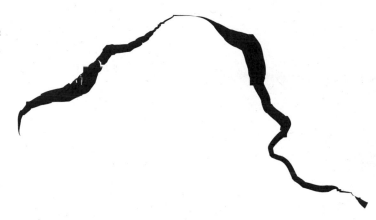

When you use PowerLines, keep in mind what's beneath the surface. They aren't as simple as they look!

*Figure 33.24.*
*The pressure PowerLine*
*exposed.*

*Figure 33.25.*
*The error message that*
*appears when you*
*attempt to weld a pres-*
*sure PowerLine.*

# 34

# Lens

The lens effect gets its name from its counterpart in the photographic world. When a lens is applied to an object, the lens distorts the object in some fashion. CorelDRAW's lenses can provide transparency, magnification, brightening of color, inversion of colors, limiting of color, addition of color, conversion to grayscale, infrared imaging, mapping to custom colors, wireframe and fish eye views.

You can find all the lenses in the Lens roll-up (see Figure 34.1), which you access through the Effects pull-down menu (the shortcut key is Alt+F3). The roll-up contains a crude sample of what an effect will do to the selected object, as well as a choice of lenses, the rate at which they will be applied, and, on some lenses, a color selector. All the lenses have the option of being frozen or being linked to a viewpoint.

You apply lenses to an object that covers an object or objects that the lens will affect. The object to which you apply the lens can't be part of a group, but you can apply the lens to a whole group at once. Each object then acts as a separate lens. You can't apply more than one lens to an object, but you can have multiple objects stacked on top of each other with a different lens effect in each one. Be forewarned that stacking lenses makes it more difficult to print the image; therefore, it is not a good idea to stack them too deep.

All the screen shots of the Lens roll-up in this chapter show it as being separate from the Effects roll-up, as in a default configuration. To separate the Lens roll-up, simply click its name in the list and drag it away from the Effects roll-up group.

## Transparency

The first lens is Transparency. When an object with this lens applied to it is floated over other objects, it gives the illusion that the lens object is transparent. If you apply a color, the objects behind the lens are affected by that color. You can adjust this lens by changing the rate at which it is applied. When you set the lens to 100 percent, the object is completely transparent, and the color setting has no effect. On the other hand, a setting of 0 percent makes the object opaque, and the color setting becomes its fill. Figure 34.1 shows the Lens roll-up with the transparency.

*Figure 34.1.*
*The Lens roll-up with*
*Transparency chosen.*

## Magnify

The Magnify lens makes objects behind it appear larger by the factor set in the Amount box. Any color applied to the Magnify lens object is ignored because it's always completely transparent. The amount can range anywhere from 1.0 to 100.0 and is accurate to one decimal place. Figure 34.2 shows the Lens roll-up with Magnify chosen.

*Figure 34.2.*
*The Lens roll-up with*
*Magnify chosen.*

In CorelDRAW 5, the lens had to be over the area affected, and in this case, it blocks important areas of the map. CorelDRAW 6 has two new features for lenses that address this problem. The first option is to check the Frozen check box before applying the lens. After you have applied the lens, you can move the object anywhere, and it will retain its image.

The other new feature added in CorelDRAW 6 is the ability to change the viewpoint of the lens. First, you check the Viewpoint check box; then an Edit button appears on the roll-up. Click Edit, and an × appears in the middle of the lens. Move the × to the area on the page from where you want the lens to draw its image. Figure 34.3 shows how the viewpoint is being moved on the map example.

*Figure 34.3.*
*Moving the viewpoint of*
*the lens on the map.*

## Brighten

The Brighten lens actually should be called the Brighten and Darken lens. Although you can apply a color to it, the color is not used. Instead, the lens either brightens or darkens the objects behind it by the amount set in the Rate box. Amounts between 0 and 100 brighten the object, and amounts between 0 and –100 darken it. A setting of 100 makes any lens object solid white, and –100 makes it solid black. But the rate affects each color differently because it is based on the RGB values of the colors beneath the lens. Figure 34.4 shows the Lens roll-up with Brighten chosen. Figure 34.5 shows how the Brighten lens applied to text affects the underlying image.

*Figure 34.4.*
*The Lens roll-up with*
*Brighten chosen.*

Figure 34.5.
The Brighten lens at 50
percent applied to text
over a photograph.

## Invert

The Invert lens shows the CMYK complementary colors when you place it over objects. The resulting image is basically a photographic negative. Invert is an all-or-nothing lens because there's no rate or color to adjust. Figure 34.6 shows the Lens roll-up with Invert chosen.

Figure 34.6.
The Lens roll-up with
Invert chosen.

## Color Limit

The Color Limit lens works much like the color filter on a camera. At its full strength, it allows only the color of the lens and the color black to show through. But unlike the color filter, the Color Limit lens is adjustable in strength. In the roll-up, you can choose the tint color of the lens, at a rate between 0 and 100 percent. It approaches black as you increase the strength of the lens. The only exceptions to this are white objects; they are the color of the lens itself. Objects that are the exact same color as the filtered lens are unaffected altogether. Figure 34.7 shows the Lens roll-up with Color Limit chosen.

*Figure 34.7.*
*The Lens roll-up with*
*Color Limit chosen.*

# Color Add

The Color Add lens adds the color of the lens to the color of the objects behind it. Remember that, in an additive color model (RGB colors), the sum of all colors is white, and therefore white is unaffected by this lens. If you add red to blue at full strength, you get magenta. Green added to red at full strength gives you yellow. Green added to blue at full strength gives you cyan. Coincidentally (not really), those three colors—magenta, yellow, and cyan—are the backbone of the subtractive color model. The color black is added to that model only because of impurities in printed inks.

This lens is one of the most difficult to understand because the colors that result may not be what you expect. With Color Add, as with other lenses, you can adjust the percentage of the lens color from 0 to 100 percent. Figure 34.8 shows the Lens roll-up with Color Add chosen.

*Figure 34.8.*
*The Lens roll-up with*
*Color Add chosen.*

# Tinted Grayscale

The Tinted Grayscale lens changes a color object to its grayscale equivalent. Giving the lens a color makes that color the darkest shade in the object, and makes all other colors lighter shades of the lens' color. For example, you can easily change a color photograph into a sepia-tone one by putting a brown lens over the bitmap. When you place the Tinted Grayscale lens over objects with black as the color, this lens produces an effect similar to what you get by printing a color image on a black-and-white laser printer.

Note that, if you use spot colors with this and other lenses, they will be converted to CMYK colors for output; therefore, you should not use this method to get a duotone effect. Figure 34.9 shows the Lens roll-up with Tinted Grayscale chosen, and Figure 34.10 shows the effects of three rectangles with the Tinted Grayscale lens applied to them.

*Figure 34.9.*
*The Lens roll-up with*
*Tinted Grayscale chosen.*

*Figure 34.10.*
*Three examples of the*
*effects of the Tinted*
*Grayscale lens.*

## Heat Map

The Heat Map lens enables you to produce the effect of infrared imaging. A color palette of white, yellow, orange, red, blue, violet, and cyan is used to map the various "heat" levels. By adjusting the rotation setting, you can control which colors are "cool" and which are "hot." Basically, hot colors in the original image are mapped to red and orange; cool colors, to violet and cyan. Figure 34.11 shows the Lens roll-up with Heat Map chosen, and Figure 34.12 shows the effect of applying a 50 percent rotated Heat Map lens over a rainbow gradient fill.

*Figure 34.11.*
*The Lens roll-up with*
*Heat Map chosen.*

*Figure 34.12.*
*The effect of the*
*Heat Map lens.*

## Custom Color Map

The Custom Color Map lens enables you to choose two colors, and all colors of the underlying image will be mapped to the range of colors between those two. If you want to reverse the order of the colors, simply click the <> button. Where this lens really gets interesting is that you can use Forward Rainbow or Reverse Rainbow. This means that colors will be mapped using a rainbow of colors between the two colors you have chosen. Figure 34.13 shows the Lens roll-up with Custom Color Map chosen, and Figures 34.14 and 34.15 show the effect of applying this lens to a photograph.

*Figure 34.13.*
*The Lens roll-up with*
*Custom Color Map*
*chosen.*

*Figure 34.14.*
*The effect of the*
*Custom Color Map*
*with a Direct Palette.*

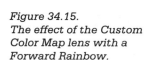

*Figure 34.15.*
*The effect of the Custom*
*Color Map lens with a*
*Forward Rainbow.*

## Wireframe

The Wireframe lens shows the outline of any objects behind it just as with
CorelDRAW'S wireframe view. Options in the roll-up enable you to choose the
color you want for both the outline of objects and their fill. If you don't want to see
either the outline or fill, then simply uncheck the appropriate check box. Figure
34.16 shows the Lens roll-up with Wireframe chosen.

*Figure 34.16.*
*The Lens roll-up with*
*Wireframe chosen.*

## Fish Eye

The Fish Eye lens outwardly distorts and magnifies the objects behind it when you specify a positive amount. But you also can enter negative amounts that shrink and inwardly distort the objects. You can specify up to 1000 percent in either the positive or the negative direction. Figure 34.17 shows the Lens roll-up with Fish Eye chosen, and Figure 34.18 shows the effects of the Fish Eye lens on a square group of objects.

*Figure 34.17.*
*The Lens roll-up with*
*Fish Eye chosen.*

*Figure 34.18.*
*The effect of the Fish Eye*
*lens on a radially filled*
*square with grid lines.*

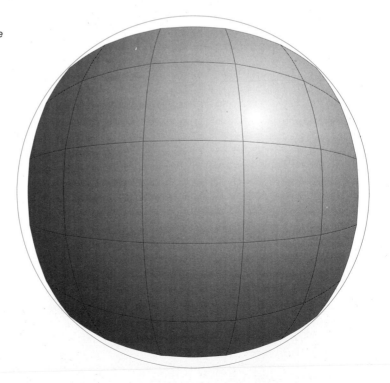

# None

The last lens type is None. You use None when you want to remove a lens effect from an object. Note that objects with lenses applied to them don't behave the same way that normal objects behave.

# 35

# PowerClip

The PowerClip command is used to insert an object inside another object. You must decide which object becomes the *contents*, and which object becomes the *container*. The container can be created from Artistic text, a group of objects, or a closed path. You can choose from these types of objects to create the contents: Artistic or Paragraph text, a group of objects, a closed path, or a bitmap.

The PowerClip command can also be used to create interesting effects with scanned photo files and text objects. If you need to create an effect such as placing photos into text, you can insert a photo of the Grand Canyon into the word Arizona.

Place a PowerClip container in another container to produce a nest of PowerClip objects, which can have up to five editable levels.

PowerClip is selected from the Effects pull-down menu and has a submenu with four options: Place Inside Container, Extract Contents, Edit Contents, and Finish Editing This Level. (See Figure 35.1.)

Select the content object to place inside the container. Choose PowerClip from the Effects pull-down menu and then select Place Inside Container from the submenu. The cursor changes into a large black arrow. Use it to select the container object. Use the following steps when using the PowerClip effect:

1. Choose the object you want to act as the contents.
2. In the Effects pull-down menu select PowerClip.
3. From the submenu select Place Inside Container.
4. Click the object you want to act as the container. (See Figure 35.2.)

*Figure 35.1.*
*The Effects pull-down*
*menu PowerClip com-*
*mand and submenu.*

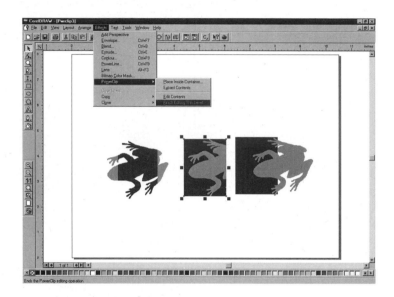

*Figure 35.2.*
*A telephone icon and the*
*group of rectangles that*
*will be used as the*
*container.*

By default, the contents are centered within the container. Change the default in the Options dialog box. The Options command is found in the Tools pull-down menu. To remove a content object from the PowerClip container object, select the container and choose the Extract Contents command from the PowerClip submenu in the Effects pull-down menu.

If you save your drawing to an earlier version of CorelDRAW, such as 3 or 4, the PowerClip object will appear grayed out when viewed.

# Corel *TIP!*

An object can be placed inside an open path such as a line. However, the contents won't be displayed until the open path is closed up.

You can manipulate a PowerClip object the same as you would any other object. This includes commands such as Rotate and Skew, Stretch and Mirror, Resize, Add Perspective, and so on. A more advanced manipulation can be achieved with the PowerClip command to create a jigsaw puzzle. First select an object to Place inside a group that will become the container. Ungroup the container to create an effect like a puzzle.

Each section of the ungrouped PowerClip object now contains a copy of the content object and displays a specific section of it. You can use bitmap images for the contents of the previously mentioned puzzle, but using bitmaps creates a large file because the number of bitmaps in your drawing is equal to the number of ungrouped PowerClip objects. (See Figure 35.3.)

*Figure 35.3.*
*The telephone icon after being placed inside the group of rectangles and after the objects have been ungrouped and moved away from each other.*

You can use the Blend and Contour effects on PowerClip objects. Once you separate them, each step of the contour or blend group contains a copy of what was in the original PowerClip object.

If the contents object is a black-and-white, line art bitmap, you might not want to give it a fill color. The fill surrounds the bitmap, which is rectangular in shape. This might create an undesirable result. To work around this result, change the outline color of the bitmap and change the fill color of the container object.

When the fill of a container is removed, the container (not the contents) becomes transparent. Objects placed behind the container will show through it, but they will not show through the contents.

The contents of your PowerClip container act as a single unit. If you manipulate the container, the contents are manipulated. However, you can activate a feature that allows you to move the container while the contents remain in position relative to your screen. To do this, click a container with the right mouse button. In the object menu, select Lock Contents To PowerClip. A check mark appears next to this option when it is enabled. Select it to disable this option. This allows you to move the container while the contents remain in place.

*Figure 35.4.*
*The figure on the left illustrates the results of a PowerClip container with the Lock Contents To PowerClip option turned off.*

To change the position of the contents in a container, choose the PowerClip object and select Edit Contents from the PowerClip submenu. Other objects seem to temporarily disappear while you edit a PowerClip object.

The container's outline becomes blue, select the contents and transform them. After editing the contents, select Finish Editing This Level from the PowerClip submenu. (See Figure 35.5.)

The Clone and Copy commands in the Effects pull-down menu can be used to copy or clone PowerClips to other objects. If you make changes to a master clone PowerClip object, the clones reflect those attributes.

Figure 35.5.
*The PowerClip object in*
*edit mode and the*
*PowerClip submenu,*
*displaying the Finish*
*Editing This Level option.*

The PowerClip effect can be applied to extruded objects with or without fills. If you extrude a shape with no fill, the content object can be viewed through all the extruded sides. When the Use Object Fill option is selected in the Extrude roll-up and the object has a fill, the content object will be displayed on the face of the extruded shape.

The symbol on the left side will be placed inside the extruded shape in the middle of the illustration. Because the extruded shape has no fill applied to it, the symbol can be seen from all of the sides of the extruded shape. The extruded shape on the far right has a fill applied to it. This time the symbol is placed into the face of the extruded shape. (See Figure 35.6.)

Figure 35.6.
*The symbol, shown*
*separately, and placed*
*within two extruded*
*shapes.*

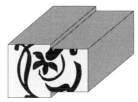

# 36

# Copying and Cloning Effects

Use the Copy or Clone command to copy or clone an effect to another object. The Copy and Clone commands are found in the Effects pull-down menu.

## Copy Effects

The Copy command permits you to copy eight different types of effects from one object and apply them to another. They include Perspective, Envelope, Blend, Extrude, Contour, PowerLine, Lens, and PowerClip.

Choose an object to which you want to apply the desired effect. Select Copy from the Effects pull-down menu. When the large black arrow appears, use it to select the object with the effect you want to copy; the effect is instantly applied. (See Figure 36.1.)

*Figure 36.1.*
*The Effects pull-down*
*menu with the Copy*
*submenu selected.*

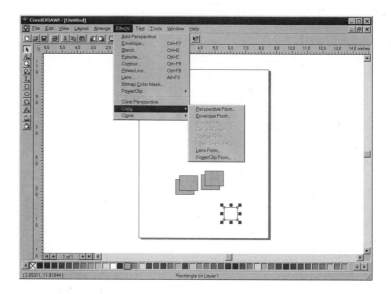

If the object you want to copy from has an effect that cannot be applied to another object, a message box is displayed on-screen and the Copy command in the menu bar becomes unavailable.

# Corel *NOTE!*

> If the last effect you apply to an object is the envelope effect, to be able to copy other effects from that object, you must select Clear Envelope first. Without doing this, the only effect you'll be able to copy from that object will be the Envelope effect.

Figure 36.2 illustrates the eight effects you can copy from other objects. The effects are arranged in two rows, which contain circles with effects copied from rectangles. The top row depicts the following effects (from left to right): Perspective, Envelope, Blend, and Extrude. The bottom row has the following effects (from left to right): Contour, PowerLine, Lens, and PowerClip.

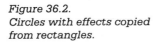

*Figure 36.2.*
*Circles with effects copied*
*from rectangles.*

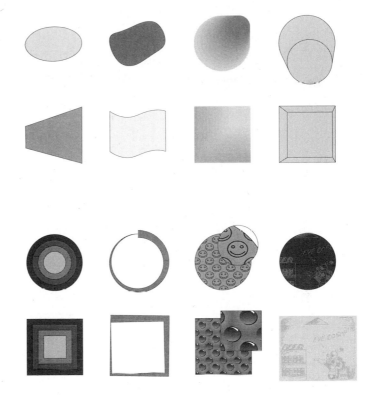

## Clone Effects

Once you've copied an effect from an object, you can promptly recopy that effect to other objects by using the Clone command in the Effects pull-down menu. (See Figure 36.3.)

There is a slight distinction between copying and cloning effects. When you copy an effect to another object, that object retains its individuality. It can be changed independently of any other objects. When you clone an effect to another object, however, that object will change if you modify the master object, such as changing the fill or outline attributes.

Figure 36.3.
*The Effects pull-down
menu with the Clone
submenu selected.*

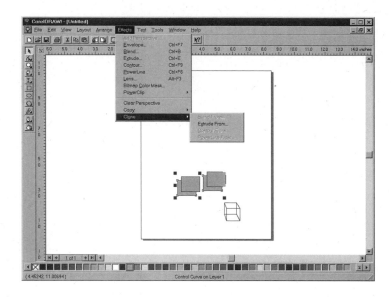

# Corel *NOTE!*

During cloning, a master/client relationship exists between the effect cloned and the
original effect. The cloned effect emulates any alterations made to the original effect. You
cannot directly alter the cloned effect. You must change the effect on the master object
and then copy (not clone) it to the client object.

Use the Clone command in the Effects pull-down menu to clone an object's Contour, Blend, PowerLine, or Extrusion effect to a selected object. After you choose
this command, a large black arrow appears. Click the object whose effect you
want to clone. (See Figure 36.4.)

Figure 36.4.
*Circles with effects cloned
from rectangles.*

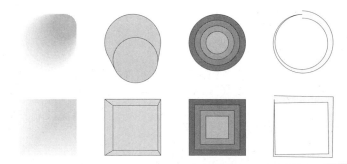

# Corel *TIP!*

A cloned object can copy the following effects only if they were applied to the object before it was cloned: Extrude, PowerLine, Blend, and Contour. Perspective and Envelope effects are cloned regardless of when they were applied to an object.

If the object you select cannot have an effect copied to it, the Clone command is grayed out and a message box will appear on-screen.

# Skill Session: Text Workshop

# 37

# Changing Text Attributes

This skill session describes how to change all attributes of individual characters and blocks of text. Many more settings are available for Paragraph text. These settings are described more fully in Skill Session 38, "Paragraph Text Attributes."

## Adjusting Text Spacing

You can adjust text kerning and spacing in two different ways: interactively and through dialog boxes. The interactive method can be useful for adjusting spacing and kerning on short text blocks, such as headlines, but can be quite maddening to use for larger blocks of text. This method uses the Shape tool and is described in Skill Session 7, "The Shape Tool."

You can work with the spacing dialog boxes through either the Text Paragraph command or the Alignment tab in the Text Character Attributes dialog box. The dialog boxes of each are shown in Figures 37.1 and 37.2.

*Figure 37.1.*
*The Spacing tab of the*
*Paragraph dialog box.*

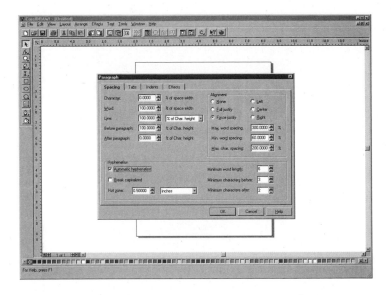

*Figure 37.2.*
*The Alignment tab of the*
*Character Attributes*
*dialog box.*

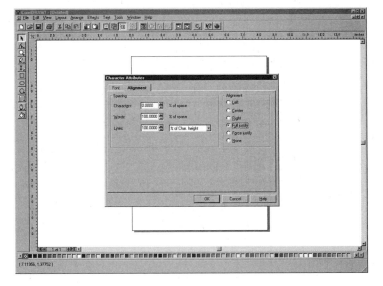

Character spacing refers to the spacing between individual characters that make up words. Each font contains a space character that has a given width. The spacing is measured as a percentage of the space character, the default value for which is zero. A positive value adds space between characters, and a negative value decreases the space between characters. Figure 37.3 shows the same line of type set with character spacing of −20, 0, and 20.

*Figure 37.3.*
*The same line of type with*
*character spacing of –20,*
*0, and 20.*

This is to demonstrate inter-character spacing.

This is to demonstrate inter-character spacing.

This is to demonstrate inter-character spacing.

Word spacing refers to the width of the space between words. It is measured as a percentage of its default width, as defined in the font. The default value is 100 percent. Values above 100 percent increase the space between words, and values below 100 percent decrease the space. Figure 37.4 shows the same line of type as Figure 37.3, but the variations are now in the word spacing. The top line is set to 80 percent, the middle line to 100 percent, and the bottom line to 120 percent.

*Figure 37.4.*
*Word spacing set to 80*
*percent, 100 percent, and*
*120 percent.*

This is to demonstrate inter-word spacing.

This is to demonstrate inter-word spacing.

This is to demonstrate inter-word spacing.

Although the first two settings can be substituted for kerning, they aren't really the same thing as kerning. CorelDRAW automatically uses the kerning pairs defined in both TrueType and PostScript fonts; therefore, if the kerning is properly defined, it doesn't need to be adjusted very often. The most obvious exception is for headlines, where the spacing between characters is critical.

Line spacing refers to the space from one baseline to another in a paragraph of text. It can be set in points, or as either a percentage of character height or a percentage of point size. The default value is either 100 percent for the two percentage measurements or the point size of the text itself. The most common value for body text is the point size of the text plus 2 points. This leaves a comfortable amount of space between the lines so that they are readable yet conserve space. Figure 37.5 shows a paragraph of 12-point text with 10-point spacing on the left, 12-point spacing in the middle, and 14-point spacing on the right.

# Corel *TIP!*

Corel's default for line spacing is measured as a percentage of character height. It is highly recommended that you change this spacing to points because you will find that spacing will be more consistent. This happens to be the measurement system traditionally used by typesetters.

*Figure 37.5.*
*A paragraph of 12-point*
*text with line spacing of*
*10, 12, and 14 points (from*
*left to right).*

The basic character in type design is determined by the uniform design characteristics of all letters in the alphabet. However, this alone does not determine the standard of the typeface and the quality of the composition set with it.

The basic character in type design is determined by the uniform design characteristics of all letters in the alphabet. However, this alone does not determine the standard of the typeface and the quality of the composition set with it.

The basic character in type design is determined by the uniform design characteristics of all letters in the alphabet. However, this alone does not determine the standard of the typeface and the quality of the composition set with it.

# Corel*NOTE!*

> You may hear line and paragraph spacing referred to as *leading* (rhymes with *sledding*). Leading refers to the strips of lead inserted by typographers back in the days of hot metal type.

The next settings can only be found in the Paragraph dialog box. Before paragraph spacing refers to the amount of space before each paragraph. Much like line spacing, it can be set either as a percentage of character height or in points. It defaults to the same type of measurement as that for line spacing. It should be set to the same amount as the line spacing, unless more or less space is desired between paragraphs. Space can also be added at the end of a paragraph. The default setting is that no space is added. Depending on the layout of your document, either or both of these settings may be desirable.

Six methods of text justification are now allowed. No justification and left justification are virtually the same. Each has a smooth left edge and a ragged right edge. Center justification centers each line of text. Right justification provides a smooth right edge to the text block while leaving the left edge ragged. Full justification provides the block with a smooth edge on both the left and the right. Force justify is the same as full justification, except that it also makes the last line of text justified. When full justification is used, extra white space is added between characters and words. This can look ugly at times; therefore, controls are provided for the minimum and maximum word spacing as well as the maximum character spacing to achieve either full or force justification. An example of each of the six types of justification is shown in Figure 37.6.

The Paragraph dialog box also enables you to turn hyphenation on or off for Paragraph text. The hyphenation is done by a hyphenation algorithm and occurs within the hot zone defined in the Paragraph dialog box. The Break Capitalized option is a way to keep words in all capital letters together. The *hot zone* refers to a measurement at the end of a line of text where hyphenation is allowed. The default value of .50 inches is normally fine, unless you're working with either very large or very small type. You can also specify the minimum number of letters that must appear before and after the hyphen, as well as the minimum length word that can be hyphenated.

Figure 37.6.
*An example of each of the
six types of justification.*

This is an example to shown each of the types of justification available in CorelDRAW! 6.                     **None**

This is an example to shown each of the types of justification available in CorelDRAW! 6.                     **Full Justify**

This is an example to shown each of the types of justification  available  in  CorelDRAW!  6.            **Force Justify**

This is an example to shown each of the types of justification available in CorelDRAW! 6.                     **Left**

This is an example to shown each of the types of justification available in CorelDRAW! 6.                      **Center**

This is an example to shown each of the types of justification available in CorelDRAW! 6.                           **Right**

The other tabs in the Paragraph dialog box are discussed fully in Skill Session 38.

## Character Attributes

The attributes of individual characters can be changed when you're using either the Text tool or the Shape tool. Use either tool to select the characters to be changed. With the Shape tool, marquee-select the characters by dragging a box around the nodes to the left of the characters. With the Text tool, select the characters by dragging the cursor over the characters with the left mouse button. Figure 37.7 shows a sentence selected with the Shape tool, and Figure 37.8 shows the same sentence selected with the Text tool.

Figure 37.7.
*A sentence selected
with the Shape tool.*

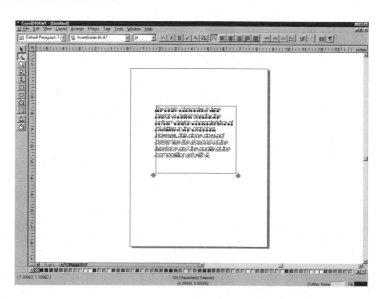

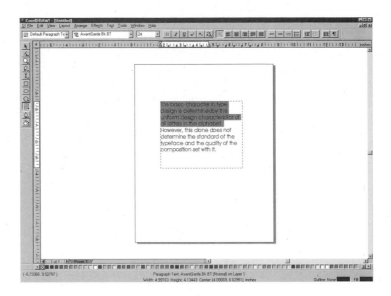

*Figure 37.8.*
*A sentence selected*
*with the Text tool.*

After the text has been selected, you can change the attributes through the Character Attributes dialog box. Either double-click one of the selected nodes and choose Text Character or use the Ctrl+T keyboard shortcut to invoke the Character Attributes dialog box shown in Figure 37.9.

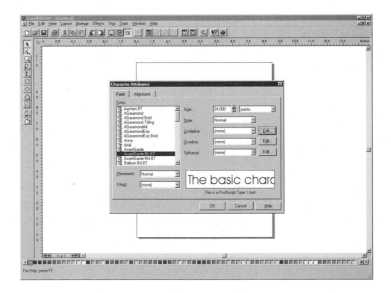

*Figure 37.9.*
*The Font tab of the*
*Character Attributes*
*dialog box.*

There's a common misconception that CorelDRAW is unable to italicize or bold-face a word within a text block. This is because the concepts discussed in this skill session are not completely understood by users.

The upper left of the dialog box controls the font to be used, its point size and style (Normal, Italic, Bold or Bold Italic), and the usage of attributes such as Underline, Overline, and Strikeout. Each of the lines can be set for Single Thin, Single Thick, or Double Thin. You can also choose whether everything is underlined or just the words are underlined. If you are not happy with the default settings for Underline, Overline, or Strikeout, you can fully customize them by clicking the Edit button next to their drop-down list. This will give you the dialog box shown in Figure 37.10. By clicking on the Units drop-down list, you can adjust the settings to percentage of character height, points, or a percentage of point size. Any of the measurements can then be adjusted.

*Figure 37.10.*
*The Edit Underline*
*dialog box.*

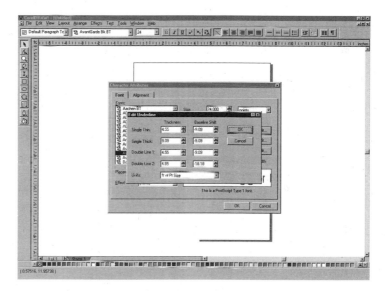

The bottom right of the dialog box shows an example of what the font will look like as well as the format of the font chosen (PostScript Type 1 or TrueType). The line attributes are shown, but other attributes, such as kerning and placement, are not.

The lower left of the dialog box contains the settings for the Placement and Effect options. Placement allows you to set text to Normal, Subscript, or Superscript. Effects has settings for Normal, Small Caps, and All Caps. Either of the "caps" settings will not permanently change the case of the text; it will only display the lowercase letters in caps. To permanently change the case, you need to use the Text | Change Case command described in the next section.

The fill and outline of the characters can also be changed easily by using all of the methods described in Skill Sessions 15, "The Outline Tool," and 16, "The Fill Tool." Again, note that any changes you make apply only to the characters selected, and not the whole text block.

The settings in the Character Attributes dialog box work exactly like the controls found in the Text toolbar. Many times you will find it easier to use the Text toolbar instead of the dialog box. Skill Session 4, "Customizing and Setting Preferences," shows you how to access the Text toolbar. The icons are fairly self-explanatory, but if in doubt, hold your cursor over a button for a second or two and you'll see the pop-up help, which tells you what the button does.

## Changing Case

The Text Change Case command, which is found in the Text pull-down menu, allows you to permanently change the case (uppercase or lowercase) of the currently selected text. The dialog box is shown in Figure 37.11. The Sentence Case option capitalizes the first letter of all other text as is. The Lowercase option changes everything to lowercase, and the Uppercase option capitalizes everything. The Title Case option capitalizes the first letter of each word. And the Toggle Case option changes everything from its current setting to the opposite setting.

*Figure 37.11.*
*The Text Change Case*
*dialog box.*

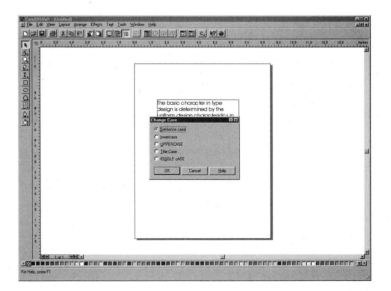

# Paragraph Text Attributes

Paragraph text has many attributes that are not available to Artistic text. One of the most important attributes, in relation to page layout, is the capability to set up multiple columns within a text frame. To do this, select either the Columns command in the Text pull-down menu or click the Columns Format button in the Text toolbar. Either of these will bring up the Columns dialog box, which is shown in Figure 38.1.

The number of columns can range anywhere from a single column to as many as eight, with the default being one. When you check the Equal column widths check box, each of the columns will be made the same width. If this box is not checked, you can use the Column # and Width text boxes to enter the width of each column and gutter individually. The gutter width controls the amount of gutter (white space) placed between each column of text. This defaults to a value of zero, but can be as large as 2 inches. The column width can be automatically adjusted to fit within the frame by choosing the Maintain current frame width radio button. If you select the Automatically adjust frame width radio button, the frame will be sized, as needed, to hold the column widths chosen. Figure 38.2 shows a text frame with three columns of text.

Figure 38.1.
The Columns dialog box.

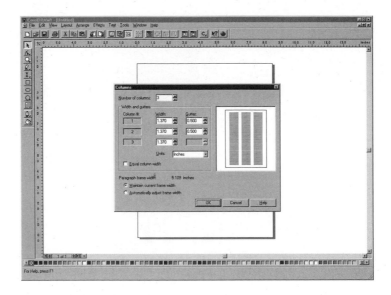

Figure 38.2.
A text frame with three
columns of text.

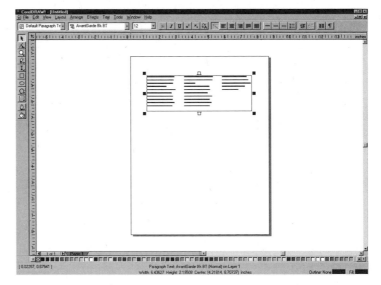

## Spacing

Paragraph text spacing is discussed in depth in Skill Session 37, "Changing Text
Attributes." To change the spacing, you must access the Spacing tab in the Paragraph dialog box shown in Figure 38.3.

*Figure 38.3.*
*The Spacing tab of the*
*Paragraph dialog box.*

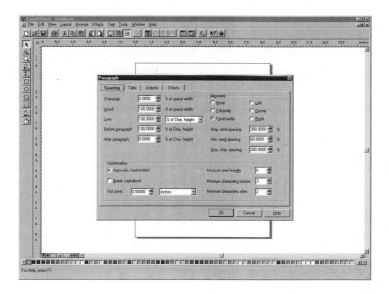

## Setting Tabs

You can easily set tabs using the Paragraph dialog box. This dialog box is accessed with the Paragraph command in the Text pull-down menu. Choose the Tabs tab in the Paragraph dialog box, and you will be presented with the dialog box shown in Figure 38.4.

*Figure 38.4.*
*The Tabs section of the*
*Paragraph dialog box.*

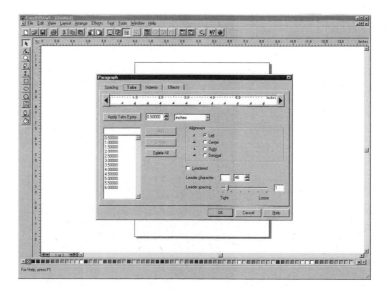

Left-aligned tabs are automatically set at half-inch increments. These can easily be changed or deleted. You can select individual tab settings from the list box in the middle of the dialog box by clicking the appropriate value. You can also choose them by clicking the tab marker sitting on the ruler at the top of the dialog box. Once the desired tab has been selected, you can either delete it by clicking the Delete button or you can move it by typing a new value into the list box or by manually dragging it along the ruler. The tab alignment can be set by choosing the Left, Right, Center, or Decimal option button. To clear all the tabs, choose the Delete All button.

You can add tabs by typing a new value into the text box on top of the list box and then clicking the Add button, or you can click along the ruler where the new tab should appear.

Support for leadered tabs has been added to CorelDRAW 6. To make a tab leadered, simply check the Leadered check box. Now you are able to select a leader character and adjust the spacing between the leader characters with the slider control. An example of leader tabs is shown in Figure 38.5.

*Figure 38.5.*
*Example of leader tabs.*

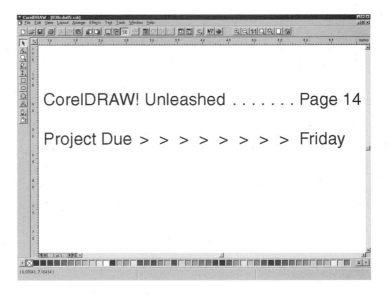

CorelDRAW also has the capability to edit tabs directly on-screen. Figure 38.6 shows the tabs, which are fully editable, on the top ruler. Also notice that the rulers are lighter in color in the area where the active text column is located.

*Figure 38.6.*
*Tabs can be edited*
*manually on the ruler.*

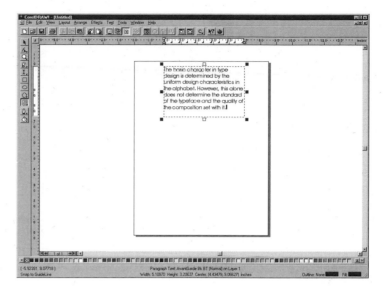

## Setting Indents

Indents can be set in two different parts of the Paragraph dialog box. The settings for the indents for First line and Rest of lines can be adjusted in the Tabs section of the dialog box by dragging the ruler's First line and Rest of lines icons (they look like a small right triangle). Either of the icons will always move independently of the other. Remember that the top-left triangle is for the indent and the bottom-left triangle is for the rest of lines.

These settings can also be adjusted numerically in the Indents section of the Paragraph dialog box. (See Figure 38.7.) You call up this dialog box by clicking the Indents tab.

The Indents section of the dialog box also allows you to set the right margin. The margin settings are measured from the edge of the text box, not from the edge of the page.

Figure 38.7.
The Indents section of the
Paragraph dialog box.

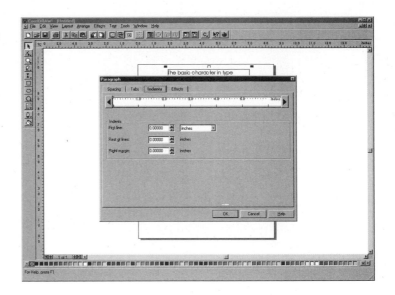

## Adding Effects

You access the Effects section of the Paragraph dialog box by clicking the Effects tab, which brings up Figure 38.8.

Figure 38.8.
The Effects section of the
Paragraph dialog box.

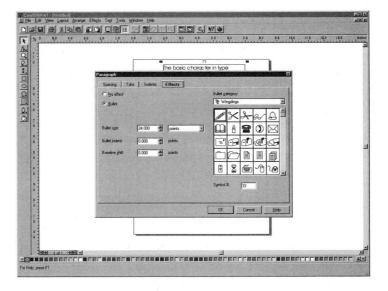

At the top of this section are radio buttons for selecting the type of effect you desire. To use bullets, select the Bullet radio button, or everything else will be grayed out. The list of available bullet fonts is displayed just below the check box. These are the same fonts that are available in the Symbols roll-up. Fonts included are those that have the symbol character set in either TrueType or PostScript format.

The right half of the dialog box shows examples of each of the available characters; the symbol number is just below the samples window. The Bullet size box indicates the size of the bullet character, and the Bullet indent box contains the same value as that shown in the Indents part of the Paragraph dialog box. This value indicates the amount of space between the bullet and the rest of the text. The Baseline shift box indicates the amount of space above the baseline where the bullet will sit. A negative number places the bullet's baseline below the paragraph's baseline.

## Styles

Most of the attributes covered in this skill session are best used with defined styles within a template. For more information about creating and modifying styles and templates, see Skill Session 58, "Styles and Templates."

# 39

# Word Processing Tools

This skill session discusses several of the tools found on the Text menu that relate to word processing functions. While CorelDRAW is certainly not a word processor, it has many of the same features as popular word processing software on the market. These features make it easier to work with larger amounts of text without leaving CorelDRAW.

## Find and Replace

The Text | Find command provides the capability to search for text strings anywhere within a document. The search can be for Artistic text, Paragraph text, or both. Clicking the Match case check box (shown in Figure 39.1) will limit the search to only text that matches the case of the text you've entered. Once text is entered, just click the Find Next button, and the next occurrence of that particular text will be highlighted. If the text is not found, you will be presented with the error message "Search text not found."

Figure 39.1.
The Find dialog box.

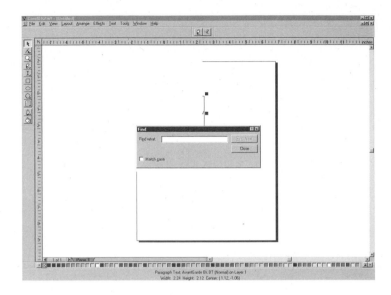

# Corel*NOTE!*

When text is found within a Paragraph text frame, the whole frame will be highlighted rather than just the text within the frame.

Instead of just finding the text, you can use the Text | Replace command so that once the text is found, it can be automatically replaced. Using this option, you can choose to find the text and replace the next instance, or you can replace all instances of the text. Again, you can make the search case sensitive or not. The Replace dialog box is shown in Figure 39.2.

Figure 39.2.
The Replace dialog box.

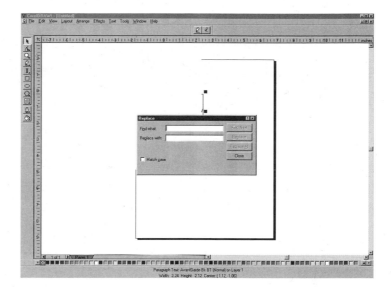

## Type Assist

The Type Assist feature performs several different functions. Each of these functions serve to improve your typing skills. For example, Type Assist can correct mistyped characters for you. It also can help speed up your typing by replacing a short abbreviation with longer text. Type Assist works with both Artistic and Paragraph text.

Figure 39.3 shows the Type Assist dialog box, with all of its options checked. The first option is Capitalize first letter of sentences (the shortcut key combination is Alt+F). This capitalizes the first letter of a sentence—that is, the first letter following a period (.), exclamation mark (!), question mark (?), or the Spanish symbols ¿ and ¡.

The next option is Change straight quotes to typographic quotes (the shortcut key combination is Alt+T). This option automatically converts the (') and (") keystrokes to their "curly" equivalents on the fly. This can be quite handy, because you don't need to remember the keystrokes required to get the typographic quotes. Be careful, though, because there are times when this feature can get in the way. For example, notice that curly quotes were not wanted in the first part of this paragraph.

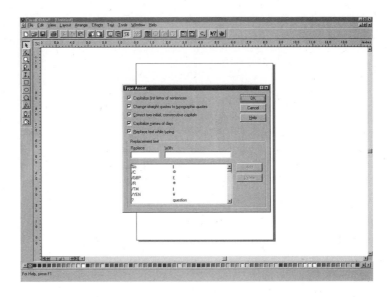

Figure 39.3.
The Type Assist dialog
box.

The next option, Correct two initial consecutive capitals (the shortcut key combination is Alt+C), is for those times when you accidentally capitalize two letters at the beginning of a word. When activated, this feature automatically changes the second letter to lowercase if it's not followed by a space or period. This option doesn't apply to two-letter words.

The next option, Capitalize names of days (the shortcut key combination is Alt+R), is self-explanatory. It automatically capitalizes the names of any days typed. Note that this also applies to months. It's multilingual, so feel free to type names in your favorite language.

The last option, Replace text while typing, is the most powerful Type Assist option. This comes in handy if there's a word you have trouble typing. An example is typing "teh" instead of "the." You enter the incorrect spelling in the Replace text box (the shortcut key combination is Alt+E) and the correct spelling in the With text box (the shortcut key combination is Alt+W). Click the Add button to put the word in Type Assist's database. This database is saved when you exit CorelDRAW, not immediately after you click the Add button; therefore, the additions won't be made if the program crashes. Another way to use this feature is to associate an abbreviation (for example, E.T.A.) to be spelled out (estimated time of arrival). If something is in the database that you don't want, just select it in the bottom window and click the Delete button. It will no longer be "corrected."

The Type Assist feature stores this database in a file named CORELDRW.TPA, which is found in the \COREL60\CUSTOM directory. It cannot be edited outside of CorelDRAW. If you have a large database of corrections and abbreviations, you can distribute it to other CorelDRAW users quite easily.

## Spell Checker

A full-featured spell checker is also included for checking the spelling of both Artistic and Paragraph text, as shown in Figure 39.4. When spell checking, you can choose which range to check: Selected Text or Full Text.

*Figure 39.4.*
*The Spell Checking dialog box.*

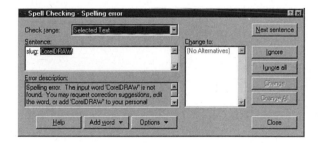

When an error is found, the whole sentence is displayed in the Sentence text box and the misspelled word is highlighted. Just below the text box is the Error description box, which explains the error to you. For most words, suggested alternatives are listed in the Change To list box. In Figure 39.4, no Alternatives were found for *CorelDRAW*. If you select a word, then the Change and Change All buttons are ungrayed. The Change button only changes the current instance, while the Change All button changes all instances. You can also use the Ignore button to ignore the current instance or the Ignore All button to ignore all instances.

If the word found is one you use often and it is correctly spelled, the Add Word button will allow you to add it to a personal dictionary. The default is USERPD, although you can create more than one and use whatever name you desire. The Options button lets you choose a dictionary or create a new one. It can also be used to choose the formality level—from Formal to Standard to Informal. The default setting is Standard. By choosing the Advanced Options selection from the Options menu, you will get the dialog box shown in Figure 39.5.

There are three different drop-down lists from which you choose a language. By default, they all use US English (for the English-language version of CorelDRAW), but they can easily be changed to UK English.

The Spelling Correction section provides two check boxes. The Always provide alternate spelling check box specifies that the spell checker will always try to find a correctly spelled word for any word it finds that it does not understand. You can also choose Use personal dictionaries check box and, if so desired, you can choose which personal dictionary to use.

Figure 39.5.
The Advanced Options
dialog box.

The Maximum sentence elements box is the maximum number of words and punctuation elements allowed in a sentence for the chosen language. It is highly suggest that you stick to the default setting.

The Rule Manager button brings up the dialog box shown in Figure 39.6.

Figure 39.6.
The Rule Manager dialog
box.

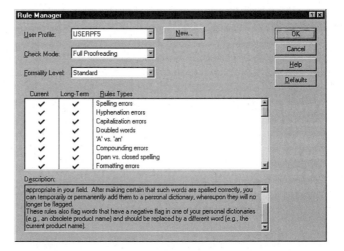

The Rule Manager lists many rules of grammar and whether or not they are checked in the various levels of formality. Unless you are very persnickety about your grammar, it is suggested that you stick to the default settings.

## Grammar Checker

Options are given in the Text | Proofreading menu for both a Quick Proofread and a Full Proofread. These modes are supposed to check for stylistic and grammatical errors. But in the release version of CorelDRAW, these functions were only to be found in the documentation and not in the program itself.

## Thesaurus

The Text | Thesaurus command brings up a fully functional thesaurus, as shown in Figure 39.7.

*Figure 39.7.*
*The Thesaurus dialog box.*

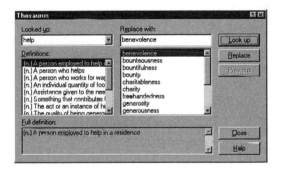

To use the thesaurus, simply type a word in the Looked Up text box and then click the Look Up button. A list of replacement words and definitions will be provided for you. In cases where the word you looked up is not found, you will receive an error message.

## Statistics

Text | Statistics provides you with many statistics, such as the number of linked frames, paragraphs, lines, words, and characters in the text block you have selected. Note that it does not check the whole document. An example of these statistics is shown in Figure 39.8.

*Figure 39.8.*
*The Statistics dialog box.*

# 40

# Fitting Text to a Path

Fitting text to a path involves dynamically linking the text to a specified path. The path can be an ellipse, rectangle, line, or curve. You can even use text that has been converted to curves as a path. You can edit the text on the path, including modifying the spacing of the text and changing the direction of the path.

Fitting text to circles and ellipses is one of the most common uses of this effect. The procedure for fitting text to a path, such as a curved line, is different than fitting text to an ellipse. CorelDRAW senses whether you're trying to fit text to an ellipse or a line. Notice that the Fit Text To Path roll-up changes depending on which type of path you apply the text to. Figures 40.1 and 40.2 show the differences between Fit Text To Path for an ellipse and for a line.

Figure 40.1.
The Fit Text To Path roll-
up for an ellipse.

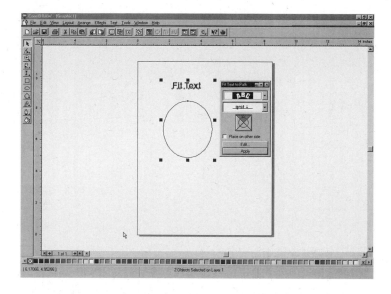

Figure 40.2.
The Fit Text To Path roll-
up for a line.

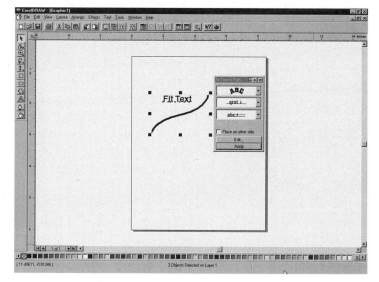

## Fitting Text to a Circle (Ellipse)

Fitting text to a circle can be very frustrating to many CorelDRAW users. Often the text is placed backwards or upside-down. However, it's really not that complicated if you follow the correct sequence of steps.

## Part One

The following steps illustrate how to fit a single word to a circle. When you understand the concepts involved, you can apply them to multiple words on the same
path.

1. To begin, select Fit Text To Path from the Text menu. The Fit Text To Path
   roll-up appears on-screen.

2. Type a word on-screen.

3. Draw a circle with the Ellipse tool.

4. Select both the text and the circle, either by marquee-selecting both objects
   or by selecting the text with the Pick tool and then selecting the circle while
   holding down the Shift key. The Fit Text To Path roll-up is now active.

5. From the Fit Text To Path roll-up, choose the orientation in which you want
   the text to appear on the path. For this example, choose the default setting:
   Vertical. The text orientation box is the top box containing the letters *ABC*.

6. From the parameters box below the text orientation box, choose the side of
   the line on which you will lay your text. By scrolling in this box, you see
   several visual choices. Each choice shows how the text will fit on the circle.
   The default shows the text resting on top of the line with the descenders
   below the line. The other options are self-explanatory, with the exception of
   the last choice. In reality, the letters *qrst* are blurred in the box because there
   are three copies of these letters on top of each other. This is a variable mode.
   When you choose this option, you can manually move the text inside or
   outside the path line. For this first example, choose the default.

7. Your next choice is whether you want your text on top of the circle, along the
   sides of the circle, or at the bottom of the circle. The box sectioned into four
   quadrants, in the center of the dialog box, defaults to the top quadrant. If you
   want the text to appear at the sides or bottom, click the appropriate quadrant. For this example, keep the default selection.

8. Now you can click the Apply button. Figure 40.3 shows the result.

## Part Two

You're now ready to learn how to apply a second word to the same circle.

1. Type a second word on the screen.

2. Select the word with the Pick tool, hold the Shift key down, and select the
   circle.

3. Keep the default orientation, as you did in Step 5 of Part One.

4. From the second parameters box, scroll down to the example showing the letters *qrst* below the baseline.

5. Click the bottom quadrant of the sectioned box located in the center of the dialog box.

6. Click the Place on other side check box to place a check mark in it.

7. Click the Apply button.

*Figure 40.3.*
*Fitting text to a path*
*using the default settings.*

Figure 40.4 shows the final result—the words "Fit Text" are at the top of the circle and the words "To Path" are at the bottom.

If your figure doesn't look like Figure 40.4, you left out Step 6. If you did it right, try the same exercise and skip Step 6. Notice that the word is placed backwards inside the circle. The purpose of this exercise has been to illustrate how important it is to follow the steps exactly to get the desired results.

## Part Three

This exercise illustrates how to put text inside a circle instead of outside a circle.

1. Repeat Steps 1 through 5 of Part One.

2. From the second parameters box (discussed in Step 6 of Part One), select the option that shows the baseline above the text.

3. Click the top quadrant of the sectioned box.

4. Click the Apply button.

*Figure 40.4.*
*Text fitted to the top and*
*bottom of the circle.*

Figure 40.5 shows the result—the words "Fit Text" are placed inside the circle and at the top.

*Figure 40.5.*
*Text placed inside the*
*circle.*

## Part Four

This final exercise shows you how to place a second word inside and at the bottom of the same circle.

1. Repeat Steps 1 through 3 of Part Two.
2. From the second parameters box, click the default setting with the letters *qrst* on top of the baseline.
3. Click the bottom quadrant of the sectioned box in the center of the dialog box.
4. Click the Place on other side check box to place a check mark in it.
5. Click the Apply button.

Figure 40.6 shows the final result—the words "Fit Text" are inside the top of the circle and the words "To Path" are inside the bottom of the circle.

Figure 40.6.
Text fitted to the inside of
the circle.

## Editing Text on a Circle (Ellipse)

After you've placed text on your circle, you might want to adjust the spacing of the letters or even move the entire text to a location other than one of the default locations. You can change the color of individual letters with the Shape tool, just like you can with normal text. You can also change the text using the Edit Text dialog box. The key to editing the text is to isolate individual words.

The procedure for editing text must be followed exactly. The number of steps required to edit a specific word depends on how many separate pieces of text are attached to the path.

The following steps describe how to change the spacing of the letters in the example from Part One. Figure 40.7 shows the results.

1. Click the word you typed with the Pick tool. The status line will indicate that you have selected text on a path.

2. Hold down the Ctrl key and click the text again. The status line now indicates that you've selected the text, and it also tells you the font name, point size, and so on.

3. With the text still selected, click the Shape tool. The text now displays the nodes for each letter and two spacing handles.

4. Click and drag the spacing handle on the right. How far you drag determines how much you change the spacing between letters.

*Figure 40.7.*
*Changing the spacing of*
*text fitted to a circle.*

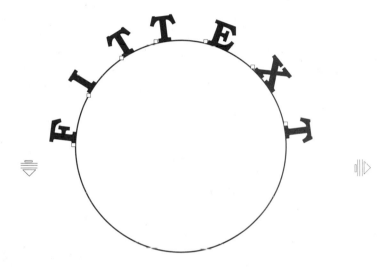

# Corel*NOTE!*

When you're editing two or more blocks of words that have been placed on the circle, you must click the word or words you want to edit three times while holding down the Ctrl key. The status line will indicate the following:

First click: Compound object of $x$ elements (where $x$ equals the number of words on the circle plus the circle itself)

Second click: Text on a path

Third click: The text

## Moving Text Along the Path

# Corel*NOTE!*

When you click the Edit button in either Fit Text To Path dialog boxes, you can move the text horizontally along the path (or around the path in the case of an ellipse) or vertically away from the path by entering the appropriate numbers in the parameters boxes.

You might want to move the text manually to a location on the path other than one of the default locations. Follow these steps to move text on a path. You can also use the Edit button at the bottom of the roll-up. (See the previous note.)

1. Select the text using the methods described previously.
2. With the text still selected, click the Shape tool.
3. Marquee-select the entire word so that each node of each letter is selected.
4. With the Shape tool still selected, click one of the nodes and drag the entire word to the desired location along the path. Notice that when you move the text around the circle, the cursor changes to crossed arrows and there is a "marching ants" selection box around the text. The original text stays in place until you release the primary mouse button.
5. Release the primary mouse button when you're satisfied with the placement.

# Corel*NOTE!*

If you want to move individual letters within a word, repeat Steps 1 and 2 and then select only the node of the single letter you want to move.

## Fitting Text to a Single Path

Fitting text to a path differs in several ways from fitting text to an ellipse. The first difference you'll notice is that the dialog box is different. Refer back to Figures 40.1 and 40.2 to see the difference.

The first steps required to fit text to a single path are the same as those to fit text to an ellipse:

1. Draw a straight or curved line.
2. Type a word on the screen.
3. Select the text and the line, either by marquee-selecting both objects or selecting them one at a time while holding down the Shift key. The Fit Text To Path dialog box displays three parameter boxes.

4. The top parameters box enables you to choose the orientation of the text on the path. Choose the default setting.

5. The second parameters box enables you to choose the vertical placement of the text on the path. You can choose between having the text on the line or below the line, just as you did when you fitted text to an ellipse. Choose the default setting.

6. The third parameters box enables you to choose the justification of the text on the path. *This option is only available if it's an open path.* Choose the default setting.

7. Click the Apply button.

Figure 40.8 shows the words *text on a path* applied to a single path. Notice that the first letter of the text string in the top example in Figure 40.8 is on the far left end of the line. This is the default setting you chose in Step 6. The second setting places the text on the center of the line. The third setting places the text at the end of the line. This placement method is the same as the left, center, and right justification used in word processing programs.

*Figure 40.8.*
*The three default settings*
*for placing text on a open*
*path.*

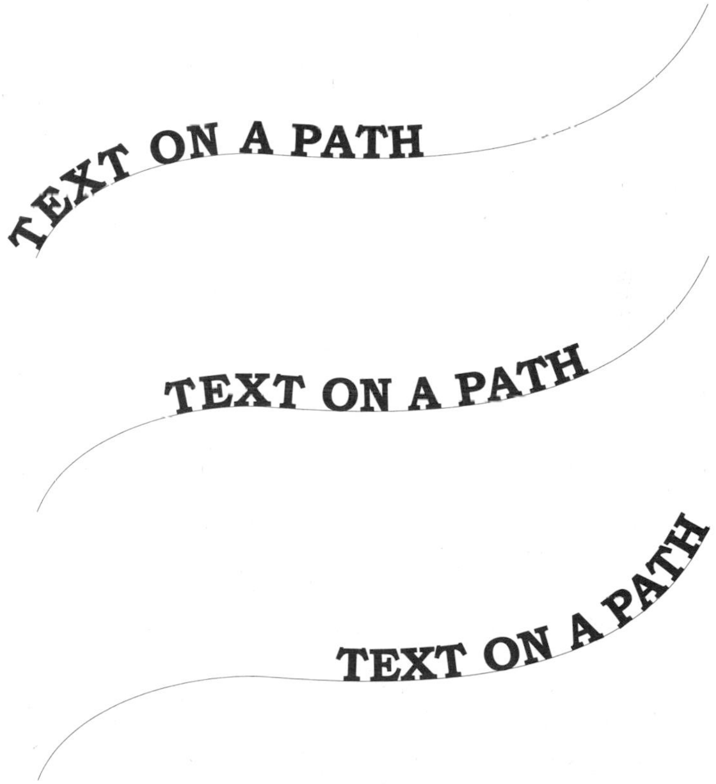

# Corel *NOTE!*

Left-handers take note: The line in Figure 40.8 was originally drawn from left to right. Had it been drawn from right to left, the text string would have been placed upside-down below the right end of the line. If this happens, click the Place on other side check box to place the text correctly. This also applies if a closed path is drawn from right to left.

Figure 40.9 illustrates how the text can be spaced evenly over the entire length of the line. Click the Shape tool and then drag the right-hand, text-spacing handle to the right to stretch the text string to the desired length.

Figure 40.10 illustrates how the shape of the text on the line can be dynamically changed. Select the Shape tool and click the line. Use the line, nodes, or handles to reshape the path.

The Edit box in the Fit Text To Path dialog box enables you to type in the parameters to move the text away from the path, either horizontally or vertically. (See the previous note.)

*Figure 40.9.*
*Spacing the text along the*
*length of a path.*

*Figure 40.10*
*Changing the shape of the*
*path dynamically.*

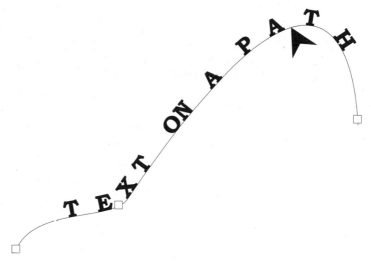

**41**

# Extracting and Merging Back Text

You can use the Extract and Merge-Back features on CorelDRAW's Tools menu to edit large text documents or just to do a quick spell-check routine in your favorite word processor. In some cases, such as in the example shown in Figure 41.1, editing text in a word processor is simply easier to do. You can edit the text, save your changes, and then use Merge-Back to return your text to CorelDRAW. You can then apply text attributes such as styles, colors, outlines, fills, and so on in CorelDRAW.

Figure 41.1.
*A initiation certificate of author Foster D. Coburn with a large amount of Artistic and Paragraph text.*

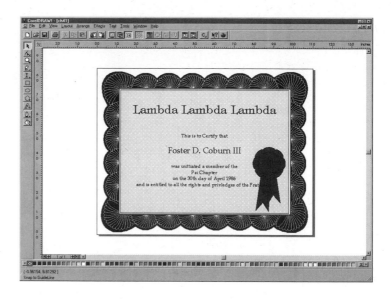

## Tools Extract

Notice that the word *initiated* is misspelled in Figure 41.1. You can use Extract and Merge-Back to fix this type of error.

First, extract your text. You can find Extract Text under Tools on the main menu bar. (See Figure 41.2.) If you haven't saved your design, you will be prompted to do so before extracting the text and saving it to a file. For minor text editing, use the Edit Text command. If your file contains graphic elements, they won't be extracted to the text file.

## Corel*NOTE!*

You don't have to select text to extract it.

The CorelDRAW file that you want to extract can contain a mixture of Artistic and Paragraph text. One of the things that makes Artistic text different from Paragraph text is your ability to resize Artistic text the same way you would resize an object or graphic element. With Paragraph text, however, you must change the point size of the text in the Text roll-up or in the Edit Text dialog box if you want to resize it.

*Figure 41.2.*
*The Extract dialog box*
*with the extracted file*
*saved in ASCII format.*

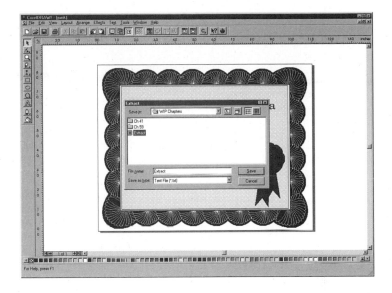

# Corel *TIP!*

Before you use Tools | Extract, save any changes that you make. If you do not,
CorelDRAW will prompt you with a warning, telling you that you must save your latest
changes before you can extract.

# Corel *NOTE!*

Make any non-text changes before you extract text; otherwise, you may have problems
merging back the edited text.

After you save the file in ASCII format, open your text file in the word processor of
your choice. The example in Figure 41.3 uses Microsoft Word.

You'll notice that the Artistic text in the word processing file is prefaced with
@ATXT; the Paragraph text is prefaced with @PTXT. This order differs from the original
order in the CorelDRAW file, but it doesn't affect the positioning in the
CorelDRAW document. Edit the text as needed.

Figure 41.3.
Using Microsoft Word to
edit text.

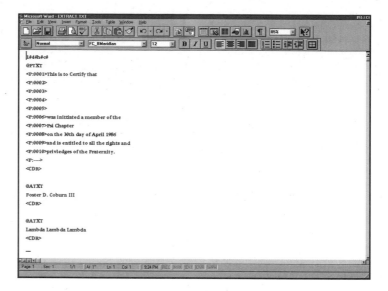

# Corel*NOTE!*

When you edit your file in the word processor, do not change the very first line of the file or the first and last lines of each paragraph or text string. These lines contain codes that CorelDRAW uses to interpret the text file.

Also, the order of the items within the file is not important. All lines will be merged back to their original position.

## Merge-Back

After you edit the text, switch back to CorelDRAW and then select Merge-Back from the Tools menu. The Tools Merge-Back dialog box appears. Select the text file and click OK. The extracted text then replaces the text in your file automatically. (See Figure 41.4.)

Attributes (such as font type, size, character spacing, or point size) and alignment (such as justified, centered, left, right, or none) are not altered when text is merged back. Some of the individual character attributes (character angle, vertical shift, bold, and so on) are not maintained when text is merged back. Text that has been fitted to a path, extruded, or blended can be altered when merged back. For more information about Tools | Extract and Tools | Merge-Back, see the "Command Reference" section.

Figure 41.4.
*The edited text after being*
*merged back to the*
*CorelDRAW file.*

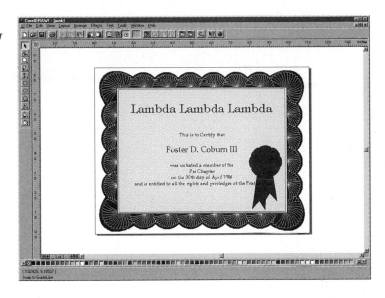

# Corel*NOTE!*

If you make numerous additions to text, be sure to check for overlapping of text or
objects in your file after you merge back the extracted text.

# 42

# Creating Your Own Fonts

CorelDRAW 6 gives you the capability to create custom fonts. It's very easy to turn a set of simple drawings and logos into a font that can be used in almost any Windows program. The most difficult part of this process is creating the template used to create the fonts.

## Creating the Template

Create a new file. Select Page Setup from the Layout menu and change the page size to Custom. The measurement system should be changed to Points, both horizontally and vertically. Set the width and height to 720 points, which is approximately the same as 10 inches. This provides enough room for the detail that's needed to design a character. It's also half the size of the largest point size available in CorelDRAW (through Version 6).

Right-click the rulers to bring up the Grid & Ruler Setup dialog box. Change the grid frequency to 1 per point, both horizontally and vertically. The Grid Origin should be set to 0 points horizontally and 240 points vertically. Make sure Snap To Grid and Snap To Guidelines are both enabled. Insert two horizontal guidelines—one at 480 points (to indicate the cap height) and another at 0 points (to indicate the baseline).

You set the cap height to 480 points because it's two-thirds of the 720-point design size you're using. Making the cap height two-thirds of the point size is a standard throughout the type foundries of Europe. It provides for consistency between typefaces.

Insert a vertical guideline at 60 points to indicate the left sidebearing. This just happens to be a good round number that doesn't sit on the edge of the page; there's no real significance to this number. Deselect the Snap To Grid option, because you won't need it.

Type the text string HOqdx. Highlight the text and then change it to a font similar in design to the one you plan to create. Choose a font that has characteristics very close to the one you're designing; for example, serif or sans serif, x-height, descenders, and so on.

Adjust the text so that it sits flush with the baseline and just to the right of the guideline. Stretch the text so that the top of the *H* is even with the cap-height guideline. Drag out horizontal guidelines for the x-height and the descenders. Delete the text string and save the file. This is now the template you'll use to create new fonts.

In the future, most of these steps will be unnecessary if you keep the template file you just created. Figure 42.1 shows the font-creation template.

*Figure 42.1.*
*The font-creation*
*template.*

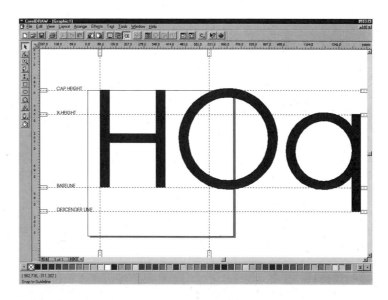

Now it's time to start creating some characters. Font characters can be made up of a single object only; therefore, you need to combine the pieces of characters that contain more than one path. For now, create an *O* by combining two ellipses.

Enlarge the *O* so it extends from the baseline to the cap height. Choose File Export and either the PostScript or TrueType font format. If there's more than one object on-screen, make sure to choose Selected Objects Only. When you export the first character to a new font, the Font Export Options dialog box appears. (See Figure 42.2.)

*Figure 41.2.*
*The Font Export Options*
*dialog box.*

Put the font's name in the Family name field. This name will appear in the Windows font menus. It should be no more than 32 characters long. Choose the style of the font you're creating. CorelDRAW provides only four choices: Normal, Italic, Bold, and Bold Italic. If this font is to be used as a standard text typeface, the Symbol Font check box should be disabled. If you want the font to appear in CorelDRAW's Symbols roll-up, make sure Symbol Font is checked. The Grid Size and Space Width fields should both be kept at their defaults—2048 for TrueType fonts and 1000 for PostScript fonts—unless there's an obvious reason to do otherwise. These numbers come straight from the font specifications for TrueType and PostScript Type 1. After everything is checked, click the OK button. The Export dialog box shown in Figure 42.3 appears.

*Figure 42.3.*
*The Font Export*
*dialog box.*

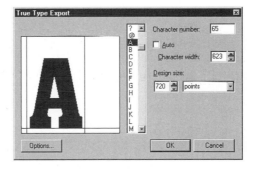

Set Design Size to 720 points, because this is the size used to design the characters. If you have deviated from the instructions in this chapter, this might need to be adjusted. Character Number indicates the position in the font in which the current character will be placed. Alphabetic and other keyboard characters are displayed to the left of the ANSI number. Consult the character chart that accompanies your CorelDRAW package for the ANSI numbers of other characters. The

Character Width field can be adjusted by clicking the up and down arrows, and the right sidebearing will move accordingly. For most characters, it's much simpler to accept the default value by checking the Auto check box. After you've made all your selections, click the OK button.

When you export a character to a font that already has that character, the Options dialog box appears. (See Figure 42.4.)

*Figure 42.4.*
*The Options dialog box*
*that appears for an*
*existing font.*

The Options dialog box adds a button for Load Font Metrics. This button can be used to import an Adobe Font Metrics (.AFM) file from an existing typeface so you can mimic its spacing and kerning. Unless the typeface you're creating is very close to an existing typeface, this is usually unnecessary. When you click the OK button to export a character to an existing font, an extra dialog box appears if there's already a character in the position you've selected. The dialog box asks whether you want to overwrite the existing definition.

Repeat this process until all of your characters are in the font. This font doesn't contain any kerning information unless you choose the Load Font Metrics option. At this point, you might want to import the "finished" font into a program, such as Altsys Fontographer, where you can optimize the spacing and add kerning and hinting information.

Once you've made all the adjustments, you can install the font, either through Adobe Type Manager for PostScript fonts or Control Panel Fonts for TrueType fonts (or you can use Corel FONT MASTER for either type). It can then be used in any Windows program that supports scaleable fonts, including CorelDRAW itself. Not only can you create fonts for yourself, but you can create them for clients so that a logo, signature, or other symbol can be used in any of their Windows applications.

# 43

# Font Formats

CorelDRAW has traditionally supported three different font formats: WFN, TrueType, and PostScript. Starting with CorelDRAW 6, the WFN format is no longer supported. Each of the other formats has several advantages and disadvantages. These are pointed out as each font format is described, and the installation process for each is described in detail.

## WFN Format

This format was developed by Corel for use in early versions of CorelDRAW. The format is no longer usable by CorelDRAW 6. If you have fonts in the WFN format that you would like to continue using, Ares FontMonger can convert them into either PostScript or TrueType format.

## TrueType Format

TrueType was co-developed by Apple and Microsoft to challenge PostScript Type 1's then-proprietary format. Support for TrueType fonts is built directly into Windows 3.1 and higher, as well as the Macintosh's System 7.0 and higher. This ensures that the format has a very large user base. It has proven to be quite successful on Windows since the release of Windows 3.1. Unfortunately, the many advantages of the TrueType format are vastly underutilized by current software, and CorelDRAW 6 in particular.

The biggest advantage of TrueType fonts is the fact that they are directly supported by Windows, and therefore can be used by almost all Windows-compliant applications without the need for an additional utility. At this point, that is the only practical advantage the TrueType format provides.

One advantage that could be very beneficial to CorelDRAW users is the capability to embed TrueType fonts in data files. This means that if a drawing is made that includes a nonstandard font, it can be shared with other users without distributing the font (which could be illegal). This would be especially beneficial for sharing a drawing between several systems and/or sending the file to a service bureau. The embedding specifications provide for several different types of embedding, but unfortunately Corel has decided to wait until a future version to implement these important services.

## Installing TrueType Fonts

Click the Windows 95 Start button and select the Settings flyout and then the Control Panel as shown in Figure 43.1. Now double-click the Fonts icon in the Control Panel dialog box shown in Figure 43.2. This will open the Windows 95 folder where fonts and font shortcuts are stored. An example of this directory is shown in Figure 43.3. Note that your folder might look different, depending on the view you have chosen in the View menu. From the File menu, select the Add New Fonts command and you will see the dialog box shown in Figure 43.4. Select the drive and then the folder on that drive where the fonts you wish to install are located. Select the fonts you want to install by clicking their names while holding down the Shift key (to select all fonts between clicks) or the Ctrl key (to select only names clicked). The bottom of the dialog has the option of copying the fonts to the Windows 95 Fonts folder. If you wish to leave the fonts in their current location, then make sure that this box is not checked. Once you've selected all of the fonts that you wish to install, click the OK button and they will be installed.

An easier way to install fonts is to use the Corel FONT MASTER utility, which is included with CorelDRAW 6. It is explained in more detail in Skill Session 95, "Corel FONT MASTER."

*Figure 43.1.*
*The Control Panel icon in*
*the Start menu.*

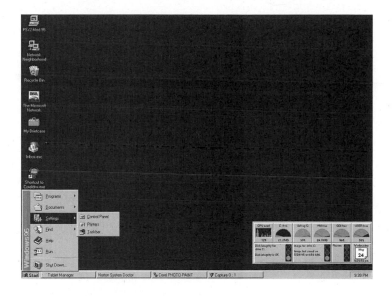

*Figure 43.2.*
*The Fonts icon in Control*
*Panel.*

Fonts icon

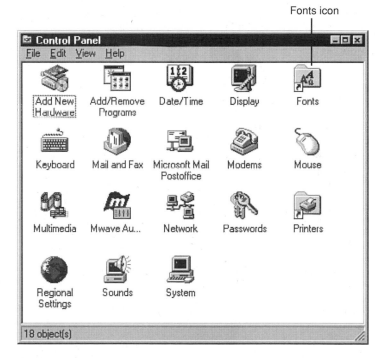

*Figure 43.3.*
*The Fonts folder.*

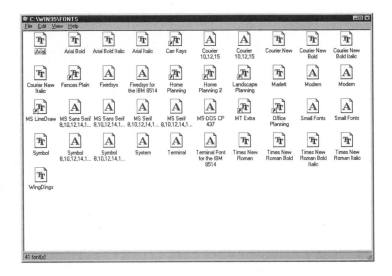

*Figure 43.4.*
*The Add Fonts dialog box.*

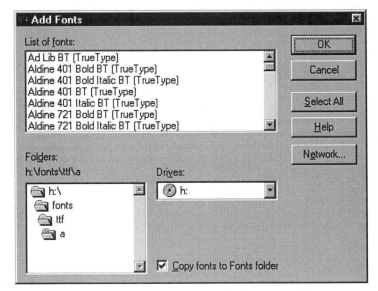

# PostScript Fonts

PostScript fonts were developed by Adobe Systems to be used with its PostScript
Page Description language. PostScript Type 1 fonts are commonly confused with
the PostScript Page Description language. You don't need to use the language in
order to use the fonts. Under Windows, Adobe Type Manager gives you full use of
PostScript fonts, both on-screen and on any Windows supported printer.

For users with PostScript output devices (which range from laser printers to imagesetters) there is really no logical choice but to use PostScript fonts. Although the other formats will work fine, the PostScript fonts are the output devices' native format, and therefore are the preferred format to use. Users with PostScript printers can download the fonts directly to their output devices rather than converting characters to curves or bitmaps. TrueType fonts can only be downloaded to a PostScript device after they have been converted on-the-fly, causing a loss in quality.

The biggest advantage to PostScript fonts is that they are the native format of many high-end devices. They are also the most popular format, with well over 20,000 different fonts available from numerous vendors.

One of the most interesting advantages for CorelDRAW users is that fewer nodes are required to render a PostScript font than a TrueType font. Figure 43.5 shows two copies of the same character—one in each format. When the characters were converted to curves, the PostScript version had three fewer nodes.

*Figure 43.5.*
*TrueType versus*
*PostScript character*
*node count.*

TrueType
24 nodes

PostScript
21 nodes

Three nodes might seem to be a negligible difference in this case, but consider that when a page full of graphics is converted to curves, the difference can be thousands of nodes. This can make a significant difference in the size of print files and the time it takes to print them.

The last major advantage is the fact that PostScript fonts are much more reliable at larger sizes. Due to bugs in the TrueType rasterizer, many of the fonts will just explode or disappear, and characters will be represented by a hollow square. Sometimes this appears only on the printout, which can be even more frustrating.

For these reasons, PostScript is the format of choice for those who really care about their output.

## Installing PostScript Fonts

Because the use of PostScript fonts in CorelDRAW requires Adobe Type Manager (ATM), the fonts themselves can be installed either by following the directions in the next section for ATM or by using the Corel FONT MASTER utility that is included with CorelDRAW 6. See Skill Session 95 for more information on Corel FONT MASTER.

## Adobe Type Manager

Adobe Type Manager (ATM) is an essential utility for professional users of CorelDRAW. Because it can work with Type 1 fonts, it is almost mandatory for users of PostScript printers, because the fonts can be directly downloaded to the printer. Service bureaus are also very reluctant to work with anything except PostScript fonts; PostScript is the standard output format for most high-end devices. Adobe Type Manager provides users with the ability to use PostScript Type 1 fonts in most Windows applications, including CorelDRAW. It is essential that you use Adobe Type Manager 3.0 or higher in order to work correctly with CorelDRAW. The current version as of this writing is 3.02 and is not included with CorelDRAW 6.

Many users confuse the ATM Control Panel (see the icon in Figure 43.6) with the Windows Control Panel fonts (see the icon in Figure 43.1). ATM Control Panel is one way that PostScript Type 1 fonts can be installed into Windows; However, Corel FONT MASTER is a much better way (see Skill Session 95). Information is copied into both the ATM.INI file and WIN.INI file so that the fonts can be used on both the screen and the printer. Figures 43.7 and 43.8 show the ATM screens for installing fonts. Note that fonts installed through the ATM Control Panel are not visible in the Windows Control Panel. During the installation of ATM itself, two multiple master fonts are installed into Windows. These will not show up in any font list, but will be used by products such as Adobe Acrobat.

CorelDRAW 6 supports dynamic updating of the font list; therefore, it is possible to minimize CorelDRAW and install fonts that will be immediately available. This can be very beneficial should you find that you need a font in the middle of working on a project.

*Figure 43.6.*
*The Adobe Type Manager*
*Control Panel icon in the*
*Start menu.*

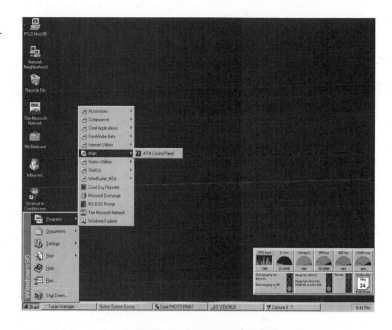

*Figure 43.7.*
*The initial Adobe Type*
*Manager Control Panel*
*screen.*

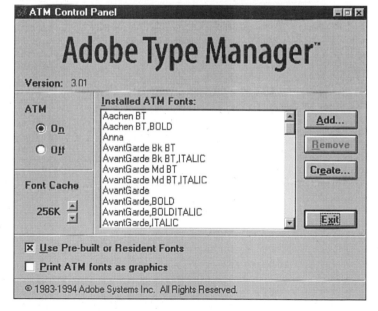

*Figure 43.8.*
*The Add ATM Fonts*
*dialog box.*

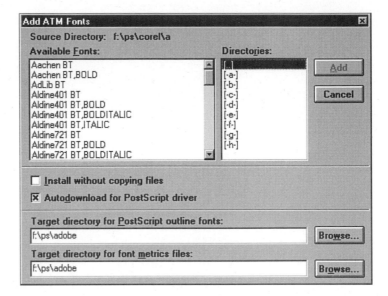

The fonts that come with CorelDRAW are all provided in PostScript Type 1 format; therefore, exactly the same fonts are available as the TrueType fonts that the default install adds. The spacing and kerning should be identical for both formats, so there should be no compatibility problems when you decide to switch from one format to another.

# 44

# Basic Typography

## Typographical Terms

Figure 44.1 contains examples of several basic typographical terms. The *baseline* is an imaginary horizontal reference line on which the characters align. Note that some characters extend slightly below this line. The *cap-height line* is another imaginary line that defines the height of the capital letters. Notice how some characters extend slightly above this line. The cap-height is usually about two-thirds of the point size, but this is not true of fonts from all foundries. The *x-height* is defined as the height of a lowercase letter without ascenders or descenders. An *ascender* is a lowercase letter that extends above the x-height. Characters with ascenders include *b, d, f, h, k, l,* and *t*. A *descender* is a lowercase letter that extends below the baseline. The descenders include *g, j, p, q,* and *y*. In old Roman typefaces, the ascenders extend above the cap-height. Descenders are not necessarily always the same; some may descend farther than others.

Figure 44.1.
Common typographical
terms.

## True Italic Versus Skewing

With a program like CorelDRAW, users commonly use skewing when they actually
want italics. Unfortunately, the two are not the same in many typefaces. An italic
typeface is meant to be the "cursive" version of the Roman typeface. In a sans serif
typeface, the italic is normally called *oblique*, because it's just a slanted or skewed
version of the Roman typeface. But in serif faces and some sans serif faces, the
italic weight has different curves and can even have different letter shapes. Figure
44.2 shows two different typefaces, each with the Roman weight, a skewed
version of the Roman, and the true italic face. Notice in the sans serif version (the
one on the left) that there is little difference between the skewed version and the
italic version. The serif version shows a dramatic difference. Although sometimes
it might seem appropriate to create a false italic, it is strongly discouraged, especially on serif faces.

## Bold Versus Outlining

Many people feel that a bold weight can be created by adding an outline to
characters. Figure 44.3 shows two different faces, each with the Roman weight,
the Roman weight with a thin outline, and the true bold weight. Notice how the
true bold weight has a much crisper look than the outlined version. CorelDRAW 6
also offers a contouring feature that can be used to create a pseudo-boldface font.
Use this feature cautiously.

Figure 44.2.
Roman, skewed Roman,
and true italic typefaces.

abciABC     abciABC

*abciABC*     *abciABC*

*abciABC*     *abciABC*

## Condensed and Extended Fonts Versus Stretching

You can create a pseudo-condensed typeface by stretching Artistic text by less
than 100 percent. This can come in handy when you're trying to fit that extra little
bit of text into a tight area. Before you use this feature, check whether a true

condensed version of the typeface is available. Figure 44.4 shows how a character may become distorted when it's condensed. Notice how the width of the stem on the pseudo-condensed *O* is not of a uniform thickness when compared with the true-condensed weight of the font.

*Figure 44.3.*
*Roman, Roman with an*
*outline, and true bold*
*typefaces.*

abciABC abciABC
abciABC abciABC
**abciABC** **abciABC**

The same applies to extending a font by stretching Artistic text more than 100 percent. Figure 44.5 shows the same text block found in Figure 44.4, with both a true-extended and a pseudo-extended weight. Again notice how the thickness of the letterforms is not uniform on the pseudo-extended face.

*Figure 44.4.*
*Distortions may occur*
*when you use stretching*
*to condense a font.*

*Figure 44.5.*
*A true extended font and*
*the same text extended by*
*stretching.*

Ligatures are two or more characters combined into one character for better legibility. Figure 44.6 shows several of the more common ligatures, with the same characters typed in the normal way below them. There are five different ligatures: *fi*, *ff*, *fl*, *ffi*, and *ffl*. Note that Windows currently does not support these characters unless they are remapped into nonstandard locations, which is commonly the case in expert-set typefaces. Ligatures were created for these characters so that they could be set closer together. They also have been shown to increase legibility. Diphthongs (see Figure 44.7) also are considered ligatures. There are occasionally several other ligatures within a typeface (such as the *ct* in Figure 44.6), but they are not very common.

*Figure 44.6.*
*Several ligatures and their*
*equivalents.*

fi fl ffi ffl ct
fi fl ffi ffl ct

*Figure 44.7.*
*Common diphthongs and*
*their equivalents.*

æ Æ œ Œ
ae AE oe OE

## Old-Style Numerals

Numerals come in two styles, as shown in Figure 44.8. The top examples are *old style* or *nonaligning*, and the bottom examples are *modern* or *aligning*. These should be used in a style consistent with your document. Numbers under 100 are usually spelled out, unless they relate to references, and they should always be spelled out at the beginning of a sentence. Some style books change this rule to ten and under, so consult the style book for your particular project.

*Figure 44.8.*
*Two styles of numerals.*

0123456789
0123456789

## Small Capitals

Small capitals (see Figure 44.9) are designed to match the x-height of a particular typeface. Many fonts don't include true small capitals; therefore, they're created by reducing the point size by two sizes (to 80 percent). These characters often appear lighter and look out of place, such as the reduced characters in the first line of Figure 44.9. True-cut small caps are the same height as the x-height and are usually equal to the normal cap width. Small caps should be used for abbreviations that follow a person's name (awards, decorations, honors, titles, degrees, and so on). They should also be used for time, as shown in Figure 44.9.

*Figure 44.9.*
*Reduced point size versus*
*true small capitals.*

8 A.M.  8 A.M.

8 A.M.  8 A.M.

## Swash Characters

Swash characters (the second line in Figure 44.10) are alternative characters with extra flourishes on them. They are meant to be used for an initial capital or an occasional alternate character, but they should be used prudently.

*Figure 44.10.*
*Regular characters and*
*swash characters.*

ABCDEFGHIJKLMNOPQRSTUVWXYZ
ABCDEFGHIJKLMNOPRSTUVWXYZ

## Ornamental Drop Capitals

Ornamental drop capitals are generally used for the first character of a large block of text to indicate the beginning of a passage. Many of these ornamental capitals are too complex to fit within the bounds of a TrueType or PostScript font. Therefore, they're provided as clip art files. This can create problems when you're trying to make the character fit within the text block. In CorelDRAW 6, you can do this by wrapping the text block around the ornamental character. Figure 44.11 shows an example of this technique.

*Figure 44.11.*
*An ornamental drop cap.*

nce upon a time there was a software company in Ottawa, Canada that made an illustration package for use on a PC. Then new versions were released that enabled the software to run on many other types of computers thus making the world a happier place to live.

## Common Kerning Pairs

Kerning pairs are used to move various pairs of characters closer together or farther apart than the normal spacing allocated to the characters. Figure 44.12 shows two examples of the letter pair *AV*—the first one set with the normal spacing and the second one kerned together with the built-in kerning pair. CorelDRAW 6 supports up to 1500 kerning pairs per font. These pairs are stored within a TrueType font's TTF file or a PostScript font's AFM and PFM files. While these pairs are not necessary for every font, they can be helpful. Decorative faces, such as Script, normally do not contain kerning pairs, because the exact spacing is needed to make the letters connect properly.

*Figure 44.12.*
*An example of kerning.*

## Tips for More Attractive Documents

Following are a few typographical tips that will help you create more attractive documents. They will also help you avoid mistakes that will brand you as a novice to typography.

> *Quotation marks and apostrophes*   Do not use the " and ' keys to indicate quotation marks and apostrophes. Instead, use ALT-0147 for open quotation marks and ALT-0148 for closed quotation marks. The single quotation marks are ALT-095 for open and ALT-039 for closed. Using the Type Assist function in CorelDRAW 6 will allow you to have the quotes converted to "curly" quotes automatically.

# Corel *NOTE!*

To create extended characters, hold down the Alt key and type the character's number on the numeric keypad. The Corel character chart shows all the keys and their numbers.

*Dashes* The em dash, ALT-0151, is used to separate two thoughts in a sentence. An en dash, ALT-0150, is used to separate two dates or times. Some typographers add space before and after an em dash or an en dash. This is uncommon. If you must have space, use a thin space.

*Spaces* Always put a single space between sentences. Two spaces are a good idea when you're using a typewriter with a monospace type, but when you're using proportional type, it looks horrible.

*All Caps and Underlining* Again, it was necessary to use these features on a typewriter to give emphasis to a section of text. However, it looks hideous when you're using proportional type. Use bold or italic type instead; if you must have all caps, set them in small caps.

*Bullets* No more asterisks, hyphens, lowercase *Os*, and so on. Now you can use real bullets. But don't go overboard. Stick to bullets, circles, and squares. Avoid pointy fingers, arrows, snowflakes, and so on (unless you have a good reason to use them). For example, you might use a snowflake bullet for a skiing brochure.

*Numbers* Don't type a lowercase *l* when you need a one (1), or an uppercase *O* when you need a zero (0). This not only looks bad, but it creates problems for the spell checker.

*Abbreviations* Whenever possible, spell out words rather than abbreviating them. It's rarely necessary to abbreviate a word or a state name. If you do abbreviate a state, use the postal form—two capital letters with no period.

## Where to Get More Information

This skill session presents a brief overview of typography as well as several situations that often confuse electronic publishers. Should you need more information, check your local bookstore for books on typography and style.

# Skill Session: Bitmap Workshop

# 45

# Transparency and Coloring

One useful feature in CorelDRAW is that you can modify black-and-white bitmaps, either by making parts of them transparent or by adding color to parts of them.

## Transparency

The purpose of making part of a black-and-white bitmap transparent is to allow a background image to show through. There could be times when you have a grayscale bitmap image you want to superimpose over another image. If you simply imported the grayscale image, it would cover up the underlying image. By converting the grayscale image to black and white, it allows part of the underlying image to show through. Only the white pixels of the bitmap can be made transparent. Follow these steps to make the white pixels of a black-and-white bitmap transparent:

1. Import a black-and-white bitmap into CorelDRAW by using the Import command in the File pull-down menu.

2. Select the bitmap and click the × icon in the Fill flyout menu. This is the same as removing the fill of an object.

3. Place the modified bitmap over any background you desire. Resize as needed.

In Figure 45.1, the bitmap image on the left shows the original. The image on the right has been placed on top of a background image to show that the white background of the bitmap image has been made transparent.

*Figure 45.1.*
*A transparent bitmap*
*superimposed over an*
*underlying image.*

## Coloring Bitmaps

When you change a black-and-white bitmap to colors, you change black to one color and white to a different color.

Follow these steps to change the color of a black-and-white bitmap:

1. Select the bitmap with the Pick tool.
2. Change the black pixels by clicking the color palette with the right mouse button.
3. Change the white pixels by clicking the color palette with the left mouse button.

The first example in Figure 45.2 shows the original bitmap. The second example shows the bitmap with just the black pixels changed. In the third example, both the black and white pixels have been changed to different colors.

*Figure 45.2.*
*Changing the colors of a*
*bitmap.*

# 46

# Cropping and Hiding Bitmaps

## Cropping Bitmaps

There are three basic methods for cropping bitmaps in CorelDRAW. The method you choose depends on what effect you're trying to accomplish. When you import a bitmap into a new or existing file, it comes in as a rectangle or square. If the image doesn't have a definite background that fills the entire image area, the image you import will have a white background defining the area. This extra area of white background can sometimes interfere with other objects on-screen. It can also conflict with your page background color.

There will be times when you want to crop a portion of an image that has a background filling the entire area and you want to cut out just a particular part of the image.

The three basic methods for cropping bitmaps are described in the following sections. Bitmaps are always imported into a CDR file.

# Cropping When Importing

This method allows you to eliminate portions of an image before the image is actually imported.

1. Choose the Import command from the File pull-down menu.

2. When the Import dialog box appears, select the folder where your bitmap is located and choose a file.

3. After you have selected the file, click the down arrow beneath the preview window. Choose Crop from the drop-down menu. (See Figure 46.1.)

*Figure 46.1.*
*The Import dialog box*
*with Crop selected.*

4. Click the Import button.

5. A new dialog box will appear showing the bitmap image. Use the selection handles to crop the image of unwanted areas (see Figure 46.2). If you want the cropped image to be a specific size, enter the numbers in the Height and Width parameters boxes. The dimensions are measured in pixels by default. When the selection handles move to the desired size, click and drag the selection box over the portion of the image you wish to crop.

6. Click the OK button. Your cropped image will be imported into your CDR file.

*Figure 46.2.*
*The Crop Image*
*dialog box.*

*Figure 46.3.*
*The cropped image.*

## Cropping Using the Bitmap Color Mask

# Corel*NOTE!*

**Special Final release note!**

Prior to the final release of CorelDRAW 6, the Bitmap Color Mask roll-up contained a Remove Holes button. (See Figure 46.4.) When Corel released the final version, this button was removed. The removal of this button and the function it provided severely degrades the usefulness of the Bitmap Color Mask. It is everyone's hope that this function will be put back in the roll-up with the first maintenance release. Because we are confident that this problem will be fixed, we have left the instructions for using the Bitmap Color mask as written. Use of the Bitmap Color Mask is very limited until this problem is fixed.

As a workaround to this problem, try filling the background of the bitmap image with a color you know is not in the image you want to mask prior to importing the image into CorelDRAW.

*Figure 46.4.*
*The Bitmap Color Mask*
*roll-up prior to final*
*release.*

A new feature in CorelDRAW 6 is the Bitmap Color Mask. It functions much like the color tolerance settings in Corel PHOTO-PAINT. Figure 46.5 shows a bitmap image of contributing author, James "Homer" Simpson, with a white background. The image on the left is the original imported image (a dotted line has been placed around the image to show the background area). The image in the center has the background removed using the Bitmap Color Mask. A duplicate of the center image has been placed on a new background on the right with a gradient fill. Notice that the previous white background has indeed been removed.

# Corel*NOTE!*

Technically the background has not been removed, but rather it has been made transparent. (See Step 7 in the following list.)

*Figure 46.5.*
*Cropping an image with a*
*solid background using*
*the Bitmap Color Mask.*

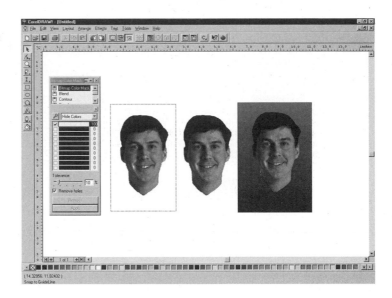

The following steps are required to remove a solid background color from a bitmap image:

1. Open the Bitmap Color Mask roll-up from the Effects pull-down menu.
2. Select the bitmap image with the Pick tool (it is very important that the bitmap be selected).
3. Click the top color bar (beneath the Hide Color parameters box).
4. Click and drag the slider to 10 percent on the Tolerance setting. A setting of ten percent is to allow for any slight variance in the background color.
5. Click the Eye Dropper tool. Using this tool, click on the background color of the bitmap. The color white will fill the color bar and an × will be placed in the adjacent box.
6. Click the Apply button.

7. In this example the white background will be made transparent, allowing any object behind it to show through. A small part of the subject's teeth, eyes, cheek, and nose were made transparent because they too were white.

8. Place a check mark in the Remove Holes box and click the Apply button again. This action will remove the transparent portions on the face.

9. Use the completed image as is or place it on a new background.

Figure 46.6 shows co-author Foster Coburn with a gradient-like background. The process to remove a multicolored background is a little more difficult than with a solid background. Remember, it was only necessary to sample the solid background in Figure 46.5 once with the Eye Dropper tool.

The example in Figure 46.6 would require sampling the background three separate times or more with the Eye Dropper tool because of the various hues in the gradient fill. The tolerance setting was set in the 50 percent range on each background area sampled. This was done to collect similar hues of each sample. You will have to experiment with the percentage settings with each individual image you mask. Remember to select a new color bar for each color sampling.

The center image in Figure 46.6 shows the results after applying the color mask using the 50 percent settings. As in Figure 46.5, a portion of the face was masked. To remove the transparent portions of the face, place a check mark in the Remove Holes box and click the Apply button again. By not having the Remove Holes button in the release version of CoreDRAW 6, it is impossible to completely mask out the background without masking part of the face.

*Figure 46.6.*
*Cropping an image with a*
*gradient background*
*using the Bitmap Color*
*Mask.*

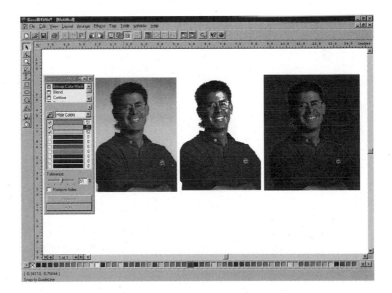

CorelDRAW supplies thousands of clip art images. You should take advantage of them to create some interesting and humorous images. The clip art image on the left is called Karate.cmx. The head was removed from the clip art image and replaced with a scanned photo. The photo was cropped using the bitmap color mask that shipped with the final release of CorelDRAW 6. The background of the image was filled with green prior to importing the image. Using green as a background color removed the possibility of masking part of the image itself.

## Cropping Using the PowerClip Effect

Another method of cropping bitmaps is to use the PowerClip effect. This effect enables you to place the bitmap inside a predefined target object so that only a portion of the bitmap is displayed and printed.

The image in Figure 46.7 was imported from one of Corel's Photo CDs. This particular image was selected because the background colors are very similar to the swan's colors. Using the color mask method described previously would be very difficult because of these similarities. You could spend a very long time trying to mask the swan and still not end up with an accurate mask. When you have an image of this type, you should use the PowerClip method.

Here is the procedure for placing a bitmap inside another object:

# Corel*NOTE!*

Before you recreate the steps below, click the Tools pull-down menu and choose Options. In the Options dialog box, remove the check mark from the Automatically center new PowerClip contents check box. If you leave this box checked, CorelDRAW places the bitmap in the center of your target object, and this is not what you will want to do in most every case.

1. Make sure the bitmap is not selected! Trace around the portion of the bitmap you want to mask using the Pencil tool, either in freehand mode or Bézier mode. This will be your target object.
2. Select the bitmap with the Pick tool.
3. Click the Effects menu and select PowerClip. Next, select Place Inside Container from the flyout. The cursor becomes an arrow.
4. With the arrow, click the target object where you want the bitmap to go. The bitmap is placed inside your tracing.
5. Use the Shape tool to tweak the traced image so that none of the background shows. This step can take some time depending on how complicated the image is.

Figure 46.7 shows the original bitmap image on the left and PowerClipped object in the center. The image on the right has a rectangle with a solid fill placed behind the PowerClipped swan.

*Figure 46.7.*
*Using the PowerClip effect*
*to crop a bitmap.*

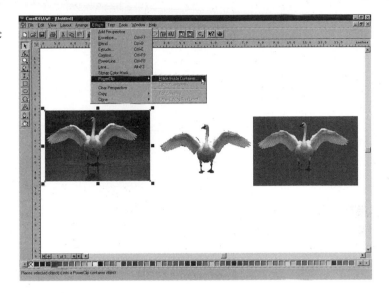

## Hiding Bitmaps

*Hiding a bitmap* means that the bitmap will not show in preview or wireframe mode. The reason for doing this is to reduce the time it takes to redraw the screen. To hide a bitmap, you have two options. The first method is to click Bitmaps in the View menu and remove the check mark from the Visible check box in the flyout. You must be in wireframe mode to remove the check mark. The bitmap will still appear in preview mode, but it will be hidden in wireframe mode. You should only use this method if you're going to spend a lot of time in wireframe mode.

The second method requires you to put the bitmap on its own layer and to make it invisible. You do this by adding a new layer using the Layers Manager and moving the bitmap to this new layer. The next step is to click the eye icon to make the bitmap invisible. Because both preview and wireframe modes are affected by this change, don't forget that you still have an image on your page. (See Skill Session 21, "Layers," for information about using layers.) To preview the entire page with bitmaps, choose Full Screen Preview from the View menu (or press F9).

# 47

# Manual Tracing Versus Autotracing

Tracing bitmap images is required when you need a vector image to replace a bitmap image. The most common need to trace a bitmap image is when reproducing a logo. A client will supply you with his logo, usually on a business card, and expect you to reproduce it with sharp clean lines. The first thing you have to do is scan the logo and save it as a bitmap image. After creating the bitmap, you have to convert it to a vector image to produce the sharp image the client requires. The two methods of tracing bitmap images are outlined in the following sections.

## Manual Tracing

Manually tracing bitmaps involves using the Pencil tool to actually draw lines around the portion of the image you want to trace. To begin, import your bitmap and place it in a convenient place on the page.

# Corel*NOTE!*

> Before beginning to trace, make sure that the bitmap is not selected. If it is selected, you will enable the Autotracing tool.

Using the Pencil tool, trace around the portion of the bitmap you want to use. You can use either the Freehand tool or the Bézier tool. If you use the Freehand tool, hold down the right mouse button the entire time you're tracing. If you release the right mouse button while you're tracing, you'll have to go back and connect the nodes after your trace is completed. If you use the Bézier method, click once with the right mouse button and then move to another point on the image you're tracing and click again. Continue this point-to-point method of tracing until you finish the trace. Your last click of the mouse button should end on the first node. If you don't connect the first node with the last, you'll have to join them. (See Skill Session 7, "The Shape Tool.")

If the object you traced has lots of curves, marquee-select all of the nodes using the Shape tool and right-click one of the nodes to bring up the Object Properties menu. Choose Cusp from the menu. Choosing Cusp puts two handles on each node, allowing you to more accurately manipulate the lines around the shape of the bitmap. If your object has mostly straight lines, select all the nodes and click To Line in the Object Properties menu. This method enables you to adjust the tracing more easily.

All this may sound complicated, but it really isn't. For those of you who use tablets with pens, it's easy to manually trace any object. It's more difficult to manually trace with a mouse.

## Autotracing

Unless you're tracing a very simple black-and-white bitmap, you might consider using Corel OCR-TRACE (see Skill Session 91, "Corel OCR-TRACE"). Figure 47.1 shows the results of tracing a black-and-white logo using the autotrace and freehand method. The image on the left is the original bitmap. The center image is the autotraced image, and the image on the right was traced freehand. The autotracing of the logo produced very poor results. The stylized letter M lacked the necessary straight lines, and the curves did not follow the original image. The circle surrounding the letter M was too fine to trace. On the other hand, the freehand traced image produced very good results on the letter M. The circle was simply drawn with the ellipse tool as a separate object.

*Figure 47.1.*
*Examples of autotraced*
*and manually traced*
*bitmaps.*

Here is the procedure for using the Autotrace feature:

1. Choose Import from the File menu.
2. Change the directory to the one where your bitmap file is located and then select the bitmap to import. Be sure to use the correct extension in the Import dialog box for the type of bitmap you're importing (.PCX, .TIF, and so on). Select a black-and-white image for the best results.
3. Click the OK button.
4. When the bitmap appears on-screen, select it with the Pick tool.
5. With the bitmap still selected, click the Pencil tool. The Pencil tool changes to a crosshair cursor with the right-hand line extended. The crosshair is not displayed unless the bitmap is selected.
6. Click the center of the bitmap. An outline of the object is drawn as a vector object.
7. If the lines are not connected for some reason, you need to join them with the Shape tool. (See Skill Session 7.)

# Corel*NOTE!*

> If you don't want to manually trace or autotrace an object, by all means use Corel OCR-TRACE. It's an excellent tracing program for most solid filled images. Refer to Skill Session 91 to learn more about CorelTRACE.

## Part VII

# Skill Session: Output Workshop

**48**

# Import Filters

## Vector Formats

### Adobe Illustrator (AI, EPS)

Full support is provided for all Adobe Illustrator formats, up to and including 3.0, Illustrator 88, and 1.1.

Imported files come in as a group of objects that can be ungrouped using Arrange Ungroup.

### AutoCAD (DXF)

AutoCAD files can be converted to DXF format using the DXFOUT utility included with AutoCAD. For 3D images, choose the view you wish to convert before running DXFOUT. Polylines should be used whenever possible rather than regular lines because they reduce the complexity of the file. Files from AutoCAD v11, v12, and v13 are not fully supported.

### DXF File Complexity

DXF files that are too complex to import can be output as Plot-To-File files and then imported using the HPGL import filter.

## Notes and Limitations on DXF Files

- An attempt is made to center the imported image in an 18"×18" area. This is not guaranteed, especially with 3D images. All drawings will be scaled to fit within an 18"×18" area.

- Dashed lines are converted to a similar dashed-line pattern.

- Dimension entities might scatter when imported. In these cases, explode the dimension entities in the original AutoCAD file and re-export to DXF.

- Imported polylines retain only their minimum line width as specified in AutoCAD. This width may be up to 4 inches.

- Solid and trace entities are filled for all non-3D fills (that is, they are filled on an x/y axis view only).

- Points are imported as ellipses, whereas extruded points come in as line segments with two nodes each.

- If a file was exported as an entities-only file, it might import incorrectly due to lack of header information.

## AutoCAD Features Not Supported by CorelDRAW

- Shape entities (CorelDRAW does not read SHX files)

- Polylines, including variable-width polylines, elevation (Group 38), mesh M and N vertex counts (Groups 71 and 72), smooth surface M and N densities (Groups 73 and 74), and smooth surface type (Group 75)

- 3D shapes such as cones, spheres, and tori as well as extrusions of circles, arcs, text, polylines with width, and dashed patterns

- Invisible lines in 3D face entities

- Automatic wireframes

- Hidden line removal

- Extrusion direction assumed to be parallel to the z-axis

- Binary DXF format

- Paper space entities within a model space

- Layers information

## Text in the DXF File

AutoCAD-generated text will show the following differences:

- The justification of text might not be preserved. Text that specifies no justification will work best.

- Because of its limits regarding point size and skew, CorelDRAW might adjust the values to stay within those limits.

Here are some points regarding special characters in text strings:

- Control characters will be ignored.
- Overscore and underscore will be ignored.
- If a character is referred to by number, the number must be a three-digit number, such as %%065 for character 65.
- The character %%010 is a carriage return and line feed.
- CorelDRAW replaces any nonstandard characters with a question mark (?). These characters include the degree symbol, the +/- tolerance symbol, and the circle dimensioning symbol.

Typefaces specified in DXF files will be remapped by the Panose font matching system to the closest available font. If a font cannot be remapped, it will use the default font.

## Computer Graphics Metafiles (CGM)

### Bitmaps

Bitmaps are not supported.

### Markers

Only markers supported by the CGM standard are imported; private-use markers are ignored.

### Text in CGM Files

- Text is editable only if the correct options were used when the file was exported.
- The typefaces will probably change in the import process. This can be changed when the file is in CorelDRAW.

## CorelCHART (CCH)

To import CorelCHART files, you must choose Save Corel Presentation Data when saving your CorelCHART file. This will not maintain links between objects in the CorelCHART file and underlying data. CorelCHART files not saved with presentation data will open Chart via OLE and extract the presentation data. Unfortunately, the presentation data will add to file sizes.

## CorelDRAW (CDR)

CorelDRAW files import as a group of objects. You may ungroup them using the Arrange Ungroup command.

### Text in Earlier Version Files

Text that is contained in files from earlier versions might import with intercharacter spacing that is slightly off. This problem affects only certain typefaces and is not always noticeable. It is most noticeable when the text is close to another graphic element. It can be corrected by using the Shape tool to adjust the spacing. If the text is fit to a curve, straighten it and then use the Fit Text to Path option of the Text menu again.

## Corel MOVE (CMV, MLB)

Actors and cells can be imported for editing.

## Corel SHOW (SHW)

Presentations can be imported for editing.

## CorelTRACE (AI, EPS)

CorelTRACE files import as a group of objects. You can ungroup them using the Arrange Ungroup command.

## Corel Metafile (CMF)

This format is a predecessor to the CMX format and can be imported for full editing.

## Corel Presentation Exchange 5.0, 6.0 (CMX)

Corel Presentation Exchange format is used for exchanging information between Corel applications. It is similar to the native CDR format but does not maintain links to objects or other data. You can save CDR files with the Presentation Exchange data attached, but this will add to your file size.

## Encapsulated PostScript (Placeable EPS)

This format of EPS will not try to translate the data in the EPS file, but will display a thumbnail of the file (if one exists) on-screen and send the EPS file itself to the printer. If no header is included in the file, then it will be displayed as a gray box with an × through it. If an EPS file is printed to a non-PostScript printer, then the low-resolution header will be printed. This filter will not work with the All Files import option because there are multiple types of EPS files and it is not able to distinguish between them.

## Enhanced Windows Metafile (EMF)

This is a format used by newer Windows programs. Any missing fonts will be substituted by similar fonts available at the time of import.

## GEM Files (GEM)

### Object Interior Fills

Objects with custom fills, such as grids, hatches, and ball bearings, are not supported. They are imported with a tinted color fill corresponding to the color of the pattern fill of the original object.

### Line End Styles

Caps or corners created in GEM Artline do not import. For files created in GEM Draw, the following occurs:

- Round end caps will be successfully imported.
- Lines with arrows import with no end caps.

### Symbols

Symbols created in GEM Artline are converted to curves when imported into CorelDRAW.

### Text in GEM Files

- GEM Artline files convert all text to curves. Text contained in other GEM files comes in fully editable.
- If a font is not available on your system, the Panose system remaps it to the nearest available font.
- The text alignment might not be exactly the same as that in the original file because of differences between the formats in font sizes and spacing. This can be corrected when the file is imported into CorelDRAW.
- Characters not supported by CorelDRAW appear as question marks. Underlined text is not supported.

## HPGL Plotter File (PLT)

CorelDRAW supports only a subset of the HPGL and HPGL/2 command set. It uses a stepping factor of 1016 plotter units = 1 inch.

### Image Size

A dialog box appears that allows a drawing to be scaled when importing. If a drawing is bigger than what CorelDRAW supports, it is automatically scaled to fit within CorelDRAW's maximum page size.

## View

3D files should be changed to the desired view before exporting because that will be the view imported into CorelDRAW.

## Pen Information

HPGL files define colors by pen numbers. The pen numbers can be mapped to colors in the dialog box shown in Figure 48.1. Up to 256 definitions can be entered. You can change a color assignment by selecting a pen number and choosing a color from the Pen color field. You can also choose the color from the color definition dialog box by entering RGB values.

You can also change pen widths in this dialog box by selecting a pen and changing the value in the Pen width field.

*Figure 48.1.*
*The HPGL Options*
*dialog box.*

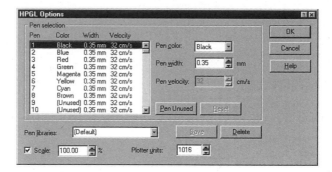

## Fills

Not all objects in an HPGL file will be filled in CorelDRAW.

## Line Types

HPGL dotted, dashed, and solid-line types are remapped to a CorelDRAW line pattern, as shown in Table 47.1.

**Table 47.1. Converting HPGL lines to CorelDRAW line types.**

| HPGL Line | CorelDRAW Line Type |
|-----------|---------------------|
| #0        | Solid               |
| #1        | Dotted              |
| #2        | Small dash          |
| #3        | Large dash          |
| #4,5      | Dot-dash            |

| HPGL Line | CorelDRAW Line Type |
|-----------|---------------------|
| #6 | Double dot-dash |
| #7 and over | Same as #2 |

### Text in HPGL Files

- Text will be editable only if the exporting application is capable of exporting text as text.
- Text will be assigned to the monospaced font, but it can be changed to any typeface and size once imported.
- Imported text will have a fill color based on its pen number, but it will not have an outline color.

## IBM PIF (PIF)

### Unsupported Functions

- Set Background Mix, Set Foreground Mix, Call Segment, and Set Character set orders are not processed. Objects are overlaid in the order in which they are read. Each non-overlapping object has its own defined color.
- Set Paper Color and Set Pattern Symbol are not supported.

### PIF Line Types

- Line types 1, 3, 4, and 6 map to CorelDRAW's "three-unit dash followed by a five-unit space" line type.
- Line types 2 and 5 map to CorelDRAW's "one-unit dash followed by a five-unit space" line type.

Line type translations are not controlled by the CORELDRW.DOT file because all the translations are hard-coded into the PIF import filter.

### Text in PIF Files

Text strings are assigned the monospace typeface if available. In its absence, Toronto will be used. Otherwise, the first font in the font list will be used. The font can easily be changed once the text is imported.

## Lotus PIC (PIC)

### Color

A color in a .PIC file is translated into one of eight colors.

445

**Text**

- All text comes in as editable text.
- All Title text maps to the Toronto typeface and all non-Title text maps to the monospaced typeface.

## Macintosh PICT (PCT)

### Objects

Objects with both a fill and an outline will import as a group of two objects, one being the outline and the other the fill.

### Colors

Many PICT fills are actually bitmap patterns, and CorelDRAW tries to maintain them as bitmap patterns.

### Pattern Outlines

A pattern outline is converted into a solid color.

### Arrowheads and Dashed Lines

Arrowheads and dashed lines are not supported.

### Text

- All text comes in as editable text.
- The Panose font-matching system remaps typefaces not available to the closest available fonts. Unsupported Macintosh fonts are remapped to CorelDRAW's default font.
- Text might not be aligned properly because of changes in font size and spacing. This can be adjusted in CorelDRAW.
- Question marks replace all unsupported characters.
- Bold, italic, outline, and shadow text styles and any combinations are fully supported. Underlined text is not supported.

## Micrographx 2.*x*, 3.*x* (DRW)

- Clip regions are not supported.
- Most raster operations are not supported.
- Gradient and fountain fills are converted to a series of polygons.

## PostScript Interpreted (PS)

This filter utilizes an internal PostScript interpreter to import PostScript files. This allows for all forms of EPS to be fully imported into CorelDRAW and gives users without PostScript printers access to the many PostScript fills.

- If text was exported as text, it should import as editable text. Point size and font information should be properly maintained. Figure 48.2 shows the dialog box that lets you choose how you wish text to be imported.

- Importing a file with large or complex gradient fills might generate a very large number of objects, which can lead to large files and possibly an inability to import the file due to memory limitations.

- The line VMSize=x in the CORELFLT.INI file controls how much memory is allocated for Virtual Memory. The default value is 2, which indicates 2 MB. Increasing this will allow more complex files to be imported.

This format can not be imported using the All Files option, because CorelDRAW is unable to distinguish between the various PostScript formats.

*Figure 48.2.*
*The Import PostScript*
*dialog box.*

## Windows Metafile (WMF)

The Panose font-matching system remaps unavailable fonts to the closest available font.

## WordPerfect Graphic (WPG)

- WPG Version 2 is not fully supported.
- Graphics Text Type 2.
- WPG Version 6 is not supported.

# Bitmap Formats

You can import black-and-white, color, and grayscale bitmap graphics. If you save a color or grayscale bitmap as part of a CDR file, the color and shades of gray are retained.

When importing bitmaps, you can choose to crop or resample the file while importing. Choosing Crop will bring up the dialog box shown in Figure 48.3, which allows you to specify which part of the image to retain.

*Figure 48.3.*
*The Crop Image dialog*
*box.*

Choosing Resample will allow you to enlarge or reduce the file while importing. You'll get the dialog box shown in Figure 48.4.

*Figure 48.4.*
*The Resample Image*
*dialog box.*

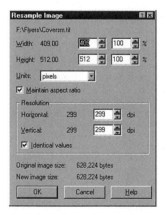

You can adjust the width and height of the image either by measurement or percentage. You can also choose to distort the image by unchecking the Maintain aspect ratio check box.

## Adobe PhotoShop (PSD)

PhotoShop files are fully supported in monochrome, grayscale, and color (including 32-bit).

## CALS Compressed Bitmap (CAL)

CAL files are in a monochrome (1-bit) compressed format.

## Corel PHOTO-PAINT Image (CPT)

CPT files are an RGB TIFF 6.0 format. Support for "floating objects" in a CPT file is only found in Corel PHOTO-PAINT.

## CompuServe Bitmap (GIF)

GIF files conforming to the 87A and 89A specifications can be imported. Interlaced GIF files can not be previewed.

## GEM Paint File (IMG)

GEM IMG files are fully supported.

## JPEG Bitmap (JPG)

The JPEG standard format was developed by the Joint Photographers Experts Group, and it offers superior compression techniques—albeit in a lossy format. This allows large color files to be easily transported between a wide variety of platforms.

## Kodak Photo CD (PCD)

Photo CD format was developed by Eastman Kodak as a way to store 35mm photographs on a compact disc. The files contain multiple resolutions of the same picture, stored in a single compressed file. Some images might be subject to copyright, although CorelDRAW will not display a warning about this.

The dialog box shown in Figure 48.5 enables you to choose which of the following sizes you would like to import:

- Wallet (128×192)
- Snapshot (256×384)
- Standard (512×768)
- Large (1024×1536)
- Poster (2048×3072)
- Billboard (4096×6144)

449

*Figure 48.5.*
*The Photo CD Image*
*dialog box.*

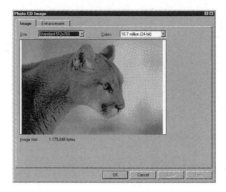

The high-resolution file requires extremely large amounts of memory or disk space to be used as the Billboard file—approximately 48 MB when uncompressed.

You are also given the following choices of color depth:

- 16.7 million colors (24-bit)
- 256 colors (8-bit)
- 16 colors (4-bit)
- 256 grayscale (8-bit)

Images can also be color-corrected (the Enhancement tab) when imported. You have a choice of GamutCD correction or Kodak color correction. These methods are described in the following paragraphs.

GamutCD uses gamut mapping to enhance the color fidelity and tonal ranges of the CD image. The Photo CD Image Enhancement dialog box is shown in Figure 48.6.

The Set active area option allows you to use the mouse to specify an active area within the image in the view field. GamutCD bases its color correction on the selected area so that any black borders left over from the original scan do not affect the correction process.

You can use the Set neutral colors option to define neutral colors by clicking on pure whites, blacks, and grays within the active area.

The Adjust white in image option is for when you have good white elements in the photo. Do not use this option if you do not have a white area, because the picture will be overbright. This option assists GamutCD in enhancing the tonal range of your image and removing color cast. If your white is not pure white, you might want to lower the value in the number box to the right.

*Figure 48.6.*
*The Photo CD Image*
*Enhancement dialog box*
*with GamutCD color*
*correction selected.*

The Adjust black in image option is for when you have good black elements in the photo. Do not use this option if you do not have a black area, because the picture will be overdark. This option assists GamutCD in enhancing the tonal range of your image and in removing color cast. If your black is not pure black, you might want to raise the value in the number box to the right.

Choosing Fast Preview will display the effect that the GamutCD settings you have chosen has on the image.

Choosing Best Preview also will display the effect that the GamutCD settings you have chosen has on the image. This is more accurate than Fast Preview, but it takes longer to display.

An example of the GamutCD correction is shown in the color pages.

Kodak Color Correction enables you to alter color tints, adjust brightness and color saturation, and make adjustments to the level of contrast. The dialog box for making adjustments is shown in Figure 48.7.

You can select the Remove scene balance adjustment option to turn off the scene balance adjustment rather than use the photofinisher when the original image is scanned and placed on the Photo CD disk.

*Figure 48.7.*
*The Photo CD Image*
*Enhancement dialog box*
*with Kodak Color Correc-*
*tion selected.*

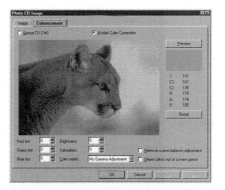

Selecting Color metric allows you to adjust contrast by preset amounts.

Selecting the Show colors out of screen gamut option shows any changes you've made that are too extreme as pure red or pure blue pixels.

Various other settings can be adjusted by moving the sliders for Red tint, Green tint, Blue tint, Brightness, and Saturation.

Be sure that you do not have a version of Kodak's PCDLIB.DLL in the Windows directory, because it will result in an error message or crash with CorelDRAW.

## MACPaint Bitmap (MAC)

MACPaint files are fully supported monochrome bitmaps.

## PaintBrush (PCX)

PCX files of specification 2.5, 2.8, and 3.0 can be imported. They may contain either one-, two-, or four-color planes. Those containing three-color planes cannot be imported.

## Picture Publisher 4 (PP4)

Picture Publisher files are fully supported in monochrome, grayscale, and color.

## Scitex CT Bitmap (SCT)

This filter supports full 32-bit color images and grayscale .ct files.

## Targa Bitmap (TGA)

You can import 16- and 24-bit Targa files in the following variations:

- Uncompressed color-mapped images
- Uncompressed RGB images
- RLE compressed color-mapped images
- RLE compressed RGB images of types 1, 2, 9, and 10 (as defined by AT&T Electronic Photography and Imaging Center)
- Some 32-bit TGAs (but the last 8 bits will be ignored)

## TIFF Bitmap (TIF)

Black-and-white, color, and grayscale TIFF files can be imported up to and including the 6.0 specification. The files can be compressed using the CCITT, Packbits 32773, or LZW compression algorithms. Loading times might be longer on compressed files, because these files must be decoded. TIFF 6.0 files using JPEG compression and CMYK data are supported. Those using the YCbCr are not valid.

## Wavelet Compressed Bitmap (WVL)

Wavelet files are full-color files and are fully supported.

## Windows and OS/2 Bitmaps (BMP)

All BMP files are imported following the Windows BMP specification. Color, grayscale, black-and-white, and even compressed bitmaps (RLE) can be imported.

If the RLE has "bands" that appear where they should not, some editing is required in CORELFLT.INI. In the CORELFLT.INI file's [CorelBMPImport] section, add the following line: `Import Corel30RLE=1`. If this section does not exist in CORELFLT.INI, simply create it.

## Windows 3.x/NT Bitmap, Cursor and Icon Resources (EXE, CUR, ICO)

This imports the bitmaps inside of EXE files. These bitmaps are 32 pixels square at not more than 16 colors. Colors can be selected for transparent and inverse masks.

# Word Processing Filters

Imported text files mirror the original document as much as possible, although not all formatting attributes and layout features are supported. If possible, the features will be simulated. The following features are not supported:

- Headers, footers, footnotes, and endnotes
- Underlining
- Embedded graphics
- Columns
- Tables
- Macros

### Fonts and Character Sets

CorelDRAW attempts to match fonts when importing the file for any format that includes accessible font family information.

All RTF files are converted into the Windows ANSI character set. The Macintosh Character Set and Standard IBM PC Code Page 437 are also supported.

Due to the differences in character sets, not all characters can be properly translated. In these cases, an underscore character will be substituted for the undefined character.

Table 48.2 shows how the various word processor formats translate fonts in CorelDRAW.

**Table 48.2. CorelDRAW word processor font support.**

| Word Processor | From RTF to CorelDRAW |
| --- | --- |
| WordPerfect | All fonts supported |
| Microsoft RTF | All fonts supported |
| Microsoft Word PC | All fonts supported |
| Ami Professional | All fonts supported |
| Microsoft Word for the Macintosh | Limited font support |
| Microsoft Word for Windows | All fonts supported |

*All fonts supported* means that CorelDRAW can support all the font family information provided by that format. *Limited font support* means the application is unable to read some of the font family information because CorelDRAW cannot work with extended font families. Formats that are not listed in Table 48.2 map to the best font available.

## Proportional Fonts Versus Nonproportional Fonts

Because of the spacing differences between proportional and nonproportional fonts, imported documents that specify a proportional font may have more text per page than the original.

## Page Size and Margins

Imported documents do not retain the page size specified in the original document and are fit to the current page size in CorelDRAW.

## Anchored Text and Frames

Anchored text can be properly converted from WordPerfect 5.*x*, Microsoft RTF, Microsoft Word for Windows, Microsoft Word for the Macintosh 4.0 and 5.0, and Ami Professional. All other formats convert the anchored text to regular text.

## Miscellaneous Formatting

- Because CorelDRAW relies on RTF for importing, paragraph alignment applies to the whole paragraph and not to individual lines.
- Documents containing tables of contents and indexes convert into the appropriate functions in RTF.

- Automatic outlining data converts to regular text.
- Style sheets specified in the original document do not import into CorelDRAW styles; however, the formatting specified by the styles applies to the imported text.
- Text contained within a frame or a positioned object is retained.

## Ami Professional 1.1, 1.2, 2.0, 3.0 (SAM)

There are no special considerations.

## ANSI Text (TXT)

This filter imports only true ASCII files. If your word processor is not supported by another filter, export the files to ASCII, specifying text only. All attributes such as bold, italics, and underlining will be ignored. Tabs and indents will be converted to spaces.

## Legacy 1.0, 2.0 (LEG)

There are no special considerations.

## Microsoft Word 3.*x*, 4.*x*, 5.0, 5.5 (DOC)

Endnotes and footnotes are not supported.

## Microsoft Word for Mac 3.0, 4.0, 5.0 (DOC)

Endnotes and footnotes are not supported.

## Microsoft Word for Windows 1.*x*, 2.*x*, 6.0 (DOC)

### General Notes and Limitations

- The embedded field method for building indexes is supported, but the style-implied method is not.
- Word's Normal text style is converted to CorelDRAW's default text style, which is set in the Preferences Text dialog box.
- Characters that are available in the sets Symbol or MS Linedraw are converted to the corresponding PC character set entries when possible.
- Soft line and page breaks often appear in new locations when you convert a monospaced font to a proportionally spaced font.

## Rich Text Format (RTF)

### Unsupported Features

- Table of contents and indexing data
- Frames/positioned objects

## WordPerfect 4.2, 5.x, 6.x for DOS and Windows (*.*)

### General Notes and Limitations

- CorelDRAW does not support text in WordPerfect's table of contents and index functions.
- WordPerfect style sheets are not supported.
- CorelDRAW converts equations and formulas created in WordPerfect's equation language to regular text.
- Graphic features such as HLine and VLine are not supported.

## WordStar 1.x Windows (WS1), 2.0 Windows (WS2)

### Unsupported Features

- Merge dot commands
- Printer dot commands
- Display commands
- Footnotes and endnotes

## WordStar 3.3, 3.31, 3.45, 4.0, 5.0, 6.0, 7.0, 2000 (WSD)

### Unsupported Features

- Merge dot commands
- Printer dot commands
- Display commands
- Footnotes and endnotes

## XyWrite III, III Plus, IV (XY)

There are no special considerations.

# Other Formats

## Lotus Freelance (PRE)

Fonts will be substituted for a similar font available on your system or the default font. Objects in the file will be grouped together and you will have to ungroup them with Arrange Ungroup to edit the individual objects.

## Microsoft PowerPoint (PPT)

Fonts will be substituted for a similar font available on your system or the default font. Objects in the file will be grouped together and you will have to ungroup them with Arrange Ungroup to edit the individual objects.

**Table 48.3. Recommended import formats.**

| Program | Recommended Import Format |
| --- | --- |
| Adobe Illustrator | AI |
| Arts & Letters | AI , Clipboard |
| AutoCAD | DXF, HPGL (PLT files) |
| ASCII text | Clipboard and Paragraph text import |
| CorelDRAW | CDR, Clipboard |
| CorelTRACE | CorelTRACE AI |
| GEM Artline | GEM |
| GEM Graph | GEM |
| GEM Draw Plus | GEM |
| Harvard Graphics | CGM |
| Lotus 1-2-3 | Lotus PIC |
| Lotus Freelance Plus | CGM |
| Macintosh-based vector packages | Macintosh PICT, AI |
| Micrografx Designer, Graph Plus | DRW, AI |
| Scan Gallery | TIF |
| WordPerfect | WPG |

**49**

# Export
# Filters

## Vector Filters

### Adobe Illustrator (AI, EPS)

AI is the native format of Adobe Illustrator and is a subset of the Encapsulated PostScript file format. Not all of the effects CorelDRAW produces are available in the AI format. This export filter uses the dialog box shown in Figure 49.1.

### Limitations

- Fountain fills are exported as a series of filled bands in much the same way as CorelDRAW's blending feature. You can control the number of bands created by using the Preview Fountain Steps option in the Preferences menu.
- Texture fills are exported as solid gray fills.
- Arrowhead line caps are exported as separate objects.
- Fit Text to Path exports each character as a separate text string.
- Text objects containing characters with special attributes (kerning, rotation, typeface changes, and scaling) are exported as separate text objects.

*Figure 49.1.*
*The Adobe Illustrator*
*Export dialog box.*

## Outline Attributes

For accurate reproduction of calligraphic outlines, corner styles, and line caps, select the Calligraphic Text box in the Preferences Text dialog box. Outlines export as a group of polygons to match the outlines in CorelDRAW at the expense of larger file size.

## Bitmaps

Bitmaps are not supported.

## General Notes and Suggestions

- Objects should not be combined so the export conversion is easier.
- If the drawing will require future editing, you should do it in CorelDRAW to avoid the complexities added during the conversion.
- Files that will be imported into layout packages should be exported as EPS files. They will print much better this way.

## Text

Exported text can be sent as editable text if the necessary fonts are available in Illustrator. Otherwise, the text should be sent as Curves.

# Adobe Type 1 (PFB) and TrueType (TTF) Fonts

These filters use the dialog boxes shown in Figures 49.2, 49.3, 49.4, and 49.5. The dialog boxes are almost exactly the same for PostScript and TrueType except for the values they use. See Skill Session 42, "Creating Your Own Fonts," for more information on how to use these dialog boxes.

*Figure 49.2.*
*The Adobe Type 1 Export*
*Options dialog box.*

*Figure 49.3.*
*The Adobe Type 1 Export*
*dialog box.*

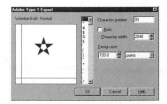

*Figure 49.4.*
*The TrueType Export*
*Options dialog box.*

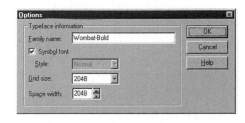

*Figure 49.5.*
*The TrueType Export*
*dialog box.*

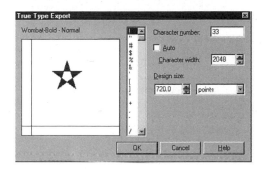

## Limitations

- Type 1 and TrueType fonts are exported with no hinting.

- Exported characters must be composed of only one object each. This can be accomplished by combining the various pieces using Arrange | Combine.

- Avoid lines that intersect. Objects should be either completely inside or outside other objects.

- Fill and outline attributes are not supported.

- Adobe Type 1 fonts can be used only with Adobe Type Manager Version 2.0 and higher.

## AutoCAD (DXF)

### CorelDRAW Features

- Calligraphic pen effects, dashed and dotted lines, and all line weights are converted to solid lines, 0.003 inch thick.
- Bitmaps are not supported.
- Layers information is not supported.

### Texture Fills

Texture-filled objects are filled with a solid gray fill. All other fills are not supported.

### Objects with No Outlines

Filled objects that have no outlines have an outline added when they're exported.

### File Size

Files can grow quite large when they're exported from CorelDRAW to the DXF format. An increase in size of more than ten times is not uncommon.

When you export to DXF, you are presented with the dialog box shown in Figure 49.6, which allows you to adjust several settings.

*Figure 49.6.*
*The DXF Export dialog box.*

### Colors

- Standard Colors (7): Matches colors in the CorelDRAW file to the seven colors available in DXF.
- Full Colors (255): These files may most closely represent the original CorelDRAW file, but they are heavily dependent on the video driver being used by AutoCAD.

### Curve Resolution

The curve resolution factor can be set to a value between 0.0 and 1.0 inch, with an accuracy of up to eight decimal places. A setting of 0 provides the best resolution, at the cost of file size. The default value of 0.004 inches is recommended.

### Text

Text is exported as curves to maintain its appearance. Therefore, it is not editable.

## Computer Graphics Metafile (CGM)

The CGM Export dialog box is shown in Figure 49.7.

*Figure 49.7.*
*The CGM Export dialog*
*box.*

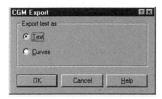

### Unsupported CorelDRAW Features

- ■ PostScript textures (converted to solid gray fills)
- ■ Bitmaps

### Fountain Fills

You can control the number of bands used when exporting fountain fills by using the Preview Fountain Steps setting in the Preferences View dialog box.

## Corel Presentation Exchange (CMX)

This format is transportable between various Corel applications. Version 5 is a 16-bit implementation and version 6 is a 32-bit implementation. The only difference between CMX and Corel's native CDR format is that any live effects will not transfer to CMX. As an example, blends would be converted to three separate objects: one for each end and a group of objects between the two ends.

## Encapsulated PostScript (EPS)

Although CorelDRAW can import the EPS files it creates as editable files using the Interpreted PostScript import filter, it is a good idea to save the original CDR file if you want to edit it later. The EPS Export dialog box is shown in Figure 49.8.

Figure 49.8.
The EPS Export dialog
box.

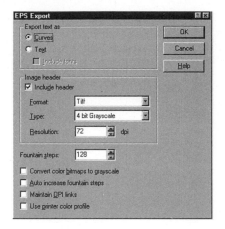

## Image Header Size

An image header can be included with your EPS file. It will be displayed on-screen for placement purposes. Supported headers include the following: TIFF 5.0, 1 KB, monochrome; TIFF 5.0, 2 KB, monochrome; TIFF 5.0, 4 KB, color; TIFF 5.0, 8 KB, color; TIFF 4.2, 1 KB, monochrome; TIFF 4.2, 2 KB, monochrome; TIFF 4.2, 4 KB, color; and TIFF 4.2, 8 KB, color. CorelDRAW 6 has added the ability to include a WMF header as well. This is very useful because it will give a much better representation on-screen, as well as printing better to non-PostScript printers. The downfall is that it is not supported in all software when importing, such as Corel Ventura 5.0.

Some programs have a limitation on the size of the image header they are able to import, and therefore you may receive an error message stating that the file you're trying to bring in is too large. To minimize file size, choose a low-resolution image header, such as the TIFF 4.2 (mono) when exporting.

## Corel*NOTE!*

> Remember that the header is only for display purposes and does not affect the resolution of the output whatsoever. Also note that EPS files print only on PostScript devices. On non-PostScript printers, the header will be printed instead.

## File Contents

EPS files exported from CorelDRAW contain the filename, the program name, and the date. CorelDRAW automatically determines the size of the bounding box.

## Text

- If you want to use PostScript typefaces in place of CorelDRAW's typefaces, make sure all the necessary fonts have been downloaded to your printer.

- CorelDRAW embeds the fonts used in the EPS file if you choose the Include Fonts check box. No fonts are downloaded if Text as Curves is chosen.

- Fonts that are not found in the printer output as Courier or else they do not print.

# Enhanced Windows Metafile (EMF)

## Unsupported CorelDRAW! Features

- PostScript functions, including PostScript texture fills and halftone screens, are not supported.

- Two-color and full-color patterns appear as gray in the EMF file.

- Texture fills exported as solid gray fills.

## EMF File Complexity

An EMF file can be very large if the drawing contains several curves or large amounts of text. Some programs, such as Ventura Publisher and PageMaker, impose limits on the size of imported files and can have problems with these files.

# GEM File (GEM)

GEM saves files in a vector format usable in GEM Artline, Delrina Perform, and Ventura Publisher (versions 2.0 through 4.2). When you export GEM files, you see the dialog box shown in Figure 49.9.

*Figure 49.9.*
*The GEM Export dialog box.*

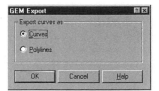

## Limitations

- Fills, outlines, arrowheads, and segments in dotted and dashed lines are exported as separate polygons.

- Fountain fills are very grainy because of the limited color availability in GEM.

- Texture fills are exported as solid gray fills.

- Breaks may occur when outlines come to a point. This depends on the size of the objects, the thickness of the outline, and the angle at which the outline meets at the point.
- Text is exported as curves and is not editable.
- Colors are mapped to the 16 colors GEM supports.
- Because of limits in the number of objects the GEM format supports, some files are not completely exported. Decreasing the complexity of the drawing may alleviate this problem.

### Unsupported Features

- Bitmaps
- Bitmap pattern fills
- PostScript textures (converted to uniform mid-gray fills)
- Corners (joins) appear round in GEM Artline
- Dotted and dashed lines

### Bézier Curves

Not all applications can work with Bézier curves; therefore, they are converted to line segments. Curves with more than 128 segments are broken into smaller grouped objects.

When the objects are broken and imported back into CorelDRAW, construction lines appear. These show only in wireframe mode and do not print.

In GEM Artline, the objects that appear to be individual are actually groups of smaller objects.

## HPGL Plotter File (PLT)

This format is very handy for those who will be using sign and glass cutters. You are presented with a dialog box containing three separate sections, as shown in Figures 49.10, 49.11, and 49.12.

*Figure 49.10.*
*The Pen Options section of the HPGL Export dialog box.*

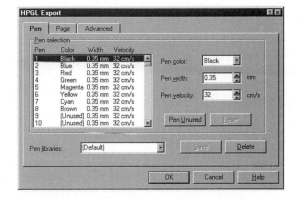

*Figure 49.11.*
*The Page Options section of the HPGL Export dialog box.*

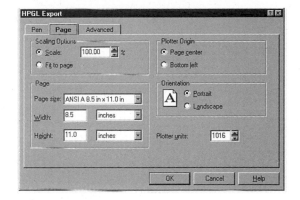

*Figure 49.12.*
*The Advanced Options section of the HPGL Export dialog box.*

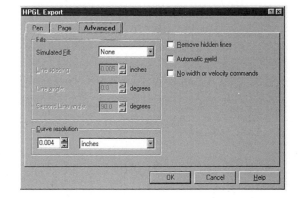

### Unsupported Features

■ All fills are ignored except for texture fills, which are converted to solid gray fills.

■ Bitmaps are not supported.

### Limitations

■ Dotted and dashed lines convert to the standard HPGL line types.

■ Bézier curves are converted to line segments.

■ Outlines are exported with a pen width of 1.0. Thickness and calligraphic settings are not supported.

### Colors

The colors exported to HPGL files are controlled by the pen numbers assigned to the file. These pen colors can be controlled in the Pen Options section of CorelDRAW's HPGL Export dialog box, which is shown in Figure 49.9. Adjust the settings so that they correspond to the colors of the pens in the plotter.

### Page Size and Orientation

To properly position the image when plotting it, verify that the page size and orientation specified in CorelDRAW match those of the plotter. You can change the page orientation in the Page Options section of the HPGL Export dialog box, shown in Figure 49.10.

### Unoutlined Objects

Any filled object that has no outline has one added when it is exported.

### Text

To maintain its appearance, text is automatically converted to curves when it is exported.

## IBM PIF (PIF)

The PIF Export dialog box is shown in Figure 49.13.

Figure 49.13.
The PIF Export dialog box.

## Limitations

- Colors are mapped to the best available color from PIF's 16-color palette.
- Because of the limited palette, fountain fills do not render well.
- Texture fills are converted to solid gray fills.

## Outline Attributes

For accurate reproduction of calligraphic outlines, corner styles, and line caps, select the Calligraphic Text box in the Preferences Text dialog box. Outlines export as a group of polygons to match the outlines in CorelDRAW, at the expense of a larger file size.

- Objects created using the calligraphic pen
- Line caps
- Custom outline thicknesses

## Unsupported CorelDRAW! Features

- PostScript textures
- Bitmaps
- Two-color and full-color pattern fills

## Text

To maintain its appearance, text is automatically converted to curves when it is exported. This text is not editable. The text can be exported as text if you check the Export Text As Text radio button.

# Macintosh PICT (PCT)

The PICT Export dialog box is shown in Figure 49.14.

*Figure 49.14.*
*The PICT Export dialog*
*box.*

### Outline Attributes

For accurate reproduction of calligraphic outlines, corner styles, and line caps, select the Calligraphic Text box in the Preferences Text dialog box. Outlines export as a group of polygons to match the outlines in CorelDRAW, at the expense of a larger file size.

- Calligraphic pen effects
- Line caps

Calligraphic effects and line caps appear as separate objects grouped with the line to which they are applied.

### Unsupported CorelDRAW! Features

- Bitmaps
- PostScript texture fills (exported as gray fills)
- Two-color and full-color pattern fills

### Objects with Fills and Outlines

A filled object with an outline exports as a group of two objects: one object is the outline, and the other is the fill.

Outlines on text are exported only when you convert the text to curves prior to export by choosing Arrange | Convert to Curves

### Fountain Fills

You determine the number of steps in fountain fills by using the Preview Fountain Steps setting in Preferences.

### Colors

The colors available on the Mac are dependent on the type of display used. A display that uses eight-bit color is limited to 256 colors. A display that uses 24-bit color displays colors that are virtually identical to those of the original file.

## Text

To maintain its appearance, text is automatically converted to curves when it is exported. This text is not editable. The text can be exported as text if you check the Export Text As Text radio button.

# SCODL (SCD)

The SCODL Export dialog box is shown in Figure 49.15.

*Figure 49.15.*
*The SCODL Export*
*dialog box.*

## The Outline Attributes Option

For accurate reproduction of calligraphic outlines, corner styles, and line caps, select the Calligraphic Text box in the Preferences Text dialog box. Outlines export as a group of polygons to match the outlines in CorelDRAW, at the expense of a larger file size. The following attributes are affected by this setting:

- Corner types
- Calligraphic pen effects
- Line caps and arrows
- Fountain fills

## Unsupported CorelDRAW Features

- PostScript textures
- Bitmaps
- Two-color and full-color pattern fills

## Producing Slides with Full PostScript Effects

Agfa-Matrix offers an Adobe PostScript RIP (Raster Image Processor) for their film recorders. This virtually eliminates the limitations above. Check to see if your service bureau offers this option.

## Aspect Ratio

For proper slide output, the page size should be set to 7.33"×11". If the page size is set to another value, change to this page size option and resize the elements on the page to fit within the page borders.

### Working in Portrait Orientation

To produce slides in portrait orientation, follow these steps:

1. Select Slide as the page size in the Page Setup dialog box.
2. Select Custom and change the orientation to Portrait. Do not change the page dimensions.
3. After you complete the drawing, change the orientation back to Landscape.
4. Select all objects and rotate them 90 degrees in the drawing.
5. Choose Export.

## Windows Metafile (WMF)

The WMF Export dialog box is shown in Figure 49.16.

*Figure 49.16. The WMF Export dialog box.*

### Unsupported CorelDRAW Features

- PostScript functions, including PostScript texture fills and halftone screens
- Bitmaps
- Two-color and full-color patterns (appear as gray in the WMF file)
- Texture fills (exported as solid gray fills)

### WMF File Complexity

A WMF file can be very large if the drawing contains several curves or a large amount of text. Some programs, such as Ventura Publisher and PageMaker, impose limits on the size of imported files and can have problems with these files.

### Image Header

An image header can be included with the exported WMF file. This makes it possible to view the contents of the file in programs such as PageMaker, Ventura, and Word for Windows. This can make the WMF file impossible to read by certain applications not designed to handle it.

### Fountain Fills

The number of steps in fountain fills is determined by the Preview Fountain Steps setting in the Preferences View dialog box.

## WordPerfect Graphic (WPG)

The WPG Export dialog box is shown in Figure 49.17.

*Figure 49.17.*
*The WPG Export*
*dialog box.*

### Outline Attributes

For accurate reproduction of calligraphic outlines, corner styles, and line caps, select the Calligraphic Text box in the Preferences Text dialog box. Outlines export as a group of polygons to match the outlines in CorelDRAW, at the expense of a larger file size.

### Fountain Fills

Fountain fills tend to contain coarse banding.

### Unsupported CorelDRAW Features

- PostScript texture fills and halftone screens
- Bitmaps
- Texture fills

### Colors

The number of colors exported is set in the Export WPG dialog box.

- 16 Colors: Matches colors in the CorelDRAW file to a standard set of 16 colors. Choosing this option usually yields acceptable results on a VGA display.
- 256 Colors: Provides a truer representation of your CorelDRAW file, although the results vary depending on the video adapter and driver used in WordPerfect. The colors may appear as shades of gray. In this case, export the file again with the 16 colors option selected.

### Text

To maintain its appearance, text is automatically converted to curves when it is exported. This text is not editable. The text can be exported as text if you check the Export Text As Text radio button when exporting.

## Bitmap Filters

### Scaling Bitmaps

Due to the nature of bitmaps, they degrade in quality when they are enlarged. Shrinking them usually does not degrade the quality, but disk space is wasted. All bitmap exports use the dialog box shown in Figure 49.18.

# Corel *TIP!*

Rather than exporting from CorelDRAW to a bitmap, you will receive better results by opening the CDR file in PHOTO-PAINT and saving to the desired format.

*Figure 49.18.*
*The Bitmap Export*
*dialog box.*

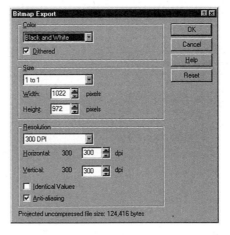

### File Size

Bitmaps should be exported in the correct size according to where they will be placed. A full-page bitmap exported at 300 dpi can take over 24 MB of disk space. Many times, 300-dpi resolution is overkill for the intended use.

## Compression Schemes

Compression applies only to images that are 16 color, 256 color, 16 gray, or 256 gray (that is, four- or eight-bit images).

## Fountain Fills

The number of steps in a fountain fill is controlled by the Preview Fountain Steps setting in the Preferences View dialog box.

## CALS Compressed Bitmap (CAL)

CCITT Group 4 compression

## CompuServe Bitmap (GIF)

After the Bitmap Export dialog box shown in Figure 49.18, you will see the dialog box shown in Figure 49.19. By checking the Interlaced image option from this dialog box, you can save the GIF file in an interlaced format for use on the Internet. You can also specify that a particular color of the image becomes transparent by checking the Transparent color option and then selecting the desired color from the palette. All GIF files use the LZW compression method.

*Figure 49.19.*
*The GIF Transparent*
*Color dialog box.*

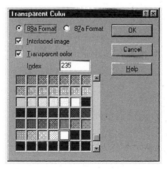

## Corel PHOTO-PAINT Image (CPT)

One-bit files (black and white) use Huffman, CCITT Group 3-Dim-1, CCITT Group 3-Dim 2, or CCITT Group 4 compression. However, four-bit files (16 colors) and higher use RLE/Packbit or LZW compression.

## GEM Paint File (IMG)

RLE encoding

## JPEG Bitmap (JPG)

After the Bitmap Export dialog box shown in Figure 49.18, you will receive the dialog box shown in Figure 49.20.

CorelDRAW supports two flavors of JPEG: JPEG File Interchange Format and JPEG TIFF. Each of them has subformats that control the amount of compression. The Quality Factor that you choose controls the size of the file, but the size is inversely related to the quality. To get a high-quality file, you will need more hard drive space. Note that JPEG is a "lossy" format, meaning that some of the quality is lost, and so reopening a JPEG file will not produce a file as good as the original.

*Figure 49.20.*
*The JPEG Export*
*dialog box.*

### MACPaint Bitmap (MAC)

RLE encoding

### OS/2 Bitmap (BMP)

All files use RLE encoding. You can choose between Standard v1.3 and Enhanced v2.0 in the dialog box shown in Figure 49.21.

*Figure 49.21.*
*The OS/2 BMP Export*
*dialog box.*

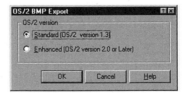

### Paintbrush (PCX)

RLE (PCX version 3.0) encoding

### Scitex CT Bitmap (SCT)

No compression

## Targa Bitmap (TGA)

Either RLE-compressed color-mapped images or RLE-compressed.

■ RGB images (types 9 and 10, as defined by AT&T Electronic Photography and Imaging Center) 24-bit color TGA files are exported as RLE-compressed RGB bitmaps. Compressed TGA files are supported by few applications.

You can choose between Normal and Enhanced file format in the dialog box shown in Figure 49.22.

*Figure 49.22.*
*The TGA Export*
*dialog box.*

## TIFF Bitmap (TIF)

Supports either LZW v4.2, 5.0, or 6.0. CMYK files will automatically use v6.0; 24-bit files automatically use v5.0, and eight-bit files will automatically use v4.2.

## Wavelet Compressed Bitmap (WVL)

Wavelet files use their own WVL compression which can be specified in the dialog box shown in Figure 49.23. The higher the number, the lower the quality of the image.

*Figure 49.23.*
*The Wavelet Export*
*dialog box.*

## Windows Bitmap (BMP)

RLE (Run-Length Encoding)

This format is not universally supported and may cause problems in many applications.

# Clipboard Pasting Limitation

## Features

Objects containing the following effects are not supported when they are pasted into non-Corel applications:

- PostScript textures
- Pattern fills

## Unsupported Metafile Features

Objects using the following Windows Metafile features, cut-and-copied to the Clipboard from other programs, are not supported when you try to paste them into CorelDRAW:

- Background commands (SetBkMode and SetBkColor)
- Pattern fills (only uniform fills are currently supported)
- Clipping regions
- Flood fills
- Individual pixel manipulations
- ROP2 modes, except R2_COPYPEN (that is, you cannot combine pen colors)
- WINDING polygon fill mode (ALTERNATE mode is supported)

## Pasting Text

The number of characters, their spacing, and the text attributes that are assigned by CorelDRAW vary depending on the font used and available memory.

Artistic text uses CorelDRAW's default spacing, which is zero percent for intercharacter, zero percent for interword, and 100 percent for interline. The attributes assigned are the current defaults. Paragraph text spacing is the default, just as with Artistic text, unless changes have been made in the Text Spacing dialog box.

Pasted text is automatically treated as Paragraph text, unless you first click on the Text tool and then on the page.

# Recommended Export Formats

**Table 49.1. Recommended export formats for layout and word processing packages without editing capabilities.**

| Program | PostScript Printers | Non-PostScript Printers |
|---|---|---|
| Ami Professional | EPS | WMF |
| Delrina Perform | GEM | GEM |
| PageMaker | EPS | WMF |
| Corel Ventura | EPS | CMX |
| WordPerfect | EPS | WPG |

**Table 49.2. Recommended export formats for page layout and desktop publishing packages with graphics editing capabilities.**

| Program | Recommended Format |
|---|---|
| Adobe Illustrator | AI |
| Arts & Letters | WMF, EPS (using Decipher) |
| AutoCAD | DXF |
| GEM Artline | GEM |
| Macintosh-based vector programs | Macintosh PICT, AI |
| Micrografx Designer | CGM |
| PC Paintbrush | PCX |

**Table 49.3. Recommended export formats for graphics devices.**

| Device | Recommended Format |
|---|---|
| Matrix, Genegraphic Solataire film recorders | SCODL (if PostScript compatibility is not available) |
| Computer-driven cutters, machines, and plotters | HPGL or DXF outlines |

# 50

# Printing

Printing is probably the most important function of CorelDRAW because it isn't feasible to haul a computer around everywhere to show off a drawing. Printing is also one of the most difficult topics to fully understand, especially with all the new pre-press functionality that has been added to CorelDRAW 6.

## Print Dialog Box

The appearance of the Print dialog box (see Figure 50.1) is dramatically different than in earlier versions of CorelDRAW. The dialog box now lets you quickly print something, and most of the extra settings have been moved to the Options dialog box.

The top third of the dialog box relates to the printer to which you will be printing. The Name drop-down list shows all the printers currently installed on your machine. Just because a printer is installed does not mean that you actually have that printer. Quite often you will have several extra printers installed that are used when creating files for services bureaus. Just below the Name drop-down list is an area that describes the status, type, connection, and any comments regarding the selected printer.

At the bottom right of the Printer section of the dialog box are two check boxes, labeled Print to File and For Mac. The main use for the first check box is to prepare a file for outputting at a service bureau. The For Mac check box strips the Ctrl+D characters from the files being printed to disk. Because the Ctrl+D is the Macintosh end-of-file character, these files *will not output properly from a Macintosh* unless this box is checked. You can always check For Mac, because the lack of the Ctrl+D characters has no effect whatsoever on files that are output from a PC.

Figure 50.1.
*The Print dialog box.*

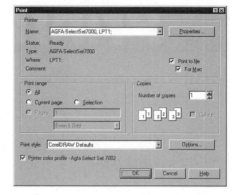

The Properties button to the right of the Printer name is for making changes to the printer's settings. The dialog box you see will depend on the printer you have selected, because each printer's properties are different. Figure 50.2 shows the properties for an Agfa SelectSet 7000 imagesetter, Figure 50.3 shows the properties for a Hewlett-Packard LaserJet 4 Plus laser printer, and Figure 50.4 shows the properties of an Epson Color Stylus ink jet printer.

Figure 50.2.
*Properties dialog box of an Agfa SelectSet 7000 imagesetter.*

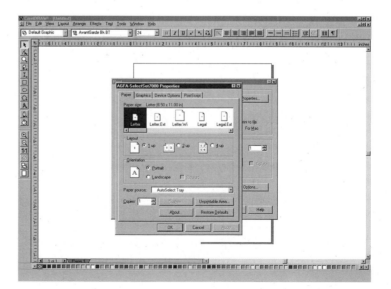

*Figure 50.3.*
*Properties dialog box of a*
*Hewlett-Packard LaserJet*
*4 Plus laser printer.*

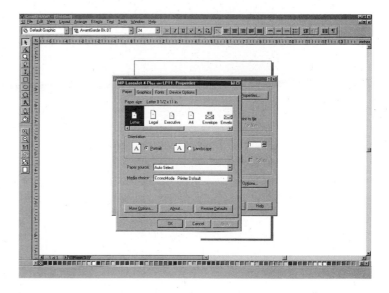

*Figure 50.4.*
*Properties dialog box of an*
*Epson Color Stylus ink jet*
*printer.*

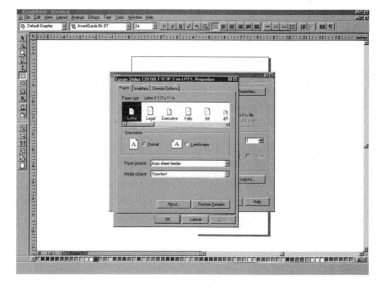

Note that many of the settings for each printer are the same. Two of the more important things that you should set are the size of the paper to be used and the orientation of the page. If you will be printing a page to a printer and you want items such as crop marks and registration marks to print, you must choose a paper size larger than the document you have created.

# Corel*NOTE!*

There are times when you will print a page indicated as Portrait even though the page is wider than tall, and vice versa. Some imagesetters and software programs expect you to print this way. Adobe Acrobat Distiller will definitely need all files printed as Portrait no matter what their size, or the page will automatically rotate the page 90 degrees, thus making it sideways on-screen.

The Print Range section of the dialog box is where you choose which pages and objects you want to print. This can include the whole document, the current page, selected objects on the current page, or a range of pages specified in a text box. If a hyphen (-) is used between page numbers, all pages from the first number to the last number are included. Commas can be used to separate individual page numbers or ranges of page numbers. You can also choose whether to print Even and Odd pages, just Even, or just Odd. This allows you to manually print on both sides of paper. To do this, print all the odd pages, flip the paper over, and then print all the even pages.

# Corel*TIP!*

Selecting certain objects and then printing can help you find a complex object that isn't printing. Select fewer objects until the offending object(s) can be identified and then rework them until they print reliably. You can find stray spot colors the same way.

To the right of the Print range section is the Copies section. Here you will find the setting for the number of copies to be printed. The copies are collated if you check the Collate Copies check box at the bottom right. The graphic will give you a visual clue about how the pages will emerge from your printer.

If you have predefined a Print style, you can chose that style from the drop-down list at the bottom of the dialog. The creation of Print styles is discussed later in this Skill Session. Below the Print Styles setting is the name of the color profile being used and a check box to disable the color profile. This is defined in the Color Manager dialog box, discussed in Skill Session 68, "Color Management."

The very bottom of the dialog box contains three buttons: OK, Cancel, and Help. OK starts the printing, Cancel takes you back to your drawing, and Help provides you with information on printing.

Just above these three buttons is the Options button. The Options button brings up the Print Options dialog box, shown in Figure 50.5. The right half of the dialog box is actually separated into three different sections, labeled Layout, Separations, and Options. The Layout section is pictured in Figure 50.5. Other sections are shown and discussed later in this skill session.

The left half of the Print Options dialog box remains static, regardless of which section is chosen. Most of this half is taken up by the preview of the image to be printed. The preview portion of the dialog box is bounded at the top and the left by rulers. A dotted line around the page indicates the printable area of the page and is shown as a white rectangle with a folded-down corner. These boundaries indicate, before printing, whether all the objects will appear on the printout. Below the preview are left and right arrows to manipulate the view to other pages on multipage documents.

*Figure 50.5.*
*The Layout section of the*
*Print Options dialog box.*

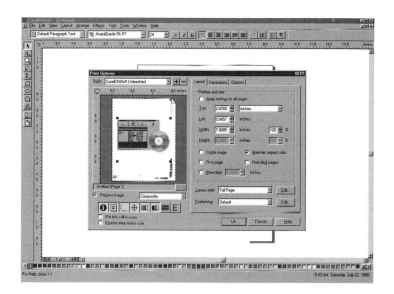

Initially your image will be displayed as a gray box with an X through it. This indicates the bounding box for your image. If you want to see the actual image, place a check in the Preview Image check box. This image is not always necessary, so turning the Preview Image check box off can significantly save time during the print cycle. To the right of Preview Image is a drop-down list of the color you want to preview. This defaults to Composite and can be changed only if you have selected to print color separations. If so, you can choose to view any of the colors contained in the drawing separately.

Below the preview image is a series of eight buttons. From left to right, they are File Information, Page Number, Crop Marks, Registration Marks, Color Bar, Densitometer, Negative, and Emulsion. These control the printing of many marks that are useful when you output to imagesetters and color separations. It's a good idea to turn on the first six attributes even when only one of them is required. All six of these marks appear outside the document page, and therefore will not interfere with the drawing.

You use the File Information button to print the filename, date and time, color profile, and screen and color separation information. This information normally prints outside the document page, but if you check the File info within page check box, it's printed within the page. The Page Number button will print the page number at the bottom of each page. Crop marks are used to indicate the edges of the document page. These are especially useful when you are printing to imagesetters that use continuous rolls of paper. Without crop marks, it can be very difficult to tell where the page falls. Add crop marks by pressing the Crop Mark button. When printing multiple copies of the same image on the same page, you can check the Exterior crop marks only check box so the internal crop marks do not print on the image. You use registration marks to align the various sheets of color separations so the colors properly align. They are added when the Registration button is pressed. Note that you can control the type of registration marks used by making an adjustment to the Registration Mark Type in the Option Special Settings section of the Print dialog box. You use the Color button to print the colors red, green, blue, cyan, magenta, and yellow for calibrating the color output with actual color swatches. This can be used to make sure that the color is being produced properly on a particular output device. You use the Densitometer button to print a scale of each color from 0 to 100 percent so the consistency of output can be checked from one sheet of film to another.

# Corel *NOTE!*

It's common for users to suspect a bug in the print function when the reference marks don't show on the printed page. This is normally because the marks show only when the printable area of a page is larger than the document page.

Use the Negative button to create a negative version of the file, which is very useful when you're outputting film for color separations. When you press the Emulsion button, the image prints with the emulsion side of the film down; when the Emulsion button is not pressed, the image prints with the emulsion side up. The choice of negative is a value that your offset printer should provide when asking for film. Note that your service bureau might want to do this part themselves. If the printer were to make a negative of your negative, you would get a positive and would probably be upset. Ask before using these last two settings.

# Corel *TIP!*

> The Emulsion button can be very handy for screen printers who need to print a reverse image to press onto a shirt or a mug.

By checking the Apply settings to all pages button, all changes you make will affect all pages. Otherwise, your changes will affect only the currently displayed page. The Top, Left, Width, and Height text boxes can be used to precisely position the objects on the page. If Maintain Aspect ratio is checked, adjusting either the width or height automatically adjusts the other measurement. If it isn't checked, the height and width can be changed independently, which distorts your image. Either of these measurements can be adjusted with exact amounts or percentages relative to the original drawing.

The Center image check box centers the printable objects on the page. This controls both horizontal and vertical centering. The Fit to page check box stretches the image to fill the printable area of the page. This provides the largest possible size without requiring you to make adjustments manually, but will be distorted if the Maintain aspect ratio check box isn't checked. The Print tiled pages check box can tile an object that's larger than the printable area on multiple pages so it can be pieced back together. This can come in very handy for proofing tabloid pages or banners. By checking the Bleed limit check box, you can specify the amount your image can bleed past the edge of the page.

The Layout box gives you the choice of several specialized printing formats for producing cards, books, and booklets. These impose pages onto a page of film so that all pages are rotated and moved without making you do a lot of extra work in CorelDRAW. Each panel is created as a separate page in CorelDRAW, and the print engine pieces them together in the appropriate places and rotations. By clicking on the Edit button, you can create your own custom imposition. The Edit Layout Style dialog box is shown in Figure 50.6.

At the top of the Edit Layout Style dialog box, you can specify the number of pages across and down that will appear on a sheet. If you want to have white space between the pages, change the Horizontal and Vertical gutter values to the amount of space that you desire.

After you've added pages, you can adjust their appearance. Click on a page, and now you can assign a page number to it and rotate the page 180 degrees. In the example shown in Figure 50.6, pages 1 and 4 will be on the outside when folded, and pages 2 and 3 will be on the inside.

*Figure 50.6.*
*The Edit Layout Style*
*dialog box.*

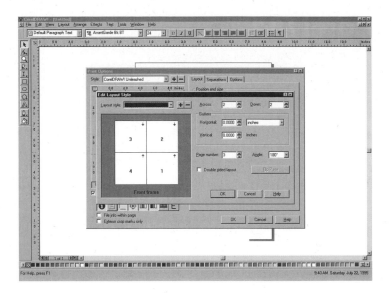

You might want to create a custom imposition for both the front and back of a sheet of paper (or film). In this case, choose the Double sided layout option. The Flip Page button will switch between the Front frame and Back frame as they are labeled in the preview window.

Once you've created the imposition you want, click on the Add (+) button at the top of the dialog box, and you will be prompted for a name. This will permanently add your custom imposition design to the list of Layout styles. If you want to delete a particular style, click on the Delete (-) button.

You can also edit the positioning of your images on a page. Initially, the only listing for Positioning is that of Default. After you've customized some settings for Positioning, they will be listed here as well. Customize settings by clicking on the Edit button next to Positioning. You will see a dialog box similar to that shown in Figure 50.7.

At the top of the Edit Positioning dialog box are text boxes for the number of rows and columns of the same object that will be printed. The best example of this is for printing business cards. Quickly create a custom page, 2 inches high and 3.5 inches wide (hint: Layout Page Setup). Put a couple of pieces of text and a graphic on the page so that it resembles a business card. Now enter 4 in the Rows box and 2 in the Columns box. Check the Clone Frame check box, and you'll have 8-up business cards all ready to print. If you have enabled crop marks, the cards will have the individual crops next to them as well. The Gutter Width setting enables you to place a gutter between the various items, but in this case it would be best to leave it at 0. The Maintain document page size check box means that the page you are cloning will not be enlarged or reduced.

Figure 50.7.
*The Edit Positioning
dialog box.*

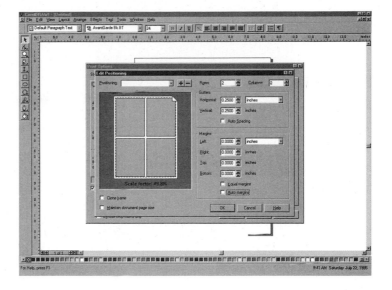

The Separations section of the Print Options dialog box is shown in Figure 50.8.
The first check box is Print Separations. This controls whether the document is
printed as a composite drawing on one page or separated into individual colors on
multiple pages. By checking the box just below it, each separation can be printed
in color rather than in black and white. This can be useful if you're outputting to a
transparency. This option is available only when you print to a color device;
otherwise, it's grayed out.

Figure 50.8.
*The Separations section of
the Print Options dialog
box.*

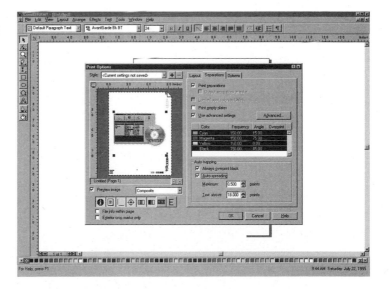

The Convert spot colors to CMYK check box automatically converts a spot color into the four process colors. This is very useful when you're printing a piece that has previously been specified in spot colors. Changing the drawing might take several hours, whereas this check box enables you to do the work on the fly, without affecting the original drawing. Note that this conversion process can produce colors that are much different than the spot colors—and therefore should be used with great caution. This option is grayed out if no spot colors were used in the image. If you want to have colors printed even if they are not used, check the Print empty plates check box.

Checking the Use advanced settings check box ungrays the Advanced button, which enables you to enter custom screen angles and frequencies. The Advanced Separations Settings dialog box is shown in Figure 50.9.

*Figure 50.9.*
*The Advanced Separa-*
*tions Settings dialog box.*

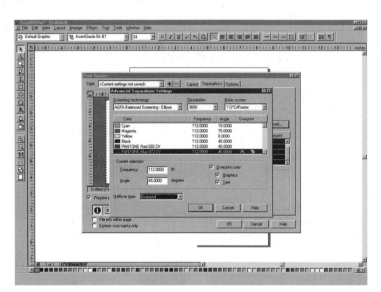

Many custom screening technologies are included with CorelDRAW. You can access them through the drop-down Screening technology box, such as the AGFA Balanced Screening–Ellipse method shown. Choose the technology to be used, and the angles are reflected in the bottom part of the dialog box. After you choose a technology, you can select an output resolution and basic screen resolution in the other drop-down list boxes. For those who want to edit the frequencies and angles themselves, select the color you wish to change (now including spot colors) and enter the desired frequency and angle. You can also set any color to overprint either graphics or text by simply checking the check boxes at the right of the dialog box. At the bottom of the dialog box is the Halftone Type drop-down list box, which controls the shape of the halftone dots.

The Screen Frequencies and Angles section controls the screen angles of each of the process colors and the screen frequency at which they print. These numbers are usually loaded from the various INI files found in the COREL60\PROGRAMS\DATA directory to optimize the angles and frequencies for the screen frequency specified in the Options dialog box. Many imagesetters automatically substitute their preferred angles for whatever is included in the file, so using specialized angles and frequencies is not always necessary.

In the Separations section, a list box lists all the colors used in the drawing and shows a swatch of each color, its frequency, angle, and whether or not it will overprint. When process colors are used, all four colors are automatically listed, even if some are not used. Only the colors used in the document are highlighted and therefore printed. You can select and deselect individual colors by clicking on their names, and you can add multiple colors by clicking on the names while pressing the Ctrl key or the Shift key.

Auto Trapping provides the capability of automatically creating traps. Always Overprint Black controls whether the color black always prints on top of other colors. This can be useful for overlapping black outlines and black type on a colored background. Auto-Spreading automatically creates spread traps, where the inside object is enlarged slightly to overlap the outside object. When this option is activated, the Maximum parameters box becomes enabled. This specifies how much the objects are allowed to spread. The default setting is 0.5 points. New to CorelDRAW 6 is another parameters box that determines the minimum point size of text the auto-spread traps will affect. The default value is 18 points.

The Options section of the Print Options dialog box is shown in Figure 50.10. It contains settings for adjusting the quality and complexity of the image.

*Figure 50.10.*
*The Options section of the*
*Print Options dialog box.*

The Fountain Steps setting controls how many levels of gray are printed. This value can range anywhere from 1 to 2000, but the limit for most PostScript devices is 256. This also is dependent on the output resolution of the printer and the screen frequency. Skill Session 53 "Preparing for Printing," discusses the relationship between these numbers.

# Corel*NOTE!*

> Increasing the number of fountain steps increases the complexity of a file. This can cause problems in outputting complex files to a high-resolution device and can also significantly increase print times.

The Screen Frequency text box controls the density of the line screen for outputting the image. This value depends on the output resolution of the device on which the file will be printed. This option is grayed out if you are not printing to a PostScript printer. For more information on setting a proper line screen, see Skill Session 53 or ask your printer. Because this setting can be changed elsewhere, it might display Custom; you should not change it here. Just below these two settings is the PostScript Preferences button. Clicking on it will produce the dialog box shown in Figure 50.11. The PostScript Preferences button is only available if you are printing to a PostScript printer.

*Figure 50.11.*
*The PostScript Preferences*
*dialog box.*

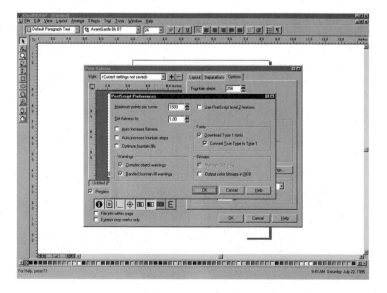

The setting Maximum points per curve is the same as the PSComplexityThreshold setting found in the CORELPRN.INI file. It breaks curves that are more complex than what is set in this box so that they print more reliably. It does not affect the look of an object, only its complexity. However, it causes jobs to take longer to print. This trade-off is a good one because complex objects might not print at all if this is not lowered. Although this number can be lowered to as low as 20, it is not recommended to lower it below 600 as objects may begin to disappear.

Just to the right of the Maximum points per curve setting is the Use PostScript level 2 features. If you will be printing to a PostScript level 2 printer, you definitely want to check this box. If you are not sure if the printer supports PostScript level 2, you should leave it in the default unchecked state.

The next setting controls the flatness of the image. This is especially useful for complex images. Because of limitations in the PostScript language, files with complex fills, such as gradients, textures, and bitmaps, can cause the PostScript output device to produce limitcheck errors. The Set Flatness To setting actually flattens out the curves of the object to try to decrease this complexity. On high-resolution imagesetters, this change in flatness is not noticeable until it gets over 12 to 16. Laser printers are much more likely to be affected by this setting. The maximum value is 100, but this produces a completely distorted image. The Auto Increase Flatness check box automatically increases the flatness up to 10 over the setting in the Set Flatness To box until the graphic outputs properly.

# Corel *NOTE!*

Increasing the flatness also causes images to print much faster. Therefore, it's a good way to proof draft pages very quickly.

The Auto increase fountain steps will be used if the number of fountain steps specified in the Options section of the Print dialog box is less than the optimal number calculated from the current resolution and screen frequency. Therefore, the output looks as good as it possibly can when printed (but might increase the printing time). In the opposite fashion, Optimize fountain fills will reduce the setting for the number of fountain steps if it exceeds the optimal number and can therefore speed up the printing time without degrading the quality of the image.

Download Type 1 fonts tells CorelDRAW to automatically download any PostScript fonts used in the document to the PostScript output device or file. If this box is not checked, the fonts are converted either to curves or to bitmaps. Convert TrueType to Type 1 converts any TrueType fonts into PostScript and then downloads the PostScript font to the output device or file. These two items are almost always a must unless a drawing contains a large number of fonts on the same page.

Complex object warnings will present you with a dialog box similar to the one in Figure 50.12 if you try to print an object with complex outlines, complex fills, texture-filled text, or complex clipping paths. Similarly, the Banded fountain fill warnings will present you with a dialog box similar to the one in Figure 50.13 if you try to print an object that will output with banded fountain fills. Using both of these options can be very helpful in catching objects which may cause you problems at the service bureau. By catching these errors, you can avoid wasting film and therefore save some money.

*Figure 50.12.*
*Printing Alert dialog box*
*for texture-filled text.*

*Figure 50.13.*
*Printing Alert dialog box*
*for banded fountain fills.*

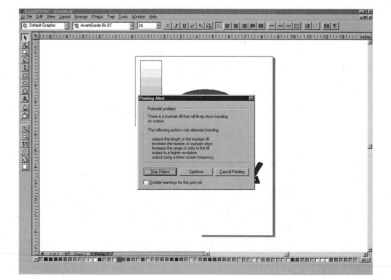

Maintain OPI links is available only if you have imported an image and told CorelDRAW to maintain the OPI links. To do this, you will import either a TIFF or a CT file and then link that file to a high-resolution version stored on your hard drive. When the file is output, only a link itself will be output and not the low resolution file you imported. If you uncheck this option, the low resolution file will be output and not the link. Note that the OPI links are different that the use of DCS bitmaps. Those are to be imported through the Placeable EPS filter. OPI links should only be used if you or your service bureau has OPI server software to substitute the high-resolution image for the comments in the PostScript. If Output color bitmaps in RGB is checked, any 24-bit bitmap imported will not be converted into CMYK color space when output. This means that the conversion will be done by the output device and not CorelDRAW.

The Proofing options section of the Print Options dialog box gives you many ways to output your file. On the left side are three check boxes, labeled Print vectors, Print bitmaps, and Print text. If any of the options are checked, all objects of that type will be output. The default is that they are all checked. If you want all of your text objects to output in black, check the Print all text in black check box. This can be handy if you've filled some text with a complex fill and you just want to get an idea of how your page will look. The Fit printer's marks and layout to page will squeeze all the reference marks onto the paper size that you have selected. Again, this is handy for proofing on a laser printer, but not a good idea for final output.

On the right side of this section are three radio buttons. The Full color button will output everything in the colors you have chosen. But if you want all objects to print in solid black (which speeds output), you can select All colors in black. To see all objects in grayscale, choose All colors in grayscale. Note as you select these options, the preview window in the right half of the dialog box will update to show you the changes.

Checking the Print job information sheet will output a file listing the options you chose when printing. You can control exactly what is printed. Simply click on the Info Settings button and you will be presented with the dialog box shown in Figure 50.14. The Information section enables you to choose exactly which sections get printed. The destination section lets you send all the information to a file or to a printer. Note that the printer this information prints on can be different from the printer the main file prints on.

# Corel*NOTE!*

> If you are going to be taking a file to a service bureau for output, you should take a printout of your job information sheet so that the service can output your file properly.

Figure 50.14.
The Print Job Information
dialog box.

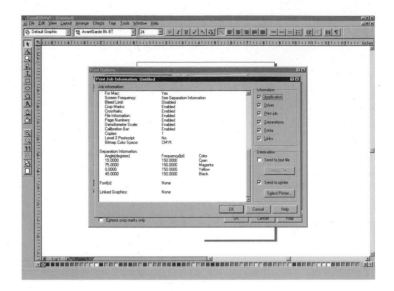

The Special settings section gives you many options that can affect output. These settings have previously been stored in the CORELPRN.INI file, but are now more easily accessible. A list of the Options will appear when you click on the drop-down list, as shown in Figure 50.14. After you have selected an option, you can change the setting. Each of the options is described in the following sections.

Figure 50.15.
The Special Settings drop-down list.

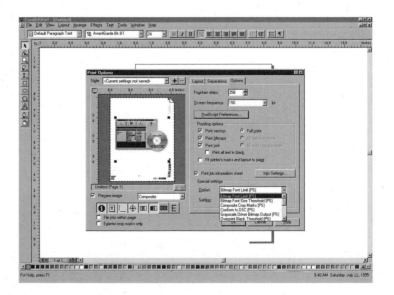

## Bitmap Font Limit (PS)

This specifies the size at which a font will be printed as a bitmap on a PostScript printer. The benefits of printing fonts as bitmaps are that they will look better at small sizes and will print faster than when the font is converted to curves. Bitmap fonts tend to use quite a bit of memory and should be used sparingly to avoid PostScript errors when printing. Only certain fonts qualify to be converted to bitmaps, and they must meet the following criteria:

- The font is not a resident font as specified in the WIN.INI file.
- The size, in pixels, of the printed character is no more than that specified by PSBitmapFontSizeThreshold (normally 75 pixels). On a 300-dpi device it is 18 points, at 600 dpi it is 9 points, and so on.
- The text has not been scaled or skewed.
- The text has no outline and its fill is a uniform fill.
- The text has not been enveloped or nonlinearly transformed in any way.
- The document is not being printed by using either the Scale or the Fit To Page options in the Print dialog box.

The value of PSBitmapFontLimit can range from 0 to 250, and its default value is 8. If you are having trouble printing PostScript fonts, change the value to 0 and the problem may go away.

## Bitmap Font Size Threshold (PS)

This specifies the maximum height, in pixels, of text that will be printed as bitmaps on a PostScript printer. Larger values indicate that bigger bitmaps can be created, which can take a longer time to print. Any text larger than this value is converted to curves if the font is not a resident font as specified in CORELFNT.INI's [PSResidentFonts] section. The value of PSBitmapFontSizeThreshold can range from 0 to 32,767, and its default value is 75.

## Composite Crop Marks (PS)

Choosing Output in black (normal) will output all crop marks in black while choosing Output in all colors will output the crop marks in each of the colors. The default value is to Output in black.

## Conform to DSC (PS)

This specifies whether the output will conform to Adobe's Document Structuring Convention. The default setting is On.

## Grayscale Driver Bitmap Output (PS)

This setting applies when you're outputting color bitmaps on monochrome PostScript devices. A setting of Send color bitmaps as color indicates that the print engine will send bitmaps with full-color information to monochrome devices. A setting of Send color bitmaps as grayscale indicates that the color images will be converted to grayscale before being sent. This is done to conserve disk space and virtual memory and to limit processing time. The default value is to Send color bitmaps as grayscale.

## Overprint Black Threshold (PS)

This specifies the percentage of black trap that will be added when you print color separations. It has an effect only when Always Overprint Black is checked in the Print Separations dialog box. The default value is 95 percent and can range from 0 to 100 percent. Anything less than 95 percent will enable white space to appear on separation layers.

## PostScript 2 Stroke Adjust (PS)

This is only for PostScript Level 2 output. The command `setstrokeadjust` allows for a special adjustment, although using this option is rare.

## Resolve DCS Links (PS)

Substitute Plates at Print Time, Leave DCS Links Unresolved.

## Registration Mark Type (PS)

This indicates the type of registration mark that will be used. You have a choice between Corel's logo, an elongated bullseye, a half inverted bullseye, a square and circle, or a standard bullseye. The default setting is a standard bullseye.

## Bitmap Printing

This setting specifies how bitmaps are printed to Hewlett-Packard LaserJet Series IV printers. If this is set to Output in 64 KB chunks, the bitmap will be sent one raster line at a time to ensure that the bitmap prints correctly. Incorrect printing can occur if the printer driver's graphics mode is set to print raster images as transparent. Output entire bitmap sends the whole bitmap at once, which is faster but less reliable. The default value is to Output the entire bitmap at once.

## Driver Banding

Let Driver Handle Banding will send the full image to the driver and let it create the bands. Send Bands to Driver means that CorelDRAW's print engine will create the bands and sent them to the driver.

## Fill Clipping

Use Driver Clipping for Fills means that any clip regions used in your file will be handled by the print driver. You can select Use Software Clipping for Fills which means that CorelDRAW's print engine will clip the regions for you.

## Page Orientation Warning

This specifies whether CorelDRAW issues a warning message when the page orientation of the printer does not match that of the page being printed. The default value is On.

## Preview Image Default

This setting controls the default value of the Print Preview in the Print Options dialog box. The original default setting is to have it turned off.

## Print Preview Drag Mode

This determines what visual indicator you will get as you drag an image in the Print Preview window. Drag full image will move the whole image with the cursor, whereas drag marquee will show you the bounding box only after you have stopped moving the image. The default is to drag the full image.

## Text Output Method

The default value is on. This means that text will be printed using text bands. If set to off, each character is sent to the printer as a graphic object, which decreases the quality and speed of your output.

After you've made changes in the Print dialog box, you can save these settings to be reused so that you don't have to enter them each time. At the top of the Print Options dialog box is a Style drop-down list. Click on the + button to get the Save Print Style dialog box shown in Figure 50.16.

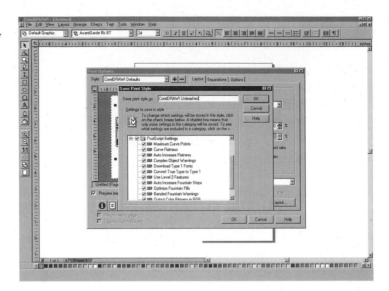

*Figure 50.16.*
*The Save Print Style dialog*
*box.*

In the Save Print Style dialog box you can give your print style a name and select which settings you want to have saved in the style. This uses a Windows 95 style tree list. Click on the + next to a folder, and it will show you all of the settings within that folder. If an option is checked, it will be saved. If you want to delete a style, you can select it and click the - button in the Print Options dialog box.

# How CorelDRAW Handles the Printing of Fonts

In past revisions of CorelDRAW, there was no such thing as the handling of fonts. All text was converted either to curves or to bitmaps unless a font was resident in the output device. There were ways to manually make fonts resident, but that was rather difficult for most users. This situation has finally been addressed, and the following sections explain when a font is used and when the objects are instead converted to curves or bitmaps.

## Printing PostScript Fonts

Fonts that are registered as being resident in the PSResidentFonts section of CORELFNT.INI are not downloaded. They are re-encoded, however. This works the way earlier versions of CorelDRAW did, except that the look-up table in CORELFNT.INI is much shorter. For a font to be treated as always resident, enter it in this table. The next stages are ignored.

For nonresident fonts, the printer driver is first given an opportunity to download the font. If the driver sees the font as resident or already downloaded, CorelDRAW re-encodes the font and treats it as being resident. This works with any PS driver (including the Adobe PostScript driver) just the way it does for other Windows applications.

If the printer driver fails, the print engine in CorelDRAW downloads the font, re-encodes it, and uses it as a resident font. Therefore, in general, the fonts are not converted to curves (unless the text has nonlinear transformations or a link to some other object).

## EPS Export

The default setting is that all text is converted to curves. If the Text As Text button in the Export dialog box is selected, all Type 1 fonts are treated as being resident and are called using their PostScript FontNames (as found in a font's .PFM file). This is similar to the now-defunct (version 4) All Fonts Resident, except that it affects only PostScript fonts. It's different from printing because it doesn't involve the look-up table in CORELFNT.INI.

If the Include Fonts check box is selected, all PostScript Type 1 fonts are embedded within the .EPS file. This is the opposite of the old All Fonts Resident.

## Printing TrueType Fonts

If nonlinear transformations such as envelopes have been used or if the text is linked to another object (such as text on a path), the text is converted to curves.

For fonts that have been mapped to a PostScript FontName in the PSResidentFonts section of CORELPRN.INI, the font is re-encoded and the text is printed using the PostScript font named in the look-up table.

For text whose point size falls within the threshold (defined by PSBitmapFontSizeThreshold in CORELPRN.INI) and for which there are no transformations on the text, a PostScript Type 3 font is created and downloaded. If the text's point size is outside the threshold or if there are transformations on the text, a PostScript Type 1 font is created, downloaded, and re-encoded. This is not the same as other Windows applications that enable the printer driver to do this. CorelDRAW adds only the necessary characters to the font, builds an accurate encoding vector, and is more efficient than the normal driver.

If none of the previous conditions are met, the text is converted to curves, just as in the past.

# Pipeline Optimized PostScript

Pipeline Associates, the developer of the PowerPage PostScript clone technology, has created a special version of PowerPage that speeds up the printing of PostScript files created by Corel applications. PowerPage Level 2c is found in quite a few of the newer printers on the market; it would be best to contact Pipeline for further information of which printers contain the technology.

This technology embeds parts of Corel's PostScript prolog into the printer itself. Because this technology is build into the printer, the PostScript can be processed much faster. Pipeline claims that some files print up to ten times faster. For further information on this, contact Pipeline at (201) 267-3840.

# 51

# Selecting a Printer

Selecting a printer is an important job on any printing project. There are probably hundreds, if not thousands of companies from which to choose and many variables need to be considered in order to select the right company to produce your finished piece. Your reputation may depend on it, so choose wisely!

## Finding Prospective Companies

The first step in selecting a printing company is to obtain a group of prospective printers that you can evaluate and compare in order to make a final selection. If you plan to produce a medium to large volume of printing, you should think in terms of narrowing this list down to three companies. These three companies will produce the majority of your work and will bid to obtain your business. If you expect to have a small number of printing projects, selecting one primary company is probably the best choice.

The following sections discuss some excellent sources for prospective printing companies.

## Referrals

The best way to find prospective printing companies is to ask for referrals from someone who has experience in dealing with several of the companies. This will save you a great deal of research and hopefully eliminate companies that produce substandard work. Individuals in the following businesses work with printers on a consistent basis:

- Graphic designers
- Advertising agencies
- Service bureaus
- Photographers
- Print buyers at large companies

## Directories

Most metropolitan areas have directories listing local printing companies. These directories are usually created by printing related magazines and can be found at public libraries. They normally provide specific information about equipment, company size, and specialty products.

## Printing Brokers

Printing brokers coordinate projects with a very large group of printers on a local and national scale. Many times they work with "trade" companies that have no salespeople and sell exclusively to brokers and other printing companies. Printing brokers constantly evaluate this network of companies to purchase printing at the best price for their customers and take their fees in the form of markups added to the wholesale pricing they receive. Brokers get large discounts based on the volume of printing they purchase and can usually save you money on your printing.

In addition, because brokers work with a large pool of companies, they are not limited by equipment and can produce almost any type of printing. This is a tremendous advantage, because it reduces the number of printing companies with which a buyer must work and saves costly hours of research.

## Printing Organizations

Various printing trade organizations exist to promote the business and education of their members. These organizations usually produce a directory containing information about their members and can refer you to several quality companies. If no local organizations exist, you can contact Printing Industries of America (PIA) located in Alexandria, Virginia, (703) 519-8100, for information on local member companies.

## Special Interest Organizations

Many cities have special interest groups that meet on a regular basis to discuss computer design or desktop publishing–related interests. An excellent example would be a local Corel users group, such as those listed in the Corel Approved Partners file that is part of CorelDRAW 6. These groups have individuals that are very experienced in graphic design and can refer you to several qualified companies.

## Advertisements

Whether it is by television, radio, or direct mail advertising, it will not be long before you see an advertisement for printing companies. Examine the ads carefully for clues about the quality and area of expertise of the advertising business. If the ad is printed, is it the quality you would expect on your project? These advertisements can provide leads to a quality company but are much less reliable than other sources.

# Evaluating Prospective Companies

Once you have selected some prospective companies, you will need to qualify them in order to determine if they are the right company for your printing project. You should ask for samples of other projects they have produced, references from other customers, and conduct a plant tour to see their facilities.

The prospective printing companies should be compared and evaluated using the criteria discussed in the following sections.

## Equipment

The most important factor in choosing a printer is finding someone who has the right equipment for the particular project. In an effort to gain business, some printing companies will take work that is above the capability of their equipment. Yes, they probably can "print" it, but will the quality be up to your standards? See Skill Session 55, "The Printing and Binary Process," for information on selecting the proper equipment for printing.

## Quality

Quality is a relative term. The level considered acceptable for the daily newspaper, for instance, is substantially different from that of an annual report for a major corporation. The level of quality for a project does not classify a project as good or bad, but determines what is acceptable for the particular use of the piece. When overseeing the print production for someone else, always discuss quality expectations and the associated costs before starting the design. For clarity in communications, quality can be categorized into the four levels discussed in the following sections.

### Average Quality

Average quality printing should be used on basic projects such as business forms, newsletters, return postcards, and fliers. They are usually printed in one color and do not contain complex images, tight registration, or large solids. A small variation of ink density and registration should be expected. These items are the meat and potatoes of the quick printer and are generally printed on small presses at a very low cost.

### Medium Quality

Medium quality printing is the standard for catalogs, brochures, and business materials. They may contain solids, tight registration, and complex images, but are not perfect. The number of ink colors will usually vary from one-color to four-color process, and good quality control should be performed by the printer to ensure a consistent image. These projects should be printed on medium-size presses and will command a higher cost than average quality.

### High Quality

High quality printing should be used for annual reports, marketing materials for more expensive products, and for particular clients. When image is everything, choose high quality. Ink colors are primarily four-color process and may utilize additional spot colors, varnishes, and complex images. The final piece should appear nearly perfect to an average person and have tight registration, flawless solids, and colors that equal the match print. High quality projects should be printed on expensive, medium- to large size- presses by expertly skilled pressmen. Great attention to detail should be expected from the printing company and a press proof should normally be performed. See Skill Session 56, "The Press Check," for information. The cost for high quality printing is much greater than average or medium quality.

### Museum Quality

The highest level of quality is reserved for products that must be flawless, including limited edition prints, marketing materials for luxury products, and a few annual reports. These projects are printed only on the finest papers and printing presses under extremely strict quality control. Only the finest materials are used, and ink colors are almost exclusively four-color process with additional spot colors, varnishes, and specialized bindery for additional impact. It is not uncommon for the pricing in this category to be four to ten times that of the high quality standard; therefore, very few companies or individuals are willing to pay such a price.

## Service

Good service does not just happen—it is the result of careful planning as well as the personnel found at the printing company. Interview the key people involved in the production of printing to make sure that they are skilled, knowledgeable, and can be relied upon to keep their commitments.

Although others certainly contribute, there are three key individuals who must coordinate to effectively deliver good service.

### Salespeople

Salespeople are your interface with the company. They should act on your behalf and be knowledgeable on the printing process, offer alternatives to save costs and raise quality, and promptly return phone calls. They should be willing to provide samples, create dummies, and discuss the project in detail. Look for salespeople who write things down—they are much more likely to avoid forgetting an important detail. A salesperson with more seniority at the company might also have additional leverage when it comes to job scheduling.

### Customer Service Representatives (CSRs)

Customer service representatives, also called CSRs, oversee the production of the printing internally. They coordinate the various tasks that must be accomplished for the project and balance the schedules in order to accommodate the expected delivery time. Because salespeople are usually out of the office working with their customers, the CSR should be available to answer technical questions, provide production scheduling updates, and coordinate delivery.

### Press Operators

The best press in the world will not produce quality printing if it is not run by a knowledgeable, skilled operator. Look for a press operator who is experienced, has pride in his work, and understands both the printing and prepress operations. Experience has shown that the cleanliness (or lack thereof) of the press area is a strong indicator of the attention a press operator pays to detail and the pride he takes in his work.

## Price

Every printing project is a custom piece, and the price can vary tremendously from company to company. It is not uncommon for the bids from printers to vary as much as 100 percent! To obtain the lowest cost, you should develop relationships with about three printing companies. This should ensure competition among the firms, but also allow enough volume with each to gain priority press times, courteous service, and a working knowledge of delivery and packaging expectations. Limiting the number of printing companies will also allow for convenient reorders and the building of good communication, which eliminates costly errors. See Skill Session 53, "Preparing for Printing," for information on how to obtain competitive bids on your printing project.

## Delivery Schedule

Sometimes a company must be selected because of its ability to get the work done within a very tight delivery schedule. This practice is not advisable except in extreme situations because it may cost substantially more for rush charges, you might not be able to use the lowest bid, and the odds for making a mistake increase dramatically with no time for any correction. On more than one occasion, I have produced projects where the goal was to rush something into the customer's hands first, and worry about the correctness of the information later. Consult with your printing companies about what is a reasonable turnaround time for your project. Do not fall into the trap of always expecting a rush delivery.

After evaluating the companies with this criteria, you should be able to select a printer for your job. Strive to develop a relationship with the company you have selected. This will improve communication, reduce the number of errors, and enable you to obtain preferential press scheduling.

# 52

# Paper Selection

After the selection of the printing press for a project, the next most important decision you will make is which paper to use. Recently, sharp increases in the cost of paper have made this a critical decision. In many projects the cost of paper can be half the cost of production.

When specifying paper for any project, be sure to include the following information:

- Number of sheets
- Brand name of paper
- Grade
- Weight
- Size of paper
- Grain
- Color
- Finish

This information will describe the paper to the printer or bindery so they can adequately bid or produce your project. Each of these specifications are discussed in the remainder of this chapter.

# Characteristics

The characteristics of a sheet of paper ultimately determine its cost, appearance, and ability to be printed. By considering these factors, you will be able to select the right paper for the project, reducing costs and avoiding mistakes.

## Grades

Paper manufacturers categorize their products into several different grades. This is extremely useful, because it allows buyers to clearly communicate the type of paper needed for a project and also aids in comparing the prices of different brands.

### Bond

Bond paper is designed for letters, forms, and correspondence pieces that are printed on one side. For this reason, it has a much lower opacity than other grades and should generally not be used for two sided printing. Some bond papers contain partial or 100-percent cotton fiber content and may also have a translucent logo, called a watermark.

Bond is available in weights of 9 to 28 pound, with 20 or 24 pound typically being used for photocopying and 24 or 28 pound for stationary.

### Uncoated Book

Uncoated book is the general use paper of the printing industry. It is used to produce most books, flyers, direct mail pieces, and other projects that do not require a high quality sheet.

Uncoated book is available in weights of 30 to 80 pound. Lower basis weights (30 to 50 pounds) are excellent choices for web-fed printing, where production costs and mailing weight are very important. Higher basis weights (60 to 80 pounds) are commonly used for most sheet-fed printing.

Two finishes are commonly available: smooth and rough. A smooth finish will not absorb ink as rapidly as the rough finish, thus producing a better ink holdout.

### Text

Text paper is an uncoated sheet that usually contains a textured surface. It is commonly used for brochures, flyers, mailers, and projects in which a texture can produce an added appeal. Text is available in weights of 60 to 100 pound in three primary categories: laid, linen, and felt.

The laid and felt finishes are produced by rollers while the paper is still wet. This process does not compress the paper, and therefore the paper has additional stiffness and bulk. A linen finish is created by slightly embossing the dry sheet. This produces a pattern that varies from mill to mill.

## Cover

Cover paper is normally a heavier version of the corresponding bond, book, or text paper. Because of its thickness and durability, it is used for the cover of books, postcards, business cards, tickets, and brochures. Cover paper is available in basis weights of 60 to 120 pound and a caliper of .007 to .015.

## Coated Book and Coated Cover

Paper mills produce book and cover papers that are coated with clay and smoothed in a process called *calendering*. This technique smoothes the paper by filling in the peaks and valleys created by its fibers. The flat surface enhances ink, improves ink holdout, and limits dot gain. Three common finishes are available: dull, matte, and gloss.

Dull and matte finishes are not heavily calendered; therefore their appearance contains little gloss. They are ideal for projects that require extensive reading or where a high contrast with a glossy ink or varnish is wanted.

Gloss finishes are highly calendered, polished sheets that have a very reflective surface. This polishing process produces a sheet that has substantially less opacity and bulk than a similar weight of dull or matte finish. Gloss-coated papers are excellent for process color printing, producing the sharpest and cleanest ink dot of all papers.

Coated book paper is available in basis weights of 60 to 100 pound for sheet-fed printing and 40 to 100 pound in web rolls.

Coated cover is available in basis weights of 60 to 100 pound and calipers of .007 to .015 and may ordered with coating on one side (designated as C1S for coated one side) or two sides (C2S).

Paper mills use a rating system to describe their coated paper based on opacity, brightness, and fiber. This scale goes from 1 to 5, with 1 being the finest grade and 5 the lowest quality. Some mills also have grades they consider to be better than a typical number 1 and call them premium number 1 or super premium number 1. These ratings are assigned by the manufacturer and should be used to loosely categorize the quality of a paper.

## Cardstock and Board

Several varieties of cardstock are produced for lower cost and unique projects. They are specified by caliper in a range from .007 to .06. Lighter weight stocks include tag, bristol, and index papers that are used for tags, business reply cards, warranty cards, and inexpensive direct mail pieces. Extremely heavy basis weight papers, used for specialized applications such as packaging, signage, and displays, are referred to as board or blanks. Be careful when ordering heavier weights of board for offset printing as they might not be flexible enough to run through the printing press.

## Specialized Papers

A few types of specialized papers have been created that do not fit into any of the previous categories. They are unique papers with unusual qualities created for specific applications.

### Synthetic Papers

Synthetic papers, such as Tyvek and Teslin, are waterproof, tear-resistant, and very durable. They are created from petroleum products, plastic fibers, and materials of the polyolefin family. Consult with an experienced printer when using any synthetic papers, because they do not react to printing and bindery like other papers.

### Carbonless

Commonlycalled by the brand name NCR, carbonless papers house invisible micro capsules that rupture when pressure is applied. This fluid is converted into a blue or black ink by the sheet underneath, creating a copy of the impression.

Sheets may be coated on the back (designated CB), front and back (CFB), or front only (CF). The specification of coating is very important and determines which sheet will have the duplicate image. A typical three part form would contain a top sheet that is coated on the back, a middle sheet that is coated front and back, and a bottom sheet that is coated front. Carbonless paper is usually precollated in either straight or reverse order with a standard color sequence. Consult with your printer concerning the collating sequence preferred and make certain that the brand you have selected will work with their glue adhesive.

### Newsprint

Newsprint is a veryinexpensive paper made of ground wood pulp. Because of the low basis weight and the many impurities it contains, it is normally only used on web-fed presses. As anyone who has forgotten to pick up the morning newspaper knows, newsprint is not a durable sheet and will yellow with age or exposure to light.

### Label

Many types of paper are available with an adhesive back for label use. Most are designed for printing; however, some labels have been created for use with photocopy machines and laser printers. Do not try to run label stock designed for offset printing through your laser printer. The adhesive will build up on the interior of the printer and you will get a very large repair bill for cleaning! Stock labels can be found with die cut shapes, perforations, and other features that make them ideal for short production runs.

## Color

Although white is the most common color used for printing, paper is available in almost every color of the rainbow. Even a choice of white becomes more complex when you must decide between names such as polar white, natural white, oyster, bright white, pearl, and more.

Colored papers are created by dyes that are added in the production of paper to achieve the various hues that are popular at any given time. There is no standard that has been established for color matching between the mills, so paper sample books are the best source of information for specifying color. Like many materials, paper color will vary slightly from production run to production run. If a color match is critical in a project, be sure to complete it with as few different paper orders as possible.

## Opacity

Opacity is the capability of a paper to prevent printing on one side from showing through to the other side. Manufactures have created a scale of 1 to 100 to measure opacity, with 100 being completely opaque and 1 being virtually transparent. Be sure to select a paper that has the opacity needed for a particular project. Projects that include large solids or need detailed reading require much more opacity than simple, low-cost flyers.

## Brightness

Brightness is the amount of light reflected from a sheet of paper, expressed as a percentage on a scale from 0 to 100, where 100 represents a paper that reflects all light. Most papers have a brightness rating of 65 to 95.

## Weight

Paper weight is measured by the number of pounds found in a stack of 500 sheets (called a *ream*). This weight is referred to as the paper's basis weight. A ream that weighs 100 pounds would be a basis weight of 100 and may be abbreviated as 100# or BS 100. A ream of much thinner sheets that weighs 50 pounds would have a basis weight of 50.

Each grade of paper has a unique size for the 500 sheets that are used to determine basis weight. Below are the various sizes used for each grade:

- Bond: 17×22
- Uncoated book: 25×38
- Text: 25×38

- Coated book: 25×38
- Cover: 20×26

What this means is that a 60# sheet of text paper is much thinner than a sheet of 60# cover paper. This is a result of the difference in size of the 500 sheets used to determine the basis weight. The text paper is measured in sheets of 25×38, while the cover paper is measured in a much smaller sheet size of 20×26. Because both weigh 60 pounds, the cover paper is much thicker.

## Caliper

Caliper is the thickness of any particular paper measured in thousandths of an inch (called *points*). One point is equal to .001; therefore, a paper measuring .010 is termed ten point. Caliper is used to specify cover papers, cardstocks, and board.

## Size

Large sheets of paper are usually ordered and then cut down into smaller sizes to be used for printing. The larger size sheet is referred to as the parent sheet, and the smaller size as the cut sheet. A typical parent sheet size is 23×35 inches, where width is specified first and then height. Standard sizes of parent and cut sheets are available, and the design of any project should be tailored for efficient paper use. To reduce paper costs, design projects to fit into a multiple of 8 1/2×11. For more information on page layout considerations, see Skill Session 53, "Preparing For Printing."

Paper is shipped in cartons or on skids. Cartons are used for smaller orders and skids for medium to large quantities. When ordering cartons, it is usually cheaper to order even cartons. Partial cartons, also called broken cartons, cost more because of the additional handling involved.

## Grain

Paper grain is the tendency of paper fibers to align themselves in one direction. It is caused by the manufacturing equipment and is an important consideration in the printing and bindery process. Most pressmen prefer to have the grain run across the direction of the press, because this prevents stretching of the paper sheet while it is being printed. The bindery will prefer to have the grain run parallel to the fold; paper folds easier in this direction, and it greatly reduces cracking as well.

Often times there will be a conflict between the direction needed for printing versus the grain needed for folding. In this case, select the grain needed for printing and score the paper prior to folding.

Paper manufacturers indicate the direction of the paper grain by underlying the dimension parallel to it. A sheet specified as 23×*35* would have the grain running parallel to the 35 inch side. This is called grain long. A sheet specified as *23*×35 would have the grain running parallel to the 23 inch side. This is called grain short.

## Recycled Paper

With landfills in our country overflowing with garbage, it's no wonder that a trend has developed for using recycled paper. Experts might disagree about the energy consumption between recycled and virgin fiber, and whether it is good or bad to cut down trees. However, where are we going to live if everything becomes a garbage dump? Two sources of recycled paper exist, and it is important for the environmentally concerned buyer to know the difference.

*Preconsumer waste* is paper waste created in the manufacturing of paper and includes some printed stock that never reaches the end consumer. It includes the paper wasted in cutting, damaged in shipping, and books or magazines that were never sold to consumers. This is not a new technique; manufactures of paper have always "recycled" these types of papers. Preconsumer waste is a relatively inexpensive method for reusing paper because the cost of collection is much lower than that of postconsumer waste.

*Postconsumer waste* is paper that has been used by the consumer and brought back to the manufacturer, usually through a recycling program. It includes newspapers, packaging, and the memos thrown away by our corporations. When the average citizen thinks of recycled paper, he or she visualizes postconsumer waste.

The paper characteristics for recycled paper are slightly different from than that of virgin pulp. This occurs because of the shortening of the paper fibers in the recycling process, and the difficulty of removing all the ink. Most recycled papers will perform adequately; however, personal experience has shown that when it comes to very high-end color printing on premium coated paper, virgin fiber produces a better image than recycled paper.

If you are truly concerned about the environment and have decided to do your part, we offer the following suggestions:

- Whenever possible, specify uncoated paper.
- Limit the amount of ink coverage used in your projects.
- Limit the number of bleeds.
- Design printing projects to limit paper waste.
- Specify recycled paper.
- Look for high postconsumer waste.
- Recycle paper from your own home and office.

## Paper Effects on Printing

Paper can have a tremendous effect on the look and feel of the printed project. Not only will the texture change with different papers, but the integrity of the printed dot and the contrast of the printed images can also. The two key areas affected by paper are dot gain and contrast.

### Dot Gain

*Dot gain* is the increase in size of the printed dot from separation to the reproduced image. It naturally occurs because of image exposure on printing plates, pressure in the printing press, and the spread of ink as it penetrates the paper. Dot gain causes the middle tones to become much darker. This affects the contrast and makes the image appear flat or plugged.

Lower uncoated papers have high dot gain, because the ink is allowed to heavily penetrate the paper. Coated papers have a much lower dot gain because the ink penetrates the sheet only enough to bond the two together.

Higher line screens naturally have higher dot gains because of the increase in the total number of dots. To achieve the best looking image, it is important to use coated paper for high line screen projects.

### Contrast

Contrast is the difference between the whitest white and the darkest black on any project. A large difference between the darkest elements, middle tones, and highlights will produce good contrast and the best image. Projects with little or reduced contrasts will appear lifeless and flat.

Paper will affect the contrast of any given printing project. Coated paper produces the highest contrast of all paper grades, followed by uncoated stock, and then newsprint. Papers that are colored or have low brightness ratings will also reduce the contrast, because the whites of the highlights are limited by the color of the paper. When contrast is important, select the highest grade that your budget will allow.

## Practical Tips on Paper

In any endeavor there are suggestions for improving things that are usually learned only from experience. The following list provides real life ideas to help you with specifying and ordering paper:

- When ordering paper, it is a good idea to have it arrive about three days ahead of the scheduled press date. This allows enough time for the paper to "climatize" or adjust to the new environment. It also gives the paper supplier room in case there is a problem with delivery and allows the printer to prepare the paper for printing.

■ Some papers are considered "mill items," meaning that the supplier must order this stock for you directly from the mill. Try to avoid using these stocks because they are more expensive, must be ordered in even cartons, and there can be long delays in delivery.

■ When printing short production runs, use a higher quality of paper for appeal. Since the cost of paper in the project will be very small, it will cost very little to go from a standard to a high-end sheet. When printing long production runs, use paper that is of lower quality to reduce costs.

■ Many times the cost of a project can be reduced by slightly modifying its dimensions. If size is not critical, ask your printer if any small adjustments can be made to reduce the paper sheet size.

■ Like everyone else, printers must make a return on their investment. For this reason, all products purchased for a particular printing job will have a markup associated with them, usually between 20 and 30 percent. Ask your printer if you can purchase the paper needed for the project yourself. This can typically save you about 10 percent of the total project cost.

■ Paper companies often discontinue or modify their lines of paper products. In order to move out the old stock, they reduce the prices and have closeout specials. If paper specifications allow substitutions, consult with your printer or paper sales representative for current closeouts.

# 53

# Preparing for Printing

The image created when printing will be only as good as the preparation work you do for the process. The old adage "garbage in, garbage out" is just as applicable in printing as it is in computer work. If you take time to plan your design and prepare it for printing, your finished project will look more professional and will actually take fewer hours to complete.

## How Many Colors?

A basic decision must be made at the beginning of a project as to the number of colors to be used. Most of the time this is dictated by the use of the project and the projected budget to be spent. Using four-color process on a typical office form would probably be money wasted, whereas using only black ink to appeal to an audience of graphic designers would be ineffective. These can be tough decisions, but the rest of the design will hinge upon them.

## Spot Color or Process Color?

The term *spot color* literally means printing an ink only on portions of the project as opposed to completely covering the sheet. In the printing industry, the term spot color is commonly used to mean *flat color*, where a color is created by printing only one ink instead of building it through screens as in four-color process. *Four-color process* uses four colors (cyan, magenta, yellow, and black) to build colors. Spot color has the advantage of solid, dense ink colors that can be premixed to the exact hue. Process colors have an advantage in that almost any color can be imitated by using a combination of just four inks. The decision must be made as to whether the project will be composed of one or more spot colors or using four-color process. Usually, when you use less than four colors you will be using spot color. When using four or more colors, process color is usually used to reduce costs.

## Color Palettes

After you have selected the number and type of ink colors, you must decide which color palette is to be used for the project. Although many color palettes exist, the most popular are Pantone and Trumatch. The *Pantone Matching System* (commonly referred to as PMS), invented by Pantone, Inc., was the first of its kind and remains the standard of the printing industry today. The Pantone system includes thousands of spot colors; swatch books are available showing printing on coated stock, uncoated stock, and their four-color process approximations. The Trumatch system is based on colors created by four-color process printing alone and does not incorporate spot color.

These color systems will help you communicate to the printer the exact color desired for a particular project. Instead of just requesting a teal, you are able to better identify the color as Pantone color 327. This specification leaves no question about the particular hue you are requesting. To aid in working with different color palettes, these color-matching systems and others have been built into CorelDRAW.

When using color palettes, you must understand there will be a difference between the color displayed on the monitor and the color that will be used for printing. The colors used by your computer monitor are red, green, and blue. Using various combinations of these three colors, the monitor can imitate hues in almost any color system. Notice the word *imitate*, as many times there can be a substantial difference between the red, green, blue (RGB) image on your monitor and the flat or four-color process (CMYK) printed version of a particular color. In order to minimize the difference between the color on your monitor and the hues used by any color system, you should calibrate your monitor and use reference swatch books for exact matching.

## Project Layout

The next step in creating the project is to plan the layout of the piece. In order to maximize the dollars spent on a project, it is wise to plan your layout to fit the standard sizes used by most printing presses. The standard sizes are almost always built around multiples of 8.5×11 inches. A sheet that is 11×17 contains two 8.5×11 sheets, a 17×22 contains four, and a 23×35 contains eight with room for the gripper. Additional paper sizes such as 25×38 have been created to accommodate bleeds based upon multiples of 8.5×11. This is not to say that you cannot use a nonstandard size of, say, 4×13. You must evaluate the design of a specific project and realize that if you specify an odd size there will be more paper waste and a higher cost versus using a more standard size.

# Imposition

You can lay out a project for a printing press in several different configurations. This process is referred to as *imposition* and should generally be left to the printer and his prepress personnel. This process is very press-specific and requires some expertise in order to achieve the most economical imposition. In order to aid the printer in this layout, mockups are very important and should always be used for complicated projects.

# Terminology

Printing, like almost every other industry, has its own terms to describe elements commonly found in a project. By knowing and using the following terms, you can prepare your project in terms that describe exactly what you want in the printer's own language.

## Bleeds

A *bleed* is simply an ink that extends to the very edge of the sheet after it has been trimmed. In order to achieve this effect, you must print an additional area past the trim line, generally about one-eighth of an inch, in order to accommodate the inaccuracy of the bindery equipment. Be sure to ask your printer ahead of time how much room is needed to accommodate a bleed on his equipment.

## Built Color

A *built color* is the opposite of a spot or flat color. It is a color created by overlapping colors or screens of colors to create a hue different from the colors used. A simple example would be combining yellow and red to create orange. In this example, the yellow and red would be spot colors and the orange would be the built color.

## Camera-Ready Art

*Camera-ready art* is any artwork that has been prepared to the point that it is ready to be photographed by the camera. Copy that requires additional work, such as pasteup or other alterations, is not camera ready. The letters CRA are often used by printers to abbreviate camera-ready art.

## CMYK

The abbreviation *CMYK* is used to describe the four process colors: cyan, magenta, yellow, and black.

## Coverage

The term *coverage* is used to describe the amount of ink used on any project. The three levels are generally described as light, medium, and heavy coverage.

## Dummy

A *dummy* is a mockup that simulates the layout and composition of the project to be printed. It is used to communicate exactly what the piece should look like, and aid in the layout of the project on the printing and bindery equipment.

## Dot Gain

The term *dot gain* is used to describe the growth or enlargement of a halftone dot from the image on the film to the printed image. It is caused by the pressure of the press rollers and the absorption of the ink into the paper. Large amounts of dot gain will cause plugging and reduce the amount of contrast in a printed image.

## Flood

An ink *flood* is a sheet completely painted with an ink or varnish.

## For Position Only (FPO)

A piece of artwork that is intended only to show position and is not to be used for reproduction is termed *for position only*. It is usually abbreviated on the page as FPO.

## Ganging

*Ganging* is a technique that combines two projects onto one sheet and prints them at the same time. It is an effective alternative for reducing cost, but will usually compromise the color of one or both of the projects. Do not gang projects that are dramatically different in ink coverage and hue, or that have critical color matches.

## Gripper

The portion of the press that holds onto the paper is called the *gripper*. The term also loosely describes a small area of the sheet that cannot be printed with ink because it is the area used by the press to hold the paper.

## House Sheet

When specific paper information is not provided, the printer will use the *house sheet*—the standard paper used by the printing company for general-purpose printing.

## Loupe

The *loupe* is the glass lens used to inspect printing. The magnification of the loupe is generally 10 times, abbreviated 10×, or eight, abbreviated 8×.

## Metallic Inks

Inks containing flakes or pigments that imitate metals such as gold or silver are referred to as *metallics*. Because these inks are very different from the standard mix, they are more expensive and generally cannot be used in process color printing.

## Photomechanical Transfer (PMT)

*Photomechanical Transfer* (PMT) is a brand name used to describe a process usually used to create camera-ready artwork in which a positive image is created on paper.

## Plate Change

When a project has an image that is changed by switching plates in the middle of a single production run, the process is referred to as a *plate change*. This technique is useful for modifying copy or images to produce different versions of a particular project. There is an additional cost due to lost time on the press, and you will usually be limited to a change of only one color or plate.

## Registration Marks

Small lines used by the pressman to register colors are referred to as *registration marks*. They are printed on the sheet, but outside of the trim area.

## Solids

*Solids* are images on the sheet with almost 100-percent ink coverage. Any type or images created within the solid by using negative space are referred to as *reversing out* of the solid.

## Printing Trade Customs

In addition to terminology, many printing trade customs have been in use for over 70 years. These practices are guidelines followed by most printing companies and attempt to clarify issues related to the printing process.

# Corel*NOTE!*

The information in the following sidebar is from Printing Industries of America, Inc., originally formally promulgated, Annual Convention, United Typothetea of America, 1922. Revised and updated and repromulgated, Annual Convention, Printing Industries of America, Inc., 1945 & 1974. Updated and adopted by the Graphic Arts Council of North America, 1985.

The full title of work is *Printing Trade Customs*, published by Printing Industries of America (703) 519-8100.

**Quotation**

A quotation not accepted within sixty (60) days is subject to review. All prices are based on material costs at the time of quotation.

**Orders**

Orders regularly placed, verbal or written, cannot be canceled except upon terms that will compensate the printer against lost incurred in reliance of the order.

**Experimental Work**

Experimental or preliminary work performed at the customer's request will be charged at current rates and may not be used until the printer has been reimbursed in full for the amount of the charges billed.

**Creative Work**

Creative work, such as sketches, copy, dummies, and all preparatory work developed and furnished by the printer, shall remain his exclusive property and no use of same shall be made, nor any ideas obtained therefrom be used, except upon compensation to be determined by the printer, and not expressly identified and included in the selling price.

**Condition of Copy**

Upon receipt of original copy or manuscript, should it be evident that condition of the copy differs from that which had been originally described and consequently quoted, the original quotation shall be rendered void and a new quotation issued.

**Preparatory Materials**

Working mechanical art, type, negative, positives, flats, plates and other items when supplied by the printer shall remain his exclusive property unless otherwise agreed in writing.

**Alterations**

Alterations represent work performed in addition to the original specification. Such additional work shall be charged at current rates and be supported with documentation upon request.

**Pre-press Proofs**

Pre-press proofs shall be submitted with original copy. Corrections are to be made on "master set" and returned marked "O.K." or "O.K. with Corrections" and signed by customer. If revised proofs are desired, request must be made when proofs are returned. Printer cannot be held responsible for errors under either or both of the following conditions: if the customer has failed to return proofs with indication of changes, or if the customer has instructed printer to proceed without submission of proofs.

**Press Proofs**

Unless specifically provided in printer's quotation, press proofs will be charged at current rates. An inspection sheet of any form can be submitted for customer's approval, at no charge, provided customer is available at the press during the time of make-ready. Lost press time due to customer delay, or customer changes and corrections, will be charged at current rates.

**Color Proofing**

Because of differences in equipment, processing, proofing substrates, paper, inks, pigments, and other conditions between color proofing and production pressroom operations, a reasonable variation in color between color proofs and the completed job shall constitute acceptable delivery.

**Over-Runs and Under-Runs**

Over-runs and under-runs not to exceed 10% on quantities ordered or the percentage agreed upon, shall constitute acceptable delivery. Printer will bill for actual quantity delivered within this tolerance. If customer requires guaranteed exact quantities, the percentage tolerance must be doubled.

**Customer's Property**

The printer will maintain fire, extended coverage, vandalism, malicious mischief and sprinkler leakage insurance on all property belonging to the customer while such property is in the printer's possession; printer's liability for such property shall not exceed the amount recoverable from such insurance. Customer's property of extraordinary value shall be insured through mutual agreement.

### Delivery

Unless otherwise specified, the price quoted is for a single shipment, without storage, F.O.B. local customer's place of business or F.O.B. printer's platform for out-of-town customers. Proposals are based on continuous and uninterrupted delivery of complete order, unless specifications distinctly state otherwise. Charges related to delivery from customer to printer, or from customer's supplier to printer, are not included in any quotations unless specified. Special priority pickup or delivery service will be provided at current rates upon customer's request. Materials delivered from customer or his suppliers are verified with delivery ticket as to cartons, packages, or items shown only. The accuracy of quantities indicated on such tickets cannot be verified and the printer cannot accept liability for shortage based on supplier's tickets. Title for finished work shall pass to the customer upon delivery to carrier at shipping point or upon mailing of invoices for finished work, whichever occurs first.

### Production Schedules

Production schedules will be established and adhered to by customer and printer, provided that neither shall incur any liability or penalty for delays due to state of war, riot, civil disorder, fire, labor trouble, strikes, accidents, energy failure, equipment breakdown, delays of supplier or carriers, action of government or civil authority, and acts of God or other causes beyond the control of customer or printer. Where production schedules are not adhered to by the customer, final delivery date(s) will be subject to renegotiation.

### Customer-Furnished Materials

Paper stock, inks, camera copy, film, color separations, and other customer-furnished material shall be manufactured, packed, and delivered to the printer's specifications. Additional cost due to delays or impaired production caused by specification deficiencies shall be charged to the customer.

### Terms

Payment shall be whatever was set forth in quotation or invoice unless otherwise provided in writing. Claims for defects, damages, or shortages must be made by the customer in writing within a period of fifteen (15) days after delivery of all or any part of the order. Failure to make such claim within the stated period shall constitute irrevocable acceptance and an admission that they fully comply with terms, conditions, and specifications.

### Liability

Printer's liability shall be limited to stated selling price of any defective goods, and shall in no event include special or consequential damages, including profits (or profits lost). As security for payment of any sum due or to become due under terms of any agreement, printer shall have the right, if necessary, to retain possession of, and shall have a lien on, all customer property in printer's possession including work in process and finished work. The extension of credit or the acceptance of notes, trade acceptance, or guarantee of payment shall not affect such security interest and lien.

## Obtaining Competitive Bids

Now that you have properly planned your project and understand the industry-specific terms and customs, you are ready to bid your job with the printing companies. If you have not selected a group of printers, see Skill Session 51, "Selecting a Printer," for more information on how to properly evaluate prospective printing companies.

The biggest mistake made in obtaining pricing is the failure to get comparable quotations. It is very difficult to evaluate printing bids when you are comparing apples and oranges. The best way to obtain comparable quotations is to list your specifications on a bidding form. A sample of a bidding form can be found on the enclosed CD.

Using this form is very simple and will eliminate most of the common problems in bidding. Complete this form and send it to the printing companies you have selected for the project. Inform the companies that these are the specifications for bidding, but alternative methods and materials may be suggested. If you receive any suggestions for changing the specifications, revise the form and contact the other printing companies for a revised quotation.

Be sure to reward companies for providing cost-saving alternatives or they will have little incentive to continue doing so in the future. It is very frustrating for a printer to spend a great deal of time laying out a project to save a customer money, and then lose the job by a few dollars to someone else who didn't spend the time to find a cost-saving solution. Paying a little more on a project or allowing the printer to match the lower price of a competitor can be a nice way of rewarding a knowledgeable, cost-saving company.

## Print Order

After you have evaluated the bids and awarded the project, it is important to use a print order to communicate the exact specifications of the job. This form details any changes from the requested quotations and acts as a reference for you and the printer. A sample print order form can be found on the enclosed CD.

You submit the print order to the printer along with the artwork for the project.

# Prepress Proofs

Before printing your job, the printer might create a *prepress proof* for your approval. This might be as simple as a laser output, or the printer could incorporate a more complicated method. Three types of proofs are commonly used; they are detailed in the next sections.

## Bluelines

A *blueline* is a paper proof used to verify layout and text. It is extremely useful for checking position and registration, but is limited because you cannot verify color.

## Color Key

The *color key* is a full-color proof created from overlaid sheets of acetate. It is normally used to check color breaks and registration when using four-color process.

## Matchprint

The *matchprint* proof is made from working film and resembles a glossy color photograph. It is an excellent choice for checking registration and color and is normally used for projects using four-color process.

Regardless of the method used, evaluate the proof very carefully. This is the image you are buying, and it should accurately portray the project you will receive. If you are representing someone else on the project, make sure that that person also carefully reviews the proof and ask him or her to sign it. By asking for a signature, you will get his or her attention and make it more likely that he or she will spend the time necessary to make sure it is correct.

By following the steps outlined in this skill session, you will eliminate most of the problems found in printing. Proper preparation will not only save you time and money, but will also give you confidence that everything will look right when it is finished.

# 54

# Service Bureaus

CorelDRAW provides the capability to create many different kinds of artwork. This artwork, however, cannot always be conveniently shown to others on a computer screen. The final media type can vary widely depending on the reason for the project. For example, many projects are needed only for black-and-white output, and a laser printer output will suffice. Others require color, high-resolution film, vinyl, and many other materials.

This is the reason service bureaus exist. They buy all that expensive equipment that you can't afford or don't need on a regular basis and then "rent" that equipment and their expertise to you so your project can be output on the desired medium.

This process can lead to a great business relationship if handled properly. Unfortunately, it doesn't always work out perfectly. The key is a clear line of communication in both directions. This will help prevent problems and alleviate those that can occur in preparing and outputting the project.

## When to Start Looking

Just as you wouldn't look for an obstetrician a week before your due date, you shouldn't look for a service bureau on the eve of an important project. Create a simple project ahead of time and use it to test all aspects of the service bureau's work. You might even want to run the same project through several service bureaus and compare the quality of service and output. Although this might cost a little money in the beginning, it will definitely be worth it in the long run. This project can also give you a good sample to show clients. Clients want to see that you've done a project similar to what you will do for them. Show them that you've not only done something similar, but that you've also done research to provide the highest-quality product for them.

## Where to Start Looking

The best way to find a good service bureau for outputting the project at hand is to ask fellow CorelDRAW users who have produced similar jobs. These users might already have tried several service bureaus and found a good one, or they might not have found a good one but are able to steer you away from the bad ones. So before you look through ads, contact the users who have already been there. If you can't find another user with a good reference, ask the service bureau for references from their clients who are CorelDRAW users. If they don't have a good CorelDRAW reference, they might not be used to working with that type of file. Remember that *service* is what is being provided, and if they aren't willing to give references, they might not be worth using.

Another thing to consider is what type of output you require. Some service bureaus offer many types of output, but most bureaus specialize in a certain output medium. A service bureau that produces great film negatives might only produce so-so 35mm slides. It is not uncommon to use several different service bureaus, depending on your needs.

Service bureaus have traditionally been dominated by Mac-centric shops. Although they might be able to output your project, they might not be interested in working with PC files. If they aren't interested in helping you, send your business where it will be appreciated.

The output medium is one of two things that your service bureau must properly support. It also must be able to support your input media. For many users this is a floppy disk. When the files get too big for a diskette, a compression program such as PKZIP can make the files fit on that same floppy. But can the service bureau unzip the files? If it runs Macintosh, the answer is maybe. If it runs PCs, the answer is probably. But what if that file is much larger? The answer really varies at this point. The Syquest line of removable drives is by far the most popular device at service bureaus. It might be worth considering what type of media the service bureau supports before you look into purchasing something for your system. If the service bureau considers you an important enough client, it might purchase the device you need it to have.

## Coordinating Specifications

In addition to working with the service bureau to prepare files for output, it is important to consult your printer for the specifications he will require. Clean film with sharp images will be of no value if it cannot be used by the printer. See Skill Session 53, "Preparing for Printing," for the specifications you need to consider prior to having your film output.

## What to Provide

Now that you've chosen a service bureau, you must decide what type of file to send. Service bureaus will prefer one of two types of files. The first is the native application file, in this case a CorelDRAW file. But you also must consider what is contained in that CorelDRAW file. Are there any nonstandard fonts? Which fonts are standard? Just because you can pull one of those 1,000 fonts off of CorelDRAW's CD doesn't mean that your service bureau has that particular font loaded or even has a CD drive from which to load. These don't even approach the problems that could occur if you use fonts from a third-party vendor.

For these reasons, the best way to send a file to the service bureau is as a Print to Disk file. With this approach, the only worries are the type of media the service bureau can accept and the type of output device for which you should create the file. It is not necessary for the service bureau to have any special files, fonts, or applications. All it will need to do is send the Print To Disk file directly to its output device.

Unfortunately, service bureaus don't always like to work with this type of file because the file must be created a certain way for it to output without error. Many times a mistake is made in creating the file, and then the customer holds the service bureau accountable. Although the service bureau could make a mistake, it is most likely the customer's fault. Skill Session 50, "Printing," covers the steps necessary to produce a file that should be acceptable to almost any service bureau.

After you have created your file in the preferred format, you should create an imagesetting work order to clearly communicate what you would like to be produced with your file. A sample imagesetting work order can be found on the CD; you might want to modify it for your own use. Using a form like this enables you to communicate what you want to be done and gives you a checklist to review your file.

## Checklist

To aid in the preparation of a print file, use the following checklist of things to include in a Print to Disk file.

## Paper Size

Should the printout be larger than the final page size to accommodate crop and registration marks?

## Paper Orientation

Is thepage oriented as landscape or portrait?

## Scaling

This should realistically be set to 100 percent for anything sent to a service bureau; other settings could cause problems.

## Tiling

Tiling is a process of dividing a single piece of output into several different pages. This can be very problematic for a service bureau. Look into whether a larger paper size is available that could accommodate the full image.

## Film Negative

This is usually necessary only for film. Ask the printer who will be printing the piece what is desired. The service bureau will probably prefer to do this themselves.

## Emulsion

Check with the printer. The emulsion side of film is the side that has been developed. The service bureau will probably prefer to do this themselves.

## Reading

Check with the printer. This specifies whether the image is right reading (looks normal) or wrong reading (everything is backward) when you hold up the film. The service bureau will probably prefer to do this themselves.

## Color Separations

Does the project contain more than one color? If so, should it be color separated or just output as a composite? Color printers and slides need a composite, whereas film negatives need the separation.

## Crop and Registration Marks, Calibration Bar, and Densitometer Scale

These are a must for color separations—the only way to make sure the pieces line up correctly and to verify accuracy.

## Image Information

This is a must for color separations. It contains the name of the color output on each piece. The printer will scream trying to figure out what is yellow and what is cyan when this step is forgotten.

## Fountain Steps

Resolutions over 2400 dpi should always use 256 for the best results, although when using higher levels you should realize that it will cause jobs to become more complex, take longer, and cause an increased risk of crashing. See Skill Session 68, "Color Management," for more information on the correct setting.

## Screen Frequency

This is a number that should be supplied by the printer. See Skill Session 68 for more information on the correct setting.

## Print To File

This function should always be turned on when you are going to Print to File.

## For Macintosh

This should always be checked, even if the file is to be output from a PC! This changes the first character of the file from a Ctrl+D (Mac end-of-file) character to a space. Removing this character will not affect the file in any way other than to make it more compatible with service bureaus.

## Disks

Remove all other files from the disk!

- In addition to the print file, provide a copy of the file in native format. Remember, print files cannot be changed. Should there be a problem with the file, the file in native form will allow for corrections and save time.

- On the disk, provide a list of all the fonts used as well as the screen and printer used. Also list the maker and version. Beware of third-party fonts from little-known companies.

- Label the disk and provide platform, program and version number, your personal and company name, and telephone number. Dating the diskette can also be helpful to eliminate confusion with other similar versions of the file. Use a label and do not use sticky notes.

- If the file is too large for one diskette, do not use the restore backup program provided with DOS. Instead, try using a compression program such as PKZIP, which is available as shareware.

## Files

- Output a final laser printer proof that has NO changes to it! This gives the service bureau a reference point to check the file. The following are also important file considerations:

- Use a consistent naming convention with your files. Include extensions!

- Don't change filenames after you have imported graphics files. If you must, make sure you re-establish the links.

- Keep all files pertinent to a particular job in one folder. You'll be more organized and it will print faster.

- Include TIFF and EPS files.

- Put the job in an envelope and your diskettes in sleeves.

## Colors

- Check that all of the colors you use in graphics and page layout are either all spot or all process separated (CMYK) Make sure the color model is consistent with the printing plan. Testing of your color separations and spot colors can be performed on your own printer. This will save you time and money wasted on incorrectly set-up files.

- Avoid using RGB except when preparing slides for output. Although these colors are available in many defaults, they don't mean anything in the printing industry.

- When finished, makes sure you clean out your color palettes in any graphics file and in your page-layout program. Delete any that are not used.

## Images

- Create proper trapping with chokes and spreads. Check for fills on outlines and objects. If using spot colors, do not select process black, because this might lead to having more than one color of black on the project.

■ When placing images, cut-and-paste works well within the computer, but it might cause problems on the output from another machine. To avoid problems, select place/export as EPS OBJECT instead of cut-and-paste.

■ Do not enlarge or greatly reduce scanned images because this can create problems with the resolution of the image.

Use correct resolutions:

■ Photos—line screen × 1.5 to 2.0

■ Line art at 1200 dpi

■ Keep all images as simple as possible without sacrificing design quality.

■ Limit use of blends, graduated fills, patterns, masks, and compound/composite paths.

■ Keep paths simple (reduce the number of points or nodes).

■ Don't try to hide or cover up a large amount of unwanted design with white rectangles. This is a poor technique and complicates the file, making it larger than is needed.

■ Use CorelDRAW to crop and rotate images. Do not modify them after placing them into a page layout program.

■ Don't import another image from the same draw package.

■ Check all type on the project for correctness. Pay special attention to addresses and phone numbers that cannot be checked by a spell checker. It is also important to verify that the last line of output exists and is in the correct position. Small differences in versions of output drivers and typefaces can cause large problems, which are most evident on the position of the last line of type.

■ Check all images to make certain they are in the correct position and that they are facing the direction you had intended.

If you are supplying a file with loose halftone images,

■ Label halftones using PG-Alpha

■ Indicate crops on photocopy

■ Do not attach loose halftones to anything with paperclips. Sooner or later, this will scratch an image and you will end up looking foolish to the client and much poorer for having made this common mistake.

## Miscellaneous

■ When requesting bids from service bureaus, provide pertinent information about your file including estimated file size, vignettes, and any additional scanning that must be performed.

535

## Turnaround Time

It always seems that the project has to be finished right now, but by planning ahead just a little bit you can save quite a lot of money. Normally, service bureaus have various rates, depending on whether they must immediately drop everything for your job or can run it late at night when the machines aren't as busy. The rates for rush jobs are significantly higher, and by finishing a day or more early, you can save a notable amount of money.

**55**

# The Printing and Bindery Process

After you have completed a design, you might need to have your project printed. An understanding of the printing and bindery process will help you select the proper equipment and techniques needed to create the finished piece. These variables are very important, as they are a major determinant of the cost and quality level of any project.

## The Printing Process

Selecting the proper press for a project is the key to obtaining a quality reproduction at an acceptable price. Remember, a printed piece can only be as good as the press on which it is printed. If a project is produced on a press that is too large, unnecessary costs will result from excessive paper waste and the premium charged for a larger machine. Printing produced on a press that is too small will result in poor reproduction quality.

The following methods for printing are the most popular in use today.

## Offset Lithography

When people use the term *printing*, they are probably referring to offset lithography. Offset lithography is the most common method used for reproduction because it can produce a quality image at an affordable price with a reasonable delivery schedule.

*Offset lithography* is a method of printing in which an image is inked onto a metallic plate, offset onto a rubber blanket, and then transferred from the blanket onto paper. Many people watching a printing press operate do not realize that the metal plate never comes in contact with the paper. This provides a longer plate life and avoids water coming in contact with the delicate paper.

Offset lithography can be divided into two primary groups by the way paper is designed to feed through the printing press. The two categories are web-fed offset and sheet-fed offset.

### Web-fed Offset

*Web-fed printing*, also known as *roll-fed*, uses paper supplied in the form of a roll. Paper feeds through the press in a continuous sheet, the *web*, and is imprinted with an image. Most web presses have additional bindery equipment added onto the end of the press so that cutting, folding, gluing, and binding can be done in-line immediately after printing. These additional pieces of equipment offer the advantage of having finished materials roll off the end of the press without going through any additional processes.

Web-fed presses are categorized by the size of the paper designed to feed through the press:

- Form Web—paper is 8 $1/2$" to 10" wide
- Mini Web—paper is 11" to 14" wide
- Half Web—paper is 17" to 20" wide
- Three-quarter Web—paper is 22" to 27" wide
- Full Web—paper is 35" to 40" wide

The page layout and the size of the printed piece dictate the correct press size. For short production runs, select the press that best fits the size of the project. For longer runs and multiple-page projects, selecting a press that is capable of printing several copies at once will reduce the time on press and eliminate unnecessary cost.

#### Advantages of Web-fed Printing

The following are some of the advantages of using web-fed presses:

- Best method for longer printing runs—50,000+ impressions

- Operates at higher speeds—up to 50,000 impressions per hour
- Paper costs are lower because of inexpensive bulk rolls
- Newsprint and paper under 50-pound basis weight can be used
- In-line bindery saves time and money

### Disadvantages of Web-fed Printing

The following are some of the disadvantages of using web-fed presses:

- Cannot produce lower printing runs cost effectively
- Longer setup and make-ready times
- Generally produce products of a fixed length
- Higher paper waste

## Sheet-fed Offset

*Sheet-fed* printing uses paper cut into sheets and fed through the press one at a time. Unlike paper for web presses, these sheets can vary in size from very small to as wide as the press. Bindery and finishing operations are not in-line and occur as separate operations.

Sheet-fed presses are categorized according to the widest size of the paper designed to feed through the press.

### Small—Press Size up to 18"

Small printing presses print one or two colors and are commonly found at "quickie printers." They are a good choice for press runs under 5000 impressions, where quality is not critical, but are not recommended for projects that require large solids, line screens above 133, or tight registration. Delivery of a printed piece is fast and can be expected in one to five working days.

### Medium—Press Size up to 40"

Medium printing presses generally print from two to four colors, although some have the capability to print up to six. They are recommended for general commercial projects up to 50,000 impressions that require high quality, utilize process color, or have larger paper sizes. These presses produce excellent solids, have tight registration, and can handle line screens up to 300. Delivery of a printed piece can be expected in five to 10 working days.

### Large—Press Size up to 74"

Large printing presses vary in the number of ink colors they can print and are used in the production of large runs (from 50,000 to 150,000 impressions). They are recommended for extremely large paper sizes, long production runs, posters, and book publication.

### Advantages of Sheet-fed Printing

The following are some of the advantages of using sheet-fed presses:

- Best method for shorter printing runs—up to 50,000 impressions
- Highest quality
- Lower paper waste
- Shorter setup and make-ready times
- Various paper sizes can be used
- Can utilize more expensive paper stocks with heavier basis weights

### Disadvantages of Sheet-fed Printing

The following are some of the disadvantages of using sheet-fed presses:

- Cannot produce longer printing runs cost effectively
- Higher paper costs
- Cannot use low-basis-weight paper
- Bindery and finishing are an additional operation

## Other Printing Methods

Several other methods can be used as an alternative to offset printing. Most of these techniques have specialized applications, print on unusual materials, or produce a unique finish.

### Letterpress Printing

*Letterpress printing* is a relief-printing method that transfers images or impressions by placing the paper in direct contact with raised, inked surfaces. This process was developed in the 15th century by Johannes Gutenberg. Three basic letterpresses are rotary, platen, and flatbed cylinder.

#### Rotary

If you want speed and efficiency, the *rotary letterpress* should be your choice. This press is built for long runs. It has cylindrical surfaces for impression and printing; the plate cylinder holds the plates, and the impression cylinder provides the pressure. With each revolution of the impression cylinder, a sheet is printed. Specialized locking devices hold curved plates onto the cylinder that have the same circumference as the plate cylinder.

#### Platen

If you need short-run printing, the *platen letterpress* should be your choice. It is extremely versatile, performing embossing, scoring, and die-cutting. It uses platen and bed surfaces that open and close like an oyster to carry the paper and type form through the press. Most platen letterpresses enable *impression-lever control*, which means the depth of the impression when embossing or debossing is controlled by a lever.

### Flatbed Cylinder

The *flatbed cylinder letterpress* has a moving flatbed that holds the form; the pressure is provided by a stationary, rotating impression cylinder. In the vertical version of this press, the cylinder and the form move up and down in the same manner as a cylinder in a car engine. This means that a printed impression can be produced in one revolution, as opposed to the two revolutions required with a horizontal press.

## Screen

*Screen printing*, commonly known as *silk-screen printing*, uses a stencil made of metal, silk, or nylon. Ink is forced through this screen with a rubber-edged device, called a *squeegee*, onto the imprinted product. It is commonly used for printing items such as T-shirts, notebooks, product bottles, promotional items, billboards, and other objects that cannot be run through a printing press. Screen printing can also be a cost-effective method for printing extremely low quantities.

## Thermography

*Thermography* is a process for producing raised-ink printing that imitates engraving. The project is first printed using an offset technique; then a resin powder is sprayed onto the wet ink. This powder adheres to the wet ink, and any excess is then vacuumed off by a machine. Finally, the piece is moved into a heating unit that melts the powder and causes it to swell, producing the raised-ink surface. Thermography is primarily used on business cards, stationery, and invitations.

Be very careful in using thermography in laser printers, however, as the high temperatures can cause the thermography ink to melt and leave a mess on the rollers of the printer. Several new powders are now available to correct this problem, but you must be certain to request them as they are generally not used as the standard powder.

## Digital Printing

The newest technology in print reproduction is *digital printing*, also called *printing on demand* or *electronic printing*. This method enables the reproduction of electronic files in full color without film, and in some cases without printing plates. It can be used on almost any type of paper from newsprint to coated gloss, but paper thickness is limited to about 8 points. Many machines are equipped with additional bindery equipment so that collating, folding, stitching, and face trimming can be performed in-line.

Currently, the quality of this method is not equal to that of traditional offset printing, and line screens are generally limited to 133. Because of the elimination of costly prepress labor and materials, digital printing can produce cost-effective, full-color printing on short production runs.

This technology is extremely new, but many experts feel it will replace offset printing as the most common technique for printing. Even if digital printing does not live up to the predictions of market dominance, it is sure to create large changes in the expectations of consumers. Individuals will be able to create brochures in smaller quantities, and production times will change from weeks to hours. Projects that were previously produced in only one or two colors will be replaced with full color, and the storage of printed materials will be drastically reduced.

# Bindery

The final step in the production process is that of bindery. After a project has been printed, there are many processes needed to convert it into the finished, usable form. These finishing operations are called *bindery work* or *bindery*. Often, print buyers focus on the prepress and printing operations and feel that bindery is of secondary importance. This is a common mistake that has ruined many projects.

Bindery equipment is very specialized and expensive. For this reason, many complicated bindery operations are *outsourced* by the printer—that is, sent to companies that specialize in bindery work. It is important to find out who will be performing the bindery in order to better coordinate the project and ensure that quality expectations will be met.

## Cutting

The majority of printing runs utilize paper that is larger than the finished piece. This extra paper provides room for the gripper mechanism of the press to hold onto the paper and for ink to bleed off the edge of the finished project. Larger sheets, referred to as *parent sheets*, also are used to print several copies of the image at one time, reducing the overall length of the press run. When the printing is completed, this extra paper must be removed through the process of *cutting*.

Large stacks of paper are cut at one time using either manual or electronic cutters. Almost all printing companies have cutting equipment that is sized to accommodate their printing presses and will perform this operation in-house. A slight variation in the finished size is inevitable with today's equipment; however, a large variation should not be accepted. When coordinating printing projects, be careful to allow sufficient time for the ink to dry or the pressure used in the cutting process will cause the ink to offset and mark the adjacent sheets.

## Scoring

The *scoring* process creates a crease in the paper so that it will fold correctly. A dull metal blade, called a *scoring rule*, is pressed against the paper to create the crease. Scoring is recommended for projects that utilize heavy paper stocks (above 80-pound basis weight) or a large amount of ink coverage across the fold, or that fold against the grain of the paper. It can also be used to precede a complicated folding operation. Scoring can be performed on an offset printing press by the addition of metal strips on the impression cylinder, or off-press on specialized letterpress equipment. Letterpress equipment is the preferred technique as it produces a consistent score and has better registration.

## Perforation

*Perforation* is performed in much the same way as scoring, except a blade with sharp teeth, called a *perforating rule*, is used in place of a dull blade. This process creates small holes in the paper to aid in tearing apart or folding the project.

## Die Cutting

*Die cutting* uses sharp steel rules, the *die*, to cut paper into irregular shapes. The die operates much like a cookie cutter, producing any shape from a simple presentation folder to a more complicated image such as the outline of an automobile. The dies used in this process can be used many times; however, it is important to allocate them as part of your printing budget the first time a project is produced. Letterpress equipment is used for this process because most other printing presses cannot perform this specialized operation.

## Foil Stamp

Film with a metalized color can be applied to the project using a process called *foil stamping*. Foil stamping uses letterpress equipment to strike the foil with a heated die, releasing it from its plastic backing and transferring it onto the surface of the paper. A wide variety of colors are available. Gold, silver, and copper are the most common, so it is important to select the exact color shade you require beforehand. Consult with your printer regarding the ink formulas used to print the project, as foil might blister or not adhere to many standard printing inks and varnishes.

Foil stamping can be used with embossing to create dramatic images using a process called *foil embossing*. This technique first applies foil to the paper and then raises the image using embossing, discussed in the next section.

## Embossing and Debossing

Several types of bindery equipment utilize a matched pair of heated dies to press an image into the paper. An image raised higher than the rest of the paper is called *embossing* or *cameo and tool*. An image pressed below the surface of the paper is called *debossing* or *tool*.

The heat used in this process can dramatically change the appearance of the paper, giving it a smooth or shiny look. If a heavily textured paper is used, the smooth appearance of the embossed or debossed image will provide a strong contrast to the rest of the paper.

The dies used in this process are etched into magnesium or brass using acidic chemicals or by hand. Brass dies are more expensive, but are recommended for long-term use or long production runs. The production and design of these dies can be complicated. Consult with the die manufacturer for recommendations on the height, angle, number of levels, and detail of the image die.

## Folding

Most printing companies have equipment to produce the common folds used on projects and perform this operation in-house. Complicated folding, however, is typically outsourced to bindery companies that own the specialized equipment needed. Whenever a project requires more than four folding operations, consult with the bindery company for specifications and tolerances for layout and design.

The options for folding seem limitless, but the most common are detailed in Figure 55.1.

*Figure 55.1.*
*Several folding*
*configurations.*

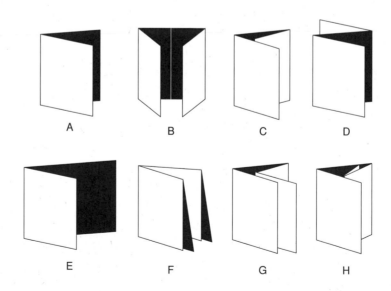

The following are common names for the folds pictured in the figure; use them to clarify specifications on print orders and quotations:

- ■ Configuration A—4-page
- ■ Configuration B—8-page Gate
- ■ Configuration C—6-page Letter
- ■ Configuration D—6-page Accordion
- ■ Configuration E—4-page Short
- ■ Configuration F—8-page French
- ■ Configuration G—8-page Double Parallel
- ■ Configuration H—8-page Scroll

Supply a folded dummy to the bindery to further demonstrate the folding required.

An important design consideration is that folding cannot be exact and will vary within certain tolerances. Most of the time registration can be held within $1/16$" on either side of the fold. This might be critical in projects requiring accordion or roll folds, where page sizes must vary and each consecutive fold is dependent on the previous one. Plan for this as you lay out your project by creating dummies with simulated folds. On complicated folding projects, consult with the bindery company and even request test folding runs prior to creating film for your project.

Paper with a basis weight of 50 pound to 80 pound book can be easily folded with bindery equipment. Paper with basis weights less than this might not feed correctly through the equipment; heavier paper will probably need to be scored prior to folding.

Paper grain direction is also an important consideration in folding. The grain of the paper should run parallel with the fold or the project may develop small wrinkles, have a cracked appearance, or might not lie flat. See Skill Session 52, "Paper Selection," for more information on paper grain.

## Binding

Many options are available for binding loose sheets together in a finished piece. To select the proper method you must consider the use of the finished piece, its appearance, printing on the spine, durability, and cost. The most common methods, except the specialized bindings used in the publication business for hardbound books, are generally listed in order of cost from cheapest to the most expensive.

## Padding

*Padding* is a simple technique used to bind loose sheets of paper together with a thick glue on one edge. Paper is loaded into a vise-like machine, called a *padding rack*, and glue is applied by hand on one edge. After the glue has dried, the sheets are cut apart in pads of usually 50 or 100 sheets. This is the least expensive binding method and is used to produce scratch pads or other lower-quality items.

## Saddle Stitching

In the *saddle stitching* method, collated sheets are placed under a mechanical stitcher and wire staples are then forced through the center of the spine. This technique is similar to the stapler on your desk and is often the choice for binding magazines, booklets, catalogs, and brochures. It can be used to bind up about 80 pages (20 sheets) together and is a very cost-effective alternative.

The saddle-stitched piece can lie flat, but it does not produce a spine that contains any printing.

## Perfect Binding

*Perfect binding* is the technique used to create many magazines, catalogs, and paperback books like the one you are reading now. Collated sheets are placed on edge and ground to produce a rough surface along the binding side. This roughened surface enables better adhesion of a flexible glue that is then applied. The project's cover is wrapped around the sheets, forcing the adhesive glue between the pages and binding everything together.

Perfect binding produces a spine that can be imprinted and enables the project to lie somewhat flat when opened. A major disadvantage is that the spine can break with wear, or the adhesive glue can melt if the project is exposed to high temperatures.

## Spiral Binding

*Spiral binding* uses a wire or plastic coil that is threaded through a series of round or slotted holes punched in one edge of the paper. It is an excellent choice for calendars, books, and manuals up to about two inches in thickness that do not require printing on the spine. The spiral-bound piece lies flat, but the pages will not line up across the gutter because of the spiral nature of the coil.

## Wire-O

*Wire-O* is similar to spiral binding, except that double loops of wire are used to bind the sheets together. It produces a more finished-looking result that will line up across the gutter.

## Plastic Comb

The *plastic comb* technique, also commonly known by the trade names *GBC* and *Plastico*, uses a plastic comb that is inserted by hand into a series of rectangular holes. Plastic comb machines can be found in most small print shops; you might even have one in your office. The bound piece lies flat, and the plastic comb can be imprinted with silk-screen inks. This method produces a result that is lower-quality in appearance but works well for cookbooks, presentations, or information packets up to about three inches thick. It is not a good choice for large quantities because of the cost of the plastic combs and the handwork involved in this process. A major disadvantage is that the plastic comb can break or separate on larger pieces.

## Loose-Leaf Notebooks

Loose-leaf notebooks are not commonly thought of as a binding technique, but they are an excellent alternative for many projects. Initially they are expensive, but can provide large savings on documents that will be updated. Selected pages can be replaced, and new versions inserted, at a cost far less than reprinting the whole document. The notebooks can be silk screened or made from custom vinyl materials. Notebooks with clear plastic pockets on the exterior, often called *viewbinders*, enable you to insert custom sheets to create unique covers that can be changed. Manufactures of notebooks describe the size of notebooks by the measurement of the rings inside and not the width of the outer spine. In order to get the correct size when specifying a particular notebook, use the measurement of the diameter of the rings inside and not the width of the spine.

# The Press Check

# 56

When your project is ready to print, you might want to request a *press check*. This procedure enables you to examine your project as it is being printed in order to make certain it looks as close to the mockups or proofs as possible. The press check is used to make slight adjustments on the press and is not a time to check for typographical errors.

If you have never been to a press check, it is highly recommended that you ask your printer if you can watch one to gain experience. When attending a practice press check, remember that you are just an observer, as this is someone else's project.

## When to Request a Press Check

The press check can be a time-consuming venture and is not needed for every printing project. A press check is recommended under the following circumstances:

- To gain experience and understanding about the printing process
- Projects for critical clients
- Expensive projects with high quality requirements
- Long printing runs
- Projects that require critical color matches
- Whenever you use a new printer

# Preparing for the Press Check

By making just afew quick preparations, you can streamline the press-checking process and make the experience better for yourself and everyone else involved. The following preparations will reduce the number of miscommunications and enable you to present yourself in a professional manner.

## Ask for an Estimated Time

If possible, try to schedule your press check at a convenient time. Many printers run more than one shift and some run 24 hours a day, so your scheduled time could be 10:00 a.m. or 10:00 p.m. Personal experience has shown that Tuesday through Thursday are the best days for press checks. Avoid being the first job in the morning, especially on Monday morning, as the press has probably sat idle for some time and many adjustments might be needed to achieve ideal color.

## Keep Your Schedule Open

Keep your schedule open and flexible and do not schedule meetings or other potential conflicts the day of the press check. The schedule of your project will depend on the jobs ahead of it on the press. If everything goes flawlessly with the previous projects, you might be called early. If there are problems on press, you might be delayed a substantial amount of time.

## Be Available

You will normally be contacted about one hour before the press check. Make sure you can be reached when the notification for the press check comes so that you can arrive in a timely manner. Press time costs hundreds of dollars per hour, and you might be charged if the press is delayed because of an inability to contact you.

## Make Certain You Have the Necessary Tools

Assemble the materials you need for the press check prior to the scheduled time. You should bring the following items:

- Reading material to keep you occupied while waiting
- Viewing loupe
- PMS book or other color-matching swatches
- Printing specifications with any alterations noted
- Mockups and other proofing materials

## Make Certain the Printer Has the Necessary Tools

Your printer should have the following items available for you to aid in the press check:

- Densitometer
- Viewing booth with color 5000K color-corrected lighting

# Conducting the Press Check

After you have sufficiently prepared for the press check, you are ready to proof your project. Realize that you might be nervous, especially if you do not have a great deal of experience. Stay relaxed and focus on the task at hand. Your printer wants the image to look as good as you do, and everyone involved is there to help. To help ensure you have a successful press check, use the following checklist:

1. Arrive promptly and introduce yourself to the individuals who will be involved.

2. Review the project specifications so that every detail is fresh in your mind.

3. Check the paper to make certain it is the correct stock. This information can be easily found on the package, roll, or skid that contained the paper.

4. Review the printed sheet in the viewing booth. Make certain that any alterations you have specified have been made.

5. Check the printed sheet for flaws such as those mentioned in the "Common Printing Problems" section later in this skill session.

6. Check the registration to make sure it is within accepted tolerances for the project. Look carefully at the edges of heavy solids, reversed type, and white areas of the sheet.

7. Compare the printed sheet to the match print or proofs for color consistency. Do the ink colors and overprint colors match the proofs? Colors should look strong and even across the sheet. Critical colors should be examined carefully for color match.

8. Use the printed sheet to create a rough mockup of the finished piece with folding and bindery. Check the bleed and trim size of the project. Does everything seem to fit correctly?

9. Pull an additional two sheets and examine them as you did the previous one. Does the printing seem to be consistent?

10. When you are satisfied with the printed sheets, sign one with your name, the time, and date. Do not sign a sheet until you are completely satisfied. Take another sheet with you as a reference to compare with the delivered product.

Be very careful, as the ink on these printed sheets will be wet and you do not want to ruin the sheet, your clothing, or the interior of your vehicle!

11. Thank everyone, especially the press operator and any assistants, for their help. Ask when the finished product will be ready and make arrangements for delivery.

## What to Do when Something Goes Wrong

Most of the timeyour press checks will last from 15 minutes to an hour, and you will have only a few adjustments. Occasionally, however, there will be a problem. When something does go wrong, it is important to focus on the item causing the problem. The people working on the project want you to be satisfied with the image; getting upset will only decrease the chances for a solution.

Explain why you are dissatisfied and ask the pressman to correct the situation. Unless you are very experienced and understand the technical elements of the press, do not try to suggest solutions. If the problem cannot be corrected by the pressman, ask for the production supervisor or the owner of the company. Explain the situation calmly and ask for help.

This technique will solve 99 percent of all problems on the press. If the situation cannot be corrected, pull the job off the press and make arrangements to solve the problem. If you are representing a client, immediately notify them of the situation, the steps you will take to correct the problem, and changes in the expected schedule for delivery.

## Common Printing Problems

The most common printing problems are listed in this section to help you identify and communicate your concerns to the press operator. Illustrations have been created to help you identify these common printing problems.

### Scratches

Small scratches or streaking might be found in the ink of the printed sheet. Usually, this is only a result of the pressman pulling the sheet out of the press for your viewing. If this occurs, just explain the situation and ask for another one. If the marks still exist, there is a problem and the source of the scratching within the press should be identified and corrected.

### Hickies

*Hickies* are small, round circles in the ink of a project. They are caused by paper dust, dirt, or fibers on the plate or blanket of the printing press. A few small hickies are almost unavoidable, especially with large solids. A good pressman will look for hickies and clean the press as soon as they are identified. Figure 56.1 illustrates this problem.

*Figure 56.1.*
*Hickies in an ink solid.*

## Scumming

*Scumming* is an adhesion of ink to non-image areas of the plate. It occurs when the printing plate does not receive enough water and appears as streaks across the paper or as fuzzy-looking type. Figure 56.2 illustrates type with a scumming problem.

*Figure 56.2.*
*Scumming around type.*

## Gloss Ghosting

A phenomenon called *gloss ghosting* can occur when printing a solid on one side and another image in the same area of the opposite side of a sheet. Fumes given off by the ink on the front can accelerate or slow the drying of the ink on the back, creating an image within its gloss. In order to avoid this problem, allow plenty of drying time between printing the two sides of the sheet. Use of a varnish might also help this situation. Figure 56.3 illustrates gloss ghosting on a solid.

*Figure 56.3.*
*Gloss ghosting on a solid*
*caused by ink fumes.*

## Ghosting

Another type of *ghosting* can be caused by ink starvation on the roller of the press. This situation usually results from the combination of an image requiring heavy ink coverage followed by an ink solid. The first image, requiring a great deal of ink, starves the roller of ink and creates a ghosted image on the impression of the ink solid. Good production personnel can identify this potential problem in the layout of a project. The only real solutions are to either redesign the layout of the project or print it on a larger press.

## Offsetting or Set-Off

An ink transfer from the top of one sheet to the back side of an adjacent sheet is called *offsetting* or *set-off*. It is usually caused by handling or cutting the paper before the ink has completely dried. Some inexperienced print buyers misdiagnose this problem as a bleed-through from the opposite side. Figure 56.4 shows how the ink from one sheet can transfer to another if it is handled roughly or cut before the ink has completely dried.

*Figure 56.4.*
*Offsetting ink from one*
*sheet to another.*

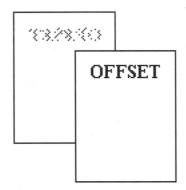

## Chalking

*Chalking* is an ink-drying problem that leaves loose pigment on the surface of the paper where it might be rubbed off when pressure is applied. Changing the combination of paper or ink used will correct this situation. If the project has already been printed, it might be possible to save it by overprinting with a varnish. Figure 56.5 shows a printed sheet with ink chalking.

*Figure 56.5.*
*Ink chalking created by*
*poor ink/paper combina-*
*tion.*

## Excess Powder

Just before a printedsheet leaves the press, it is sprayed with a very light powder to help the ink dry and prevent the sheets from offsetting. If too much powder is used the sheet will have a gritty, rough feel and the ink might have an uneven appearance. Reducing the amount of powder applied will correct the problem, but be careful not to reduce the amount too much or offsetting will occur.

**57**

# Cross-Platform Support

Many users don't realize that CorelDRAW is available on more than just the Windows 95 platform. Currently, versions of CorelDRAW are running on OS/2, UNIX, and the CTOS operating system. Unfortunately, each of these programs requires special treatment before it can use files created in CorelDRAW 6 running under Windows.

## OS/2

The latest version of CorelDRAW for OS/2 is 2.5. It's basically a 32-bit version of CorelDRAW 2.01 for Windows. Therefore, the OS/2 version can read only CorelDRAW 2.0 for Windows files. You cannot create these directly from CorelDRAW 6 for Windows 95.

To work with a file from CorelDRAW 6, you must first save the file as a CorelDRAW 5 file. You then can save this 5 file as a CorelDRAW 3 file if you still have CorelDRAW 5 loaded on your system. In CorelDRAW 3, you can then save this file into something the OS/2 version can read. Why would you go to all this trouble? You wouldn't.

The latest word from Corel on this issue is that they are seeking a partner to do the OS/2 or Warp port.

## UNIX

The current version of CorelDRAW for UNIX is 3. It can read up to 4.x files saved from versions 3, 4, or 5 of CorelDRAW for Windows.

One very viable alternative is to run Sun Solaris's WABI 2.0 (Windows Applications Binary Interface). WABI 2.0 supports versions 3 and 4. It does not support 5 or 6. Sun is working on the next version of WABI, and you will probably see it sometime in mid '96.

## Macintosh

Here's some good news for your Mac friends! Soon they will be able to run CorelDRAW 6.x. It is scheduled for delivery sometime in '96. This release will probably be labeled something like 6.5 because Corel has stated in a recent press conference that it will contain some of the new features of CorelDRAW 7. (Did you think there wouldn't be a 7?)

In the meantime, you are left with several alternatives. One is to buy a "Houdini" like card with an Intel chip and hotkey over on your Mac. The second, although untested by anyone I have talked to, is to run CorelDRAW in Insignia's SoftWindows. Doing so would probably be dreadfully slow on anything less than a 132 MHz Power Mac. The third alternative is to have the Mac read the exported file on a DOS disk.

The biggest hurdle in transporting files between a Macintosh and a PC is the actual format of the disks. A Macintosh can read PC-formatted disks with the aid of utilities such as Apple's PC File Exchange or Insignia Solutions SoftWindows. SoftWindows is probably the most flexible utility because it can also read removable media, such as SyQuest cartridges, Bernoulli cartridges, and many of the optical cartridges. This capability can be very handy when you're working with large files.

Utilities that allow PCs to read Macintosh diskettes are available, but they aren't always seamless. Having the Macintosh read and write to a PC disk is much easier.

## General

Another way to share files between platforms is to convert the files to another format, such as Adobe Illustrator. The resulting files don't retain all the features that a CDR file can retain, but they produce very good results in most cases. (See Skill Session 48, "Import Filters," and Skill Session 49, "Export Filters.")

Part

# VIII

# Skill Session: Advanced Topics Workshop

# 58

# Styles and Templates

The Styles feature enables you to modify objects that have similar features, such as fill, outline, font, and various effects, by redefining the styles associated with the objects. Many users might already be familiar with the concept of styles from using a word processor or page-layout program. CorelDRAW goes one step further; its styles can be applied to graphic objects as well. The style definitions are saved in a template file, which is commonly referred to as a style sheet.

The most important thing to remember about styles is where to find the functions for creating, modifying, and applying styles. These functions are found in two different places: the Styles roll-up and the Object menu. To access the Styles roll-up, select Styles Manager from the Layout menu or use the Ctrl+F5 shortcut key combination. Figure 58.1 shows the Styles roll-up, Figure 58.2 shows the Object menu for Artistic text, and Figure 58.3 shows the Object menu for a graphic.

Figure 58.1.
The Styles roll-up.

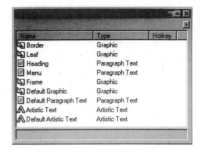

Figure 58.2.
The Object menu for
Artistic text.

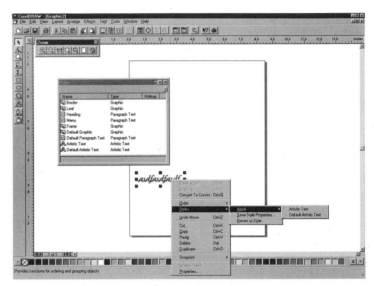

Figure 58.3.
The Object menu
for a graphic.

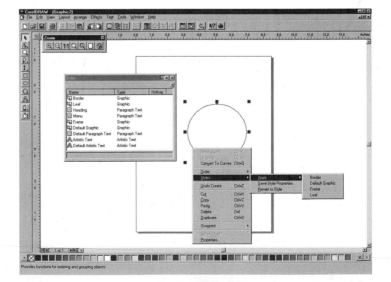

The Styles roll-up can be viewed in several different ways, just like other lists within Windows 95. If you would prefer to see icons (and thus waste screen space) instead of a text listing of your styles, click the outward pointing arrow at the top of the roll-up and choose View Large Icon from the menu, as shown in Figure 58.4.

*Figure 58.4.*
*Changing the view of the*
*Styles roll-up.*

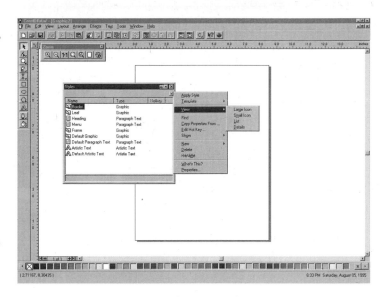

Once you have chosen View Large Icon, the Styles roll-up will look similar to the example shown in Figure 58.5.

*Figure 58.5.*
*The Styles roll-up with*
*large icons.*

## Creating and Using Styles

Styles are created by first applying the desired style attributes to Artistic text, Paragraph text, or a graphic object. Once you've selected all the appropriate attributes, bring up the Object menu. The Object menu can be activated by clicking an object with the right mouse button.

Once the Object menu appears, select the Save Style Properties command from the Styles flyout menu (if this is the first time this style has been used). The Save Style As dialog box, shown in Figure 58.6, contains a list of style options. Options that are to be saved are checked. Enter a name for the style in the text box at the top of the dialog box. Uncheck any attributes you don't want to save before you click the OK button. The style options available depend on what type of object is being defined and the modifications made to the object.

*Figure 58.6.*
*The Save Style As*
*dialog box.*

Once a style has been created, it's automatically shown in the Styles roll-up. You can view styles of each type individually, or you can turn them all on or off by selecting the appropriate choice from the flyout menu, as shown in Figure 58.7.

*Figure 58.7.*
*The flyout menu, showing*
*style types to be dis-*
*played.*

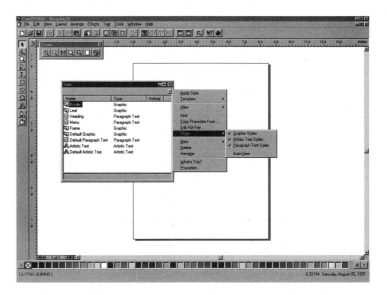

To apply a style to a new object, select the object, click the desired style in the Styles roll-up, and choose Apply Styles from the same flyout menu shown in Figure

58.7. You can also use the Styles Apply command in the Object menu, as was shown in Figures 58.2 and 58.3. A third way to apply styles is through keyboard shortcuts, which can be assigned to various styles.

# Corel*NOTE!*

Only one style can be applied to a paragraph. Apply paragraph styles by selecting any part of the paragraph and clicking the appropriate style.

Bring up the Customize dialog box, shown in Figure 58.8, to define keyboard shortcuts. You can access this dialog box by selecting the flyout menu at the top of the Styles roll-up and choosing the Edit Hot Key command.

*Figure 58.8.*
*The Customize*
*dialog box.*

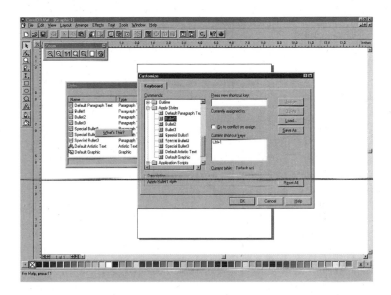

Choosing Edit Hot Key simply brings up the Customize Keyboard dialog box, which is explained in depth in Skill Session 4, "Customizing and Setting Preferences." Some of the styles already have a keystroke assigned to them, as does the Bullet1 style highlighted in Figure 58.8. If you are not using the Styles extensively, it is probably best not to worry about setting up custom hotkeys.

## Templates

Templates hold a collection of styles. To load them, use the Styles roll-up flyout menu command Template Load. More commonly, though, you will open a new file using a template from the File | New From Template command. This can be helpful if someone else has created a template. A good example is the templates that are included on the CorelDRAW CD. Figure 58.9 shows the New From Template dialog box.

*Figure 58.9.*
*The New From Template*
*dialog box.*

When you open a template, you have the option to bring it in with contents or not. If you check the With Contents check box, then all the objects within the file as well as the styles will be imported. But, if you just want the styles, make sure not to check With Contents.

You can also save templates with the Template | Save As command in the Style roll-up's flyout menu.

The Delete command, also in the Style roll-up flyout, enables you to delete any excess styles so they don't cause confusion. You can also search for objects that are tagged with that style. Select the style to be found and choose the Find command. The first object of that particular style is selected. The menu command now changes to Find Next, and you can search for additional objects with that style.

# Corel *NOTE!*

There's no need to use a template because the same information is always stored within the CDR file. It's unfortunate that the style templates in CorelDRAW aren't as flexible as those in Corel Ventura Publisher.

# 59

# Object Database

CorelDRAW's object database is precisely that—a database of graphical objects. Anything that CorelDRAW recognizes as an object can have information assigned to it. You can then summarize this information to keep track of cost, for example, or in the case of a complex object, all the inputs that make up that object.

Although applications for this object database may be limited, it really can be a useful way of organizing graphical attributes including text, dates, and numbers. Its power really becomes evident when you begin to group individual objects. By Shift-clicking individual objects, you can instantly compile summary statistics such as total cost.

In this example shown in Figure 59.1, I have taken a few things out of my refrigerator in preparation of inviting the other authors over for dinner.

*Figure 59.1.*
*Multiple objects represent-*
*ing the contents of my*
*refrigerator.*

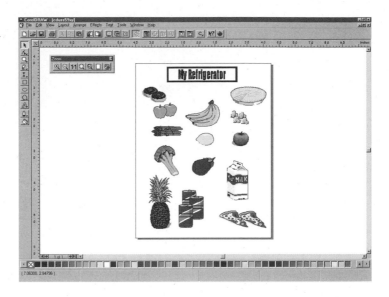

By just clicking the individual food items (see Figure 59.2), I can instantly arrive at the total cost of the meal. (See Figure 59.3.)

*Figure 59.2.*
*All about my pizza slices.*

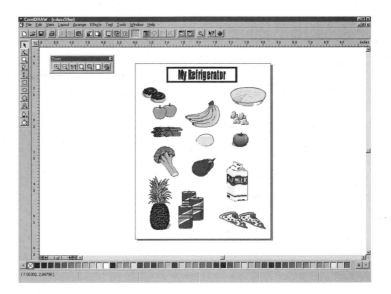

Other applications of this object database might include estimating the cost of a house's floor plan or perhaps in arriving at the total cost of a landscape design.

Figure 59.3.
Total cost of the meal.

So now you're ready to look at how this object database works. Open the Object Data roll-up by first selecting an object and then right-clicking it (see Figure 59.4).

Figure 59.4.
The Object Data roll-up.

At the upper-left portion of this roll-up is a button that looks like a spreadsheet. Clicking this button opens the Object Data Manager, which is essentially a simple spreadsheet. After you combine several objects in the example in this chapter, you will go to this Data Manager to view the summary information. More on it later.

At the top right of this roll-up is a right arrow, which allows you to edit the fields of information that you want to summarize later. (See Figure 59.5.) With an object selected, you can also clear a single field, clear all fields, or with the Copy Data From feature, you can copy all the attributes of another object. This feature can save you a great deal of time if many of the objects you are working with have similar properties.

Figure 59.5.
More choices.

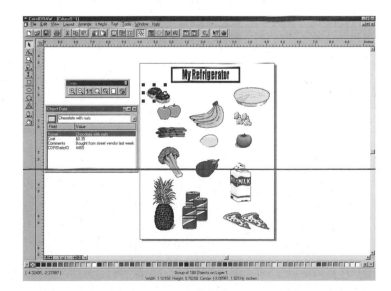

## Attaching Data to an Object

Now you're ready to enter some information. You can either highlight an individual line and type in the data, or you can go to the Object Data Manager. Spreadsheet users will probably find the Object Data Manager easier. To simplify viewing, set the Show Group Details option to 0 in the Preferences menu of the Object Data Manager.

For now, use the Object Data Field Editor. Click the right arrow in the upper-right corner of the roll-up and then choose Field Editor. In the Object Data Field Editor, you can see that four fields appear in the database by default: Name, Cost, Comments, and the CorelDRAW unique identifier, CDRStaticID. (See Figure 59.6.)

*Figure 59.6.*
*The Object Data Field*
*Editor dialog box.*

# Corel *TIP!*

Double-clicking with the left mouse button on an item in the list in the Object Data roll-up also opens the Field Editor.

## Adding New Fields

In the Object Data Field Editor, click the Create New Field button. A field named Field 0 appears. Type a new name in the text box.

The current format of the selected field is applied to all fields that you create. To change the format, click the Change button in the Format section of the Field Editor.

# Corel *NOTE!*

When you add fields to currently selected objects, hold down the Shift key and click the fields you want to add. Click a field while holding down the Ctrl key to deselect it.

## Renaming and Reordering Fields

If you want to rename the field of an object, click the right arrow in the Object Data roll-up and choose Field Editor. When the Object Data Field Editor appears, locate the field you want to rename, type a new name, and click the Close button.

To reorder fields, click on the field you want to move and continue holding down the mouse button. Drag it to the new position and release the mouse button.

To change a name or make corrections, highlight the Field Name and make your edits. Select a field and click the Delete Field button in the Field Editor if you want to remove it.

## Changing a Field's Format

To change the format definition, click the Change button in the Format section of the Object Data Field Editor. In the resultant Format Definition dialog box, choose a new format or create your own using required criteria. (See Figure 59.7.)

*Figure 59.7.*
*The Format Definition*
*dialog box.*

Built-in formats are assigned to certain types of data. When you type in the cost field, for example, the dollar sign automatically appears. Other formats are designations for dates, percentages, linear measurements, times, and a general format for text.

## Changing Column Widths

You may need to change column widths if the columns are too narrow. Use your mouse to resize the columns in the Object Data Manager and the Object Data roll-up by first selecting the column header bar and then dragging the bar separating the fields left to increase the width of a column, or right to decrease it.

## Copying Data from One Object to Another

When you want to copy data from one object to another, click the right arrow in the Object Data roll-up and choose the Copy Data From command. A large arrow then appears; it enables you to pull the attributes from another object and assign them to the object you previously selected. This arrow also enables you to append new data to an object.

# Corel*NOTE!*

> Data attached to individual objects in a group remains unchanged when you copy data from another object to the group.

## Creating Customized Formats

To create a customized format, select the object that you want to apply the custom format to and open the Field Editor. Click the Create New Field button to assign a custom format to a new field. Then click the Change button. In the Format Definition dialog box, select the format you want to create or edit under Format Type. After you edit the format, click OK. The fields now have the selected format applied to them, and the format is added to the list.

# Corel*NOTE!*

> When you edit an existing format, the original format is retained, and the edited version is added to the end of the list. The new version doesn't overwrite the old one.

## Clearing Fields and Data

Select the object from which you want to delete the data, and click the right arrow in the Object Data roll-up. Choose Clear All Fields to delete data in all the fields or Clear Field to delete data only in the selected field.

## Okay, Now What?

After you've created the database, accessing information on objects is as simple as clicking the objects. Shift-click multiple objects to get summary information.

What good is all this information if you can't share it? You can share in two ways: you can either print it from the Object Data Manager (see Figure 59.8), or you can copy the information to the Clipboard and then into a spreadsheet.

*Figure 59.8.*
*The Object Data Manager.*

# 60

# Select By Properties

Use the Select By Properties command to pick out objects in your drawing by the type of characteristics the object has. This command is found in the Edit pull-down menu. When Select By Properties is chosen, it brings up the Select By Properties roll-up. First, determine the type of attribute of the object you want to select, then select those attributes from the various lists in the roll-up. These properties include fill, outline, special effects, and so on.

Select one of the four buttons and properties from the General and Detail sections, respectively. The figure shows three objects, one with no outline attribute. The Select By Properties roll-up has the New Selection button pressed. Outlines are selected in the General section along with No Outline selected in the Detail section. With these settings, the two objects without outlines are selected. (See Figure 60.1.)

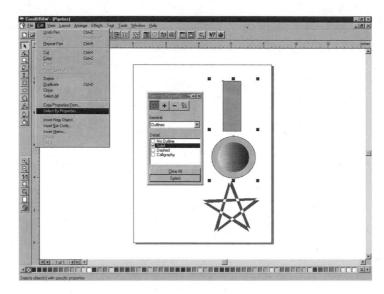

*Figure 60.1.
The Edit pull-down menu
with the Select By
Properties roll-up.*

## The Select By Properties Roll-Up

There are four buttons at the top of the roll-up. They are New Selection, Add to
Selection, Remove from Selection, and Select from Selection.

The next option in the roll-up is the General section. Press the arrow to see a list of
general properties. These properties include object types, fill types, outlines,
colors, and special effects.

The Detail section displays a list for each of the general properties. The list for
object types includes rectangle, ellipse, polygon, curve, artistic text, paragraph
Text, dimension, bitmap and OLE. And the list for fill types includes no fill, uniform
fill, fountain fill, two-color bitmap fill, full-color bitmap fill, vector fill, texture fill,
and PostScript fill.

The list of outlines includes no outline, solid, dashed, and calligraphy. The list of
colors includes CMYK, RGB, HSB, L*a*b, Grayscale, HLS, YIQ, PANTONE Spot,
PANTONE Process, TRUMATCH, FOCOLTONE, SpectraMaster, TOYO, and DIC.
The list of special effects includes blend, extrude, contour, text on a path, perspective, envelope, PowerLine, PowerClip, lens, and clone.

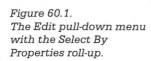

Objects that are part of a group (known as *child objects*) can also be selected as if they
were not grouped.

Along with the General menu and Details list, the four buttons give you quite a variety of choices from which you are able to select any object in your drawing.

## New Selection

Here is how to pick out objects based on object attributes:

1. Choose the Select By Properties command in the Edit pull-down menu.
2. Press the New Selection button from the Select By Properties roll-up.
3. In the General section, pick a search trait (for example, special effects or fill types).
4. In the Detail pull-down menu, choose the properties or attributes you want to find.
5. Click the Select button.

## Add to Selection

Here is how to add objects based on their attributes to your current selection:

1. Choose the Select By Properties command from the Edit pull-down menu.
2. Press the Add To Selection button from the Select By Properties roll-up.
3. In the General section, choose the search property (for example, colors or outlines).
4. In the Detail section, select the feature for which to hunt.
5. Press the Add To Selection button.

## Remove from Selection

Objects from your collection can be excluded based on the object's makeup. Here is how:

1. Choose the Select By Properties command from the Edit pull-down menu.
2. Click the Remove From Selection button from the Select By Properties roll-up.
3. In the General section, select the criteria for which you are looking (for example, object types or fill types.)
4. In the Detail section, pick out the features for which to look.
5. Click the Unselect button.

## Select from Selection

You can choose objects from a selection, based on object features. Here is how:

1. From the Edit pull-down menu, choose the Select By Properties command.
2. Press the Select From Selection button from the Select By Properties roll-up.
3. In the General section, choose the attributes of the object (for example, colors or fill types).
4. In the Detail section, choose the specific features for which to search.
5. Press the Edit Selection button.

# 61

# Presets

The Presets roll-up in CorelDRAW 6 provides a user-friendly way to create and record certain CorelDRAW effects without having to go through the many steps needed to create them from scratch each time. The Presets roll-up lets you to play back previously created effects by selecting them from a list. A thumbnail view of the selected effect is displayed in the preview window.

A number of presets come with CorelDRAW, and you can add many more by creating your own.

## Applying Presets

To apply an existing preset, do the following:

1. Create or select an object. An object can be any single object such as text, an ellipse, a rectangle, a symbol, or any freehand-drawn object. For this first example, type the word PRESET.

## Corel*NOTE!*

The object you select or create is referred to as the *seed* object. The object cannot be a group of objects or an object that has had other effects applied to it.

2. Open the Presets roll-up from the Tools menu. (See Figure 61.1.)

*Figure 61.1.*
*The Presets roll-up.*

3. Scroll through the list of existing presets. A thumbnail view is displayed in the preview box each time you pause on a preset name. If any notes are associated with the preset, they are displayed in a flyout box. The notes give you the information to create the preset so that it looks like the preview. For example if you choose Emboss, the flyout notes will tell you which Font was used. You can use a different font than the one used in the preset, but it will look somewhat different when the preset is applied.

4. Choose Emboss and click Apply.

Figure 61.2 shows the effect of applying the preset Emboss. Your results might look a little different depending on the font you used.

*Figure 61.2.*
*The preset Emboss*
*applied to text.*

Many of the presets in the Presets roll-up were created using text as the seed object. You can use any font in any point size, but you are not restricted to using only fonts. You can just as well apply a preset to a single object, such as a symbol taken from the Symbols roll-up. Figure 61.3 shows the preset Ice On Chrome applied to a symbol of a bear.

*Figure 61.3.*
*The preset Ice On Chrome*
*applied to a symbol.*

## Creating Presets

Creating your own custom presets can be exciting as well a practical. You can create a preset of a special effect you use frequently in different projects, saving you from recreating it each time. You can save your custom presets in their own folder so they can be copied to another system and shared with others.

To create a custom preset, do the following:

1. Choose the Presets roll-up from the Tools menu.

2. Create or select an object (the seed object).

   The seed object must be either a rectangle, ellipse, text, symbol, or freehand curve.

3. Click Start Recording.

4. You can now perform one or more of the following transactions on the seed object:

   Create additional single objects (rectangles and ellipses only).

   Change fill and outline properties.

   Create, copy, clone, or clear an extrusion.

   Create, copy, clone, or clear a contour.

   Create, copy, or clear a lens.

   Edit Artistic or Paragraph text.

   Overprint fill and outline.

   Undo and redo.

   Delete.

   Duplicate and clone.

   Copy attribute from.

   Move, stretch and mirror, skew, and rotate; clear transformations.

   Align and order.

   Group, combine, weld, intersect, and trim.

   Add, copy, edit, or clear a perspective.

   Create, copy, clone, or clear blend.

   Convert to curves (you cannot node-edit a curve).

# Corel*NOTE!*

Remember that the first object acted upon after you start recording is the seed object. When you later play back the preset, all transactions will be relative to the size and location of the seed object. For more information on proportional transactions, see the section titled "Understanding Basic Preset Concepts," later in this skill session.

Once you're in recording mode, you can select multiple objects you have created during the recording session and apply any of the supported transactions to them. If you select an object created before you started the recording session, the transaction will be applied but it will not re-recorded, and therefore will not be part of the playback.

5. Click Stop Recording.

6. The Edit Preset dialog box appears (See Figure 61.4). You are offered a default preset name. It consists of the word *Preset,* to which a sequentially assigned number is added. You can accept it or enter a name of your own. Below the name box is a note box. Attach a few descriptive comments in the note box. You can also assign a color key to your new preset. (See "Assigning Color Keys" later in this skill session.)

*Figure 61.4.*
*The Edit Preset*
*dialog box.*

# Corel*NOTE!*

Although adding notes is optional, they can be useful in telling the user what type of seed object is required to achieve the finished preset. For example, if you created a fancy pattern that started with an ellipse, you should tell the user that an ellipse was the seed object.

7. Click OK. A thumbnail of your new creation is created automatically.

You can now use your new preset in any future projects by selecting it from the Presets roll-up and applying it to a seed object.

Follow these steps to create a preset for a fancy pattern:

1. Select the Presets roll-up from the Tools menu.

2. Using the Ellipse tool, draw a vertical ellipse.

3. With the ellipse selected, click the Start Recording button.

4. Fill the ellipse with a solid color and change the outline to a color lighter than the fill.

5. Click the ellipse again to display the rotation arrows.

6. Using the Pick tool, move the center of rotation thumbtack to the bottom of the ellipse.

7. Click the Arrange menu and choose Transform. From the flyout, choose Rotation. The Rotation roll-up will appear.

8. Type the number 30 in the Angle of Rotation parameter box.

9. Click the Apply to Duplicate button.

10. Continue to click the Apply to Duplicate button until you have completed a 360-degree circle.

11. Marquee-select all 12 ellipses with the Pick tool.

12. Click the Arrange menu and choose Combine.

13. Click the Stop Recording button in the Presets roll-up.

14. Give your new pattern a name when the Edit Preset dialog box appears.

15. In the notes section, explain what type of object needs to be created for the seed object (an ellipse).

That's all there is to it. Your new preset pattern will now appear in the Presets roll-up so you can use it over and over again. Figure 61.5 shows the preset you should end up with after following the previous steps.

*Figure 61.5.*
*Creating a fancy*
*pattern preset.*

## Editing Presets

You can change an existing preset's name, assign an identifiable color key, or delete the preset entirely from a preset file.

## Changing a Preset's Name

To change the name of a preset, follow these steps:

1. From the Presets roll-up, choose a preset and click the Edit button. The Edit Preset dialog box appears. (See Figure 61.4.)

2. Enter a new name for the preset or edit the notes. Caution: Entering a new name does not create a second preset under the new name. It changes the current preset's name.

3. Click OK.

## Assigning a Color Key

To assign a color key to a particular preset, follow these steps:

1. From the Preset's roll-up, choose a preset and click the edit button. The Edit Preset dialog box appears.

2. Click the No Key Color button and choose a color from the drop-down color palette.

3. Click OK.

The Key Color button under the preview window will now reflect the color you assigned to that particular preset. If you want to change the color of the Key Color button using a color from an object on-screen, click the Color button next to the Thumbnail button. An arrow will appear and enable you to click the object on-screen. The object you select must be filled with a solid uniform color.

Possible uses of assigning color keys are to identify certain presets that should or should not be used in certain projects—and of course, custom presets that have been merged with the Coreldrw.PST master file.

## Deleting Presets

To delete a preset do the following:

1. Select the preset you want to delete.

2. Click Edit in the Presets roll-up. The Edit Presets dialog box appears.

3. Click Delete. The Delete Preset dialog box appears. (See Figure 61.6.)

*Figure 61.6.*
*The Delete Preset*
*dialog box.*

4. Choose one or more presets from the list and click Delete.

5. Click OK.

## New, Open, Save As, Merge With

Four new options have been add to the Presets roll-up in CorelDRAW 6. To access these options, click the arrow button at the upper right of the Presets roll-up. A flyout will appear (see Figure 61.7). Each option is described below.

*Figure 61.7.*
*The Presets roll-up with*
*the Options flyout.*

### New

This option allows you to create a completely new file for presets you want to keep separate from the master file. You might want to store custom presets in a custom file so they can be shared with others or keep the size of the file manageable. The master filename for all the default presets is Coreldrw.PST and is located in the Corel60\Draw folder. To create a New file follow these instructions:

1. Click NEW from the flyout. A New Presets File dialog box appears.
2. Type a new name in the File Name parameters box. Leave the .PST extension attached to the new name.
3. Do not make any changes in the Save As Type parameters box.
4. Click Save.

## Corel*NOTE!*

> You should create a new file before you create any custom presets for the new file.

Once you create your new file, the Presets roll-up will appear with the Start Recording button as the only option available. You can now create a custom preset, and it will be added to your custom filename.

### Open

This option lets you open the Coreldrw.PST default file and any custom files you have created.

### Save As

This option lets you save an existing file with a new filename.

### Merge With

This option lets you merge one preset file with another preset file. For example, you could merge several custom preset files into one master custom file.

To merge a preset file with another, do the following:

1. Open the file you want to merge.
2. Click Merge With from the flyout.
3. Click a new file (the file you want to merge with the open file).
4. When files are merged, a copy of the target file is merged into the file that is currently opened. The target file will still remain.

## Corel*NOTE!*

To delete a preset file, click Open from the flyout, select the file you want to delete and press the Delete key (one of the wonders of Windows 95).

## Understanding Basic Presets Concepts

When creating your own custom presets, the following are some things to keep in mind.

## Transaction Sequence

1. If the first thing you did in creating a preset was to create an object, the size and placement of objects upon playback will be absolute. This means that when you apply an existing preset to an object and that preset was originally created (by creating an object) as its first action, the new object (with the preset effect applied) will be placed in the same spot on the page where the person who created the original preset placed it.

2. If the first thing you did in creating a preset was anything other than creating an object; the size and placement of the preset will be proportional to the size and placement of the seed object on playback. (This is described in the next section.)

## Proportional Transactions

Transactions are applied proportionately if the seed object was created prior to Start Recording. When you play back a preset, the size and placement of any created object during the recording is relative to the bounding box of the seed object.

If you make a duplicate of the seed object and then move the duplicate, the proportions of each transaction are maintained upon playback. This feature enables you to add drop shadows to objects of different sizes and maintain the proportions of each object.

## Unsupported Transactions

Some transactions have not been built into presets, as in the following:

- Starting a recording with multiple objects selected
- Using any type of group as a seed object
- Using two-color and full-color pattern fills
- Attaching arrowheads to lines or curves
- All node-editing except Perspective Edit
- Text editing applies only to an entire string, not to individual characters within it

# Corel*NOTE!*

A warning message will tell you if you attempt to record a transaction that is not supported.

## Auto-Grouping of Objects upon Playback

When a preset is applied that results in the creation of more than one object, all objects created are automatically grouped.

# 62

# Creating Custom Arrowheads, Patterns, and Symbols

## Creating Custom Arrowheads

CorelDRAW provides many different arrowheads that can be attached to the ends of lines (see Skill Session 15, "The Outline Tool"). Invariably, you need an arrowhead that isn't provided. When you are presented with this dilemma, you will need to make your own.

Creating custom arrowheads is extremely simple. There are only two rules you must follow when creating an arrowhead. First, the object used to create the arrowhead must be a single object (this includes objects that have been combined). And second, create the original object approximately two and a half times as big as you want the finished arrowhead. A good rule of thumb is to create the original object at least four inches square.

To create your own custom arrowhead, follow the steps below.

1. Draw an object on the page. You can also use any of the symbols from the Symbols roll-up. The airplane used in Figure 62.1 was taken from the Symbols roll-up.

2. Stretch the object so that one dimension is at least four inches.

3. Select the Create command from the Tools pull-down menu. From the flyout, select Arrow.

4. You will get a message dialog box that asks if you want to create an arrow from the selected object. Click the OK button.

That's all there is to it. You just created an arrowhead.

To view you new arrowhead, click the Outline tool in the toolbox and select the Outline tool icon (the fourth icon from the left in the upper row on the flyout) to bring up the Outline Pen dialog box. Click either the left- or right-arrowhead preview window at the upper-right corner of the dialog box. Your new arrowhead will appear at the bottom of the drop-down list. Selecting the arrowhead from the list in the left window puts the outline on the beginning of the line, and selecting from the list in the right window puts the arrowhead on the end of the line.

*Figure 62.1.*
*The Outline Pen dialog box with the Arrowhead drop-down list showing a new custom arrowhead.*

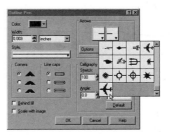

Figure 62.2 shows an interesting way of applying custom arrowheads—using them on a map.

*Figure 62.2.*
*Using a custom arrowhead*
*on a map.*

## Editing Arrowheads

There are four ways to edit an existing arrowhead. To access the Edit drop-down menu, click the Option button below the arrowhead preview window. Here is a description of the different options:

**None**   Choosing this option changes the selected line with an existing arrowhead to a straight line.

**Swap**   Choosing this option switches the arrowhead from one end to the other.

**Edit**   Choosing this option allows you to edit the size of the arrowhead (see the section "Arrowhead Editor" in this skill session).

**Delete From List**   Choosing this option deletes the selected arrowhead completely from the list.

**Arrowhead Editor**   The Arrowhead Editor allows you to change the overall size of an arrowhead and position it on the end of the line. It also allows you to mirror the arrowhead so that it points in the opposite direction.

To access the Arrowhead Editor, click the Option button beneath the arrowhead preview window and choose Edit. Figure 62.3 shows the Arrowhead Editor dialog box. Here is a description of the different options:

**Size**   To change the size of an arrowhead, click and drag one of the corner selection handles.

**Move**   To move the arrowhead on the line, click one of the arrowhead's nodes and drag it left or right.

**Mirror**  To mirror the arrowhead horizontally, click the Reflect in X button. To mirror the arrowhead vertically, click the Reflect in Y button.

**Center**  To center the arrowhead on the line, click the Center in X and Center in Y buttons.

**Zoom**  To zoom in on the arrowhead, put a check mark in the 4× Zoom check box.

*Figure 62.3.*
*The Arrowhead Editor*
*dialog box.*

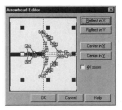

## Creating Custom Patterns

CorelDRAW's vector pattern fills (VECTOR) is probably one of the most underutilized features of the program. Vector patterns fills are repeating patterns of images created in CorelDRAW. The pattern files (.PAT) are essentially CDR files under another name. In fact, CorelDRAW ships with many predefined patterns. This skill session discusses how to create your own custom patterns and how to modify the existing patterns. To see how they are used, refer to Skill Session 16, "The Fill Tool."

# Corel*NOTE!*

> You are not relegated to using just vector patterns. You can just as easily use a bitmap image as a pattern fill. Learning how to use bitmaps as patterns is described at the end of the pattern section.

The hardest thing about creating your own patterns is making them so that they will tile correctly. First, a template needs to be created to make the process easier. Place horizontal guidelines at 10 and 6 inches. Place vertical guidelines at 1 and 5 inches. This will define a square of 4 inches. This is not a magic number; if you prefer a larger or smaller area, feel free to use that instead. The key is to have a square area. Other guidelines can be added as needed to accurately place objects. Make sure to turn on Snap to Guidelines when necessary.

For a quick example, you are going to create a star pattern. Draw a square with the Rectangle tool that covers the predefined square you made with the guide-lines. Now draw five stars that are 1 inch square using the Polygon tool. After making sure Snap to Guidelines is active, place one of the stars in each corner of the square as shown in Figure 62.4. The last star is placed in the center of the square. We know the center of the star should be at 3 inches horizontally and 8 inches vertically by looking at the rulers. Using the Transforms Position roll-up and using the absolute positioning coordinates (see Skill Session 26, "Transform"), place the last star in the middle of the square. The example shown has a blue background with white stars. Feel free to use any colors you want.

Figure 62.4.
Star pattern under
construction.

Once you have created everything, it is time to make a pattern. Make sure you have Snap to Guidelines activated and then click the Tools pull-down menu. Click Create in the menu and then choose Pattern from the flyout. You will get the dialog box shown in Figure 62.5. Choose Full Color and click the OK button.

Figure 62.5.
The Create Pattern
dialog box.

You will be presented with a large crosshair cursor in order to designate the pattern's area. Because Snap to Guidelines is active, you don't have to be precise in defining this area. Click and drag out a square delineated by the guidelines and you should see marching ants running along the guidelines. Release the mouse button and you will be prompted to name your pattern. In this case, name the pattern BADSTAR.PAT and click Save. Figure 62.6 shows the Save Vector Pattern dialog box.

*Figure 62. 6.*
*The Save Vector Pattern*
*dialog box.*

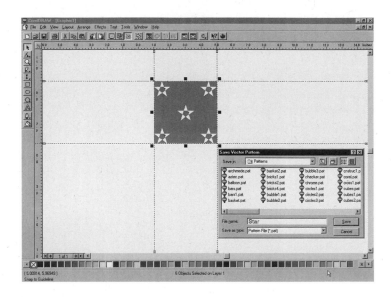

Before opening a new drawing, it would be a good idea to save the existing drawing as a CDR file, because the PAT files do not retain the guidelines and it is much easier to do editing on the original CDR.

# Corel *TIP!*

It is a good idea always to leave the 8 KB full-color header turned on when saving patterns. Otherwise, there is no way to preview them when filling. It is also good to save them in a directory other than /COREL50/CUSTOM. This way, you can differentiate your patterns from those that came with CorelDRAW.

Open a new drawing and draw a rectangle. Select the Vector Fill icon from the Fill tool flyout and fill the rectangle with the newly created pattern (see Skill Session 16 if you need more information on how to do this). You will get a pattern similar to the one shown in Figure 62.7. While this is an attractive pattern, it is not what one would expect from the original drawing. Therefore, some changes will have to be made.

The previous pattern did not work because the stars in each of the corners need to be centered on the corner rather than butted into the corner. Therefore, use the Transform roll-up again and position each of the four stars so they are centered on the guidelines. Use Absolute Coordinates in the Transform/Position roll-up to center them perfectly (see Skill Session 26 for more information on the Position roll-up). Now the pattern should look similar to the one shown in Figure 62.8. A gray background is used in this example for display purposes only (so that the white stars can be seen).

*Figure 62.7.*
*Object filled with*
*BADSTAR.PAT.*

*Figure 62.8.*
*The new, improved star*
*pattern.*

Follow the previous steps to create the PAT file and name it STAR1.PAT. Start a new drawing and draw another rectangle. Fill the rectangle with STAR1. It should look similar to the pattern shown in Figure 62.9. You'll notice that the dots tile correctly this time and everything looks good.

*Figure 62.9.*
*An object filled with*
*STAR1.PAT.*

Now it's time to create something a little more difficult. Create an interesting shape that is approximately 1.75 inches square. Make four extra copies of it. Use the Transform/Position roll-up again. These shapes are going to be placed at equal distances, as shown in Figure 62.10. Notice that the shapes at the left and right end of the top row are outside the background rectangle. If you look carefully, you'll notice that the part outside of the rectangle on the left side is inside the rectangle on the right side and vice versa.

*Figure 62.10.*
*A new pattern being constructed.*

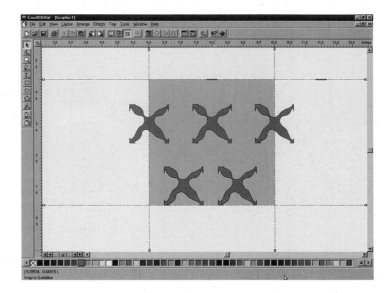

# Corel *TIP!*

The size 4 inches was chosen for the background square to make it easier for objects to tile correctly. Anything that hangs over one edge can be moved 4 inches so that it overlaps the other edge perfectly.

Again, use the Tool | Create | Pattern command to finish this pattern. Figure 62.11 shows a rectangle filled with this pattern.

*Figure 62.11.*
*An object filled with a*
*new pattern*

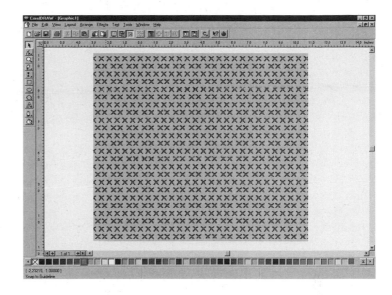

## Editing Pattern Fills

Keep patterns in mind anytime you create an interesting shape. By moving the object around, you can make great backgrounds and fills without a lot of work. And once the pattern is created, it can be edited for when you want to use a different color scheme. For example, take one of the patterns included with CorelDRAW itself, FISH1.PAT. This pattern looks like the fish scales. To change the colors used in this pattern file, use File | Open to open the existing pattern. At the bottom left of the Open dialog box is the List Files of Type box. Change this so it reads Pattern File (*.PAT). By selecting the FISH1.PAT, you'll see a small preview of it on the right side of the dialog box just as you do when opening a CMX or CDR file.

Once the file has been opened, you'll see that it is nothing but a group of circles. Unfortunately, there is no way to tell where the square defining the pattern is located. Luckily, that doesn't matter. Select the circles and ungroup them. For this example, all the circles were changed to two shades of gray, alternating between each row of circles. Figure 62.12 shows the original FISH1.PAT on the left and the edited file on the right (showing two separate views of the file was done for illustrative purposes only). When you've finished editing your pattern file, select File | Save As and name this new pattern FISH2.PAT so that it won't overwrite the original pattern. Now fill a new rectangle with the FISH2.PAT, and you'll see a fish with the yellow scales you just made. The nice thing about editing existing patterns is that the bounding box does not need to be drawn.

*Figure 62.12.*
*The original FISH.PAT on*
*the left and the edited*
*FISH1.PAT on the right.*

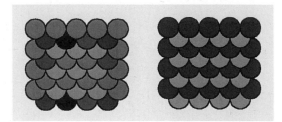

One of the best things about vector patterns is that they do retain attributes of the CDR file. So, if you need to fill an object and have it trapped, just trap the pattern when it is created. For example, if you are creating various shirt designs for a clothing catalog and need a paisley shirt, you could create a paisley shape and then apply the necessary trapping. Make a few duplicates and arrange them in a pattern, much like the pattern in Figure 62.11. Now, when you fill a shirt shape with that pattern, it will be already trapped. (This cannot be done with other fills, such as bitmap fills, texture fills, and PostScript fills.) This process is very easy. You could even hand your pre-made patterns to someone who knows nothing about trapping and he or she could produce something ready to take to the printer. Don't underestimate the power of vector pattern!

## Creating Custom Symbols

CorelDRAW provides hundreds of symbol characters that you can access from the Symbols roll-up. But, just as with custom arrowheads, there will be times when the special symbol you need is not available. This is the time to create your own custom symbol.

Creating custom symbols is easier than creating custom arrowheads, because you don't have to be concerned with the original object's size. When you create a symbol, you are actually creating an object that can be resized. Therefore, there is only one rule you must follow when creating a symbol—the object used to create the symbol must be a single object (this includes objects that have been combined).

Follow these steps to create a custom symbol:

1. Draw or create an object on the page.
2. With the object selected, click the Tools menu and choose Create. From the Create flyout, choose Symbol.
3. You will receive a message dialog box that asks if you want to create a symbol with the selected object. Click the OK button.
4. The Create Symbol dialog box appears. (See Figure 62.13.)

*Figure 62.13.*
*The Create Symbol*
*dialog box.*

At the top of the dialog box is a Symbol Category parameters box. You can choose an existing category or you can type in a new name. We recommend using a new category name for your custom symbols. The new category with your symbol will appear in the Symbols roll-up. When you first look at your new category in the Symbols roll-up, your new symbol will be shown in each preview window. However, as you add more symbols, the preview window will fill up with each new symbol.

# 63

# Bar Codes

Bar codes are used for different purposes, but they all contain certain information regarding a product or item, such as destination, location, and pricing.

The Bar Code Wizard (which you access through the Edit pull-down menu) enables you to put seven kinds of industry-standard bar codes on the objects in your drawing. The UPC and EAN codes are set industry standards, and the rest of these codes are data languages. The seven bar codes included with CorelDRAW 6 are as follow:

- **UPC-A:** UPC stands for Universal Product Code and is used mostly in North America. This type of bar code is used for retail and point of sale. It is basically a product ID number.

- **UPC-E:** This code is similar to the UPC-A, except that it is mainly used by large corporations that manufacture small products. These products, such as gum and candy, have limited label space.

- **EAN-13:** EAN stands for European Article Numbering and is mostly used in Europe. Lately, other countries outside Europe have been using this code and calling it International Article Numbering, but most still refer to it as the EAN. Both European Article Numbering and International Article Numbering are very much like the UPC code. Along with the UPC-A code, EAN-13 is the preferred code for use with books.

- **EAN-8:** This code is similar to the EAN-13, except that books or product numbers that end with zero cannot use this code. This code uses compression technology to fit larger product code numbers into the space of eight digits.

- **Interleaved 2 of 5.** This code is used in conjunction with UPC codes. You will find these codes utilized for marking large corrugated cardboard boxes. These boxes contain multiple packages of a single product such as paper towels. This code tells you what type of product and the quantity.

- **Postnet:** You will find this code on envelopes sent through the mail. It contains the 9-digit zip code information (5+4).

- **Code 39:** This code is similar to the Interleaved 2 of 5 code. It is used for shipping containers. It is also used by warehouses such as those that carry a large inventory of auto parts and by the military.

Figure 63.1 shows all the different bar codes.

*Figure 63.1.*
*The seven industry-standard bar codes provided with CorelDRAW 6.*

## The Insert Bar Code Command

You use the Insert Bar Code command to place bar code objects into your drawings. Typical bar code readers can understand these codes. You can create and edit your own bar codes in CorelDRAW using the Bar Code Wizard.

From the Edit pull-down menu, choose Insert Bar Code (see Figure 63.2), or you can choose CorelBarCode Object from the Insert New Object dialog box. Either way, you wind up opening the Bar Code Wizard. The Bar Code Wizard directs you through the procedure for creating your bar codes. Using industry-standard bar-coding formats, you can enter your bar code string, pick out a font and point size, and set readability.

In the Bar Code Wizard, select one of the industry-standard bar-coding formats—UPC, EAN, and so on. (See Figure 63.3.) Then click the Next button.

*Figure 63.2.*
*The Edit pull-down menu*
*with Insert Bar Code*
*highlighted.*

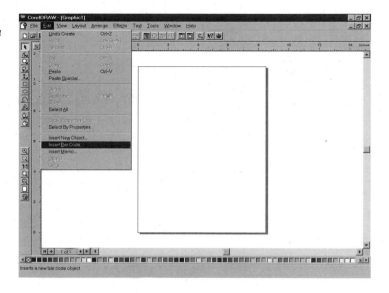

*Figure 63.3.*
*The Bar Code Wizard.*

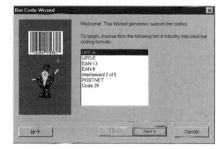

In the next wizard window, enter your product number and click Next again. In the next window, choose one of the subsequent options:

- **By Bar Code Attributes:** This option enables you to establish readability and bar width reduction choices.
- **By Font Name:** This option enables you to pick a font for the bar code.

# Corel *NOTE!*

> The bar width reduction helps to compensate for dot gain or the spreading of the ink.

Click Next to advance to the next step. Now select a suitable font for the bar code from the two available choices. Choose how you wish to select the fonts: By Font

Name or By Bar Code Attributes and click the Next button. Preview your bar code and check to see if the product number is correct, modify it if necessary. Once you are satisfied with the bar code press the Finish button.

## Corel *NOTE!*

Changing the size of the font for the bar code modifies the height of the bars and not the size of the font.

## Corel *NOTE!*

Click the Back button at any time to alter a section from a previous step.

To transform a bar code into an icon, pick out a bar code object you want to alter and choose Corel BARCODE 6.0 Object from the Edit pull-down menu. To access this command, you must first select the bar code inserted in your drawing. Choose Convert from the flyout menu. Select Display as Icon to change your bar code into an icon.

To choose a different icon display for a bar code, pick a bar code object you want to open and choose Corel BARCODE 6.0 Object from the Edit pull-down menu. To access this command, you must first select the bar code inserted in your drawing. Choose Convert from the flyout menu. In the Convert dialog box, ensure that Display As Icon is enabled and choose Change Icon. In the preview area, select an icon or use Browse to pick a new one from EXE or ICO files.

## Corel *NOTE!*

You can right-click any object to display a context menu that you can use to make changes.

## Editing Bar Codes

If you want to return bar code icons back into images, choose a bar code object you want to alter and choose Corel BARCODE 6.0 Object from the Edit pull-down menu. Choose Convert from the flyout menu. This time deselect Display As Icon to change your bar code from an icon into a bar code object.

You can revise bar codes by selecting a bar code object that you want to open. Choose Corel BARCODE 6.0 Object from the Edit pull-down menu. Then choose Edit from the flyout menu. The Bar Code Wizard opens, and you then can edit the selected bar code object.

To open bar code objects, first select a bar code object. Then choose Corel BARCODE 6.0 Object from the Edit pull-down menu. Choose Open from the flyout menu. The Bar Code Wizard opens the selected bar code object you can modify this bar code or replace it with a new one.

## Corel*NOTE!*

You can also double-click any bar code object with the left mouse button to open the Bar Code Wizard and modify the bar code that is currently selected.

After you create a bar code object, you need to position it accordingly. For books, the bar codes usually appear on the back cover in the lower section. This spot on the cover is not utilized to emphasize any benefit from the book, so it is a safe area to use for bar code placement.

## Corel*NOTE!*

On other packages, you should place bar codes, if possible, in a manner that is convenient for the scanner that reads in the code to locate. For instance, a bar code on a 50-pound bag of dog food is easier for the person at the cash register to use if it is located near the top of the bag.

You can output your bar code on a laser printer, but after proofing, you should always have your bar code output at a minimum of 2400 dots per inch.

Colors are an important aspect of the bar code. Because most scanning devices emit a red light beam, any bar code colored red will be canceled out by the scanners beam and won't be readable. Choose high contrast colors such as black for the code and white for the background. The more contrast, the better. On some packages, you can use a reflective surface for the bar code. Most soda can labels utilize this type of bar code. Black, blue, green, dark brown, and so on are good colors for the code; just remember to keep the background color at a high contrast from the bar code color.

# CorelMEMO

# 64

CorelMEMO is a separate application that works not only in CorelDRAW but in other Windows applications that support OLE (object linking and embedding). You use CorelMEMO to create graphic notes (called memos) that can be placed on-screen and printed with the document in order to leave comments for others. You can place memos in many programs, such as CorelDRAW, Corel PRESENTS, Word for Windows, and so on. To open the CorelMEMO program from CorelDRAW, open the document you want to contain the memo, and then choose Edit | Insert Memo from the menu bar. The CorelMEMO screen appears in the CorelDRAW screen and a new memo appears in the middle of the page in its default size (2 inches square).

Alternatively, you can choose Edit | Insert New Object or right-click anywhere in the drawing window and select Insert New Object or Insert Memo from the Object Properties menu. Using this method causes the Insert New Object dialog box (see Figure 64.1) to appear on-screen. Use the scroll arrows for the Object Type list box to display the CorelMEMO 6.0 Object option. Highlight CorelMEMO 6.0 Object and click OK. The CorelMEMO screen will appear in the CorelDRAW screen, and a new memo appears on the page in its default size. (See Figure 64.2.)

# Corel*NOTE!*

To open CorelMEMO in other programs, select the Insert Object command, which is usually found in the Edit menu. This action displays the Insert New Object dialog box from which you can choose CorelMEMO 6.0 Object. Some of these programs will give you a crosshair cursor called an insertion point to click the screen where you want the memo. Others will place the memo on the page for you.

*Figure 64.1.*
*The Insert New Object*
*dialog box.*

*Figure 64.2.*
*The CorelMEMO screen*
*with the default memo*
*displayed.*

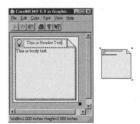

When the CorelMEMO screen appears, enter your text in both the header box and body text area. Format the memo using the options described in the following sections. When you're finished creating your memo, open the File menu in the CorelMEMO screen and choose the Update command. Open the File menu again and choose the Exit and Return command. Your memo is now complete and appears on-screen.

## Formatting a Memo

By default, a memo is two inches square. If you want your memo to be a different size, click the Edit menu on the CorelMEMO screen, and choose CorelMEMO Size to access the Size of CorelMEMO dialog box. You can change the size of both the horizontal and vertical dimensions. The maximum size in either dimension is eight inches. Enter the dimensions you want in the Width and Height text boxes, and then click OK. After you change the size, you must choose File | Update from the CorelMEMO screen before the changes will take effect. Figure 64.3 shows a memo with a width of two inches and a height of six inches.

*Figure 64.3.*
*The Size of CorelMEMO*
*dialog box and new memo*
*size displayed on-screen.*

You also can change the picture displayed in the upper-right corner of the memo. In the CorelMEMO screen, choose Edit | CorelMEMO Picture. Figure 64.4 shows the Select Picture in CorelMEMO dialog box that appears. Use the scroll arrows to select a new picture from the Please Pick a Picture list. Highlight the picture you want and click OK. If you choose View | Display as Picture, CorelMEMO uses this picture to represent the memo on-screen.

*Figure 64.4.*
*The Select Picture in*
*CorelMEMO dialog box.*

You can change the color of the header text, body text, and the paper by opening the Color menu and choosing the appropriate command. Open the Font menu to change fonts and point sizes for both header and body text.

## Customizing the CorelMEMO Screen

Selecting the Toolbar and Status commands in the View pull-down menu will enable or disable the toolbar (the shortcut icons beneath the menus) and the status line on the CorelMEMO screen.

Choosing the Adjust Window command in the View pull-down menu automatically adjusts the size of the CorelMEMO screen to fit the size of the memo (if you have resized the memo to be larger or smaller than the default size of two inches square). A reason for resizing this screen would be to view the entire memo when you have created a large memo. You change the size of a memo by dragging the small black rectangle at the lower-right corner of the memo outward or inward (depending on whether you're making the note larger or smaller).

# Editing an Existing Memo

You can edit a memo's content and the way it's displayed by right-clicking an existing memo. Right-clicking displays the Object Properties menu from which you can choose CorelMEMO or CorelMEMO 6.0 Object. The following sections describe these options.

## CorelMEMO

When you select CorelMEMO, a flyout appears with the following options:

> The Display Content option displays the entire memo if it is displayed as a picture or icon.
>
> The Display as Picture option displays the memo as a bitmap. The default picture is a light bulb.
>
> The Display as Icon option displays the memo as an icon. The default icon is the Corel Balloon.
>
> The Change Icon option allows you to change to a different icon.
>
> Choosing the Display All Memo Content option displays all the memos as complete memos if they are displayed as icons or pictures.
>
> The Display All Memos as Pictures option uses pictures to represent all memos.
>
> The Display All Memos as Icons option uses icons to represent all memos.
>
> The Change All Icons option enables you to change the icons for all displayed memos at once.

## CorelMEMO 6.0 Object

When you select CorelMEMO 6.0 Object from the Object Properties menu, a flyout appears showing the Edit and Open options. Selecting Edit brings up the CorelMEMO screen with the existing memo displayed. You can edit the memo using any of the tools described earlier. Selecting Open functions the same as selecting Edit.

# Using CorelMEMO with OLE

Because CorelMEMO is OLE-compatible, you can drag and drop memos into another application, including the Windows Desktop. Placing a memo on the Desktop puts it where it can be read each time Windows is opened. To drag a memo onto the Windows Desktop, you need to first reduce the size of the open application window. You do this by clicking the middle icon at the far right of the title bar. When the window has been reduced in size, click the memo and drag it out of the application window and onto the Windows Desktop while still holding down the left mouse button. When you release the left mouse button, the note will be placed on the Desktop.

When you first drag the memo to the Desktop, it displays a memo icon (strictly a coincidence) entitled *Scrap*. You can rename the icon by either right-clicking it and selecting Rename from the menu that appears or clicking the title box and typing in a new name.

To read the contents of the memo, the user right-clicks on the icon and selects Open from the menu that appears. The memo can be edited and updated and then returned to the Desktop. Putting memos on the Desktop is a great way to leave messages for coworkers (or your spouse) that share the same system. Each time memos are exchanged the user could change the picture on the memo to identify the author. The memos will stay on the Desktop even after you exit and restart Windows. To delete a memo from the Desktop, right-click the memo and choose Delete from the drop-down menu.

# 65

# Creating
# Maps

CorelMAP is a new addition to the Corel product suite this year. Its function is to allow a user to display data geographically. Various maps are included with the base product. More will be available soon for you to import through CorelMAP's Import feature.

A common use of this product might be to show a company's sales by state. Various color schemes could represent various sales levels such as between $250 and $500 thousand or greater than $1 million. Actual values would label each state. Another idea might be to show sales by salesperson geographically.

## Corel*NOTE!*

> You can use CorelMAP in any application that supports OLE, such as Microsoft Word or PowerPoint.

## Creating a Map

In CorelDRAW, select Edit | Insert New Object. Inside the Insert New Object dialog box, select CorelMAP 6.0 Object (see Figure 65.1).

Figure 65.1.
Inserting a new CorelMAP
Object into CorelDRAW.

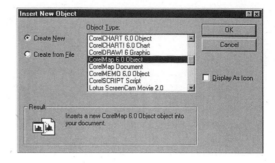

Once you select the CorelMAP Object, the Map Wizard dialog box appears so that you can choose a map overlay. The example in Figure 65.2 shows the USA by State overlay. If you are unsure of the look you want, check the Use Sample Data box in lower left corner of the Map Wizard dialog box. CorelMAP overlays sample data, which you can easily replace with your own data, on the map. After you select the map overlay you want from the list box, click the Next button.

Figure 65.2.
Selecting a map overlay
from the Map Wizard.

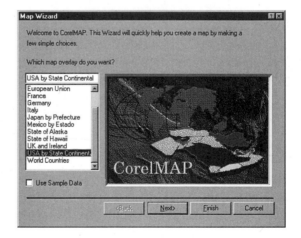

In the next dialog box, shown in Figure 65.3, various formats are displayed. Choose the one that matches the look you are after. In this example, the map title will be placed at the top with the legend along the right side.

If you check the Use Sample Data box in the dialog box shown in Figure 65.2 and choose the Next button in the dialog box shown in Figure 65.3, the dialog box shown in Figure 65.4 appears. (If the Use Sample Data box is not checked, the

Next button is grayed out.) This dialog box allows you to choose either just the data value or the data value and its attributes. In simple terms, you're choosing either color only or color and textures according the data values.

Figure 65.3.
Choosing a map layout.

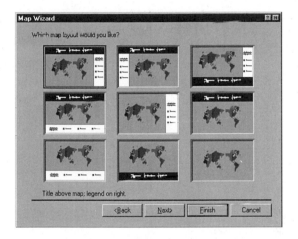

Figure 65.4.
Selecting data values only
or data values and their
attributes.

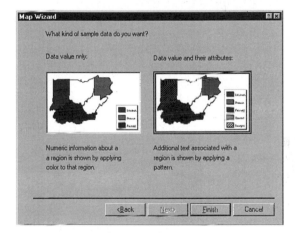

Click the Finish button to insert the map object into the current document. Figure 65.5 shows a basic map with Corel's sample data values and their attributes.

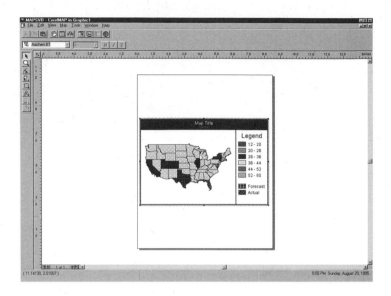

Figure 65.5.
A CorelMAP object.

# Customizing a CorelMAP Object

Once the object is in CorelDRAW, you can right-click it to edit the data values. Notice that CorelDRAW's menus have been replaced with CorelMAP's menus. The following sections explain how you can use these menus to change the CorelMAP object.

## Changing the Data

To change your map's data, select Map | Edit Data. The dialog box shown in Figure 65.6 appears.

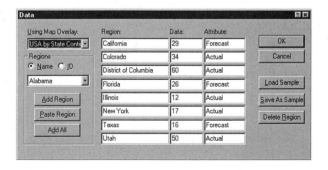

Figure 65.6.
CorelMAP's Data
dialog box.

Within this dialog box, you can add or delete regions, load sample data (if not previously loaded), or save the data you have entered as a sample. The one major drawback of CorelMAP is its inability to import data from a spreadsheet. You have to enter all data manually.

## Changing the Overlay

By choosing Map | Customize Overlays, you can add overlays as they become available (see Figure 65.7). You can also remove overlays.

*Figure 65.7.*
*The Customize Overlays*
*dialog box.*

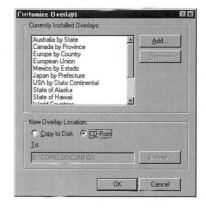

You can also add one overlay to another by choosing Map | Add Overlay. Multiple overlays are difficult to read unless you print your map on very large paper (11×17 or larger). Multiple overlays might be used when the detail is very small or dispersed. After all, why would you show a map of the entire world when you only have data for Hong Kong and France?

## Formatting Map Elements

For additional customization options, select Map | Format. The four-tab Format dialog box appears on-screen. The Layout tab of the Format dialog box is identical to the dialog box shown in Figure 65.2.

In the Display tab of the Format dialog box (shown in Figure 65.8), you can customize the colors and patterns used in the map object. You can also edit and format the map title and its subtitles by using the options in the Title area of the Display tab.

The Legend tab is shown in Figure 65.9. Data values may either be exact matches or fall within ranges. The Steps list box allows you to set the number of items contained within the legend. In Figure 65.9, this number is set to six. Notice that there are six color ranges that will be displayed on the legend. You can also set the colors, patterns, and font for the legend from this tab. To change the attribute labels, click in the Label box and edit the text.

*Figure 65.8.*
*The Display tab of the*
*Format dialog box.*

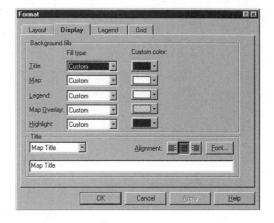

*Figure 65.9.*
*The Legend tab of the*
*Format dialog box.*

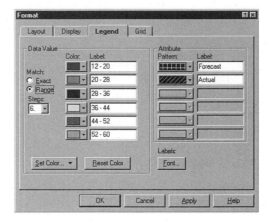

The Grid tab (see Figure 65.10) allows you to customize the grid if you intend to show latitude and longitude (see "Adding Map Accessories"). You can also customize the frame color and the font used to label degrees on the map.

## Adding Map Accessories

Choose View | Map Accessories to display latitude, longitude, degrees, and even a checkered box frame. Simply choose the item you want to display from the Map Accessories submenu. To turn off the display, choose the item again. To display all the accessories, choose View All (see Figures 65.11 and 65.12).

Figure 65.10.
The Grid tab of the Format
dialog box.

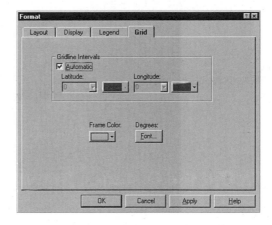

Figure 65.11.
Map Accessories menu.

Figure 65.12.
A map with all Map
Accessories enabled.

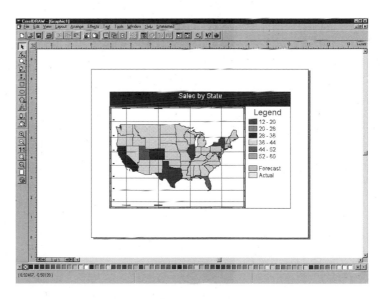

## Changing Map Options

You can use the Map Options dialog box (see Figure 65.13) to further customize
your map.

*Figure 65.13.*
*Map Options dialog box.*

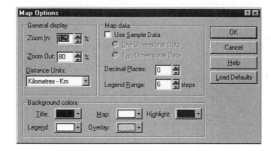

## Figuring Out the Distance Between Two Points

Because the map overlays are scaled, you can easily discover the distances between two points using your mouse to designate the points, as shown in Figure 65.14.

*Figure 65.14.*
*The Distance dialog box.*

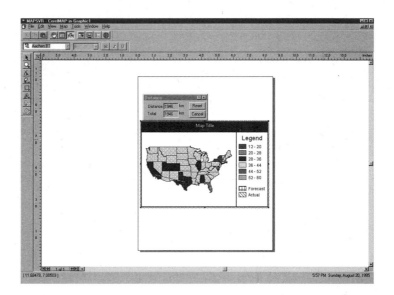

# 66

# Equation Editor

One of the utilities included with Corel is the Equation Editor. Use this utility to insert simple to complex equations into your drawings. The equations are placed into Corel as OLE objects. When you double-click an OLE object, it takes you back to the application that created it originally. (For more information on OLE, see Skill Session 73, "OLE.")

Although you can place equations into Corel documents as OLE objects, the Equation Editor cannot insert equations into strings of text created in Corel. This includes both Artistic or Paragraph text. The best way to have equations in strings of text is to use the Equation Editor in a word processing program such as Corel VENTURA. Then you can import or insert the text with the equations already in them into Corel.

## Corel *NOTE!*

When you first open the Equation Editor, the Equation Editor warning box appears. It states that the equation editor will use the fonts available on the default printer. If you wish, you can change the fonts by selecting define from the Style pull-down menu.

## Inserting Equations

To insert an equation, select Edit | Insert New Object. The Insert New Object dialog box appears on-screen. (See Figure 66.1.) Choose Corel Equation 1.0 Equation from the list. If desired, select any of the other available options. Click the OK button when you are done.

*Figure 66.1.*
*The Insert New Object*
*dialog box.*

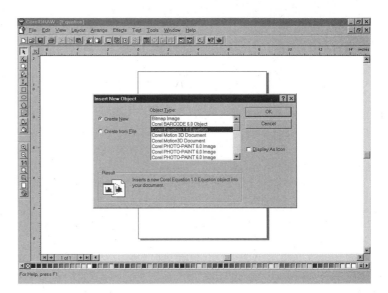

The Corel Equation Editor window is now on-screen. (See Figure 66.2.) Pick out the specific equation format you need by clicking one of the buttons under the menu bar. The format selected is the fraction format. Then type in your equation at the insertion point. In this example the insertion point starts in the fractions numerator. To move the insertion point to the denominator section of the fraction, press the Tab key on your keyboard.

Equation Editor's blinking insertion point, which appears in the single empty slot when you open the Equation Editor window, can be positioned in any slot in an equation. To move from one section of an equation to the other, press the Tab key. Type characters into the Equation Editor window the same way you would in most applications. To delete text, use the Undo command, the Backspace key, Delete key, or marquee-select the text and press Delete from the keyboard.

Once you are done creating your equation, select the File pull-down menu from the Equation Editor and choose from these two choices, Update or Exit and Return.... If you made changes to the equation, select Update to leave the Equation Editor open and see the changes applied in your applications document.

*Figure 66.2.*
*The Equation Editor*
*and a fraction displayed.*

To close the Equation Editor, select Exit and Return To (name of the current application you are using). For example, if you are inserting an equation into Corel, the File pull-down menu will say Exit and Return to Graphic1, where Graphic1 represents the name of the document you are working with.

If you have not chosen to update the changes made to the equation when you select Exit and Return, the Corel Equation Editor brings up a warning asking you "Update changes to Equation in (name of your file)?" You can choose from three available buttons: Yes, No, or Cancel.

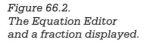

To see an equation object's properties, right-click it and choose the Object Properties command from the menu that appears.

## Object Properties

In the Object Properties dialog box there are three tabs. The first two are the General and Detail tabs. The third tab changes depending on what type of object you have selected. Because you are inserting an equation through the Equation Editor into a Corel document, the third tab reads OLE Object.

The General tab supplies information such as how many objects are selected, which layer the objects are on, and the type of objects. You can also choose if you want Paragraph text to wrap around other objects in your document.

The Detail tab informs you about the selected object's width, height, center of selection, and center of rotation.

The OLE Object tab gives you information about the type of OLE object and the location or name of the document the OLE object is found in. (For more information about object properties see Skill Session 60, "Select By Properties.")

## Equation Manipulation

Once the equation is inserted into your drawing, you can position and resize it just like any other object. You cannot rotate, mirror, or skew it, however. To edit the equation, select it and choose Edit | Corel Equation 1.0 Equation Object. Then select Edit from the flyout menu. You can also double-click the equation to bring up the Equation Editor dialog box. Or select the equation and right-click it. From the pop-up menu that appears, select Edit Corel Equation 1.0 Equation Object.

The Math style is the default style and is applied to any characters you type. This style means most characters will be in italics and the spacebar will not be enabled. To insert text into an equation, switch to text mode in the Equation Editor dialog box by choosing Styles | Text, and then type in the characters. (See Figure 66.3.)

*Figure 66.3.*
*The equation with text*
*entered into it.*

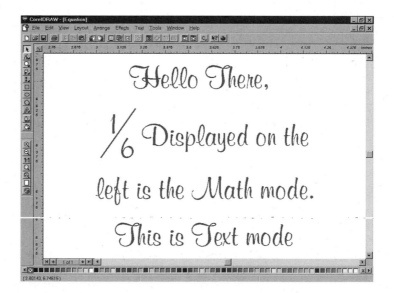

## Equation Editor Control Menu

Take a look at the commands available from the menus in the Equation Editor. To display the Control menu, right-click the horizontal bar (called the Control Bar) over the File menu. Most of the commands on this menu are standard Windows commands that alter the location, status, and size of the Equation Editor window. Commands that display the Windows Control Panel and Clipboard are also available.

Select Close to shut down the Equation Editor window and exit the Equation Editor program (if other equation windows aren't open). If you opened the Equation Editor through your word processor's Insert Object command, the equation will be inserted into the text in your word processing file. This command is comparable to the Exit command on the File menu or double-clicking the Control Bar.

Pick the Clipboard command to see what's on the Windows Clipboard, an interim storage area used when moving graphics or text. For more information, see your Windows manual. The Control Panel command reveals the Windows Control Panel, which allows you to install select printers, choose fonts, and modify a assortment of settings. For more information, please see your Windows manual.

## Equation Editor File Menu

The File menu has commands that are used to insert equations into your drawing or to finish your Equation Editor session. The Update command inserts your equation into the document without shutting the Equation Editor window. This command won't be active unless you opened the Equation Editor window with your word processor's Insert Object command.

The Exit command closes the Equation Editor window and quits the Equation Editor when no other equation windows are open. If you open the Equation Editor with your word processor's Insert Object command and then select Exit, the equation is then placed into your word processing document.

Commands from the Edit menu alter the equation in different ways. Use them to relocate sections of the equation from one area to a different one by putting them on the Windows Clipboard.

The Undo command reverses the last maneuver you completed. If it was an Undo, choosing this command reinstates the action that was reversed.

Cut will place the presently selected item(s) to the Windows Clipboard and remove them from the equation. Select Copye to place a duplicate of the currently chosen item(s) onto the Clipboard without removing them from the equation.

Choose the Paste command to insert the objects on the Clipboard into the equation at the insertion point. The Paste command is unavailable if Equation Editor can't use the Clipboard's objects. (For more information on Undo, Cut, Copy, and Paste, see "Edit Menu Commands" in the "Command Reference" section of this book.)

Pick the Clear command to delete the selected items from the equation. This command will not influence the contents of the Clipboard.

Invoke the Select All command to select the whole equation, including any segments that are not visible. This command is useful for putting a duplicate of the selected equation onto the Clipboard for placement into a document.

## Equation Editor View Menu

Use the View pull-down menu commands to modify the mode equations are shown in the Equation Editor window. 100% reveals the equation in the window at its true size, which is the size it will be in a document or when printed. 200% displays the equation at twice its true size. For most work, this command is a good compromise between actual size (100%) and maximum magnification (400%). This command has no effect on the final size of the equation. 400% shows the equation in the current window at four times its true size. This command is useful for inspecting small characters or for performing minor adjustments using the Nudge commands. This command has no effect on the final size of the equation.

The Redraw command redisplays the equation in the open window at the present magnification. This command clears the display of screen fragments that appear after making edits. Select the Show All command to turn off and on the display of specific special symbols within the equations, including explicit spaces and tab characters.

## Equation Editor Format Menu

The Format menu is used to control the positioning of equations or portions of equations. The first five commands control the horizontal alignment of lines in piles. In order for you to use these commands, the current selection or insertion point must be in a pile.

Choose Align Left to reposition lines horizontally to adjust their leftmost characters. Select Align Center to move lines horizontally and align their centers. Choose the Align Right command, and the lines move to align their rightmost characters horizontally. Pick the Align at = command to reposition lines horizontally to align equal signs and other equality and inequality signs with one another. Choose the Align at Decimal command to align decimal points horizontally. The decimal points can be commas or periods, depending on the conventions used in your country.

Pressing the Matrix command alters an earlier created matrix. You use this command to either choose the matrix to change or position the insertion point inside it. The dialog box that is displayed is the same one you used when originally creating the matrix. Choose Spacing to invoke the Spacing dialog box. Use it to define the dimensions that govern the position of items within an equation.

## Equation Editor Style Menu

Use the Style menu commands to allocate fonts and styles to chosen characters or characters that are typed subsequently, either through Equation Editor's system of styles or a specific font choice.

The Math command assigns the Math style either to chosen characters or to characters that are typed subsequently. When making equations, use the Math style at first. You can switch to other styles if the standard formatting isn't desirable. The Math style distinguishes between variables, numbers, symbols, and functions, and adjusts the characters accordingly.

Select the Text command to assign the Text style to specific characters or to characters that are subsequently typed. This style enables the spacebar on your keyboard, formats characters in Text style (which usually means plain roman), and disables Equation Editor's self-acting spacing, making it easy to type regular text with Equation Editor.

Choose the Function command to assign the Function style to certain characters or to characters that are typed in afterward. Use this command to apply the Function style to a function abbreviation that isn't acknowledged by the Equation Editor.

The Variable command allows you to apply the Variable style to selected characters or characters that are typed in later. This command is useful in circumstances where Equation Editor identifies a succession of characters as an abbreviation function, when, in the context of your equation, the characters should be reconfigured as variables.

Choose the Greek command to designate one of the two Greek styles to characters that you type later or to chosen characters. Uppercase characters are assigned the U.C. Greek style, and lowercase characters are assigned the L.C. Greek style. If you select Ctrl+G, the next character you type will be given the Greek style; after only a single character, Equation Editor will proceed with the earlier style. Press Ctrl+Shift+G to fully invoke the Greek style command.

Choosing the Matrix-Vector command assigns the Matrix-Vector style either to selected characters or to characters that you later type in. Press Ctrl+B, and then the next character you type will be assigned the chosen Matrix-Vector style; after one only character, Equation Editor will revert to the prior style.

The Other command allows you to select a different font and character style either to selected characters or to letters that are typed thereafter.

The Define command displays the Styles dialog box. In this dialog box, you can modify the font and character style designations for the Equation Editor's styles. (See Figure 66.4.)

*Figure 66.4.*
*The Styles dialog box.*

## Equation Editor Size Menu

Use the commands in the Size menu to assign a typesize either to a selected group of characters or to characters that you type subsequently. The Full command assigns the Full typesize to selected characters or to characters that you type in afterwards.

Choose Subscript to apply the Subscript typesize to chosen characters or to characters that you type in afterwards. The Sub-subscript command applies the Sub-subscript typesize to specific characters or to characters that are later typed into the equation.

Select the Symbol command to bestow the Symbol typesize to characters that are selected or to characters subsequently typed in. Choose Sub-symbol to specify the Sub-symbol typesize to currently selected characters or to characters that you type following the modification.

The Other command lets you to decide on a point size for selected characters or characters that are typed in afterwards. The Define command displays the Sizes dialog box, through which you can change the typesizes assigned to the first five size commands. (See Figure 66.5.)

*Figure 66.5.*
*The Sizes dialog box.*

## Equation Editor Help Menu

The Help menu commands furnish information about Equation Editor. The first five commands demonstrate topics in Equation Editor's Help file. The Index command provides Help topics for the Equation Editor. Select the Keyboard command to describe keyboard procedures for using Equation Editor, as well as keyboard shortcuts for many Equation Editor processes. Pick Commands to receive descriptions of each of the commands on the Equation Editor's menus. Choosing Procedures displays the step-by-step exercises for working with the Equation Editor.

Selecting Troubleshooting gives you information concerning problems you may experience while using the Equation Editor. Using Help furnishes a brief tutorial and other facts about utilizing Windows Help. Finally, About shows you the version number of your copy of the Equation Editor.

# 67

# Color Models and Color Palettes

This skill session has been included to help you understand the difference between the many color models and palettes that you can use in your projects. Deciding which is better than the other is a choice you will have to make. The CorelDRAW help files contain a voluminous amount of information on the subject. This skill session condenses the information so that you can make an intelligent decision about which model or palette to use. This skill session does not include many figures because the topic is color and the screen shots would be in grayscale. This skill session also assumes you are familiar with the location of the color models and palettes in the Uniform Fill dialog box. For additional information on the Uniform Fill dialog box and color models and palettes, see Skill Session 16, "The Fill Tool."

Regardless of the color model or palette you use, when you're ready to print, your drawing will be converted to either CMYK process color, Spot color, RGB color, or all three. The question you should be asking is, "If everything is converted to CMYK, Spot, or RGB, why should I be concerned with the other models and palettes?" First, using one of the other color models or palettes may display a truer representation of color on your monitor. Second, the special models and palettes provide an even greater color variance, which gives you more choice of color.

# Color Models

Color models are representations of color derived from a mathematical formula. This formula provides a standard that you can measure color against. Most color models are based on three primary colors called RGB colors (red, green, and blue). Models are divided into two types, additive and subtractive. To access the color models, click Color Models in the Uniform Fill dialog box.

## Additive Models

Additive models are made up of RGB colors. When you use an additive color model, you are using light to create the color. When you add light to a color, the color intensity increases. If the three RGB colors were set to their highest intensity setting of 255, you would get white. Your computer monitor displays color as RGB.

HSB (hue, saturation, and brightness) is a variation of RGB. The colors displayed in the HSB model represent the colors the human eye sees more accurately than any other model. Hue is the color. Saturation is the purity of the color. Brightness is the amount of lightness in the color. You can think of brightness as the amount of white in the color. Many designers prefer to work with the HSB color model.

The additive color models in CorelDRAW are RGB, HSB, HLS, LAB, and YIQ. The difference between all of these additive models is that they have been developed by different companies using their own mathematical formulas to display color using RGB color.

## Subtractive Models

Subtractive models use pigments to create color. The more pigment that is used, the darker the color becomes, which means that less light is reflected off the paper surface. These color models are used when you are outputting to process color printers.

The colors making up subtractive models are either CMY (cyan, magenta, and yellow) or CMYK (cyan, magenta, yellow, and black). These particular colors are used because they are the colors of process inks. Spot colors are subtractive colors as well, but they represent a specific color of printer's ink that is printed on a separate plate. As was noted earlier, the choice of color models and palettes is up to you. You may find one that is more intuitive to use than another or one that offers more colors than the other.

# Color Palettes

The default palette is the custom palette containing CMYK colors. This palette appears at the bottom of the screen when you launch CorelDRAW. To make another palette the default palette, choose View | Color Palettes. When the flyout appears, check one of the palette types. To use a color from a palette other than the default palette at the bottom of the screen, click Palettes in the Uniform Fill dialog box.

Color palettes provide predefined colors that you can use in your drawings or PHOTO-PAINT images. The palettes are comprised of colors that either have been mixed from a color model or supplied by a particular provider. The Uniform Colors palette is made of RGB colors. All the remaining color palettes FOCOLTONE, PANTONE PROCESS, TRUMATCH, SpectraMaster, TOYO, and DIC are CMYK process colors.

The Pantone Spot color palette is made up of colors that correspond to premixed printers' inks. Spot colors are often used when an exact color is needed to print without the possibility of variation that could occur if process colors were used. When you use Spot colors, you can choose the color by the name and number given to it by the manufacturer of the inks. You need a color swatch book containing all the Spot colors with their names and numbers if you'll be working in Spot colors.

# Corel *NOTE!*

Because Spot colors are opaque, do not use them for anything other than specific areas in your drawings. They are printed on a completely separate plate and will not mix with process colors. A common use of Spot color is on a company logo where the company would be very upset if their company color did not look like it should. IBM's Blue is a good example of when to use Spot color.

The Custom palette on the right side of the Uniform Fill dialog box is context-sensitive. The color you select in this palette displays the additive or subtractive color equivalents for the model or palette you are currently using. If you are using the default CMYK color model, you will see the CMYK equivalents of the selected color in the boxes just above the Custom palette. If you chose the HSB model, the RGB color equivalents will display in the boxes.

The purpose of the Custom palette is to provide a palette that you can fill with your own custom colors. The default custom palette contains over 100 colors. Most users will only use these colors, but the number of colors that you have available is unlimited. To add a custom color to the Custom palette, choose a color from any of the other palettes or models and click the Color Options button at the lower left of the Uniform Fill dialog box. Choose Add Color to Palette from the drop-down menu. Your new color will appear as the last color in the Custom palette.

If you want to take advantage of the capability to create your own custom colors, you should start with an empty palette and then add your new colors to it. To create a new palette, click the Palette Options button at the lower right of the Uniform Fill dialog box. Choose New Palette from the drop-down menu. A dialog box will appear so that you can give your new palette a name. Click the Save button. You can now use the default custom palette or your new palette by selecting Open Palette from the Palette Options drop-down menu.

## Creating a Master Print

If you have read this far, you've learned a lot about color models and palettes. That's the good news. The bad news is, no matter what lengths you go to in choosing the right colors and making sure you have a perfectly calibrated color profile (see Skill Session 68, "Color Management"), the printed colors will look different from what you see on the monitor. The reason for this difference is that the colors you see on-screen are back-lit, similar to looking at a 35mm slide on a light table. The colors you see on the printed page are reflective colors; the light reflects off the ink pigments and the paper itself.

Creating a color profile will help a great deal, but it won't solve everything. Blues and greens are notorious for creating problems. If you require exact colors when printing process colors, only two methods can predict the outcome. The first method is to use Spot colors. You have already learned that Spot colors should be used sparingly. The second method is to create a master print.

A master print is a printout of all the colors in the CMYK palette onto the material on which you will be printing. This printout should include the CMYK values for each color. Figure 67.1 shows a sample of the CMYK palette with each color defined by CMYK values. (You can find this CDR file on the CD included with the book.) If you're printing on T-shirts or cups, you should print the CMYK palette on a shirt and a cup. If you're printing to film, you should have a match print made of the CMYK palette. This may sound like a lot of trouble and money for wasted T-shirts, cups, film, and match prints, but it will pay real dividends later on.

The concept behind printing the CMYK palette colors on the final destination material is that you choose your colors from the print using the CMYK values for each color, instead of choosing from the screen palette. This system ensures that the color you have chosen from the print will print the same for every job on that material.

*Figure 67.1.*
*A sample of a master print*
*using CMYK colors.*

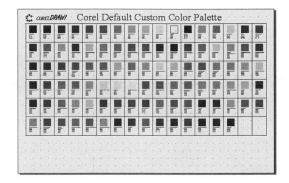

As a way of explaining this concept further, the following is a real-world job we were given. The client wanted a specific teal blue color used in their logo. We were printing on T-shirts using a Seiko sublimation printer. We printed the CMYK palette and ironed it on a sample shirt. The client chose the teal blue they wanted from the sample shirt. We looked at the CMYK values for the color they chose from the shirt and used those values for their logo. The color we saw on the monitor (using the values chosen) was chartreuse, but when we printed the shirts for the client, they got the teal blue they wanted. We would have never been able to print a teal blue color by looking at the monitor because of the tremendous color shift that occurred. This was not an extreme case. As was pointed out earlier, blues and greens are difficult colors to print accurately. If you decide you like to use palettes other than CMYK in your designs, you will need to create a master print using the colors found in those palettes.

## What Has This Skill Session Taught You?

You have learned that if your project will be printed in process colors, you can design in any color model or color palette that suits your taste. Remember, Corel's print engine will convert every color you use to process color (CMYK) unless you have used Spot color. The one exception to this rule is that if you have used a bitmap image, you can check the Output Color Bitmaps in RGB box, located in the Postscript Preferences section of the Print dialog box (see Skill Session 55, "The Printing and Bindery Process"). You have also learned that the colors you see on your monitor will not perfectly match the printed copy unless you follow the master print recommendations described in the preceding section. The science of color and color printing is a complicated subject. If you would like to learn more about color and color models, the CorelDRAW online help files are a good place to start.

# 68

# Color Management

Color management is a monumental task that only a powerful computer can handle. The goal is to have all devices calibrated to a central color model so that colors can be properly mapped from scanner to monitor to printer. The reason this is so difficult is that each device measures color in a different manner. Each individual type of monitor, scanner, and printer is different from every other one, even though they may use similar technology.

## Color Manager Wizard

The Color Manager Wizard in the Corel suite takes all this into account so that What You See Is (almost) What You Get. With all the differing technologies, you can't get exact color matching, but the gap has decreased dramatically.

In most cases, taking advantage of this technology is quite easy. The Color Manager Wizard can be started by choosing Color Manager | Run Color Wizard from the Tools menu. The initial screen is shown in Figure 68.1.

This initial screen really doesn't do anything except offer you a way to cancel or move on to the next screen. Choosing Next will bring you to the screen shown in Figure 68.2.

Figure 68.1.
The initial Color Manager
Wizard dialog box.

Figure 68.2.
The Color Manager Wizard
dialog box for deciding
what to do regarding a
color profile.

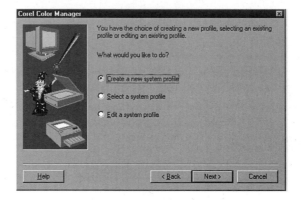

At this point, a decision needs to be made about whether you want to create a new profile, to select a previously created profile, or to edit a previously created profile. Because at some point you need to create one from scratch, we'll start with the first option and click Next.

The next dialog box prompts you for a name and description for the new profile, as shown in Figure 68.3.

The profilename can be any valid filename. In the past, the name has been limited to eight characters, but with Windows 95 that limit has increased to 255 characters. Therefore, you can type in a more descriptive name. But, since you are also given the ability to give a full description, don't make the filename too long. In the description field, you may want to list the devices you will be profiling and any other specific conditions of the profile so that it will be easier to identify later.

Clicking the Next button will bring you to the dialog box shown in Figure 68.4.

*Figure 68.3.*
*The Color Manager Wizard*
*dialog box for naming and*
*describing a profile.*

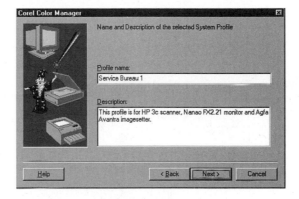

*Figure 68.4.*
*The Color Manager Wizard*
*dialog box for choosing the*
*method of color matching.*

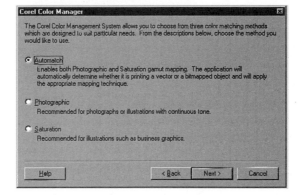

Each of the three settings is fully described right in the dialog box. The Photographic and Saturation options should only be chosen if you know that you will only use bitmaps or vectors, respectively. The best choice to make is to use Automatch and let the color manager use the best technique for each type of artwork automatically.

## Calibrating a Scanner

The next section of the Color Manager Wizard deals with calibrating a scanner. The first choice you must make, as shown in Figure 68.5, is whether you want to choose a scanner profile, create a scanner profile, or not include a scanner at all. If you choose not to include a scanner, you will go directly to monitor calibration.

If you choose to select a scanner from the list, you will be presented with a list of all the devices for which Corel supplies a profile. This list is shown in Figure 68.6.

Figure 68.5.
*The Color Manager Wizard
dialog box for choosing
how to calibrate your
scanner.*

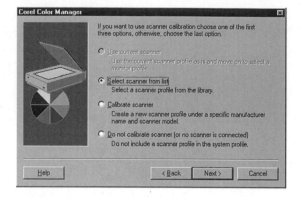

Figure 68.6.
*The Color Manager Wizard
dialog box for selecting a
scanner profile.*

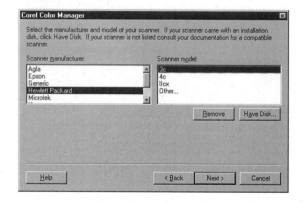

If you don't find your scanner on the list of profiles and your manufacturer has
provided one for you, then click the Have Disk button and select the profile that
was supplied to you. You'll see that the Hewlett Packard 3c scanner was selected
for the profile being generated. Once you've found a scanner profile, you'll move
on to profiling your monitor. If you are creating your own scanner profile, you'll get
a dialog box like the one shown in Figure 68.7.

Figure 68.7.
*The Color Manager Wizard
dialog box for naming your
own scanner profile.*

This dialog box simply lets you enter the manufacturer and model name of the scanner that you will be profiling. Once you've entered this information, you'll move on to the dialog box shown in Figure 68.8.

*Figure 68.8.*
*The Color Manager Wizard*
*dialog box for inputting a*
*target file.*

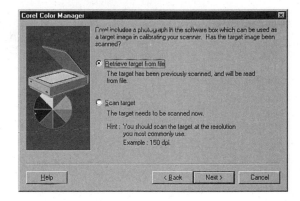

If you have not previously scanned the target file, then you will need to scan one now. In your CorelDRAW box was a photograph of a woman with a bowl of fruit along with lots of color swatches. This is the color target to scan. Simply stick it on your scanner and scan it, making sure to use no color correction whatsoever and saving it in TIFF format.

Once you've scanned in the file, you will be prompted for the name of the TIFF file to which you saved the scan. This dialog box is shown in Figure 68.9.

*Figure 68.9.*
*The Color Manager Wizard*
*dialog box for entering*
*scanner target filename.*

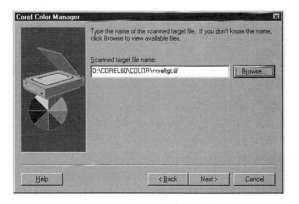

Here you can either type in the filename or use the Browse button to find the file using the File Open dialog box. The next step is to tell the Color Manager Wizard the source of the target you are using, as shown in Figure 68.10.

Figure 68.10.
The Color Manager Wizard
dialog box for the source of
the scanner target you are
using.

If you choose that the target is from another vendor, you'll see the dialog box shown in Figure 68.11.

Figure 68.11.
The Color Manager Wizard
dialog box asking for the
name of the scanner
reference file.

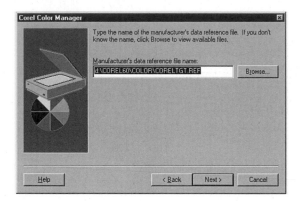

Now, regardless of the target you are using, you'll be presented with the dialog box in Figure 68.12.

The scanned target should now be showing in the dialog box. If it is not oriented correctly, use the clockwise or counterclockwise buttons to rotate it to the correct orientation. Each time you click these buttons, the image will rotate 90 degrees.

Now, you need to mark the corners of the image. If you look closely at Figure 68.12 (or the photograph you scanned), you'll see white markers in each corner. Click the button that has the Zoom icon on it and then click in the upper-left corner of the scan. You'll see an enlarged view of that area and your cursor will now be the same shape as the corner marker. Line up your cursor with that marker and click once. Now repeat this procedure for each of the other three corners so that all of the corners have been marked. Now click the Calculate button. The scanner profile will be created for you, and you'll be ready to calibrate your monitor.

Figure 68.12.
The Color Manager Wizard
dialog box for profiling the
scanned target.

## Calibrating a Monitor

Calibrating your monitor is important if you want to have the colors you see on-screen closely match the colors coming from your printer. It is still not perfect; therefore, you should never trust that the colors on-screen will match your output exactly.

You have four choices when calibrating your monitor, as shown in Figure 68.13.

Figure 68.13.
The Color Manager Wizard
dialog box for choosing
how to calibrate your
monitor.

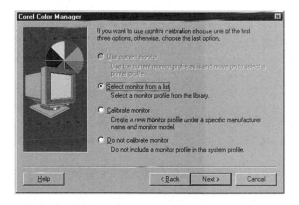

The Use current monitor selection is grayed out in Figure 68.13 because we are creating a new profile. If you are editing an existing profile, then this option would not be grayed out. The Select monitor from a list selection will allow you to choose from the list of monitors for which Corel provides profiles. The Calibrate monitor selection will allow you to create your own profile for a monitor or to edit a current one. Lastly, you have the option not to calibrate your monitor.

If you choose the Select monitor from a list selection, then you will be presented with the dialog box shown in Figure 68.14.

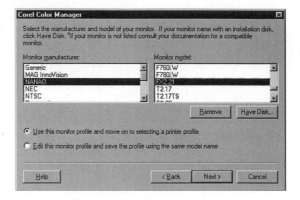

*Figure 68.14.*
*The Color Manager Wizard*
*dialog box for selecting a*
*monitor profile.*

Select a monitor manufacturer and a model from the lists provided. If your monitor manufacturer has provided you with a profile on disk, you can also use that profile by clicking the Have Disk button and selecting the profile from the disk. The default method is to just use the profile as is, but you can also choose to edit the profile. If you choose to edit the profile, you will get the dialog box shown in Figure 68.14, which is discussed later in this skill session. Otherwise, you'll move on to calibrating your printer.

If you chose the Calibrate monitor selection, then you will be presented with the dialog box shown in Figure 68.15.

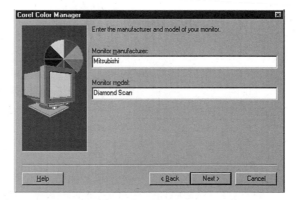

*Figure 68.15.*
*The Color Manager Wizard*
*dialog box for naming a*
*monitor profile.*

Enter the name of the manufacturer and the model name for the monitor you are calibrating. When you click the Next button, you'll be presented with the dialog box shown in Figure 68.16.

Figure 68.16.
The Color Manager Wizard
dialog box for monitor
characteristics.

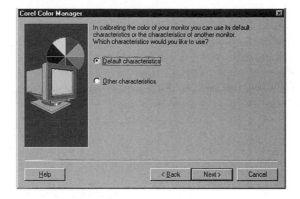

Here you have the choice of using the default monitor characteristics or choosing the characteristics of a particular monitor to begin your calibration. If you have chosen Default, the next screen you see will be Figure 68.18. But, if you choose Other, you get the dialog box shown in Figure 68.17.

Figure 68.17.
The Color Manager Wizard
dialog box for copying
monitor characteristics.

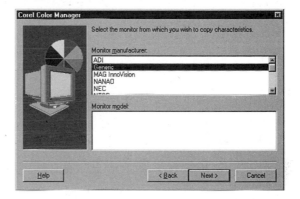

This dialog box is very similar to the one where you choose the monitor to use in a profile. The difference is that you are just choosing a profile to modify. Try to choose a monitor that is very similar to yours, or if your monitor has aged, select your monitor profile to edit. Once you've made a selection, click the Next button and you'll get the dialog box shown in Figure 68.18.

*Chromaticity* relates to the number of saturated colors that a monitor is capable of reproducing. The values provided by Color Manager are more than likely correct, because the numbers are nearly identical for all monitors. You can modify the numbers either by dragging the slider within the window to the right of the numbers or by adjusting the numbers manually. If you look in the Phosphors drop-down list, you will see manufacturers of various monitor tubes. You might just want to choose from this list. There is also a list for setting the ambient light level.

Figure 68.18.
The Color Manager Wizard
dialog box for adjusting
monitor chromaticity.

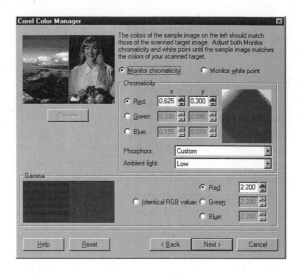

You can adjust the Gamma values for each individual color, or, by clicking on the Identical radio button, you can give them identical values. When making Gamma adjustments, you should sit at least four feet from your monitor to get the best results. Click the arrows to the right of the swatch box to adjust the settings until the color of the right half of the swatch matches that of the left half.

White point values can be adjusted by clicking the Monitor white point radio button. The dialog box will change to the one shown in Figure 68.19.

Figure 68.19.
The Color Manager Wizard
dialog box for adjusting
monitor white point.

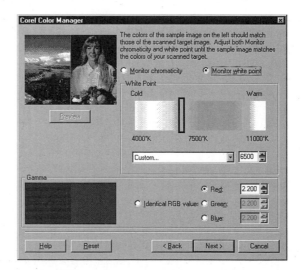

The white point can be adjusted by sliding the temperature slider between Cold and Warm. You should only make these adjustments after you adjust the contrast and brightness on your monitor and make sure that the room light is adequate. The idea is for the preview image to have quality levels of white. If the temperature is too cool, the image will have a blue tint in the white areas; settings that are too warm will cause a yellow tint in the white areas. The default is 7000; natural sunlight is approximately 6500.

After making all adjustments, you can click the Preview button to see how it will affect the preview picture of the woman standing at the dessert buffet table. When all the settings are adjusted correctly, the two pictures should look identical.

## Calibrating a Printer

The last step in creating a color profile is to calibrate your printer. As with the first two steps, the first choice is the method of calibration, as shown in Figure 68.20.

*Figure 68.20.*
*The Color Manager Wizard*
*dialog box for choosing*
*how to calibrate your*
*printer.*

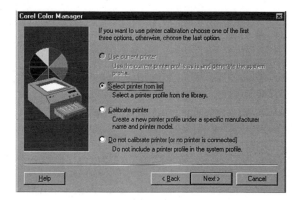

Here you have four choices for how to calibrate your printer. The first option is grayed out in Figure 68.19 because we are creating a new profile rather than editing an existing one. The Select printer from list selection will provide a list of all printers for which Corel has supplied a profile and allow you to choose your printer. The Calibrate printer selection will walk you through the steps for calibrating a printer that is not listed or for customizing one that is already listed. Lastly, you can choose not to calibrate your printer.

If you choose the Select printer from list selection, you will get the dialog box shown in Figure 68.21.

Scroll through the list and find the printer you want to include in your system profile and then select it. If your printer is not listed and you have a disk supplied to you by the manufacturer, simply click on the Have Disk button and select the profile from the disk. You also have the option of editing the selected profile if you wish. This will be described later in this skill session. If you've chosen a printer and have clicked the Next button, you'll be ready to finish creating the profile. If you have chosen to create your own profile, you'll get the dialog box shown in Figure 68.22.

*Figure 68.21.*
*The Color Manager Wizard*
*dialog box for selecting a*
*color profile for your*
*printer.*

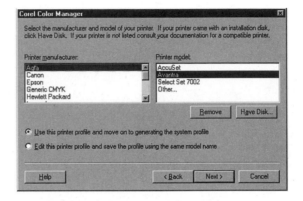

*Figure 68.22.*
*The Color Manager Wizard*
*dialog box for entering the*
*name of the printer to*
*profile.*

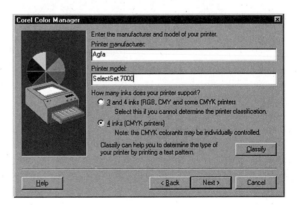

Enter the manufacturer and model name of the printer for which you are creating a profile. Next, you need to select the number of inks that your printer supports. If you do not know, then just click the Classify button, and the Color Manager will print a file to your printer for you. This file is shown in Figure 68.23.

When you print the file, if you can see the Corel C logo, then your printer is a CMYK device. If all you see is a solid blob, then you should select the 3 and 4 inks option. Once you've made your selection, click the Next button, and you'll get the dialog box shown in Figure 68.24.

*Figure 68.23.*
*The file that determines*
*the classification of your*
*printer.*

# Printer Classification Method

If all or part of the Corel C Logo is visible,

select your Printer as being a CMYK Device

*Figure 68.24.*
*The Color Manager Wizard*
*dialog box for printer*
*characteristics.*

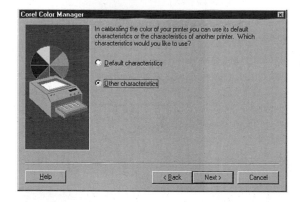

If you select the Default characteristics option, then the generic profile will be used as a starting point for your profile, and you'll move on to the dialog box shown in Figure 68.26. Choosing the Other characteristics option will allow you to specify an existing printer profile as the starting point for your new profile, as shown in Figure 68.25.

Double-click the name of the printer manufacturer and a list of the models will be displayed. Choose the model from which you want to copy the characteristics and then click the Next button. This will give you the dialog box shown in Figure 68.26.

Figure 68.25.
The Color Manager Wizard
dialog box for copy printer
profile characteristics.

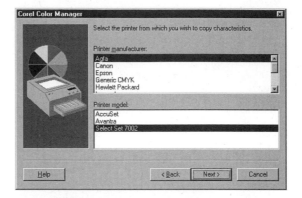

Figure 68.26.
The Color Manager Wizard
dialog box for choosing the
method of printer calibration.

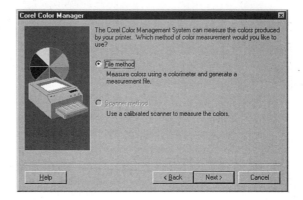

The file method requires that you use a colorimeter and generate a measurement
file from a printout. This is a very expensive device and this option is therefore not
for the average user. The other option is to scan in a target file that you've printed.
This requires that you use a calibrated scanner. Because we've yet to calibrate our
scanner, this option is grayed out. If you choose the File method and click the Next
button, you'll get the dialog box shown in Figure 68.27.

Figure 68.27.
The Color Manager Wizard
dialog box for printing a
test pattern file.

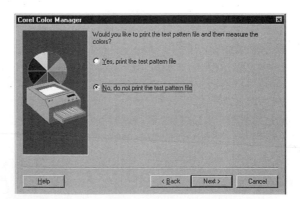

If you choose to print a test pattern, then it will automatically send the file to your printer so that you can then measure the printed file with a colorimeter. Choosing the No option will skip the printing and take you directly to the dialog shown in Figure 68.28.

Figure 68.28.
*The Color Manager Wizard*
*dialog box for specifying a*
*color management file.*

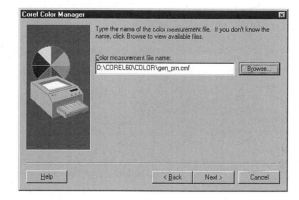

Type in the name of the color measurement file you created or use the Browse button to search for it on your disk. Once you've entered the filename, click the Next button to get the dialog box shown in Figure 68.29.

Figure 68.29.
*The Color Manager Wizard*
*dialog box for adjusting*
*the printer profile.*

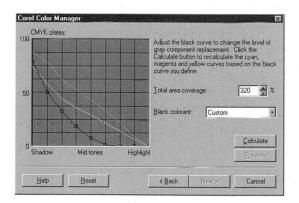

The TAC text box is for entering the total ink coverage that is allowed. The Black colorant setting in this dialog is for gray color replacement (GCR). You have several settings from which to choose. If you choose Custom, then the black curve can be manually adjusted at as many as nine different points along the line. The other settings range from None, which takes out all black, to Heavy, which uses lots of black. The initial setting shown in Figure 68.29 is the same as the Medium setting. There is no setting for dot gain—the Candela technology figures this automatically for you. Once you've made all the adjustments, click the Calculate button. When the calculation is finished, click the Next button. Now you'll see the dialog box shown in Figure 68.30.

*Figure 68.30.*
*The Color Manager Wizard*
*dialog box for finishing*
*your profile.*

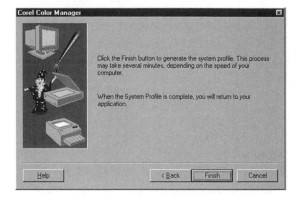

Once you've gotten to this dialog box, you are just one click and a coffee break away from being finished. Click the Finish button and the Color Manager will take a few minutes to create your system profile. The speed of this will depend on the speed of your system.

## Using a Color Profile

When the Color Manager Wizard finishes creating a system profile, it automatically makes the profile the active one in all applications that support the Color Manager. But, if you've created several different profiles, you might want to switch profiles from time to time. If you choose Color Manager | Select Color Profile from the Tools menu, then you'll get a dialog box similar to the one in Figure 68.31.

The list of profiles will show all of the profiles that you've created. Simply click the one you want to use. It will show the devices defined within the profile at the right of the dialog box and the description of the profile will be at the bottom. Click the Finish button, and the chosen profile will now be the active profile in all Corel programs that use it.

To use the color adjustments for your monitor, select Color Correction Accurate. Now go back and select Color Correction Simulate Printer, and you'll notice a drastic change in the colors on your screen. The redraw time will be noticeably slower, but this is a good way to proof things on-screen before printing. It is not a good idea to leave this on at all times, though, due to the slowness of redraw.

Lastly, the printer color profile can be activated by simply checking Printer Color Profile in the Print dialog box. More information on how to do this is found in Skill Session 50.

*Figure 68.31.*
*The Color Manager dialog*
*box for choosing between*
*system profiles.*

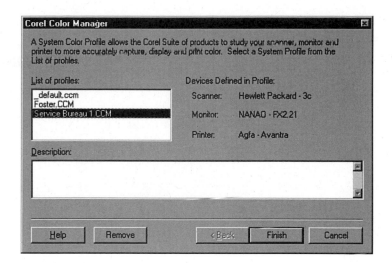

# 69

# Page Setup

When you begin a new project, the first thing you need to do is define the paper size and orientation.

## Setting Up the Page

You begin by choosing Layout | Page Setup to display the Page Settings dialog box. The default page size is Letter Portrait. Figure 69.1 shows the Page Settings dialog box with the default settings.

The following list describes the settings in this dialog box:

- For Page Size, you can choose either Portrait or Landscape. The large preview window at the right displays a graphic of the size you choose.

- The default Paper setting is Letter. Click the down arrow in the Paper drop-down list to select other sizes. Figure 69.2 shows the drop-down menu selected.

- When you choose Custom from the Paper drop-down list, you can type sizes in the Height and Width parameters boxes. (See Figure 69.3.) The new limit in CorelDRAW 6 is approximately $150 \times 150$ feet (that's not a typo) with an accuracy of one-tenth of a micron. You also have the option of several measurement systems, such as inches, millimeters, and points.

*Figure 69.1.*
*The Page Settings*
*dialog box.*

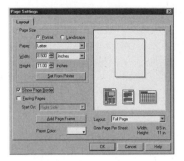

*Figure 69.2.*
*The Paper drop-down*
*menu.*

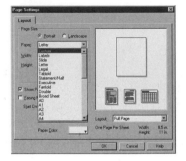

- The Set From Printer button sets the paper size to the default setting of your printer.

- Putting a check mark in the Show Page Border box displays the page border with a drop-shadow effect.

- Putting a check mark in the Facing Pages box lets you see facing pages if you have multiple pages in your document.

- The Start On option is only applicable when you have enabled Facing Pages. You can choose to display your multiple-page documents by starting on either the Right or Left page.

- Putting a check mark in the Add Page Frame box places a rectangle on the page the size of the page. The rectangle is just like any other object and is printable. The color of the rectangle uses the default settings of your Fill and Outline colors.

- Click the Paper Color button to display the default color palette. Choose a color for your background paper color. The color you choose here differs from the Page Frame setting in that it is for display purposes only and does not print. An example of its use would be that you're printing on colored paper and you want to see what your document will look like before you print.

# Choosing a Page Layout Style

Click the down arrow in the Layout drop-down list box to display the six choices of custom page layout styles (layout styles are not to be confused with other CorelDRAW styles), which are described in the following list:

- Full Page is the default page layout style. One full page is printed per sheet.

- In the Book layout, two pages per sheet are printed so that the document can be cut in the middle.

- In the Booklet layout, two pages per sheet are printed so that the document can be folded vertically for a side fold.

- In the Tent Card layout, two pages per sheet are printed so that the document can be folded horizontally for a top fold.

- In the Side-Fold Card layout, four pages per sheet are printed so that the document can be folded horizontally for the top fold and vertically for a side fold.

- In the Top-Fold Card layout, four pages per sheet are printed so that the document can be folded vertically for the side fold and horizontally for the top fold.

*Figure 69.3.*
*The Page Settings dialog*
*box with Book selected*
*from the Layout drop-*
*down list box.*

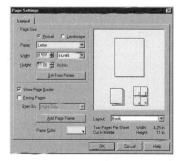

Below the Layout drop-down list box are two context-sensitive status lines telling you the number of pages per sheet required for the particular layout style and the page sizes that will be created. The benefit of using page layout styles is that when you choose a style and add the necessary pages, the images on each page will print in their appropriate orientation on the single sheet of paper. Figure 69.4 shows the Page Settings dialog box with the Side-Fold Card layout selected. Notice the graphic representation of the card at the bottom of the preview window. In this example, each numbered page is depicted by location on the sheet. Also, there are page numbers at the bottom of the screen just above the color palette. When you want to work on a new page, simply click the page number.

Figure 69.4.
The Page Settings dialog
box with Side-Fold Card
selected from the Layout
box.

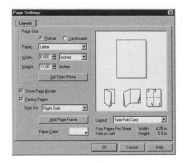

# Adding Pages

You can always add pages to your documents as needed by selecting Layout |
Insert Page. Figure 69.5 shows the Insert Page dialog box that appears.

Figure 69.5.
The Insert Page
dialog box.

To add pages to an existing document, type in the appropriate number in the
Insert box. You can choose whether the page or pages should be added before or
after a particular page by scrolling or typing that page number in the Page box.

You can also add pages by using the page controls at the bottom-left corner of the
drawing window. Click the plus buttons to add pages before or after the currently
displayed page. You can also jump to a specific page by clicking the page number
tabs. Figures 69.6 and 69.7 show the page controls with a single-page and multiple-page configuration.

Figure 69.6.
The page controls show-
ing a single page.

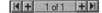

Figure 69.7.
The page controls show-
ing multiple pages.

If you have selected a page layout style (see the preceding section), the status lines beneath the Layout box in the Page Setting dialog box will tell you the number of pages required. In the case of a side-fold card, for example, you would need to add three additional pages.

# Corel*NOTE!*

Press the spacebar to quickly return to the first page when you are working with multiple pages.

# Scanning

Scanners come in three basic types: hand-held, flatbed, and drum. They all work on the same principle to capture images. The most common scanners are the hand-held and flatbed types. Drum scanners are reserved for high-end users and service bureaus.

Scanning an image is similar to taking a picture with a camera. Instead of using natural light or flash bulbs, a scanner uses a light bar to illuminate the subject. In the case of flatbed scanners, the object to be scanned is placed on the scanner glass and exposed to a traveling light bar. (If you're familiar with office copy machines, it's the same process.) Instead of being recorded on film (in the case of cameras) or selenium-coated drums (in the case of copy machines), the scanned image is stored in the computer's memory by the scanner's software and then placed on a hard drive or removable drive.

Photographers choose between color and black-and-white film, and then they must rely on the proper exposure and lighting conditions to get the perfect picture. They can change the contrast, brightness, and tones in the darkroom, but this can be very costly and time-consuming.

The computer scanning process also gives you a choice between black-and-white and color. The scanner's software enables you to automatically expose the image with the click of a button, and you can choose between different settings to allow the scanner to pick up particular information from the image.

The scanning software is similar to the photographer's darkroom but is much faster. It also enables you to alter the information from the image before it's stored in the computer or placed in an application. You can change just about anything relating to the image: image size (resolution), contrast and brightness, color hues and saturation, and light and shadows.

A photographer plans his shot before he presses the shutter on the camera. He has to decide what the final picture should look like and how it will be used. Similarly, you will be more successful if, before you scan an image, you know the requirements and limitations of the applications and printer you'll be using.

## Scanning Basics

You can scan just about any kind of image, including drawings, original photos, previously printed images, and small three-dimensional objects (if you're using a flatbed scanner).

It's important to know how the image will be used before you scan. For example, will the image be used in a flyer? Will it be saved on disk for multiple uses? It's a good idea to scan at the optimum scanning resolution the first time and then lower the resolution if the situation calls for it. If your original is a color image but you'll be using it as a grayscale image, you might consider scanning in color in case you need a color version at a later time. You can use Corel PHOTO-PAINT to convert the color image to grayscale for the first use.

The limitations of your desktop printer also need to be considered when you scan an image, along with the requirements of the service bureau you use. Your desktop printer will more than likely output at a relatively low-line screen. Therefore, scanning at a very high resolution is a waste of disk space because the extra data sent to the printer will simply be discarded. If your sending your image for output to an image setter by a service bureau, you want to scan at the optimum highest resolution based on the formulas later in this skill session.

Scanning falls into three basic categories: line art, halftones (grayscale), and continuous-tone.

## Line Art

A piece of line art is a purely black-and-white image. If you're going to use CorelDRAW's AutoTrace feature or CorelTrace, scan the line art at a minimum of 300 dpi for best results. (See Skill Session 47, "Manual Tracing Versus AutoTracing.") There may be times when the line art contains very fine lines. Try scanning this type of image in grayscale mode.

## Halftones

Halftones can come in two different forms. The first form is made up of black-and-white or color photos and original art, which are really continuous-tone images consisting of many different shades of gray or color. The second form of halftone is made up of grayscale or color images that have been previously printed as halftones. This form presents problems because you're scanning an image that's made up of tiny halftone dots created by the four-color printing process. A lithograph that has been four-color processed also falls into this category.

You have only two options when you scan a halftone image made up of halftone dots. The first option is to experiment with different dpi settings until you get a good result. This is time-consuming and doesn't guarantee a perfect scan. The second option is to scan the halftone at a relatively high dpi, 300 or greater, and then use a paint program to get rid of the moiré pattern that results. All paint programs, including Corel PHOTO-PAINT, have filters and effects that can help you eliminate the moiré patterns. Some work better than others. Try using the Gausian Blur effect in Corel PHOTO-PAINT to eliminate the moiré patterns. After using the effect, remember to sharpen the image again before doing any editing or printing. The Unsharp Mask filter in Corel PHOTO-PAINT is a good filter for sharpening an image.

## Continuous-Tone

Continuous-tone images come in two flavors: grayscale and color. Grayscale images require you to make fewer adjustments in the scanning software and paint program because you're dealing only with resolution, brightness, contrast, and (of course) sharpness. If your scanning software is deficient in any of these areas, you can usually fine-tune the image in a paint program such as Corel PHOTO-PAINT.

When you scan a continuous-tone color image, you're presented with several more decisions to make, such as color balance, hues, saturation, and so on. This book can't provide an in-depth discussion of the many considerations that are involved in color scanning. Your own scanning software manual should be of some help, as well as the third-party books that cover color scanning in depth.

## Tips on Scanning

If you scan an image at too low a resolution, the image will become pixelated. Pixelated means the edges of elements within the image will appear very jagged. If you scan too high, the printer will try and throw away information that it cannot use. This results in halftone images suffering a loss of subtle detail.

To produce the best quality prints or film, use the rule of thumb for scanning an image using a dpi setting of twice the screen frequency (line screen).

You can use either of two methods in determining the correct scanning resolution. The first is by measuring in pixels and the second by measuring in inches.

The first method is to first determine the size of the output image in proportion to the original image being scanned, then multiply the longest dimension of the final image by twice the line screen of the output device (printer); for example, your original image is 8"×10" and you are printing to a 300 dpi laser printer, which has a line screen of 60, and you want your final image to be half the original size or 4"×5". In this case, you would multiply 5×120 (twice the line screen), which will make the correct image size 480×600 pixels. In your scanning software you would scan the image with a setting 120 dpi and then scale down 50 percent using pixels as the unit of measurement until the size equals 480×600 pixels. If your original is smaller than the final output image, you would scale up instead of scaling down. This method works regardless of the size of the original image being scanned.

The second method is to determine the size of the output image (in inches) and use the formula `(LDOxLS) x2 =OSR LDI`

where

```
LDO = Longest Dimension of Output Image
LS = Line Screen to be used in final output
LDI = Largest Dimension of the Input Image
OSR = Optimum Scanning Resolution in dpi
```

**Example 1**   Suppose you are scanning a photo that is 8"×10" and you want to output your halftone at 150 Line Screen at 4"×5". LDO=5, LS=150, LDI=10; plug these numbers in the formula above.

```
 (5 x 150)x2 = 150
```

**Example 2**   Suppose you are scanning a photo that is 5"×7" and you want to output your halftone at 100 Line Screen at 10"×14". LDO=14, LS=100, LDI=7; plug these numbers in the formula.

```
(14 x 100)x2 = 400
 7
```

# Corel*NOTE!*

Ppi (pixels per inch) is the same as dpi (dots per inch).

The chart below shows the maximum line screen of output devices rated by dpi. (For example, a 300 dpi laser printer produces a maximum line screen of 60.) The chart will help you determine the correct resolution for scanning.

**Table 70.1. Comparing printer line screens to dpi of printer.**

| Maximum DPI of printer | (Default) Line Screen |
|---|---|
| 300 | 60 |
| 600 | 80 |
| 1000 | 100 |
| 1200 | 133 |
| 1270 | 133 |
| 1693 | 150 |
| 3386 | 200 |

# Panose

## The Panose Type–Matching System

Because no two users have the exact same fonts installed, ElseWare of Seattle has developed the Panose type-matching system to make intelligent font substitution choices. Limited support for Panose is built into Windows itself, and much broader support is added in programs such as CorelDRAW 6.

Some font-matching problems are rather easy to solve by defining the different names applied to similar fonts. For example, the font Optima is very similar to CG Omega and Zapf Humanist. This is something that only the most font-savvy user would know, but the Panose system includes a database that can automatically substitute the appropriate font for you. However, because the Panose database isn't always complete, you can customize the list.

Another common problem you might encounter when converting documents from the Macintosh to the PC is that the Mac font names rarely have spaces in them, whereas the PC version includes spaces. The Panose database also takes this into account. Substitution by name is only the beginning of the Panose technology.

Panose can also assign numbers to fonts based on their attributes so fonts can be substituted by these attributes rather than just their name. The attributes used are x-height, midline, letter form, arm style, stroke variation, contrast, proportion, weight, serif style, and family kind.

Each of these attributes provides a number to the Panose matching system. The Panose system then produces a 10-digit number to classify the font.

When a font is not available to a document, the Panose matching system will try to find the available font that has a classification number which is the closest to that of the missing font. This, combined with the alternative spellings and matching exceptions databases, can provide very accurate substitutions. In earlier versions of CorelDRAW, font management was basically non-existent. Crude font substitution was available as long as you didn't mind having all your missing fonts substituted by Avant Garde Bk BT. You could download your fonts as long as you were willing to edit the CORELFNT.INI file and download them manually. Otherwise, you were stuck twiddling your thumbs as CorelDRAW converted all text to curves or bitmaps when printing. Luckily, things changed in CorelDRAW 5. Rather than managing fonts worse than every other Windows application, CorelDRAW is now one of the leaders in font management.

By including support for the Panose typeface-matching system, CorelDRAW can make relatively intelligent guesses when substituting fonts. This system is also quite easy to customize so that it makes exactly the substitutions you desire. The print engine has also been updated to automatically download fonts to a PostScript printer.

## How CorelDRAW Implements Panose

The Panose Font Matching button is found in the Text Options dialog box's Text tab shown in Figure 71.1. Click this button to access the Panose Font Matching Preferences dialog box shown in Figure 71.2. Checking the Allow font matching box activates the Panose system. If this box is not checked, all missing fonts will automatically be substituted by the default font.

*Figure 71.1.*
*The Text tab of the Text*
*Options dialog box.*

*Figure 71.2.*
*The Panose Font Matching*
*Preferences dialog box.*

The Show mapping results check box displays the substitutions for approval before making them using the dialog box shown in Figure 71.3. If this check box is not checked, CorelDRAW will make substitutions based on Panose automatically, without letting you know that substitutions have been made.

*Figure 71.3.*
*The Panose Substitution*
*dialog box.*

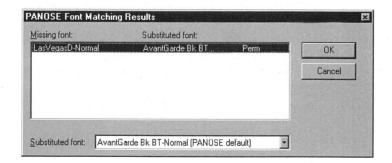

The Substitution tolerance slider tells the Panose system how closely matched the classification numbers need to be to allow a substitution. As the slider is moved toward the right, substitutions will be much less accurate. If a match cannot be found within the given level of tolerance, the default font selected at the bottom of the dialog box will be substituted instead.

# Corel *TIP!*

> You might want to change the default font to one of the symbol fonts so that any automatic substitution will be extremely obvious when you open the file.

Click Spellings to bring up the dialog box shown in Figure 71.4. Windows spellings are shown on the left side of the dialog box and their corresponding Macintosh spellings are on the right. If a particular spelling exception is not shown, you can easily add it by clicking the Add button and entering the spellings for both Windows and Macintosh in the dialog box shown in Figure 71.5. You can also edit existing names if there is an incorrect spelling exception. Note that this database has a one-to-one relationship, meaning that a font can be listed only once.

You can also enter font matching exceptions in the Font Matching Exceptions dialog box shown in Figure 71.6, which is accessed by clicking the Exceptions button in the Panose Font Matching Preferences dialog box. The Font Matching Exceptions dialog box will initially be empty, but again it is quite easy to add and edit the fonts shown in the list using the dialog box shown in Figure 71.7. The dialog box shown has an exception entered to give you an idea of how the exceptions work.

Figure 71.4.
The Alternate Spellings
dialog box.

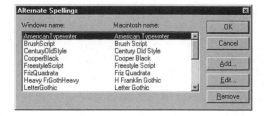

Figure 71.5.
The Add Alternate
Spelling dialog box.

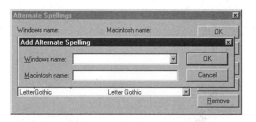

Figure 71.6.
The Panose Font Matching
Exceptions dialog box.

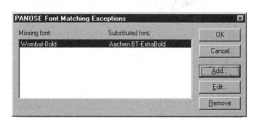

Figure 71.7.
The Add Matching
Exception dialog box.

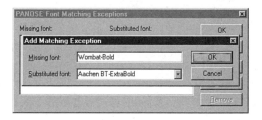

The Missing font list can have a font listed only once, but the Substituted font box
can list a font name many times if necessary. When you open a document that
contains fonts that are not currently available, you will be presented with the
dialog box shown in Figure 71.3. For each font listed as missing, you are given the
choice of accepting the substitute font listed on the right side of the dialog box, or
you can change the substitution on the fly.

Unfortunately, Corel provides no easy way to find out which fonts are used in a document before the user attempts to open the file. This capability existed in CorelMOSAIC but was dropped in Corel MULTIMEDIA MANAGER. Hopefully, someone will write a little utility program to do just that function.

# 72

# Multiple Document Interface

The Multiple Document Interface, or MDI as it will be referred to in the rest of this skill session, gives you the ability to view more than one document at a time on the CorelDRAW screen. You use MDI in Windows every time you open multiple applications or documents in Program Manager. Corel PHOTO-PAINT has enabled you to open separate files or duplicates of the same file since its inception. Now you can do the same in CorelDRAW 6.

## Working with Multiple Views of the Same File

Figure 72.1 shows a normal CDR file opened in CorelDRAW 6. Figure 72.2 shows a zoomed-in view of the same file next to the original file. One of the advantages of working with multiple views of the same files is that it enables you to edit a particular portion of a file in a zoomed-in state and see the changes reflected immediately in the original file.

The steps required to open duplicate files are as follows:

1. Have a file already opened in CorelDRAW.
2. Click the Window pull-down menu at the top of the screen.
3. Click New Window from the drop-down menu.
4. A duplicate of the original file will appear exactly on top of the original.
5. Click the Window menu again and choose Tile Vertically.

Your screen will now show both files vertically tiled next to each other. To work in either of the windows click their respective title bars to make them active. You can view the active file in either a zoomed in, zoomed out, or wireframe view. The window on the right in Figure 72.2 shows the file in a zoomed-in state.

*Figure 72.1.*
*A basic CDR file opened in CorelDRAW.*

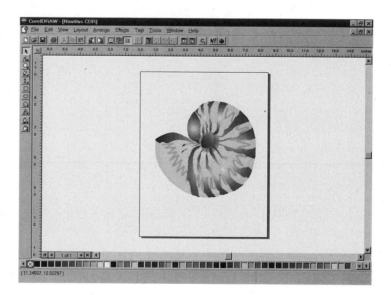

*Figure 72.2.*
*Two vertically tiled*
*windows showing the*
*same file. The window on*
*the right is in a zoomed-in*
*state.*

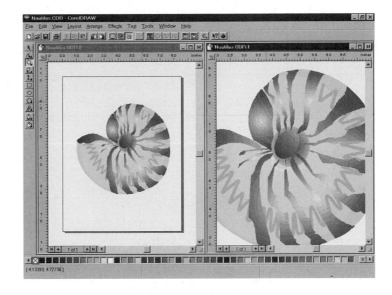

Figure 72.3 shows three open windows of the same file. The window on the left is zoomed in 400 percent and in wireframe view. The window in the middle is zoomed in 300 percent on the front of the car. The window on the right is at full view. The ability to view your files in this manner makes it easier to work on a small portion of the drawing and see the results immediately in the full view.

*Figure 72.3.*
*Three open windows of*
*the same file showing*
*different views.*

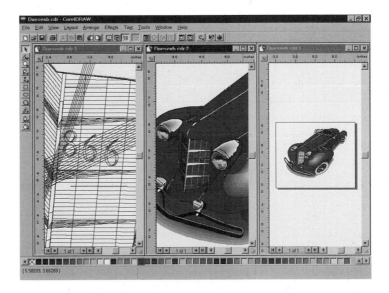

## Working with Multiple Windows Containing Different Files

Another advantage to working with an MDI is that you can steal parts of one file and put them into another. You can also select part of an image from one file and drop it into a completely new file. Figure 72.4 shows a CDR file with several pieces of office furniture. Tiled next to this file is a basic new file.

*Figure 72.4.*
*An existing CDR file next to a new file.*

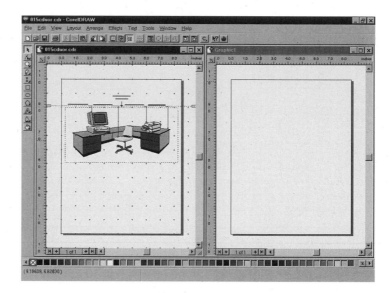

Take the following steps to open an existing CDR file alongside a new file:

1. Open a new file by choosing New | Document from the File menu.
2. Open a previously saved CDR file.
3. Click the Window pull-down menu and choose Tile Vertically from the drop-down menu.

## Corel*NOTE!*

You can reverse the sequence in steps 1 and 2 in the preceding list to accomplish the same thing.

Figure 72.5 shows a chair taken from the file on the left and dropped into the new file on the right. Follow the next steps to learn how to move part or all of one file into another:

1. Select an object or objects in the original file.

2. With the object selected, hold down the left mouse button and drag across the window into the new window. Release the mouse button to drop the object onto the page.

*Figure 72.5.*
*A chair moved from the*
*original CDR file and*
*dropped into a new file.*

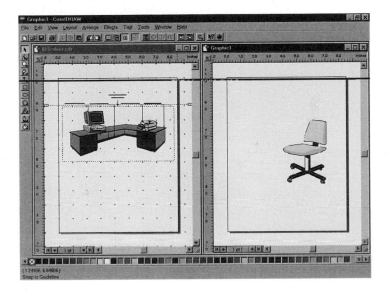

## Tiling Landscape Mode Files

You have been working with portrait mode files, but landscape mode files work in the same manner as portrait mode. When you are working with landscape mode files choose Tile Horizontally from the Window drop-down menu. Figure 72.6 shows a landscape file in the original view and a second copy in a zoomed in view.

*Figure 72.6.*
*Two landscape files tiled*
*horizontally.*

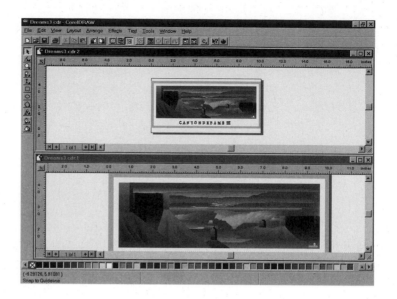

# OLE

The idea behind OLE (object linking and embedding) is that applications need to perform only one job well. For example, CorelDRAW specializes in graphics; it doesn't need word-processing tools because the text can be brought into a drawing using an OLE link to a text editor such as Microsoft Word that supports OLE. The benefit is that a graph created in Microsoft Excel or a text table from Microsoft Word may be placed within a CorelDRAW drawing.

File sizes are also reduced using OLE because no duplication occurs. The data of a linked object is stored in the original document (in this case, Microsoft Word) rather than in the client document (in this case, CorelDRAW).

## Advantages of OLE

One strong benefit of OLE is that linked objects can be updated automatically. When you update the original source, all of the other copies of the linked object are also updated.

Linked objects inserted with CorelDRAW's Paste Special command in the Edit menu can be scaled, moved, mirrored, and have other simple effects applied to them. OLE objects can also be duplicated and placed into PowerClip containers.

## Disadvantages of OLE

First and foremost, OLE is somewhat slow on anything less than a supercomputer with 1 GB of RAM. You are also limited in terms of what you can do to OLE objects.

OLE objects cannot be rotated, skewed, or cloned. They cannot be combined, welded, intersected, or trimmed with any other objects. They also cannot have any of the effects in the Effects menu applied to them.

## Hands-On Examples

Knowing all of this, let's look at an example. First let's create a table of this book's projected sales by region created in Microsoft Excel 5.0. (See Figure 73.1.)

*Figure 73.1.*
*A Microsoft Excel 5.0*
*spreadsheet.*

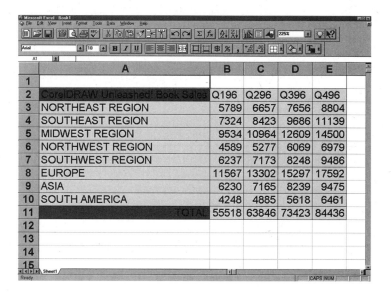

Within Excel, select the range of cells to copy. In this case copy A2...E11 by selecting Edit, Copy. (The shortcut is Ctrl+C.) This table is now on the Windows 95 Clipboard.

Using the keys Alt+Ctrl, switch back to CorelDRAW. In CorelDRAW, select Paste Special under the Edit menu. (See Figure 73.2.)

Choose Paste Link from the dialog box in Figure 73.3. Notice that CorelDRAW knows that this is an Excel 5.0 object. By selecting Paste Link instead of Paste, we are only creating a link to the original source, not actually embedding the file. If Paste were chosen, the worksheet would be embedded, increasing the size of the CorelDRAW file and preventing any further updates as the original changes. The result is shown in Figure 73.4.

*Figure 73.2.*
*Using Paste Special to*
*embed the Excel 5.0*
*spreadsheet.*

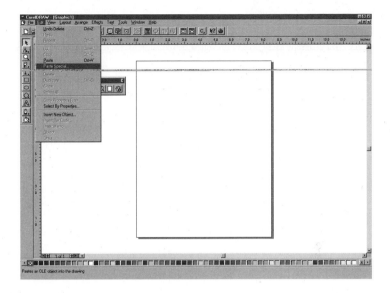

*Figure 73.3.*
*Choosing OLE options.*

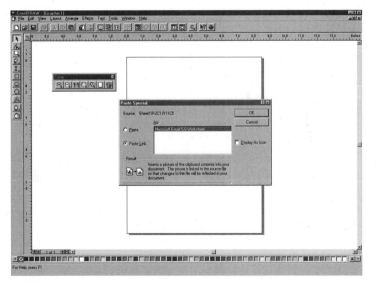

When the object—in this case an Excel 5.0 worksheet—arrives into CorelDRAW, very often it is quite small. Fixing this is simple, however. Grab one of the corners, like any other object, and stretch it. Figure 73.5 shows one possible use of numbers by our marketing department. To arrive at the numbers that Finance will use, divide them by two.

*Figure 73.4.*
*The Paste Linked*
*worksheet now in*
*CorelDRAW.*

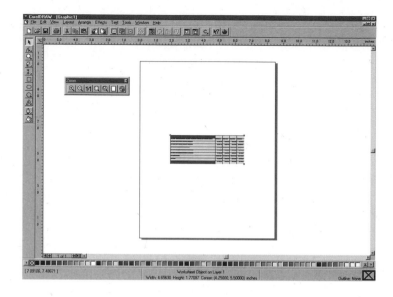

*Figure 73.5.*
*Merging graphics with an*
*OLE linked object.*

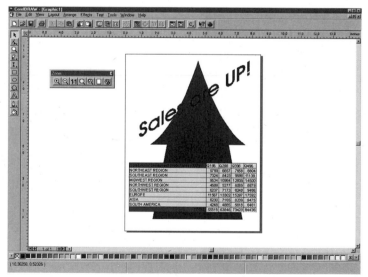

If you have several linked objects within a file and would like to locate their source or even alter the link, select Edit | Links from the main menu bar. The dialog box shown in Figure 73.6 will appear.

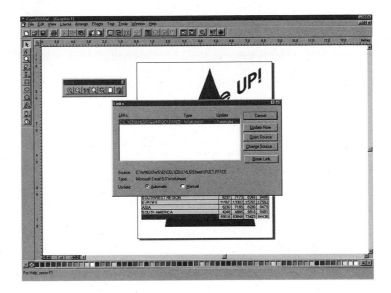

*Figure 73.6.*
*The Links dialog box.*

From this dialog box, you can easily break the link or change the link's source. You can also change the link from being updated automatically to being updated manually.

For the grand finale, double-click the object. It will open the application that created the linked object and enable you to edit it in its native environment.

# 74

# Tweaking Windows 95

CorelDRAW asks a lot from a computer, and many times its performance is slow because the computer is improperly prepared to run CorelDRAW. This skill session suggests an optimum configuration for a computer running CorelDRAW. Most of these tips are applicable to other Windows programs as well.

Most of the tweaking to improve your system performance is done through the System option in Control Panel. Choose the Performance tab and you will see something similar to Figure 74.1.

## Which Windows?

CorelDRAW 6 requires Windows 95 or Windows NT 3.51. Although either of them is required, you will probably find that CorelDRAW 6 works best under Windows 95 because this was the target operating system. Microsoft has announced that tune-up packs will be available for Windows 95 on a quarterly basis, and you might want to keep up-to-date for the best performance and reliability. Also note that Windows NT will get the user interface of Windows 95 in early 1996. This will increase its desirability as the platform of choice for CorelDRAW 6.

Figure 74.1.
*The Performance tab of
the System Properties
dialog box.*

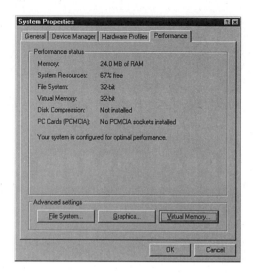

The biggest problem with either of these operating systems will be the availability of drivers for your existing hardware. Check with the hardware vendors or Microsoft before upgrading so that you don't run into any surprises. Also note that Adobe Type Manager (and therefore PostScript fonts) is not available for Windows NT. You can still print PostScript fonts, but the screen display leaves a lot to be desired.

## Hard Drive or CD?

CorelDRAW's footprint on a hard drive can be quite large (177 MB), and many users with CD-ROM drives choose to run CorelDRAW directly from the CD. This causes a general slowdown in all the applications because the CD-ROM drive is more than ten times slower than a hard drive. Not only the performance issues should be considered; accessing other CDs while CorelDRAW is running will be a major problem (and all the clip art is on a separate CD). If you don't have enough space to install CorelDRAW on the hard drive, it's time to shop for a new hard drive.

Storing the fonts on the hard drive is also a very good idea. This way you are not dependent on having the CD in your machine when you want to use the fonts. All of the fonts will require about 50 MB, but that is space well spent. This is also important because of the fact that you will be annoyed by the Autorun feature every time you start your machine or access the CD.

## Memory

The CorelDRAW box states that the program will run with 8 MB of memory. In reality, you can run CorelDRAW with less. Unfortunately, even with 8 MB your computer will be really slow. A more realistic minimum amount of memory is 16 MB, and you'll find that many power users will complain that they have only 32 MB. If you are using Photo-Paint to manipulate large images, buy as much memory as your machine will hold. It is worth it in the time you will save. Even though a file might be only 5 MB on disk, it usually requires 5–10 times that amount of memory to work with it. This is due to the fact that the image on disk might be compressed, and you will need extra room for undo and filter processing.

If you are not sure how much memory you have, the Performance tab of the System Properties dialog box shown in Figure 74.1 will tell you.

## Virtual Memory

For users who don't have the actual chips, memory should be simulated with virtual memory. This is accomplished by creating a swap file. Windows 95 automatically creates a swap file for you, but you can make adjustments to it. From the Performance tab of the System Properties dialog box in Figure 74.1, click the Virtual Memory button and you will get a dialog box similar to the one shown in Figure 74.2.

*Figure 74.2.*
*The Virtual Memory*
*dialog box.*

The default setting is Let Windows manage my virtual memory settings. If you choose to specify the settings yourself, you can set a minimum and maximum amount. You can also specify the location of the swap file for maximum performance by locating it on the fastest drive on your system.

## Processor

CorelDRAW lists a 486 as the required processor, although it can run on a 386 system. Again, the better the processor and faster the clock speed, the faster CorelDRAW will operate. Occasionally, users will disable their turbo switch and wonder why their machine is dragging along. Make sure that you are using your machine to its fullest potential.

## Video Cards

Video cards can often be the weakest performer in a system. They are also a frequent cause of crashes within CorelDRAW. Makers of video cards tend to design their cards to win speed contests rather than for real-life performance, and this can cause numerous problems. When shopping for a card, make sure to check the speed, but also check the reliability of the drivers used by Windows to run the card. The drivers are updated fairly regularly, so you might want to check with your vendor (through an online service) to make sure you are using the latest drivers.

If you tend to crash often in CorelDRAW, then switch to a generic VGA driver running at 640×480×16 colors. If the problems disappear then the video drivers for your card are most likely the cause of the crashes.

One way to try and correct the problem is to adjust your graphics settings in Windows 95. From the System Properties dialog box shown in Figure 74.1, click the Graphics button. You'll now see the dialog box shown in Figure 74.3.

*Figure 74.3.*
*The Advanced Graphics*
*Settings dialog box.*

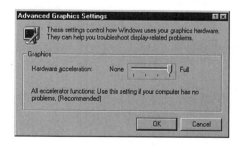

If you move the setting from the Full setting to the first notch from the right, it will correct any mouse pointer display problems you might be encountering. The next notch over will prevent bit-block transfers and disable memory mapped I/O on some display drivers. The last setting, None, will run your video card in safe mode. This is useful if your computer frequently stops responding to input.

## Running Multiple Applications

One of the biggest benefits of Windows is its capability to run multiple applications at the same time. Unfortunately, this can hinder the performance of larger applications such as CorelDRAW. For the best performance, try to keep the number of applications running to a minimum.

## System Resources

System resources have always been scarce in previous versions of Windows. Windows 95 alleviates most of the problems with resources, but it does not eliminate them. CorelDRAW uses a large amount of resources, and each additional roll-up will use even more resources. If you keep the number of roll-ups to a minimum and don't run large numbers of applications at the same time, you should have no problem with the amount of resources that Windows 95 provides. To see the amount of free resources, bring up the Performance tab of the System Properties dialog box, as shown in Figure 74.1.

## Fonts

CorelDRAW includes over 1,000 fonts in the box, and many users are tempted to install them all. This will render Windows 95 useless because it is limited to no more than 1,000 fonts. Even with half that many, it will make a system perform much slower than a system with no more than 100 fonts. By using a font management program such as Corel FONT MASTER or the much superior Ares FontMinder, it is easy to have access to all your fonts while not keeping them installed in the system. Ares can be contacted at (800) 783-2737 or (415) 578-9090.

## Wallpaper, Screen Savers, and So On

Windows provides many ways to customize a system. You can install bitmapped wallpaper, screen savers, patterns, sounds, animated cursors, and many other cute utilities. All of these things take time to load and use up memory that could be put to better use. Therefore, you should weed out those extra Windows utilities that aren't needed.

## Printing

Printing can be one of the most frustrating tasks under Windows, and especially with CorelDRAW. Windows 95 makes it more bearable through multitasking between applications and multithreading within applications. Multithreading enables printing to take place in the background. A frequent problem with

PostScript printers is that they "time out." This is because the default transmission retry setting is much too low. From Control Panel Printers, right-click the printer icon you wish to change and choose Properties. Select the Details tab and change the Transmission retry setting to 999 as shown in Figure 74.4.

*Figure 74.4.*
*PostScript printer Proper-*
*ties dialog box.*

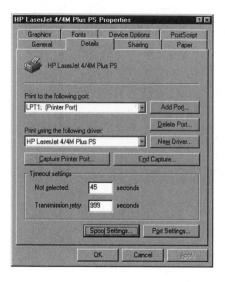

To adjust the spool settings, click the Spool Settings button and you'll get the dialog box shown in Figure 74.5.

*Figure 74.5.*
*The Spool Settings*
*dialog box.*

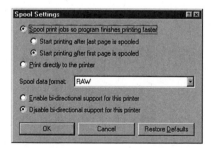

If you choose Print directly to the printer, Windows 95 will not return you to your programs as fast. Therefore, make sure to check the Spool print jobs so program finishes printing faster check box. You then have the choice to start printing after the first page is printed or after the last page is printed. The default setting is after the first page and that is probably your best bet for daily use. The bi-directional support has shown problems in our use of Windows 95 and therefore is disabled on our systems.

Another way to dramatically increase your print times is through the PrintCache utility program from LaserTools. It has a spooler that functions similarly to the one built into Windows 95, but the performance is much better. LaserTools can be reached at (510) 420-8777.

## Disk Access

CorelDRAW really puts a hard drive through its paces, and if the hard drive is not taken care of, CorelDRAW slows dramatically. Depending on use, hard drives should be optimized at least once a week to pack data into contiguous clusters. The Disk Defragmentor program that comes with Windows 95 does a good job of this, although you might want to use a third-party utility such as Speed Disk from Symantec's Norton Utilities. Make sure you do not use a utility if it wasn't written specifically for Windows 95. It can damage your data.

Both hard drives and CD-ROMs can also be cached to improve their performance if you are using 32-bit drivers. The System Properties dialog box shown in Figure 74.1 will tell you if you are using 32-bit drivers. If so, choose the File System button and you'll see the dialog box shown in Figure 74.6.

*Figure 74.6.*
*The File System Properties*
*dialog box for Hard Disk.*

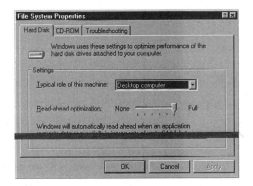

You have three choices for the typical role of this machine: Desktop Computer, Mobile or Docking System, and Network Server. The Desktop Computer setting assumes that you have more than the minimum RAM and are running from AC power rather than a battery. Mobile or Docking Station assumes that you have low memory and you are running from batteries. This means that it will flush the cache more frequently to prevent data loss. Finally, the Network Server option assumes that you have frequent disk activity. Because CorelDRAW uses the disk quite often, this might be the optimum setting for most users. You want to set the Read-ahead optimization setting to Full for the best performance.

To adjust your CD-ROM settings, choose the CD-ROM tab in the dialog box shown in Figure 74.6. You'll get the dialog box shown in Figure 74.7.

*Figure 74.7.*
*The File System Properties*
*dialog box for CD-ROM.*

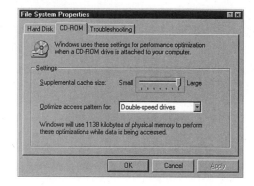

For best performance, slide the Supplemental cache size slider to the far right so that it is as large as possible. In the Optimize access pattern for: drop-down list, choose the speed of your drive. These two settings in combination determine how much memory Windows 95 will set aside for caching purposes. If you are running in a machine with less than 16 MB of memory, you might want to decrease the size of the supplemental cache.

## Invalid Page Fault

One of the problems you might run into occasionally is the Invalid Page Fault (IPF). You might remember these faults as general protection faults (GPF) from Windows 3.1. These usually mean that memory has been corrupted in some fashion. Users tend to blame these problems on the program that was running when the fault occurred, but quite often the blame lies elsewhere. Following are some of the most common things that can be done to avoid the dastardly IPF.

First, if you are using a video driver other than the generic VGA driver that came from Microsoft, switch to the VGA driver. This might mean that your picture is awful, but it is the best way to test whether your proprietary video driver is the cause of the problem. If the problem disappears, then call your video-board manufacturer and get its latest drivers to see if the problem has been solved. Some boards are known to have unstable drivers, and you should check around before buying a new card.

Also, make sure that you have enough free space on your temporary drive. The biggest problem users face is when they place the temporary drive on a compressed drive. This is not a good idea at all. Rather than compressing your drives, you will find better stability if you just buy a new drive. The prices are very low right now for very large drives. If you are having problems with your disk, it is a good idea to run Scandisk or Norton Disk Doctor.

# 75

# Understanding the INI Files

This section provides a general overview of the numerous settings contained in the initialization files. Before you make any changes to the files manually, it is a very good idea to make a backup copy in case you make a mistake. Incorrect settings can prevent CorelDRAW from loading. Additional settings that are not documented as this book goes to press might appear in your INI files. If you do not understand them, check in the help files for additional information or contact Corel.

## CORELAPP.INI

CORELAPP.INI contains settings for customizing Corel-DRAW. Following are a listing of those settings that you may wish to adjust. Make sure that you have a backup of this file in case you make a mistake.

### *[Config]* Section

#### *ProgramsDir=*

This shows the path to the folder where all program files are stored. This setting is usually `..\Programs`.

#### *DataDir=*

This shows the path to the folder in which all data files are stored. This is usually `..\Programs\Data`.

### CustomDir=

This shows the path to the folder in which all data files that can be customized are stored. This is usually `..\Custom`.

### ColorDir=

This shows the path to the folder in which CorelDRAW stores color-specific files. This is usually `..\Color`.

### DrawDir=

This shows the path to the folder in which CorelDRAW-specific files are stored. This is usually `..\Draw`.

### Dream3DDir=

This shows the path to the folder in which Corel DREAM 3D–specific files are stored. This is usually `..\Dream3D`.

### FontMasterDir=

This shows the path to the folder in which Corel FONT MASTER–specific files are stored. This is usually `..\FontMstr`.

### MediaMgrDir=

This shows the path to the folder in which Corel MULTIMEDIA MANAGER–specific files are stored. This is usually `..\MediaMgr`.

### PhotoPaintDir=

This shows the path to the folder in which Corel Photo-Paint–specific files are stored. This is usually `..\PhotoPnt`.

### PresentsDir=

This shows the path to the folder in which Corel PRESENTS–specific files are stored. This is usually `..\Presents`.

### TraceDir=

This shows the path to the folder in which CorelTRACE-specific files are stored. This is usually `..\OCRTrace`.

### FontsDir=

This shows the path to the folder in which fonts are stored. This is usually `..\Symbols`.

### FiltersDir=

This shows the path to the folder in which filters are stored. This is usually `..\Filters`.

### MapDir=

This shows the path to the folder in which Corel Map Server–specific files are stored. This is usually `..\MapView`.

### ScriptsDir=

This shows the path to the folder in which Corel SCRIPT–specific files are stored. This is usually `..\Scripts`.

### DepthDir=

This shows the path to the folder in which CorelDEPTH-specific files are stored. This is usually `..\Depth`.

### FountainPresets=

This specifies the name of the file used to store fountain fill presets for radial, conical, rectangular, and linear fills. It is created when CorelDRAW is loaded for the first time. The default value is CORELDRW.FFP.

### Language

This specifies which language version of CorelDRAW you are using. The default value is English for the release used by the authors.

### FontRasterizer=

This specifies whether the internal font rasterizer is enabled or disabled. The rasterizer improves the appearance of fonts printed at small sizes. A 0 indicates that the rasterizer is disabled, which might be necessary for printer drives that conflict with the rasterizer. A disabled rasterizer is indicated by text that prints incorrectly. A 1 indicates that the rasterizer is enabled. The default value is 1.

### TTFOptimization=

This specifies whether CorelDRAW will use its own internal TrueType rasterizer or the one provided with Windows. A 0 indicates that the Windows rasterizer will be used; this is slower than CorelDRAW's own rasterizer. Some printers and screen drivers have problems with CorelDRAW's rasterizer and therefore should use this setting. A 1 indicates that CorelDRAW's internal TrueType driver will be used. The default value is 1.

### *TextureMaxSize=*

This specifies the maximum width (in device pixels) that an object being filled with a texture can be before the resolution of the bitmap is reduced. The maximum resolution of the bitmap is 120 dpi. To increase the resolution you must enlarge an object, fill it with a texture, and then shrink the object back to its original size. The texture generator is optimized for thresholds that are a power of 2 plus 1 (for example, 257, 513, 1025, and 2049). The default value is 257.

### *UseClippingForFills=*

This specifies whether Windows clip regions are enabled or disabled. Video drivers for some accelerator boards do not work well when clipping regions are enabled. Disabling Windows clip regions results in slower redraw speeds, but provides better compatibility. A 0 indicates that Windows clip regions will never be used, a 1 indicates that they are used in previewing only, a 2 indicates that they are used for printing only, and a 3 indicates that they are always used. The default value is 3.

## Color Calibration Section

### *SystemColorProfile=*

This specifies the default color profile used by the Color Manager. The default is `_DEFAULT.ccm`.

### *ProfileMatchMode=*

This specifies the mode of operation used by the Color Manager. A 0 indicates Automatch, a 1 indicates photographic, and a 2 indicates illustration. The default value is 0.

### *GamutAlarmColor=*

This specifies the color used by the gamut alarm. The default is `RGB255,0,255,0,USER`.

## *[TempPaths]* Section

### *Cleanup=*

This line tells Corel applications if they were terminated abnormally so that TMP files can be automatically deleted. A 0 indicates that an application is running, a 1 indicates that it shut down properly. Therefore, if an application is started and this line equals 0, it will automatically delete TMP files that are no longer necessary.

***x=***

This line indicates the directories in which the TMP files can be stored. The first line (and the only line necessary) will start with the number 0 replacing the x. Any additional directories will be added on separate lines. An example would be `0=C:\TEMP`.

## *[ClipboardCorelMetafile]* Section

This section specifies the contents of the CorelMetafile, which is placed on the Clipboard by CorelDRAW. None of the settings in this section have been documented. The default values are listed here:

```
CalligraphicPen=0
1BitBitmaps=1
8BitBitmaps=1
24BitBitmaps=1
CompressedBitmaps=1
MonoBitmapFills=1
FountainFills=1
FountainSteps=20
VectorFills=1
BezierCurves=1
HoleSubpaths=1
RectsAndEllipses=1
RotatedRectangles=1
RoundedRectangles=1
RotatedEllipses=1
EllipticalArc=1
PenStyle=1
TextCharacter=1
Text=1
RotatedText=1
TextInRectangle=1
TextInParallelogram=0
TextInPerspective=0
ExactText=0
OutlineSeperate=0
BinaryBitmaps=1
WireFrameOnly=0
VectorMaxPolygonSize=4096
CurveFlatness=0
MiterLimit=0
```

## *[Directories]* Section

### *ImportVector=*

The default value is `..\CUSTOM\PATTERN`.

## *[Applications]* Section

### *CorelDRAW=*

This shows the path to CorelDRAW. This is usually `..\PROGRAMS\CORELDRW.EXE`.

### *Corel PHOTO-PAINT=*

This shows the path to Corel Photo-Paint. This is usually `..\PROGRAMS\PHOTOPNT.EXE`.

### *Corel PRESENTS=*

This shows the path to Corel PRESENTS. This is usually `..\PROGRAMS\PRESENTS.EXE`.

### *CorelDREAM 3D=*

This shows the path to Corel DREAM 3D. This is usually `..\PROGRAMS\DREAM3D.EXE`.

### *CorelMOTION 3D=*

This shows the path to Corel MOTION 3D. This is usually `..\PROGRAMS\CORELM3D.EXE`.

### *Corel OCR-TRACE=*

This shows the path to Corel OCR-TRACE. This is usually `..\PROGRAMS\OCRTRACE.EXE`.

## *[Registration]* Section

### *UserName=*

This specifies the user name entered during the installation of CorelDRAW.

### *SerialNumber=*

This specifies the serial number entered during the installation of CorelDRAW. It is in the format *xxxx-xxxx-xxxx*, where each *x* is replaced by a digit.

### *PhoneNumber=*

This specifies the phone number entered during the installation of CorelDRAW. It can take any form that a user enters.

### *Organization=*

This specifies the organization name entered during the installation of CorelDRAW.

## *[DisplayInfo]*

### *ScreenScaleFactorX=*

This is the number used to scale the horizontal screen rulers to measurements in the real world. The default value is 3355.000000.

### *ScreenScaleFactorY=*

This is the number used to scale the vertical screen rulers to measurements in the real world. The default value is 3413.000000.

# CORELDRW.INI

All of the settings in the CORELDRW.INI file can be controlled from within CorelDRAW itself. Corel suggests that this file not be altered by users. A figure will be shown for each section of the file so that you will know where to make changes, and the default values will be shown for each entry. This file is found in the *drive*:\COREL60\DRAW directory. If you have noticed strange behavior in CorelDRAW or the inability to run the program, delete this file and it will regenerate itself with the default settings.

## Connector Tool

The Connector Tool settings can be changed in the dialog box shown in Figure 75.1. You access it by right-clicking the Connector tool and choosing Properties. These settings are discussed in Skill Session 10, "The Dimension Tool."

*Figure 75.1.*
*The Connector Tool*
*Properties dialog box.*

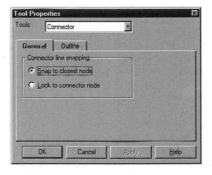

```
SnapToClosestNode=1
```

## Curve, Bézier Tool

The Curve and Bézier tool settings can be changed in the dialog box shown in Figure 75.2, which is accessed by right-clicking the Pencil tool and choosing Properties. These settings are discussed in Skill Session 9, "The Pencil Tool."

*Figure 75.2.*
*The Curve and Bézier Tool*
*Properties dialog box.*

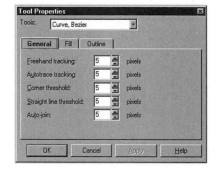

```
FreehandTracking=5
Autojoin=5
AutotraceTracking=5
StraightLineThreshold=5
CornerThreshold=5
```

## Ellipse Tool

The Ellipse Tool settings can be changed in the dialog box shown in Figure 75.3. You access this dialog box by right-clicking the Ellipse tool and choosing Properties. These settings are discussed in Skill Session 12, "The Ellipse Tool."

*Figure 75.3.*
*The Ellipse Tool Properties*
*dialog box.*

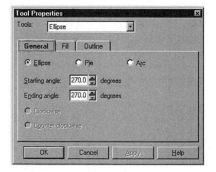

```
CreateArc=1
Clockwise=1
StartingAngle=270000000
EndingAngle=270000000
```

## Eraser Tool

The Eraser tool settings can be changed in the dialog box shown in Figure 75.4. You access this dialog box by right-clicking the Eraser tool and choosing Properties. These settings are discussed in Skill Session 7, "The Shape Tool."

*Figure 75.4.*
*The Eraser Tool Properties*
*dialog box.*

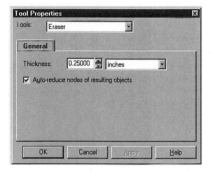

```
HairlineEraser=0
AutoReduceNodes=1
Thickness=63500
```

## Graph Paper Tool

The settings for the Graph Paper tool (sometimes called the Grid tool) can be changed in the dialog box shown in Figure 75.5. You access this dialog box by right-clicking the Graph Paper tool and choosing Properties. These settings are discussed in Skill Session 13, "Polygon, Star, Spiral, and Grid Tools."

*Figure 75.5.*
*The Graph Paper Tool*
*Properties dialog box.*

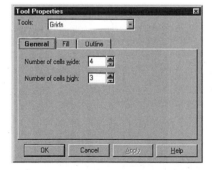

```
GridDimens=4,3
```

## Knife Tool

The Knife Tool settings can be changed in the dialog box shown in Figure 75.6. You access this dialog box by right-clicking the Knife tool and choosing Properties. These settings are discussed in Skill Session 7.

*Figure 75.6.*
*The Knife Tool Properties*
*dialog box.*

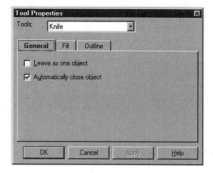

```
AutoReduceResult=1
AutomaticallyCloseObject=1
LeaveAsOneObject=1
```

## Node Edit Tool

The Node Edit Tool settings can be changed in the dialog box shown in Figure 75.7. You access this dialog box by right-clicking the Shape tool and choosing Properties. These settings are discussed in Skill Session 7.

*Figure 75.7.*
*The Node Edit Tool*
*Properties dialog box.*

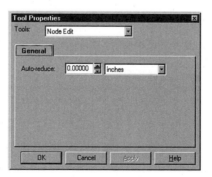

```
AutoReduce=4
AutoReduceUnits=0x1
```

## Pick Tool

The Pick Tool settings can be changed in the dialog box shown in Figure 75.8. You access this dialog box by right-clicking the Pick tool and choosing Properties. These settings are discussed in Skill Session 6, "The Pick Tool."

*Figure 75.8.*
*The Pick Tool Properties*
*dialog box.*

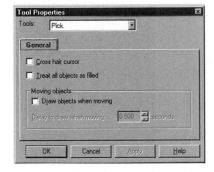

```
CrossHairCursor=0
DrawObjectsWhenMoving=0
DelayToDrawWhenMoving=500
TreatAllObjectsAsFilled=0
```

## Polygon Tool

The Polygon Tool settings can be changed in the dialog box shown in Figure 75.9. You access this dialog box by right-clicking the Polygon tool and choosing Properties. These settings are discussed in Skill Session 13.

*Figure 75.9.*
*The Polygon Tool Proper-*
*ties dialog box.*

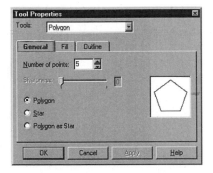

```
Sides=5
Sharpness=0
Type=0
```

## Rectangle Tool

The Rectangle Tool settings can be changed in the dialog box shown in Figure 75.10. You access this dialog box by right-clicking the Rectangle tool and choosing Properties. These settings are discussed in Skill Session 11, "The Rectangle Tool."

*Figure 75.10.*
*The Rectangle Tool*
*Properties dialog box.*

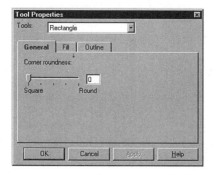

```
CornerRoundness=0
```

## Spiral Tool

The Spiral Tool settings can be changed in the dialog box shown in Figure 75.11. You access this dialog box by right-clicking the Spiral tool and choosing Properties. These settings are discussed in Skill Session 13.

*Figure 75.11.*
*The Spiral Tool Properties*
*dialog box.*

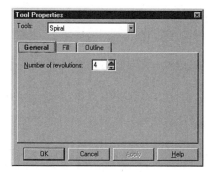

```
NumofRevolutions=4
```

## Zoom, Pan Tool

The Zoom and Pan Tool settings can be changed in the dialog box shown in Figure 75.12. You access this dialog box by right-clicking the Zoom or Pan tool and choosing Properties. These settings are discussed in Skill Session 8, "The Zoom Tool."

*Figure 75.12.*
*The Zoom and Pan Tool*
*Properties dialog box.*

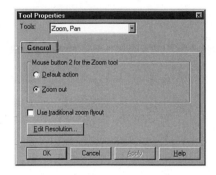

```
Button2ForZoomOut=1
TraditionalZoomFlyout=0
```

## Options—General

The Options General settings can be changed in the dialog box shown in Figure
75.13. You access this dialog box by selecting Options from the Tools menu and
choosing the General page. These settings are discussed in Skill Session 4,
"Customization and Setting Preferences."

*Figure 75.13.*
*The Options General*
*dialog box.*

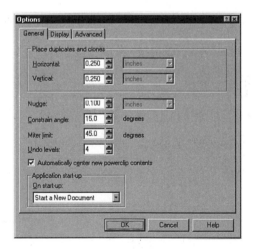

```
DupOffset=63500,63500
DupOffsetUnits=1,1
NudgeOffset=25400
NudgeOffsetUnit=0x1
MiterLimit=45000000
ConstrainAngle=15000000
UndoLevels=4
AutoCenterPowerClip=1
StartUpAppDisplay=1
```

## Options—Display

The Options Display settings can be changed in the dialog box shown in Figure 75.14. You access this dialog box by selecting Options from the Tools menu and choosing the Display page. These settings are discussed in Skill Session 4.

*Figure 75.14.*
*The Options Display*
*dialog box.*

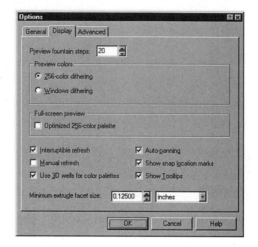

```
Fountain=50
WindowsDithering=0
OptimizedPalette=0
InterruptableRefresh=1
AutoPan=1
ManualRefresh=0
HighlightSnapNodes=1
ShowPopUpHelp=1
MinExtrudeFacetSize=31750
MinExtrudeFacetSizeUnits=0x1
```

## Options—Advanced

The Options Advanced settings can be changed in the dialog box shown in Figure 75.15. You access this dialog box by selecting Options from the Tools menu and choosing the Advanced page. These settings are discussed in Skill Session 4.

*Figure 75.15.*
*The Options Advanced*
*dialog box.*

```
MakeBackupWhenSave=1
AutoBackupMins=10
SaveTextures=1
IntrruptibleIO=0
CustomActionSelection=0
MultiThreading=0
```

## Text Options

The Text Options settings can be changed in the dialog box shown in Figure 75.16. It is accessed by selecting Text Options from the Text menu. These settings are discussed in Skill Session 4.

*Figure 75.16.*
*The Text Options dialog*
*box.*

```
EditTextOnScreen=1
ShowFontSample=1
MinLineWidth=3
GreekTextBelow=9
DisplayCharsDuringKern=25
CalligraphicText=1
TextInMetafile=0
```

## Display Settings

These settings indicate the state of various commands found in the View menu. For more information on these commands, see Command Reference 3, titled "View Menu Commands."

```
DrawInWireframe=0
GridFlags=0x2A
ShowBitmaps=1
HighResBitmaps=1
Window=0,0,-32768,-32768,0
ScreenSize=1024,768
```

## Page Setup Settings

These settings indicate the last settings used in the Page Setup dialog box. Skill Session 69, "Page Setup," discusses each of these options.

```
PaperSize=2159000,2794000
PageSizeUnits=1,1
PaperSizeType=0x3
PaperOrientation=0x0
PaperColor=RGB255,255,255,255,USER
ShowPageBorder=1
PageLayout=0x1
FacingPages=0
LeftPageFirst=0
```

## Ruler and Grid Settings

These settings indicate the last settings used in the Grid and Ruler Setup dialog box. Skill Session 19, "Grid and Ruler Setup," discusses each of these options.

```
GridOrg=-1079500,-1397000
Units=1,1
WorldUnits=0x1
WorldPageUnits=0x0
WorldScaleInUse=0
WorldScale=1.000000
```

## Palette and Color Settings

These settings indicate the last settings used for the color palette and color model. Skill Session 67, "Color Models and Color Palettes," discusses each of these options.

```
ColorModel=0x2
OnScreenPaletteIndex=5
DefPaletteMethod=0
ColorCorrection=0
```

# CORELFLT.INI

The CORELFLT.INI file controls all of the import and export filters for each of the Corel applications.

## [TXT]

This is the filter for TXT files. Each of the entries controls an aspect of the filter. Some of the filters will have multiple lines dealing with compression. In the TXT filter there is no compression (NoOfCompressions=0) and therefore the CompressionX line is blank. Also, you might see multiple extensions on the Extensions line if a particular format can go by different names. This line can be edited by the user, but make sure you have a backup.

```
Signature=CORELFILTER - A
FilterEntry=0
Description=ANSI Text (TXT)
Extensions=*.TXT
CorelID=0x800
FilterCapability1=0x13000
FilterCapability2=0x0
NoOfCompressions=0
CompressionX=
```

## [Corel DRAW 6.0]

These are the filters for CorelDRAW 6. Each of the applications will have a similar section listing all of the filters it uses. The order of the filters in this file determines their order in the import and export dialog boxes. Therefore, you might want to reorder them so that the most-used formats are listed first. Make sure to have a backup file before editing.

```
FilterNo1=PS,\IEVCT60.FLT
```

# CORELPRN.INI

The CORELPRN.INI file controls everything related to printing for all of the Corel applications.

## *[Config]*

All of the settings in this section can be changed within the Special Settings section of the Options tab in the Print Options dialog box, as shown in Figure 75.17. Each of the settings is described in detail in Skill Session 50, "Printing."

*Figure 75.17.*
*The Options tab of the*
*Print Options dialog box.*

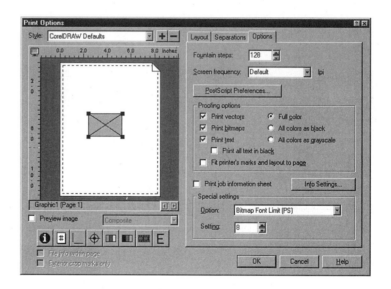

```
AllTextAsGraphics=0
TextAsClip=0
PreviewImage=0
UseColorProfile=0
DumpEntireBitmap=0
WarnBadOrientation=1
PSBitmapFontLimit=8
PSBitmapFontSizeThreshold=75
PSComplexityThreshold=1500
PSOverprintBlackLimit=95
PSRegistrationMarkType=0
PSCompositeCMYKMarks=0
PSDownloadType1Fonts=1
PSConvertTrueTypeToType1=1
PSSpotFountainsAsProcess=0
PSColorBitmapsAsGrayscale=1
PS2StrokeAdjust=1
PSConformToDSC=0
```

```
FullImageDrag=1
DoBanding=0
Unit=1
```

## [PSDrivers]

This section lists PostScript drivers that can be used with CorelDRAW. A 1 indicates that the driver is a PostScript driver, and a 0 indicates a non-PostScript device. Three drivers are listed in a standard configuration: MGXPS for the Micrografx PostScript driver, PSCRIPT for the standard Windows PostScript driver, ADOBEPS for the Adobe PostScript driver, and AGFAPS for the Agfa PostScript driver. To add additional drivers, use the filename preceding the period, followed by an equal sign and a 1. (For example, USPC.DRV would be shown as USPC=1.)

```
pscript=1
```

## [PSScreenSets]

Before the equals sign is the DOS filename of the INI file for specific screen set data. After the equals sign is the technology name to be loaded into the selection list box.

```
AGFAD.INI=AGFA
```

The left side of the equals sign is the DOS filename for the file that contains the custom screen information. The right side of the equals sign is the name that will be loaded into the selection list box.

## [PSScreenFreqDefaults]

Before the equals sign is the printer resolution. After the equals sign is the associated default screen frequency. In the following list, the left side of the equals sign is the printer resolution. The right side of the equals sign is the default screen frequency for that particular printer resolution.

```
300=60
600=80
1000=100
1200=133
1270=133
1693=133
2540=150
3386=200
```

# WIN.INI

## *[CorelGraphics6]* Section

### *Dir=*

This specifies the full path to the folder in which the initialization files for all Corel programs are located. The default value is *drive*:\COREL60\CONFIG, where *drive* is the hard drive on which the programs are located.

# Skill Session: Graphics Toolkit Workshop

# 76

# Introduction to PHOTO-PAINT

Welcome to the world of pixels! This is the section of the book that shows you how Corel PHOTO-PAINT works and more importantly, how to make it work for you. My name is David Huss, and as one of the world's leading practitioners of PHOTO-PAINT, I am going to be your guide for the next few Skill Sessions. I would love to jump right in and start showing you how to do dazzling photo effects, but you need to have a brief tour of the Paint program in order to understand some terms.

## It's the Same, Except It's Different

Can I tell you a story? Early one spring afternoon in Minneapolis (that means the temperature was hovering just above freezing), I visited the garden department of a local store. While trying to pay for my item, a sweet lady in front of me was asking the clerk what the difference was between the two brands of insecticide she held. His answer was classic. "They're exactly the same, except they're different." Her response was even better: "Thank you, that's what I thought." That story illustrates the difference between CorelDRAW and PHOTO-PAINT. Corel has gone to a great amount of effort to make its user interface (UI) the same—except they're different. The reason they're different is that the base programs are completely different. Therefore, let's take a quick tour of the PHOTO-PAINT screen and then talk about how things work in PHOTO-PAINT's pixelated, bitmapped world.

## A Quick Tour of the Screen

Figure 76.1 shows the screen with two images already loaded. The concept of toolbars and roll-ups was explained in previous Skill Sessions, so let's look at features, beginning with the toolbox on the left side of the screen.

*Figure 76.1.*
*The PHOTO-PAINT screen*
*with a few photographs*
*already loaded. The*
*toolbox located on the left*
*is our first stopping point*
*on the tour.*

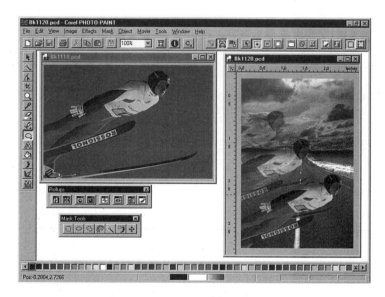

# Corel *TIP!*

This is a big tip for PHOTO-PAINT 5 users. If you have spent some time learning PHOTO-PAINT 5 you are in for a big surprise. PHOTO-PAINT 6 has been changed substantially.

## Object Pointer

At the top of the toolbox is the Object pointer. You might think you know what this is because you probably are familiar with CorelDRAW. The Object Pointer in PHOTO-PAINT is used to select and move objects. You will learn more about this tool later, so for now just remember its name.

## Mask Tools

The little black arrowhead on the lower corner of the next tool tells you it contains a flyout. In this figure I have already dragged the Mask tools out as a toolbar. (It is the second toolbar below the skier.) Like the other tools, you will learn to use them a little later on. For the moment, remember where the Mask tools are parked.

## Crop Tool

The Crop tool is used to crop images.

## Zoom/Hand Tools

These tools contain short flyouts that have a Zoom tool and a Hand tool used for quick panning in an image.

## Eyedropper Tool

The Eyedropper tool is a very handy tool used to select colors in existing images.

## Eraser/Local Undo/Color Replacer Tool

Don't worry about these tools; you won't be using them as often as you might first imagine.

## Pen Tools

Don't worry about these tools; you won't be using them as often as you might first imagine.

## Rectangle/Ellipse/Polygon Tools

These are a handy collection of the tools that are used to produce filled or unfilled polygons. You will use these tools often.

## The Text Tool

The Text tool in PHOTO-PAINT is the same concept as the Text tool in CorelDRAW. It is used to add text in an image with very limited type control.

## Fill Tool

The Fill tool is used to flood a defined area with either a solid color, gradient, pattern, or bitmap tile. This is the same tool as in CorelDRAW, except the operation is somewhat different for some of the options.

### Brush Tools

Major parking garage for a majority of the freehand tools you will use. Contains over 26 different brush types and styles. Version 6 of PHOTO-PAINT has expanded the number of paintbrushes. Now you can paint with a spray can, air brush, pencil, pen, or marker, among others.

### Effects Tools

You'll use these tools for image correction and touch-up. PHOTO-PAINT has a wide range of professional-quality effects you can use to enhance or customize your image. Effects provide access to the entire range of PHOTO-PAINT effects.

### Clone Tools

The Clone tools are the tools used primarily to clean up photographs and other images. Disappointed? You can also use it for crazy special effects, but restoring photographs is its primary function.

### Tour's Over

Everyone out of the bus. I could spend pages showing you where all of the unique (think weird) stuff is located (there are 19 toolbars and roll-ups), but let's get on with the business of learning how to use PHOTO-PAINT.

## What's New in PHOTO-PAINT 6?

The following is a list of the important features incorporated in Corel PHOTO-PAINT 6.

- **32-Bit power**   Is it just me, or does this sound like an ad for a video game? Because PHOTO-PAINT 6 is a Windows 95 (WIN95) application, it is nearly three times faster than PHOTO-PAINT 5. This speed improvement is especially evident in some of the filters that used to take forever to complete their action.

- **Unlimited file size**   This is easily the biggest improvement for those using the product professionally. PHOTO-PAINT 5 could load only a 16 MB image file; actually, you were lucky if it loaded a 12 MB file. PHOTO-PAINT 6 can load any size image file.

- **Unlimited undos**   What more can I say? You are no longer limited to being able to undo only the last command. Don't break out the champagne yet, it has limitations.

- **New filters**   Many new filters have been added to the robust set of filters that were part of PHOTO-PAINT 5. There is a filter to automatically remove scratches and imperfections in a photograph, another that adds lighting effects and many, many more.

■ **Improved mask capabilities** With PHOTO-PAINT 6 you will experience a much larger selection of mask options. You can now feather masks, make them grow and shrink, or add borders to them. You can take objects and convert them to masks or convert objects to masks. You can now automatically remove those small pieces of masks that occurred when you used a Magic Wand mask tool on a multi-colored background. If you worked with PHOTO-PAINT 5, you will find the new selection of masks will dramatically increase your ability to control effects and image selections.

■ **Improved text editing and handling** Now when text is placed on an image it remains as text that can be edited at a later time. There still is no control of leading or kerning, which gives us something to look forward to in PHOTO-PAINT 7 or 8.

■ **Support for 16-bit, plug-in filters** Many of the more popular plug-in filters have not been converted to operate in the 32-bit environment. PHOTO-PAINT 6 can work with existing 16-bit plug-in filters as well as enjoy the power of the new 32-bit filters as they become available. Commercially available plug-in filters can be your gateway to a world of incredible digital effects. The plug-in filter concept was introduced by Adobe with Photoshop. Today, many third-party developers make products that can tap directly into the powerful Corel PHOTO-PAINT program to produce effects such as making a photograph look like an oil painting. Filters can take a picture of a stationary bus sitting in a parking lot and make it look like it is rocketing down the road at warp-factor four. PHOTO-PAINT already comes with an impressive set of built-in filters, while support of the plug-in standard means that you can purchase third-party filters such as Aldus Gallery Effects, Andromeda Series, or Kai Power Tools and achieve even greater graphic effects.

■ **Improvement of object handling** The Object/Layers roll-up of PHOTO-PAINT 5 has been completely redesigned. The new interface offers improved control of objects in an image. A favorite feature of mine is the new ability to protect (lock) a layer without the necessity of hiding it from view.

## Classroom Time

You are now going to learn a few things about the type of images that PHOTO-PAINT works with. If you don't learn it now, you will always be wondering why the photograph fills your screen in PHOTO-PAINT and looks like a postage stamp when you import it into CorelDRAW. I am not kidding about this. I answer the same basic questions on the Corel PHOTO-PAINT Forum and the PHOTO-PAINT page of CorelNET all of the time.

## Understanding Digital Images and Color

By now you have figured out that Corel PHOTO-PAINT works with bitmapped images. Even if a vector-based (non-bitmap) file is loaded into PHOTO-PAINT, it is converted (rasterized) to a bitmap when it is loaded. To work effectively with bitmap images, it is necessary to understand why they act differently than the object-based images in CorelDRAW. Let us begin by defining our terms.

### Pixels

These are not little elf-like creatures that fly through the forest at twilight. The term "pixel" is short for *picture element*. Bitmap images are composed of pixels. They are the individual squares that make up an image on a computer screen or on hard copy. One way to illustrate the idea of pixels is to think of a wall mural created with mosaic tiles. When you get close to a mural made of mosaic tiles, it looks like someone had a bad Lego day. This is because you are so close you are looking at individual tiles. However, step away a few feet from the mosaic and the individual tiles begin to lose their definition; they visually begin to merge together. The tiles have not changed their size or number, yet the further back you move, the better the image looks. Pixels in bitmaps work much the same way.

I have created a sample image in Figure 76.2 to illustrate how pixels make up an image. Figure 76.2 shows that as you zoom in on an image, the individual pixels begin to stand out more and the image they produce becomes less and less evident. Returning to our mosaic tile illustration, there are, of course, major differences between pixels and mosaic tiles. Pixels come in a greater selection of decorator colors (more than 16.7 million, to be exact). And pixels don't weigh as much as tiles. However, tiles and pixels operate in the same way to produce an image.

*Figure 76.2.*
*This photograph of a young girl is shown at three different zoom levels. Notice how the pixels begin to appear at the 440-percent zoom level. At the 1600-percent zoom level, it is difficult to identify what we are viewing.*

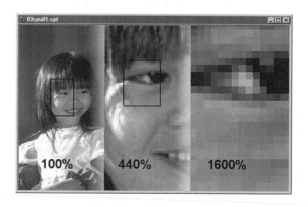

## Image Size and Resolution

These two terms represent some of the more elusive concepts of digital imaging. An image's *size* describes the physical dimensions of the image. Image size is measured in pixels. The reason for using pixels is because the size of an image in pixels is fixed. Therefore, when I speak of an image being 1200×600 pixels, I know approximately how big the image is. If I use a system other than pixels—inches, for example—the size of the image is dependent on the resolution of the image. If I receive an image that is described as being 3 inches by 1.5 inches I must ask "At what resolution?"

## So What Is Resolution?

*Resolution* is the density of pixels-per-inch (ppi) that make up an image; it is measured in dots-per-inch (dpi). The "Resampling" section of Skill Session 77, "Basic Image Manipulation," explains a more detailed exploration of resolution, so for now, the following is a brief explanation of resolution.

Assume we have an image that has a width of 300 pixels and a height of 300 pixels. The size of the image is described as being 300×300 pixels. How big will the image be when I import it into CorelDRAW? This is a trick question! There is not enough information to determine the size. This is where resolution comes in. If the resolution of this image is set to 300 pixels per inch, then the image dimensions are 1 inch by 1 inch when imported into CorelDRAW. If the resolution is doubled (set to 600 dpi), the image would be half the size or .5 inch by .5 inch. If the resolution is reduced by half (150 dpi), the image size doubles, or is 2 inches by 2 inches. It is an inverse relationship, which means that if one value increases the other decreases.

# Corel *TIP!*

> Image size is expressed as the length (in pixels) of each side. Resolution tells you how many pixels are contained in each inch.

Figure 76.3 shows a file saved at four different resolutions; each one was then imported into CorelDRAW.

*Figure 76.3.*
*The file size of each block*
*of bricks is identical; only*
*the resolution was*
*changed.*

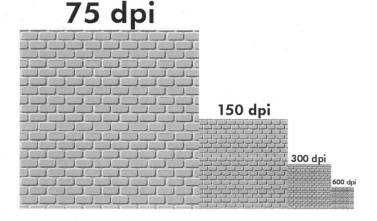

## Image Resolution or Hey! Why Is My PHOTO-PAINT Image So Tiny?

If you work with a PHOTO-PAINT image that fills your screen and then import that same PHOTO-PAINT file into CorelDRAW and discover it is now only one inch wide, you have experienced image resolution. If you have always worked in vector-based programs such as CorelDRAW (which is resolution-independent), you never had to know this before. Don't get discouraged, it isn't as difficult to understand as it might first appear. Look at Figure 76.3 again to see what a difference changing the resolution can make.

## Corel *TIP!*

> The greater the resolution of an image in PHOTO-PAINT, the smaller the image will be in CorelDRAW.

## Enough Already!

We could go on for many more pages, but it is time to actually use the program. Turn the page and see how much you can learn in a short span of a few pages. See you on the next page.

# 77

# Basic Image Manipulation

It seems that everyone I talk to wants to start creating an incredibly complicated photo montage when they begin to work with Corel PHOTO-PAINT. The truth is, Paint's greatest asset to the CorelDRAW user is its capability to do basic image manipulation. Don't groan. You can always skip this skill session, but be warned that the material in this skill session is the heart of most day-to-day PHOTO-PAINT operations. Did I scare you?

## Why You Need to Know This Stuff

Understanding image manipulation is important because for all of the fancy things that CorelDRAW can do with bitmap images—and it's a lot— you cannot properly resize images in CorelDRAW or any other vector-based program. Many page-layout programs such as Corel Ventura, PageMaker, and QuarkXPress offer the capability to resize and crop graphics as part of the tools of the program. They are usually fine for very minor adjustments, but to make any significant changes to the image you should open the files in PHOTO-PAINT to make the changes there. There are several reasons for doing so; here are a few:

■ If you crop a large image file in these programs, the file size remains unchanged. Even if you use only 5 percent of a 16 MB image file, the entire file remains as part of the document file. Large document files create problems with lengthy print times and difficulty in transport to a service bureau. If you crop that same 16 MB file in PHOTO-PAINT, it becomes an 800 KB file.

■ Resizing bitmap files in these applications can cause the image to become distorted; in many cases this distortion shows up as unwanted moiré patterns over the entire image.

## Before You Start...

I am assuming if you have gotten this far into the book, you know how to launch PHOTO-PAINT and use the File menu to open an existing file.

## Changing the Size of an Image

Images are rarely provided to you in the exact size that is required for your project. In the old days, when you needed to change the size of an image you made a *PMT* (photo-mechanical transfer) of the image, which was reduced or enlarged as required. Fortunately, PHOTO-PAINT provides several much simpler ways to change both the size and the surrounding working area of an image. There are two ways to change the size of an image in PHOTO-PAINT: resampling and cropping. I have listed the three commands in PHOTO-PAINT that are used to accomplish this.

| | |
|---|---|
| Resampling | Makes the image larger or smaller by adding or subtracting pixels. It can also change the resolution of the image, which affects the printed size without adding or subtracting pixels. |
| Crop tool | New to PHOTO-PAINT 6, this tool acts like a traditional cropping tool. It enables you to define a specific area of an image and remove all of the area outside of the defined area. |
| Changing paper size | A very handy command that uses a combination of both techniques. The Paper Size command increases overall image size by increasing the size of the base image. It is as if you put a larger sheet of paper under the original. It can also be used to crop the image. |

## Resolution—the Key to Resampling

To use resampling, you need to know how it works. Before you can understand how resampling works, you need to understand some fundamentals of bitmap images. Before that, you need to explore the "Big Bang" theory...just kidding! If you learn how this part works, you will amaze your friends at user group meetings, because very few people understand this stuff.

Unlike images in CorelDRAW, which are composed of vectors, PHOTO-PAINT files are bitmap images composed of millions of tiny picture elements called *pixels*. In Figure 77.1, I have enlarged part of a photograph by zooming in at 600 percent so you can see the pixels that compose that portion of the picture. Bet you didn't know pixels were square!

*Figure 77.1.*
*The portion of the photograph surrounded by the darker rectangle is shown zoomed at 600 percent to show the individual pixels that make up the photograph. Courtesy of PhotoDisc Food Essentials collection.*

The spacing between pixels is called *resolution*. It is correctly measured in pixels per inch (ppi), although almost everyone refers to resolution measurements in dots per inch (dpi). (I know that sounds dry, but there isn't any other way to say it.)

Resolution is one of the most misunderstood terms in the desktop-publishing arena; this is because its meaning changes depending on the subject. When you are talking about the resolution of a laser printer being 600 dpi, you are referring to something that is completely different from the resolution of an image or the resolution of a monitor.

When I talk about resolution in PHOTO-PAINT 6 (or any other bitmap editing program), I am always referring to the distance between pixels. So why should you care how close the pixels are to each other? Good question. The pixel spacing (resolution) in a bitmap image affects how large the image will appear when it is printed and the amount of detail the image possesses.

## Resolution and Size

Simply stated, resolution in Paint affects the size of the image when imported into another program. Here is the part that's weird: Because Paint maps each pixel in an image to a screen pixel, resolution changes in Paint have no apparent effect. I have included a visual demonstration. In Figure 77.2 I have loaded three separate images. The resolution of the photographs are (from left to right) 75, 150, and 300 dpi. They are all at the same zoom factor (100 percent). All of the images appear to be the same size. Look closely at the rulers that were enabled in each of the images and you can see that although they look to be the same size, they are not. In Figure 77.3, the same three files have been imported into CorelDRAW 6 and labeled. The difference in size caused by the change in resolution can now be seen very clearly.

*Figure 77.2.*
*The resolutions of the photographs are, from left to right, 75, 150, and 300 dpi. They appear to be the same size, but close examination of the rulers shows that they are not.*

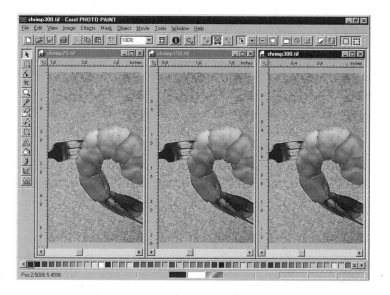

*Figure 77.3.*
*The same three files have been imported in CorelDRAW 6. The difference in size caused by the change in resolution is now obvious.*

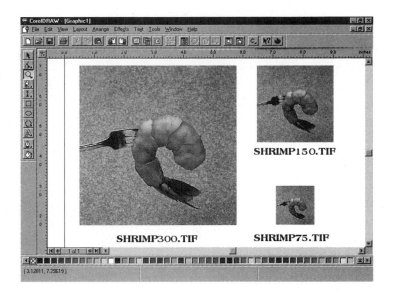

## Changing Size with the Resample Command

This is a simple technique, but one I use all the time. The photograph I want to use in the Photo-CD is not the correct size. The photograph is roughly 2.5×3.8 inches. I need a 5×8 inch photo. I'll use PHOTO-PAINT's Resample command to resize it:

1. Launch PHOTO-PAINT by double-clicking its icon.

2. From the File menu, select Open. When the dialog box appears, choose the file CAT.CPT from the companion CD-ROM. The file CAT was originally a Photo-CD format file from the Corel Professional Photos Cats and Kittens collection that has been converted to the native PHOTO-PAINT format (CPT) to save space.

3. Press the F4 (Zoom to Fit) key and then turn on the rulers (by pressing Ctrl+R) so you can see how big this image is.

4. To see the resolution and other information about the image, open the Image menu and select Info. A window appears as shown in Figure 77.4. In this case, you see that the image has a resolution of 200 dpi. Normally, you would not want to go much below that, but you know that the final output will not be a high-resolution device and the printer says you can go down to 96 dpi and still look acceptable. Click the OK button to close the Info screen window. (Alternately, you can get this information by right-clicking your pointing device on the image and selecting Info from the Property flyout menu.)

Figure 77.4.
*All of the information you
need about an image is
displayed when the Info
command is invoked or its
button in the toolbar is
enabled.*

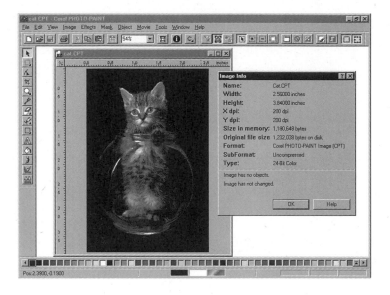

5. From the Image menu, choose the Resample command. This opens the
   Resample dialog box as shown in Figure 77.5. Check the Maintain Original
   Size check box. This instructs the Resample command to change the resolu-
   tion to achieve the requested size.

Figure 77.5.
*The Resample dialog box
enables you to make
images larger and smaller
by adding or subtracting
pixels or changing
resolution.*

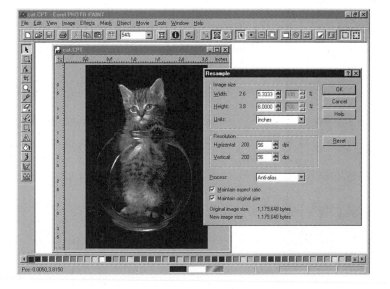

6. Enter the new Height value of 8 inches. (The Width value changes automatically.) Click the OK button and—instantly—the action is complete. The reason this happens so quickly is because the only change made was the resolution value in the image file. The only indication you have that the action was completed is by looking at the rulers, which indicate the figure is now 5.3×8.

7. Open the File menu and select the Save As command. Save the file as Cat In Progress.CPT.

## Using the Paper Size Command to Crop the Image

At this point, the cat is almost the correct size. The project called for a specific image size of 5×8. You didn't use the Resample command to change the aspect ratio, as this would have created different horizontal and vertical resolutions. You won't use the Crop tool because it is difficult to be precise with it. You will use the Paper Size command.

The Paper size command increases the overall image size by increasing the size of the base image. It is as if you were to put a larger sheet of paper under the original. It can also be used to crop the image, as you are about to see.

1. Open the file Cat In Progress.CPT if it is not already open.

2. From the Image menu, choose Paper Size. The Paper Size dialog box opens as shown in Figure 77.6.

*Figure 77.6.*
*You can use the Paper Size*
*dialog box to increase or*
*decrease the size of the*
*background on which the*
*image sits.*

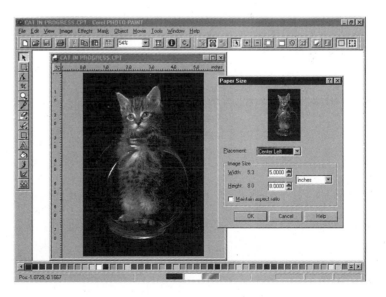

3. To use the Paper Size as a cropping tool, disable the Maintain Aspect Ratio button (so the Height will not be changed when you change the Width value). Enter 5.0 in the Width box.

   Because there is image information in the background on the left side of the photo, you want the .3 inches of width to be taken off of the right side. You select this with the Placement setting. Choose Center Left for the placement setting and click the OK button. The image is now 5×8 inches as indicated either by the rulers or the Info command.

   The Placement setting determines the position of the image on the resized paper. The drop-down list box has the following options: Top Left, Top Center, Top Right, Center Left, Centered, Center Right, Bottom Left, Bottom Center, Bottom Right, and Custom. If you choose Custom, use the hand cursor in the Preview window to move the image to the correct location.

4. Save the file using the Save command in the File menu.

## More Tricks with the Paper Size Command and Some New Tools

After completing resampling and cropping the photograph, you are feeling good. Until, that is, the client returns and explains that they need the same cat picture as a 15-inch banner for the top of a larger sign for the lobby. Well, there is no way to stretch the cat picture to 15 inches wide, but using the best tool in PHOTO-PAINT, the one located between your ears, there is some magic that can be done quickly and easily:

1. Open the file Cat In Progress.CPT if it is not already open.

2. From the Image menu, choose Paper Size. The Paper Size dialog box opens.

3. Disable the Maintain Aspect Ratio button (so the Height will not be changed when you change the Width value). Enter 15.0 in the Width box, choose Center Left again for the placement setting, and click the OK button. The image is now 15×8 inches, as shown in Figure 77.7.

4. Next, you need to place a duplicate copy of your furry friend at the other end of the image. Select Paste From File from the Edit menu. This opens the Paste an Image From Disk dialog box. Select the same figure you currently have open, Cat In Progress.CPT, and click the OK button. The result looks like Figure 77.8.

   The Paste From File command pastes a copy of the selected image on top of the existing image. The pasted image will be an object, which means it can be rotated, resized, or moved to wherever it is needed.

*Figure 77.7.*
*Using the Paper Size command, the width of the photograph has been increased by adding 10 inches to the right of the original photograph.*

*Figure 77.8.*
*A copy of the photograph has been pasted on top of the existing image using the Paste From File command.*

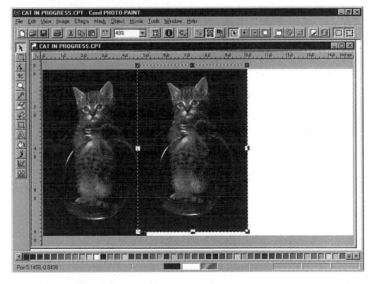

5. To move the object to the opposite end of the image, use the Object Picker located on the top of the toolbox. Click the object with the Object Picker tool to select it (if it is not already selected).

   New in PHOTO-PAINT 6 is a large selection of alignment options for objects. Open the Align dialog box (Ctrl+A) and you will recognize the Align dialog box from CorelDRAW 5. Select the Vertical and Horizontal settings shown in Figure 77.9 and click the OK button. The object aligns to the vertical center and the horizontal right.

*Figure 77.9.*
*The Align dialog box*
*provides extensive control*
*over the alignment of*
*objects.*

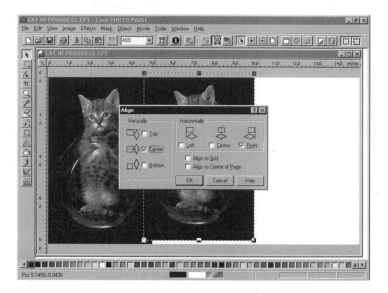

6. To give the cat banner some symmetry, you need to flip the image of the cat horizontally. In the Object menu, select the Flip command and choose Horizontal. The object has now been flipped and is facing the opposite direction of the original, as shown in Figure 77.10.

*Figure 77.10.*
*After aligning the object*
*with the background, you*
*can use the Flip command*
*to horizontally flip the cat*
*object.*

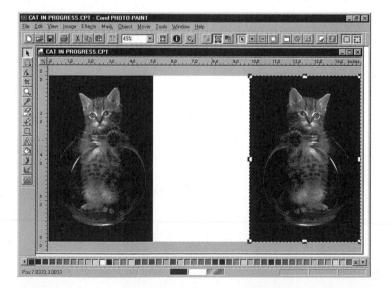

7. The next step is simple but needs some explanation. Because you no longer need to apply any more effects to the object and it is in position, you will combine it with the background. After it is combined (called Merge in Paint 5) with the background it can no longer be rotated, resized, or moved because it is no longer an object—it has become part of the background image. In the Object menu, select Combine and choose Object(s) with Background. The blue marquee that surrounded the object disappears, indicating that the object has combined with the background.

8. Great—now you have two symmetrical cats with a white rectangle in the middle. The last step is to fill the white rectangle with the background color, which is easier than you might imagine. First, select the Fill tool from the toolbox. (It looks like a paint bucket.)

9. Next you must make the fill color identical to the current background color with the Eyedropper tool. You could select the tool, but a quicker way is to place the cursor over it and hold down the E key. The cursor becomes an eyedropper. The Eyedropper tool samples the image area under the cursor and makes the paint color the same color. To select the fill color, click the right mouse button while holding down the E key with the cursor over the black background near the edge of the center. Now the fill color has become the same color as the background, as indicated in the Status Bar at the bottom of the screen. Release the keys and massage your fingers.

# Corel *TIP!*

The Status Bar gives you a quick, visual way to confirm what colors and styles (types of fills) are currently selected through three very small preview windows. The three preview windows (from left to right) are Paint (foreground) color, Paper (background) color, and Fill color.

10. Click the Fill cursor anywhere in the white rectangle in the center of the photograph; after a moment, it fills completely with the fill color. The finished photograph is shown in Figure 77.11.

   The Fill tool is used to fill masked areas or the entire image with a color, fountain, texture, or bitmap fill. The tolerance setting (found in the Tool Settings roll-up) determines how much of the image or area is filled with the selected color or texture. Choosing a tolerance value of 100 percent causes the entire area under the Fill tool to be filled. Lower values, however, restrict the application of the fill to those pixels adjacent to the starting pixel with colors that fall within the tolerance range.

*Figure 77.11.*
*The completed cat banner.*

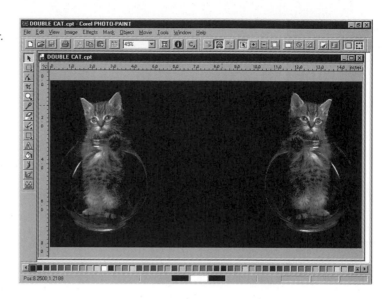

11. Here is a final use of the Paper Size command and a nice finishing touch. Place the cursor over the blue in the kitten's eyes. Hold down the E key and the Ctrl key (are you starting to feel like you're playing Twister?) and click the left mouse button. The Paper color is now a nice blue-gray.

12. Select Paper Size in the Image menu, disable Maintain Aspect Ratio, and add one inch to the Width and Height values. Click the OK button. After a few moments you will have a nice blue border as shown in Figure 77.12.

*Figure 77.12.*
*The Paper Size command can also be used to create borders for images.*

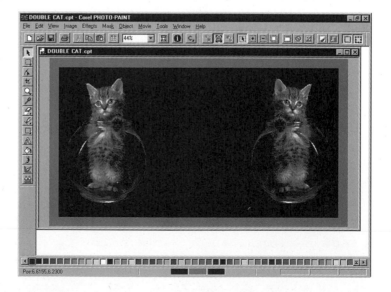

13. Save the file as DOUBLE CAT.CPT. You will use it in another exercise.

# Image Conversion

PHOTO-PAINT does not have an export command like the one found in CorelDRAW. It can, however, convert images in two ways: by saving files in a wide variety of different formats (.EPS, .TIF, and so on) and by converting open images to different color modes (such as 256-color, grayscale, and others) using the Convert To command in the Image menu.

Converting color images to grayscale can save enormous amounts of disk space when producing graphics that will be printed in grayscale. Converting a 24-bit color image to grayscale reduces the image file to one-third of the original size. For example, if the original 24-bit color image is 1.1 MB, converting it to grayscale will result in a file size of approximately 250 to 300 KB.

Another use of this feature is viewing color images for pages that will be printed in grayscale. This book is a classic example of that type of work. All of the examples that are shown were originally color. I have learned that it is very important to convert the images to grayscale so I can see what they will look like when they appear in the book. Many times in my previous book, I would find an excellent example to show an effect or technique only to discover that the results did not show up when printed in grayscale.

To convert an image, select Convert To in the Image menu. A drop-down list opens with the following choices:

**Black and White (1-bit)** Converts the image to black and white (not be confused with grayscale). This selection opens another drop-down list with the following choices:

**Line Art:** Use this if you do not want a halftone applied.

**Printer Halftone:** This is for fating a halftone. (Fating is the process by which the half-tone cells are enlarged to compensate for the distance between the dots on low resolution printers.) Use it if you are going to print the image on a low-resolution printer.

**Screen Halftone:** This is for a diffused halftone. Used if the image is only for display use.

**16 color (4-bit)** Converts the image to 16 colors.

**Duotone** This is new in PHOTO-PAINT 6. This converts a grayscale image into a Duotone image.

**Grayscale (8-bit)** Converts the image to grayscale.

**256 Color (8-bit)** Opens the Convert to 256 Colors dialog box. Converts the image to 256 colors. (See additional discussion under color resuction.)

**True Color (24-bit)**   Converts the image to 24-bit color (also called True-Color or 16.7 million color). It uses eight bits of data for each of the three channels of Red, Green, and Blue (RGB).

**CMYK (32-bit)**   Converts the image to 32-bit color. This is a 24-bit color image that is separated into four channels: Cyan, Magenta, Yellow, and Black (CMYK), which is the standard separation for four-color printing.

## Understanding Color Reduction

Before I discuss the Convert to 256 Color dialog box, you must understand some more basics of color images. When you reduce a color image from a palette of 16.7 million colors (24-bit) to a palette of 256 possible colors, something has to give. It is much like putting 16.7 million pounds of flour in a 256-pound sack. The way conversion is accomplished is by using a color table. All 256-color graphic images contain information about how color is supposed to be mapped; this is called a *color table*. This produces a 256-color image that is indexed to the color table. This type of file (256-color image) is also referred to as an *indexed color file*.

The explosive growth of online services demands 256-color images. If you don't do a good job converting your image from 24-bit to 256 colors, it can look terrible. File-size savings in color publications can be accomplished by using 256-color images since the are one-third the size of 24-bit color files. Believe it or not, you can use some of the 256-color images in color publications and have them look as good as (or at least very close to) 24-bit quality.

## Corel *TIP!*

Don't be too quick to dismiss the 256-color option because of previous bad experiences with a 256-color palette. Corel uses a proprietary 256-color palette that produces color that can be very close to 24-bit color, but without the system overhead. (Image files in 256-color mode are two-thirds smaller than 24-bit files).

## Corel *TIP!*

When converting an image to 256 colors, always select the Optimized Palette and Error Diffusion to create the best color.

Well, that covers the basics of image manipulation with PHOTO-PAINT 6. In the next Skill Session, you will be introduced to masks and all of the neat things you can do with them.

# 78

# An Introduction to Masks and How to Use Them

## What Is a Mask?

The most important part of PHOTO-PAINT! Finish this chapter and you will agree. The following definition of a mask is provided with Corel's online help:

"A mask is a tool much like a stencil that allows you to isolate an area so that you can apply color and special effects to that area without altering the rest of the image."

Everything inside a mask can be altered; everything outside a mask is protected from change. If you have ever used Adobe's Photoshop be advised that a PHOTO-PAINT Mask is the same as a Photoshop Selection.

## What Can You Do with a Mask?

Most operations in PHOTO-PAINT require the use of a mask. You will use the mask to isolate one area from an effect—such as Contrast—being applied to the rest of the image. You use a mask to define areas to be removed or modified.

There are many different types of masks in PHOTO-PAINT, such as Rectangle, Freehand, and Magic Wand. Basically, all of the masks fall into one of two categories: regular masks, which define areas based on shape; and color-sensitive masks, which define areas based on color. Once a mask has been defined, you can paint on the image; apply a solid, fountain, or texture fill; and apply special effects such as smudging or blending—all without altering the area outside the mask marquee.

## Working with Masks Based on Shape

In this first session, we are going to take a test drive with the Rectangle mask tool to get familiar with it.

1. Launch PHOTO-PAINT and open the file PUBSIG1.CPT.

2. From the toolbox, select the Rectangle Mask tool from the flyout of mask tools.

   The Rectangle Mask tool defines rectangular masks. Holding down the Ctrl key before defining the mask constrains the shape to a square. Holding down the Shift key expands or contracts the mask from the center.

## Corel *TIP!*

A quick way to open any flyout is to click the tiny black arrow in the lower-right corner of the tool.

3. Click a corner of the pub sign and, holding down the left mouse button, drag a rectangle that covers most of the sign. There is no need to be exact about the placement of this mask. The marquee of the mask is composed of moving black-and-white dashes. These dashes were first called "marching ants" in Photoshop, and people have been calling them that ever since. Figure 78.1 shows the approximate location of the mask.

   The Marquee Visible Command is new to PHOTO-PAINT 6. It enables you to turn off the marquee, which can be distracting at times. It has no effect on the mask's operation, only the display of the mask. There is also a button on the Mask toolbar that turns the marquee on and off.

*Figure 78.1.*
*The rectangle mask*
*marquee of "marching*
*ants" is shown around the*
*sign.*

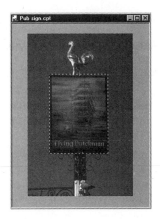

4. With the Rectangle mask tool still selected, place the cursor inside the mask. Click the left mouse button and drag the mask to the lower-right corner, as shown in Figure 78.2. What happened? When a mask is created and moved with any mask tool other than the Mask Transform tool, the pixels surrounded by the mask "float" and are replaced with the Paper (background) color. You can move the mask all over the image and the contents of the mask will continue to move with it. In other words, it is the same as if you used the Cut command to remove the contents and place them in the Clipboard.

*Figure 78.2*
*The mask after it is*
*dragged to the lower-right*
*corner of the image.*

5. Now let's remove the mask and see what happens. Select None in the Mask menu. The contents of the mask have merged with the background and have become a permanent part of the image.

6. Let's revert the image back to the original state. Select the Revert command in the File menu.

The Revert command restores the currently selected image back to its last saved state. A message box advises you that PHOTO-PAINT is about to replace your existing image with the last saved version.

Click OK and the original image returns.

7. Now select the Rectangle mask tool again. This time, select the entire top of the image as shown in Figure 78.3.

# Corel *TIP!*

> You can mask to the edge of an image by dragging the cursor outside of the image. You might need to expand the size of the image window to prevent the cursor from interacting with the edge of the image window.

Figure 78.3.
*Here we have masked the entire upper part of the image.*

8. Place the cursor in the masked area. Click and drag the mask to the position shown in Figure 78.4. If you find the mask has shifted to the left or right while you were repositioning it you can either drag it in position or, if it is only a small amount, use the arrow keys to "nudge" the mask and its contents.

# Corel *TIP!*

> When you make fine position adjustments it is recommended that you turn off the mask marquee either through the Mask menu or by using the button on the toolbar. The mask is still present, it is just invisible.

Figure 78.4.
In this figure we have
dragged the masked area
down to cover the iron
scroll work below the sign.

9. Remove the mask by choosing None from the Mask menu. The contents of the mask are merged into the image.

10. Select the Crop tool from the toolbox and drag a rectangle that includes the entire image excluding the white area. Double-click inside the selection area and PHOTO-PAINT will crop the image to the boundaries you selected. If all went well your image should look like Figure 78.5.

Figure 78.5.
The pub sign image is now
two inches shorter and the
scroll work has been
removed.

11. Save the file using the Save As command as PUB SIG2.CPT.

## Using the Freehand Mask Tool

Now you are going to learn how to use the Freehand mask tool and some more about mask properties. This exercise starts where the last one left off. I do that because I don't like an exercise that has 300 steps.

1. Launch PHOTO-PAINT and open the file PUB SIG2.CPT.

2. From the toolbox, select the Freehand mask tool from the flyout of mask tools. It is the one that looks a little like a hairy amoebae.

   The Freehand Mask tool is a combination of the Polygon and Freehand tools of PHOTO-PAINT 5. The Freehand mask tool defines irregular mask shapes. You can use the Freehand mask tool to either draw the mask freehand (like a Pen tool) or click to establish anchor points around the area.

   In the next step we want to create a mask that surrounds the picture inside of the pub sign. If you tried to do this with the Rectangle mask tool it would not work because the sign is slightly skewed.

3. Place the cursor in the upper-left corner (it can be any corner) of the painting in the sign and click once. This action anchors the mask. Next, place the cursor over the upper-right corner of the painting and click again. Click a third time in the bottom-right corner. Notice that there is a geometric figure being created.

4. Click the fourth point somewhere in the iron gridwork. This is a deliberate mistake for this exercise. To remove the last point made on the mask press the Delete key. The point is gone. You can continue to remove successive points along the mask each time you press the Delete key. Nice touch, don't you think? Place the fourth point in its correct location at the bottom-left by double-clicking it there. The double-click informs PHOTO-PAINT that you are finished and to connect this point to the original anchor point. That's it—the mask is complete as shown in Figure 78.6.

*Figure 78.6.*
*The Freehand mask was*
*used to create the mask*
*shown in this figure.*

# Corel*NOTE!*

**Note for PHOTO-PAINT 5 Users**

In PHOTO-PAINT 5 the Backspace key was used to delete points on a polygon mask. In PHOTO-PAINT 6 the Delete key is used.

5. To actually see the mask you have created you can select the Mask Overlay command in the Mask menu or click the Mask Overlay button in the toolbar (it looks like a red square with an "S").

   The Mask Overlay command superimposes a translucent color over everything in the image except the currently selected mask. It is useful for identifying where the regions of a complex mask are located on an image. You can change the color of the overlay in the Preferences dialog box (Advanced tab). The screen turns red everywhere that is protected by the mask.

   Enabling Mask Overlay doesn't interfere with the operation of the mask—it might get a little confusing, but you could leave it enabled. Therefore, by looking at the mask you can see that in our little exercise the picture is not protected and everything else is protected.

6. This step is to give you a better few of the image on which you are working. In the View menu change your Zoom to 100%. Use the scroll bars to position the picture in the sign so that it can be seen.

7. We are going to use one of the built-in filters in the Effects menu to enhance the picture a little. In the Effects menu select 3D Effects and another drop-down list will appear. From that list, choose the Emboss filter. When the dialog box for this filter opens use the default settings: Original Color, Light direction: Up, and Depth setting of 1. Click the OK button.

   The Emboss filter creates a three-dimensional relief effect. Directional arrows point to the location of the light source and determine the angle of the highlights and shadows. Although the Emboss filter is designed to give images an appearance of depth, it can also be used to enhance some images as we have done here. Figure 78.7 shows the results.

8. You are finished with that mask, so to remove it select None in the Mask menu.

9. Next, we want to replace the background. To do that we will be using one of the second type of masks discussed earlier—the color-sensitive mask. Open the Color Mask roll-up (Ctrl + F5).

*Figure 78.7.*
*The Emboss filter applica-*
*tion was limited to the*
*perimeter of the mask*
*shown in Figure 78.6.*

The Color mask is one of PHOTO-PAINT's color-sensitive masks. This means that if the colors you pick clash with each other, the mask will become upset (just kidding). The Color Mask roll-up lets you mask portions of an image with colors that you choose using the color picker (Eyedropper tool). The Color mask is applied to the image based on colors you select using the color picker (eyedropper) and the color tolerance established by the tolerance slider. The Color Mask roll-up lets you create complex, intricate masks that would otherwise be extremely difficult to define using any of the standard mask tools.

10. We want to use the Color mask to select all of the shades of blue in the sky. To pick the first color use the Color mask eyedropper. Click the Eyedropper button on the Color Mask roll-up and click the sky in the lower-right part of the photograph. This is one of the darker areas of the sky. The color appears in the roll-up and the next sample area becomes active. Next, click the sky above the golden rooster's back, which is one of the brightest areas of the sky. Two samples should do the trick, so click the Eyedropper button again to turn it off.

    Set the roll-up to Modify Colors. Modify Selected Colors lets you isolate the selected color(s) so that any changes will affect only the selected colors. Protect Selected Colors lets you protect the selected color(s) so that the changes will affect only the color(s) that are not selected.

11. Set the Tolerance value for both colors to 24. There is nothing magic about the number 24, I tried several settings and that created the color mask I was looking for in this demonstration.

By adjusting the tolerance in the Tool Settings Roll-Up, you can select how many shades of a color are masked, thus expanding or contracting the boundaries of the mask. Increasing the tolerance value increases the number of color shades included in the mask. To change the tolerance value for a color shade, select the color sample on the roll-up and either use the Tolerance slider to change the value or enter the number directly.

After you have both numbers entered, click the Create Mask button. Your image will look something like Figure 78.8. Notice that the blue sky is masked but so is the blue in the sign. Not to worry, that was why I had you increase the Tolerance setting—so you could see another mask mode. Close the Color Mask roll-up.

*Figure 78.8.*
*This mess-of-a-mask is brought to you today by the Color mask and all of the other color-sensitive mask tools.*

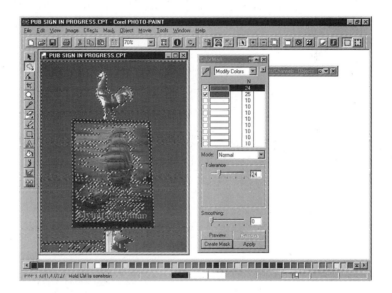

12. Select Mode in the Mask menu and choose Subtract From Mask from the drop-down list.

    When the Subtract From Mask mode is enabled, any mask created is subtracted from an existing mask. The dimensions and shape of the area removed are determined by the mask created.

    Now, any mask you make will be subtracted from the existing mask. Select the Freehand mask tool again from the toolbox. Repeat the same mask procedure you did to create a mask around the picture in the previous session. When you double-click the last point, the portions of the mask inside the sign will be removed. When you have removed the portions of the mask inside the sign, open the Mask menu and return the Mask Mode to Normal.

# Corel *TIP!*

Any time you enable the Subtract From Mask mode, make sure you take it out of that mode when you are finished. If you leave it in this mode, you will go to create a new mask and will scratch your head in wonder when no mask appears. This is one of the biggest "gotchas" in PHOTO-PAINT. You have been warned!

13. Finally, with the mask protecting everything in the image except the sign, we are going to paste another image on top of this one. Because the image we are pasting is rather large, in the View menu change the zoom level to 50 percent (maybe 33 percent depending on the size and resolution of your display).

14. Select Paste From File in the Edit menu. Select the file PUBBACK.CPT and click the OK button.

   The Paste From File command is used to bring an existing image file into the image as an object. An object is a bitmap that floats on its own layer above the image.

   The image we have pasted is much wider than the original photograph, as indicated by the control handles on either side. (See Figure 78.9.) Also, notice that you can see the mask (because the mask is always on top) but not the original photograph (because it is underneath the object we just pasted on top). By grabbing the PUBBACK object with the Object Picker tool, you can move the image to the left or right until it looks correct to you.

*Figure 78.9.*
*Because the mask is on the top we can see it, but not the image underneath.*

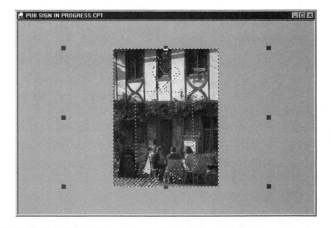

15. Once you are satisfied with the position of the PUBBACK object, select Clip Object to Mask in the Object menu.

The Clip Object to Mask command lets you change the shape of an object using a mask as a clipping tool. Use a mask tool to define the area of an object you want to maintain and choose this command. The area outside of the mask will be deleted.

# Corel *TIP!*

Practitioners of PHOTO-PAINT 5 used to be able to merge an object through a mask. This has been changed in PHOTO-PAINT 6. You must use the Clip Object to Mask command.

16. Finishing touches. The background is in clear focus and is therefore a little distracting. Because the mask is still protecting the sign we can apply a little blurring to the background without affecting the pub sign. Making the background slightly out of focus gives it a feeling of depth. Select Blur in the Effects menu and choose Gaussian Blur.

The Gaussian Blur effect produces an out-of-focus effect. It can significantly improve the quality of images with sharp edges and is great for what we are using it for in this session. Gaussian refers to the bell-shaped curve that is generated by mapping the color values of the affected pixels. The higher the percentage value, the greater the blurring effect.

When the Filter dialog box opens use the default setting of 5 and click the OK button. This will take a moment or two to accomplish. Figure 78.10 shows the final result.

*Figure 78.10.*
*This final image is the*
*result of multiple masks*
*and a few other tools.*

17. After it has completed its action, it is time to do the housekeeping. Remove the mask. Next, select Combine all objects with Background from the Objects menu.

18. Save the image if you want.

## Other Things About Masks

We have only scratched the surface in our working with masks. Here is a quick run-around of some of the other features and operating rules of masks. In Figure 78.11 I have used the Rectangle mask tool to create a single mask. It appears to be four masks, right? There can be only one mask on an image at a time. This mask that I made is composed of four parts. By clicking the Mask Overlay button, you get the image shown in Figure 78.12. This shows more clearly that it is one mask and not four. The Mask Overlay displays the areas protected from effects being applied to them in red (the default color). The Mask Overlay does not affect the operation of any tool.

*Figure 78.11.*
*How many masks can you see in this picture? The answer might surprise you.*

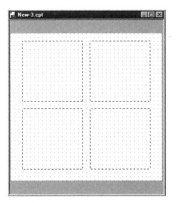

*Figure 78.12.*
*Using the Mask Overlay feature we can see that there is only one mask.*

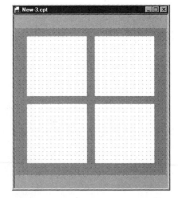

# Corel *TIP!*

Remember that there can be only one regular mask on the image at a time. An image can support several different masks (such as color mask and a regular mask) at the same time.

## Other Mask Tools

There are so many things you can do with and to a mask it is almost scary. Let's look at some other color-sensitive masks: the Lasso and Magic Wand mask tools. When you want to mask a specific color within an image, such as a blue sky in a landscape, using a color-sensitive mask can give you the best results with the least amount of effort. You can specify the range of color to be masked by selecting a tolerance value in the Tool Settings roll-up. The following tools can also used to create color-sensitive masks:

## The Lasso Mask Tool

The Lasso mask tool is used to define a colored area within an image. You can draw freehand around an area or click to establish anchor points. Double-clicking sets the mask, causing it to shrink until it reaches its color tolerance limit. Unlike the Color mask tool, this mask tool works only with pixels that are connected together. Look at Figure 78.13. The Mask Overlay is enabled so you can see the mask more clearly. The character had a mask placed around it, because the two areas inside of the ampersand were not connected to the white in background there were not included.

*Figure 78.13.*
*The Lasso mask tool is used to mask all the pixels in the area of a specific color. Unlike the Color mask, the selected pixels must be connected.*

### The Magic Wand Mask Tool

Like the Lasso mask tool the Magic Wand is also used to define a colored area within an image. You click the color you wish to mask, and the mask expands until it reaches its color tolerance limit. In Figure 78.14 I have clicked the Magic Wand tool to have the mask include the two areas not selected using the Lasso mask tool.

*Figure 78.14.*
*By clicking the Magic*
*Wand Tool in the two*
*areas not selected by the*
*Lasso mask tool, we are*
*able to include them in the*
*mask.*

## A Brief Discussion On Mask Logic and Modes

You need to understand how masks work logically to be able to control them. Referring back to Figure 78.14, the area outside of the ampersand is protected and everything inside of the ampersand, including the white areas, is unprotected. To modify the mask with the Magic Wand tool so that only the ampersand character is selected, it is necessary to remove the portion of the mask that is covering the white areas. To do that you use the Subtract From Mask mode. Figuring out what is inside or outside of a mask sometimes becomes difficult.

## Feathering and Other Neat Stuff

Up until now we have been dealing with regular masks; that is, masks that are straight black-and-white without any variation in shade. Now let's look at a different type of mask, a transparency mask. The term *transparency mask* might be confusing to those who are used to PHOTO-PAINT 5 because there used to be a specific mask called the Transparency mask. In PHOTO-PAINT 6 we have the ability to make any mask into a transparency mask, as you shall soon see. First, let's discuss what transparency in a mask actually is.

## Transparency in a Mask

Regular (black-and-white) masks isolate areas in an image so that you can control where on the image color and effects are applied. If you have a photograph of a landscape and you want to apply a special effect to only the sky, you can use a mask tool to isolate the sky. However, if you want the edges of that sky to receive 100 percent of the effect and the edge of the horizon to receive only 50 percent, you can achieve that level of control by adjusting the mask's transparency.

## Transparency Explained

In a regular mask, every pixel in the mask has a value of zero or 255. Every pixel in a transparency mask has a transparency value between 0 and 255 corresponding to the 256 levels of gray. The transparency of a pixel determines how much or how little it can be changed. If a pixel has a transparency value of zero, none of the effects you apply will change it. On the other hand, if a pixel has a transparency value of 255, all of the effects you apply can change it.

## Adjusting the Transparency of a Mask

The are many ways to control the transparency of a mask. You adjust transparency automatically by feathering the mask (explained next) or by painting the pixels inside the mask with different shades of gray. When you select the Paint on Mask command (from the Mask menu), a grayscale copy of the image displays. White represents the 100 percent transparency of pixels inside the mask, whereas black represents the 100 percent opaqueness of pixels outside the mask. You apply the paint by selecting the paint tool, selecting a shade of gray from the Color roll-up, and brushing over the white pixels in the image. The darker the shade, the less the color or effects you apply later on change the affected pixels. You can also use the Fill tool to adjust the transparency of the entire mask by applying a uniform, fountain, texture, or bitmap fill. The possibilities are almost limitless.

When you return to the image by deselecting Paint on Mask, the changes you've made to the mask might not be readily apparent. The mask marquee cannot accurately reflect the different shades of transparency because it is only a bunch of dumb marching ants. The way to see the effect of the mask is to use the Mask Overlay.

## Feathering

The Feather command creates a gradual transition between the pixels along the mask's edge or directly inside the mask and the surrounding pixels. You can control the direction and hardness of the feathered edge by selecting different options in the Feather dialog box.

In Figure 78.15 I have used the Feather command in the Mask menu to add a 10-pixel soft feather to the existing mask. When the Mask Overlay button is enabled it gives the character a distinct glow.

*Figure 78.15.*
*Applying a feather to the*
*mask gives it a soft edge*
*that creates the appear-*
*ance of a glow when*
*viewed with the Mask*
*Overlay button enabled.*

## Mask Logic Again

As nice as Figure 78.15 looks, if I had applied a rectangle fill across the entire mask I would not have a glow but rather a large, fuzzy-looking ampersand. That is because everything inside of the mask is unprotected. To make the image shown in Figure 78.16, it was necessary to first invert the mask.

## Invert Mask

This is one of the most useful commands in the toolbox. The Invert Mask command reverses the area affected by the mask. In a regular (black-and-white) mask, the area inside the mask can be altered. When the mask is inverted, the area outside the mask can be altered.

With a transparency mask (a mask containing a grayscale element, such as feathering), the degree to which the image can be altered depends on the level of mask transparency. For example, a gradient transparency has black areas that protect the image, white areas that enable the image to be altered, and graduated shades of gray that let varying degrees of effect on the image, which depends on how dark or how light the gray. When the transparency mask is inverted, the light areas become dark and the dark areas become light. This changes the areas of the image that can be altered.

After the mask is inverted I applied a colorful bitmap texture fill with the Rectangle tool as shown in Figure 78.16. In this case we have taken advantage of the fact there was a strong contrast that existed between the ampersand and the background. It still resulted in a great glow.

*Figure 78.16.*
*Unlike the previous image,*
*which showed the mask,*
*this image is the result of*
*applying a fill on top of the*
*inverted mask of Figure*
*78.15. The feathered mask*
*produces an excellent*
*glow.*

There is so much more you can do with masks, but time and pages demand that we move on to the next topic. Congratulations, you are finished, you have survived the Skill Session. Well done. This Skill Session has only scratched the surface of what you can do with masks. I hope you will spend time to learn more about how they work. If at times it seems hard and frustrating learning how to use some of these features, just remember that all of us who wrote this book worked on the beta software for almost three months without any documentation. And you thought you had it bad. See you in the next Skill Session.

# An Introduction to Objects

The use of objects falls into a category I call fun stuff. There is a tabloid sold in the United States called the *Sun*, which is one of the leading forums for unique photo-editing. If you live in the United States, you might have seen the *Sun* while standing in grocery lines. Last year it used clone tools to superimpose the image of the devil over a towering column of billowing smoke, which was displayed under the headlines "Scientists Drill Hole into Hell." They also have aliens (the UFO variety) talking with heads of state and famous celebrities. Last night, the headline was "Mother Refuses to Give Up Her Dog-Faced Baby." The photograph showed a woman holding an infant who had the face of a dog. I am not saying it was an ugly child. It had the face of a dog! Someone at the *Sun* staff had masked the face of a small dog, made it an object, and placed it over the face of the infant. Like I said, this is the fun stuff. If you are an avid reader of the *Sun*, do not take what I say as criticism of the tabloid. I love the *Sun*! I stand in a lot of grocery lines, and believe me, it provides entertainment to an otherwise boring wait.

## Fundamentals of Objects and Layers

Before you can properly work with objects, you need to understand what they are and what makes them unique. To accomplish this, let's review the fundamental differences between bitmap images and vector images. To help us, we are going to use an image from the Sampler photo CD and a clip-art image from CorelDRAW.

The photograph of the ruins of the Parthenon built on the Acropolis in Athens is shown in Figure 79.1. The photograph is a bitmap (also called paint) image. The image that you see originally came from a photograph. There is only one layer to the image. Although it appears to be a photograph of the magnificent ancient structure sitting atop a hill against a blue sky (background), it is actually an area composed of hundreds of thousands of tiny picture elements called *pixels*. To the PHOTO-PAINT program, the building, the hill Acropolis, and the background are all one great sea of pixels.

*Figure 79.1.*
*A bitmap (also called paint) image. It is composed of a sea of multicolored pixels.*

The Parthenon shown in Figure 79.2 is a vector (also called draw) image. Like the bitmap, it looks like a single image, but in fact it is composed of over 478 separate elements called *objects*. Figure 79.3 has been separated so that many of the objects that make up the image in Figure 79.2 can be seen. You probably noticed that the vector-based drawing of the Parthenon was CorelDRAW clip art, whereas the other image was a Corel Photo-CD. CorelDRAW is a vector-based program; PHOTO-PAINT is a bitmap-based program.

*Figure 79.2.*
*A vector (also called draw)*
*image of the Parthenon.*

*Figure 79.3.*
*The vector image has been*
*separated so that many of*
*the 478 objects that make*
*it up can be seen.*

## Sticky Paint

When an image is placed in a bitmap program such as PHOTO-PAINT, it becomes part of the background of the image. Traditionally, bitmap programs had only one layer. With these one-layer programs, if we were to take a brush from the toolbox and draw a wide brush stroke across the entire bitmap image of the Parthenon, every pixel the brush touches would change to the color assigned to the brush. If we then removed the brush color, the original image would not be there because the brush color did not go on top of the original color; it replaced it. It is as if every pixel that is applied has crazy glue on it. When an action is applied to an image, it "sticks" to the image and cannot be moved. This is why the Undo command can only "remember" what color(s) it replaced in the last action. Each Undo operation requires the entire image area to be replaced, a process that consumes vast amounts of system resources. Anyone who has spent hours and hours trying to achieve an effect with these older style programs, such as PHOTO-PAINT 4, will testify that the process by which bitmaps merge into and become part of the base image was the major drawback to photo-editing programs.

## Objects Defined

What is an object? Here is the official Corel definition:

"An object is an independent bitmap selection created with object tools and layered above the base image."

Let's expand that definition. In PHOTO-PAINT, an object is a bitmap that "floats" above the background, which is also called the *base image*. It is part of the background only in the sense that all of the 478 parts of the vector-based Parthenon in Figures 79.2 and 79.3 are part of that image. Because it is not a part of the base image, but instead floats above the image, it can be moved as many times as needed without limit. Objects can also be scaled, resized, rotated, and distorted.

PHOTO-PAINT 5 had simple and complex objects. PHOTO-PAINT 6 has only one kind of object. The best part is, objects are much easier to create in PHOTO-PAINT 6 than they were with PHOTO-PAINT 5. You are about to learn how to do some amazing things with objects. Most of the rules that apply to masks also apply to objects.

## The Object Roll-Up

The Object roll-up is the control center for all object manipulations. With the Object roll-up, you can do the following:

- Select objects
- Lock or unlock objects
- Make objects visible or invisible
- Create objects from masks
- Create masks from objects
- Move objects between layers
- Control the transparency/opacity of objects
- Select merge modes for individual objects
- Label different object layers
- Combine objects with the background
- Combine individual objects together
- Delete objects

## Corel *NOTE!*

The Object roll-up has been changed substantially from the Layers/Objects roll-up of PHOTO-PAINT 5. The feathering control has moved and been placed in the Object menu.

To explain how the roll-up operates I have prepared an introductory skill session.

## Introductory Skill Session Using Objects

In this project we are going to take a photograph of a martial arts instructor, convert it into an object, and create a composite photograph for use in a brochure for the Academy of Street Defense.

1. Open the file MARTIAL ARTS MAN.CPT from the accompanying CD-ROM. Open the Objects roll-up through the Roll-ups section of the View menu or use the keyboard combination Ctrl+F7. Your screen should look like Figure 79.4.

*Figure 79.4.*
*The background image for the project. At this point the Object roll-up shows the background image and there are no objects in the image.*

The Object roll-up display is divided into five columns, described next."

**Layer Title**

The column on the far right shows the name of the layer. PHOTO-PAINT assigns new objects the title Object # until the user changes it.

**Lock Icon**

The second column to the left contains an icon that shows whether a layer is locked or unlocked. If a layer is locked, it cannot be selected and effects cannot be applied to it. In PHOTO-PAINT 5 the rule was that any object that is visible is subject to effects being applied. In PHOTO-PAINT 6 an object that is locked is protected even if it is visible.

### Visible/Invisible Icon

The eye icon in the center column is either open or closed, indicating the object is either visible or invisible. If an object is invisible, it is protected and cannot be selected.

### Thumbnail View

The next column to the left displays a thumbnail of the object in the layer. The size of the thumbnail is determined by the size setting that is selected by the right arrow button to the right of the Number of Objects display.

### Group Indicator Icons

The column on the far left is active only when the objects are grouped together. It displays what objects are grouped together.

The status line, Total number of objects, shows the total number of objects in the image, which in the case of Figure 79.4 is zero. To the right of the status line is a small arrow button. Pushing it opens a drop-down list that can be set to display small, medium, or large icons. The roll-up in Figure 79.4 is set to display small, which shows five lines (or layers).

The buttons at the bottom of the Object roll-up are not available because there are no objects in the image at this time.

The Edit Selected Only and Edit All button at the bottom of the roll-up are used for selecting grouped objects.

2. Our first task is to make the man in the photograph into an object. To make him into an object, we must first surround him with a mask. There are two ways you can do this. Either load the mask mask.cpt provided on the accompanying CD-ROM or create your own mask using the Lasso mask tool. Select the Lasso Mask tool and click at several points around his figure. When he is completely surrounded double-click the mouse button to complete the mask.

   If you choose to make your own mask, try a Tolerance setting of 79 in the Toll Settings roll-up. Because there is a white background, you do not need to be fancy about where you place the points with the Lasso mask tool. Be careful to observe he is wearing white socks. Therefore, after you have created the mask with the Lasso mask tool, change the mask mode to Add to Mask. Then, using the Brush mask tool (control the size of the brush with the Toll Settings roll-up), add the portions of his white socks that the Lasso tool didn't include.

3. With the mask in place notice that a new button has become active on the Object roll-up. It is the Convert Mask to Object button. Click the Convert Mask to Object button and watch what happens. The results are shown in Figure 79.5.

*Figure 79.5.*
*The man is now an object*
*(no comments please). A*
*thumbnail of him appears*
*in the Object roll-up,*
*which is highlighted to*
*indicate it is selected.*

The masked figure became an object as indicated by the blue marquee surrounding his shape. The figure now appears as Object 8 (yours will have a different number) on the top (and only layer) in the Object roll-up.

■ The thumbnail of this layer is highlighted, indicating the object is selected. It can be selected only if the Object picker tool in the toolbox is active.

■ The thumbnail of the background layer has been updated to show the figure is no longer part of the background.

■ The mask that surrounded the figure is now gone, so the Convert Mask to Object button is no longer available.

■ Three new buttons near the bottom of the roll-up became available. They are, from left to right: Convert Object to Mask, Merge Object with Background, and Delete Object (the trash can).

Obviously, a lot has happened. When converting a mask to an object, we have discovered that the mask disappears and an object made from the contents of the mask appears.

# Corel *TIP!*

When you use the Convert Mask to an Object command, remember that the mask is lost. I recommend that you save masks that might be required at a later time before you use this command.

4. The next step is to remove any part of the background that remains. With PHOTO-PAINT 5 you would have had to hide the figure. Not so with PHOTO-PAINT 6. In the Objects roll-up box click the lock icon so that it appears locked. The icon works as a toggle. Each time it is clicked, it will change from locked to unlocked, or vice versa. With the object locked, nothing that you will apply to the image will affect that layer. Next, unlock the background by clicking its lock icon.

5. Clear the background with the following procedure. Select the current mask tool in the toolbox (it doesn't matter which tool, we are only doing this to put PHOTO-PAINT into a mask mode of operation). Choose All from the Mask menu. There should now be a mask surrounding the entire image area. Select Clear from the Edit menu or use the Delete key. The image background is clear and the figure is not affected. Finally, remove the mask by choosing None from the Mask menu.

# Corel *TIP!*

If you worked with PHOTO-PAINT 5 you are accustomed to the area behind a visible object being protected from effects applied to the image. This is not true with PHOTO-PAINT 6.

6. At this point nothing appears to have changed. We have a man doing a martial art kick against a white background. Let's learn how to edit the name of a layer, even though it is not necessary with an image that has such a small number of objects. Place the cursor over the title Object and double-click the left mouse button. The name is highlighted. Now, give the subject a name. I chose something very dull: Man. You can use something more imaginative. Figure 79.6 shows the results of the name change.

7. Our next task is to remove the not-completely-white background so we can add a different background. We could skip this step because when we merge the new background with the existing background it will disappear. I added this step to give you practice in the technique of clearing an image area.

The selection of a background requires some careful decisions. Because this is a school for street defense, a background of a lovely garden would appear out of place. We can use a brick wall, which gives a stronger image, but you need to ensure that the bricks are in scale with the person. It can't look like each brick is six feet long, nor can it be so small that it is difficult to determine that it is a brick wall.

Figure 79.6.
*The man is no longer an object. By using the layer labeling capability of PHOTO-PAINT we are able to name each layer/object in an image.*

I have included a brick wall for the background, which I created using a bitmap fill and a brick seamless tile. It is called brick.cpt and can be found on the accompanying CD-ROM. Select Paste from File in the Edit menu. When the dialog box opens, locate the brick.cpt file and click OK.

8. Your image should now look like Figure 79.7. Yep! We buried the sucker under a brick wall to demonstrate a point. To move the brick wall to the bottom of the heap (so to speak), click the name of the object in the Object roll-up and drag it between the man and the background.

# Corel *NOTE!*

> The background is always on the bottom so that the object can only be placed above, and not behind, the background.

9. The next step is to combine the brick wall with the background. This is a very simple action. Make sure that only the brick wall object is selected and click the Combine with Background button near the bottom of the Object roll-up (it's the one next to the trash can). The object will merge into the background, as shown in the Object roll-up in Figure 79.8. Notice that there is no other indication that the two have merged. This is why the roll-up is so valuable for viewing the objects in layers.

*Figure 79.7.*
*Pasted objects are*
*automatically placed on*
*the top of all existing*
*objects.*

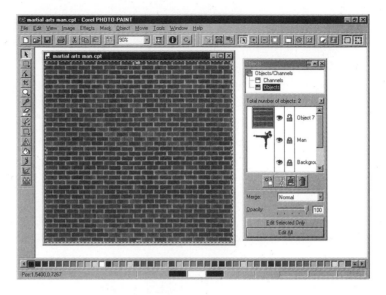

*Figure 79.8.*
*Our man is now out from*
*under the wall thanks to*
*PHOTO-PAINT's capabil-*
*ity to move objects*
*between layers with*
*the Object roll-up.*

10. It turns out that the man is facing in the wrong direction for the brochure. We could have used the Flip command in the Image menu to reverse the image before making him into an object. However, we can flip objects just as easily. Open the Objects menu, select Flip, and choose Horizontally from the choices. The result is shown in Figure 79.9

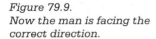

*Figure 79.9.*
*Now the man is facing the*
*correct direction.*

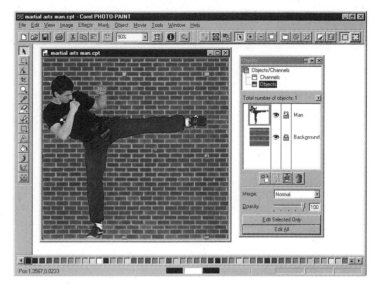

**11.** With the Object picker from the toolbox, click the man. If he wasn't selected before, he will become selected now. If you cannot select the object, see the following tip.

# Corel *TIP!*

> If you cannot select an object by clicking it, check the Objects roll-up and see whether the object is locked. If it is, unlock it and then select the object.

**12.** Now, select the Text tool from the toolbox and enter the text you want to have on this martial arts photograph. The text I placed on the image is two separate objects. The word MASTER is one object and the words STREET DEFENSE is the second object. Figure 79.10 shows the results.

**13.** This step is optional. I say this because I have a pretty darn fast machine and it took it a few minutes to accomplish the last parts. You have been warned. To make the text stand out, I wanted to put some dark, semi-transparent, black paint behind the letters. To accomplish this I selected one of the text objects and clicked the Create Mask from Object button (the one on the far left). From the Tool Settings roll-up I set the Air Brush tool to a high transparency setting (80). Then I used the Stroke Mask command from the Mask menu, selecting the air brush when the dialog box appeared. After that finished, I did the same thing to the second character block. Figure 79.11 shows the finished product.

Figure 79.10.
*The man is now in the*
*right position.*

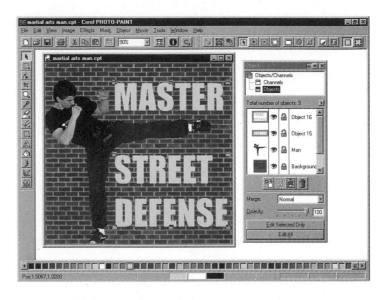

Figure 79.11.
*The finished photograph*
*ready for insertion in a*
*brochure.*

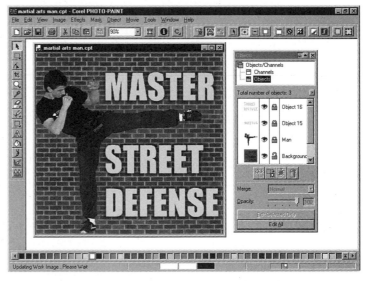

14. At this point, you have two choices. You can save the file with all of its objects as a PHOTO-PAINT file (*.CPT), or you can choose to combine all the objects in the background, as shown in 79.11. Be aware that although this produces a smaller file, you will not be able to go back and make minor adjustments to the position of the objects.

# Corel *TIP!*

It is generally a good practice to save work files both in their original CPT format (for archive purposes) and in the desired format of the client.

## A Work Session in Object Creation and Manipulation

In this session you will work with the tools we have already learned, plus a few other tools. The project is a simple one. The former Soviet Union is holding an air show. They have a very limited budget and need you to make a nice postcard for it. Unfortunately, they have only one picture of a single MIG jet, and it is decided that the postcard needs three. On top of all that, the sky is too dark and needs to be enhanced or replaced. Sound tough? It's a walk in the park.

1. Open the Jet.cpt file from the accompanying CD-ROM. For those who don't want to go through all of the work to make the mask, there is a copy of the completed mask on the accompanying CD-ROM. The name of the mask to load is jetmask.cpt. After loading the mask, skip to step 10.

2. Select the Lasso mask tool. Open the Tools Setting roll-up and change the Tolerance setting to 14.

3. Click at points around the plane, as shown in Figure 79.12. There really isn't anything special about the points I have chosen except the point on the right (upper) wing of the jet. I deliberately made the Lasso mask as close to the wing as possible because the cloud and the wing are similar colors. When you have finished, double-click the left mouse button to complete the mask action. Wait a few moments for PHOTO-PAINT to calculate the mask boundaries.

*Figure 79.12.*
*The points of the Lasso*
*mask tool.*

4.  No mask is ever perfect, and this one is no exception. We could try it again at different tolerance settings, but it will take less time to fix the mask that is shown in Figure 79.13.

*Figure 79.13.*
*The Lasso mask tool was*
*able to produce a nearly*
*perfect mask of the jet.*

# Corel*TIP!*

If your mask doesn't look similar to Figure 79.13, simply remove the mask by selecting None in the Mask menu and try again at a slightly different point. For its starting point, the Lasso mask uses the color value of the pixel under the cursor at the time it is clicked. Different starting points produce slightly different masks.

5.  To make the project in this session, we need a mask that surrounds only the jet. What we have now is a mask that surrounds the jet and some other things we don't want and does cover some things we do want. Therefore, before we do anything else, let's clean up the mask a little. Click the Subtract from Mask button in the Mask toolbar or choose Subtract in the Mode section of the Mask menu. We need to remove part of the mask created by the Lasso mask tool. Adding and subtracting masks can get confusing. Keep in mind what the mask is surrounding. In this case, the mask is surrounding the jet. To remove the mask surrounding the little cloud in front of the right wing, we need to subtract it from the existing mask. (If you're still confused, just follow the directions and it will make sense. Really.)

6.  Open the Mask tool flyout and select the Mask Brush tool. When the Mask Brush tool is selected the cursor changes to the size and shape of the currently selected brush.

7.  Open the Tool Settings roll-up (Ctrl+F8) and change it to a round shape and a size of 20 pixels.

8. With the Mask Brush tool, paint over the small cloud until the mask is even with the wing. When you are finished with the mask, click F4 (Zoom to Fit) and the image returns to its original zoom ratio.

# Corel *TIP!*

When working with masks, you sometimes need to get in close to the area on which you are working. The quick way to do this is to hold down the Z (for Zoom) key. As long as the Z key is pressed, the cursor is a magnifying glass. Continue to hold down the Z key and the left mouse button and drag the magnifying-glass cursor over the area to be zoomed. A rectangle is created. Release both keys and wait for a moment as the image area is refreshed on the screen. Learning to use the Zoom tool will enable you to quickly produce accurate masks, even with a mouse.

9. Click the Add to Selection button in the Mask toolbar. Using the Mask Brush tool, add the parts of the mask that are missing in the tail section of the jet and one in the cockpit area. You probably won't need to zoom in to do this but if you do, use the same technique described in the previous tip. At this point, we have masked all of the jet, as shown in Figure 79.14.

*Figure 79.14.*
*The completed mask shows the result of adding to and subtracting from the mask. Now the jet is masked, and the back-ground is protected.*

10. From here, we will use the mask to make an object. Before we do, select Checkpoint from the Edit menu. The progress bar indicator moves quickly across the bottom of the work area, indicating that a file has been made. No matter what happens to the image, we can always return the image to this point in time.

11. There are three ways to make the jet into an object. You can

    ■ Click the Create Object button on the Mask Tools toolbar

    ■ Select Create Object(s) from Mask in the Mask menu

    ■ Click the Create object from Mask button near the bottom of the Object roll-up

Regardless of how you do it, convert into an object the mask surrounding the jet. The mask disappears and is replaced by a blue marquee. The jet is now an object in the Object roll-up.

# Corel *TIP!*

Many people find the blue marquee distracting. To turn off the blue marquee, open the Object menu and click Marquee Visible. This action will turn off the blue object marquee. To return the marquee open the Object menu and click it again.

12. If it is not already open, open the Objects roll-up (Ctrl+F7). The status line at the top informs us that there is one object in the image: the background and the newly created object. Double-click the text describing the jet object and replace it with the words JET 1.

13. Next, we are going to want to erase the existing sky. We want to protect the jet from being erased while we do this. There are two ways to protect the jet. First, we can click the Lock icon in the Objects roll-up. Second, we can click the Eye icon to make the jet invisible. When an object is not visible, it is automatically locked. In PHOTO-PAINT 5 we had to hide the objects to protect them, so to get used to the new way we do things in Paint 6, click the Lock icon in the Object roll-up to lock it. It looks as if nothing has changed.

14. To quickly erase the sky, choose All in the mask menu. This masks the entire image. Select any mask tool. Press the Delete key or choose Clear from the Edit menu. After the background has become white (assuming your paper—background—color is white), remove the mask by selecting None in the Mask menu. Nothing to it. The sky is now all gone and you have an empty background. Jets need a sky in order to look realistic, so we are going to quickly add one. Your image should now look something like Figure 79.15.

15. To place a sky in the picture, from the Edit menu select Paste from File. When the dialog box opens, locate the file CLOUD.CPT on the accompanying CD-ROM. Once you have selected the file, click OK. After the file loads, label the object layer "Cloud" in the Object roll-up.

*Figure 79.15.*
*Great jet, but where's*
*the sky?*

Depending on your display, you might not be able to see all of the image. When files are pasted onto an image, they do not always align themselves with the image. The sky in Figure 79.16 is such an example. Although you cannot see that the Cloud object is not centered on the background, it is actually above and slightly to the left of the white background. In PHOTO-PAINT 5, you would have had to grab the object and attempt to center it on the background. In PHOTO-PAINT 6, Corel has provided complete object alignment control. Its appearance and operation are identical to the Align window that is in CorelDRAW. Figure 79.17 shows the Align window.

*Figure 79.16.*
*The sky covers the jet, of*
*course, but the Cloud*
*object is not centered on*
*the page.*

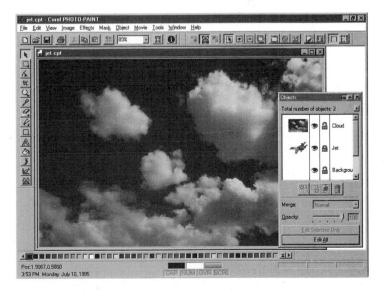

To use the Align command, you must select the objects that are to be aligned. To align the sky, you must click the sky object (Cloud) in the Objects roll-up (see Figure 79.17) so that it and not the jet is selected. In the Object menu click the Align to Center of Page check box and then press OK. When PHOTO-PAINT has finished, the object containing the sky will be centered on the background image.

*Figure 79.17.*
*New in PHOTO-PAINT 6 is*
*the Align dialog box.*

16. Click the layer named Cloud. The cursor becomes a hand. Drag the name down between the background and the jet. When you have it there, release the left mouse button. The cloud object layer is now just above the background and behind the jet. This is one of the ways in which we can move objects between layers in an image. We could have also used the Order command in the Object menu.

17. Because we know that the photograph of the sky will become the background, go ahead at this point and combine it with the background. The quickest way is to click the Combine Object with Background button (next to the trash can button). The image should now look like Figure 79.18.

*Figure 79.18.*
*Now we have the jet flying*
*in a much more interest-*
*ing sky.*

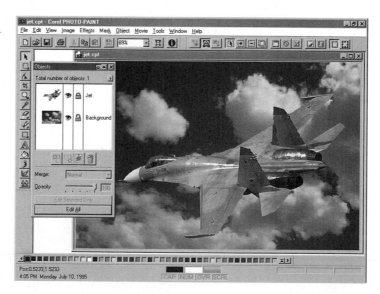

What happened to the name Cloud? When you combine objects, the only layer label or name that remains after a combine operation is the name of the background, or the bottom object if you are combining objects.

# Corel *TIP!*

Always double-check that only the objects you want to combine with the background are selected before you click the Combine button on the Object roll-up.

A quicker way to have accomplished steps 16 and 17 would have been to select the sky and choose the Combine button. Any object(s) can be merged from any layer without affecting the objects in between. So why did we choose to take the scenic route? So you could work with moving objects between layers.

18. We now need to make duplicate copies of the jet. Before we can do that we must first unlock the jet in the Object roll-up. Always remember that an object that is locked cannot be selected. Use the Object picker to select the jet and move it down and to the right so it looks like Figure 79.19. We now have a jet in the sky. To see the image without the clutter of the Corel PHOTO-PAINT screen, press the F9 key (full-screen preview).

*Figure 79.19.*
*The jet has been*
*moved into a new*
*position to make room*
*for the other jets.*

# Corel *TIP!*

If the full-screen preview doesn't work when you press the F9 key, you probably have a roll-up active instead of the image. If so, just click the image and try again.

19. Open the Tool Settings roll-up. Select the Object Scale dialog box by clicking the middle tab. This dialog box (in this mode) enables us to scale an object and make mirror images or mirror copies of an object. For this session, make sure the Maintain Aspect check box is enabled. With the cursor click either the H (horizontal) or V (vertical) setting and change it to 80 percent. The other setting will change automatically because Maintain Aspect is selected. Click the Apply To Duplicate button. A copy of the jet will appear slightly above and to the left of the original.

20. Now click the Apply to Duplicate button again. When we created the duplicate image of the jet in step 19, two things happened. First, the duplicate object (jet) is placed on the top layer. Second, the copy is always selected. The result of clicking the button the second time is the creation of a third object (jet) that is 80 percent of the size of the second object, which is 80 percent of the size of the original. Are you getting dizzy? Figure 79.20 shows the results.

*Figure 79.20.*
*Talk about flying in*
*tight formation!*

21. In the Object roll-up, double-click the object containing the mid-size jet and label it the Middle Jet. Do the same for the top jet, except label it Small Jet.

Next, using any of the techniques previously described, put the small jet on the bottom of the layers and the middle jet in the middle (where else would you put it?) Figure 79.21 shows the completed labeling and layering in the Object roll-up.

*Figure 79.21.*
*The duplicates are now in the proper order (smallest in the back and the largest in the front).*

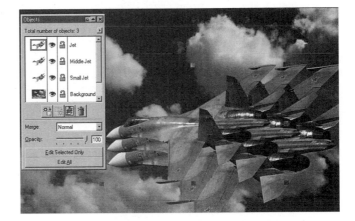

22. We are now going to change the position of the middle and small jets. Before we do, in the Objects roll-up lock the background and the original jet objects. This prevents them from being accidentally selected and moved. Click the small jet and move it to a position in the sky as shown in Figure 79.22. Next, click and select the middle jet and do the same.

*Figure 79.22.*
*Now the three jets look like they are real.*

23. Select the Text tool from the toolbox. From the Tool Settings roll-up, change the font to Futura XBLKCN BT at a size of 36 points. Using the palette at the bottom of the screen, pick a pale yellow for the paint color by clicking it with the left mouse button. Type in the text AIR SHOW '96. When you have finished,

773

click the Object Picker tool in the toolbox and move the text to the top of the page, as shown in Figure 79.23.

*Figure 79.23.*
*With the Text tool and the merge mode in the Object roll-up, we have created an unusual typeface effect for the name of the air show.*

24. With the text still selected, open the Objects roll-up (if it was closed) and change the Merge setting to Lightness. I explain more about the merge mode later.

25. Change the paint color to black by placing the cursor over the appropriate square of the on-screen palette and clicking with the left mouse button. Change the font size setting in the Tool Setting roll-up to 24 points.

26. Type in the word MOSCOW in the lower-left corner of the image. The results should look similar to Figure 79.24.

*Figure 79.24.*
*The photograph is finished. This figure shows the Object roll-up with all of the layers labeled.*

**27.** Save the file as jetfinal.cpt. After it has finished saving use the F9 key to see a full-screen preview of the session as shown in Figure 79.25. You can use the Esc key to return to PHOTO-PAINT.

# Corel *TIP!*

When the image is saved as a PHOTO-PAINT file, all layers, objects, and masks of the image are preserved. When the image is saved as a bitmap image, such as a TIFF, PCX, or GIF format, PHOTO-PAINT displays a warning message that all of the layers/objects will be merged into the image. All layers and masks will be lost.

*Figure 79.25.*
*The completed project.*

Now that you have an idea about how objects work, the following sections describe all of the dull reference details that Corel did not have room put into its PHOTO-PAINT manual.

## Object Tool Settings Roll-Up

The functionality of the Transform roll-up from CorelDRAW was added to PHOTO-PAINT with the release of PHOTO-PAINT 5. It is structured so that when you have the Object Picker selected and bring up the Tool Settings roll-up (Ctrl+F8), the Transform roll-up is displayed as shown in Figure 79.26. The Tool Settings roll-up for objects provides a very powerful and easy way to make precise manipulations of objects. There are five tabs that control the following:

- Object Position
- Object Rotation
- Object Scaling/Mirror

- Object Resizing
- Object Skewing

*Figure 79.26.*
*The Tool Settings dialog*
*box for objects provides a*
*wide range of manipula-*
*tions to objects. The*
*Object Position tab is*
*shown open.*

Each of the tabs within the Tool Settings dialog box when used for objects have several common functions. They are

- Apply To Duplicate button. When this button is selected it creates a copy of the selected object with the effects applied, while leaving the original object unchanged.
- The Apply button. This button applies the effect to the original.
- The Anti-aliasing check box. When enabled, this check box causes PHOTO-PAINT to process the image through a more sophisticated process to produce smoother lines and prevent jaggies. Use of this feature might take a little longer to process than if it is not used.

## Object Position

Viewing the tabs from left to right, clicking the first tab accesses the Object Position page. The controls in this page are used to reposition or move objects. The default units are pixels, but you can change the units in the Preferences dialog box. (See Figure 79.27.)

*Figure 79.27.*
*Object positioning.*

If you attempt to move an object with a setting that will place the object outside of the image area, nothing will happen when you apply the setting. When these controls are used in conjunction with the rulers, you can position objects very precisely and quickly anywhere within the image.

## Absolute Positioning

When the Relative Position option is unchecked, the Horizontal listing displays the far-left position of the object and the Vertical listing displays the topmost position of the object in relation to the 0,0 point of the image (upper-left corner). You move the object by changing these values. If negative numbers are used nothing will happen because negative numbers would position the object outside of the image area.

Although precise positioning, such as centering an object on the page, can be done with this roll-up, use of the Align command in PHOTO-PAINT 6 is much simpler. Objects of equal size can be positioned on top of one another by entering the same values for each object in these settings.

## Relative Position

When the Relative Position option is checked, the Horizontal and Vertical settings start out at zero pixels in both the horizontal and vertical axis in reference to the object. Movement is applied relative to the apex of the topmost and far left lines of an object. Entering a positive value for the Horizontal setting moves the image to the right, and a negative value moves the image to the left. Entering a positive value for the Vertical setting moves the object down, and a negative value moves the object up. After a setting is applied the settings both return to zero. Values that place the object outside of the image area will move the object off of the page.

# Corel *TIP!*

> You can create a duplicate object directly over the original by pressing the Apply To Duplicate button, without changing the Horizontal and Vertical settings. This is important when you use multiple layers with merge modes to achieve an effect.

## Object Rotation

The are many times it is necessary to rotate objects with precision. At that time, you need to use the Object Rotation page of the Tool Settings roll-up.

### Angle of Rotation

The second tab on the Tool Settings roll-up, as shown in Figure 79.28, provides access to the Object Rotation controls. Control of rotation is divided into two parts. The first set controls the amount of the angle of rotation. There is nothing mystical here; the value is in degrees. The range of rotation is +360 degrees through –360 degrees. It is important to note that you can enter a number for the angle of rotation as low as one one-thousandth of a degree. Regardless of what rotation values are entered into this setting, the Center of Rotation setting remains centered on the object.

## Center of Rotation

The next set of controls is a little more interesting. With the Center of Rotation controls, you can precisely position the center of rotation. With the Relative Center option turned off, the controls for Center of Rotation report where the center of rotation is located on the currently selected object. Whenever you need to reposition the center of rotation, simply use the rulers to locate the new position and enter those values into the Center of Rotation controls. For example, if your currently selected object has a center of rotation at the horizontal and vertical position of one inch each, you could easily change that to, perhaps, two inches horizontal and three inches vertical by simply entering those values in the Center of Rotation controls.

## Relative to Center

When the Relative to Center option is turned on, the controls for Center of Rotation start off at zero. Units are controlled by the Preferences dialog box. Values entered in the Center of Rotation controls will move the center of rotation according to the values relative to its current position. For example, if you are working in inches and you enter Center of Rotation values of one inch for both the Horizontal and Vertical settings, the center of rotation would be repositioned one inch down and to the right of the current center of rotation.

*Figure 79.28.*
*The Object angle of*
*rotation and Center of*
*rotation settings give you*
*precision control of object*
*rotation.*

# Corel *TIP!*

A quick way to rotate an object is to select it with the Object Picker and then click the object a second time. The control handles will change to indicate it is in rotation mode. By holding down the Ctrl key on the keyboard while dragging the handles, you get rotation in 15-degree increments.

## Object Scale/Mirror

Object Scale, shown in Figure 79.29, enables you to do exactly what its name suggests: scale objects. This is the function we used to make the duplicate jets smaller in the previous work session. An object can be scaled by percentages of the object's size. You cannot enter negative numbers for the Object Scaling settings. Instead, numbers larger than 100 percent scale the object larger than its current size; numbers smaller than 100 percent scale the object smaller than its current size.

When Maintain Aspect is selected, the Horizontal and Vertical settings within Object Scaling remain the same. The Object Mirror buttons flip the objects horizontally and vertically. The Object Scale settings and the Mirror buttons can work in conjunction with one another. For example, if you have 50 percent Horizontal and Vertical settings for Object Scale with the Vertical Mirror button on, the selected object will be flipped vertically at 50 percent of its original size when the Apply button is pressed.

*Figure 79.29.*
*The Object Scale and*
*Mirror settings enable you*
*to resize and flip objects.*

# Corel *TIP!*

You can create a duplicate object exactly over another by hitting the Apply To Duplicate button with 100-percent Horizontal and Vertical Object Scale settings and the Mirror buttons not selected.

## Object Size

The Object Size settings, shown in Figure 79.30, are a more accurate way to resize an object than Object Scale. The Object Size settings list the dimensions of the currently selected object. To change the dimensions of the currently selected object, simply enter the new values and select Apply or Apply To Duplicate. Units are determined by the default setting in the Preferences dialog box. Negative numbers cannot be entered for the Object Size settings.

## Maintain Aspect

When the Maintain Aspect option is checked, the aspect of the object will be maintained when you enter a new value in one of the Horizontal or Vertical settings. For example, if you have an object that is one inch horizontal and two inches vertical and you enter 2 inches in the Horizontal setting with the Maintain Aspect option checked, the Vertical option will automatically maintain the aspect ratio of the object by changing to four inches.

*Figure 79.30.*
*The Object Size settings*
*provide a more accurate*
*method of resizing objects*
*than the Object Scale*
*settings.*

## Object Skew

Object Skew settings shown in Figure 79.31 enable you to numerically skew objects. Like all of the other settings in the Object Tool Settings roll-up, Object Skew simply provides a way to accurately enter values for alterations that could otherwise be performed manually. Negative degree values can be used. Once new values are entered into this setting, the Object Skew settings will remain the same until they are changed, even if the file you are working on is closed and another is opened.

*Figure 79.31.*
*The Object Skew settings*
*enable you to skew objects*
*accurately.*

## Additional Tips for Working with Objects

Here are some general points to remember when working with objects:

- Transform Options will be unavailable when anything other than the Object Picker is selected from the toolbox.

- Objects do not have to be the same size as the page. You can paste or drag and drop an object that is larger than the page size.

- Although PHOTO-PAINT does not have a paste inside feature, you can emulate this effect by creating a compound object with a hole or holes in it. For instance, if you have an image with a TV screen on it and you want to change what's on the TV, simply create an object with a hole where the TV screen is, and then position the new image behind it. With this functionality, a paste-inside feature is unnecessary.

- The capability to create, modify, and position objects makes Corel PHOTO-PAINT 6 such a powerful photo-editing program. We have only covered the basics to this point.

## Summary

Objects are the greatest thing to happen to bitmap photo-editing since desktop publishing. Objects enable the greatest degree of freedom regarding placement and arrangement of subjects and backgrounds in an image. The following is a summary of the points covered in this Skill Session:

- An object is an independent bitmap that is layered above the base image.

- There are two types of objects: simple and complex.

- Objects cannot be selected with mask tools, and masks cannot be selected with object tools.

- Objects are surrounded by a blue marquee.

- There are many ways to create an object, as follows:

  1. Mask an area, and then select Create Object from Mask.

  2. Paste an image as an object.

  3. Paste a file into an image as an object.

- Each object occupies its own layer.

- The Object roll-up can control objects and layers by locking or unlocking them. In this way it is possible to selectively apply effects in an image composed of many layers/objects.

- Images saved as PHOTO-PAINT format files (*.CPT) preserve their layers and objects. All other file formats lose this information as the layers/objects are combined into the image background.

# 80

# Using CorelDRAW and PHOTO-PAINT Together

Corel PHOTO-PAINT and CorelDRAW enjoy a powerful relationship, which began with the release of the 5.0 versions of these products in 1994. Corel PHOTO-PAINT imports CorelDRAW CDR files as well as other industry-standard vector files; you no longer are required to export your CorelDRAW files into bitmap format. Furthermore, Corel PHOTO-PAINT can export with clipping paths, creating increased flexibility with bitmaps in prgrams such as CorelDRAW, PageMaker, and Corel Ventura. In this case, a clipping path is a boundary formed by the mask rather than by the rectangular edge of the image.

This skill session explores the powerful relationship between Corel PHOTO-PAINT and CorelDRAW. You will learn the best ways import files CorelDRAW files into PHOTO-PAINT and techniques for saving images in PHOTO-PAINT so that they will be the correct size and shape when brought into CorelDRAW.

Although Corel PHOTO-PAINT's capabilities have increased dramatically, CorelDRAW and Corel Ventura are still much better suited for layout and text placement. Avoid falling into the one-program-does-all mentality. You will see that it is by combining each program's strengths that the best results are achieved. Many of the people that I talk with are trying to do everything in PHOTO-PAINT or CorelDRAW. I have two words for you if you are doing this: Stop it!

## To Use PHOTO-PAINT or Not to Use PHOTO-PAINT...That Is the Question

Use PHOTO-PAINT to enhance bitmap images and then bring them back into CorelDRAW for adding text. The exception to this rule is when you are applying special effects to the text. The reason I encourage placing text in CorelDRAW is because the outputted text will be much sharper. When text is created in PHOTO-PAINT, it is a bitmap image that is resolution-dependent. Text in a program like CorelDRAW is resolution-independent. This means that text placed in PHOTO-PAINT will be the resolution of the image. If it is 300 dpi (dots-per-inch), then the text will be a bitmap image that is 300 dpi regardless if it is printed to a 300 dpi laser printer or a 2450 dpi imagesetter. If the same text is placed in CorelDRAW, it remains text. If it is output to a 2450 dpi imagesetter, then the resolution of the text will be 2450 dpi. The result is sharper text.

Printing of bitmaps is easier to control with CorelDRAW than it is with PHOTO-PAINT. This is because PHOTO-PAINT sees a page as one single bitmap image. In CorelDRAW, the bitmap image is seen as an object on the page, making it easier to control placement of the image in CorelDRAW than in PHOTO-PAINT. I think you have the idea.

## Moving Images Between CorelDRAW and PHOTO-PAINT

Before I begin demonstrating neat tricks and effects, I will cover some basic concepts about transferring images between these two programs. It is a highly advertised fact that the entire Corel line of products, beginning with CorelDRAW 4, supports OLE 2.0 (Object Linking and Embedding). Corel PHOTO-PAINT 6 and CorelDRAW 6 now both support in-place editing. OLE is a powerful inter-application discipline in which you drag an image from one application and drop it into another. This is great, right? Well, sort of. The drag-and-drop method does work. The only reservation is that the image quality isn't as good with this method as it is with others. OLE is given a lot of hype by Microsoft and the press. On paper, OLE looks great, but in practical application it carries a lot of overhead. In-place editing means that when you place a PHOTO-PAINT image into a word processing application, such as Microsoft Word, you can right-click the image and PHOTO-PAINT will open up within Word. For the average PHOTO-PAINT user, this isn't a big issue. Because of the resources needed for photo-editing in PHOTO-PAINT, I cannot recommend using OLE's in-place editing unless you have a really powerful system, and even then I am not sure what the great advantage is.

So, what is the best way to get an image from CorelDRAW to Corel PHOTO-PAINT? Glad you asked.

## The Three Paths from CorelDRAW to PHOTO-PAINT

There are three different ways to transfer images between CorelDRAW and PHOTO-PAINT. The first method is drag-and-drop (which we just mentioned). This method is the quickest of the three. The second method is the traditional approach, which was used until the introduction of PHOTO-PAINT 5. An image is exported as a bitmap file from CorelDRAW and imported into PHOTO-PAINT. The third (and best) way to transfer images between the two programs is to save an image in the native Corel CDR file format and then open the CDR file with PHOTO-PAINT. Each of the three methods offer advantages and disadvantages. The following sections look at the rules for each one and explore the options and limitations for each method.

There is a fourth method. You can copy an image to the Clipboard and paste it as an object into Photo-Paint. If you choose to use the Clipboard, it occupies memory while the image is in the Clipboard—thereby reducing available memory for Photo-Paint.

## Defining Rasterization and Dithering

When you go from CorelDRAW to PHOTO-PAINT (or any other bitmap application), it is necessary to convert the vector (or line) format into bitmap (or paint) format. This process is called *rasterization*. It is how the rasterization is accomplished that determines how faithfully the image you import into Corel PHOTO-PAINT is reproduced.

When a color in the original image cannot be produced precisely (either because of display or color mode limitations), the computer does its best to make an approximation of the color through a process called *dithering*. With dithering, the computer changes the colors of adjacent pixels so that to the viewer they approximate the desired color. Dithering is accomplished by mathematically averaging the color values of adjacent pixels. The use of dithering can also affect the process of getting from CorelDRAW to PHOTO-PAINT.

That's enough prelude for now. Let's look at our first method: drag-and-drop.

## The Drag-and-Drop Method

The drag-and-drop method is limited to screen resolution, which for a standard VGA monitor is 96 pixels per inch. Don't let the low resolution associated with screen display put you off on the drag-and-drop method. The most noticeable loss in image quality results from the way the fountain fill information is rasterized.

### When to Use Drag-and-Drop

One of the big advantages of using the drag-and-drop method is the speed at which it operates. Without going into the technical details of how rasterization is accomplished with the drag-and-drop method, I simply say that it is not the best choice for importing images that have fountain fills or that have a large number of colors, such as color photographs, because of dithering.

So what good is drag-and-drop? Multimedia applications are all limited to screen resolution; therefore, they are an ideal candidate. Drag-and-drop is an excellent way to import items with solid or no colors, such as symbols, or items with a limited number of diagonal lines. (Diagonal lines are a particular obstacle to any form of rasterization.)

### Using Drag-and-Drop

If you do decide that drag-and-drop is the best choice for your project, you should follow these guidelines:

- Both applications must be open. This means that neither one can be reduced to a little icon at the bottom of the screen.
- PHOTO-PAINT does not need to have an image area open. If an existing image is not open, a new image will be created.
- To drag an image from CorelDRAW, you must click it and drag it into the PHOTO-PAINT application. When the cursor is over the paint application, the icon will turn into an arrow-rectangle icon.

## Corel *TIP!*

> When dragging an image into PHOTO-PAINT, be patient. It sometimes takes longer than you might expect for the cursor to change into the arrow-rectangle icon.

■ When you let go of the left mouse button, two things happen:

The image is rasterized and placed into PHOTO-PAINT. If there was not an existing image file open, the object dragged into PHOTO-PAINT is rasterized at 300 dpi. If there is an existing image, it is rasterized at the resolution of the image.

The image in CorelDRAW disappears. To restore the image that was dragged kicking and screaming out of CorelDRAW, just click anywhere in the CorelDRAW window (which makes it active again) and select Undo Delete from the Edit menu or press Ctrl+Z.

## The Downside of Drag-and-Drop

I have included some examples of what you can expect when using the drag-and-drop method of moving images from CorelDRAW into PHOTO-PAINT.

Figure 80.1 shows an image that was loaded in CorelDRAW from the Symbol library. I used a solid black fill. Next, using the drag-and-drop technique, I dragged it into PHOTO-PAINT. Figure 80.2 shows a comparison between the original CorelDRAW symbol and the rasterized version of the same symbol. Don't panic. It isn't as bad as the figure makes it look. If it were viewed on-screen, I doubt you would notice the difference. However, when it is printed out, you notice the difference.

*Figure 80.1.*
*A symbol in CorelDRAW*
*with 100 percent black fill.*

In the next series of figures, you will move the same symbol with a fountain fill instead of a 100 percent black fill. Figure 80.3 is the original, and Figure 80.4 is the same image at the same zoom level after it is dragged into PHOTO-PAINT. Notice that the image in PHOTO-PAINT is smaller than the original in CorelDRAW. That is because the image in CorelDRAW is at a screen resolution of 72 dpi. It was brought into PHOTO-PAINT at 300 dpi, resulting in a smaller image. To correct for this reduction caused by resolution change, you must resample the image in PHOTO-PAINT.

*Figure 80.2*
*The original symbol is*
*placed alongside the*
*resultant symbol after it*
*was rasterized using drag-*
*and-drop.*

In Figure 80.5, the resampled image from Figure 80.4 is saved as a CPT file and imported into CorelDRAW, where the images are displayed next to each other. The original is the one in the upper-left corner. What doesn't show on the screen shot, but appears when the figure is printed, are the moiré patterns that result from this type of rasterization. Moiré patterns are distortions that appear as wavy patterns.

*Figure 80.3.*
*The original symbol with a*
*radial fill in CorelDRAW.*

*Figure 80.4.*
*The rasterized symbol*
*after it is dragged into*
*PHOTO-PAINT.*

*Figure 80.5.*
*The differences between*
*the three methods.*

## Exporting CorelDRAW Files as Bitmaps

Yes, you can still export CorelDRAW images as bitmap files using the following steps:

1. As a safety precaution, when you have the drawing the way that you want it in CorelDRAW, save it as a CDR file using the Save command in the File menu.

2. Select the Export command in the File menu. You will be presented with a series of choices at this point. Figure 80.6 shows the CorelDRAW Export dialog box. It operates just the same as the Save dialog box for images. It fact, it is the same dialog box with a different title. You may consider using the Corel PHOTO-PAINT format (CPT) if you are going to be opening the file with Corel PHOTO-PAINT. If you are going to use the exported bitmap in

another document, I would recommend using the TIF, BMP, or PCX format. These formats are more widely used than most of the other formats. For use with exported images in applications other than PHOTO-PAINT, Corel has provided the following recommendations for selection of file formats. (See Table 80.1.) These recommendations are based on the type of printer you are using. Generally, if you have a PostScript printer and the program you are exporting to supports PostScript, use the EPS format. Otherwise, use the format shown in the table.

**Table 80.1. File format recommendations for bitmap files based on output device.**

| Program | PostScript Printers | Non-PostScript Printers |
|---|---|---|
| Ami Professional | EPS | WMF |
| Delrina Perform | GEM | GEM |
| PageMaker | EPS | WMF or TIF |
| Corel Ventura | EPS | CMX |
| WordPerfect | EPS | WPG |

Table 80.2 provides recommendations for placement in other graphic applications.

**Table 80.2. File format recommendations for graphic applications.**

| Program | Recommended format |
|---|---|
| Adobe Illustrator | AI |
| Arts & Letters | WMF, EPS (using Decipher) |
| AutoCAD | DXF |
| GEM Artline | GEM |
| Macintosh-based vector programs | Macintosh PICT, AI |
| Micrografx Designer | CGM |
| PC Paintbrush | PCX |

3. Click the Save button, and the Bitmap Export dialog box opens, as shown in Figure 80.7. You have a large selection of commands to choose from in this dialog box. The commands are explained in the next section. Not all of the options are available—it depends of the type of bitmap file that is selected. Make your selections and then click the OK button.

*Figure 80.6*
*The CorelDRAW*
*Export dialog box.*

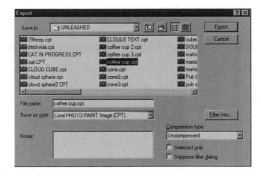

# Corel*CAUTION!*

Beware! Converting an image to a bitmap, especially a large one, can take a significant amount of time. Don't be surprised if it takes minutes to complete. My next book will be called *101 Neat Games to Play with Your Hourglass.*

# Corel*TIP!*

In the Bitmap Export dialog box, you select the format of the bitmap file (CPT, TIF, PCX, GIF, and so on.) In this dialog box, you select the type of file (color, grayscale, black and white, and so on).

4. Once the file has been converted, you may open it with PHOTO-PAINT or place it as a bitmap in any application that supports placement of bitmap graphics.

## The CorelDRAW Export Dialog Box

This dialog box is used to convert the current selection to a format other than CorelDRAW (CDR) for use in other programs.

### Filename

The program provides a default name for the export file. Either accept it, or type your own filename. The file extension corresponds to the export file format selected from the List Files of Type box.

## Drive/Folders

This is used to select the drive and folder in which the file you want to export is stored.

## Save as Type

Use to choose the type of file to export.

## OK

Displays the CorelDRAW Bitmap Export dialog box.

# The CorelDRAW Bitmap Export Dialog Box

Use this dialog box, shown in Figure 80.7, to specify how you want to export files in any of the bitmap export formats—PCX (PCC), TIFF, TGA, GIF, Windows BMP, OS/2 BMP, SCITEX CT, and third-party filters.

*Figure 80.7*
*The Bitmap Export dialog box, used to specify how you want to export files in any of the bitmap export formats.*

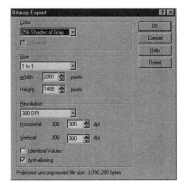

# Dialog Box Options

There is a large selection of dialog box options that control how CorelDRAW will convert the current image or selection.

## Colors

Although I have listed all of the color choices available, you should only consider 24-bit color for color photographs or 256 color if the image you are working on is going to end up as a GIF file on the Internet. Color settings determine in what format CorelDRAW will export your drawing—as shades of gray or color. From the list box, choose the number of shades of gray or the number of colors that you want to use in the exported file.

The greater the number of colors, the larger the exported file. Table 80.3 lists the available color choices and the color depth of each choice.

**Table 80.3. The available color choices and their color depth.**

| Colors | Color Depth |
|---|---|
| Black and white | 1 bit |
| 16 shades of gray | 4 bits |
| 256 shades of gray | 8 bits |
| 16 colors | 4 bits |
| 256 colors | 8 bits |
| 16 million colors | 24 bits |

Not all levels of color or grayscale are supported by all bitmap formats. If you have chosen a bitmap format that does not support a gray or color format, the option will not appear in the list box. For example, SCITEX CT is only exportable in 16-million color, 24-bit format.

## Dithered

This is not always the best choice unless you are making a graphic for use on the Internet. Selecting this button dithers the colors and gray shades in the exported file. Dithering may produce better results when exporting fewer colors than the original image. If the image contains fountain fills or color blends, dithering can cause obvious banding in the exported bitmap. Here are some guidelines to help you decide whether to dither the bitmap:

- If you are exporting 16 or 256 colors or grays, use dithering.
- If you intend to scale the bitmap in another application, dithering is not recommended.

## Size

This function is used to specify the dimensions of the exported bitmap. You can choose one of the preset sizes from the list box or select Custom and enter the dimensions in the Width and Height boxes.

If a size is not selected, the size of the image in CorelDRAW is used. Smaller bitmaps (with lower resolution) or larger bitmaps (with higher resolution) can be created by scaling the image up or down in CorelDRAW prior to exporting.

# Corel*NOTE!*

If you choose one of the preset sizes from the list box, the dimensions you choose may not be proportional to the bitmap's original aspect ratio. The exported bitmap will distort unless you place an empty border around your bitmap with the same ratio as the preset. For example, create a rectangle around your image 6.4"×4.8" if you are exporting at 640×480. Then, assign No Fill and No Outline to the rectangle. Now the aspect ratio of the image will be maintained when you export.

## Resolution

This setting specifies the resolution (in dots per inch) for bitmaps exported at a size of 1 to 1. Choose one of the preset resolutions from the list box, or choose Custom and enter a resolution in the DPI box.

# Corel*NOTE!*

As resolution increases, so does the size of the export file and the time required to convert the image.

# Corel*TIP!*

Don't use a value larger than 200 dpi for this option unless you have a specific reason for doing so. It will make a ridiculously large file, take lots of time, and will not look any better.

## Identical Values

There are applications where small differences in resolution allow the bitmap to fit a specific size without visible distortion. Did you catch the key words? SMALL DIFFERENCES. There is another situation where you can enter larger differences in resolution and not cause visible distortion. That is when the object contains natural repeating patterns, such as clouds or rocks. They can be distorted, and you would never know it unless you looked at the original. When the Identical Values check box is enabled, any values entered in the either the Horizontal or Vertical value box are automatically reflected in the other box. Use this to keep the resolution uniform.

## Anti–Alias

This check box, when enabled, uses a process that produces smoother bitmap rasterization. There is a small increase in the amount of time this feature takes. It is on by default and it is strongly recommend that you keep it enabled. Let me restate that—there is no reason in this solar system to turn it off.

## Reset

You will use this box more than you might imagine. It returns the settings in the dialog box to what they were originally before you began making lots of changes.

## Projected Uncompressed File Size

The displayed value shows the estimated size of the exported file before compression. Compressed files will be smaller than the value displayed.

## The Best Way...Finally

No, I didn't get lost. The best way to bring an image from CorelDRAW into PHOTO-PAINT is to save the file as a CDR file. To keep the file size from becoming ridiculously large, select the objects that are to be imported into PHOTO-PAINT. Use the Save As command and check the Selected Only option when saving the file. This way, only the CorelDRAW image and not a lot of white paper is converted into a bitmap.

Using PHOTO-PAINT, open the CDR file. When a non-bitmap file is opened, PHOTO-PAINT will automatically display the Import Into Bitmap dialog box. This dialog box is identical to the CorelDRAW Bitmap Export described in the previous section—well, except for the title.

## So What's the Difference?

It would seem that it does matter which way you do it. After all, the bitmap conversion engine in Corel does both the exporting from CorelDRAW and the importing for PHOTO-PAINT. I can't explain it, but the results achieved importing with PHOTO-PAINT are superior to the results achieved when the image is exported from CorelDRAW. Go figure.

# 81

# DREAM 3D

Before we begin to talk about CorelDREAM 3D, it would be helpful to discuss what a 3D program is and what it is not. When I was growing up, 3D was low-budget, sci-fi films watched while wearing cardboard glasses that had one red lens and one blue lens. The films were not three-dimensional; the glasses gave the viewer the illusion of depth. There are several roll-ups in CorelDRAW that also provide the illusion of depth to two-dimensional objects. So what is the difference between something that is really three-dimensional and something that appears three-dimensional? Much more than you might imagine.

With CorelDRAW you are working with two-dimensional objects on a two-dimensional display. With CorelDREAM 3D you are working with three-dimensional objects on a two-dimensional display. Because of the nature of constructing objects in three dimensions, the user interface (UI) for creating and displaying 3D objects on a 2D display is unique. That's my cute way of saying confusing. The first change you will encounter is working with a multitude of windows, which are called Browsers. Figure 81.1 shows the interface for CorelDREAM 3D.

*Figure 81.1.*
*For some of you, this*
*might be your first*
*glimpse of the*
*CorelDREAM 3D interface.*

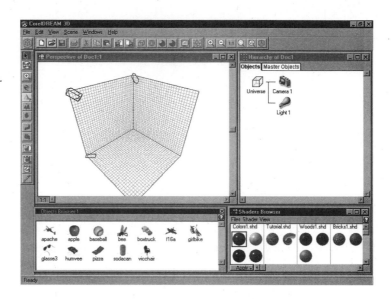

Although learning how to work in this environment is not overwhelming, it is a major change in how CorelDRAW approached things. For those who like to jump in and begin using a program without reading the manual, you might get very frustrated. If it will be any consolation, using this program was so difficult for the beta testers that Corel actually had to send out the documentation for this program so it could be tested.

3D programs encompass a different methodology and vocabulary than their 2D counterparts. In CorelDRAW, all objects are flat. They posses height and width but they lack depth. Figure 81.2 is an example of a 2D drawing created in CorelDRAW 6. Although it creates the illusion of depth, the drawing has only two dimensions: height and width. The view angle cannot be changed without completely redrawing the object from scratch. Figure 81.3 shows similar text created using CorelDREAM 3D. After the text object is created, it can be rotated to any angle (view). 3D has a great advantage over 2D but the positioning of the object is a little more complicated than it is in 2D.

*Figure 81.2.
An example of extruded
text created in two
dimensions using
CorelDRAW.*

*Figure 81.3.
The same text created
using CorelDREAM 3D.*

3D applications have an additional dimension, called depth. Every object in the program possesses depth. In 3D programs all objects, even two-dimensional ones, exist in three-dimensional space. You can move objects and view them from different vantage points—from above, behind, below—just as if you were floating in space around them.

In addition to depth, most 3D programs enable the user to apply and manipulate other real-world attributes. For instance, you can control lighting. Controlling how many lights, what types of lights, and where the lights are located enhances the realistic appearance of the objects.

Like objects in the real world, objects in 3D programs can be made from different materials. These materials (referred to as shaders in CorelDREAM 3D) range from smooth gold to rough granite. Figure 81.4 was a Corel Art Show winner by Chris Purcell. Chris used various colors to make the lizard appear to be real. Figure 81.5 was created by Mark Siegel using the original Ray Dream Designer. Because the objects in this image contain photo textures, the pictures look real.

*Figure 81.4.
Great lizard, right? This
fellow was created with
CorelDRAW.*

*Figure 81.5.*
*An even better lizard*
*created using the original*
*version of CorelDREAM*
*3D, Ray Dream Designer 3.*

Some of the better programs produce images that are so realistic that you must decide if they are real or computer-generated. If the images in this chapter don't convince you how realistic the output of these programs can be, watch the movie *Jurassic Park*. Remember the charming over-grown lizards in the kitchen scene? Could you tell which Raptors were models or humans in costumes from the computer-generated ones? You probably couldn't because they did such a good job.

Once you get used to the idea of multiple windows, you will encounter rendering. All of the images you work on will be little better than wireframes. In CorelDREAM you are offered two different levels of previews. But when you want to see the "real stuff," you then must render the object (called a model) that you have created. This is where the 3D programs make you pay for the realistic effects. It can take an enormous amount of time to render an image. The amount of time that is required to render your creation depends on how complex the model is, how much horsepower is in your computer, and what type of rendering you want done. Now that we have finished scaring you, let's look at using CorelDREAM 3D with CorelDRAW to create some unusual effects.

## Getting Started

If you already went through the two tutorials in the Corel manual, congratulations. If you are like me, you finished them and then as you sat there with your completed castle-in-a-fishbowl and fork, you wondered how to use the program. In this chapter we are not going to teach you to do complicated model building or how to create exotic shaders. You are going to learn how to create some very basic stuff.

First of all, using CorelDREAM 3D requires three basic parts. First, you must make the object. The object can be a shape such as a cone or cube, or it can be text. That's the easy part. Next, you must position it where it needs to be. Believe it or not, this is the part that drives everyone bats, including yours truly. I will show you some tricks that make the positioning part a little simpler. The last step is rendering. This is the part that converts all of the vectors into bitmap, which can consume vast quantities of CPU time. One of the great advantages of Windows 95 is made evident while rendering objects in CorelDREAM 3D. As I am writing this chapter, I am rendering one of the images in the background.

## A Quick Tour of CorelDREAM 3D

Referring again to Figure 81.1, you see that when CorelDREAM 3D is opened there are many windows staring back at you. If you are like a lot of users, you want to get out at this point and return to good old friendly, familiar CorelDRAW. Everything you see here isn't necessary to have in view. The Object Browser is in the lower-left corner of the main screen.

## Object Browser

The Object Browser is a catalog of 3D clip art objects. You can add objects from the Browser simply by dragging them into your scene. The Browser is a visual catalog of your clip art library. You can select one of the 3D libraries via the Browse 3D Clipart command in the File menu. When you select an object in the Browser, the name of the object appears at the top-right corner of the Browser window. The 3D clip art images are complete 3D models that can be used to create almost anything your heart desires.

There is a small collection of 3D clip art placed on your drive when you install CorelDREAM 3D. There is a much larger collection of 3D clip art on Corel CD-ROM # 1. In fact, Viewpoint Datalabs International has produced almost 400 pieces of clip art. Look in the clip art book (the one that looks like a Manhattan phone directory) in section "N" to see all of the clip art that has been included on the disk.

We won't be using the Object Browser in this chapter, so you can close this window and get it off the screen until you need it.

## Shaders and Shaders Browser

The Shaders Browser provides a visual display of all currently available shaders. Shaders have nothing to do with shadows or things in the shade. In CorelDREAM 3D, you control the appearance of objects by applying shaders to them. A *shader* is simply a set of surface characteristics. Shaders are complicated things that can contain settings for one or more of the following attributes: color, highlight, shininess, bump, reflection, transparency, and refraction.

Each object you create in CorelDREAM has a base shader called the primer, which covers the entire object. By applying a shader to an object's primer, you can easily control the appearance of the object's surface.

You'll use the Shaders Browser to apply one of the many shaders provided for you by CorelDRAW. You can also create new shaders, delete shaders, organize shaders in families, save shaders in files, and load saved shader files. Because you are going to use the Shader Browser in this chapter, keep it open for the moment.

## Perspective and Hierarchy Windows

The Hierarchy window provides a way to manage the contents of a scene (which is what the total 3D picture is called). Although it is possible to work without using the Hierarchy window, you will find it handy as you develop more complex scenes someday, but not in this chapter. The Hierarchy window shows a logical (as opposed to visual) representation of the scene. All objects, cameras, and lights that you bring into the Perspective window on the left are represented by icons in the hierarchy. In Figure 81.1 the Hierarchy window shows that the default perspective has one camera and one light.

Now about the Perspective window, which is the main work window in CorelDREAM 3D. This window shows a view of the 3D workspace, where objects are created and arranged in three dimensions to create a scene. The workspace itself is called the *universe*.

By default, CorelDREAM opens new scenes with one camera and one light in the universe. This camera provides the point of view for the display in the Perspective window. You can zoom in or out of the Perspective window with the magnifying glass to get a better view of your scene. Like the Zoom in other Corel applications, the setting of the Zoom tool does not affect the final output.

## How the Perspective Window Thinks

See the box in the Perspective window that looks like three sheets of graph paper? It is called the *Working Box*. The Working Box is a set of three intersecting grid planes. It is a reference floating in the Perspective window. It helps you visualize the spatial relationships of your objects.

One of the first major misconceptions users have about CorelDREAM 3D is that the Working Box determines the part of the image that is finally seen, much like the edge of the paper in CorelDRAW. Actually, it doesn't. It is a visual reference to help you see where objects exist in 3D space. The grid walls of the Working Box do not confine your scene in any way. You can place objects anywhere in the universe, within or beyond the grid planes of the Working Box. You can choose to display or hide all the planes or select which planes are displayed and which is the active plane. Furthermore, the Working Box is mobile; you can rotate it, resize it, and move it to different positions in the universe. Therefore, if the Working Box doesn't define the "edges" of the image, what does? The Production Frame. Once you understand the Production Frame, you will understand the heart of how to do things in CorelDREAM. Look at Figure 81.6.

*Figure 81.6.*
*A look at some of the*
*parts of the Perspective*
*window.*

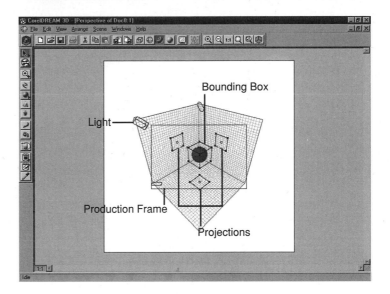

## The Production Frame

I have expanded the Perspective window to make things a little clearer. I turned on the Production Frame (Ctrl+R) and placed an object (sphere) in the Working Box. The Production Frame determines what will be there when the scene is rendered. Anything inside the Production Frame will be rendered when the Render command is selected. You can change the size of the Production Frame, although its minimum size is 300×300 pixels. You will want to change the size of the Production Frame because rendering takes time and the larger the Production Frame the longer it takes to render. Therefore, you want the Production Frame to be only as large as necessary. Can you move the Production Frame to change its position? No. You can change its size, but the Production Frame always remains centered in the Perspective window. To summarize: you must ensure the Production Frame is the size required for the final project and then create the object. Then, you must position the object in the Production Frame. Let's do it.

## Creating a Text Object in CorelDREAM 3D

In this skill session we are going to create a three-dimensional text object for use in PHOTO-PAINT.

1. Launch CorelDREAM 3D.

2. Select the Text tool from the toolbox on the left.

3. Maximize the Perspective window. Place the cursor over the point shown in Figure 81.7. Exactly where you put the cursor isn't critical; don't sit there and count squares in the grid to make it match mine, just try and place it in the general area. Click the left mouse button, and a new screen will open up.

4. Using the Text dialog box is the way all text is entered in CorelDREAM 3D. The operation of the text dialog box is fairly obvious. To make it match what I am using select PTBarnum BT. To create a bevel on the text you must click one or both of the boxes in the upper-left corners of the dialog box. Here are the settings I selected or changed: Font, On Front, Type, and Face Depth. There is one other, which you will see in the next step.

5. From the menu bar select Geometry and pick Surface Fidelity (the only choice). The dialog box that appears controls how well the rendered object follows the contour of the original wireframe object. Look at Figure 81.7. This character was set to a Surface Fidelity of 75 percent (the default), whereas Figure 81.8 was set to 400 percent. Look at the edges of the bevel on the character. In Figure 81.7, because the Surface Fidelity was set low, you can see the small segments that make up the curve of the *S*.

*Figure 81.7.*
*The tiny line segments that make up the character are apparent when the Surface Fidelity is set at 75 percent (default).*

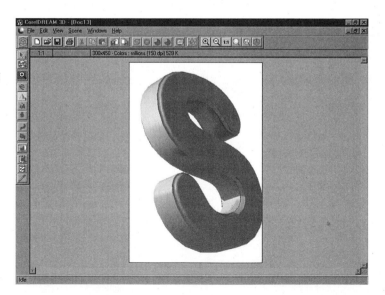

*Figure 81.8.*
*The curve of the character*
*looks much better when*
*the Surface Fidelity*
*setting is increased to a*
*larger setting like the*
*maximum of 400 percent.*

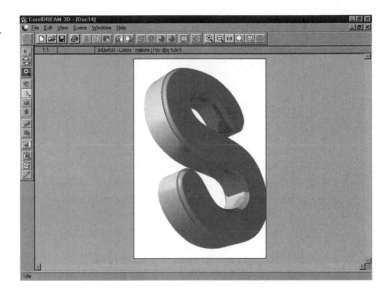

# Corel *TIP!*

> Always set the Surface Fidelity setting to at least 200 percent to get smooth lines on objects.

6. For this project, we want the text tilted back. Before we can rotate the text we need to understand hot points.

   The *hot point* is the single point of an object that identifies the object's location in the universe. Look at Figure 81.9. There are several hot points identified. Each object shown on the grid walls has a hot point. If you look at the numerical position of an object, the x, y, z coordinates refer to the hot points. You can move the hot point to any point in the object, on the surface, or at some distance from the object. Returning again to Figure 81.9, note that there are three rectangles (called *bounding boxes*) on the Working Box (grid). The bounding boxes represent the projections of the object in all three dimensions. It is these projections that should be used to manipulate the object.

*Figure 81.9.*
*The text object shown*
*with the bounding boxes*
*and their hot points*
*identified.*

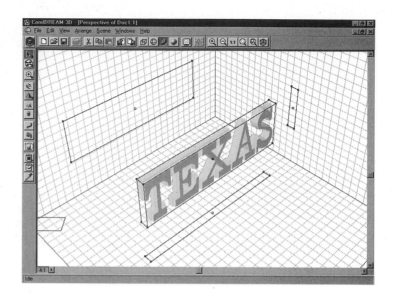

CorelDREAM provides two tools on a flyout in the toolbox to rotate 3D objects. The first is the Virtual Trackball. This tool provides rotation in multiple axes at the same time. For now, ignore this tool; there are times and places for this tool, but not in this chapter. The other rotation on the flyout is the One Axis Rotation tool. This tool rotates an object on only one axis at a time. With the One Axis Rotation tool selected, make sure the object is selected and rotate the text object about 45 degrees by clicking a corner and dragging the bounding box as shown in Figure 81.10. The text in the figure might look a little different from yours because I have selected a higher preview level so the screen shots would look better. I don't recommend doing that at this point because it slows down the operation.

7. Next, rotate the upper-left corner of the rear bounding box (projection) as shown in Figure 81.11. Notice after the rotation has completed how much the shape of the bounding box has changed. That is because they are projections that act like shadows. As the position of the object in 3D space changes, the projections, like shadows, change their shape.

*Figure 81.10.*
*The text has now*
*been rotated 45 degrees*
*using the One Axis*
*Rotation tool.*

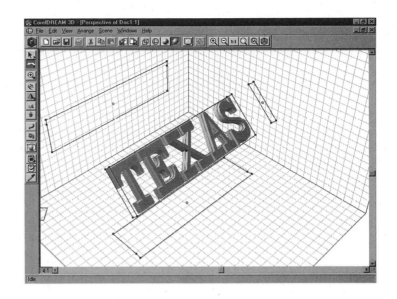

*Figure 81.11.*
*The rear bounding box*
*is rotated next.*

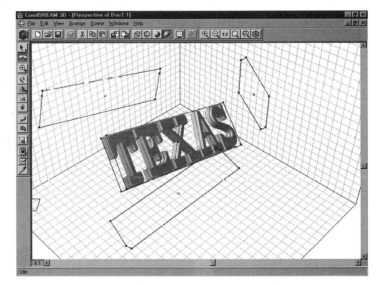

8. We want the text to be viewed from the front, and there are two ways to do that. First, we can rotate the object, as we have been doing up until now, or we can change camera positions. You have probably guessed that is what we are going to do—use the camera.

   Cameras provide viewpoints for the Perspective window and for renderings. You can position several cameras in your scene and switch among them to get various perspectives. You can even create a second Perspective window to view your scene from two angles at once. When you're ready to render, choose a camera as the viewpoint. The camera position and settings combine with the rendering format to determine the scale and framing of the scene. Open the Camera Settings dialog box (Ctrl+E).

9. In the Camera Settings dialog box change the following settings: Position to FRONT and Type (of camera) to CONICAL.

   The Conical camera is patterned after the standard 35 mm camera. The Isometric camera provides views of the object(s) that do not reflect the distance from the camera (that is, there is no vanishing point).

   Figure 81.12 shows the results of the new position. This setting box enables you to make many different changes to the way the objects are viewed. Changes made to the camera, unlike the Zoom tools, affect the final output.

*Figure 81.12.*
*The full frontal view of Texas made possible by changing the camera position.*

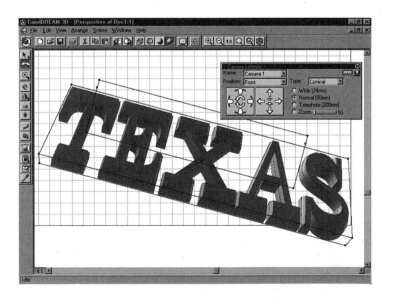

# Corel *TIP!*

When working with a scene that contains many objects, it is easier to move the camera than it is to move all of the objects.

**10.** We are getting close to being finished. Click the 1:1 button in the Zoom menu. Then, in the View menu select the Production Frame I talked so much about in the first part of the chapter. You might have to use the Zoom tool to adjust your display to see all of the Production Frame. Figure 81.13 shows the results. As you can see, the text is outside of the Production Frame so if we were to render it now we would cut off the bottom of several characters. Because we cannot move the Production Frame, we can move the object or the camera. Choose the camera again.

*Figure 81.13.*
*When we zoom back and look, we see the text is outside of the Production Frame.*

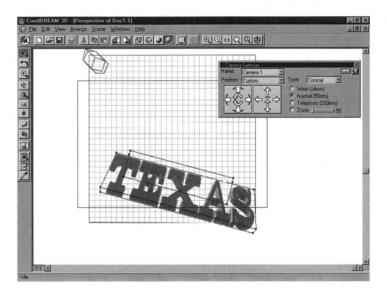

**11.** There are two sets of buttons in the Camera Settings dialog box. The one on the left is the Rotate and Translate button, which is used to change the orientation and position of the camera. The other button is the Tracking button, which moves the camera without changing its current attitude. Click the bottom arrow (Pan Down) of the Rotate and Translate button three times. The results should look like Figure 81.14.

Figure 81.14.
*Using the panning
controls of the camera we
are able to get the text
into the Production Frame
without moving the
object.*

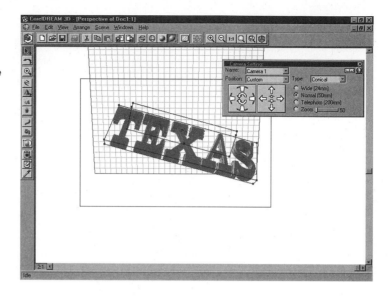

12. Save this camera position by selecting Save Position from the Position Box. This opens the Save Position dialog box. Name the position Texas. We are almost finished. The next step is to change the lighting.

    By default, your 3D scene will contain two kinds of light sources: ambient and directional light. Lighting effects are not shown in the regular Preview display mode. When you create a ray-traced rendering of your scene, it will show color, shading, and all of the complex lighting effects, including reflection, shadows, transparency, and refraction.

13. You might have noticed that the lighting seems to be coming from behind the text; in fact, that is exactly where it is coming from. Click the 1:1 button again until you can see the Light object as shown in Figure 81.15. If your display looks all jumbled, select Isometric and then reselect Conical.

14. The height of the light is fine; we need to place it so it shines on the front of the text. To make that easier we need to pick a different camera view. In this case choose TOP in the Position setting of the Camera Settings dialog box. Figure 81.16 shows the result. Do not worry about the Production Frame because this is not the camera position we will be using for rendering the text.

*Figure 81.15.*
*The object up in the*
*corner is the light source.*

Light ——

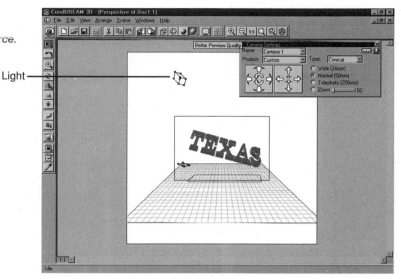

*Figure 81.16.*
*This is the view from the*
*top, so to speak. The light*
*source is shinning from*
*behind the text.*

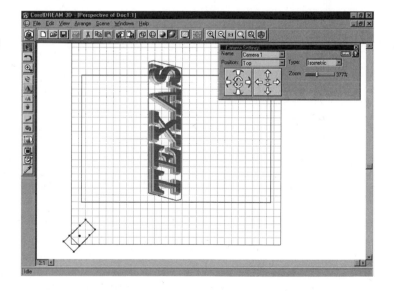

**15.** With the Object Selector tool (top of the toolbox), click the light and drag it to the right corner. Now the problem is that the light is facing in the wrong direction. We could rotate the light, but there is a better way. With the light still selected, hold down the Shift key and select the Text object. Now we have two objects selected. From the Arrange menu choose Point At. This command causes the light (or camera, if a camera is selected) to point at the hot point of the selected object. The results are shown in Figure 81.17.

*Figure 81.17.*
*Now the light is in the*
*correct position and we*
*have finished playing with*
*the lights.*

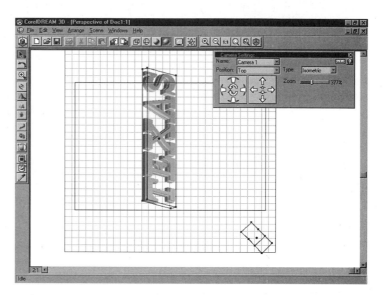

# Corel *TIP!*

The Point At command is the best way to position lights and cameras, but it should be noted that it is not dynamically linked to the object. In other words, if the Point At command is used to position a light and then the light is moved, the Point At command should be used again after the movement.

16. Change the Camera setting to Texas; make sure the Type does not change to Isometric. If it does, change it back to Conical and close the Camera Settings dialog box. From the View menu choose Default Quality and select Better Preview from the drop-down list. This will take a few minutes to create. I am using a DX4/100 with 32 MB of RAM, and it takes about 10 to 15 seconds to show a Better Preview. Your results should look like those in Figure 81.18. If your grid portion of your Working Box is in a different position, you can change it by clicking the icon in the upper-left corner of the Perspective window. Each time you click the portion of the icon, one of the three grids (planes) of the Working Box becomes visible or invisible.

*Figure 81.18.*
*The camera and lights*
*are now in the correct*
*position.*

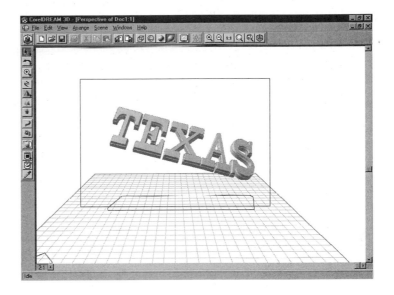

**17.** Reduce the size of the Perspective window so that you can see the Shader Browser and the Hierarchy window. Use the Object Picker and select the Text icon. Now choose one of the shaders in the Shader Browser. In my example, I have selected one of the shaders that was included on the Corel CD-ROM, Hammered Gold. Pick any shader you want and click the Apply button at the bottom of the Shader Browser. If you cannot see the Apply button, lift the shader up a little. Because Better Preview is still selected, it will take a little more time for the text to display the shader setting.

*Figure 81.19.*
*Applying the shader to the*
*object further enhances*
*the photo-realistic*
*appearance of the text.*

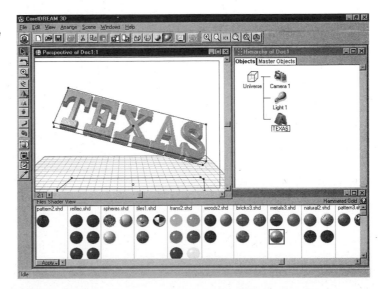

*Rendering* is the process of capturing a view of your three-dimensional scene and saving it as a 2D image. You can think of a rendering as taking a photograph of your scene. You can take any number of renderings of your scene—from different angles and, perhaps, under different lighting conditions. The rendered image does not contain objects. It is an image, comprised entirely of colored dots called pixels. A rendering is distinct from the scene from which it was taken. It is a separate file, stored on disk, in a different format. CorelDREAM lets you save renderings in many of the popular image formats: BMP, TIFF, Adobe Photoshop, TGA, and PCX. You must render the image before it can be printed or opened in a photo retouching or page-layout application.

# Corel *TIP!*

Before you begin the rendering process, you can see accurate light source effects while working in your scene by using the Render Preview tool to render a marqueed area of your scene.

From the Scene menu choose Render Setup and then select Final from the next drop-down list. We are going to use these settings to tell CorelDREAM 3D how to render the text. From the first dialog box (Size) change your settings so that they match those shown in Figure 81.20. You can change the size of the Production Frame with this dialog box.

*Figure 81.20.*
*The Artwork Settings are*
*used to control the size*
*and resolution of the*
*Production Frame.*

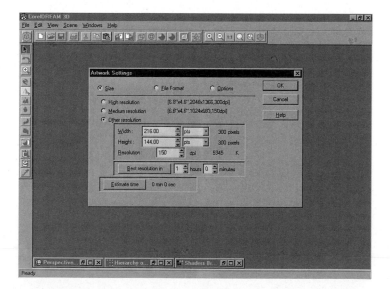

18. Now click the File Format button. Under the Save Format list, change the file format to Photo-Paint(Cor). Check the Mask box so it will include mask information. Click OK.

19. Finally, we get to render the image. Be warned! This is going to take some time. On my system, it will take over five minutes. I once rendered a complex image that took two hours.

    In the Scene menu choose Render and then choose Final from the next drop-down list. When the process begins, you will discover one of the sneaky tricks of this program. It will begin to render the objects in the Perspective window in a separate window. The window will be buried somewhere on the screen under another window. Wasn't that a clever idea? My recommendation is to maximize the window that is being rendered and then use the "cool switch" (Alt+Tab) to go to some other program (like Solitaire) and use it until the rendering is finished. The result is shown in Figure 81.21.

*Figure 81.21.*
*The finished rendered text*
*is now a bitmap image.*

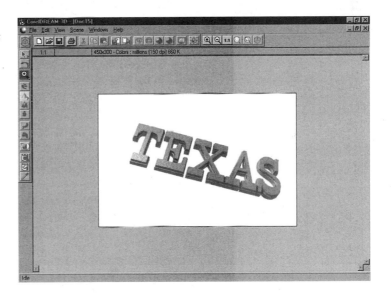

20. It's time to clean up after ourselves. Save the rendered file as a PHOTO-PAINT image (TEXAS TEXT.CPT) and then save the original CorelDREAM 3D object as a CorelDREAM 3D file (TEXAS TEXT.D3D). We're finished! We will use the rendered in the next two chapters.

This chapter has only scratched the surface of what can be done with CorelDREAM 3D. However, it is a start. In the next two chapters we will briefly look at things that can be done by combining the power of CorelDREAM 3D with CorelDRAW and PHOTO-PAINT.

# 82

# CorelDRAW
# and
# CorelDREAM
# 3D

One of the first things that I learned about using CorelDRAW with CorelDREAM 3D was that many objects created in CorelDRAW cannot be brought into CorelDREAM 3D and made into 3D objects. Maybe we can do it in CorelDREAM 7.

## Getting CDR Files Into CorelDREAM 3D

Most objects cannot be brought into CorelDREAM 3D, but there is a way. It is long and complicated, and is described here:

1. Launch CorelDRAW and open a new drawing.
2. Create a shape like the one shown in Figure 82.1 and save it as STAR.CDR.

*Figure 82.1.*
*A simple star shape in*
*CorelDRAW.*

3. Minimize or close CorelDRAW and launch CorelDREAM 3D.

4. In CorelDREAM 3D select the Freeform tool (below the Zoom tool) in the toolbox. Click in the Perspective window near the corner of the working box closest to you. The Perspective window changes into the Modeling window. A dialog box opens asking you to name the new object. Name it star (how original) and click the OK button.

5. From the File menu select Import and select the STAR.CDR file. Click the Import button and you will receive the message box shown in Figure 82.2. Click the Proceed button.

*Figure 82.2.*
*This warning message is*
*of questionable use. The*
*general recommendation*
*is to click Proceed.*

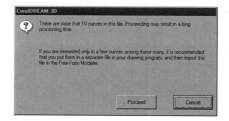

6. When CorelDREAM finishes, you will have a strange small blob in the middle of your Modeling window, shown (zoomed in) in Figure 82.3. It is not yet an object; it is a free-form model. It is also ridiculously long. You are finished with the Modeling window, so click the Return button at the bottom-left corner.

7. All you have is a tiny blob in the Perspective window. Don't touch it—I will show you how to fix it. The CorelDRAW file came in so small because of the reference system that the two programs use to talk to each other. Hopefully, they will have it cleared up by the next release. In the Perspective window right-click on the object. From the large drop-down list that appears, select Properties. The Object Properties dialog box opens, as shown in Figure 82.4.

Admittedly, it looks a little intimidating, but we are only interested in changing a few values. At the bottom of the dialog box, make a note of the smallest value of the three. Make sure the Keep Proportions box is checked and change the X value to a number that is about 20 times the size. For example, if it reads 3.0 change it to 60. Next, turn off the Keep Proportions check box and enter the Y value you noted earlier in the Y value. Click Apply. You now have a 3D object, which is shown rotated and rendered in Figure 82.5.

*Figure 82.3.*
*The CorelDRAW file has*
*been imported but needs*
*some work to be useful.*

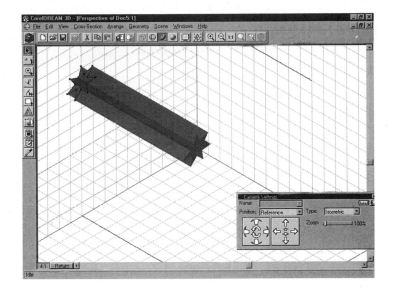

*Figure 82.4.*
*The Object Properties*
*dialog box.*

*Figure 82.5.*
*The final result of import-*
*ing a shape from*
*CorelDRAW.*

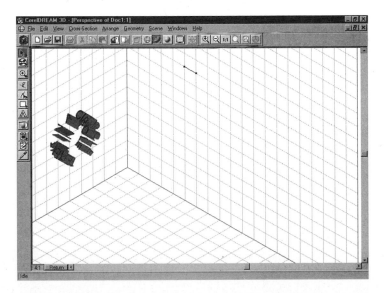

# Corel*NOTE!*

The current release has some restrictions you should be aware of. First, any text that is imported using the procedures described will have the counters filled. The counter is the area inside the characters "A, B, D, O, P, Q, R, 0 and 8. Next, the objects created using this method don't always accept shaders correctly. You will just have to experiment.

## Bring CorelDREAM into CorelDRAW 6

A general rule to follow when you are rendering files for use in CorelDRAW is to use the Medium resolution setting in the Render Setup file.

Although the interrelationship between CorelDRAW and PHOTO-PAINT isn't very strong, the ability to bring CorelDREAM objects into CorelDRAW is very robust. Experiment with bringing 3D objects into CorelDRAW and you will see some really exciting effects.

# 83

# Corel PHOTO-PAINT Meets DREAM 3D

If there were ever a marriage made in heaven, it has to be Corel PHOTO-PAINT and DREAM 3D working together. Unlike the relationship between CorelDRAW and PHOTO-PAINT, which was, for the most part, a one-way relationship, the inter-application workings of DREAM 3D and PHOTO-PAINT are bi-directional. We are going to look at a few of the things that can be done with the two programs.

## Bringing Objects from DREAM 3D into PHOTO-PAINT

In Skill Session 81, "An Introduction to DREAM 3D," you created and saved the file Texas Text.CPT. You are now going to learn how to bring that work into PHOTO-PAINT and use it.

1. Launch PHOTO-PAINT. (Did I really have to tell you to do that?)
2. Open the file TEXAS.CPT. If you did not make this file in Skill Session 81, you can find it on the companion CD-ROM as TEXAS.CPT. Figure 83.1 shows the rendered DREAM 3D object with the mask visible.

*Figure 83.1.*
*When you load the*
*rendered DREAM file, it*
*shows the mask that was*
*created by DREAM 3D.*

3. Because the text is masked to place a photograph in the background you need to first invert the mask. Either click the Invert Mask button in the toolbar or choose Invert in the Mask menu.
4. Select Paste from File in the Edit menu. When the dialog box opens locate the file labeled RODEO.CPT from the companion CD-ROM and click OK. When the file is loaded it will be an object that is larger than the existing image, so you will not be able to see the entire photograph, as shown in Figure 83.2. You can, however, see the mask.
5. Select the Object Picker tool from the toolbox and position the photograph by clicking and dragging it down and to the right, as shown in Figure 83.3.

# Corel *TIP!*

When positioning objects larger than the viewing area you do not have any visual indication that the movement is actually taking place. It is best to click and drag the object a short distance and let the program "catch up."

*Figure 83.2.*
*The photograph is larger than the image, so part of it falls outside of the viewing area.*

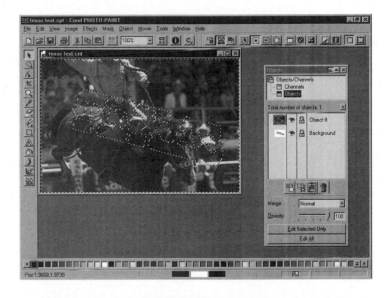

*Figure 83.3.*
*The photograph now looks like it is a little better composed with the new position.*

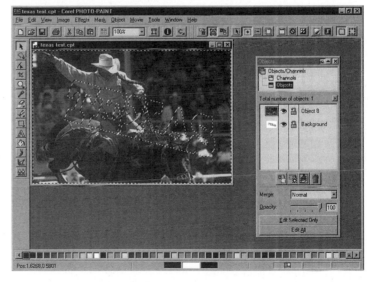

6. From the Object menu choose Clip Object to Mask. The advantage of this approach is speed. The disadvantage is the text cannot be moved. The results are shown in Figure 83.4.

*Figure 83.4.*
*The photograph has been*
*clipped to the mask.*

7. Next, you need to select Combine from the Object menu and select Combine objects with background from the drop-down list that appears. You have now combined all the objects with the background.

8. For the next step, invert the mask again. Make sure that the paint color of your brush is black by clicking the black color on the on-screen palette. The far left square (of the three at the bottom-middle of the screen) will be black.

9. Now add a dark blur behind the text. To do that you must first make an object of the text. This could be difficult because when an object is created from a mask, the mask is lost. To get around this, from the Mask menu select Save Mask, but when the next drop-down list appears, choose Save As Channel. Accept the default name of Mask 1. For the purposes of this session think of the channel as a temporary mask storage area.

10. Pick Create From Mask in the Object menu. The masked area (the text) becomes an object. In the Objects roll-up click the text object lock icon so it is protected from all filter and other PAINT actions.

11. Restore the mask that was lost by selecting Load and selecting Mask1 when the drop-down list appears. Voila! The mask is back. Now choose Stroke Mask from the Mask menu, and the Stroke Mask dialog box opens as shown in Figure 83.5. Select the Airbrush tool (second from the left, top row) and in the Type drop-down list box choose Medium Cover. Click the OK button. Figure 83.6 shows the final photograph.

*Figure 83.5.*
*The Stroke Mask dialog*
*box. From here it is*
*possible to apply a large*
*number of effects based on*
*the brush/effect selected.*

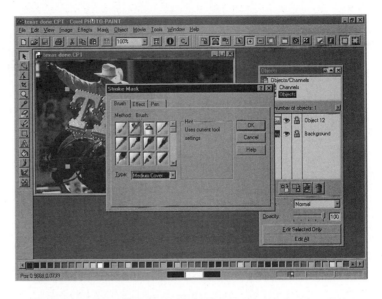

*Figure 83.6.*
*With the Stroke Mask*
*feature you can apply a*
*brush along the contours*
*of a mask.*

# Using PHOTO-PAINT in DREAM 3D

The principal use of PHOTO-PAINT as it relates to DREAM 3D is to create textures
for the shaders. Although there are other ways to use it—to modify photos, resize
images before placing them in DREAM 3D, and so on—the best use, in my opinion,
is for creating textures for shaders.

# 84

# An Introduction to Corel PRESENTS

An integrated, fully featured presentation program is the dream of thousands who, on a day-to-day basis, turn out presentations as part of their communications with clients, coworkers, and students. Whether you make slides, overheads, charts embedded in word-processing documents, or self-running presentations, Corel PRE-SENTS can help you get the task accomplished more quickly and communicating with improved clarity.

Although Corel PRESENTS is new to the suite of Corel products in the version 6 package, it is really a combination and revamping of version 5's SHOW and CHART modules with the addition of many new and interesting features. Coupled with Windows 95's power and features, this program is formidable indeed.

From the point of view that any image or drawing is part of a presentation in some fashion, the integration of the power of CorelDRAW into the PRESENTS program is a dream come true for many people who create presentations as part of their everyday jobs.

Due to space limitations and the integration of identical features, Skill Building Sessions 84, 85, 86, and 87 are not intended to introduce basic skills of either Windows 95 or CorelDRAW. If the functionality of a tool or feature is similar or covered previously in this book, it is not repeated in great detail in these exercises.

Following an introduction to the layout and tools of Corel PRESENTS, the following skill sessions, 85 through 87, walk you through a basic slide show; the use of animation and sound; and the creation of a portable, self-running presentation.

# Corel*NOTE!*

All of the text, screen views, and descriptions are based on Corel PRESENTS version 6.00.118.

After a typical installation, starting Corel PRESENTS brings up the screen shown in Figure 84.1.

*Figure 84.1.*
*The Corel PRESENTS*
*opening screen.*

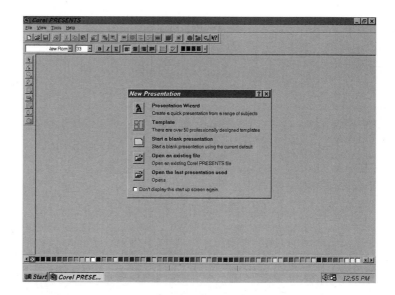

You must either use one of the choices from the dialog box in the startup screen or close it and then begin by choosing New or Open from the File menu.

# Getting Started

In the startup screen's dialog box are five options you can choose from to begin creating your presentation. There is also a check box, "Don't display this startup screen again." This requires a reinstallation of the program to re-enable the start-up screen.

## The Presentation Wizard

*Figure 84.2.*
*The Presentation Wizard*
*dialog box.*

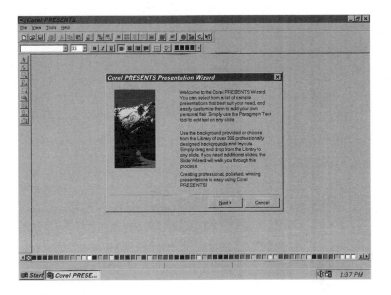

Selecting the Presentation Wizard opens a dialog box that enables you to proceed or cancel the operation.

Using the Next button enables you to proceed to the following dialog box, where you have a choice of six types of presentations.

The six styles listed in this dialog box (see Figure 84.3) are a good starting place for many different kinds of presentations:

- **Financial** opens with 10 slides with a beveled, graduated purple background.
- **General** opens with 10 slides with a graduated blue background featuring the scales of justice.
- **New Product** opens with 15 slides with a graduated blue background featuring a keyboard-like graphic element.
- **Sales** opens with eight slides with a graduated purple background featuring gears.

- **Status Report** opens with eight slides featuring a gray background with a gold-and-red line.
- **Training** opens with six slides featuring a graduated gray background with three white lines.

Figure 84.3.
*The Presentation Wizard's second dialog box.*

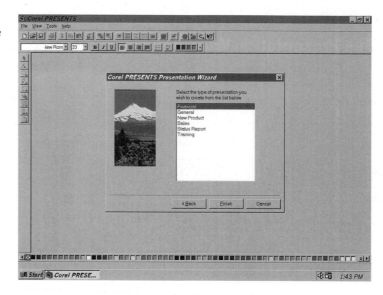

## Templates

If your choice from the startup dialog box, Figure 84.4, is Templates, the Template dialog box gives you the choice of 52 different templates, arranged in five categories:

- High Tech—13 preset backgrounds
- Business—nine preset backgrounds
- Finance—12 preset backgrounds
- Science—11 preset backgrounds
- Funky—seven preset backgrounds

*Figure 84.4.*
*The Template dialog box.*

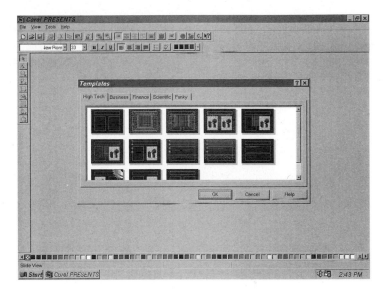

*Figure 84.4.*
*The Template dialog box.*

## Starting a Blank Presentation

This screen view is the starting point for all new presentations and uses the current default setup.

The last two choices in the startup dialog box—Open an existing presentation and Open the last presentation used—do exactly what they say they do.

## The Menu Bar

If you choose to close the startup dialog box, your next stop must be the *menu bar*. You use the menu bar to start a new presentation or open an existing one.

The menu bar layout (see Figure 84.5) responds to the presentation status of Corel PRESENTS. Without a presentation opened or under construction the menu bar view has four menu choices: File, View, Tools, and Help.

Figure 84.5.
The menu bar.

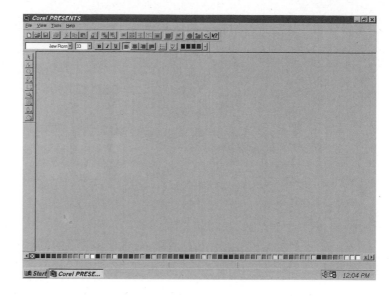

## File

Choosing File opens a drop-down menu with 12 selections and a list of the last presentations opened (maximum of four), which are detailed in the following section:

## New

Selecting New produces a flyout menu with three choices: Document, Templates, and Wizards. The last two open the same dialog boxes covered in the "Startup Screen" section of this chapter. Any item selected, in this flyout, starts a new presentation, and the menu bar changes from four items to 10 items, as you can see in Figure 84.6.

Selecting File from the extended menu bar produces the same drop-down menu with all but two, Save and Save All, of the items available. After using Save As, the remaining two items become active.

Selecting Import opens a comprehensive dialog box. (See Figure 84.7.)

There are 74 import filters listed in the dialog box. Three radio buttons control the placement of the imported item to the current slide, to new slides, or to the background. All other functions in this dialog box operate in standard Windows 95 fashion.

The Send option opens a dialog box titled Choose Profile. This selection is part of the Microsoft Exchange Windows 95 conventions.(See Figure 84.8.)

Figure 84.6.
The extended menu bar.

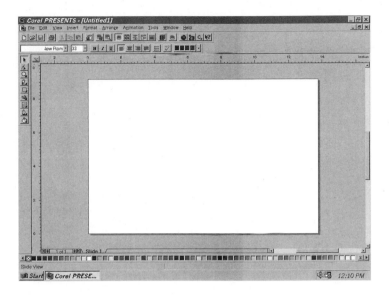

Figure 84.7.
The Import dialog box.

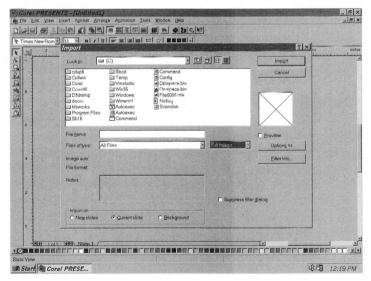

Selecting Print opens a dialog box that is almost identical to the one used in CorelDRAW. The features and functions perform in nearly identical manners. In the lower left you select from four types of output: Slides, Notes, Handouts, and Outline. The Include backgrounds check box can be toggled on and off.

Clicking the Options button opens the Print Options dialog box. Again, this dialog box is nearly identical to the one in CorelDRAW.

Figure 84.8.
The Send dialog box.

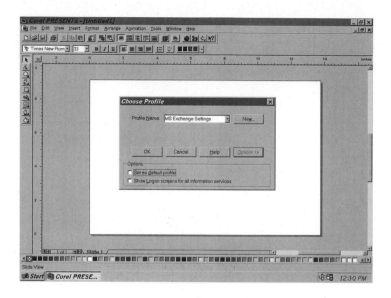

The features and functions also perform in nearly identical ways. In Corel PRE-SENTS, a function that is not expected to be used in a presentation program, Separations, has been removed.

## Page Setup

Selecting Page Setup opens a dialog box that is used to control the size and margins as well as the view of the page. All functions of this dialog box work in a typical Windows 95 fashion. One area that might lead to confusion is the selection box for paper type. Corel PRESENTS refers to all layouts as slides. Regardless of the final output style, you have a Slide View and Slide Sorter View. In the Page Setup dialog box, the "slide" available for selection is a specific shape and size of page. Slide is meant to be used for presentations that will be sent to a film re-corder or service bureau.

# Corel*NOTE!*

In the version of Corel PRESENTS, several betas through the first customer release tested, the Page Setup dialog box selections (shown in Figure 84.9) and the Slide View did not correspond in shape and size. The rulers in the slide view indicate a shape and size different from that selected in the Page Setup dialog box. Changing the paper type selection after text has been entered can result in the loss of text near margins. Page Setup and the Options selection in the Print dialog box do not correspond in shape, size, or margins. This did not seem to adversely affect output of pages or overheads to a laser printer. The size/shape mismatch effect could not be tested on a film recorder at the time this was written, due to the lack of drivers for the test film recorder.

*Figure 84.9.*
*The Page Setup*
*dialog box.*

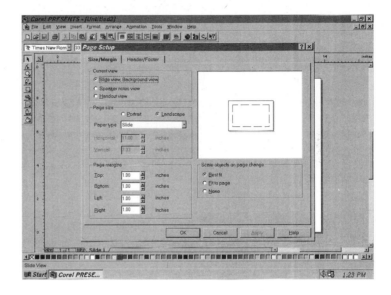

## Run Presentation

The Run Presentation selection is covered in Skill Session 87, "Presentations, Timelines, and Self-Running Presentations."

### Edit

The Edit drop-down menu is very straightforward in following Windows 95 conventions. The items in this drop-down that are unique to Corel PRESENTS are Background, Go To, and Properties.

Selecting Background produces a flyout with seven choices: Blank, Uniform Fill, Fountain Fill, Two-color Bitmap, Full-color Bitmap, Texture Fill, and Vector Pattern.

This Background tool is under the Edit menu; its effect applies to one slide at a time.

Selecting Blank returns the slide background to white.

The remaining selections on the Background flyout function identically to their counterparts in CorelDRAW.

The Go To flyout has three choices: Slide, Handout, and Speaker Note. This enables you to select the view and slide feature you want to alter.

The Properties item is useful during the creation of a runtime or animated presentation. This selection is covered in Skill Session 87.

## View

Selecting View from the extended toolbar produces a drop-down menu with 17 items. These choices alter the screen in which you are working or make changes to the overall view of the work area.

The first choice, Slide, is the default when Corel PRESENTS starts. Slide Sorter is a convenient way to view many slides in your presentation and to move quickly to a specific slide. Outline and slide views are where most of your work is accomplished while entering the data for a presentation.

## Master Layout

Selecting Master Layout produces a flyout with four items: Title Slide Master, Slide Master, Handout, and Speaker Notes.

Title Slide Master and Slide Master set up all text attributes and placement of text on slides in a presentation. There is an exception, however: If a presentation is started by using a Wizard, these selections only affect new slides added to the presentation. The last two items enable changes to the layout and the overall look of handouts and speaker notes.

## Background

Choosing Background brings up the background view. Any graphic element added here, such as a logo, will appear in all slides of the presentation.

## Speaker Notes

Selecting Speaker Notes brings up the Speaker Notes view. This view shows a thumbnail of the slide and an area where you can type in notes about this slide.

## Handouts

Choosing Handouts brings up the Handouts view, enabling you to type the notes alongside a miniature view of the slide. You can set the Print command to print this combination for your audience.

## Animation

Animation is covered in Skill Session 86, "Adding Video, Sound, and Animation and Working with Timelines."

## Object Manager and Timeline

The next two choices, Background Library and Layout Library, open the same dialog box. The dialog box has two tabs, Background and Layout. (See Figure 84.10.) In both cases, the default selection is the background layer.

*Figure 84.10.*
*The Background and*
*Layout Library dialog box.*

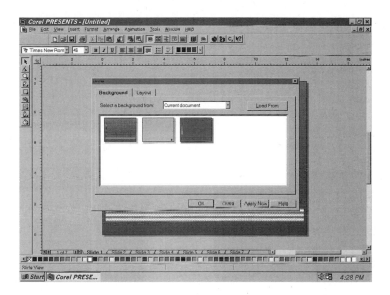

This dialog box enables you to select a background from the current presentation or from other background groups, or backgrounds loaded from different drives. The default backgrounds are from the current show. During the initial installation, five other libraries are loaded and are listed in numbered groups (the numbers indicate the number of background choices in the group). They are group01.cpb(16), group02.cpb(22), group03.cpb(20), group10.cpb(22), and group15.cpb(19). In addition, on the CorelDRAW CD-ROM number 2 in the Presents folder is another folder, called Slidebgd, where 10 new background groups are located. These 10 groups contain 205 more backgrounds of various styles, colors, and treatments.

Selecting the Layout tab enables layout choices via a radio button from the Current Presentation as well as the Preset Library. Opening the Library shows 25 different thumbnails with various styles of slide designs.

# Memo

The next item on the View drop-down menu is the Memo flyout. This flyout, with eight choices, gives you control over the memos you create under the Insert drop-down menu. You can attach these memos to various slides.

Take a look at the Memo flyout. The functions are self-explanatory; they do just what the name implies.

A similar feature is also used in CorelDRAW.

The last section of the View drop-down menu has four items: Toolbars, Status Bar, Rulers, and Color Palette. Essentially, these are identical to those found in CorelDRAW and work in the same manner.

The exceptions are the toolbars and color palette choices.

Selecting Toolbars opens the dialog box shown in Figure 84.11. Color Palette is a simple toggle on and off in Corel PRESENTS, without the selection of different color models found in CorelDRAW.

*Figure 84.11.*
*The Toolbars dialog box.*

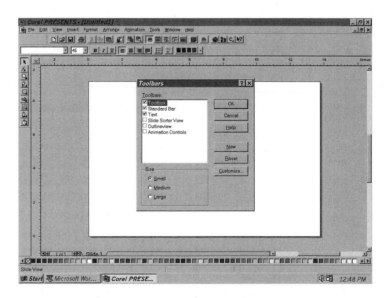

The Toolbars dialog box has six listed items and three radio buttons, along with two additional buttons: New and Customize. New and Customize open additional dialog boxes that enable the user to set up Corel PRESENTS to match his or her working style. Most of these features are covered in the CorelDRAW skill sessions. The biggest difference between the two programs is the exclusion of many specialized Corel DRAW features from Corel PRESENTS. Only three of the listed items (Slide Sorter View, Outline View, and Animation Controls) are completely new to these dialog boxes.

The choices available in this dialog boxes enable you to select which tools and buttons will be visible (that is, which ones you want to use) during slide-show creation. Turning everything on and to the large size makes for a very small work area, so you should experiment with the settings to find a compromise that works for you. (Those readers with 21-inch monitors can disregard that last statement.)

## Insert

The next item on the extended menu bar is Insert. The Insert drop-down menu contains nine items: Insert Slide, Delete Slide, Background, Memo, Sound, Video, New Object, Chart, and Map.

Selecting Insert Slide opens the Insert Slide Wizard. The first dialog box in this wizard wants to know how many slides and their placement (either before or after the current slide). "One slide and after" (the current slide) is the default insert setting.

*Figure 84.12.*
*The Insert Slide Wizard.*

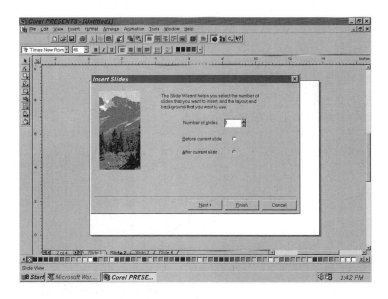

The second dialog box in this wizard is the Layout dialog box; the third is the Background dialog box. They function as expected. Selecting Finish produces the number of slides indicated in the styles chosen.

# Corel*NOTE!*

> As a performance note, the Background feature from this Wizard does not function in the same way as it does when applied from the Edit or View menu. Applied by the Insert Slide Wizard, the background is slightly too tall and slightly too narrow to fill the selected size for the background. This occurs every time and with all page size selections. It works as expected everywhere but here.

## Delete Slide and Background

Delete Slide deletes the selected slide. Selecting this background flyout opens the same flyout discussed under the Edit section of the extended menu bar.

## Memo

Selecting Memo opens the CorelMEMO dialog box (see Figure 84.13.), which enables the creation of memos. You use memos for comments or correction areas when sharing the creation of the presentation with multiple authors or more than one administrator if an approval process of the presentation is neccessary.

*Figure 84.13.*
*The CorelMEMO*
*dialog box.*

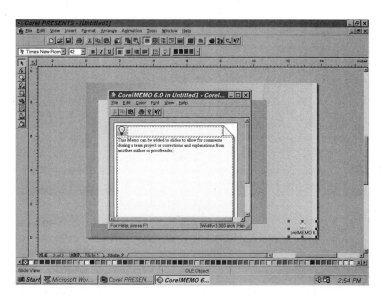

Sound and video are covered in Skill Session 86.

# New Object

Selecting New Object opens the New Object dialog box, which is similar to the Import dialog box invoked through the File menu, but does not offer as many import filters. (See Figure 84.14.)

*Figure 84.14.*
*The Insert New Object*
*dialog box.*

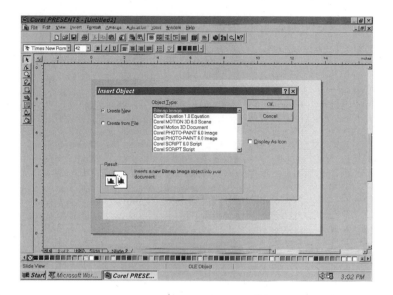

In addition, this dialog box has two radio buttons. The first, Create New, actually launches a program to create this new object. For example, if you select Bitmap Image, it will start Microsoft Paint to create the bitmap. This new object is an OLE object; double-clicking it opens the program used to create the object.

# Chart

Selecting Chart opens a dialog box that presents 22 choices with up to seven variations each, enabling you to create a chart of almost any type. (See Figure 84.15.)

This is also a link to an OLE client program. After you select a chart type, CorelCHART runs so it can create the chart to place into Corel PRESENTS. Return to Corel PRESENTS by double-clicking in an open area of the slide. If you close CorelCHART (or other OLE client) on completion of adding or editing an object, it also closes Corel PRESENTS.

See Skill Session 85, "Corel PRESENTS," for a more thorough explanation of the features and tools of CorelCHART.

Figure 84.15.
The Chart Type
dialog box.

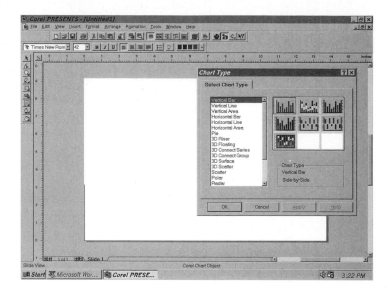

## Map

Selecting Map opens a dialog box that presents 14 choices of different geographic locations and enables you to create a map area in your slide. (See Figure 84.16.)

Figure 84.16.
The Map Wizard.

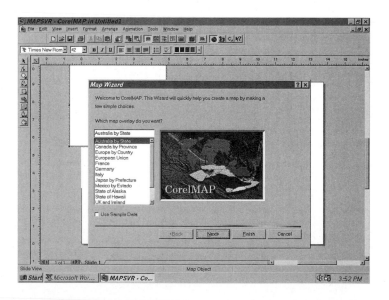

There is a limited number of maps to chose from; for example, the only individual U.S. states are Alaska and Hawaii. Although you can show just Australia, you can't select just Spain. No provisions were made for African or South American countries or land masses. Again this is a link to an OLE client program. After you select a map type, CorelMAP runs so it can create the map to place into Corel PRESENTS. Return to Corel PRESENTS by double-clicking in an open area of the slide. If you close CorelMAP (or other OLE client) on completion of adding or editing an object, it also closes Corel PRESENTS.

## Format

The Format drop-down menu has 10 items: Character, Change Case, Bullet Style, Fit Text To Path, Separate Text From Path, Straighten Text, Grid Setup, Guideline Setup, Snap To Grid, and Snap To Guidelines.

## Character

After either Artistic or Paragraph text has been entered on a slide, selecting Character opens a two-tabbed dialog box identical in functions and features to CorelDRAW. (See Figure 84.17.)

*Figure 84.17.*
*The Character Attributes*
*dialog box.*

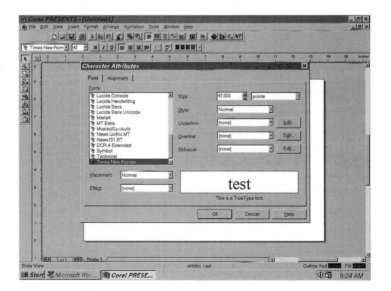

## Change Case

You can only change the case of text after it has been entered. Clicking Change Case in the Format menu, after selecting text, opens the Change Case dialog box. (See Figure 84.18.)

Figure 84.18.
The Change Case
dialog box.

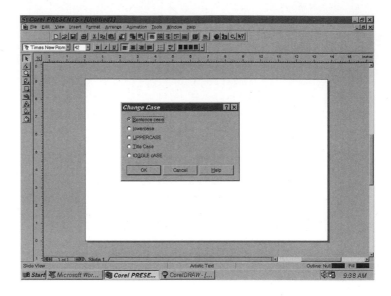

The dialog box has five radio buttons: Sentence case, lowercase, UPPERCASE, Title Case, and tOGGLE cASE.

They perform just as you would expect; but the Title Case radio button, although fairly self-explanatory, might be misnamed. It improves readability to use upper-case first letters in concise bullet items as well as titles. The Change Case feature, normally found in word-processing programs, is a nice addition to a presentation and drawing program.

## Bullet Style

In this dialog box (see Figure 84.19), there are 10 symbol file selections from which you can choose your bullet style, as well as a point-size spinner to select the size of the bullet. Use the Text tool to select the existing bullet; then select your new bullet choice from the grid, change the point size (if necessary), and click OK.

This menu item is used to select the style of bullets during changes to the Master Layout, which is found under the View menu. You can also use it to alter the size and style of bullets in slides made from templates or master layouts with bullets. You cannot use it to add bullet points to a new, blank slide.

Fit Text To Path, Separate Text From Path, and Straighten Text are the next three choices on the Format drop-down menu.

*Figure 84.19.*
*The Bullet Style*
*dialog box.*

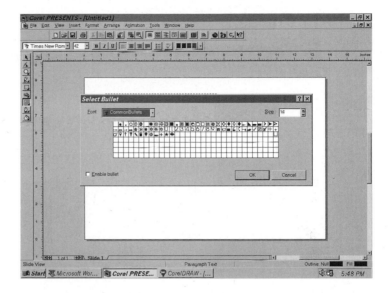

*Figure 84.20.*
*The Fit Text dialog box.*

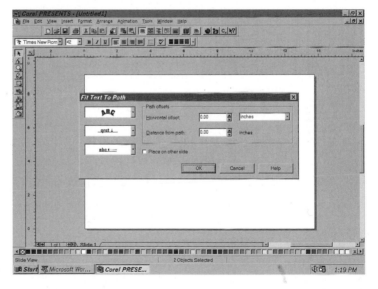

This is another dialog box out of CorelDRAW. All functions and features are the same. The two commands, Straighten Text and Separate Text From Path, that follow Fit Text To Path are applied to the text without confirmation and enable you to either return the text to its original appearance or move it away from the path, which can then be deleted, or allow for separation from another design element.

845

## Grid Setup

Why the menu item in Corel PRESENTS only mentions the grid, I'll never know. This is where you set up both the grid and the ruler. This works the same way as in CorelDRAW. (See Figure 84.21.)

*Figure 84.21.*
*The Grid and Ruler Setup*
*dialog box.*

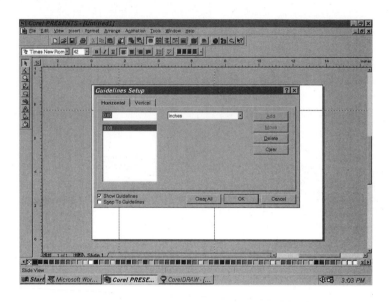

## Guidelines Setup

This is one area where the new Corel PRESENTS is at odds with its own instructions and in comparison to CorelDRAW. (See Figure 84.22.)

Based on the help file, guidelines are supposed to act just like those in CorelDRAW. "Not now" is the best comment I can make on the current functionality. PRESENTS doesn't support slanted guidelines, and the positions of the guideline are reported incorrectly. As it stands now, guidelines can be used only for placement and alignment. The Snap to Grid and Snap to Guidelines features, however, currently work as they do in CorelDRAW.

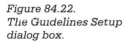

*Figure 84.22.*
*The Guidelines Setup*
*dialog box.*

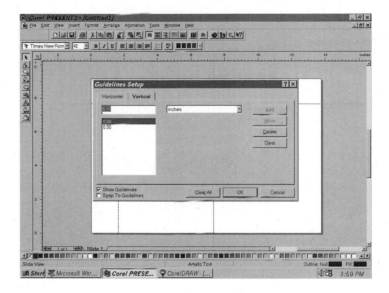

# Arrange

This drop-down menu with 10 items is usually one of the most-used sections for embellishments to spruce up any presentation. The items are To Front, To Back, Forward One, Backward One, Group, Ungroup, Combine, Break Apart, Convert To Curves, and Fit Object To Slide.

All but one of the menu items are found in, and function the same as in, CorelDRAW. The new item is Fit Object To Slide. Selecting an object or Artistic text and choosing this option changes the size and shape of the object to fill the page size from border to border.

## Animation

This drop-down menu is covered in Skill Session 86.

# Tools

The five-item Tools drop-down menu has three choices you might expect to find in your word processor. Although they have been added to CorelDRAW, where they reside in the Text menu, they are much more important to a text-intensive presentation program like Corel PRESENTS.

Selecting Proof-Reading triggers a flyout with four options: Spelling, Quick Proof Read, Full Proof Read, and Advanced Options. These are covered in Skill Session 85.

The last two items, Customize and Options, are similar to CorelDRAW, but with a few changes.

## Customize

This four-tabbed dialog box is similar in design and identical in function to the one in CorelDRAW and is covered in Skill Session 4, "Customizing and Setting Preferences." The major differences are reflected in the missing Roll-ups tab (not used in Corel PRESENTS) and in the choices of items such as Animation (not used in CorelDRAW). You will have to work in the program for a while to find if your style will require any customizing from the default setup.

## Options

This dialog box (see Figure 84.23) is unique to Corel PRESENTS. It is used during animation and presentations. (Refer to Skill Session 86.)

*Figure 84.23.*
*The Options dialog box.*

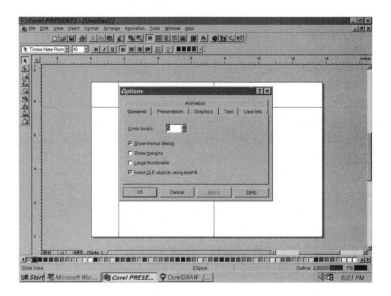

The last two menu items, Windows and Help, are standard to all Windows 95 applications.

## Toolbars

The upper toolbar that is the default when you start Corel PRESENTS contains many items that are standard to Windows 95 and CorelDRAW. Starting with the ninth button from the left, the buttons are unique to Corel PRESENTS. (See Figure 84.24.)

*Figure 84.24.*
*The default toolbar.*

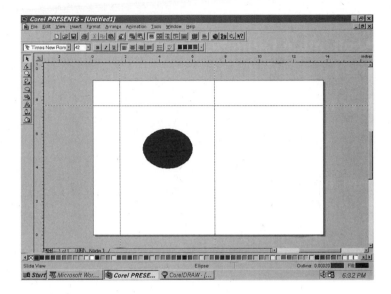

## Run Presentation and Preview

The ninth button on the bar starts a finished presentation in a playback mode, one slide at a time, according to the sequence and timeline you have defined. The right-hand button in this pair is the Preview slide button. The user can return to the presentation creation/edit mode by pressing the Esc key.

## Presentation Views

The next five buttons—Slide View, Slide Sorter View, Outline View, Master Layout, and Background View—are described in detail in Skill Session 85.

## Timelines

Opens a dialog box used for adjusting the display times of slides in a presentation.

## Libraries

Displays the dialog box you use to select backgrounds and layouts for the presentation.

## Insert Buttons

Inserts additional slides within a presentation or new objects into slides. From left to right, these buttons are Add a Slide(s), Maps, Charts, and Motion 3D Animation.

## Application Launcher

Launches any one of 10 different programs from the CorelDRAW package.

## Text Toolbar

The Text toolbar is a familiar feature to many Windows 95 applications. Because it isn't found in CorelDRAW, it needs some explanation for the first-time user.

## Font Type and Size

The left window of this pair identifies the font. The right identifies the font size in points.

## Font Style

The left button toggles bold on and off. The middle button makes text italic, and the last button underlines text.

## Justification

Left to right, these buttons are left, center, right, and full justification.

## Bullet Style

Toggles the default bullet style on and off.

## Spell Check

Runs the spell checker.

## Color

Produces a 100-color, drop-down menu and provides access to the full Color Palette dialog boxes. This selection also displays the last four colors chosen. The four 3D color wells store the last four colors used in the program can also be used to select fill colors for text and non-text items.

# Corel*NOTE!*

> Keep in mind that by using the Customize selection in the Tools drop-down menu you can alter the toolbars to fit your particular style of working.

## Toolbox

This feature and the power of the tools, common to both DRAW and PRESENTS, are a major part of what sets Corel PRESENTS apart from other presentation packages. This toolbox is covered in detail in Skill Sessions 6 through 16.

New to the common user interface is the sixth button, which invokes the Shapes flyout. This flyout offers 24 different two- and three-dimensional objects. The buttons show a representation of the shape to be pasted into the slide.

## Color Palette

The on-screen color palette gives you quick scrolling access to 100 different colors.

A left-click on a color applies a fill color to the selected object and a right-click changes the outline color. The small up arrow on the right side displays all of the colors at once.

## Configurable Status Bar

Using the right mouse button, click this area to define display attributes. This opens the status bar.

You can display information about the object details by changing the size and location, or by defining the number of regions of the status bar.

This skill session has provided a basic introduction to Corel PRESENTS for a new user. Remember, many features in Corel PRESENTS are either part of the common user interface of the CorelDRAW suite of applications or are part of the standard conventions of Windows 95. Features that are covered in previous Skill Sessions or that are common to all Windows 95 programs have not been reviewed in detail.

# 85

# Corel
# PRESENTS

The best way to learn a new presentation program is simply by doing a sample presentation from scratch. In this skill session that is what you will do, step by step. As you do these exercises, please save them to disk; they will be used in later skill sessions.

The first step in creating a presentation with Corel PRESENTS is to choose how to start. You can use the Wizard, the Templates, or Document. To start this skill session, select File | New from the menu bar. From the flyout choose Document. This opens a blank slide to begin the presentation.

## Page Setup

Next, select Page Setup from the File drop-down menu. This will open the Page Setup dialog box shown in Figure 85.1.

Select the tab marked Size/Margin. In the Current view box click Slide view, Background view. In the Page size box chose Landscape with a Paper type of Slide. Note that the size defaults to 11.00 horizontal by 7.33 vertical. Under Page margins set all four margins to 0.25 inches. In the Scale objects on page change select Best fit. No changes will be made using the Header/Footer tab. Click OK to make the changes to your presentation.

Figure 85.1.
The Page Setup
dialog box.

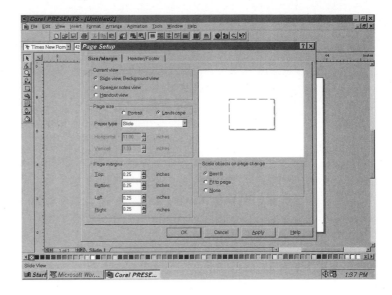

## Custom Background

The next step adds a custom background to the presentation.

Following the instructional text will take you into CorelDRAW for a portion of this skill session. Although it should be possible to make custom backgrounds from within Corel PRESENTS, this appears to be nonfunctional in the tested version.

You can launch CorelDRAW from within Corel PRESENTS, but the viability of this depends on your CPU type and RAM. You might find better results by closing PRESENTS before you run CorelDRAW. With a 486 CPU and 16 MB of RAM, the following steps work quite well.

From the toolbar, click the Application Launcher (the stylized red C), then from the drop-down menu select CorelDRAW.

In CorelDRAW select Layout from the menu bar and click Page Setup. Use the same page setup that is set in Corel PRESENTS.

From the toolbox on the left side of the screen choose the Rectangle tool. Align the crosshairs just outside a corner of the page border, hold the left mouse button down and move diagonally to just outside the opposite corner. Release the mouse button. The rectangle you have just created will fill with the default color selection.

Click the Pick tool and the rectangle you just created will be selected. Click the Fill tool and from the flyout select the Fountain Fill. In the Fountain Fill dialog box you will make several changes to the default settings. In the Options box enter -90.0 in the Angle spinner box. Note that the gradation indicator now shows a black to white vertical graduation. Within the Color blend box select the Custom radio button. In the Color selection window choose the blue that is the second item in the second row. In the Position: window enter a value of 50. In the Color window select black, the first item in the first row. Now click the small white box near the upper-right corner of the horizontal gradation display. Again, in the Color selection window choose the blue that is the second item in the second row. Click OK to return to the page view.

From the left side ruler and the top ruler, click and pull out guidelines and place them approximately one-quarter inch in from all margins. Your screen should now look like Figure 85.2.

*Figure 85.2.*
*The background screen*
*view.*

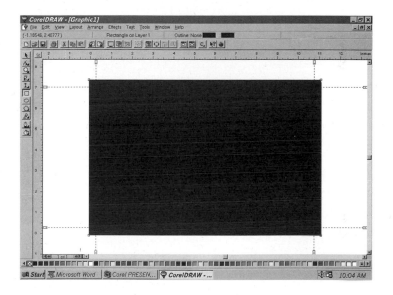

This is only half of the custom background. To finish, on the menu bar use the Layout drop-down box to toggle on Snap to Guidelines. From the toolbox on the left side of the screen choose the Rectangle tool. Align the crosshairs on the guideline intersection at one corner. Hold the left mouse button down and move diagonally to an opposite corner guideline; release the mouse button. The rectangle you have just created will fill with the default color selection. Select the Pick tool now and the rectangle you just created will be selected. Click the Fill tool and from the flyout select the Fountain Fill. Here you will make two changes to the default settings. In the Options box enter -90.0 in the Angle spinner box. Within the Color blend box click the white button to the right of the word To. From this drop-down color slider, choose the blue color that is the second item in the third row. Click OK to return to the page view.

Take a moment now to save your work. Choose the name Graphic1 to match the Skill Session as it progresses.

From the menu bar select the Layout drop-down menu and choose Guideline Setup. At the bottom of the Guideline Setup dialog box click the Clear All button and then OK.

If you look closely now that the guidelines have been removed, you might find the two rectangles have an outline. Some people might prefer to leave them, but in this example the Outline tool is selected and the No Outline button is chosen.

You must now export the graphic so that it can be used in Corel PRESENTS. From the menu bar choose File and then Export. The Export dialog box opens, as shown in Figure 85.3.

*Figure 85.3.*
*The CorelDRAW Export*
*dialog box.*

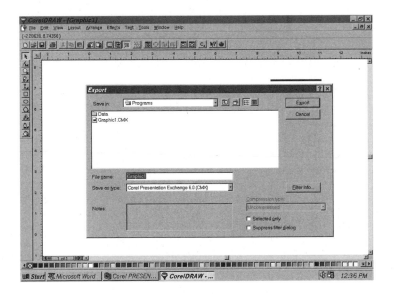

Use Corel Presentation Exchange 6.0 (CMX) as the export filter. Enter the name Graphic1. After you export the graphic, close CorelDRAW.

If you launched CorelDRAW from Corel PRESENTS, you are now back in PRE-SENTS. If you are not in Corel PRESENTS, go ahead and start it. From the menu bar, select File | New and then from the flyout choose Document. Reset the page setup as discussed previously in this skill session.

Select Edit from the menu bar and then open the Background flyout. Choose Vector Patterns to open the Vector Pattern dialog box shown in Figure 85.4.

*Figure 85.4.*
*The Vector Pattern*
*dialog box.*

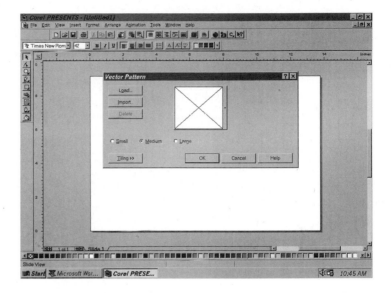

In the upper-left corner of the dialog box select Import to open the Import dialog box, which is covered in Skill Session 48, "Import Filters." In Files of type use Corel Presentation Exchange 6.0 (CMX) as the import filter. Select the file (Graphic1.CMX) and then click the Import button, and the program will return to the Vector Pattern dialog box. Of the three radio buttons choose Large. Click the Tiling>> button. See Figure 85.5.

*Figure 85.5.*
*The extended Vector*
*Pattern dialog box.*

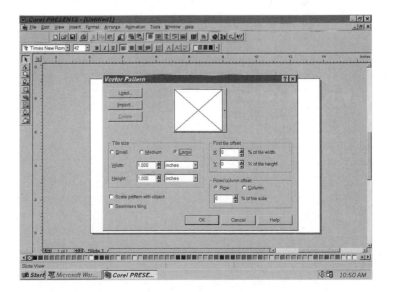

The dialog box opens further and on the lower left you will find two check boxes. Click Scale pattern with object, and then Click OK.

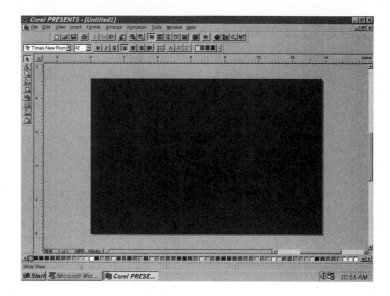

*Figure 85.6.*
*The Slide view with custom background.*

The background is a very simple design that will enhance a presentation that is to be imaged as an actual 35mm slide show or viewed directly from a computer monitor. The rich, deep colors will work well in a properly lit (very dim to no lights) room. As we add text, the color choices will also reflect this design. If, however, your presentation will utilize color overhead transparencies or will be a projected computer show, you should choose lighter variations with white or light colored text; otherwise, the readability will suffer.

## Layout Masters

From the View drop-down list on the menu bar select Master Layout and from the flyout select Title Slide Master. A title slide template replaces the slide view. Use the Pick tool to select the upper box (Title text). For this example choose Arial, 48 points, and bold from the Text toolbar. From the Fill Color selector on the Text toolbar, choose yellow for the text color. Select the lower box (Body text). Here, choose Arial, 42 points, and bold from the Text toolbar. From the Fill Color selector on the text toolbar, select light blue for the text color. From the menu bar select the View drop-down and click Slide.

From the View drop-down list on the menu bar, select Layout Library. Select the layout tab and click the Preset library radio button. This will give you a choice of 25 slide layouts; choose the first one for a title slide. Click OK. (See Figure 85.7.)

*Figure 85.7.*
*The Layout Library*
*dialog box.*

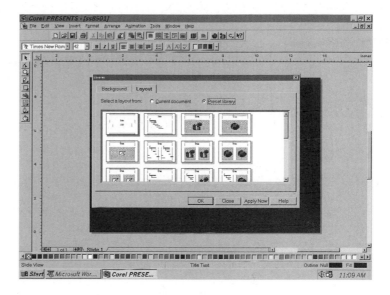

The formatting in Master layout now applies to this title slide template from the Layout library. From the toolbox select Paragraph text. In the Title text box, type Slide Show Etiquette and in the Body text box type your name. You should now have a screen that looks something like Figure 85.8.

*Figure 85.8.*
*The Title Screen view.*

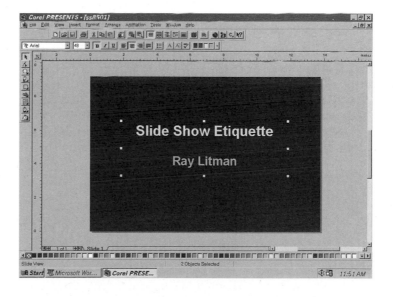

From the View drop-down list on the menu bar select Master Layout and from the flyout select Slide Master. A master slide template replaces the slide view. Use the

Pick tool to select the Title text box. Again, with this upper box selected choose Arial, 48 points, and bold from the text toolbar. From the Fill Color selector choose yellow for the text color. Select the Body text box and Arial at 30 points. From the Fill Color selector, keep the text color consistent by choosing light blue.

In a more mature version of a presentation program, I would expect that from this screen, the color, size, and style of each bullet level would also be controllable. Currently, that is not the case in this version of Corel PRESENTS.

## Inserting a Slide

From the menu bar select the View drop-down list and click Slide. You have now returned to Slide view. From the menu bar select Insert and from the drop-down list select Slide. This opens the Insert Slide Wizard. The default settings, One slide and After the current slide, are fine. Click the Next button. In this dialog box, select the Preset library and the Bullet template by clicking them. Click the Finish button to return to the slide view. From the toolbox click Paragraph text and select the title text box. Enter the following text: `Bullet Do's & Don'ts`. Select the bullet area and enter the following text: `Simple`. Press Enter to go to the next line. Type `Concise` and press Enter. Type `First Letter Caps` and press Enter. Type `No Ending Punctuation`, press Enter, and then press Tab once. Type `Except ? or !` and press Enter. Type `Best Readability` and press Enter and the Tab key once. Type `7 Lines Or Less` and press Enter. Press Tab once and type `7 Words Or Less`.

The rules of thumb you just typed can and will be broken in many of your presentations. The closer you stick to them the better you will communicate your ideas to your audience.

For added emphasis, change the color of the bullets. To do this, use the Pick tool to select the bullet text area. Select the Paragraph text tool and block the first diamond bullet only. Click yellow on the text color bar, and repeat this action with the four remaining diamond bullets. Follow the same procedure and use magenta on the second-level round bullets. Select a third color and apply it to the third-level star.

From the menu bar insert a third and fourth slide. Change the Number of slides spinner to two. Click Next. Choose the blank template and click Finish. On the third slide you will enter Paragraph text and then edit it. Type `The size of your words seldom matters to the weight of your message.`. From the toolbox select the Pick tool. In order to see your text clearly, change the color to yellow from the text toolbar. Change the font to Arial, the point size to 48, and the style to bold. Use center justification and with the Pick tool, place the text block just above center. (See Figure 85.9.)

*Figure 85.9.*
*The third slide screen*
*view.*

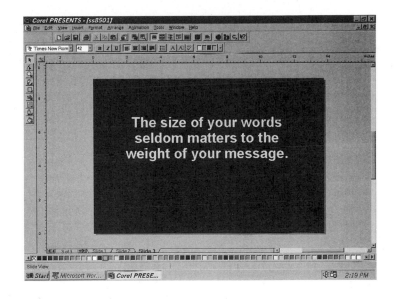

## Go To Slide

Rather than using the tabbed bar just below the Slide view, go to slide four by using the Edit drop-down menu and clicking Go To. Select Slide from the flyout. In the Goto Slide dialog box click Slide 4 and then OK. In a presentation with many slides, this is quicker than using the slide tabs below the slide view.

From the toolbar select the outline view. (See Figure 85.10.)

*Figure 85.10.*
*The outline view*
*of Slides 1–4.*

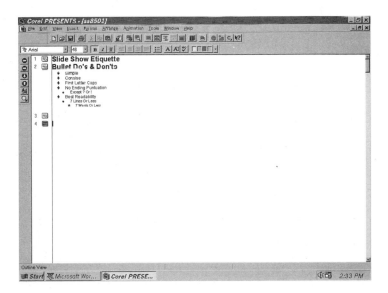

Notice in Slide 3 of the outline view, Artistic text does not register. Next to the Slide 4 icon enter Never Use Prestidigitation When Simple Magic Will Do. Using the Slide view icon on the toolbar, return to the slide view. Slides entered in the outline view might not show the entire text when viewed in slide view. Use the Pick tool and grab the center handle on the bottom of the Paragraph text box. Pull down until all text can be viewed.

## Adding Graphics

From the menu bar use Insert to add a single slide using the blank template. Slides are like billboards—keep them simple and to the point. Reading too much distracts the audience. They might miss a vital clue that can wreck your presentation. Slide five will be utilized to illustrate that point. Under File, choose Import. Select the Files of type: filter Corel Presentation Exchange 6.0 (CMX). In the clip-art folder on the Corel CD-ROM disk 4 is a folder titled Transpor. In the Transpor folder is a folder called Personal; in that folder is the file Crsh1.cmx. Import this file.

Use the Pick tool and place the clip art in the lower-right corner of the slide. From the toolbox, select the Rectangle tool and in the upper-left form a rectangle a little more than one inch high by six inches. Fill it with a light background color and use artistic text to enter Keep It Simple. The text attributes used are Arial, 42 points, and bold. Select a contrasting color for this text. Using the Artistic Text tool type Distractions Are Dangerous and place this text on the left side just below center. The text attributes used are Times New Roman, 48 points, bold and yellow. Your slide should look something like Figure 85.11.

*Figure 85.11.*
*The Dangerous Distrac-*
*tions slide view.*

## Adding Charts

From the menu bar, select Insert to add a single slide using the blank template. From the toolbar, select the Library icon. From the Library dialog box, click the Layout tab. Click the Preset library radio button. Select the third chart template and click OK. (See Figure 85.12.)

*Figure 85.12.*
*Double-click to start*
*CorelCHART.*

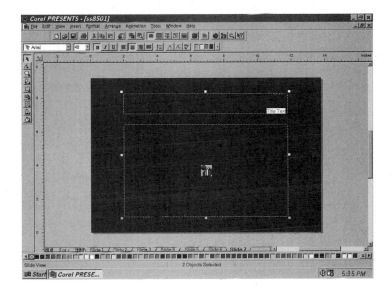

This section was meant to be an in-depth example of the power of CorelCHART. The example is a vertical bar chart rating typical audience distractions. Prior to deadline, a fully functional CorelCHART was not available. What follows is a best guess of the way CorelCHART should work.

Double-click the CorelCHART icon in the middle of Slide 6. This opens the Chart Type dialog box, shown in Figure 85.13. From here a choice of 22 different graph types with up to seven styles each is available.

Choose Vertical Bar and click OK. This opens an OLE link to the CorelCHART program, as seen in Figure 85.14.

From the menu bar use the Chart drop-down list to open the Data dialog box. Click cell A2 and type Taking Notes. Click on cell A3 and type Reading Handouts. In cells A4 and A5 enter Sales Literature and Presenter's Survey, respectively. Starting with cell B2 through cell B5 enter the values 10, 20, 30, and 35. These are the relative values of distractions. Delete the numerical values in columns C, D, and E. The Data dialog box should look like Figure 85.15.

*Figure 85.13.*
*The Chart Type*
*dialog box.*

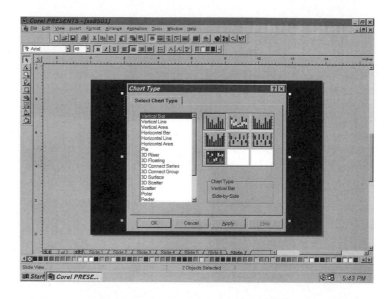

*Figure 85.14.*
*The CorelCHART main*
*screen.*

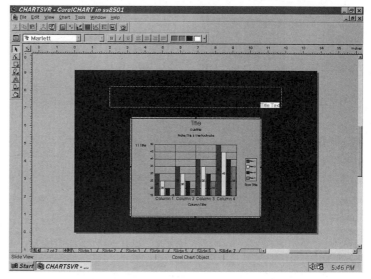

If CorelCHART displays an empty blue box instead of the chart, nothing will recover that error. You might also get a message warning that the program has performed an illegal action and will be shut down. The third result is a chart, as seen in Figure 85.15. The additional column markers should not show as they currently do.

This simple chart needs little in the way of explanation. To improve readability many small text items will be turned off or eliminated. From the Chart drop-down

list click Format. This opens the Format Chart dialog box. (See Figure 85.16.)
Choose the Titles tab and in the Chart Titles box leave Title, Subtitle, and Footnote
blank. In the Frame Titles box the Groups Title and Y1 Title can also be left blank.
All of the items are accompanied by a check box marked Display. Unchecking this
box is another quick way to hide these items. Click OK to return to the Chart view.
From the toolbar select Legend. This opens the Legend dialog box shown in
Figure 85.17. In the Legend Display box, uncheck Display Legend. Click OK.

*Figure 85.15.*
*The Chart Data entry*
*dialog box.*

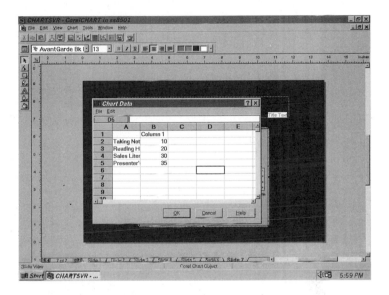

*Figure 85.16.*
*The Format Chart*
*dialog box.*

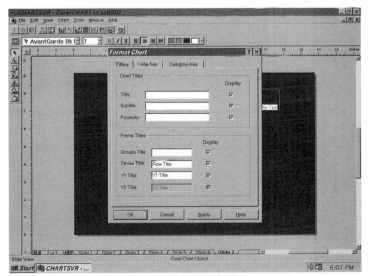

Figure 85.17.
The CorelCHART Legend
dialog box.

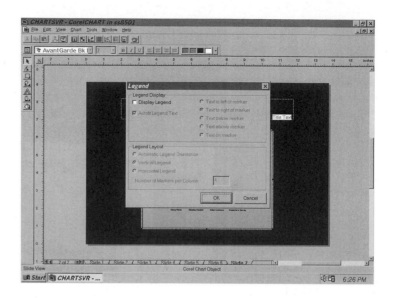

After the chart data is entered and the format is set, click in the blue area of the chart. A bonding box with handles is now available. Click a handle and expand the chart until it fills most of the area under the title. Now click the bar chart itself. A bounding box with handles will enable the chart area to be expanded until it fills the empty space of the chart. Double-clicking in the background area will return the chart to Corel PRESENTS. Enter `Audience Distractions` in the title box. The slide now looks like Figure 85.18.

Figure 85.18.
The finished CorelCHART-
based slide.

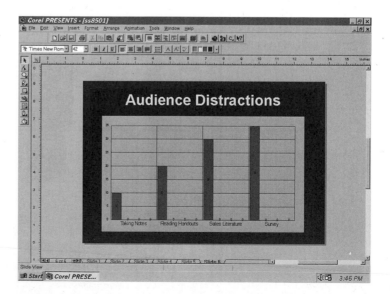

Some other features of CorelCHART that might be useful until a more stable version is ready are covered in the following paragraphs.

To change chart types, on the menu bar click Chart, and from the drop-down select Chart Type.

The Chart Type dialog box opens. The default chart type is Vertical Bar. Scroll down the Chart Type list box and click 3D Scatter. The styles of this chart type are displayed as thumbnails in the preview window. Choose Horizontal Bar and click OK. This applies the currently highlighted chart type and closes the dialog box.

Many presentations are made up of mostly data. One of the best ways to present data is in some form of a graph. You can use colors to call attention to one point or item, and the bar positions quickly demonstrate the relative merit of the data.

Click one of the bars to select all of them for that group and apply color using any of the fill functions.

There are some functions left unmentioned that will wait until CorelCHART is a better behaved OLE link to Corel PRESENTS.

## Adding a Slide from the Outline View

To add a slide from the Outline View, use the toolbar and select the Outline View icon. (See Figure 85.19.)

*Figure 85.19.*
*The Slide 7 outline view.*

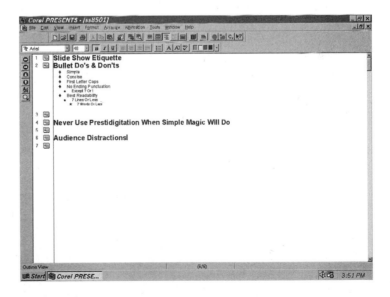

Select Insert from the menu bar and add another bullet slide. Although examples have taken you to this screen before, take a moment to become familiar with the outline view. The screen is like a sheet of paper, and there are some buttons on the left side specific to the outline view. Each slide in your presentation is represented by a number and an icon in the left margin of outline view. Double-clicking the Slide icon will quickly switch back to slide view mode. (See Figure 85.20.)

*Figure 85.20.*
*The outline toolbar view.*

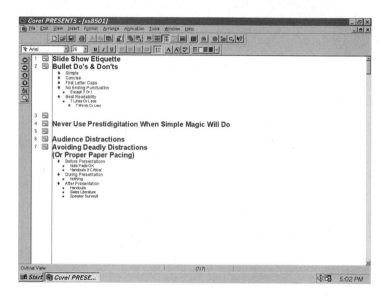

The only new screen feature in the Outline view is the toolbox on the left side of the screen. The six buttons in order are

> Promote
> Demote
> Move Down
> Move Up
> Show Formatting
> Zoom

The first four have two different functions each. When applied to text or bullet text, the effect they have is altered. Examples are given in the following text to show all of the toolbox functions.

To add text in outline view, position the cursor beside Slide 7. Type `Avoiding Deadly Distractions!`. Press the Shift and Enter keys at the same time. This moves the cursor to the next line. Next, type `Or Proper Paper Pacing`. To add a bullet after the title, press Ctrl and Enter at the same time. At the first bullet point type `Before Presentation`.

There are two ways to add a bullet item on a different level: use either the Tab key or the toolbox. Press Enter to add the next bullet. For the first time try the Tab key.

The bullet moves into the next level. Type Note Pads OK and press Enter. This adds the second bullet. Handouts If Critical is entered next. To move back to the previous bullet level try using the Promote button. Press Enter and select the Promote button with the mouse. The diamond-shaped bullet appears. Type During Presentation and press Enter. At this new bullet, use the mouse to select the Demote button and, just like when you used the Tab key, the bullet is indented and becomes a dot. Type Nothing and press Enter. To promote this bullet back to the upper level, press Shift and Tab at the same time. Now enter After Presentation. Use your choice of methods to demote the bullet from the next three lines. Type Handouts, Sales Literature, and Speaker Survey on the following lines.

The Promote and Demote buttons work as you would expect them to when it comes to bullets. They can also be applied to slides. Take a moment and save your presentation at this point. Click once on the Slide 7 icon. All items in Slide 7 are now blocked (selected). Click the Promote icon. Slide 7 is now spread across three additional slides. Be careful because pressing the Demote button now while they are all still selected transfers all the information to bullet points in Slide 6. To return to just bullets under the title and subtitle of Slide 7, click in the white space to deselect all. Hold the mouse button down and move across the slide icons to select Slides 8, 9, and 10. Press the Demote button. Slide 7 is now restored.

The Move Up and Move Down buttons can be used to move lines of text within a slide or slides within a presentation. This is simply dependent on what is currently selected.

Use the Zoom tool to enlarge the font appearance. Click the Zoom flyout in the toolbox. If you click the Zoom In button, you magnify a portion of the screen. If you click the Zoom Out button, Corel PRESENTS zooms out by a factor of two each time you click, or it returns to the screen view prior to the last zoom in.

## Applying Text Attributes in Outline View

Use the tools in outline view to apply various attributes to your text. Corel PRE-SENTS gives you default text attributes that you can modify at any time. Add emphasis to presentation text by adding bold and italic styles to call attention to key words or phrases. Color can also be used to highlight and make a word or two stand out. Keep the number of font types used to a minimum, and stay within the same family of fonts. Using too many styles and colors can distract your audience. To alter a font style in the outline view, use the same text tools from the Text toolbar used in slide view. It's important to remember that a person seated in the back row should be able to clearly see your presentation.

Take a moment and color the bullet points to match Slide 2. You will probably have to expand the title text box in three directions to see all of the two lines of text. Select the subtitle and change the point size to 36.

## Adding a Map

CorelMAP is an OLE module that seemed at first to this author as an odd choice for a program with a fully functional import section. If I want to add a map to a presentation, I just import one from the many clip-art collections I already have. Because Corel PRESENTS is bundled with the huge Corel clip-art library that has hundreds of maps to choose from, I was even more confused.

However, after a few minutes of testing I found the many features that make CorelMAP an interesting addition.

Adding a map is quick and easy with CorelMAP. First, insert a slide using the blank template and choose the Map icon from the toolbar. Place the Map tool in the upper-left corner of the slide, hold down the left mouse button, and then drag a box across toward the lower right. The Map Wizard opens, as shown in Figure 85.21.

*Figure 85.21.*
*The first screen view of*
*CorelMAP Wizard.*

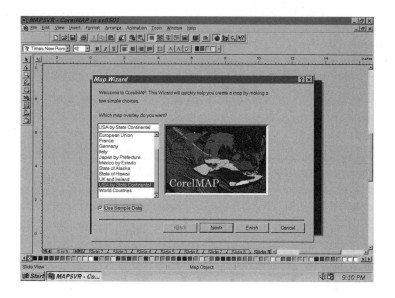

For the example, scroll down and click USA by State Continental. Then check the Use Sample Data check box. Click Next. Choose the map layout in the upper-right corner of the dialog box. Again, click Next. See Figure 85.22.

Answer the What kind of sample data do you want? question. Try the Data value and their attributes choice on the right. Click Finish.

The map is now ready to be edited. Change the map title by a right mouse button click. Choose Edit Title; this opens the Format dialog box, shown in Figure 85.23.

*Figure 85.22.*
*The third screen view of*
*CorelMAP Wizard.*

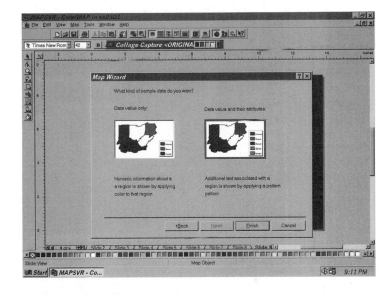

*Figure 85.23.*
*The CorelMAP Format*
*dialog box.*

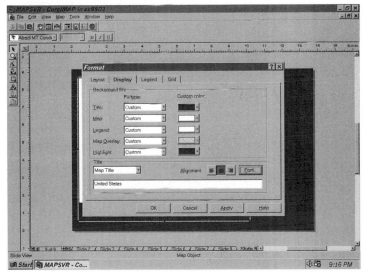

Choose the Display tab. In the Title box enter United States in place of Map Title.
Choose the Font button. This opens the Font dialog box, shown in Figure 85.24.

Now select Arial for the font, Bold for the style, and change the point size to 24. In
the Effects box change the Color to yellow. Click OK. This returns the user to the
Format dialog box. Change the Map Title selector to Map Subtitle and delete the
word Subtitle from the text entry area.

*Figure 85.24.*
*The CorelMAP Font*
*dialog box.*

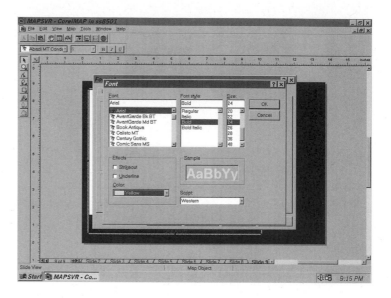

The Display box has another feature that can be used later to further customize a map. You can set the Fill type for each area of the map. The choices are None, Window Color, and Custom. When you are satisfied with the map appearance, click OK. (See Figure 85.25.)

*Figure 85.25.*
*The CorelMAP edit title*
*view.*

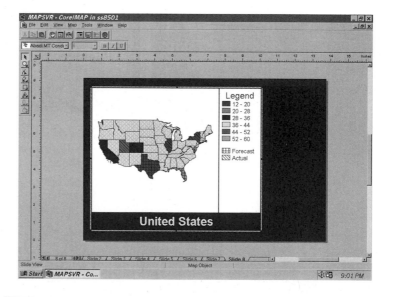

The Slide view now has a nice-looking map; you could stop here. However, that would do the map module an injustice. The power of this map module is best understood by running through the menu bar's features that are unique to CorelMAP.

Starting with View, the selections are new. (See Figure 85.26.) Listed in the View drop-down list are

> Zoom
> Entire Map
> Toolbars
> Title
> Legend
> Map Accessories
> Refresh Map

*Figure 85.26.*
*The CorelMAP View drop-down menu.*

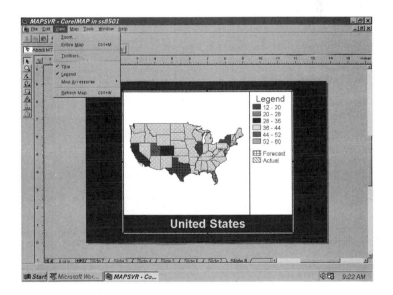

## Zoom

Clicking Zoom opens the Zoom dialog box, as shown in Figure 85.27.

Clicking Zoom Factor drops down a series of preset choices or you can enter any figure. The zoom value affects only the magnification of the map area.

## Entire Map

The Entire Map selection brings the map view back to 100 percent.

*Figure 85.27.*
*The CorelMAP Zoom*
*dialog box.*

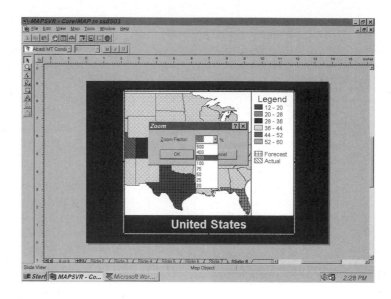

## Toolbars

The Toolbars selection opens the Toolbars dialog box, which enables you to customize the user interface to suit your style of working. (See Figure 85.28.) It functions in the same manner as all the Toolbar dialog boxes.

*Figure 85.28.*
*The CorelMAP Toolbars*
*dialog box.*

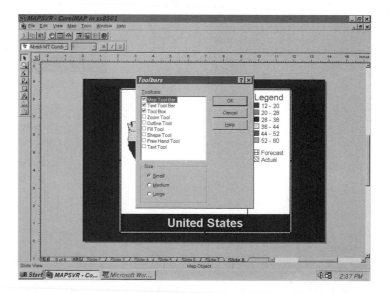

## Title and Legend

The Title and Legend items are simple toggle on and off selections for the map's title and legend.

## Map Accessories and Refresh Map

The Map Accessories flyout (see Figure 85.29) is one of the nice and powerful features of CorelMAP. This flyout enables the user to add lines of latitude, longitude, and degrees to the map. The Frame feature adds another frame just around the map area. The last two, View All and Clear All, quickly add or clear all of the features of the flyout. (See Figure 85.30.)

Refresh Map redraws the image of the map to the screen.

*Figure 85.29.*
*The CorelMAP Map*
*Accessories flyout.*

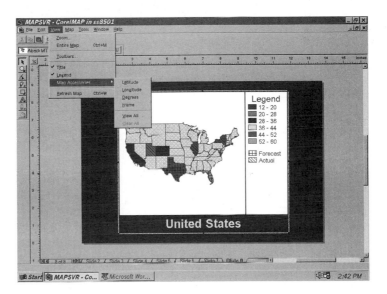

## Map Drop-Down List

Next on the menu bar is the Map drop-down list, which features three sections: Overlays, Data, and Format. (See Figure 85.31.)

Figure 85.30.
The CorelMAP United
States map with View All
applied.

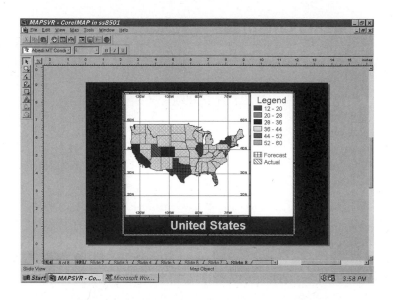

Figure 85.31.
The CorelMAP Map drop-
down list.

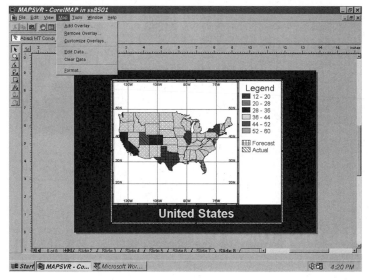

The first three selections all deal with overlays. They are

> Add Overlay
> Remove Overlay
> Customize Overlays

Choosing Add Overlay opens a dialog box that gives you the choice to add any of
the maps you aren't already using. (See Figure 85.32.)

*Figure 85.32.*
*The CorelMAP Add*
*Overlay dialog box.*

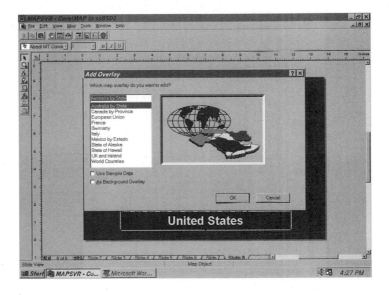

Move through the list and select countries or regions that need to be added to the map. In this example (see Figure 85.33), the United States is now all of North America. Europe has been added, along with Japan and Australia.

*Figure 85.33.*
*The CorelMAP altered*
*map view.*

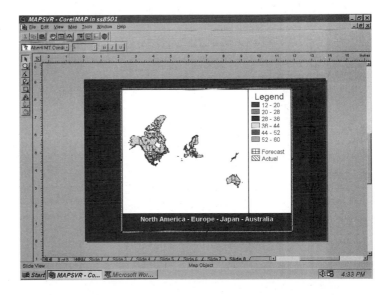

The Remove Overlay option opens a similar dialog box that works by listing the items on the map that can be removed. Only one overlay can be removed at a time.

The Customize Overlay option enables the user to add more overlays to the list of installed overlays or remove overlays from the list. Clicking here opens the Customize Overlays dialog box, as shown in Figure 85.34.

*Figure 85.34.*
*The CorelMAP Customize*
*Overlays dialog box.*

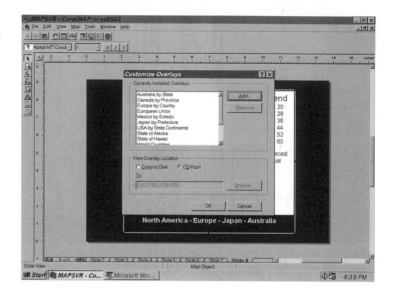

The Customize Overlays dialog box lists the already installed maps (overlays). Selecting one of them enables the Remove button so the overlay can be dropped from the list. The New Overlay Location box has two radio button choices, Copy to disk and CD-ROM. Select CD-ROM and click the Add button to open the Install Overlay dialog box. (See Figure 85.35.)

On Corel CD-ROM number 2 in the MAPDATA folder are many *.TV files. That is the extension the program is looking for.

The next two items in the Map drop-down list, Edit Data and Clear Data, enable the user to enter or edit data about the map region that is displayed. Selecting Edit Data opens a dialog box that enables the data relevant to the presentation to be entered. (See Figure 85.36.)

Clicking Clear Data opens a small dialog box that asks a very simple question: Are you sure you want to clear the data? (See Figure 85.37.) If the Yes button is selected, your data is gone.

Figure 85.35.
*The CorelMAP Install
Overlay dialog box.*

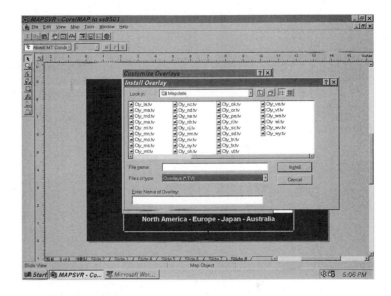

Figure 85.36.
*The CorelMAP Data
dialog box.*

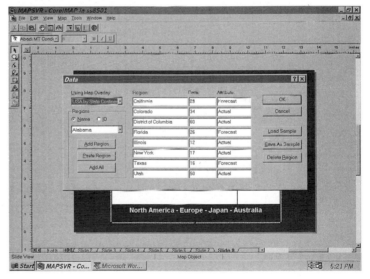

Last on the Map drop-down list, Format is part of what is used by the CorelMAP
Wizard at the start of the map building process and when the user clicks on the
map using the right mouse button. (See Figure 85.38.)

*Figure 85.37.*
*The CorelMAP Clear Data*
*dialog box.*

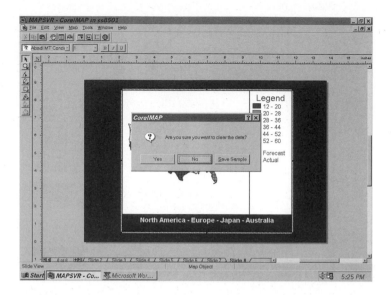

*Figure 85.38.*
*The CorelMAP Format*
*dialog box.*

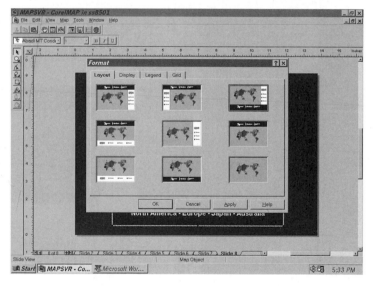

The first tab (Layout) gives the user the chance to alter the position of the map components. The second tab (Display) is covered in detail in Figure 85.24 and its accompanying text. The third tab (Legend) formats the map's legend. (See Figure 85.39.)

Figure 85.39.
*The Legend tab in the*
*Format dialog box.*

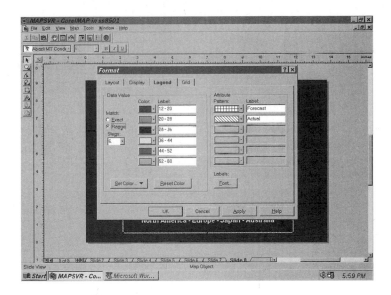

Under the Legend tab in the Format dialog box, the data, data range, and data format can be entered and altered. The data font and color of the individual areas can also be selected.

The last tab in the Format dialog box is Grid. (See Figure 85.40.) The Grid tab enables the user to select either automatic or manual placement of the lines of longitude and latitude. In addition, you can format the color of the frame and the Degrees font.

Figure 85.40.
*The Grid tab of the Format*
*dialog box.*

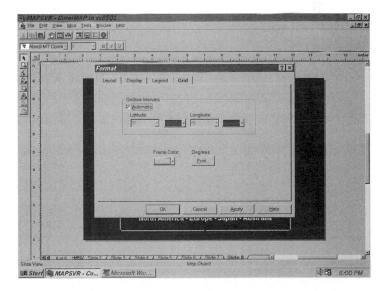

## Tools Drop-Down List

The last menu bar drop-down list that is unique to CorelMAP is Tools. (See Figure 85.41.) Four items make up the drop-down list:

> Text Label
> Distance
> Arrange
> Options

*Figure 85.41.*
*The CorelMAP Tools drop-down list.*

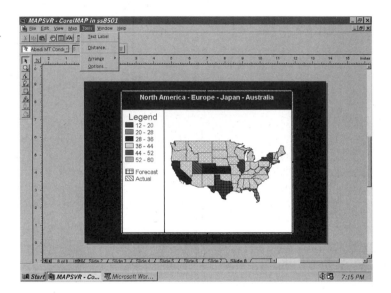

## Text Label

You can select Text Label from the drop-down as well as from the toolbox on the left edge of the screen. This tool is represented by the icon shown on the toolbox (See Figure 85.42.)

When the icon is selected, place it over an area of the map. When you click the icon it displays the name of the state or area. Right-click to open a dialog box that enables the name to be moved or anchored to the map. Several other attributes can be applied with the aforementioned dialog box. (See Figure 85.43.)

Figure 85.42.
*The Text Label icon on the*
*toolbox.*

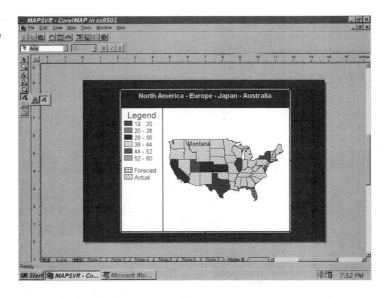

Figure 85.43.
*The Text Label right*
*mouse click drop-down.*

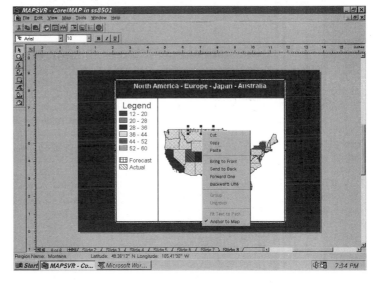

## Distance

The second item on the Tools drop-down list, Distance, is a quick way to include distance information on the map. Select Distance from the drop-down. The Distance dialog box opens and the icon changes to a ruler. (See Figure 85.44.) Click a region of the map. Keeping the mouse button pressed, move to a second location. The distance between points is now displayed.

*Figure 85.44.*
*The CorelMAP Distance*
*dialog box and icon.*

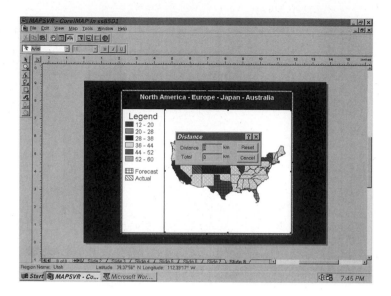

To measure the distance between several points and keep a total of all distances measured, repeat the steps between each location. Click Cancel to end the process. Use the Reset button to set the distance to zero.

## Arrange

The Arrange selection opens a dialog box nearly identical to the dialog box opened when you use the right mouse button to click on the Text Label. The Arrange dialog box allows the user to modify text labels using the following commands:

> Bring To Front
> Send To Back
> Forward One
> Backward One
> Group
> Ungroup
> Fit Text To Path
> Anchor To Map

## Options

The Options selection opens the Map Options dialog box, as shown in Figure 85.45.

*Figure 85.45.*
*The CorelMAP Map*
*Options dialog box.*

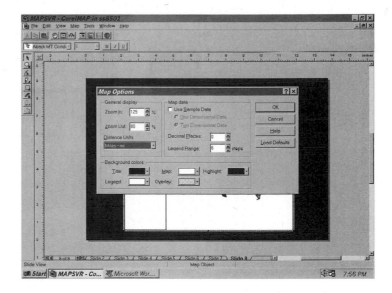

The General display box enables the user to set the Zoom In and Zoom Out percentages and the type of units of measure used by the Distance display. The next box to the right, the Map data box, sets the sample data on and off. It also sets the number of decimal points allowed in the data. The number of data ranges are also controlled here. Below is the Background colors box, which enables you to set the different colors of various regions of the map.

## Toolbar

The toolbar contains seven buttons that are unique to CorelMAP. (See Figure 85.46.)

> Pan Map
> Map Data
> Distance
> Layout
> Display
> Legend
> Grid

The Pan Map icon is the only tool not covered in the previous areas. It is useful in viewing the map when the map is displayed in a zoom mode at greater than 100 percent.

The rest of the toolbar icons perform and/or open the same dialog box as their menu bar counterparts.

Figure 85.46.
The CorelMAP toolbar.

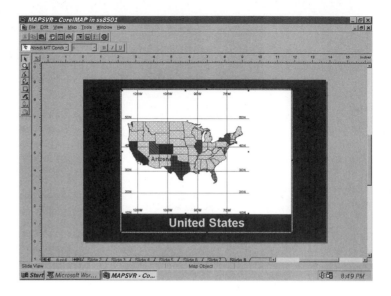

Another drop-down that is very useful is triggered by a right mouse click on the map area itself. Although the items in the drop-down can be selected in one or two other ways, the right mouse click and the grouping can be a more convenient way to utilize the features. (See Figure 85.47.)

Figure 85.47.
The CorelMAP right-click,
drop-down menu.

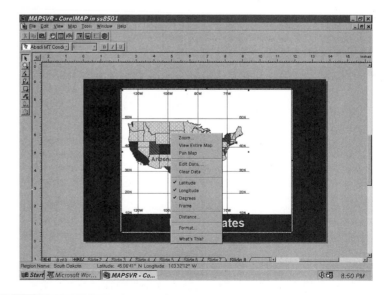

Click on the slide area outside the map to return to Corel PRESENTS.

## Slide Sorter

The next major feature in Corel PRESENTS is the slide sorter. Either the menu bar under View or the toolbar (the icon with four slides) can be used to select Slide Sorter view. (See Figure 85.48.)

*Figure 85.48.*
*Slide Sorter view.*

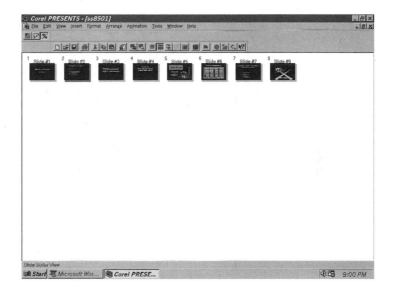

The presentation is shown as though viewed on a 35mm slide light box. The metaphor is quite accurate and performs the same function. The overall view and the ability to quickly rearrange the order is very handy. If you decide that Slide 7 would be better if presented as Slide 6, just drag the slide to its new position. Slides can be added and deleted from the Slide Sorter view.

There are three icons that are unique to the Slide Sorter view (see Figure 85.49):

> Transition
> Show/Hide Slide
> Show/Hide Jacket

## Transition

The Transition icon opens the Transition dialog box. This feature is covered in Skill Session 87, "Presentations, Timelines, and Self-Running Presentations."

## Show/Hide Slide

The Show/Hide Slide icon is very important in what it will do and how it affects many aspects of the presentation. To hide a slide, select the slide by clicking it.

Then toggle the Show/Hide icon. The slide will be marked by a gray × when it is hidden. Not only will the slide not show during the presentation, it can't be deleted. The Go To slide feature will not respond to a call to hidden slides. The tabs at the bottom of the screen view will also not respond to a hidden slide.

*Figure 85.49.*
*The Slide Sorter icons.*

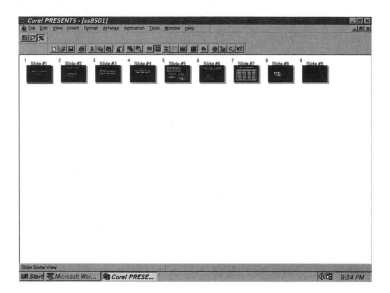

## Show/Hide Jacket

The Show/Hide Jacket feature toggles the display of the slides with a graphic that looks like the mount of a 35mm slide.

From the menu bar, select Insert and add a ninth slide to the presentation. Choose the blank background.

Double-click a slide to return the presentation to the single slide view mode.

## Shapes Flyout

The one item in the toolbox that is new is the Shapes flyout. Select it and choose the 3D arrow.

Use the Pick tool and select the arrow. Change the arrow's color to a bright red. Under the Edit menu select Duplicate. Rotate the duplicate object 180 degrees and drag it to the other side of the slide. Strangely missing from Corel PRESENTS is an alignment feature. You will need to pull down a guideline and align both shapes to the guideline. Select the Artistic text tool and type Go To Skill Session 86. Center the text and set the point size to 72. Save the presentation. This slide is shown in Figure 85.50.

*Figure 85.50.*
*Slide 9.*

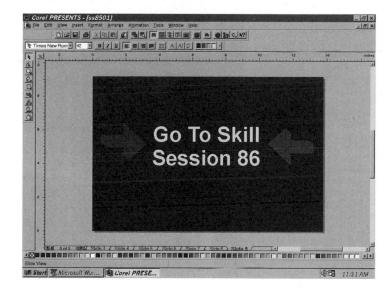

## Spell Checking On Steroids

Now that all of the text is entered into the presentation it is ready to be spell checked or proofread. Corel PRESENTS has an advanced text-checking feature. The Quick and Full Proof Read selections offer not only spell checking but punctuation and grammar suggestions as well.

Located on the menu bar under Tools is the drop-down list that contains these necessary tools. (See Figure 85.51.)

*Figure 85.51.*
*The Tools drop-down*
*menu.*

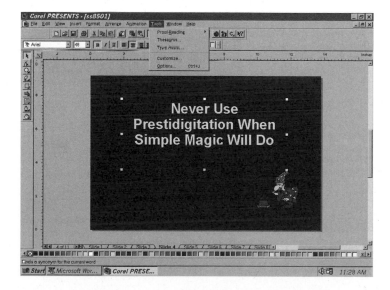

The Tools drop-down contains three items that were just touched on in Skill Session 84, "An Introduction to Corel PRESENTS." They are

> Proof-Reading
> Thesaurus
> Type Assist

## Proof-Reading

Selecting Proof-Reading triggers a flyout, as shown in Figure 85.52.

*Figure 85.52.*
*The Proof-Reading flyout.*

The user is presented with the following four choices:

> Spelling
> Quick Proof Read
> Full Proof Read
> Advanced Options

### Spelling

Spelling is available only when a text box is selected. The spell check then checks that selected text only. Using the Pick tool, select or enter text with a spelling error. Under Tools select Proof-Reading and from the flyout choose Spelling. The Spell Checking-Spelling Error dialog box opens, as shown in Figure 85.53.

Because this is a selected text item, the Check range box is set to Selected Text. This box can be changed to read Full Text. Below that window is the Sentence window with the offending word highlighted. Under the Sentence window is the Error description window, which contains a brief description of the problem and suggestion on what can be done. At the bottom on the left side are three buttons. Help and Add Word are straightforward, but Add Word is basically asking to which dictionary is the new word to be added. The last button is usually reserved for high-end word processors or dedicated spelling/grammar programs. The Options button triggers a drop-down full of power and features. (See Figure 85.54.)

*Figure 85.53.*
*The Spell Checking-*
*Spelling Error dialog box.*

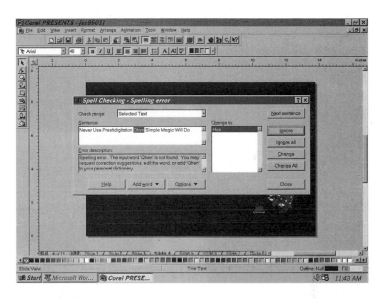

*Figure 85.54.*
*The Options button drop-*
*down menu in the Spell*
*Checking-Spelling Error*
*dialog box.*

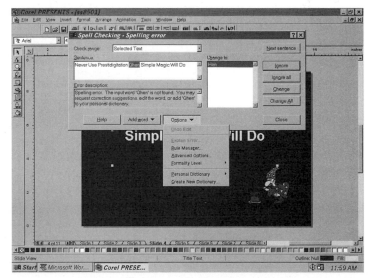

891

This drop-down contains the following seven items:

Undo Edit
Explain Error
Rule Manager
Advanced Options
Formality Level
Personal Dictionary
Create New Dictionary

The first two are simple, but from there on the real power of the module is apparent.

### Rule Manager

The Rule Manager option opens another dialog box, as shown in Figure 85.55.

*Figure 85.55.*
*The Rule Manager*
*dialog box.*

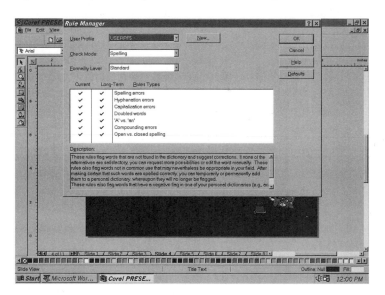

This dialog box enables the user to interact with the underlying programmed ideals that are controlling the spell checking and grammar rules that format the suggestions and corrections. Here the user can select the Formality Level: and under Check Mode: change from Spelling only to Full or Quick Proof Read. A different dictionary can be selected or a new one started.

### Advanced Options

The fourth item in the Spell Checker Options button drop-down is the Advanced Options dialog box shown in Figure 85.56. Language selection and maximum sentence length are some of the items that can be set from this dialog box. The Rule Manager can also be launched from here.

*Figure 85.56.*
*The Advanced Options*
*dialog box.*

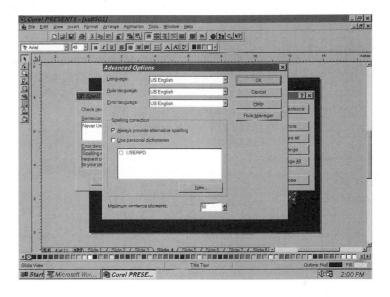

## Formality Level

The Formality Level option triggers a flyout that contains levels, which are Formal, Standard, and Informal.

### Personal Dictionary and Create New Dictionary

The next two items in the Spell Checking-Spelling Error dialog box work hand in hand. In order to select a personal dictionary, you must first create one. Selecting Create New Dictionary opens the new Personal Dictionary dialog box shown in Figure 85.57.

In the Dictionary name box type the name of the new dictionary you want to add word selections into. Click OK. This returns the user to the Spell Checking dialog box.

It should be noted that the last twelve selections were from the Spelling Checker dialog box. That dialog box is just one item on the Proof-Reading flyout.

## Quick Proof Read and Full Proof Read

The next item on the Proof-Reading flyout is Quick Proof Read, and it is followed by Full Proof Read. When working with a program that has three options for the same item, it is nice to know the difference between choices. However, there is no quick answer to this. Corel goes into great detail about the difference in the help file. What follows is a slightly shorter version.

*Figure 85.57.*
*The New Personal*
*Dictionary dialog box.*

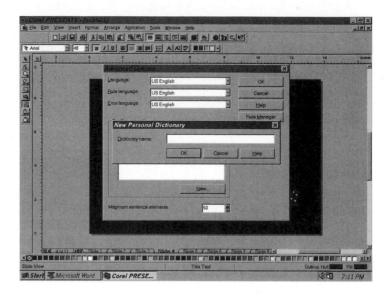

## Spelling

The International Proofreader's Spelling mode detects and corrects numerous errors, including those related to language-specific occurrences such as compound words of Germanic origin used in the English language. This mode corrects errors involving the following writing elements:

- A/An use
- Capitalization
- Spelling (typographic errors, apostrophe errors, cognitive misspellings, and abbreviation errors)
- Italics (from Indo-European or Romance languages)
- Compounding
- Double words
- Hyphenation (soft-hyphen errors and hyphenation-dependent errors in spelling)

## Quick Proof Read

The Quick Proofreading mode works with the Spelling mode. In addition, it corrects errors involving the following writing elements:

- Confused words
- Double negatives
- Format

- Homonyms
- Inappropriate prepositions
- Misspelled expressions
- Misspelled foreign expressions
- Noun-phrase agreement (Romance languages)
- Punctuation
- Spacing between words and sentences
- Ungrammatical expressions
- Uppercase/lowercase spellings of words, depending on their function or context

### Full Proof Read

The Full Proofreading (FPR) mode works in addition to the Spelling and Quick Proofreading mode. Full Proofreading identifies many categories of wording that is stylistically questionable. FPR mode offers assistance in eliminating them. Words and expressions flagged in the Full Proofreading mode might not be grammatically incorrect, but the style and grammar guides suggest that they should be avoided, except for intentional effect, in most cases. The error messages displayed are designed to give users the stylistic guidelines they need to make a subjective decision about including or omitting certain words and expressions. These categories include

> Archaic expressions
> Clichés
> Contractions
> Gender-specific expressions
> Informal expressions
> Jargon expressions
> Overused phrases
> Pretentious words
> Redundant expressions
> Sexist expressions
> Stock phrases
> Unnecessary prepositions
> Vague quantifiers
> Wordy expressions

### Advanced Options

Advanced Options opens the same dialog box that responds in the Spell Checker, Quick or Full Proof Read dialog boxes under the Options button. (See Figure 85.56.)

This is the last of the options in the Proof-Reading flyout under the Tools drop-down from the menu bar. The next item from the drop-down is the Thesaurus.

## Thesaurus

Before selecting Thesaurus, open Slide 4 and block the word Prestidigitation. The Thesaurus dialog box opens, as shown in Figure 85.58.

*Figure 85.58.*
*The Thesaurus dialog box.*

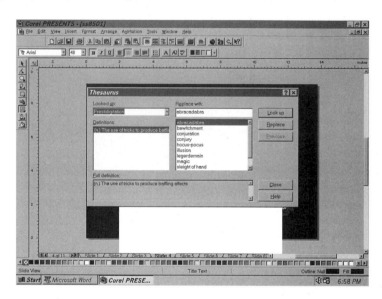

This dialog box now contains the word prestidigitation in the Looked up: window. The Replace with: window contains the word abracadabra. Below that is a list of eleven additional words, all of which appear to be good choices. To the left is the Definitions: window, complete with a valid definition. Running across the bottom is the Full definition. This is a first-rate Thesaurus. Selections made here should serve to enhance any presentation.

## Type Assist

Selecting Type Assist opens the Type Assist dialog box, shown in Figure 85.59.

This is a rather busy dialog box. It starts with five toggle on and off check boxes. They are

- Capitalize first letter of sentences
- Change straight quotes to typographic quotes
- Correct two initial, consecutive capitals
- Capitalize names of days
- Replace text while typing

*Figure 85.59.*
*The Type Assist*
*dialog box.*

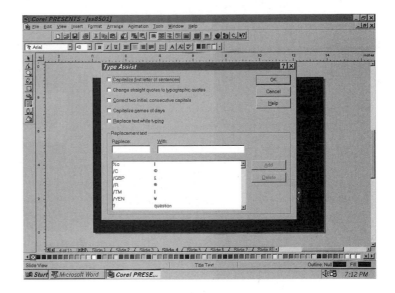

These are followed by the Replacement text box. Already listed are 111 abbreviations and the replacement word. The user can add to the list in the Replace and With windows. Provisions are made to remove words from the default list as well as those added by the user.

## Speaker's Notes

After the presentation has been entered and proofread, you now need some form of hard copy from which to review, correct, or practice the presentation. To create speaker's notes, select Speaker's Notes from the View drop-down menu. A new screen view appears. (See Figure 85.60.)

On this screen is a representation of the slide and an area to type speaker's notes about the image.

After notes about each slide have been entered, select Print from the File drop-down menu. The Print dialog box opens.

Since it will not be the default, check that the word Notes appears in the Print window. Next, check to make sure that the correct printer is selected, and that in the Print Range box the correct range of slides is selected. Then, in the Copies box indicate the number of copies needed. Clicking OK will print the Speaker's Notes.

Figure 85.60.
Speaker's notes creation
view.

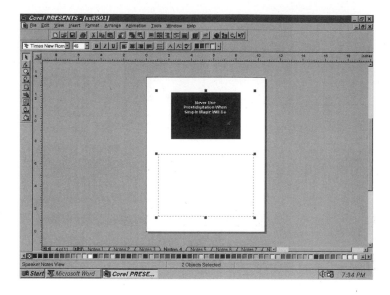

## Outline Printouts

Somewhat related to Speaker's Notes is the printing of the outline view. The biggest disadvantage to the outline view is the lack of graphics. After all slides have been entered, select Print from the File drop-down menu. The Print dialog box opens. Set the Print window to Outline. Take a moment and check that under Printer the correct printer is selected, and that in the Print Range box the correct range of slides is selected. Indicate the number of copies needed in the Copies box. Clicking OK will print the outline of the presentation. Remember that any Artistic text entered in the slide view does not appear in the outline view.

## Handouts

Handouts are very popular with an audience. Handouts enable an audience to review the material at a later date. Corel PRESENTS offers a selection of different handout formats, and the user can also create his or her own handout styles. To choose a handout layout, select Handout from the View menu. This brings up the handout view. (See Figure 85.61.)

Click the Libraries icon in the toolbar. The Libraries dialog box opens. Now click the Layout tab. Select the Preset Library button to enable that option. From the ten thumbnails choose a handout that suits your needs. Use this layout to create audience handouts. (See Figure 85.62.)

Figure 85.61.
*The handout view.*

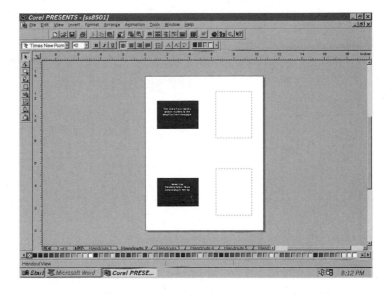

Figure 85.62.
*The Libraries Handout Layouts dialog box.*

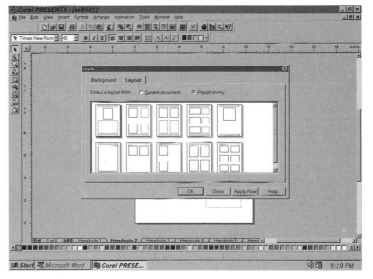

Click OK to apply the layout and close the dialog box. To create a custom audience handout (including a description), double-click a handout text box near the slide thumbnail in the handout layout view. This activates the Paragraph Text tool. Information about the slide can be entered.

Notice that you can use the Page Up and Page Down keys to move from one handout to another. The Handout tabs at the bottom of the screen work the same as they do in slide view.

After the handouts for each slide are ready, select Print from the File drop-down menu. The Print dialog box opens.

In the Print window, make sure that the word Handouts appears. Take a moment and check that the correct printer is selected, and that in the Print Range box the correct range of slides is selected. In the Copies box, indicate the number of copies needed. Clicking OK will print the handouts.

# 86

# Adding Video, Sound, and Animation and Working with Timelines

Every object or slide included in your presentation can be time-based. The Timelines feature assists in managing these objects. Included in these objects are transitions and sound effects, as well as other multimedia features. A complete animation file can be imported to help communicate an idea or to impress a viewer.

Use PRESENTS to reopen presentation SS8501, which you created in Skill Session 85, "Corel PRESENTS." Opening an existing presentation is a basic Windows 95 feature.

# Adding Video

Corel PRESENTS 6 ships with a large number of video clips. These clips are located on the Corel CD-ROM number two.

Prior to using a video clip, you must select the slide that will contain the video. As you did in Skill Session 85, add or insert a slide on the end of the presentation. This should be Slide 10. Under Insert, select Video. (See Figure 86.1.)

*Figure 86.1.*
*The Open dialog box.*

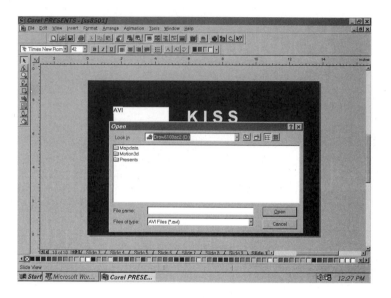

Open the Presents folder; Video is one of four folders listed there. Open the Video folder and three more folders are listed: Clips, General, and Themes. Clips contains eight compressed, live video files. General contains 32 art-based AVI files. Themes opens to reveal 26 addition folders. Each folder contains groups of AVI files based on a common theme. Open the Educate folder, and select the file listed as Edusumm. Click Open. The screen view returns with a rectangle marked AVI in the upper-right corner. Place this rectangle to the right and above the center of the slide. Using the Paragraph Text tool, add the text KISS and press Enter. Next, type Bold Graphs and press Enter. Then type Distractions and press Enter. Now, select a color and point size that fills the left half of the slide.

From the toolbar, select the Preview Slide icon. The view changes to a full screen view and the AVI file runs next to the text. A video insert is now part of the presentation. Keep in mind that when you add video or sound to a presentation, the presentation is then limited to playback from a computer. (See Figure 86.2.)

*Figure 86.2.*
*Slide 10.*

## Adding Sound to an Individual Slide

Corel PRESENTS 6 also allows the addition of sound (in the form of wave files) to a presentation. Sound effects, music, or narration can enhance a presentation and can help focus the attention of the audience. To add or record a sound, the computer must have the appropriate sound-capturing hardware installed. To hear the sound, you need a sound card and a set of speakers. To record narration, the computer needs a microphone that is compatible with your sound card.

Use the slide sorter view to move through the presentation. Select the Distractions are Dangerous slide. Double-click the slide to return to the slide view. It might seem that to add a sound effect to an individual slide, a procedure similar to adding video would be used. Not quite. Do not use Insert | Sound, but instead use File | Import. (See Figure 86.3.)

Set the import filter to Windows Wave. Open the Presents folder and find Sound, one of four folders listed there. Open the Sound folder and select the wave file Honk. An audio wave file insert is now part of the presentation. From the toolbar, select the Preview Slide icon. The view changes to a full screen view and the sound file runs in the background. The simple honk doesn't quite work with the graphic, but sounds can be added or edited. For this example, another sound file will be added. Again from the File menu, choose Import. This time select the wave file Smash. Close out the dialog box by clicking Import. From the toolbar, select the Preview Slide icon. Now the sound plays back and is more like the screen graphic.

Figure 86.3.
The Import dialog box.

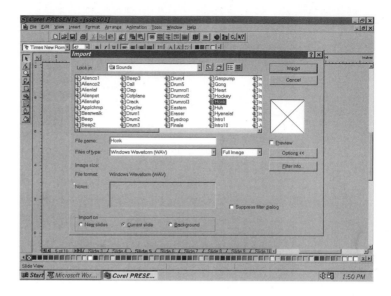

## Adding Background Music to an Entire Presentation

To add background sound to the entire presentation, change the view to slide sorter. When sound is added in slide sorter view, an imported sound automatically becomes a background sound. (See Figure 86.4.)

Figure 86.4.
The slide sorter view.

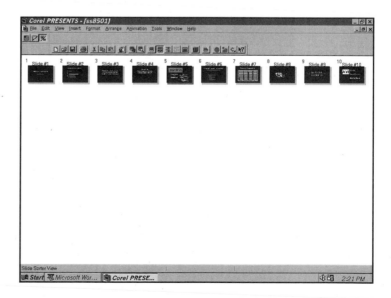

Click File | Import, and the Import dialog box will appear.

Click the Look in list check box and then click a folder where longer wave files are stored. Remember the length of the file(s) must be long enough to last for the length of the presentation. The timeline will help you with this. (If you don't have long wave files yet, then just read along.) Depending on the quality of the audio file, a wave file can be quite large. Make sure the audio file size is compatible with your computer's playback limitations. Make sure the Files of type list box is set to Windows Waveform (*.WAV). Select the sound file of your choice. The name appears in the File name text box. Click Import. From the File drop-down menu, select Run Presentation to play back your background sound.

## Music, Music Everywhere

This is probably the best place to stick the following warning: Yes, you can add sound and video to a presentation. (When doing this for practice, any OLE sound file will do.) However, when a presentation is made to an audience, proper copyright usage must be followed. For example, today's popular tunes as well as yesterday's golden oldies are both off limits. Also, it may be very tempting to use the latest technology to take a clip from a commercial video or network TV program, but these are also verboten. Depending on the audience, sound files and video clips purchased at the local computer store may not have the proper releases. Your best bet is to read the fine print carefully.

There are music and video clips from many sources that will release rights for use with presentations. Corel is one source of music clips, and the photo CDs have images that can be used for backgrounds. One source of customizable music is a program called AudioTracks Professional. The program creates music in any length the user sets, with up to six voices in more than 50 different styles. All of this is copyright- and royalty-free.

## Adding Narration: The Master's Voice

To record narration to accompany the presentation, click Insert | Sound. The Wave Editor dialog box opens. (See Figure 86.5.)

Plug a microphone that is compatible with your sound card into the Mic In jack on the computer's sound card. When you are ready to start recording, simply click the Record button before you begin. Click the Stop button when ready to stop recording, and click the Play button to hear the recording. The sound bite must be saved to be used. It can be saved at different levels of quality. The default audio quality is 11kHz, 8-bit mono. Sounds are displayed as waveforms in the Wave Editor. Waveforms are graphic representations of audio. You can perform basic editing to the sound as well as apply various sound processing effects.

Figure 86.5.
The Wave Editor (Re-
corder) dialog box.

Select Effects | Change Characteristics, and the Wave Characteristics dialog box opens. (See Figure 86.6.)

Figure 86.6.
The Wave Characteristics
dialog box.

This dialog box is broken into three sections: Sample Rate, Channels, and Sample Size. In the Sample Rate section you can select the frequency of the wave file: 11, 22, or 44kHz. The Channels section can be set to Stereo or Mono, and the Sample Size section can be set to 8 bit or 16 bit. The default settings keep the wave file size the smallest. Choosing Stereo, 16-bit, and 44kHz produces the best sound quality (not recommended for recording voice); however, these settings will produce a very large wave file.

There are more features in the Effects drop-down menu other than Change Characteristics. (See Figure 86.7.) For example, you can select a portion of the wave file from the timeline by clicking on any point within the wave file with the mouse and dragging it to the place in the wave file you want the effect to stop. Then you can use one of the following effects to alter the audio:

> Silence
> Fade In
> Fade Out
> Amplify
> Reverse
> Echo

Silence lowers the selected portion of the wave file to near zero output. Fade In and Fade Out ramp up or ramp down the volume of the selected wave. Amplify raises the volume. Reverse literally plays the audio portion in reverse. And Echo adds a delayed copy of the selection to the selected portion of the wave file at a lower volume.

Also, you can zoom in on the sound wave by using the Zoom In button, found under View on the menu bar.

*Figure 86.7.*
*The Effects drop-*
*down menu.*

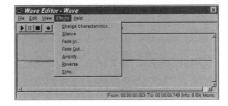

## Animation

Animation is a series of images that when played back rapidly in sequence create the illusion of movement. These static images are called *frames*. Corel refers to animated images as actors. Actors are comprised of static pictures (called *cels*). Actors can have any number of cels.

Use Go To to move to Slide 4, the slide about using magic. In the File menu, select Import, and on Corel CD-ROM number 2 in the Presents folder, open the folder Actorprp. (See Figure 86.8.) For File Type, select CorelMOVE (CMV MLB). Now, find the file Magician.

*Figure 86.8.*
*The Import dialog box.*

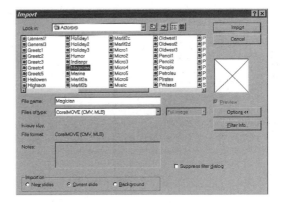

At the bottom of the Import dialog box in the Import On section, check the Current Slide radio button. Next, select Import from the dialog box. This opens a new dialog box called Import Actor/Prop. (See Figure 86.9.)

In the Import Actor/Prop dialog box, check the Preview check box. Select the actor called Explosion, and then click OK. This might take a while to import, so don't panic. When the actor is imported, drag him to the lower-right corner of the screen.(See Figure 86.10.)

*Figure 86.9.*
*The Import Actor/Prop*
*dialog box.*

*Figure 86.10.*
*Slide 4 with the actor.*

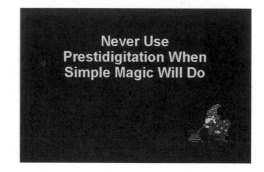

The screen should look like the one shown in Figure 86.10. From the toolbar, select Preview Slide and watch the actor work his magic.

## The Animation Menu

In the View drop-down menu, select Animation to switch to animation view. You'll notice that there is now a VCR-style toolbar located at the bottom-left corner of the screen. If you press the Play button, you'll find that the animation from the previous section runs about 18 frames and repeats five times before stopping.

From the menu bar, you can now select the Animation menu. There are sixteen commands listed in this drop-down menu. (See Figure 86.11.) The sections that follow describe these commands.

### Transitions

This command brings up the three-tabbed Transition dialog box, which is covered in detail in Skill Session 87, "Presentations, Timelines, and Self-Running Presentations."

Figure 86.11.
The Animation drop-down
menu.

## Path

This command is one of the tabs in the Transition dialog box (covered in Skill Session 87). You can use it to select the path that the animation will take across the screen. It is usually applied to text rather than to drawn animation.

## Create/Edit Actor

This command brings up the Create/Edit Actor dialog box, which is used in the creation and editing of an actor. (See Figure 86.12.)

For example, use the Pick tool to click the Magician actor in Slide 4. Next, open the Create/Edit Actor dialog box. The cels in actor box will show that Magician is made up of 18 cels of animation. You can use this dialog box to add cels to the actor as they are created or to edit cels to alter the look of the actor.

Figure 86.12.
The Create/Edit Actor
dialog box.

## Cel Sequence

This command brings up the Cel Sequence dialog box, which controls the speed of the actor as well as the direction in which the animation moves through the cels. (See Figure 86.13.)

In the Effects box, there are five choices for the direction in which the animation can move. These choices are Constant, Forward, Reverse, Ping Pong, and Random Cel. In the Speed box, the choices are Slow, Normal, and Fast. Checking the Preview check box will run the animation so that you can observe the effect that the changes have made.

Figure 86.13.
The Cel Sequence dia-
log box.

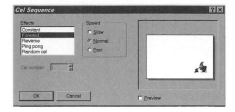

## Custom Path

When this command is selected, the mouse pointer automatically changes to a pencil, allowing the user to mark the custom path of the actor. The Custom Path command is normally used with drawn animation.

## First Frame, Previous Frame, and Play Reverse

These commands become active when the animation view's VCR controls are used. They move a stopped animation to the frame location specified by the command. They can also be triggered by the commands that are listed just below them in the Animation drop-down.

## Stop, Play, Next Frame, and Last Frame

These commands are similar to the animation view's VCR animation controls. They trigger the animation currently on-screen, whether it is selected or not.

## Set Key Frame, Advance To Next Key Frame, Advance To Previous Key Frame, and Advance Time

This set of commands also works together on the selected animation. The Set Key Frame command marks a frame of animation for reference and is helpful in locating a single point in an animation with many frames. The Advance To Next Key Frame and Advance To Previous Key Frame commands navigate through an animation from key frame to key frame. This is useful when checking animation that is being unruly during playback. The Advance Time command moves the animation one frame forward. The timeline on the VCR controls shows the frame number as well as the advance.

Now that you have had a chance to insert and work with a supplied animation, have some fun and create one of your own. You might want to try entering text that moves from one side of the screen to the other. Type the text on a template that has an animation placeholder. Apply the direction to the text and the number of steps it takes for the text to complete its move (about eighteen per second is a good guide). That's it—you are all set. Play back this simple move, and then decide to do more with it if you like.

# Corel *TIP!*

Corel PRESENTS ships with a ton of predrawn animation that can liven up any presentation. But, be sure not to overuse these effects in a presentation. Too many sound effects and too much clip art can detract from the message. Use effects sparingly.

## Timelines

The Timeline view allows you to set the sequence and timing of events in your slides. You can display and edit the time relationships among all of the elements in a Corel PRESENTS presentation. Suppose, for example, you wanted to add the sound of an explosion to match the Magician actor in Slide 4. The time at which the sound is played would be critical to the effectiveness of the sound effect. The timeline also effects the timing of all slides within a self-running presentation. Stopping the time slider shows the position and state of all the objects that are present at that point in the presentation.

## Setting the Presentation Timeline

Move to Slide 1 in slide view. Click View | Timeline, and the Timelines dialog box is displayed. (See Figure 86.14.)

*Figure 86.14.*
*The Timeline dialog box.*

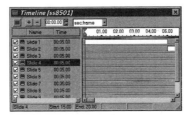

Click Slide 1 to highlight it, and then double-click to expand the slide. The displays list the number of slide objects, the position, and length of time displayed.

Click the object to which you've applied opening and closing transitions. In the upper row is a yellow box with an arrow. Click this box to return to the list of all slides in the presentation. Select Slide 4. In the expanded view, the three objects that make up the slide are displayed—five seconds for text and actor and one second for sound. Next to the yellow box (no name is given to this box in Corel literature.) is a plus and minus symbol. These symbols expand and contract the spacing of the viewable timeline.

To the right of the objects is an area that graphically displays the relative position and time of each object. Place the cursor on the left edge of the box for the actor, and the cursor changes to a set of parallel lines. Now drag the beginning of the line to the 2 second mark. Move to the right edge of the actor's timeline box and drag that end back to the 3 second mark. The actor now indicates one second. That action adjusts the object's transition timeline as well as the duration of its path. Move the cursor down to the sound timeline and place the cursor in the middle of the box. The cursor changes to a double-headed arrow. Move the sound effect over to the right under the actor. (See Figure 86.15.)

*Figure 86.15.*
*The Timeline dialog box*
*after editing.*

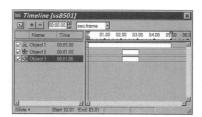

Close the timeline, return to the slide view, and then select Preview Slide. The slide appears, and then two seconds later the actor performs just one cycle of the action.

The Timeline dialog box allows you to change many of the objects' aspects within your presentation. To display an object during runtime and editing modes, click the check box beside the object identifier to place a check mark in it. To hide an object during runtime and editing modes, click the check box beside the object identifier to remove the check mark.

Any object can be removed from the timeline and at the same time from the slide. To delete an object, select it in the list and then press the Delete key. The selected object is then removed from the object list as well as the slide.

The presentation is now complete, with sound effects and animation.

# 87

# Presentations, Timelines, and Self-Running Presentations

Now that the show is complete, checked, and proofread by both human and PC, it should be ready for prime-time viewing. At this point, a decision will have been made that the presentation will stay inside the PC and not make its rounds as overheads 35mm slides or perhaps recorded to video tape.

Even with everything correct and animation added, the presentation still may not quite be ready. Why? Is it going to be presented by the creator in an open forum or is it going on tour by itself? If the presentation has music and narration that completes the show, the user can follow along in this chapter and at the end have a portable, self-running and complete presentation. A self-running presentation can also be triggered manually with the volume down; while the transitions occur smoothly from slide to slide, the presenter can add his or her own commentary to complete the presentation.

Under File select Open and then choose SS8501. By default Corel stores the presentations in the Program folder. (See Figure 87.1.)

*Figure 87.1.*
*Slide 1.*

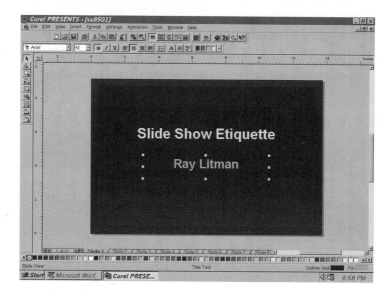

If some time has passed since you last worked on this presentation, then the following is a refresher about moving through the presentation. There are several ways to move from one slide to another in Corel PRESENTS: by clicking the numbered slide tab on the bottom of the presentation window, by double-clicking on the slide thumbnail in slide sorter view, or by selecting Go To | Slide on the menu bar under the Edit drop-down menu.

## Slide to Slide Transitions

Transitions are how one slide moves into another during presentation playback. Special effects can be assigned to a slide or to objects on that slide in order to make your screen show visually interesting. Opening and closing transitions should complement the slide content if possible. Don't overuse effects, such as wipes (where the page is gradually revealed) or random transitions (where the program chooses random effects).

To apply an opening transition, move the cursor to an open area of the slide. Right-click and then select Transitions from the drop-down menu. (See Figure 87.2.) The Object Settings Transitions dialog box will open. (See Figure 87.3.)

Figure 87.2.
The right mouse click
drop-down menu.

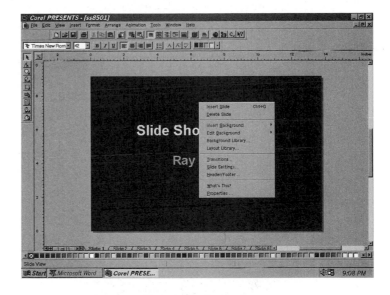

Figure 87.3.
The Object Settings
Transitions dialog box.

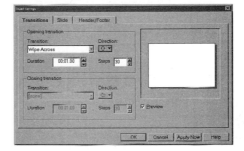

Since these are simple slides (for the most part), the five-second-per-slide default
will be left intact. Keep the total time of each slide in mind as the effects are
applied to each slide. To see the default, select the Slide Properties dialog box
from the Slide tab. (See Figure 87.4.) The duration of the slide is listed here.

Figure 87.4.
The Slide Tab of the Slide
Properties dialog box.

In the Opening transition section in the Transition tab, scroll through the list (there are forty choices) and select Iris In. Set Duration to 00:03.00. In the Closing transition section, select Fade Out, set Duration to 00:02.00 and Steps to 20. Click OK. Now move to Slide 2. (See Figure 87.5.)

*Figure 87.5.*
*The Transition tab of the*
*Object Settings dialog box.*

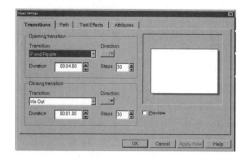

Repeat these steps to open the Transition dialog box. In the Transition window, find and select Wipe Across and set Duration to 00:02.00. The Direction window is active in this selection. Choose the up arrow from the drop-down menu. Change the Steps number box to 20. In the Closing transition window, select Fade Out. Set Duration to 00:02.00 and Steps to 20. Click OK.

Slide 1 is set to an opening transition called Iris In, which takes 30 steps and 3 seconds to complete. Slide 1 has a closing transition called Fade, which takes 2 seconds and 20 steps to disappear. Slide 2 uses an opening transition called Wipe Across, which has 20 steps and takes 2 seconds to complete. It closes with a Fade that takes 2 seconds and has 20 steps. Finish the presentation with an open and close for each slide.

You can preview or play back the presentation at any time. You can preview the entire presentation or just one slide at a time. To preview a single slide, select the Preview Slide icon from the toolbar. If you want to watch all of the presentation, select the Run Presentation icon from the toolbar. When the entire presentation plays, it is called *runtime mode*. To return to slide view mode press the Esc key.

The previous section is written from several different versions of Corel PRESENTS 6. The latest and tested version (see Skill Session 84 for the exact version number) did not function well enough to be tested fully. For example, the Slide Properties would not allow the selection of a Closing Transition.

The presentation can be run by pressing the Enter key or the mouse button to change from slide to slide. If either of these methods are used, do not enter a closing transition. The presenter can now trigger the slide changes to suit the presentation pace. The left and right arrow keys can also be used to change the direction the presenter moves through the show.

# Transition Effects Applied to Objects

Opening and closing transition effects can be applied to objects within a slide as well as the slide itself. To apply transition effects to an object in a slide, move to Slide 6, select the Pick tool, and then click on the slide's title. Right-click and then select Properties from the drop-down menu. This displays the Object Settings dialog box.

Click the Transitions tab if it is not already selected. In the Opening transitions section, click the Transition list box.

Scroll up and select Pond Ripple. Set the Duration box to 00:04.00. Leave the default setting of 30 in the Steps number box. Use the Apply Now button to apply the change and then leave the dialog box on-screen. This transition does not require a direction to be chosen.

To apply a closing transition for the title on Slide 6, in the Closing transition window scroll up and select Iris Out. Set the Duration box to 00.04.00. Leave the default setting of 30 in the Steps box. Click the Preview option check box to see the transition effect. Click OK. From slide view, select the Preview Slide icon to see the effect in full view.

An object with an assigned path can also be added to a presentation. A *path* is the route an object takes in moving from one part on the slide to another during a presentation. Change to Slide 5. To assign a path to an object, click the Pick tool and select the car and pole graphic. Click the right mouse button and select Properties. This opens the Object Properties dialog box. Select the Path tab, and the view changes to the Path page.

Scroll through the list box and select the Diagonal Top-Left Bottom-Right path option. Click the Preview option check box to see the object follow the selected path in the preview window.

Click OK to apply the path and then close the dialog box.

# Definitions of Slide Properties

The user can define or change the properties of any slide at any time. The settings affect each individual slide. To define slide properties, move the cursor to an open area of the slide. Right-click and then select Properties. The Slide Properties dialog box appears.

Select the Slide tab, and the Slide page appears. You can name the slide in the Name box. Three check boxes allow the slide, the header, and the footer to be shown or hidden. Enabling the Hide Slide option allows you to conceal a slide that contains confidential information. From this dialog box, you can also select the Header/Footer tab. (See Figure 87.6.)

*Figure 87.6.*
*The Header/Footer tab*
*of the Slide Properties*
*dialog box.*

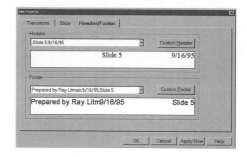

From the Header/Footer tab, you can enter custom information or accept the default header/footer information. Selecting Custom opens yet another dialog box. (See Figure 87.7.)

*Figure 87.7.*
*The Header/Footer tab of*
*the Custom Header/Footer*
*dialog box.*

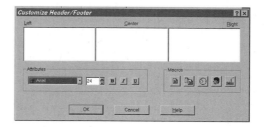

When finished entering or accepting data, click OK.

## On-Screen Annotations

On-screen annotations are similar to adding written information on an overhead during a presentation. This feature can be used when the presenter wants to emphasize important points to the audience. Filling in key information is an interesting way to help the audience retain important data.

The presenter can preselect the on-screen annotation pen features or change these features during a presenter-keyed presentation. To preset the pen's attributes, open the Tools drop-down menu and select Options. The Options dialog box opens. Now, click the Presentation tab. (See Figure 87.8.)

On the right side of the dialog box in the On Screen Annotations section are two buttons: Thickness and Color. The Thickness button allows you to select one of the three different pen thicknesses from the Line Thickness flyout. The Color button allows you to select a pen color. Press the Color button, and a color palette with 16 colors appears. Select a color that has a strong contrast to the background color in use and then click OK.

*Figure 87.8.*
*The Presentation tab in*
*the Options dialog box.*

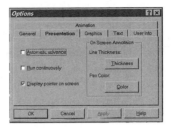

The on-screen annotation pen can be used any time during a presentation. Select the File drop-down menu and click Run Presentation (or press F5) to begin the screen show. When the presentation reaches the point that you want to emphasize, click with the left mouse button to pause the presentation and activate the on-screen annotation pen. (See Figure 87.9.)

*Figure 87.9.*
*The on-screen*
*annotation pen.*

In the lower-right corner of the screen is a small pen icon. Clicking it opens a dialog box that allows the user to modify the on-screen annotation pen. Holding down the left mouse button activates the pen. The mouse becomes the on-screen annotation pen. Use the mouse to guide the pen in order to underline or circle important points. Double-click the left mouse button or press the right-arrow key on the keyboard to continue the presentation.

A presentation creator can edit the presentation's timeline so that the presentation pauses when needed to allow emphasis for an important point.

## Making a Self-Running Presentation

What is a self-running presentation? It's a presentation that runs from a disk, which can be placed in a different computer than the one on which the show was created. How can it be put to use? Rather than making a sales presentation video (let's say that cost or time is a factor), you can simply create a presentation in Corel PRESENTS in order to cover the points needed to sway the viewer. You can grab your laptop and head to the airport—a Corel PRESENTS self-running presentation on a laptop is smaller, lighter, faster, cheaper, more compact, and has greater flexibility than a VCR and monitor. It is ready to hit the convention circuit in a moments notice. The self-running presentation automatically advances from slide to slide and begins again after the last slide; thus, running in a continuous loop. This feature comes in handy if you want your presentation to run continuously at a trade show or exhibit.

To create a self-running presentation, open the Tools drop-down menu and select Options. The Options dialog box opens. (See Figure 87.10.)

*Figure 87.10.*
*The Options dialog box.*

Select the Presentations tab and click the Automatic advance check box. Next, click the Run continuously check box to enable that option. Click OK to apply the changes and then close the dialog box. To play a self-running presentation, select Slide View from the View drop-down menu (or from the keyboard, press F5). The presentation will play over and over until you press the Esc key.

## Creating A Portable Screen Show

Here's the scenario. You have a customer on the phone who needs to know if your company's new XYZ widget will fit his needs. Well, rather than packing up and rushing across the country or sending an expensive sample, you promise to send out a demo right away. Grabbing your trusty Corel PRESENTS presentation from the last convention and making a few simple changes to customize it to suit this prospective client, you make a portable screen show and slip it in the overnight mail. While you are in the fantasy mode, imagine the prospective client calls the next day with a huge order. Almost as tantalizing is going on the road with your presentation in your shirt pocket. Perhaps, mailing out hundreds of screen shows to prospective clients is more your style.

You can create a portable version of your presentation or screen show, which can be shown on any computer running Windows 95, even if Corel PRESENTS is not installed on it.

To create a portable screen show, select File | Save As. The Save As dialog box opens. (See Figure 87.11.)

In the Save In list box, you can open or create a folder in which to store your portable screen show. Type a name for the screen show in the File name text box. Select the Save As Type list box to open it and from the drop-down choose Self Executing Presentation (*.EXE). Corel PRESENTS automatically assigns .EXE as the file extension for a portable screen show.

*Figure 87.11.*
*The Save As dialog box.*

This option saves a presentation as a non-editable file, which can only be run as a screen show. Before you save a presentation with this option, make a copy of it or save it under a new name. Without a backup copy, you won't be able to open the presentation to make changes.

## Playing a Portable Screen Show

Corel PRESENTS creates a self-executing file that runs on any computer that has Windows 95 or Windows NT installed. If animation files are included in portable screen shows, the application in which the animation was created must be installed on the computer that runs the show. If the animation files are not installed, the screen show player simply skips the animation slide and moves to the next one.

If you make a large show with lots of animation, you will be like the man who builds a boat in his basement that is too large to get out. The file size of the executable file must fit on a disk format that is acceptable to the computer that will play it back.

There are several methods you can use to play a portable screen show. Double-click the file from a Windows file management utility (for example, Windows Explorer). Create a shortcut to the Corel PRESENTS self-executing file on the Windows 95 desktop.

Skill Sessions 84 through 87 just open the door to the power of Corel PRESENTS. Now that you have the basic skills for creating effective and interesting presentations, try creating a presentation of your own.

# CorelDEPTH

CorelDEPTH enables you to create 3D text and 3D shape objects by using 2D drawing tools. Many features needed to produce full-color 3D graphics and text come standard with CorelDEPTH, including a step-by-step Wizard that directs you through the making of 3D text. As a starting point, you can select from over 30 expertly designed Template Wizards.

## Corel*NOTE!*

> CorelDEPTH calls a 3D object that is created from 2D outlines that are extruded from a shape object.

When you create shape objects and 3D text, you can apply colors, decals, and shading, and you have the capability to rotate them in 3D. Use the selection of predefined styles or create your own custom style by grouping unique lighting effects and colors. During the design procedure, the text and objects can always be edited.

By virtue of working in 3D space, you can view your document from any angle and at various degrees of magnification. To change the view and magnification of the objects in your document, rotate the objects with the Virtual Trackball and use the Zoom tool, respectively. CorelDEPTH documents can be exported in various distinct formats that are compliant with Corel VENTURA, CorelDRAW, and other graphics and desk-top-publishing applications.

You can open CorelDEPTH from within CorelDRAW. Select the Application Launcher icon from the standard toolbar, below the menu bar. (The icon is shaped like the Corel logo.) To open CorelDEPTH, select its icon from the drop-down list. (See Figure 88.1.)

*Figure 88.1.*
*Opening CorelDEPTH*
*from within CorelDRAW*
*by using the Application*
*Launcher.*

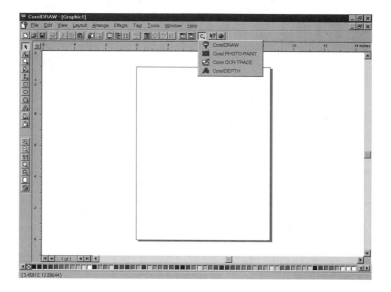

You also can start CorelDEPTH from the Windows 95 Start menu. Click the Start button and then choose the Programs folder. From there, select the Corel Graphics folder and pick the CorelDEPTH icon from the list. (See Figure 88.2.)

*Figure 88.2.*
*The Windows 95 Start*
*button displaying the*
*various folders to open to*
*get to the CorelDEPTH*
*icon.*

## The CorelDEPTH Workspace

When you first open CorelDEPTH, you are greeted by the Startup box. You are given four options from which to choose: You can create a blank new document, open an existing document, or use one of two different types of Wizards to generate 3D artwork. They include the Template and the Step By Step Wizards. (See Figure 88.3.)

*Figure 88.3.*
*The Startup box and its*
*available selections.*

The CorelDEPTH document window is comparable to CorelDRAW's. Your workspace comprises the entire window, both inside and outside the page borders. You can edit and move objects anywhere inside the workspace, but only items in the print area within the confines of the page are printed.

An interruptible, full-color preview is a characteristic of CorelDEPTH; it enables you to finish nearly any procedure without waiting for the screen to redraw. As an alternative, you can choose to work in wireframe view by selecting Wireframe from the View pull-down menu.

CorelDEPTH enables you to maneuver objects in three dimensions; instead of plainly moving objects across a flat surface, you can move and rotate them easily inside the 3D workspace. To help you navigate the 3D workspace, CorelDEPTH provides two significant features: the Perspective Box and the Working Plane.

When you select Create A Blank New Document, you get a new document titled Doc1. By default, the Styles palette and the Geometry palette are also opened. The toolbar, the Working Plane, the status display, and the Perspective Box are all part of the workspace. The Perspective Box is displayed by clicking its icon (third one down in the toolbar).

The Working Plane is denoted visually by a grid on the screen. The Working Plane is of endless size and, in fact, extends outside the edges of the grid. This applies to all planes in your document. You can fit the object to the Working Plane or vice versa. Select Working Plane from the View menu to conceal or display the Working Plane.

The status display is positioned at the lower-left corner of the main window. It gives you information about the program, specifically if it is extruding an object or if it is idle. It also informs you regarding what drawing mode you are in (2D or 3D). Because CorelDEPTH redraws and extrudes objects in the background, you can proceed to work while CorelDEPTH is applying effects to an object.

The toolbar consists of nine tools. Some of them have flyout menus that enable you to switch from one mode to another. The first five are called 3D tools. The remaining four are 2D tools. From the top working your way down, they are: 3D Selection, Virtual Trackball, Perspective Box, Magnifying Glass, 3D Box, Convert Point, Bézier, Rectangle, and Text. The Magnifying Glass has a flyout from which you can select the Hand tool. The Convert Point tool has a flyout where you can switch from Delete Point or Add Point. The Rectangle tool can switch to the Ellipse or Polygon tools. (See Figure 88.4.)

*Figure 88.4.*
*Select Create A Blank*
*New Document to get to*
*this window.*

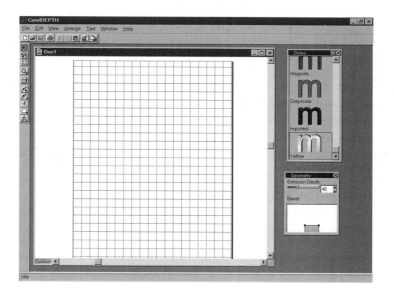

## The Template Wizard

When you choose the Use The Template Wizard button, you are presented with a window that has various prebuilt templates from which to choose. Select a template and then click the Next button.

Depending on the template you choose, you have either one, two, or three lines of text fields that you can edit. Edit the text and then click the Done button to see the template. You can then select the text or other objects and apply a different font as well as fill attributes. (See Figures 88.5–88.7.)

*Figure 88.5.*
*Select the Use The*
*Template Wizard button*
*to get to this window.*

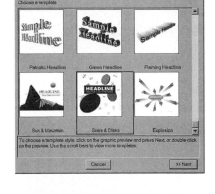

*Figure 88.6.*
*Enter the text in the text*
*fields and press the Done*
*button when you are*
*finished.*

*Figure 88.7.*
*The edited template in the*
*workspace after additional*
*text formatting.*

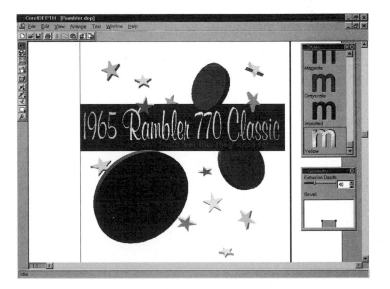

# The Step By Step Wizard

When you pick the Use The Step By Step Wizard button, you will be presented with windows that take you through several steps to create a text object. First you are instructed to select from 15 ready-made bevel and depth combinations. (See Figure 88.8.)

*Figure 88.8.*
*The Step By Step Wizard's*
*prebuilt depth and bevel*
*assortment.*

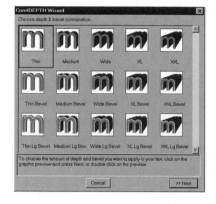

After clicking the Next button, you will come to a window where you can select from 15 ready-made rotation and perspective styles. After making your selection, click the Next button or double-click the desired style to progress to the next window. (See Figure 88.9.)

*Figure 88.9.*
*The Step By Step Wizard's*
*ready-made perspective*
*and rotation assortment.*

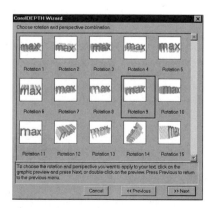

The next window is where you choose an effect style. This pertains to color and effect choices such as gradient fills. Scroll the window to select from the 25 available effect styles. Again, double-click the desired style or click the Next button to advance to the next window. (See Figure 88.10.)

*Figure 88.10.*
*The Step By Step Wizard's*
*available effect styles.*

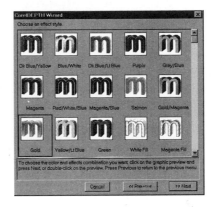

The following window enables you to choose from six different light sources. Select your light source and double-click it to proceed to the next window. (See Figure 88.11.)

*Figure 88.11.*
*The Step By Step Wizard's*
*light source choices.*

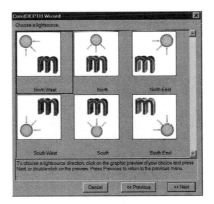

The final window is where you enter your text string. When you are done typing in the text, click the Done button. The effects applied to the text in the Step By Step Wizard's various windows are displayed in your document. (See Figures 88.12–88.13.)

*Figure 88.12.*
*The Step By Step Wizard's*
*text entry window.*

*Figure 88.13.*
*The text displayed in the*
*document.*

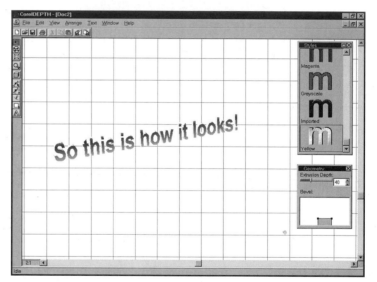

## Preferences

The Preferences dialog box enables you to predetermine several program preferences. Open it by choosing Preferences in the File pull-down menu. You can select from the following options included in the Preferences dialog box:

The Startup Dialog option defines if the Startup dialog box will be visible when CorelDEPTH is started. Turn this option off, and when CorelDEPTH is started it won't display the Startup dialog box. Choose the Nudge Value option to designate the size of the nudge increment. The Default Unit option indicates the unit of measure used in the dialog boxes that show units of size.

The Default Color Model option designates the default color model that will be utilized within the Color Style dialog box. The Working Plane option manages the visual aspects of the Working Plane grid. This includes the Grid Step, with which you can modify the dimensions of the squares in the grid; and Grid Color, which enables you to alter the color of the grid. (See Figure 88.14.)

*Figure 88.14.*
*The Preferences dialog*
*box.*

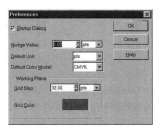

## Menu Commands

In the File pull-down menu you will find commands common to many applications such as opening new or existing documents. Other commands that you can select from the File pull-down menu include Close, Save, Save As, Revert, Import, Import/Replace Outline, Exit, Print, Print Setup, and opening previously opened files. (See Figure 88.15.)

*Figure 88.15.*
*The File pull-down menu.*

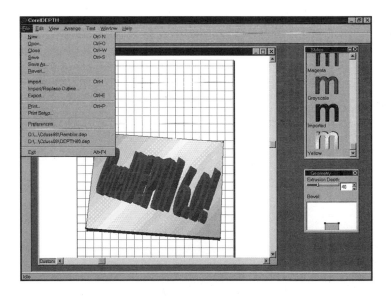

The Edit pull-down menu includes such standard commands as Undo, Cut, Copy, Paste, Delete, Duplicate, and Select All. Also available from here are the Properties, Style, and Style Library commands. (See Figure 88.16.)

*Figure 88.16.*
*The Edit pull-down menu.*

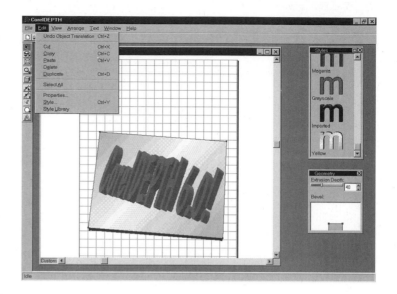

From the View pull-down menu select whether to display items such as the Status Bar, Toolbars, or Working Plane Perspective box. You can display the contents of the Windows Clipboard by selecting Show Clipboard. You can also choose Fit in Window and Wireframe drawing mode. (See Figure 88.17.)

*Figure 88.17.*
*The View pull-down menu.*

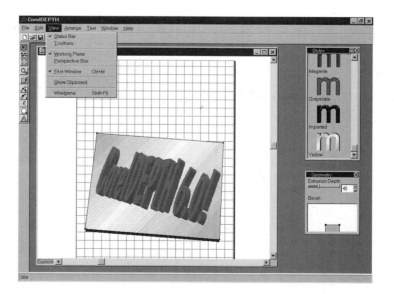

In the Arrange pull-down menu there are commands that are typical of what's found in other programs. They include Align/Distribute, Align Again, To Front, To Back, Group, Ungroup, Combine, and Break Apart. Other commands include Send To Working Plane, Set Working Plane To, and Light Source. (See Figure 88.18.)

*Figure 88.18.*
*The Arrange pull-down*
*menu.*

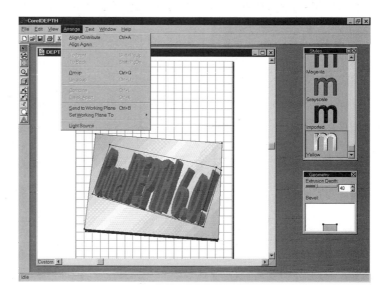

The basic text features found in the Text pull-down menu include selections for Font, Size, Style, Alignment, Leading, Edit Text, and Convert To Curves. (See Figure 88.19.)

*Figure 88.19.*
*The Text pull-down menu.*

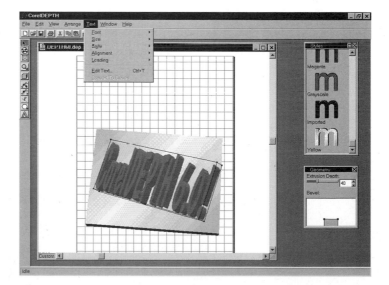

Change the way your windows are displayed with the commands from the Window pull-down menu. They consist of Cascade, Tile, Arrange Icons, Styles Browser, and Geometry Palette; a list of any currently open documents rounds out this menu. (See Figure 88.20.)

*Figure 88.20.*
*The Window pull-down menu.*

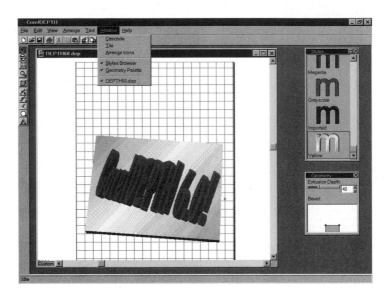

Do you need help with CorelDEPTH? If so, select from these commands in the Help Menu: Contents, Search Help On, How To Use Help, and About CorelDEPTH. (See Figure 88.21.)

*Figure 88.21.*
*The Help pull-down menu.*

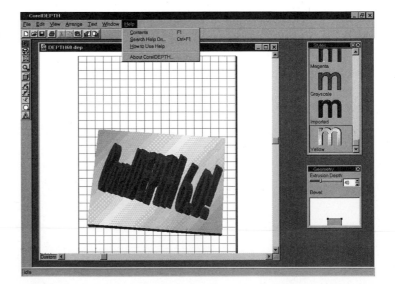

# MOTION 3D

# 89

Corel MOTION 3D is a stand-alone program that can generate AVI files, which can be made into movies using basic 3D models. You move these models to create animation effects. You will be able to use these movies in your presentation programs, such as Corel PRESENTS and other multimedia programs. You can also export a scene as a bitmap image for use in programs such as Corel PHOTO-PAINT. Open Corel MOTION 3D from the Corel Graphics flyout in the Start menu. Figure 89.1 shows the Corel MOTION 3D screen as it first appears when you start the program.

The main window of Corel MOTION 3D is comprised of four windows that show four different views of the 3D space. The name of each window view is shown in the window's title bar. The four views from left to right are Camera View, Top View, Right View, and Front View.

The Camera View window is where the final animation will be rendered. You might think of this view as showing the scene as though you were looking at it through a camcorder's view finder. The objects that appear in this view will be rendered in 3D space when you start making a movie. Unlike the three other views, the camera view can move freely in 3D space. Its movements include panning, moving in/moving out, rotating, and tilting. The camera view can also zoom in or out.

*Figure 89.1.*
*The Corel MOTION 3D*
*default screen.*

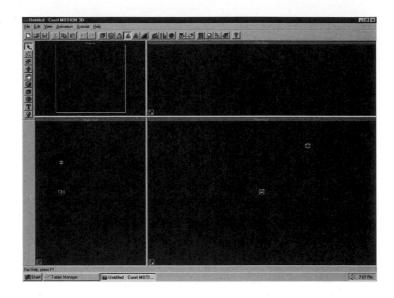

The three remaining views are fixed along specific planes in 3D space. The small icons in the bottom-left corner of each view show the specific plane for each window. Imagine that you looking into a glass aquarium. You can look down into the aquarium from the top, front, and sides of the aquarium, but you can't rotate or tilt the aquarium. The three remaining views are fixed to the following planes:

The top view is fixed along the X-Y plane.

The front view is fixed along the Z-X plane.

The right view is fixed along the Z-Y plane.

Although you can't move, rotate, or tilt the fixed views, you can rotate, size, and move the objects within these views. When you perform any of these actions, the camera view will be updated.

These windows provide the necessary views required to show a 3D perspective of space. Having these views to work with provides the information necessary to determine the relative position of all the objects in the scene, including the camera and lights. It can be difficult to translate the 2D view of an object seen on a monitor to a 3D representation. The translation process uses wireframe views of objects, mapping of color and light onto the object, and the ability to size, rotate, and move the object in a pseudo-3D space. Before you begin working in Corel's MOTION 3D, you should familiarize yourself with the tools needed to help you create your objects and movies.

# Using the Toolbox

There are 10 tools that make up the toolbox which runs down the left side of the Corel MOTION 3D window. The tools are described in the following list:

- You use the Pick tool to move objects in 3D space. Click the Pick tool and hold down the mouse button to display the flyout menu. You can choose between the following two move tools:

  The Vertical Move tool moves the selected objects left, right, up, or down along the vertical plane of the current view.

  The Horizontal Move tool moves the selected objects left, right, in, or out along a horizontal plane that is perpendicular to the current view.

- The Edit Object tool brings the selected object into the Object Editor, where you can edit Lathe or Extrude objects (see the Object Editor section later in the skill session for more information).

- The Uniform Scale tool resizes the selected object equally in all three directions when you drag it inward or outward.

- The Squash tool scales an object along one axis at a time, creating a distortion of the original shape.

- To access the View tools, click the current View tool and hold down the mouse button to display the flyout menu. Choose one of the following View tools:

  The default View tool is the Pan tool, which looks like a hand. This tool moves the position of the view window up, down, left, or right along the viewing plane.

  The Move In tool moves the position of the camera into the 3D space.

  The Zoom In tool makes objects in the view appear closer.

  The Zoom Out tool makes objects in the view appear farther away.

  The Camera Navigation roll-up (see Figure 89.2) provides additional navigational controls to the camera. You can access the Camera Navigation roll-up from the View menu or use the F4 key. The roll-up looks like a globe with directional arrows superimposed on it. Clicking the arrows rotates the camera view in the direction indicated. The six different rotation controls are rotate up, rotate down, rotate right, rotate left, tilt right, and tilt left.

*Figure 89.2.*
*The Camera Navigation*
*roll-up.*

- The Rotation tools rotate an object around its centerpoint. The following list describes these tools:

  The Vertical Rotate tool rotates the selected object vertically (up or down) in any view.

  The Horizontal Rotate tool rotates the selected object horizontally (left or right) in any view.

  The Tilt tool tilts the selected object to the left or right in any view.

- Clicking in the camera view with the Extrude Object tool selected places a cube in the camera view. You can use the Object Editor to change the shape of the cube.

- Clicking in the camera view with the Lathe Object tool selected places a sphere in the camera view. Use the Object Editor to change the shape of the sphere.

- The Text Object tool allows you to type a string of extruded text into the camera view.

- Clicking in any of the views with the Light Object tool selected places an additional point of light in each view.

## Using the Toolbar

The toolbar across the top of the view windows is divided into basic and rendering modes. The function of each button in the toolbar is described in the following sections.

### Basic Buttons

The first eight buttons (starting at the left) are for the basic mode:

- The New button creates a new scene.
- The Open button opens a previously created scene file.
- The Save button saves the current scene information.
- The Cut button removes the currently selected object from the scene and places it on the Clipboard.
- The Copy button places a copy of the currently selected object on the Clipboard.
- The Paste button places the contents of the Clipboard into the scene.
- The Undo button undoes the last operation.
- The Redo button redoes the last operation that was undone.

## Rendering Buttons

The next six buttons after the basic buttons are the rendering buttons. Each of the following buttons represents a different mode:

- The Bounding Box button represents each object as a six-sided box. This mode is the fastest for rough object placement and animation preview, but it offers the least detail.

- The Wireframe button displays the outline of all facets of an object. Wireframe mode has improved detail over the bounding box mode, while maintaining significant redraw speed.

- The Shade Fast button adds color to the facets. Each facet has its own color. This mode provides basic feedback on color and lighting effects.

- The Shade Better button provides a higher quality of shading, but it takes more time to display in the view.

- The Ray Trace button provides the highest quality of shading. It also takes the most time to render.

- The Anti-Aliasing tool provides sharper edges on the objects rendered in the shade fast, shade better, or ray trace modes. Note that the rendering time will increase when this option is activated.

## Movie Buttons

The next three buttons are the Movie buttons. They are described in the following list:

- The Preview button runs through the entire animation sequence with all objects in bounding box mode.

- The Make Movie button creates a movie based on all the attributes created in the scene setup.

- The Stop button stops a currently running animation.

## Editing Buttons

The next two buttons are used for basic editing:

- The Surface Editor button allows you to edit existing surfaces or create new surfaces. Figure 89.3 shows the Edit Surfaces dialog box.

- The Point At button points the camera or lights at the centerpoint of a specified object. Figure 89.4 shows the Point At dialog box.

*Figure 89.3.*
*The Edit Surfaces*
*dialog box.*

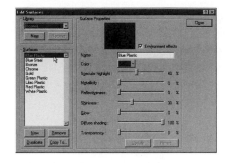

*Figure 89.4.*
*The Point At dialog box.*

## Stagehands Button

You use stagehands to apply predesigned elements into your scene that can instantly create an animation. When you click the Stagehands button, the Stagehands dialog box appears. The dialog box contains tabs for cameras, lights, and props. Click the appropriate tab to choose the different stagehands. Each stagehand is described in the following sections.

### Stagehand Cameras

Stagehand cameras provide animated effects to the scene by moving the camera through 3D space. Because you can have only one camera per scene, the current camera will be replaced when you use a stagehand camera. Figure 89.5 shows the Stagehands dialog box with a camera selected.

*Figure 89.5.*
*The Stagehands dialog*
*box with the Camera tab*
*selected.*

### Stagehand Lights

Stagehand lights generate assorted effects by setting color, intensity, and motion of the light sources. You can add multiple lights to a scene, but be careful; too many lights can wash out the surfaces. Multiple lights will also add to the rendering time, particularly when you use the ray trace mode. Figure 89.6 shows the Stagehands dialog box with the Lights tab selected.

*Figure 89.6.*
*The Stagehands dialog*
*box with the Lights tab*
*selected.*

## Stagehand Props

Stagehand props are animated objects that you can add to the 3D space to easily assemble an animated scene. Once you place them in the scene, you can edit any of the attributes for each prop to suit your needs. Using props together in one scene lets you create an animated movie. You can further customize your scene by adding your own outlines and text. Figure 89.7 shows the Stagehands dialog box with the Props tab selected.

*Figure 89.7.*
*The Stagehands dialog*
*box with the Props tab*
*selected.*

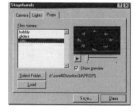

# Environment Button

The Environment button provides environmental controls to the 3D space. When you click this button, the Environment Properties dialog box appears. The Environment Properties dialog box contains the Atmosphere, Backdrop, and Sky properties. Click the appropriate tabs to control the different properties. Each property is described in the following sections.

## Atmosphere

You can control the Atmosphere property by choosing different colors for the ambient light and the background. You can also choose clear, light fog, medium fog, or heavy fog from the Visibility list box. Experimenting with different levels of fog will help provide a greater sense of depth in 3D space. As you move objects deeper into the scene, they appear to fade into the background color. The heavier the fog is, the more pronounced the effect. Figure 89.8 shows the Environment Properties dialog box with the Atmosphere tab selected and the Visibility list box displayed.

*Figure 89.8.*
*The Environment Proper-*
*ties dialog box with the*
*Atmosphere tab selected.*

## Backdrop

Click the Backdrop tab in the Environment Properties dialog box and choose a backdrop from the Files list box. If the list box is empty, click the Select Folder button to access the backdrop files. The path to the default folder is Corel60\motion3d\backdrop. Backdrops are bitmap files that you can use as background images to the animation. These bitmaps are static and remain fixed in the center of the camera view. Figure 89.9 shows the Environment Properties dialog box with the Backdrop tab selected.

*Figure 89.9.*
*The Environment Proper-*
*ties dialog box with the*
*Backdrop tab selected.*

## Sky

Click the Sky tab in the Environment Properties dialog box and choose a sky from the Files list box. If the list box is empty, click the Select Folder button to access the Sky files. The path to the default folder is Corel60\motion3d\Skies. The skies are bitmap images that envelop the 3D space. Skies are used to reflect light onto the object surfaces. Using light sources, including ambient light, helps to reflect the sky image onto the object surfaces. The effect is more apparent when the ray trace rendering mode is used. If the surfaces of objects in a scene are not bright enough, you will need to add a sky to the scene. Surfaces like chrome often require adding a sky. Figure 89.10 shows the Environment Properties dialog box with the Sky tab selected.

*Figure 89.10.*
*The Environment Proper-*
*ties dialog box with the*
*Sky tab selected.*

## Timelines Button

Click the Timelines button to activate the Timelines dialog box. This dialog box provides the time-related controls for the scene. These controls are explained later in this skill session. Figure 89.11 shows the Timelines dialog box.

*Figure 89.11.*
*The Timelines dialog box.*

## Surfaces Button

Clicking the Surfaces button opens the Surfaces roll-up, which contains all the surfaces you can apply to objects in the scene. You can use the Surface Editor to edit the existing surfaces, or create new ones by clicking the Edit button at the lower-left corner of the Surfaces roll-up. Refer to Figure 89.3 to review the Surface Editor. Figure 89.12 shows the Surfaces roll-up.

*Figure 89.12.*
*The Surfaces roll-up.*

## Working with the Different Views

If you have read this far, you should be anxious to start creating a scene. First, you need to create a few objects to learn how to work with the different views. Follow these steps:

1. Click the Lathe tool in the toolbox, and then click the camera view. A wireframe view of a sphere is created.
2. Click two more times in the camera view with the Lathe tool to place two more spheres. You should end up with three spheres in the camera view (see Figure 89.13).

Figure 89.13.
Three spheres placed in
the camera view.

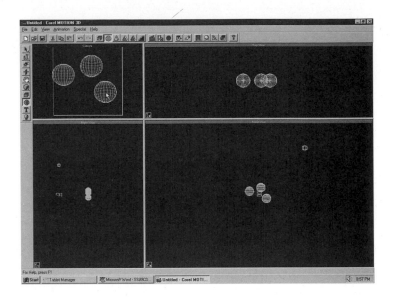

3. Click the Pick tool in the toolbox and click in the top view.

4. Drag the sphere on the right up to move it away from the camera; notice it now appears smaller in the camera view.

5. Drag the left sphere down so that it appears larger in the camera view. At this point, you can see the relative position and size of each sphere. Notice how the first sphere you moved appears smaller, and the second sphere you moved appears larger in the camera view. In 3D space, objects of the same size appear smaller the farther away they are and appear larger the closer they are. You can get an even better perspective of this situation by looking at the right view. Notice the sphere that appears the largest in the camera view is closest to the camera in the right view. (See Figure 89.14.)

6. Click the Uniform Scale tool in the toolbox. Click the right sphere in the camera view and drag it outward to scale the sphere to the same size as the middle sphere.

7. Still using the Uniform Scale tool, select the left sphere and drag it inward to scale down the sphere so that it is the same size as the middle sphere. Your screen should now look similar to Figure 89.15.

Now when you look at just the camera view, you will see that it's not possible to determine which object is bigger or which one is closest to the camera. They appear to be three objects of equal size. You can not get enough information from the camera view alone to make an accurate determination of the relative size and position of these three objects. You can, however, determine the relative size and position of all the objects in the scene, including the camera and lights, by looking at the three fixed views. Notice that in each of the fixed views the spheres are no longer equal in size because you resized them in Steps 6 and 7.

*Figure 89.14.*
*The spheres after being moved in the top view.*

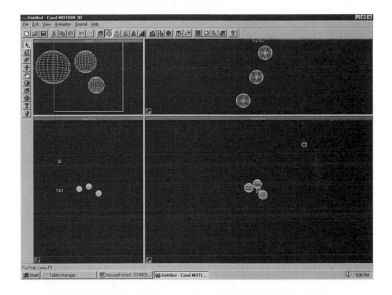

*Figure 89.15.*
*The three spheres after being resized in the camera view.*

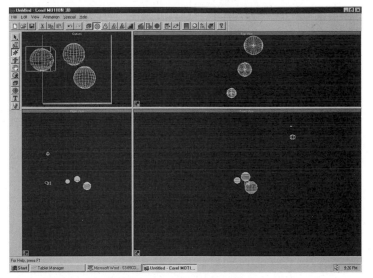

945

## Making a Basic Movie

To make a quick movie, follow these steps:

1. Click File | New to open a new scene.

2. Click the Text tool in the toolbox. Then click in the camera view. The Object Properties dialog box appears (see Figure 89.16).

3. Type the words MY MOVIE in the text box. Leave the Extrusion depth at 0.20 points, and click the Format button. The Font dialog box appears (see Figure 89.16).

Figure 89.16.
The Object Properties and
Font dialog boxes.

4. Choose a heavy font such as Bauhaus from the Font list (the point size is locked at 14 points.). Then click the OK button.

5. Click OK in the Object Properties dialog box. The name you typed will now appear in all the views.

6. Click the Pick tool and center the text in the camera view.

7. With the text still selected, click the button for the Surface Roll-Up on the toolbar. (Refer to Figure 89.12.) Choose one of the colored balls and click Apply. You text should change to the color you selected. Close the roll-up.

8. Click the Stagehands button on the toolbar. The Stagehands dialog box appears. Click the Camera tab and select Panround. Select the Show Preview box to preview the camera effect. Now click the Load button to load the camera effect. Refer back to Figure 89.5 if you need help.

9. Click the Lights tab in the Stagehands dialog box and select Spotlight from the Files names list. Then click the Load button to load the spotlight effect.

10. Click the Close button in the Stagehands dialog box.

11. Click the Environment button on the toolbar. The Environment Properties dialog box appears. Click the Backdrop tab and select Canyon from the Files names list. Click the Apply button to apply the backdrop effect. Refer back to Figure 89.9 if you need help. If you want to include a sky to add more reflection in the scene, click on the Sky tab and choose one of the available skies. Be sure to click on the Apply button if you add a sky.

**12.** Click the OK button in the Environment Properties dialog box to close it. Your scene in the camera view should now look similar to Figure 89.17. You won't see the sky if you added one because it's there for reflection only.

*Figure 89.17.*
*The completed scene.*

**13.** Choose File | Scene Setup. The Scene Setup dialog box appears (see Figure 89.18). Make sure the Rendering tab is selected. Click the down arrow in the Shading Mode list box and select Shade fast. Change the Window Size in the lower-right corner to a Width of 300 and a Height of 200. Scroll in the Number of Colors list box and choose the highest number of colors your monitor supports. High Color (16-bit) equals 64,000 colors. True Color (24-bit) equals 16 million colors.

*Figure 89.18.*
*The Scene Setup*
*dialog box.*

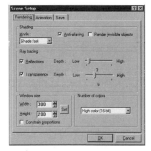

**14.** Click the Animation tab in the Scene Setup dialog box (see Figure 89.19). Type the number 3 in the Frames Per Second box (this is going to be a fast movie). Leave the other settings as they are.

*Figure 89.19.*
*The Scene Setup dialog*
*box with the Animation*
*tab selected.*

15. Click the Save tab in the Scene Setup dialog box (see Figure 89.20). Scroll in the Preview Type list box and choose Single Frame. Click the Compression Options button to display the Compression Options dialog box. Scroll in the Compressor list box and choose Microsoft Video 1. Move the Compression Quality slider over to 100. Click OK in the Compression dialog box.

*Figure 89.20.*
*The Scene Setup dialog*
*box with the Save tab*
*selected and the Compres-*
*sion Options dialog box*
*opened.*

# Corel *NOTE!*

If you chose Full Frames (uncompressed) in the Compression Options Compressor list box, your AVI files will be five times larger. If you choose Microsoft Video 1 and move the quality slider to 100, the movie will still look as good as an uncompressed movie but the file size will be much smaller.

16. Click OK in the Scene Setup dialog box.

17. Before you make the movie, click the Preview button on the toolbar. The preview will be a quick representation of the movie in Bounding Box mode.

18. Click the Make Movie button in the toolbar or select Animation | Make Movie. The Make Movie dialog box appears. This dialog box is just like any Save As dialog box. Instead of saving a file, however, you're saving a movie.

19. Choose a folder where you want to store your movie file. Give your movie a name in the Name box, and then scroll in the Save as Type list box and choose Video for Windows (AVI).

20. Click Save. You will see your scene being rerendered (based on the settings you made in the Scene Setup dialog box) during the Save process. This would be a good time to go to lunch because rendering times can take from several minutes to several hours depending on numbers of frames and the complexity of the image.

21. If you want to see your movie played back right after you have saved it, click the Play Movie button on the toolbar or select Animation | Play Movie (see

Figure 89.21). The Windows Media Player will appear along with the movie screen. Click the Play icon in the Media Player to run your movie.

*Figure 89.21.*
*The Media Player and the*
*movie screen.*

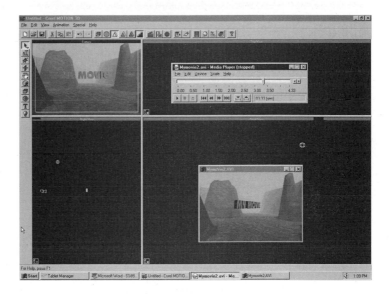

22. To play your movie anytime in the future, open the Media Player from the Start menu and play the movie from there. To access the Media Player, click Programs | Accessories | Multimedia | Media player.

## Using the Timelines Dialog Box

Click the Timelines button on the toolbar to open the Timelines dialog box. The Timelines dialog box displays a list of all the objects in a scene and provides the controls that allow you to set timed events for each object in the animation, including the camera and lights. You also can group objects into hierarchies in the Timelines dialog box. Figure 89.22 shows the Timelines dialog box. Refer to this figure as you learn about the tools and controls.

*Figure 89.22.*
*The Timelines dialog box.*

## Understanding the Parts of the Timelines Dialog Box

The Timelines dialog box contains six control buttons, which provide the following functions:

- The Preview button runs through the entire animation with all objects displayed in bounding box mode.
- The Make Movie button creates an animation from the current scene by rendering all the frames based on the information set in the Scene Setup dialog box.
- The Stop button stops the animation that is currently running.
- The Set Keyframe button moves the current time (as shown by the World Time Marker) ahead to the next time increment as defined in the Scene Setup dialog box. The default value is 1/2 second.
- If you click the Zoom In Time Scale button, less time will be visible in the timebar, and eventmarks will appear further apart. This option permits you to work in smaller increments of time.
- If you click the Zoom Out Time Scale button, more time will be visible on the timebar, and eventmarks will appear closer together. This option permits you to view a larger slice of time in the timeline.

The names of all objects in the current scene are listed in a column on the left side of the dialog box. To the right of each name is the corresponding timeline for that object. Default names are provided when an object is created, but you can edit object names in the Object Properties dialog box. Selecting a name in the list selects the object in the current view. Conversely, selecting an object in any view highlights the name of that object in the list. This feature is helpful when you're trying to locate objects that may have previously been set as invisible or when several objects appear to be identical.

The timebar runs across the top of the sequencer to display units of time. You can display time in one of the formats listed below by selecting the format from the Time list box at the top center of the Timelines dialog box.

Second/Frame

Second/Hundredths

Frames

The Time Tracker display is located just above the timebar and to the right of the Time Units list box. It displays the current time in the format that has been selected. The Time Tracker will show 00.00 before any events have been started.

The World Time Marker is the pointer that appears just below the timebar. This pointer determines the current time. You will drag the World Time Marker to the point in time where you want an object edit to take place. For example, if the marker is positioned at 2.0 seconds on the timebar, any manipulations that are performed on objects in the scene will take place two seconds into the animation.

You will notice that a symbol will be created on the timeline for the object, at the current time, only after you've performed some manipulation of the object. This symbol is called an eventmark. Eventmarks may be deleted, duplicated, or moved to another position on the timeline.

The Punch-In and Punch-Out markers are located just above the timebar. They are hardly visible before an animation is started. Look at Figure 89.24, and you will be able to see them. They consist of a bar with two handles on each end. By default, these markers start at time zero and move to track the last eventmark that was created in the timelines. These markers can be shortened by dragging the handles or repositioned by dragging on the bar portion. Shortening or repositioning the markers allow you to render only a portion of the entire scene when you make the final movie. If you plan on rendering only a portion of the timeline events using the Punch-In and Punch-Out markers, you must activate Between Punch-In and Punch-Out Markers in the Animation tab of the Scene Setup dialog box.

## Grouping Objects

You can group objects in a hierarchical model called a parent control object. This feature is important because you can create a model that consists of several individual objects that can be manipulated as one. The child objects within the parent control object may still be changed independently. When you create a parent control object, use an object that is not part of the model. This way, you can control all the objects as one by using the parent control object and maintain independent control of the individual child objects.

Right-click the parent control object to access the Object Properties dialog box. Set the object to Invisible and give it a name that describes the entire model. Now you can always locate the invisible parent in the view by selecting its name in the Timelines dialog box, yet it will not interfere with the rendered view of the model.

To create a hierarchy, drag an object's name onto the name of the object you want to be the parent object in the Timelines dialog box. Continue dragging as many objects' names as you want to be part of the hierarchy. A - sign appears to the left of the parent control object's name. Clicking this sign collapses the list of all the child object names under the parent control object and replaces the - with a +. Click the + sign to expand the object names again. Notice that the child objects names are placed below the parent and are indented. A child object may have only one parent, but a parent object can have multiple children. The order of the child object names in the list is not important. You should create any hierarchies you want before manipulating objects or creating animation.

## Making an Intermediate Movie

To incorporate the features of the Timeline dialog box into a more complex movie, follow these steps:

1. Open a new scene and click the Fast Render button on the toolbar.

2. Click the Timelines button on the toolbar to display the Timelines dialog box.

3. Choose File | Scene Setup. When the Scene Setup dialog box appears, use the same settings as you did making your first movie. You might want to increase the number of frames per second in the Animation tab settings just to make a smoother animation. Remember that the movie will take longer to render and the file size will increase.

4. Select the Lathe tool and click twice in the camera view. This will place two spheres side by side in the view.

5. Select the sphere on the left with the Pick tool and make it smaller by dragging it inward. Your scene should now look like Figure 89.23

*Figure 89.23.*
*The beginning scene with*
*the Timelines dialog box*
*displayed.*

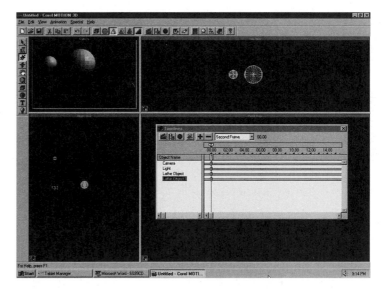

6. In the Timelines dialog box, drag the World Time Marker to the two second mark. If you hold down the Ctrl key as you drag, the World Time Marker will snap to each time scale increment.

7. Select the small sphere on the left and drag it to the right of the large sphere in the camera view. Notice that a small symbol will appear on the timeline at the two second mark. This symbol indicates that the event of moving the small sphere has taken place at that point. Your screen should now look like Figure 89.24.

*Figure 89.24.*
*The small sphere moved*
*to the right and the*
*Timelines dialog box*
*showing an event change.*

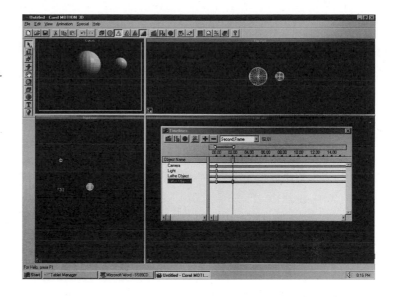

8. Click the World Time Marker again and drag it to the three second mark.

9. Select the small sphere again and drag it to the lower right in the camera view.

10. Click the Edit Object tool (its icon is a screwdriver and wrench) in the toolbox to display the Object Editor. (See Figure 89.25.)

*Figure 89.25.*
*The Object Editor dialog*
*box with the sphere*
*displayed.*

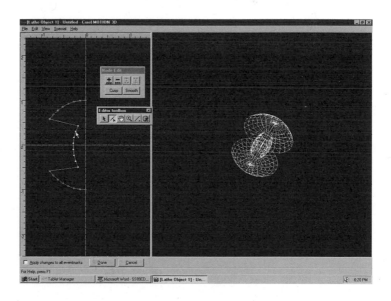

11. Click the Node edit icon in the Editor Toolbox.

12. Marquee-select the eight middle nodes on the perimeter of the circle and drag them toward the centerline. Look at the preview window to see the results in wireframe mode.

13. Click and hold on the Rotation icon in the Editor Toolbox. Select the Tilt icon from the drop-down menu that appears.

14. Click the wireframe model in the preview window and tilt the new shape to an angle similar to Figure 89.26.

*Figure 89.26.*
*The modified sphere in the*
*Object Editor.*

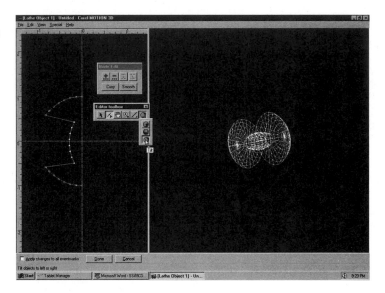

15. Click and hold the Rotation icon again and select Horizontal Rotate from the menu that appears. Click the wireframe model again and rotate the shape to look like Figure 89.27.

16. When you are finished rotating the modified sphere, click the Done button at the lower left of the Object Editor dialog box. You will be returned to the main screen. Notice another symbol has been added to the timeline and the modified sphere is displayed (see Figure 89.28).

17. Drag the World Time Marker over to the five second mark.

18. Select the modified sphere again and move it to the upper left in the camera view.

19. With the sphere still selected, click the Edit Object tool in the toolbox again.

Figure 89.27.
The sphere after being
rotated horizontally.

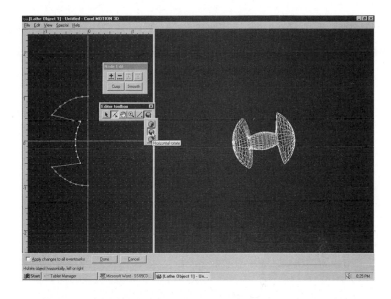

Figure 89.28.
The modified sphere and
the updated Timelines
dialog box.

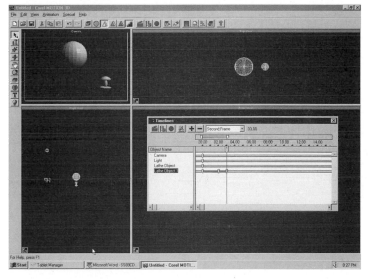

**20.** Click the Node Edit tool in the Editor Toolbox and marquee-select the four
middle nodes on the perimeter of your modified sphere and drag them to the
left (see Figure 89.29).

*Figure 89.29.*
*A newly modified shape.*

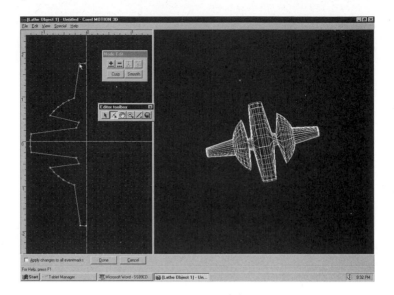

**21.** Marquee-select the two top nodes on the perimeter next to the centerline and drag them upwards. Do the same with the two bottom nodes on the perimeter. Click Done to return to the main screen. Your shape should now look something like Figure 89.30.

*Figure 89.30.*
*The newly modified shape and the updated timelines.*

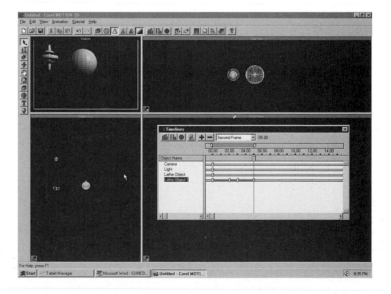

22. Click the Make Movie button in the toolbar or select Animation | Make Movie. The Make Movie dialog box appears. This dialog box is just like any Save As dialog box. Instead of saving a file, however, you are saving a movie.

23. Choose a folder where you want to store your movie file. Give your movie a name in the Name box, and then scroll in the Save As Type list box and choose Video for Windows (AVI).

24. Click Save. You will see your scene being rerendered (based on the settings you made in the Scene Setup dialog box) during the Save process.

You just created a second movie. You should now have a good start on being able to create some real masterpieces.

## Using the Object Editor

You were briefly exposed to the Object Editor when you created your second movie. The Object Editor provides separate views of objects and provides tools for editing the outlines of Lathe or Extrude objects.

Extrude objects are 3D objects created by pushing out a 2D outline to give it depth. For example, a cube is an extrusion of a square. In Corel MOTION 3D, a cube is the basic extrude object. Lathe objects are 3D objects created by rotating a 2D outline around a central axis. For example, a lathed semicircular arc is the outline that would produce a sphere. In Corel MOTION 3D, a sphere is the basic lathe object.

The Object Editor has its own separate toolbox called the Editor Toolbox. The following tools are included in the toolbox:

- You use the Pick tool to move and resize the outline.

- You use the Shape tool to node edit the outline. You can move, add, delete, break, or join nodes. When you click the Shape tool, a small Node Edit box appears above the toolbox. The Shape tool works just like the Shape tool in CorelDRAW (see Skill Session 7, "The Shape Tool").

- The Pan tool moves the Object Editor's view, as opposed to the outline itself. This tool is especially useful when zoomed into a portion of the outline.

- The Zoom tool has a flyout that contains zoom tools that let you zoom in, zoom out, or get a 1-to-1 view of the outline.

- The Outline Edit tool lets you draw lines, freehand outlines, rectangles, ellipses, open polygons, or closed polygons to edit or create a new outline. Click and hold the Outline Edit tool and choose an outline tool from the flyout.

- The Rotate tool rotates the 3D object view.

In Corel MOTION 3D, you can import other outlines into the Object Editor. These outlines must be either a Corel .CMX file or a 3D .DXF file. Corel does not recommend using a 2D .DXF file. Try using some of the outlines you have created in CorelDRAW or try using clip art. Follow these procedures to import a new outline:

1. Place an Extrude (cube) object in the camera view.
2. Double-click the Extrude object to open the Object Editor.
3. Delete the Extrude object that is currently in the Editor.
4. Import a .CMX file by choosing File | Import. From the Import flyout, choose Outline. Select the file you want to import from the Import dialog box. The imported outline will be placed in the left window and centered on the centerline. Your new outline will be instantly extruded into a 3D object in the right hand window. You can now edit the outline as you did when making your second movie. Figure 89.31 shows a CMX file of a CorelDRAW symbol imported into the Object Editor.

*Figure 89.31.*
*The Object Editor with an*
*imported DXF file.*

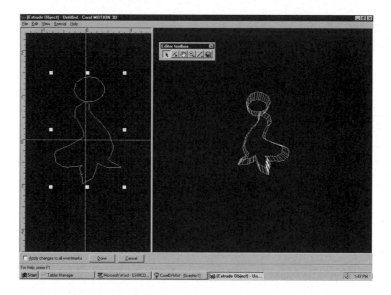

Depending on whether you have selected a Lathe or Extrude object, the behavior of Corel MOTION 3D will be slightly different. See what happens when you move an outline over the centerline when you are working in lathe mode. Remember, Lathe object outlines are rotated around the centerline, and Extrude object are extruded straight back. The object type will be displayed in the title bar to remind you which type of object you are working on.

The Apply Changes to All Eventmarks check box located in the lower-left corner of the Object Editor allows you to apply your edits to an object's shape, to all eventmarks in the scene for that object. If the box is not checked (the default state), the edits will apply only at the current time.

## Using the Surface Editor

You were briefly introduced to how to apply surfaces when you made your first movie. The Surface Editor allows you to edit the current library of surfaces and also lets you create your own surfaces or update the surfaces supplied with MOTION 3D. To access the Surface Editor, open the Surface roll-up by clicking the Surface button on the toolbar. Then click the Edit button. The Edit Surfaces dialog box will appear. (See Figure 89.32.) A list of the default surfaces are listed on the left of the dialog box. The various settings are listed on the right.

*Figure 89.32.*
*The Edit Surfaces*
*dialog box.*

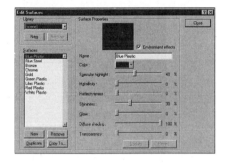

A brief description of what each setting is and what it does follows:

- Color sets the basic color of the surface.
- Specular highlight controls the brightness of the small, round white spot that is reflected at a point on the object that is closest to the light source.
- Metallicity adjusts the color of the specular highlight to match the surface color, giving a more metallic appearance.
- Reflectiveness controls how much of the adjacent objects will reflect in the object surface.
- Shininess controls how shiny the object appears by adjusting the size of the specular highlight.
- Glow makes an object appear as though it had a light inside of it, although it will not cast light onto adjacent objects.

- Diffuse shading adjusts the degree to which light is uniformly scattered over the surface of the object. The lower the value, the less illuminated the object appears.

- Transparency determines the degree to which you can see through an object. The effect of this attribute can only be seen in ray trace mode.

## Understanding Advanced Rendering Information

Rendering determines the rendering mode that will be used when the movie is created and whether anti-aliasing will be applied. Remember that the time to render the movie will be increased when you use higher quality rendering modes. Anti-aliasing also adds significant time to the rendering process. However, the quality of the finished product is much better when you use these modes. To get an idea as to the quality difference, try rendering a single frame in each mode, with and without anti-aliasing. This experiment will show you how each mode renders objects, and it will also give you an idea of the time involved.

When you work in ray trace mode, several factors will affect the time required to render the image. One is the number of lights in the scene, as well as the number of reflective surfaces. Ray tracing is a process in which the path of the light rays is calculated through each pixel on the objects being rendered. The attributes of the pixel determine how the light ray will bounce off or be absorbed by the surface. More sources of light require more calculations. Reflective surfaces also force additional calculations to determine the path of the reflected light. Additionally, objects may have a transparent surface in ray trace mode, which means that light rays will pass through the surface.

The controls to limit the ray trace calculations are located in the Scene Setup dialog box on the Rendering tab. The Reflection Depth control limits the number of times a ray will trace between two surfaces. The higher the number, the longer the rendering will take. Transparency Depth sets a limit to the number of transparent surfaces that a ray will travel through. The higher the setting, the longer the rendering process will take. If you have more transparent surfaces in a path than the depth level is set for, those surfaces beyond the depth level will not appear as transparent.

What is important to remember is that you are trying to produce a given effect in your 3D animations, and the tools needed to produce the desired effect may take considerable time. This is acceptable if the final results live up to the expectations. Use only the modes and settings that are required to produce the desired effect.

## Saving Corel MOTION 3D files

When saving your scene files, you can create a preview of the animation. This preview may be defined as Single Frame or Full Frame. Single Frame produces a single still image of the first frame of the scene. Full Frame creates a preview of the entire timeline, which can be run from the File Open dialog box. A scene file is saved with a .m3d extension.

It is important that you save the scene file if you want to edit any of the elements of the movie in the future. An .m3d scene file has all the editable data that can be modified to generate another movie. An AVI file is merely a series of rendering images (bitmaps) that are combined in a series to produce the animated effect.

# 90

# Corel MULTIMEDIA MANAGER

Corel MULTIMEDIA MANAGER is similar to what used to be Corel Mosaic, but it's more along the lines of a bookshelf-type application. At first glance, it appears to be just another Windows Program Manager, unless you noticed that it consumed 10 MB on your hard disk.

Corel MULTIMEDIA MANAGER is an electronic bookshelf designed to help you manage all of Corel's various multimedia files. Contained within each bookshelf are albums. Albums are groups of items that can represent either an embedded file or a link to another file elsewhere on the network or even on a CD-ROM. you also can create sub albums within albums.

As in the old Mosaic program, each item within an album is displayed with a thumbnail or miniature image of the original. If the object is not an image, it is represented with an icon.

Like in Microsoft Word, Excel, and PowerPoint workbooks, you can identify the contents of an album by assigning labels, keywords, and various notes about the contents of each file. With these things now labeled, you can search the various key fields for that "what did I do with that?" file. Project management has arrived in CorelDRAW 6. What could be easier? Just drag and drop the file into an album. Want a snapshot of where your project is? Print out the album's thumbnails. Want to browse through all the items? Create a slide show within the MULTIMEDIA MANAGER!

When files or *items*, as they are referred to in MULTIMEDIA MANAGER, are placed within an album, they are compressed, thus saving hard disk space. Items also only have to be saved in one location as they can be linked to another album. Each item can also have a reference to a default application saved with it in order to simplify editing. To edit a particular object, double-click it and launch the application that created it.

## Creating an Album

Create a new album. By default, the name of this album is Album1 (see Figure 90.1).

*Figure 90.1.*
*The Corel MULTIMEDIA*
*MANAGER desktop with*
*a new album.*

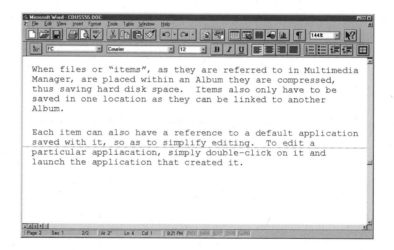

Add items to your album by choosing Edit | Insert Item. The Insert Item dialog box appears (see Figure 90.2). This example pulls in some full-color fills from the CorelDRAW Unleashed Seminar CD v. 5.1.

After inserting several more items, create a sub-album by choosing Edit | Insert Sub-Album. Press the Ctrl key and click the items you want in your sub-album. Then drag them onto the sub-album to move them. A dialog box enables you to confirm that you want to move the items. (See Figure 90.3.)

*Figure 90.2.*
*Inserting items into an*
*album.*

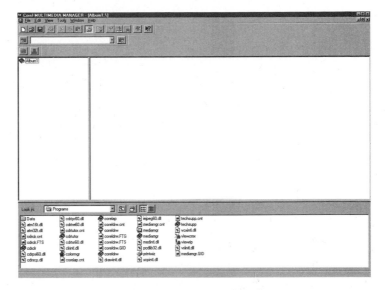

*Figure 90.3.*
*Inserting multiple items*
*into a sub-album.*

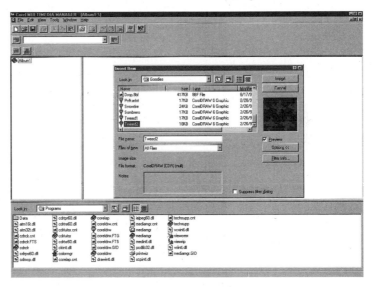

These three items, the PCX file, the TTF file, and the SCM file are now part of the
new sub-album, Sub Album1 (see Figure 90.4). Notice that Corel MULTIMEDIA
MANAGER knows what a PCX file is and creates a thumbnail of the image. It also
knows what a TrueType font is. Notice, however, that it does not recognize a SCM
(Lotus ScreenCam) file so it gave it a generic icon.

Figure 90.4.
Various contents of the
new sub-album.

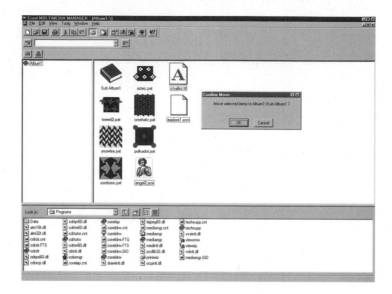

## Searching Albums

What good is MULTIMEDIA MANAGER if you still lose files? The key is hiring a librarian. Normally, this is you. Click an item and choose Edit | Properties or press Alt+Enter. The Properties dialog box (see Figure 90.5) has five sections identified by tabs.

Figure 90.5.
The Edit Properties dialog
box.

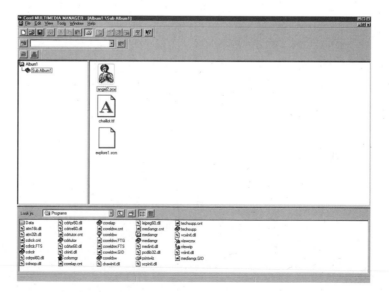

The first tab, General, provides you with a summary of the other five sections. The Link section shows you that this file is really a reference to a file existing on a CD-ROM on the F: drive. The Storage section tells you how big the file is. The Data Type is essentially what file type the object is. There are presently no Keywords entered for this item so nothing appears in the Keywords section.

Pay close attention to the Thumbnail tab shown in Figure 90.6. Notice that you can edit the image type from Black and White to say 16 Million Colors in the Type list box. In the Size list box, you can edit the image size. Other options in this dialog box include changing the image header and file compression.

*Figure 90.6.*
*The Edit Properties*
*Thumbnail dialog box.*

# Corel *TIP!*

Don't forget that you can right-click an item to quickly edit its properties, print it, or search for a particular item.

To begin a search, select all the items, including sub-albums, you want to search through. Then choose Edit | Search (or press Alt+S). The Item Search dialog box in Figure 90.7 will appear, prompting you for search criterion.

*Figure 90.7.*
*The Item Search*
*dialog box.*

In Figure 90.7, I have requested any items with a keyword like "Seminar."

Figure 90.8 shows the results of the search. From this point, the dialog box will allow you to perform many of the standard editing commands, such as copying the item or printing the item.

*Figure 90.8.*
*Results from the search.*

## Batch Editing Items

The Batch Property Edit dialog box shown in Figure 90.9 allows you to perform many of the same functions as Edit Properties, only on multiple objects. You can perform a batch edit either on items based upon certain criterion you enter (for example, change all 256 color items to 16 color items) or all items, simply Ctrl-select on the items you wish to batch edit.

*Figure 90.9.*
*The Batch Property Edit*
*dialog box.*

## Playing a Slide Show

To perform a slide show (one pass through by default), just press the Ctrl key and click the items or sub-albums you would like to be displayed. This slide show is not presentation quality, but it is a good way to browse through a project.

To change slide show options, choose Tools | Options, and then select the Slide Show tab. To find this tab, click the right arrow box in the upper right portion of the Options dialog box.

## Customizing MULTIMEDIA MANAGER

Just like CorelDRAW, any or all the menus, shortcut keys, or toolbars may be customized. The procedure for doing this in MULTIMEDIA MANAGER is the same as in CorelDRAW. See Skill Session 4, "Customizing and Setting Preferences," for more information.

## Using MULTIMEDIA MANAGER's Mini-Editors

MULTIMEDIA MANAGER contains two editors, one for bitmap images and one for vector drawings. To set the default editor for items, choose Tools | Options | Editors. The dialog box in Figure 90.10 appears. I recommend keeping the defaults as most of the time the mini-editors can only perform very simple functions. Neither of the editors is very feature-rich, but for a quick and simple edit that will do.

*Figure 90.10.*
*The Editors tab of the*
*Options dialog box.*

## Exporting Multiple Files

One of the most convenient features of MULTIMEDIA MANAGER is the capability of mass-exporting an entire group of files into a new file format. In the example shown in Figure 90.11, I have selected multiple vector files representing various color fills and mass-exported them all as JPEG files by just selecting them and then choosing Export. To accomplish the above, Ctrl-select the items to export.

*Figure 90.11.*
*Using the Export dialog*
*box to export multiple*
*files.*

# OCR-TRACE

OCR-TRACE is a program that lets you scan text from books, newsletters, and so on, and convert it to editable text for use in CorelDRAW and other word processing programs. The program also lets you convert bitmap images into vector format for use in CorelDRAW. Using OCR-TRACE is fairly straightforward. There are a number of settings that can be used to control the accuracy of the trace when you are tracing bitmap images or text.

Corel's user manual devotes five pages to the section on the TRACE module and two pages on the OCR module. Both sections describe what the modules will do but fails to tell you how to do it. In the case of the trace module, you will see sample traces using the various tracing methods such as Outline and Wood Cut. In the authors' view, you will save time and frustration by not even using the CorelTRACE module in Corel's OCR-TRACE. We say this because we have found it to be a very poor bitmap-to-vector conversion application. You might find it useful if you use the program to trace images for an abstract effect. If you do decide to give this program a try, beware of the enormous number of nodes the trace will produce when you create the vector drawing.

## Corel *TIP!*

Corel OCR-TRACE is TWAIN-compliant, which means you can scan text and images directly into the program.

# TRACE

Figure 91.1 shows the OCR-TRACE screen as it first appears when the program is opened. (The Trace Settings dialog box has also been opened and is displayed on-screen.)

*Figure 91.1.*
*The OCR-TRACE screen*
*with the Trace Settings*
*dialog box displayed.*

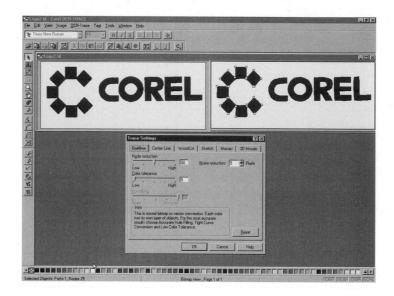

The following is a brief description of the process of tracing a bitmap image:

1. Open a previously saved bitmap image or choose the Acquire command in the File menu and scan a new image directly into OCR-TRACE.

2. The bitmap image will appear on the left of the screen with a blank screen displayed on the right.

3. Click the OCR-TRACE menu and select Trace Settings from the drop-down menu. The Trace Settings dialog box will appear. (See Figure 91.1.)

4. Click the appropriate tab for the trace you want to perform. There is a Hint box in the lower left of the dialog box suggesting certain settings for the type of trace you have selected.

5. After changing the settings in the Trace Settings dialog box, click OK. You are now ready to trace the bitmap.

6. Click the OCR-TRACE menu again and click Perform Trace in the drop-down menu. A flyout menu will appear.

7. Choose the type of trace you want to perform from the flyout menu. The vector trace will appear in the window on the right.

8. Save your vector trace by choosing Save in the File menu, and then choose Vector from the Save flyout menu.

9. You will be given a choice of several vector formats. If you want to save the trace as a CorelDRAW vector, you must save the file as a CMX file.

10. If you want to save the bitmap image you scanned, choose Save from the File menu again and then choose Image from the Save flyout. You can save the bitmap image in various bitmap formats.

That's the basics of tracing a bitmap image. If you try tracing a color bitmap in Outline mode, an object will be created for each color in the image. If the image contains the same color in different areas of the image, separate objects will be created for that color, but they will be combined as one single object. Use the Break Apart command in CorelDRAW to do any further editing.

## OCR

Although we recommend caution when using the Trace module in OCR-TRACE, the OCR capabilities are excellent. Therefore, we will devote the remainder of the skill session to learning the OCR module.

The OCR tracing method is used to trace all forms of scanned-in text or text from a fax you have received directly into your system. The purpose of OCR tracing is to convert bitmap text images into editable text. The default settings will produce excellent results if you are OCR tracing a high-resolution image. To demonstrate this fact, scan in a page of text at 300 dpi. OCR trace the image by clicking the Perform OCR command in the OCR-Trace menu. Your page of bitmap text will appear in the menu on the right, converted to editable text. When the text appears, the Verification dialog box will appear and begin spell checking your new text. The spell checker works like most other spell checkers, letting you make corrections or ignore suggested misspelled words. You can even edit the text directly by placing the cursor in the traced text page. Figure 91.2 shows the scanned text on the left and the traced text on the right, with the Verification dialog box showing on screen. Notice the word Splitter is shown in the Word box and a suggested new word to replace it.

If you're working with a low-resolution image or you want to change or retain certain formatting of the traced text, you will need to make changes in the OCR Settings dialog box before you evoke the Perform OCR trace command. The following sections explain the steps to follow and the different settings that are available to get the optimum OCR trace.

## Corel*NOTE!*

> For best results, in most cases, scan your text at 300 dpi.

*Figure 91.2.*
*The Verification dialog*
*box checking a word in*
*the traced text.*

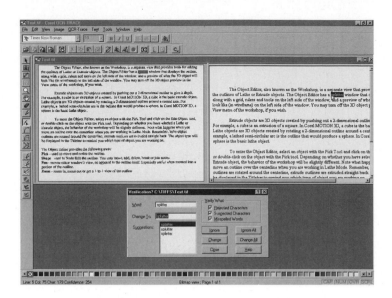

## OCR Settings

1. Open a previously scanned image or choose the Acquire command in the File menu and scan a new text page directly into OCR-TRACE.

2. Click the OCR-Trace menu and choose OCR Setting from the drop-down menu. The OCR Setting dialog box with four tabs at the top of the dialog box appears. (See Figure 91.3.) Clicking the tabs will display different setting options for Language, Content, Source, and Formatting. Each option is described next.

### Language

1. From the Language list box, choose the language to be traced. Select the appropriate language to ensure that the OCR properly traces the accents and other special symbols in the language of the document. French, German, Spanish, and Swedish capabilities are available on the CorelDRAW CD-ROM included in the box. If you use a language other than English you will need to do a custom reinstall of CorelDRAW and choose the appropriate language when you choose dictionaries. If you're not concerned about spell checking or accent characters, you can OCR trace in English and manually correct any misspelled words. Figure 91.3 shows the Setting dialog box with the language tab selected.

2. Place a check mark in the Check Spelling box to enable the spell checker.

3. Type a character in the Reject Character box. The default is the tilde (˜). This character is used as a reference character for the confidence level of the spell

checker. If the spell checker doesn't recognize a letter, the checker will replace it with a tilde character. The tilde character is used as a default because it is the least likely to be used in any text document.

4. Adjust the Confidence slider to a level of confidence. The setting you choose controls the accuracy of the spell checker. The default is 75.

5. The Hint section gives you tips on how to use the settings in the dialog box.

*Figure 91.3.*
*The OCR-TRACE Setting*
*dialog box with the*
*Language tab selected.*

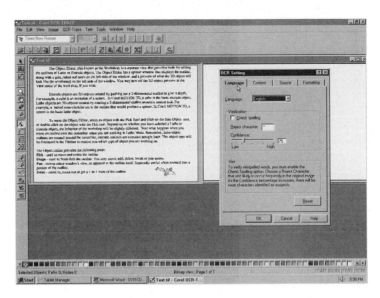

## Content

1. Choose between Multi-column text and/or graphics, Single column text, or Table. The choice of settings here are self-evident depending on the form of text you're tracing. If you're tracing a scanned image of multi-column text or any form of text that also included graphics, choose Multi-column text and/or graphics. If you scanned single-column text with no graphics, choose Single column text. If your scanned image included tables, choose Table. Figure 91.4 shows the OCR-Trace setting dialog box with the Content tab selected.

2. The Hint section gives you tips on how to use this dialog box.

## Source

1. Click the down arrow on the Source list box to choose a source that most closely represents the type of text you will be tracing. Your choices are Normal, Dot Matrix, and Fax. Normal would be text found in books, magazines. Dot Matrix is text printed on a dot matrix printer. Fax is text printed from a fax machine or received via modem into your computer system.

*Figure 91.4.*
*The OCR-TRACE setting*
*dialog box with the*
*Content tab selected.*

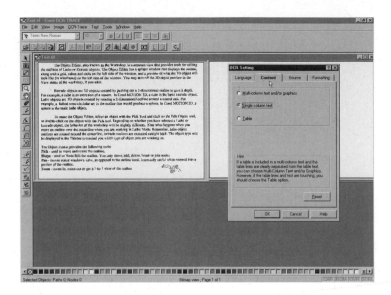

2. Choose the orientation of the document you're scanning by clicking the appropriate button. The Orientation buttons show a visual representation of the page with arrows pointing to the direction that the document was placed on the scanner prior to scanning. If you're not sure of the orientation choose Auto-detect.

3. If you check the Deskew box, the Maximum angle parameters box and Rotate Image to Portrait are lit up. Entering a number in the Maximum angle box will rotate the image by the number of degrees you enter. You will need to rotate the image only if you have scanned it in at an angle. Checking the Rotate Image to Portrait box will place the scanned text in portrait mode if it's in a different orientation.

4. The Hint section tells you what will occur if you check Auto-detect.

Figure 91.5 shows the Setting dialog box with the source tab selected.

### Formatting

1. You have three formatting choices: Retain all page formatting, Retain font and paragraph formatting only, and Ignore formatting. We have found that choosing Retain font and paragraph formatting seems to work the best. You can always change other formatting in your word processor.

2. If you have chosen Ignore formatting you can choose the font to be used in the trace by choosing a font from the font list. You can also choose the font size by entering the number in the Size box. Figure 91.6 shows the Setting dialog box with the Formatting tab selected.

Figure 91.5.
The OCR-TRACE Setting
dialog box with the Source
tab selected.

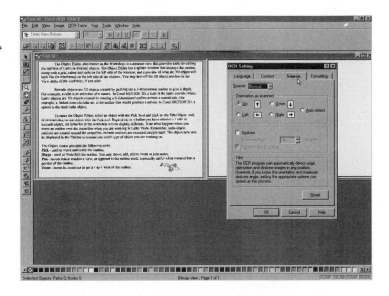

Figure 91.6.
The OCR-TRACE Setting
dialog box with the
Formatting tab selected.

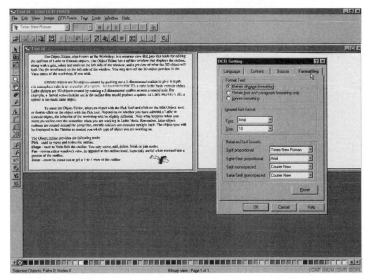

After you have completed the OCR trace of the bitmap text, you can either save
the trace by choosing the Save command in the File menu and then choosing Save
Text from the flyout, or you can choose Print in the File menu and print the new
text directly to your printer.

If you decide to print directly from OCR-Trace you must place the cursor in the
traced text and highlight the text before choosing Print from the File menu. Figure
91.7 shows the Print dialog box and the highlighted text to be printed.

*Figure 91.7.*
*The Print dialog box with*
*the selected text dis-*
*played on the right-hand*
*screen.*

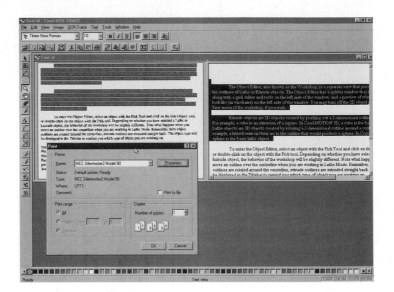

# 92

# Corel SCRIPT

Corel SCRIPT provides a scripting (or macro) language for use with CorelDRAW and CorelPHOTO-PAINT. The commands you use for your scripts are a cross between Visual Basic and application commands. If you already have a background in Visual Basic, then you should find the language fairly simple to understand. For those without a programming background, you'll be glad to know that the Visual Basic language is one of the easiest to learn.

The scripts you create will be saved with a CSC extension, but they are nothing more than ASCII text files. Therefore, you can create them in any text editor if you desire. However, the Corel SCRIPT Editor provides many features that assist you in writing scripts. The Corel SCRIPT Editor screen is shown in Figure 92.1 with one of the scripts supplied by Corel loaded.

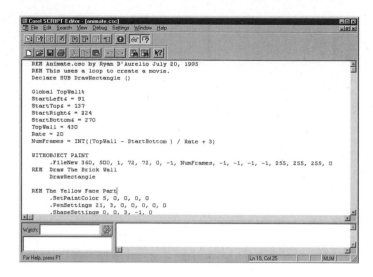

*Figure 92.1.*
*The Corel SCRIPT Editor*
*screen.*

## Creating a Dialog Box

There is not much to describe about the Corel SCRIPT Editor, and detailing all of the commands in the language is not feasible in this book. All of the commands are documented in the Corel-supplied help files. Therefore, we'll walk you through the creation of a simple script and the design of a user interface. This script will give you capabilities that the CorelDRAW application doesn't include. It will draw a rectangle of a precise size and a precise corner radius. Doing this without a script requires close watching of the status line or the placement of several guide-lines.

Most scripts will have two parts. The exceptions are scripts that don't require user input; therefore, they only include one part. But, when user input is required, a user interface must be designed. For this example, we need to get the height, width, and corner radius from the user. While the user interface can be created in code, it is usually easier to design it with Corel SCRIPT Dialog Editor. This allows you to design in a WYSIWYG environment. All this may seem complicated, but once you have created your first script and an interface, it will be much easier from then on. The Dialog Editor is described in depth in Skill Session 93, "Corel SCRIPT Dialog Editor."

The script and user interface are created in the Corel SCRIPT Dialog Editor. When you first open the Dialog Editor, you will see in the main window a blank, gray dialog box titled Corel SCRIPT Dialog. Follow these steps in order to create the entire script:

1. Drag the bottom portion of the window downward to increase the vertical size (see Figure 92.2).

*Figure 92.2.*
*Expanding the size of the*
*script window.*

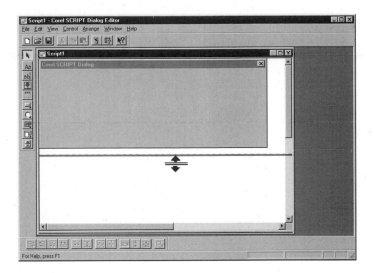

2. Place the cursor on the thin gray line just above the bottom window border (watch closely because it can be hard to find). The cursor will change to a small double-headed arrow with two horizontal lines separating the arrows (the cursor in Figure 92.2 was purposely made larger so that it would be visible).

3. After you select the line, drag it upward in the window. A thick gray line will be attached to the cursor. Drag all the way up until you reach the bottom of the blank dialog box and then release the mouse button. You will see the code generated for the dialog box. It starts with only two statements: one for beginning the dialog and one for ending it. (See Figure 92.3.)

4. The first thing you want to do is change the name of the dialog box from Corel SCRIPT Dialog to Draw Rectangle of Exact Size. To do this, click the title bar that contains the words Corel SCRIPT Dialog. With the dialog box selected, right-click in the dialog box itself and choose Attributes from the menu. The Dialog Attributes box will appear (see Figure 92.4). Changing the value (in this case the value is the name) in the Text field will change the name in the title bar.

5. You also want to give a name to this dialog box as it will be referenced within the script. Go ahead and enter DrawRectDialog in the Value field.

6. Change the numbers in the width parameters box to 204 and in the height parameters box to 57. These settings determine the size of the interface dialog box that will be created.

7. Now you can click the OK button. You will see the script changes (in the bottom half of the window) and the new dialog box for the interface. (See Figure 92.5.)

*Figure 92.3.*
*A window showing the dialog box and its associated code.*

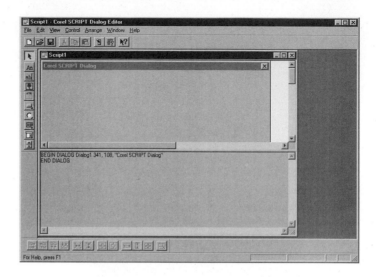

*Figure 92.4.*
*The Dialog Attributes dialog box.*

*Figure 92.5.*
*The dialog box after changing the name in the title bar.*

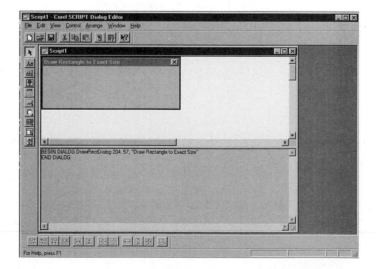

The next step is to put some controls on the interface dialog box. The first control will be a group box. This box will contain several different control items. It helps you visually group related controls on the dialog box. While it may not be necessary for this simple script, it could come in handy if this script is expanded with more controls later. Follow these steps to create the user interface dialog box:

1. The fifth icon down in the tool box (with the letters XYZ) is used to create a group box. Click this icon and then drag a rectangle onto the dialog box, the same as if you were creating a rectangle in CorelDRAW. You'll now see the group box labeled GroupBox1. We want to change the name as well as several other attributes of this box.

2. Right-click the group box and choose Attributes.

3. Change the text to Desired Rectangle Size. Change the numbers in the X and Y boxes to 0 and the numbers in the Width and Height boxes to 140 and 40. Click OK to see your group box with its new name.

4. You now need to add three boxes for user input with labels above them. Before you add the actual box, you need to add the text label above the box. The second icon down in the tool box (Aa) is for adding text. Click this icon and then drag a rectangle inside of the group box. Once you've let go of the mouse, the rectangle will be drawn with the text Text1 inside of it.

5. Right-click the Text1 rectangle and choose Attributes. Change the text to Height. Change the value of the X position to 5 and the Y position to 9. Change the Size values to 25 in the Width box and 8 in the Height box. Note that these numbers were chosen after some experimentation and are by no means "magic numbers." Click OK and you'll see the changes. Also take a look below the dialog box at the new code that's been created.

6. We now need the parameters box for the user input of the height. Choose the third icon down to create this parameter box. Drag out a rectangle below the word Height, and you'll see a white rectangle.

7. Right-click the white rectangle and choose Attributes. The Value field will be highlighted. The Value field contains the name of the variable in which the user's input will be stored. Change this to DesiredHeight$. In case you haven't done any programming in the past, the dollar sign indicates that you will be receiving a string of text. (You'll convert it to a number later.) Change the Position settings to 5, 18 and the Size settings to 35, 13. Click OK to see the new parameters box with the label above it. Figure 92.6 shows the results of all the changes that have been made.

Creating the other two labels and text boxes is done in the same way. Steps 8–15 take you through creating the rest of the boxes.

8. Click the second icon down in the tool box (Aa) for adding the label text. Click and drag a second rectangle inside the Main group box.

*Figure 92.6.*
*The dialog box with a*
*label and a text input box.*

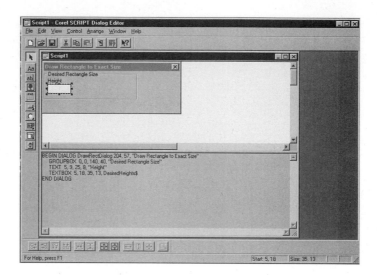

9. Right-click the Text2 rectangle and choose Attributes. Change the text to Width, the Position settings to 50, 9 and the Size settings to 25, 8. Click OK and you'll see your changes.

10. Choose the third icon down to create the Width parameters box. Drag out a rectangle below the word Height to make the white rectangle.

11. Right-click the white rectangle and choose Attributes. The Value field will again be highlighted. Change the text to DesiredWidth$ and change the Position settings to 50, 18 and the Size settings to 35, 13. That takes care of the Width parameters box. Now you can finish up by creating the Radius box.

12. Click the second icon down in the tool box (Aa) for adding the label text. Click and drag a third rectangle inside of the Main group box.

13. Right-click the Text3 rectangle and choose Attributes. Change the text to Radius, the Position settings to 95, 9 and the Size settings to 25, 8. Click OK and you'll see your changes.

14. Choose the third icon down to create the Radius parameters box. Drag out a rectangle below the word Radius to make the white rectangle.

15. Right-click the white rectangle and choose Attributes. Change the text in the Value field to DesiredRadius$ and change the Position settings to 95, 18 and the Size settings to 35, 13.

Congratulate yourself—you are almost finished. You should now see something similar to the example shown in Figure 92.7. The only things missing at this stage are the OK and Cancel buttons.

*Figure 92.7.*
*The dialog box with all*
*text boxes and labels.*

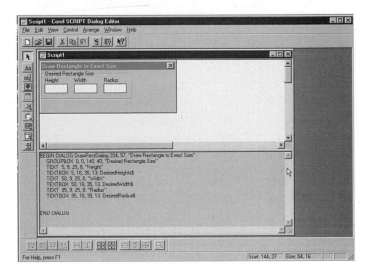

To create a button choose the Button icon (the sixth tool down in the toolbox). Click and hold down the icon to display the flyout and then choose the second button (the one with a green check mark on it). This is the tool for creating an OK button. Select the tool and drag a rectangle to the upper-right corner of the dialog box. It will draw a button with the text OK on it. Now return to the flyout and choose the third button across (the one with a red × on it). This is the Cancel button. Drag a rectangle to the lower-right corner of the dialog box to get a button with the word Cancel on it. Size and position these buttons to your liking, either by stretching and dragging or by adjusting the attributes as you've done with the other controls. You should now have a complete dialog box, as shown in Figure 92.8. Save this file as DRAWRECT.CSC in the COREL60\SCRIPTS folder, and you'll move on to the Corel SCRIPT Editor application.

Figure 92.8.
The finished dialog box.

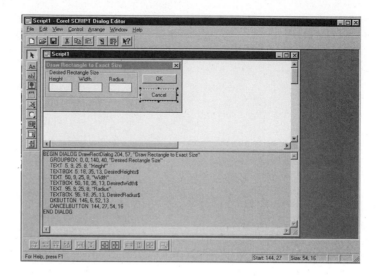

## Writing a Script

To begin, start the Corel SCRIPT Editor program. Open the DRAWRECT.CSC file in Corel SCRIPT. You'll see the code created by the Corel SCRIPT Dialog Editor, as shown in Figure 92.9.

Figure 92.9.
The script as seen in the
Corel SCRIPT Editor.

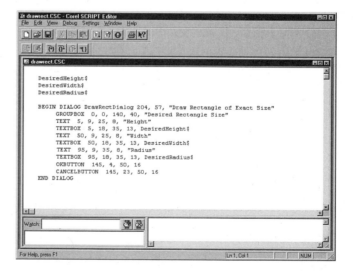

The first thing you should do in any program is put in some information about the program itself at the top of the file. Place the cursor at the beginning of the top line and press the Enter key. To add comments to a file, use the REM command. You want to add a comment telling a little about the program, so add the line REM Draw rectangle of specified size (make sure there is a space after REM). It is also quite common to add a comment regarding the ownership of the program. Therefore, you'll see that the next line is a copyright notice.

Now you want to give some of your variables a default value. This is so that when you bring up the dialog box, there will already be numbers in each of the fields. So, add the line DesiredHeight$="1" followed by the lines DesiredWidth$="1" and DesiredRadius$="0" (these will be the default numbers). You'll remember that those were the names you gave to the Value field in the text boxes created in the Dialog Editor.

Following this preliminary code is the code for drawing the dialog box. Look at the code closely. Remember, this is what you entered in the Dialog Editor. You will see the name of the control first, followed by four numbers that indicate the position and size of the control. Lastly, some of the items have text or variable names at the end of the line. At a future time, you might feel more comfortable creating your dialog boxes right here in Corel Script Editor because the syntax is fairly easy to follow. Also, notice that the dialog box definition begins and ends with the commands BEGIN DIALOG and END DIALOG. This is so the script will know where the definition begins and ends, and it also gives the definition a name. In this case, the name is DrawRectDialog, the name you assigned in the Dialog Editor.

Okay, now you're ready to do some programming. All of the drawing commands in the Corel SCRIPT language use the base measurement of one tenth of a micron. Most people don't normally work in microns, so you'll want to specify measurements in inches. Therefore, you need to declare a value for how many tenths of a micron are contained in an inch. The next line, therefore, reads CONINCH& = 254000 (CONINCH is an abbreviation for "convert to inches"). The ampersand after CONINCH indicates that this variable is a long integer, which means that the number is bigger than 32,767 and it doesn't have any decimal places.

You previously defined the look of the dialog box in Corel SCRIPT Dialog Editor, now you want to write the command to display it on screen. To do this, you will use the DIALOG command. When you call the command, you need to assign it to a variable so that you know what happened when the dialog is closed. Clicking OK will return one number, clicking Cancel will return another, and so on. For this exercise, don't worry about the number because you just want your rectangle. But, in the future, you should differentiate between the OK button and the Cancel button. The command is ret=DIALOG(DrawRectDialog). ret is the name of the variable (it's an abbreviation for "return") that will tell you what the user pushed, and the name of the dialog box is in the parentheses. The numbers entered by the user will now be stored in the variables.

You need to create a routine that draws a rectangle. To begin a routine, enter the command WITHOBJECT DRAW, where WITHOBJECT tells the routine to use a particular object (that means a program such as, DRAW, PAINT, and so on) and DRAW is the name of the object. Basically, this means to do whatever we tell you in CorelDRAW.

To draw a rectangle, use the CreateRectangle command. That's pretty simple to remember, right? What gets difficult is remembering how each of the measurements is used by the command. Therefore, you should add a REM to show how the command is used. It reads REM .CreateRectangle height, width, bottom, right, radius. This means that you need to add five numbers after the CreateRectangle command. Also note that all commands are preceded by a period.

The following section is an example of what you will find in the Help file when you look up a command. You'll see the command name followed by several variables. In this case, each of the variables has =long following it. This means that the command expects a long integer. Then, each of the variables is defined, so that you'll know what it is used for.

## The *CreateRectangle* Command

This command draws rectangles and squares. Here is the syntax:

```
.CreateRectangle .Top=long, .Left=long, .Bottom=long, .Right=long,
.CornerRadius=long
```

Each of the variables is defined as shown in the following list:

| Syntax | Definition |
| --- | --- |
| .Top | Specifies the Y coordinate of the upper-left corner of the rectangle in tenths of a micron, relative to the origin. |
| .Left | Specifies the X coordinate of the upper-left corner of the rectangle in tenths of a micron, relative to the origin. |
| .Bottom | Specifies the Y coordinate of the lower-right corner of the rectangle in tenths of a micron, relative to the origin. |
| .Right | Specifies the X coordinate of the lower-right corner of the rectangle in tenths of a micron, relative to the origin. |
| .CornerRadius | Specifies the radius used to create the rounded corners in tenths of a micron. |

Now you just need to calculate each of these numbers. The numbers entered in the dialog box are entered as text, and not numbers. Therefore, you have to convert them. The VAL command will take the numbers as text and convert them into numbers. You use the command `RectHeight=val(DesiredHeight$)` to do this conversion. This is followed by the commands `RectWidth=val(DesiredWidth$)` and `RectRadius=val(DesiredRadius$)` to convert the Width and Radius boxes.

Now, draw the rectangle. Remember that you need to multiply each of your numbers by CONINCH or you will get very tiny rectangles. Two of the numbers needed are for the bottom and right side of the rectangle. Deciding the placement of the rectangle will be left for a future exercise, so just use 0. Therefore, the command reads

```
.CreateRectangle RectHeight * CONINCH, RectWidth * CONINCH, 0 * CONINCH, 0 * CONINCH, RectRadius * CONINCH.
```

The asterisk is the symbol for multiplication. You might also wonder why you multiplied 0 by CONINCH as well. This was done so that when you have a variable for these measurements, you'll just need to replace the zeros with it.

The last thing you need to add is the END WITHOBJECT command. This indicates that you're done using whatever object (DRAW, PAINT, and so on) you were using. In this case, you're done with DRAW. When you're all done, your screen should like the one shown in Figure 92.10. You can't see the entire script listing in Figure 92.10 because it has scrolled off the screen.

Now you're ready to see if it works.

*Figure 92.10.*
*The finished script, as*
*seen on-screen.*

Open CorelDRAW and click the Tools menu. Choose Script from the flyout and then choose Run. This will bring up the Run Script dialog box. Change to the folder where your new script file is located and then open the file. You should have named the file Drawrec.CSC. Figure 92.11 shows the script's dialog box that you designed within your script. Now it's simply a matter of entering the Height, Width, and Radius values. Figure 92.12 shows the script's dialog box and a completed, rounded rectangle. The values entered in the example are 4 for Height, 4 for Width, and .5 for Radius.

*Figure 92.11.*
*The dialog box, ready for*
*user input.*

*Figure 92.12.*
*The dialog box with the*
*rectangle it created.*

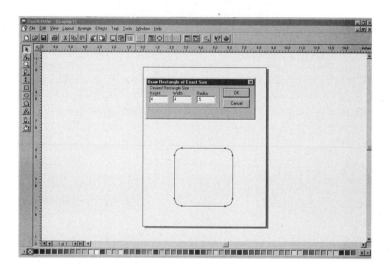

The really interesting thing about using the script's dialog box is that you can specify the radius for the rectangle's corners in inches. You can't do this in CorelDRAW itself! However, there is something else the script does that is actually a side effect. Run the script again and specify 4 inches for each of the three measurements. You should get a shape similar to the one shown in Figure 92.13. This shape you can't create without a script, because CorelDRAW limits the amount of radius to one half of the shortest side of a rectangle when you do it manually. Therefore, not only can you be really accurate, but you can also do things that can't be done any other way.

*Figure 92.13.*
*Rectangle created with*
*our script.*

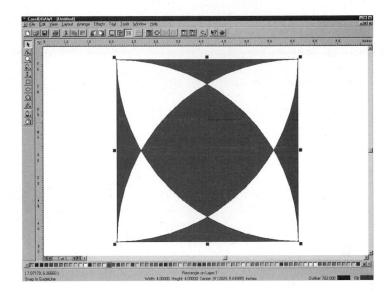

# 93

# The Corel SCRIPT Dialog Editor

The Corel SCRIPT Dialog Editor is used to create dialog boxes for use in Corel SCRIPT. Although it is not necessary to create the dialog boxes in the Dialog Editor, it is much easier to create them in this WYSIWYG environment than in Corel SCRIPT.

Not all scripts need a dialog box; they are only necessary when the script will require some form of input from the user. This input can be as simple as a single number or as complex as you want to make it.

In this skill session, you'll get a basic overview of how the Dialog Editor works. Remember to keep your dialog boxes simple so that users can easily understand them.

## The Toolbox

The tools in the Dialog Editor should look familiar if you've done any programming with Visual Basic. Icons in the toolbox work like the rest of the Corel suite as some of them are on flyouts. The toolbox is shown in Figure 93.1.

*Figure 93.1.*
*The Dialog Editor's*
*toolbox.*

## The Selector Tool

The Selector tool looks and works just like the Pick tool in CorelDRAW, but Corel decided to make things difficult and call it the Selector tool. Like the Pick tool, it can be used to select, stretch, move, and generally alter objects. As you progress through the other tools, select the Selector tool and adjust each of the other dialog elements. You'll see the similarities.

## The Text Tool

The Text tool's icon has "Aa" on it. It is used to place text on a dialog box as a label—this means it is used to create text that the user can see but cannot change. Click the icon and marquee-select a rectangular area on the blank dialog box titled Corel SCRIPT dialog. This will give you a box with sizing handles that says Text1. To change the text itself, right-click the object and choose Attributes (or simply use the Alt+Enter shortcut key). Change the text showing in the Text box and hit Enter. The changes will now be displayed. Figure 93.2 shows some text I created that says This is a text control.

*Figure 93.2.*
*Text created with the*
*Text tool.*

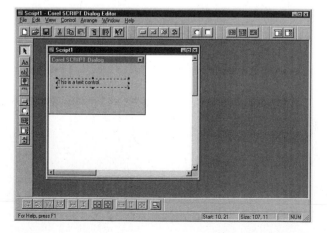

One of the limitations of the Text tool is that there is no way to change the font or size of the text. If that is important, you'll have to create your scripts in Visual Basic or some other application that supports OLE Automation.

## The Text Box Tool

The Text Box tool's icon has "ab" and the insertion cursor on it. It is used to create a box for the user to enter text. You can also enter a default value in the box by declaring a variable in Corel SCRIPT (see Skill Session 92, "Corel SCRIPT"). Create a text box just like you created text: Select the Text Box tool and drag out a rectangle to the size you want. If the box is too big or too small, simply use the Selector tool to resize it or use the Attributes dialog box to specify exact values (hint: right-click and choose Attributes). An example of a text box is shown in Figure 93.3.

*Figure 93.3.*
*A text box created with*
*the Text Box tool.*

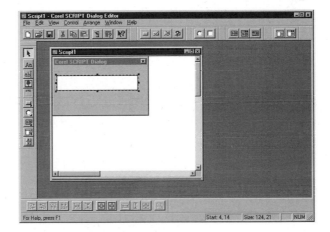

## The Image Tool

The Image tool enables you to place a static image on a dialog box. The image can be in either BMP or RLE format only. To create a placeholder for the image, select the Image tool and drag out a rectangle to the size you desire. Again, you can stretch and shape this rectangle using the Selector tool until it is the right size. You can also change the size through the Attributes menu. To use an image, enter its full path name in the Value field of the Attributes dialog box. This is initially set to a variable name so that you can control the image from within your script if you so desire. Figure 93.4 shows an Image placeholder on the dialog box. Note that it will always show the Corel balloon over the mountains until runtime.

Figure 93.4.
An image placeholder
created with the Image
tool.

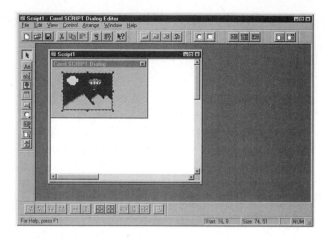

## The Group Box Tool

*Group boxes* are used to draw a border around several controls on a dialog box so
that they are visually grouped. To create one, click the Group Box icon (it has the
letters xyz on it) and drag a rectangle on the dialog box where you want a group
box to appear. You can resize it in the same manner as the other controls. In the
Attributes dialog box, the text you enter will be the title shown at the upper left of
the group box. An example of a group box is shown in Figure 93.5.

Figure 93.5.
A group box.

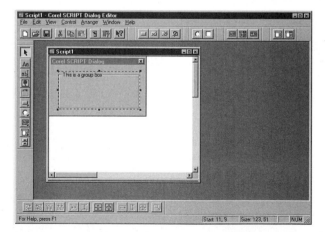

## The Button Tools

The Dialog Editor provides four different kinds of button tools. Each of these tools
has a separate icon on the toolbox flyout, as shown in Figure 93.6.

Figure 93.6.
The Button Tool flyout.

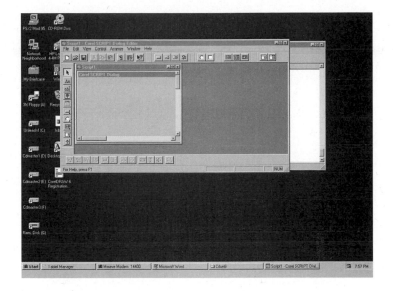

The first tool is the Button tool itself, which enables you to place a button and insert whatever text you desire on the button. The other three buttons will have predefined text and behaviors. They are the OK Button tool, the Cancel Button tool, and the Help Button tool. An example of each of the button tools is shown in Figure 93.7.

Figure 93.7.
Each of the buttons
available for use.

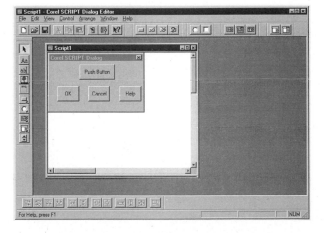

To add a button to the dialog box, simply select the appropriate button tool and drag a rectangle onto the dialog box. If you are using the Pushbutton tool, you can change the text in the Attributes dialog box. All other buttons have predefined text that you cannot change.

997

## The Value Button Tools

There are two different value buttons found in the Value Button flyout shown in Figure 93.8. The first is the Option button and second is the Check Box.

*Figure 93.8.*
*The Value Button flyout.*

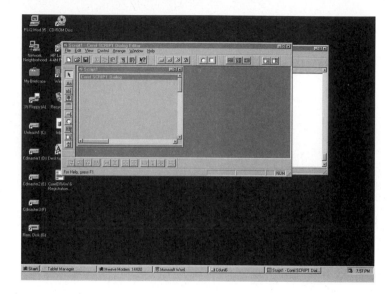

*Option buttons* work in groups. They are used when you have several items to choose from and only one item can be chosen. As you create option buttons on a dialog box, they are automatically grouped for you. You might see them referred to as *radio buttons* in other programs.

*Check boxes* are used when something is either on or off. As they are used, an × is placed in the box for on and the box is left blank for off.

Either of these tools works similarly. Click the appropriate tool and drag a rectangle onto the screen where you want the object to be. You will see either the option button or the check box along with some accompanying text. The text can be changed in the Attributes dialog box. Figure 93.9 shows an example of each of these value buttons.

Figure 93.9.
An option button and a
check box.

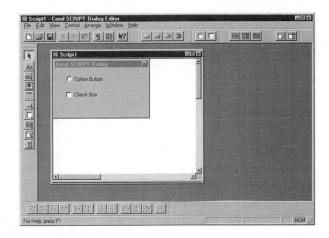

## The List Control Tools

There are three different list control tools. Each of them has a separate button on the List Control flyout, as shown in Figure 93.10.

Figure 93.10.
The List Control flyout.

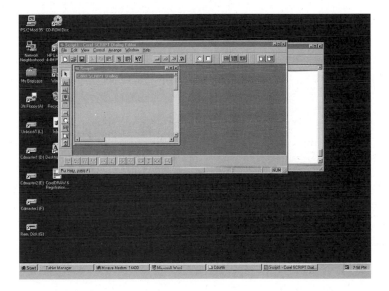

A *list box* is used to list multiple items from which the user can choose. Rather than have a short list of less than six items, you might want to use option buttons instead. When a user clicks an item, it then becomes the selection. Another form of list box is the Drop-Down (D-D) list box. The advantage of this type is that it takes up less space on the dialog box, as the user has to first click the drop-down arrow to see the list. Lastly, there is the *Image List box*, which works just like the list box except that it is used for images in either BMP or RLE format. It will resize all of the images to fit the list horizontally.

Each of the controls is added by selecting the appropriate tool and dragging out the control on the dialog box. Each of them can be resized to the desired size. Remember that the list box and Image box need space to list multiple items, whereas the D-D list box just needs room for one item because it will drop down later. The lists themselves are added within the script and not here in the Dialog Editor. Examples of each of the controls are shown in Figure 93.11.

*Figure 93.11.*
*The three types of list*
*boxes.*

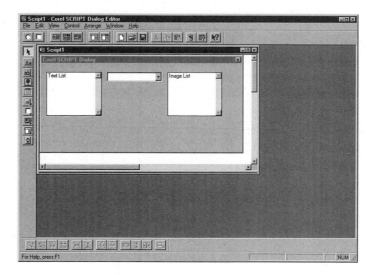

## The Combo Box Tools

A *combo box* is a combination of a list box and a text box. The advantage is that if the item desired isn't in the list, the user can type it in; if the user starts typing and a match is found, it will be highlighted immediately. There are two types of combo box tools in the flyout shown in Figure 93.12.

*Figure 93.12.*
*The Combo Controls*
*flyout.*

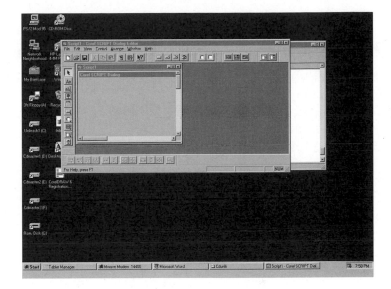

The first icon is for the combo box. It is basically a list box with a text box attached to the top of it. The second icon is for a Drop-Down (D-D) combo box. Again it is like the D-D list box with a text box attached. As with all of the other controls, you select the icon and then drag out a rectangle to the size desired. You can make editing changes in the Attributes dialog box the same as you can with the controls discussed previously. Also, like the list boxes, the lists in the combo boxes will be filled by a script. Examples of the two controls are shown in Figure 93.13.

*Figure 93.13.*
*The two types of combo*
*boxes.*

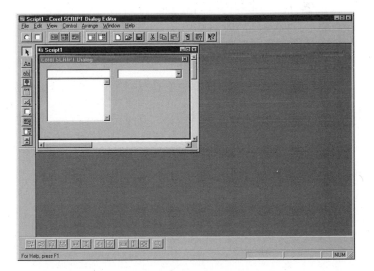

## The Spin Control Tool

The Spin Control tool is used to provide a numeric entry box that can have its number changed by either typing a new number or using up and down arrows to increase and decrease it.

To add a spin control to your dialog box, select the tool and then click and drag the control until it is the right size. As with the other controls, you can adjust its size with the Selector tool or in the Attributes dialog box. An example of a spin control is shown in Figure 93.14.

*Figure 93.14.*
*A spin control.*

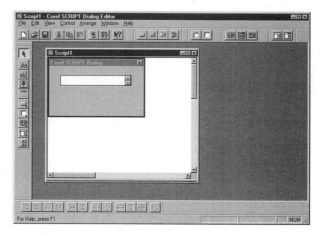

## Editing Attributes

Each object on a dialog box—and the dialog box itself—has attributes attached to it. These can be edited easily by right-clicking on the object and selecting Attributes from the menu, by using the Alt+Enter shortcut key, or by just double-clicking on the object. Figure 93.15 shows the Dialog Attributes dialog box.

*Figure 93.15.*
*The Dialog Attributes*
*dialog box.*

The Text entry is for the text that appears in the title bar of the dialog box itself. Value is the variable name used to call the dialog box when writing scripts using it. The Comment field will be ignored by the scripts themselves and is purely for notational purposes.

At the bottom of the dialog box you can control the size of the dialog box in pixels. Simply enter the width and height, and it will change accordingly. If you want the dialog box to be centered on the screen, check the Center Dialog check box.

Each of the controls has an Attributes dialog box as well. Figure 93.16 shows the Attributes dialog box for a check box. You'll see that with the controls, you can change the position as well as changing the size.

*Figure 93.16.*
*The Check Box Attributes*
*dialog box.*

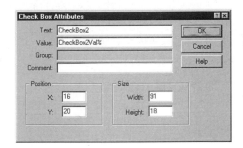

## Arranging and Aligning Objects

At the bottom of the screen are several buttons that assist you in making your controls align with each other and be sized uniformly. Figure 93.17 shows the placement bar.

*Figure 93.17.*
*The placement bar.*

The first four buttons are used to align multiple controls with each other. You can choose Left, Right, Top, or Bottom, respectively. Simply marquee-select (just like in CorelDRAW) multiple controls and click the button of your choice.

The next set of buttons is for evenly distributing controls. You must select at least three controls before the distribute buttons are available. Marquee-select the controls and click the distribute horizontal or vertical button and your controls will be evenly spaced in the direction you chose.

The next two buttons are used to center controls either horizontally or vertically. Simply choose the control or controls you want to center and click the appropriate center button.

The next three buttons are used to size multiple controls so that they are the same width, height, or size. Simply select multiple controls and click the appropriate button.

The last button is used for controls that have contents (text controls and value button controls). Select the control you want to size and then click the Size to Content button. It will resize the control so that it is perfectly sized for its contents.

## Creating a Dialog Box

Figure 93.18 shows a dialog box that has been created. You'll note that below the dialog box you can see a bunch of text that describes it. This is the code that the Dialog Editor has created. If you want to see this, choose the Split command from the Window menu. You'll get a line across the dialog box; as soon as you click, the window will split into two parts. The top part shows the dialog box and the bottom shows the code that creates it.

*Figure 93.18.*
*A finished dialog box and*
*the code that created it.*

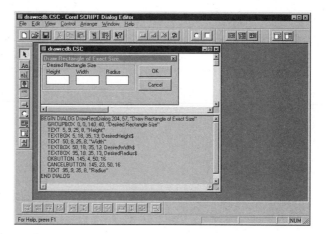

The dialog box shown in Figure 93.18 was created for drawing rectangles of an exact size and radius. It uses three text controls, three text boxes, an OK button, and a Cancel button. It is fairly simple but very functional. You saw it used in the examples in Skill Session 92.

When you've finished a dialog box, simply save it to a file. This file will be given a CSC extension and can be loaded into Corel SCRIPT and used within a script.

# Corel
# CAPTURE

Corel CAPTURE enables you to save a snapshot or movie of your screen. Once captured, the images can be saved to a file, printed, or embedded in another application.

## Activation

When you first start Corel CAPTURE, you will see the dialog box shown in Figure 94.1. The first option is the choice of the Hot Key, which begins the capturing process. Pressing the chosen key will start the countdown and eventually capture the screen. The amount of time between pressing this key and the capture can be set at anywhere from 1-60 seconds. Click the check box next to Initial Delay before the first Capture and then set the amount in the Parameters box. You can even have Capture continue to capture up to 999 more frames. Click the check box next to Repeat Captures and specify how many times you want it to repeat in the Parameters box. You can also specify the amount of time between captures in the next parameters box.

The last option on this tab is the No selection capture. When using the rectangular, freehand, and elliptical capture options, you must define the area to be captured by dragging the area with your mouse. Choosing the No selection capture enables you to do this, without your mouse affecting the underlying image. Otherwise, you might select, move, or disturb the captured area in some way. Also note that the Capture dialog box will not disappear from your screen so make sure to move it out of the way of the area you wish to capture.

Figure 94.1.
The Capture Activation
dialog box.

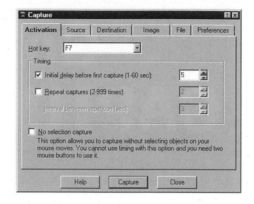

## Source

The Source tab shown in Figure 94.2 gives you six options for selecting the area of the screen to be captured. Current Window captures the full window of the currently selected application. Active Client captures the same thing as Current Windows but leaves out the menu bar, title bar, and window borders. The Full Screen option captures the whole screen. This is the same as Current Window if the current application is maximized. Rectangular Area lets you draw a rectangle of the area you want to capture. Similarly, Elliptical Area lets you draw an ellipse for the area you want to capture. The last option, Free-Hand Area, lets you specify the nodes of a polygonal area to capture.

Each left click will add a point (up to 50 can be specified), and a double-click will specify that you have finished. Figures 94.3 through 94.5 show examples of some of the options.

Figure 94.2.
The Capture Source
dialog box.

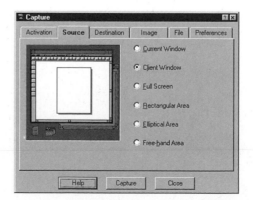

*Figure 94.3.*
*Screen captured with the*
*Current Window option.*

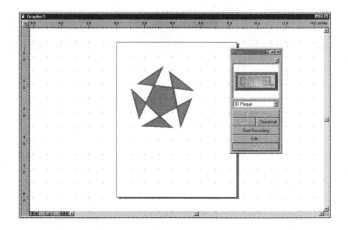

*Figure 94.4.*
*Screen captured with the*
*Client Window option.*
*Look closely to see a slight*
*border on Figure 41.3 in*
*comparison to this figure.*

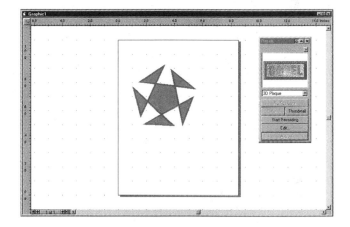

Figure 94.5.
Screen captured with the
Full Screen option.

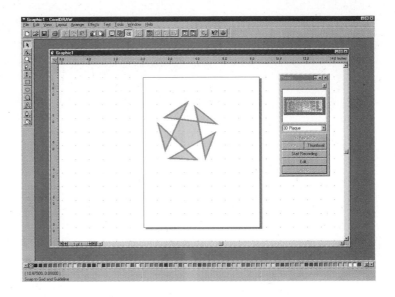

# Destination

There are five possible destinations for your capture. (See Figure 94.6.) The first option is to save the capture to a file. Simply check the box next to File, and the file will be saved according to the specifications set in the File section of the dialog box (shown later in this Skill Session). You can also save a series of captures as an Animation file. Check this option and choose Autodesk FLIC file, MPEG Animation, or Video for Windows (AVI) format.

Checking the box next to Clipboard enables you to paste the image into any of your applications from the clipboard. Checking the box next to Printer will send each capture directly to the selected Printer. If you need to specify a printer, click on Select Printer. The OLE-automated application option lets you send the capture directed to the selected application. Current only Corel PHOTO-PAINT is listed as an option. Note that you can select as many of these options as you desire, and the file will be sent to all of the selected destinations.

*Figure 94.6.*
*The Capture Destination*
*dialog box.*

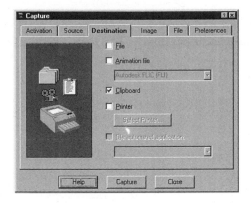

# Image

Various attributes of the saved image can be specified in the dialog box shown in
Figure 94.7. Settings lets you choose Screen, Printer, or Custom. If you choose
Screen, all other attributes will be grayed out (because all of them are taken
directly from the currently used screen driver). Selecting Printer will allow you to
choose the Type of image, but again all other options are taken from the currently
selected Print driver. By choosing Custom, however, you can specify other options.
Type lets you specify the color depth of the captured image. Choices include Black
& White, 16 color, grayscale, 256 color, and 24-bit color—with the default being the
color depth of your currently installed video driver. The Horizontal and Vertical
Resolution parameter boxes allow you to specify the resolution in dpi in either
direction. The default value is the resolution of your currently installed video
driver.

By clicking on the Resize Captured Image check box, you can choose various
options for resizing the image. Checking Keep Image Ratio keeps the same aspect
ratio when the image is resized. The Width and Height parameters box enables
you to specify an exact size in pixels of the captured image in either direction.

*Figure 94.7.*
*The Capture Image*
*dialog box.*

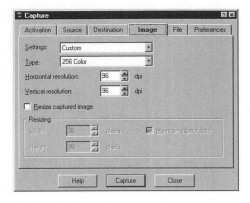

# File

The File section of the dialog box shown in Figure 94.8 determines how files are saved. The first section is the prefix that will be attached to all files. The default value is *Corel.* The Type of File drop-down list is for choosing which format of bitmap the file will use. If the file type chosen supports compression, the Type of Compression drop-down is available to choose a form of compression. The lower left contains a button for choosing the directory into which all files will be saved. Clicking on the automatic naming means that files will be saved with numbers starting at the number in the parameters box (normally 000) being attached to the Filename prefix chosen earlier. If you have chosen to save the file as an animation, you can name the prefix of the animation and the amount of milliseconds between each frame. Note that this amount of time may differ from the delay between repeated captures.

*Figure 94.8.*
*The Capture File*
*dialog box.*

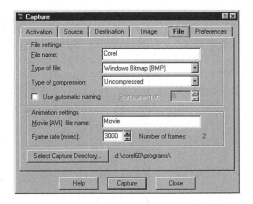

# Preferences

The Capture Preferences dialog box is shown in Figure 94.9. Selecting the Hide Icon when Capture hides the Corel CAPTURE icon so that it does not appear in any captured images. If Notify end of Capture is chosen, a message will be displayed and a beep will sound after an image has finished capturing. The Capture Under Cursor will make sure that the pixels under the cursor will be accurately captured. Borders can be added to any captured image. The size of the border can be selected in the Size parameters box, and the color of the border can be selected by clicking on the Color button and selecting the desired color.

*Figure 94.9.*
*The Capture Preferences*
*dialog box.*

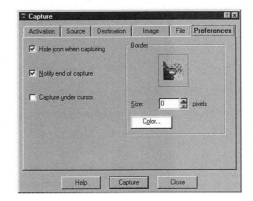

## Capturing Images

After you have selected the desired options, click on the Capture button at the bottom of the dialog box. This will minimize the program to an icon. Any time you want to capture the screen, push the Activation keystroke you selected earlier. (The default is F7.)

## Corel *NOTE!*

One of the major deficiencies of Capture is its inability to capture the cursor. In this book, many screen captures are used, and quite a few need to show the current cursor to fully explain a feature. For that reason, Corel CAPTURE was not used in the production of this book.

# 95

# Corel FONT MASTER

Corel FONT MASTER is a font management utility. It replaces the Font Minder utility from Ares Software that was included with CorelDRAW 5. Unfortunately, it is nowhere near as easy to use and lacks much of the functionality of Font Minder.

Corel provides you with more than 1,000 fonts; you undoubtedly have more fonts from other sources. Attempting to install that many fonts will cause your system to crawl if not completely crash. By using a font management utility, you can keep the fonts you need installed while easily installing and uninstalling those you use less frequently.

No Corel user should be without a font management utility; but unfortunately, FONT MASTER will not easily solve anyone's font management problems. For those who want a great utility that is easy to use, check out Ares Font Minder. For more information, contact Ares at (800) 783-2737.

## Using FONT MASTER

FONT MASTER's main window provides you with four quadrants, as shown in Figure 95.1.

*Figure 95.1.*
*FONT MASTER's main*
*window.*

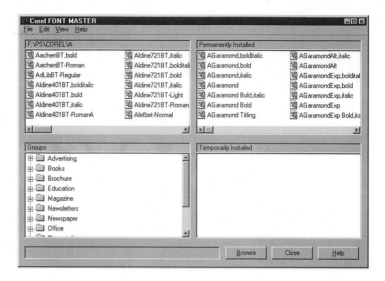

The upper-left quadrant lists all fonts in the currently selected directory. You have a choice of viewing the fonts by filename or font name. To change this, right-click on a font and choose either Display Fontname or Display Filename.

Limiting the view to only one directory really cripples the product, because Corel's fonts are located in at least 26 different directories. Even more frustrating is the fact that it displays the font name incorrectly for all PostScript fonts. This is inherited from CorelDRAW, which also incorrectly names all fonts so that they end with Regular, Italic, Bold, or Bold Italic.

The upper-right quadrant shows you the fonts that are currently installed in Windows. Below this is the temporarily installed quadrant. Any fonts you add here will be available only in your current session of Windows. If you restart your machine, you won't see these fonts any more. This can be handy if you need to use a font for a single job or for printing someone's file. Unfortunately, this window also tends to show fonts that don't exist at all.

The lower-left quadrant is for font groups. By grouping your fonts, you can easily load and unload a number of fonts all at once. Unfortunately, the groups work only if the currently selected directory in the upper-left quadrant is looking at your CD-ROM drive. The predefined groups are also defined to look only for TrueType fonts, and therefore will cause numerous error messages if you use PostScript fonts like most professional users.

## Installing Fonts

To install a font, click the font and drag and drop to either the Permanently In-stalled or Temporarily Installed window. Or, to add the font to a group, drag and drop it on the group name.

You can install groups in the same manner. Select a group and drag it to the appropriate window. I was never able to complete this successfully, so I'm not sure if the group icon will be shown or the fonts will be listed individually.

To create a group, right-click in the Groups window and choose New Group. You will get a new folder as you would in the Windows 95 Explorer, and you can type in a new name for it.

## Previewing Fonts

You can preview any font by double-clicking it. It doesn't matter which of the four quadrants a font is in. You will see a window similar to the one shown in Figure 95.2.

*Figure 95.2.*
*The Sample tab of the*
*Font Properties dialog box.*

The Font Properties Sample dialog box shows you a sentence using the font, and you can choose which point size to use. You can't, however, change the text, which can be a problem if you're trying to see how various words look such as a logo.

If you click the Info tab, you will get the dialog box shown in Figure 95.3.

Figure 95.3.
*The Info tab of the Font
Properties dialog box.*

This window will show you some basic information about the font, such as its full name, filename, type, and size.

Lastly, you can click the Character Set tab. You'll get a dialog box similar to the one in Figure 95.4.

Figure 95.4.
*The Font Properties
Character Set dialog box.*

This window shows you every character in the fonts character set. When you click a particular character, its character name and ANSI code will be displayed at the bottom of the screen. To type this character in any Windows application, hold down the Alt key, and type 0 and then the ANSI number.

# Projects
# Workshop

# Creating Artwork for a CD-ROM Disc

With the low price of CD Recorders and software such as Corel's CD Creator, many of you will need to create artwork for a CD-ROM. At first glance, it might seem difficult to do since there are many restrictions. Luckily, CorelDRAW makes it fairly easy to produce.

This project shows you how the artwork for an actual CD-ROM was created. The specifications were dictated by the company that mass-duplicates the CDs. They sent a diagram showing seven circles with exact sizes in millimeters. These circles indicate the boundaries of the areas upon which the CD can have artwork printed.

The first step is to re-create each of those circles as guidelines:

1. Drag out one horizontal and one vertical guideline that intersect at what will be the center of the disc.

2. While holding down the Ctrl and Shift keys, draw a circle measuring 120 mm. If you don't get this exact, use the Transform roll-up's Size option to resize the circle to the exact amount.

3. Repeat this process drawing circles measuring 116 mm, 45 mm, 38 mm, 34 mm, 18 mm, and 15 mm.

4. Now bring up the Layers roll-up and move all the circles to the Guides layer so they can be used as guidelines.

Your screen should now look similar to Figure PR1.1.

*Figure PR1.1.*
*The guidelines used*
*for this project.*

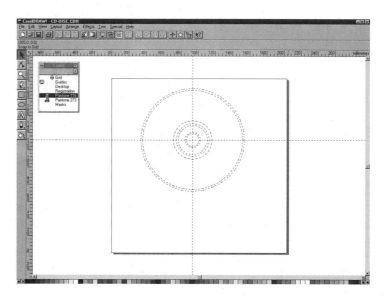

The area between the 116 mm circle and the 38 mm circle is the area upon which the artwork can be printed. In order to better visualize this area, create a new layer called Masks. Now make a copy of the 116 mm and 38 mm circles, and paste them onto the Masks layer. After they are copied, combine them using the Combine command in the Arrange menu and fill them with a light color. You'll see this depicted by the light gray area in Figure PR1.2. Now add another circle inside the printable area on the Masks layer to be used later as a path for fitting text.

You now want to create a shape that covers half of the disc and crosses it at a 45 degree angle.

5. Start by drawing a rectangle bigger than half of the circle and aligned at the bottom with the horizontal guideline at the middle of the circle. This is shown in Figure PR1.3.

*Figure PR1.2.*
*The printable area is*
*depicted by pale yellow*
*(light gray).*

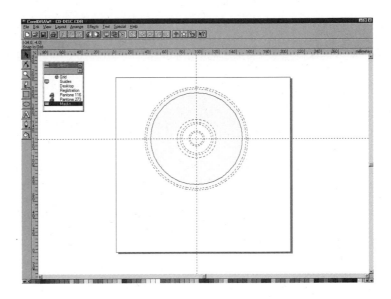

*Figure PR1.3.*
*The rectangle before*
*rotating and intersecting.*

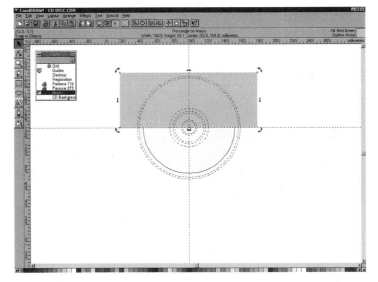

6. Select the rectangle and click again to get the rotation and skewing handles.

7. Move the center of rotation thumbtack to the center of the disc.

8. Hold the Ctrl key and rotate the rectangle 45 degrees. (Keep your eyes on the status line.)

You should see something similar to that shown in Figure PR1.4. Now it is time to make the rectangle fit on the printable area of the disc. This can be accomplished in two ways: using either Intersection or PowerClip. For this example, use the Intersection command.

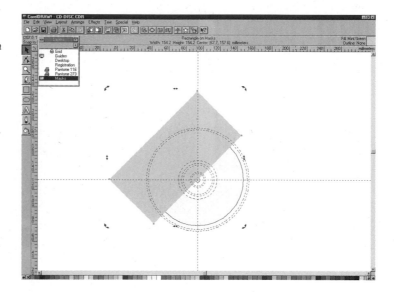

*Figure PR1.4.*
*The rotated rectangle*
*before intersecting it with*
*the printable area of the*
*disc.*

9. Select both the printable area of the disc and the rectangle, and choose the Intersection command from the Arrange menu.

You should have the desired shape (shown in Figure PR1.5). Don't forget to delete the original rectangle, because it is no longer necessary. This same technique is used later to create a shape to envelope to Paragraph text.

The next step is to add a copyright notice, the name of the company, and phone number around the bottom edge of the disc. The path for this text was pointed out in Figure PR1.2.

10. Type out the desired text.
11. Choose Fit Text to Path roll-up from the Text menu.
12. Select both the text and the path.
13. Choose the text below the baseline option and the bottom of the circle, and place it on the other side in the Fit Text to Path roll-up. Click Apply.

Now add some Paragraph text describing installation. After all the text has been entered, the shape for enveloping needs to be created. Again this is done by intersecting a rectangle (no rotation necessary this time) with the mask of the printable area shown in Figure PR1.6. This is very similar to what was done in Step 9. After you have created the intersected piece, you need to use it to envelope the Paragraph text. Again, don't forget to delete the original rectangle.

*Figure PR1.5.*
*The shape created by*
*intersecting the rec-*
*tangle with the disc is*
*shown in blue.*

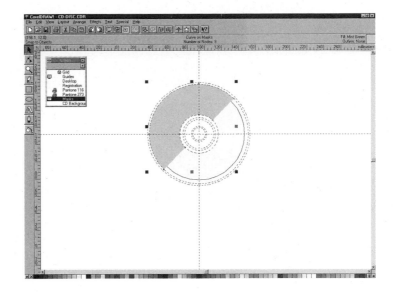

*Figure PR1.6.*
*The rectangle to be*
*intersected with print-*
*able text to create a text*
*envelope.*

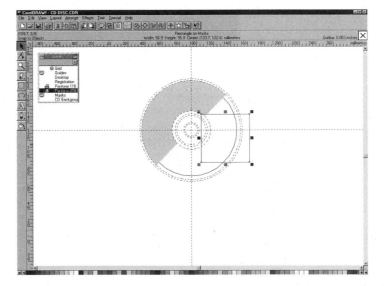

14. Select the Envelope roll-up from the Effects menu.

15. Highlight the Paragraph text and click Create From in the Envelope roll-up.

16. Now click the intersected shape with the cursor and click Apply.

The text should now be placed within the desired shape, as shown in Figure PR1.7. If it is not placed correctly, it can either be dragged into the correct position or nudged using the arrow keys. You might want to make minor adjustments to the shape of the text with the Shape tool.

*Figure PR1.7.*
*Paragraph text enveloped*
*to fit in the printable area*
*of the disc.*

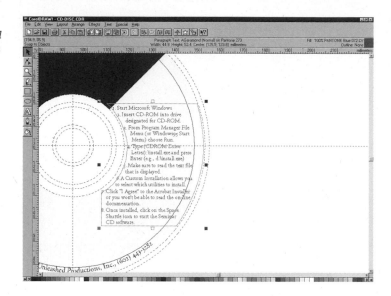

Two logos were imported to finish the artwork for this CD. The techniques to create the *CorelDRAW! Unleashed* logo are described in Project 5, "Text Special Effects."

After all the artwork is finished, a background to simulate the CD itself was created and put on a non-printing layer so that it will only be seen on screen. Figure PR1.8 shows an example of the Layers Manager roll-up.

*Figure PR1.8.*
*The Layers Manager*
*roll-up.*

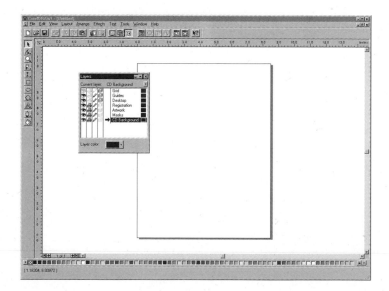

The artwork requirements called for registration marks to appear at the 3, 6, 9, and 12 o'clock positions. Creating them was easy because they are nothing more than a circle and two straight lines. The difficult part was creating them to print on each of the color separations (because spot colors were used in this project). CorelDRAW 6 makes this easy since it now supports a registration color. With the registration color used as the outline color, the registration marks will be on each piece of film. To access the registration color, click on the Color Wheel in the Outline tool flyout shown in Figure PR1.9. This will bring up the Outline Color dialog box shown in Figure PR1.10.

*Figure PR1.9.*
*The Outline tool flyout.*

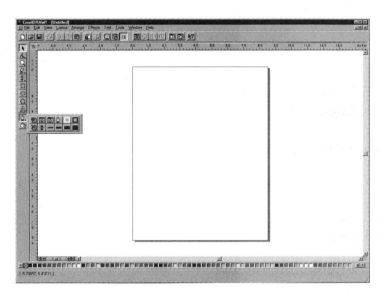

An example of the final CD is shown in Figure PR1.11.

The image at the top left is the original clip art. The image at the top right is a wireframe view of the original image. The problem you will encounter is, even though the blends looks like blends, they aren't. When the clip art was saved in .cmx format, the live effects were lost and the dynamic link between control objects and the blend group was lost.

The original blends are indicated by the arrows in the wireframe view. In order to change the color of the old blend, the old blend's intermediate objects need to be deleted. The image at the lower left in Figure PR2.3 shows the intermediate steps removed leaving the original inside and outside control objects. The control objects have a wider outline in, to indicate their location.

The lower-right view shows the modified fish recolored with new blends and solid colors. The process of recoloring requires creating new blends with the original control objects. (They will be called Curve objects on the status line.) Choose a new color for the outside control object and a different color for the inside control object, and blend them using the Blend roll-up.

There will be times when the new blend does not blend smoothly. This is caused by the fact that the nodes of the two control objects are not aligning. When this occurs, do the following:

1. Select the two control objects.
2. Choose the last icon on the right in the Blend roll-up. Click the Map Nodes button. A crooked arrow cursor will appear.
3. The nodes of one of the control objects will be visible. Click one of the nodes. Remember its location on the object.
4. After you click the first node, the nodes of the other control object will be visible. Click the node that most represents the position of the first node you clicked.
5. Now when you click the Apply button, the blend should blend correctly.

## Combing Two Images

Often you can't find the exact clip art image for a project. You might find an image that works well but is missing an element you need. In cases like this, try finding a second image that you can steal something from. Suppose you want a cook cutting a steak, but all you can find is a cook cutting a piece of fruit. Figure PR2.4 uses the cook cutting the fruit and a separate clip art image of a steak. Follow the steps below to learn how to combine the two images using elements from both images.

*Figure PR2.4.*
*Creating a new image*
*from two existing images.*

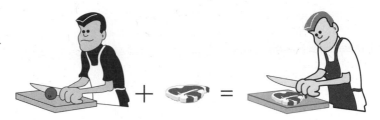

1. Import both clip art images into your page. The Cook is located in the Clip art/People/Workers folder. The steak is located in the Clip art/Food folder. Both images are found on the CorelDRAW's CD disc number 4.

2. Ungroup the first image of the cook by selecting Ungroup from the Object Properties menu.

3. Select the mouth of the cook and change the outline color by right-clicking in the color palette. *Notice the mouth has been combined with the nose, the finger separations of the hand, and the top-edge outline on the cutting board.*

4. Choose Break Apart from the Object Properties menu. This action will separate the five items into five different objects.

5. Select the cutting board, including the outline, indicating the top edge by Shift-clicking on both objects.

6. Group the two objects together by choosing Group from the Object Properties menu.

7. Move the cutting board out of the way temporarily.

8. Select the steak and place it on top of the cutting board. If your steak appears behind the cutting board, click Order in the Object Properties menu and select To-Front from the fly-out.

9. Select both the steak and the cutting board. Group them together using the Group command in the Object Properties menu. With the group still selected, click on Order in the Object Properties menu and select To-Back from the fly-out.

10. Select the fruit and delete it.

11. Select the steak and cutting board group again, and drag it to its new position under the cook's knife.

    So far so good! Now let's change the colors of the cook's clothing and change the angle of his head.

12. Click the cook's shirt and change its color. You will find out that the shirt has been combined with the cook's hair. That means you have to use the Break Apart command in the Object Properties menu again. Once the shirt and hair are separate objects, you can change their colors.

13. Click the cook's apron and change its color. Finally! There is an object that hasn't been combined with another object.

14. Before you can change the angle of the cook's head, the head has to be separated from the hands and arms. Click the face of the cook and choose the Break Apart command from the Object Properties menu.

15. Marquee-select the entire head so that you include the eyes, nose, mouth, ear, and hair and group them all together by choosing the Group command from the Object Properties menu.

16. With the group selected, click a second time to display the rotation and skew arrows. Click on the center of rotation thumbtack and move it to the back of the lower jaw area.

17. Drag the upper-right rotation arrow to tilt the head downward.

That's all there is to it. You have just created a completely new image from two clip art images.

# 3

# Drawing with Ellipses

Many people feel that they can't draw a straight line. This might be true, but I bet the majority of CorelDRAW users can draw an ellipse with the Ellipse tool. If you can draw an ellipse in CorelDRAW, you can learn to illustrate your ideas without resorting to clip art. Coauthor Peter McCormick begins most of his illustrations by first drawing an ellipse.

## Corel *NOTE!*

The secret of drawing with ellipses is to convert the ellipse to a curved object, and then add enough nodes to create the shape you want. Use the shortcut key method (Ctrl+Q) or the Convert To Curves command in the Arrange menu. (See Skill Session 7, "The Shape Tool," for more information.) The benefit of using an ellipse converted to curves is that you will get perfectly curved lines while reshaping, as opposed to jagged ones that would be created using the Pencil tool.

Figure PR3.1 shows an example of a basic ellipse that has been converted to curves. When you move the nodes and node handles on the curve, you will see an object taking shape. Remember, you can move the line, not just the nodes, to reshape an object. The only magic in manipulating the shape is your own perseverance. You will discover that you can create shapes you never thought you could. Sometimes when you manipulate a line, a completely different shape emerges. When this happens, go with it. (Any artist will tell you that *happy accidents* happen all the time.) Finish this new, unexpected gift, and save it for a future project. Then go back and create the object you originally started.

Before you begin practicing this method, you might want to review Skill Session 7. A rule of thumb is that after you convert the ellipse to curves, convert all the nodes on the object to cusp nodes. The cusp node lets you adjust the line on one side of the node without effecting the opposite side.

Begin by drawing some bananas. Follow the steps below and refer to Figure PR3.1 as you go.

*Figure PR3.1.*
*Drawing a bunch of*
*bananas.*

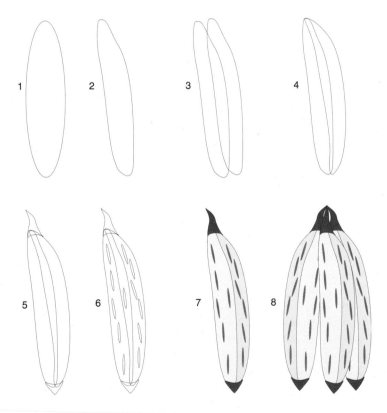

1. Draw a vertical ellipse with the Ellipse tool.
2. With the ellipse selected, choose Convert to Curves from the Arrange pull-down menu.

3. Choose the Shape tool and add four additional nodes to the ellipse.

4. Marquee-select all the nodes using the Shape tool.

5. Right-click on one of the nodes to display the Object Properties roll-up.

6. Choose Cusp from the fly-out.

7. Deselect the nodes by clicking off the page area.

8. Begin to reshape the ellipse into the shape of a banana. (See Step 2 in the illustration.)

9. Make a duplicate of the shape and move it to the right. (See Step 3 in the illustration.)

10. Reshape the duplicate shape until it looks like the figure in Step 4 in the illustration.

11. With the duplicate shape still selected, right-click on the shape and choose To-Back from the Order fly-out in the Object Properties menu.

12. Create two additional ellipses, convert them to curves, and form the shape for the darker ends of the banana. (See Step 5 in the illustration.)

13. Draw several narrow ellipses to create the brown spots of the banana, and place them accordingly.

14. Group all the shapes together by marquee-selecting all the shapes with the Pick tool and right-clicking on the selected objects to bring up the Object Properties menu. From the menu, select the Group command.

15. To make the bunch of bananas, simply two duplicates of the original, mirror one of them, and drag them into position.

## Expanding on the Basics

The cracked egg shell example in Figure PR3.2 shows how, by manipulating two ellipses, you can create the two parts of the shell. Radial Fountain fills were used to color the front and back parts of the shell.

Figure PR3.3 expands on the egg shell to create a fantasy sail boat. The creation of the sail was accomplished by converting an ellipse to curves as well. The mast and cross piece are simple rectangles. The flag was a last-minute thought obtained from the Symbols roll-up. If you are paying attention, you will notice that the sail on the boat is a mirror image of the original.

Figure PR3.4 continues on the fantasy theme. The entire frog was created using ellipses converted to curves. The individual pieces are shown below the finished piece. (See Figure PR3.5 for the completed drawing.)

Figure PR3.6 further expands on the completed drawing by incorporating more elements in the picture. The swan and mountains were both created using ellipses converted curves.

*Figure PR3.2.*
*Reshaping ellipses to form*
*an egg shell.*

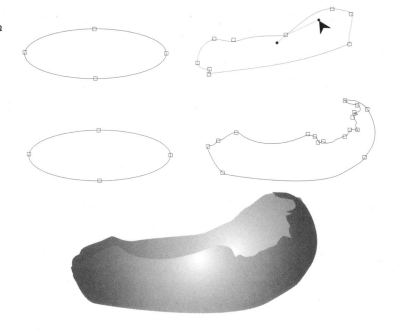

*Figure PR3.3.*
*Finishing the fantasy sail*
*boat.*

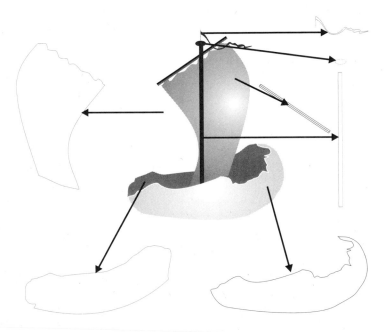

Figure PR3.4.
Variations on the basics.

Figure PR3.5.
The completed drawing.

*Figure PR3.6.*
*More elements incorpo-*
*rated into the final picture.*

# 4

# Creating a Color Separation

This project walks you through creating a color separation for a real-life project. First, the specifications of our printer and service bureau will be provided, and then we will create the separation based on those specs.

## Printer Specifications

- 225 lpi
- Right-reading emulsion down negative film
- Cut size 12.25" × 12.5"
- Bleed size 12.375" × 12.625"
- 100-lb., book-precision, high-gloss paper
- Sheet-fed, 4-color Heidelberg press
- 340-360 UCR/GCR
- Mock-up

## Service Bureau Specifications:

- Agfa SelectSet 7000 imagesetter
- 3600 dpi

- PRN file of positive
- PostScript Level 2
- Application Name and Version
- Page Orientation
- Linked Graphics
- Include all fonts
- Hard copy

## Outputting the File

You have created your piece on a custom page of 12.25" × 12.5 inches and have bled the image where necessary by 1/8". None of the objects on the page were manually trapped because you used Corel Draw's auto-trapping instead.

1. Choose Print from the File menu. You should see the Print dialog box.
2. Select the Agfa SelectSet 7000 printer driver from the Name drop-down list. If you don't have the correct printer driver installed, you will need to install it through the Windows 95 Printer's Control Panel.
3. Click the Properties button.

You should now see the AGFA-SelectSet7000 Properties dialog box, shown in Figure PR4.1. You might see something completely different depending on the driver you choose. Although the look might be different, the features and techniques are fairly similar.

*PR 4.1.*
*The AGFA-SelectSet7000*
*Properties dialog box.*

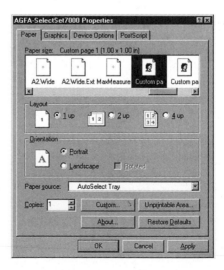

4. Scroll in the Paper size window until you come to the first Custom Page, and select it.

5. Click Portrait orientation if it not already selected.

6. Click the Custom button so that you can set a custom paper size.

You should now the Custom-Defined Size dialog box as shown in Figure PR4.2.

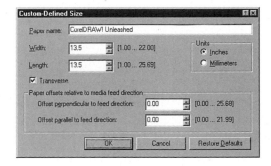

*PR4.2.*
*The Custom-Defined Size*
*dialog box.*

7. Type a name into the Paper name box if you want to give the paper a name.

8. To get an extra inch of paper for bleed and reference marks, enter 13.5 in both the width and length parameters boxes. Realistically, 13.25 would be fine in the width box, but the extra .25 inches will not cause a problem. Now click OK.

9. Click OK in the AGFA-SelectSet7000 Properties dialog box.

Now you should be back to the main Print dialog box, and it should look similar to the one shown in Figure PR4.3.

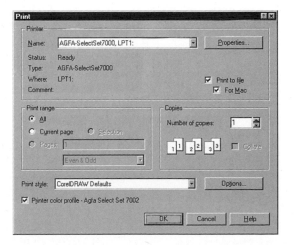

*PR4.3.*
*The Print dialog box.*

The specifications call for the provision of a PRN file; therefore, the following steps need to be taken.

10. Check the Print to file checkbox.
11. Check the For Mac checkbox. (When you are in doubt about which type of machine the service bureau will use, always check this.)

This job contains two pages, but they are stored in separate files. Therefore, the Print range is fine with its default setting of All, and the Copies is fine with 1.

The Print style setting can be useful in the future if you save all of your settings. At the end of this project, this process will be discussed so that you can make future color separations much simpler.

Next to Printer color profile is the name of the output device specified in your current profile. If this is not the device that the job will be printed on, you should Cancel the Print dialog and change this device through the Color Manager Wizard. To use the current profile, make sure this box is checked. The profile will not affect any objects already specified in CMYK color, only those specified in other color models.

12. Click the Options button.

You should now see the Print Options Layout dialog box as shown in Figure PR4.4.

*PR4.4.*
*The Print Options Layout*
*dialog box.*

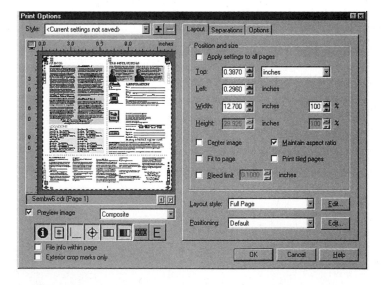

13. Click the Preview image checkbox so that a preview of the document is in the main preview window.
14. Click the File info, Page number, Crop marks, Registration marks, Calibration bar, and Densitometer buttons so that they are pressed.

You should now see all of these marks showing in the preview window.

For this particular project, no changes need to be made to the Position and size. Because no more changes are necessary, click the Separations tab. You should now see the dialog box shown in Figure PR4.5.

PR4.5.
*The Print Options Separations dialog box.*

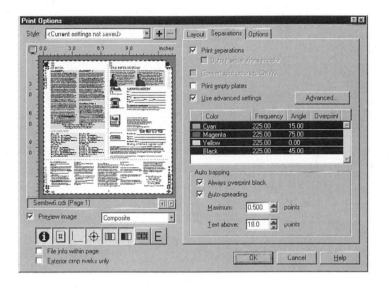

Because you are creating a color separation, you definitely want to check the Print separations checkbox. We've also created a file with no trapping included so Auto trapping is a necessity. The box in the upper left of the page has black text on a magenta background. This would be nearly impossible to trap, but when you select Always overprint black, it will not know the black out of the magenta. This will alleviate the need for trapping. For the other areas in which trapping is necessary, activate the Auto-spreading with the default settings of .5 point maximum spread and trapping on Text above 18 points.

The last change to make is in the Advanced settings dialog box. First, check the Use advanced settings checkbox and then click the Advanced button. You will get the Advanced Separations Settings dialog box shown in Figure PR4.6.

You'll want to use a screening technology native to the imagesetter used on the job. If one is not known, do not make any changes in this dialog box. In this case, the SelectSet 7000 uses Agfa's Balanced Screening. There are choices for Dot or Ellipse; choose Dot. This decision results from a discussion with our service bureau, since this was not on our list of specifications. The resolution specified was 3600 dpi, and the screen was 225 lines per inch. So, we chose each of those specifications. Now, click OK to get back to the Print Options Separations dialog box.

PR4.6.
*The Advanced Separa-
tions Settings dialog box.*

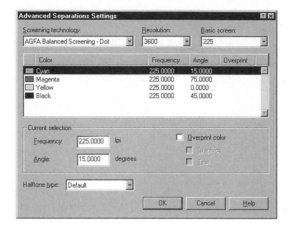

Now you're ready for the final section of the Print Options dialog box—confusingly named Options. Click the Options tab and you'll see something similar to the screen shown in Figure PR4.7.

Pr4.7.
*The Print Options Options
dialog box.*

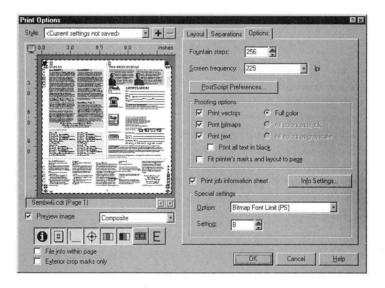

The first choice is for Fountain steps. This is a calculated number. The number you use here is derived from the resolution of the output device and the line screen used. Divide the resolution by the line screen—in this case, 3600/225. This tells how big the halftone dot is in pixels: 16. Now multiply that number by itself as the halftone dot has pixels in both the vertical and horizontal directions. That tells how many total pixels are in the halftone dot, and is also the number of fountain stripes. In this case, it is 256. That happens to be the maximum for PostScript. If the number of fountain stripes is below 256, enter the result of the equation. If it is above 256, enter 256 anyway and you won't get any more than that.

Next is the screen frequency, which was also supplied to us as 225 lpi. The only other change to make in this dialog box is to check Print job information sheet checkbox. We'll investigate this further later in the project.

Now click the PostScript Preferences button. You'll get the PostScript Preferences dialog box shown in Figure PR4.8.

*PR4.8.*
*The PostScript Preferences*
*dialog box.*

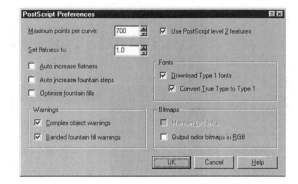

The only changes to make are to lower the Maximum points per curve to 700 so that any complex objects will be broken into less complex objects. This makes the job more likely to print. If the job is extremely complex, also check the Auto increase flatness checkbox. In this case, you are using a PostScript Level 2 imagesetter, which is virtually crashproof. Therefore, you won't need the extra protection against complexity. Check the checkbox for Use PostScript level 2 features so that the imagesetter will be used to its fullest potential. Click OK to get back to the Print Options Options dialog box.

Now click the Info Settings button. You will get the dialog box shown in Figure PR4.9.

The only selection to make is to check the Sent to Printer checkbox and then click Select Printer. This brings up a Print dialog box very similar to the one you started with. This is shown in Figure PR4.10. This dialog box specifies which printer will print the job information sheet. It can (and mostly should) be different from the original printer chosen. Send the job to your local HP LaserJet 4M+. The job information sheet is very important so that the service bureau will know what is contained in the file they are receiving.

PR4.9.
*The Print Job Information*
*dialog box.*

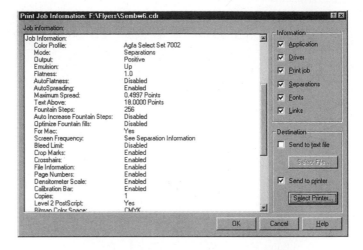

PR4.10.
*The Print dialog box for*
*the Job information sheet.*

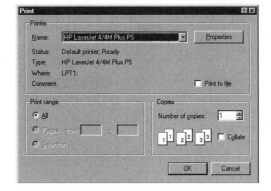

Click OK in this Print dialog. Click OK in the Print Job Information dialog. Now save all the changes you have made in these dialog boxes so that the next time you print a color separation it will be much easier. Click the + button next to the Style name. This means that you want to add something to the list of styles. You'll see a dialog box like that shown in Figure PR4.11.

You want to give it a name, so type a name into the box next to Save print style as. Make sure to give it a name that you'll remember the next time you need these settings. Now click OK to return back to the Print Options dialog box. Click OK to get back the Print dialog box. Click OK one more time to start the project printing.

You'll be confronted with yet another dialog box. This one asks for the name of the file (because you chose Print to disk). Again, give the file a name that you'll remember, and make sure to put the file on a drive with enough space as these files can get large. Never print directly to a floppy drive because it is painfully slow.

That's it; you've printed a color separation!

PR4.11.
*The Save Print Style
dialog box.*

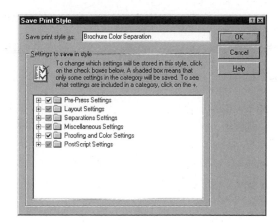

# 5

# Text Special Effects

This project illustrates several special text effects. You can re-create each of these effects by following the steps given for each of the examples.

## Neon

The Neon effect has always been popular. Basically, it requires a copy of the text placed directly on top of the original text and then blends the two together. Figure PR5.1 is an example of the Neon effect described below.

1. Type the word NEON.
2. Make the fill a solid color with an outline of .333 inches that is the same color as the fill. The outline must use rounded corners or the effect will look too squared.
3. Select the text and press the + key or the right mouse button to make a duplicate on top of the original text.
4. Change the outline width of the duplicate text to .003 inches and the outline color to white. Also change the fill to white.
5. Marquee-select both objects.
6. Open the Blend roll-up using the Effects menu.
7. Click the Apply button. (The default of 20 steps is fine.)

Figure PR5.1.
An example of the Neon
effect.

## Glowing Text

The effect of glowing text is a variation of the neon effect. You might prefer it instead of neon if your project has a black background. Figure PR5.2 shows an example of glowing text.

Figure PR5.2.
An example of the
Glowing Text effect.

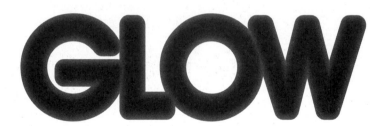

1. Type the word GLOW.
2. Make the fill a solid color with an outline of .333 inches that is the same color as the fill. The outline must use rounded corners or the effect will look too squared.
3. Select the text and press the + key or the right mouse button to make a duplicate on top of the original text.
4. Change the outline width of the duplicate text to .003 inches and the outline color to black. Also change the fill to black.
5. Marquee-select both objects.
6. Open the Blend roll-up using the Effects menu.
7. Click the Apply button. (The default of 20 steps is fine.)

## Multiple Outlines

Multiple outline text is accomplished by using two copies of outlined text with different outline widths and different colors. Figure PR5.3 is an example of this effect.

*Figure PR5.3.*
*An example of the*
*Multiple Outlines effect.*

1. Type the letter A.
2. Give it an outline of .10 inches and color the outline red.
3. Duplicate the text using the + key or the right mouse button.
4. Change the outline of the duplicate to a hairline and color it blue.

## Emboss

The emboss effect gives the illusion of the text raised above the surface of the paper. Figure PR5.4 shows an example of this effect.

*Figure PR5.4.*
*An example of the Emboss*
*effect.*

1. Draw an object and fill it with 30-percent black for a background.
2. Type the word EMBOSS and place it on the background.
3. Use the Transform roll-up in the Position configuration to move the text .05 inches horizontally and −.05 inches vertically. Make sure to click on Apply to Duplicate rather than Apply.
4. Select the duplicate created from step 3 and click on Apply to Duplicate again.
5. Select the text that is uppermost and farthest left. Change the fill color to 10-percent black.
6. Select the text that is lowermost and farthest right. Change its fill color to 50-percent black.

7. Select the remaining piece of text and change its fill color to 30-percent black (the same color as the background).

8. With this last piece of text still selected, move it to the front by selecting To Front from the Order flyout in the Arrange pull-down menu.

## Deboss

The Deboss effect is the opposite of the Emboss effect. The only difference is the way in which the different copies of the text are colored. It will give the illusion that the text carved into the background. Figure PR5.5 shows an example of the Deboss effect.

*Figure PR5.5.*
*An example of the Deboss effect.*

1. Draw an object and fill it with the Texture Fill Mineral Speckled 3-color for a background.

2. Type the word DEBOSS and place it on the background.

3. Use the Transform roll-up in the Position configuration to move the text .05 inches horizontally and −.05 inches vertically. Make sure to choose Apply to Duplicate rather than Apply.

4. Select the duplicate created from step 3 and click on Apply to Duplicate again.

5. Select the text that is uppermost and farthest left. Select the Texture Fill Mineral Speckled 3-color with the brightness changed to −30.

6. Select the text that is lowermost and farthest right. Select the Texture fill Mineral Speckled 3-color with the brightness changed to 50.

7. Select the remaining piece of text and change its fill to the Texture Fill Mineral Speckled 3-color (the same color as the background).

8. With this last piece of text still selected, move it to the front by selecting To Front from the Order flyout in the Arrange pull-down menu.

## Drop Shadow

The drop shadow effect is a common method to make an object stand out from the page by creating a shadow behind the object. Figure PR5.6 shows an example of this effect applied to text.

*Figure PR5.6.*
*An example of the Drop*
*Shadow effect.*

# SHADOW

1. Create a text object with the word SHADOW.
2. Use the Transform roll-up in the Position configuration to move the text .05 inches horizontally and .05 inches vertically. Make sure to choose Apply to Duplicate rather than Apply. Fill the original text underneath the duplicate with a dark color to emulate a shadow.

## Reflected Text

The reflected text effect uses a duplicate of the original text that has been stretched and skewed to create the illusion of the text being reflected in a mirror. (See Figure PR5.7.)

*Figure PR5.7.*
*An example of the*
*Reflected Text effect.*

1. Create a text object with the word REFLECT.
2. Make a duplicate by using the right mouse button or the + key.
3. Use the Arrange | Order | To Back command to put the duplicate text behind the original text.
4. Stretch and skew the duplicate text as necessary to get the desired effect.
5. Change the fill to a linear gradient fill to give the appropriate shadowed effect.

## Distorted Reflected Text

The distorted text effect uses a duplicate of the original text that has been stretched and skewed, and has also had an envelope effect applied to it. This technique gives the illusion of the text being reflected in water. (See Figure PR5.8.)

*Figure PR5.8.*
*An example of the*
*Distorted Reflected Text*
*effect.*

1.  Create a text object with the word DISTORT.
2.  Make a duplicate by using the right mouse button or the + key.
3.  Mirror the text by holding down the Ctrl key while dragging the middle handle down across the object.
4.  Stretch and skew the duplicate text as necessary to get the desired angle.
5.  Apply an envelope effect to the text using the single curve icon in the Envelope roll-up. Adjust the shape of the envelope to create the distorted appearance.
6.  Change the fill to a linear gradient fill to give the appropriate shadowed effect.

## Flying Text

The flying text effect gives the illusions of the text being peeled off the page. (See Figure PR5.9.)

*Figure PR5.9.*
*An example of the Flying*
*Text effect.*

1.  Create a text object with the word MAGIC.
2.  Make a duplicate by using the right mouse button or the + key.
3.  Use the Arrange | To Back command to put the duplicate text behind the original text.
4.  Add an envelope to the original text to make it appear to lift off of the page.
5.  Change the fill to a linear gradient fill on the duplicate text to give the appropriate shadowed effect.

## Split Text with Combine

The technique of creating the illusion of text that has been split in half has been available since the early days of CorelDRAW. It involves the use of the Combine command located in the Arrange pull-down menu. (See Figure PR5.10.)

*Figure PR5.10.*
*An example of the Split*
*Text with Combine effect.*

1. Draw a rectangle that is two inches square
2. Make a copy of the rectangle using the + key or the right mouse button.
3. Convert the duplicate copy to curves using Ctrl+Q.
4. Select the upper-left node with the Shape tool and delete it. Deleting the node will create a triangle.
5. Type the letter A and stretch it so that it is about 80 percent of the height of the original square. Center the A in the square.
6. Select both the A and the triangle and combine them by selecting the Combine command from the Arrange pull-down menu..
7. Now color each of the two remaining objects.

## Splitting Text with the Intersection Command

The examples in Figure PR5.11 show the different stages you will go through to create this effect, beginning at the upper left. Follow the pointing hand.

1. Open the Intersection roll-up from the Arrange menu. Put a check mark in both the Target Object and Other Object(s) boxes in the Leave Original section.
2. Type a single word on the page. Give it a white outline so the extrude will display better.
3. Draw a rectangle covering the top half of the word.

4. Select the rectangle and click on the Intersect With button in the Intersection roll-up. Use the arrow to click on the text.

5. Select the rectangle again and click on the top middle selection handle on the top side. Drag the rectangle down and over the bottom half of the text. Make sure it completely covers the text.

6. Remove the check marks from both the Target Object and Other Object(s) boxes in the Leave Original section. Repeat step 4 to intersect the lower half of the text.

7. Fill both the top and bottom halves of the intersected text with different colors.

8. As an option, you can extrude both halves for an different look. When you finish the extrudes, click on the top extrude group and bring it to the front by selecting Order from the Arrange pull-down menu and then selecting To Front from the Order flyout menu.

*Figure PR5.11.*
*An example of splitting*
*text with the Intersection*
*command.*

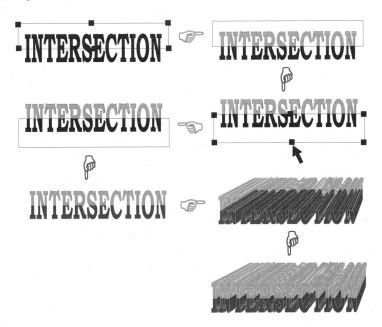

# 6

# Book Cover

Creating a book cover involves understanding certain key elements. These include the following (not in any specific order): Market, Deadline, Quantity, Binding, and Budget.

## Key Elements

Market helps focus and direct you to the appropriate type of design elements required for the design.

Deadline dictates the order or progression you should follow. This might include decisions on the type of paper and inks used, and scheduling printing time with your book printer.

Quantity helps determine the pricing and cost of a print job.

Binding leads you to the proper placement of elements on the spine. Depending on the type of binding used, there might or might not be a need for elements on the spine.

Budget is determined by the preceding items, the clients requirements, including the cost of paper, ink, and type of cover chosen.

# Bindings

Here are some distinct types of binding used for books, multi-page documents, booklets, magazines, and newsletters (not in any particular order):

- Saddle-stitched: The document is stapled through its center. Generally, about 20 sheets of paper is a good limit for this type of binding.
- Side-stitched: The document is stapled on its left side near the backbone. This is used when the size of the document is too great to be saddle stitched.
- Perfect bind: The book is cut and roughened on the left side, and then the cover is glued to it.
- Notch bind: This is similar to perfect binding except that there is a notch about 1/4 inch in from the left of the spine, which forms a grip to help prevent the loss of pages.
- Wire-O: This method uses a book that has holes punched along its edge with a continuous series of wire loops that runs through them.
- Velo bind: Holes are drilled through the book, and a flat plastic tab with teeth is placed through them. On the other side, a second piece of plastic slips over the teeth and is melted to them.
- Spiral bind: This method also uses a book that has holes punched along its edge, with a continuous series of wire or plastic loops that run through them.
- Lay flat bind: This allows the book to lay open flat, no matter where the book is opened.
- Edition bind: This starts with printed folded sheets that are assembled into signatures, collated, and sewn. The sheets are trimmed, and the sewn edges are coated with an adhesive. The sheets are passed through a rounding machine that rolls the backbone. The rolled backbone is a trait of this type of binding, and it gives the book the correct shape to close and open properly.

# Determining Cover Size

Cover size is determined by

- The dimensions, in length and width.
- Page count, which establishes the height or thickness of the spine.
- Paper type and weight, which further determine the height of the spine.

When creating a book cover, there are standard items you must have:

- Front cover panel
- Spine
- Back cover panel
- Graphic elements

Before starting any project, always contact the printer you will be working with at the beginning of the project. The printer can assist you with such questions as

- How far should any bleeds extend past the trim size? (For example, if they extend 1/8 of an inch, verify this information with your printer.)
- Can they print with spot colors, 4-color Process, or a combination of both?
- What line screen settings should you use?
- Should the film be printed with the emulsion side up, right reading? (For more information, see Skill Sessions 51, "Selecting a Printer," and 53, "Preparation for Printing.")

Remember to use a checklist and get verification or a client to sign off on agreed-upon elements before proceeding.

## Sample Cover Main Elements

The trim size, dimensions, page count, and paper type are as follows: length 8.5 inches, width 5.5 inches, and height 1 inch. Set your grid to 4 per inch vertical and horizontal. Enable the Show Grid and Snap To Grid options, and press OK. For more information on Grid Set-Up, see Skill Session 19, "Grid and Ruler Setup."

Double-click on the page border to bring up the Page Setup dialog box. Select Legal from the Paper pull-down list in the Page size section. Set to landscape and press OK. For more information on Page Setup, see Layout Menu Commands in the Command Reference section of this book.

Draw a 5 $^1/_2$ inch width by an 8 $^1/_2$ inch length rectangle for the back panel. Place it at the left side of your drawing area. Draw a 1 inch by 8 $^1/_2$ inch length rectangle for the spine. Place its left edge next to the right edge of the back panel. Draw another 5 $^1/_2$ inch width by 8 $^1/_2$ inch length rectangle for the front panel. Place its left edge next to the right edge of the spine. See Figure PR6.1.

## Corel*NOTE!*

You can also make a copy of your first rectangle by dragging it to the right side of the page and right-clicking on the mouse. This will allow you to make a copy of the original rectangle.

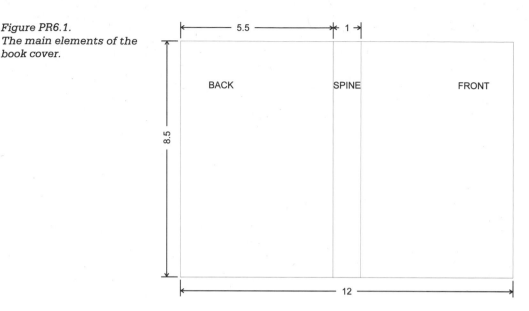

*Figure PR6.1.*
*The main elements of the*
*book cover.*

## Spine and Front Panel Elements

These items appear on the front panel and the spine:

- Title.
- Author name(s).
- Publishers name/logo.
- Graphic elements, which could be a combination of text and art. (See Figure PR6.2.)

Next, place your elements—text, graphics, author's name, and so on—on the front panel and spine. Unless the design dictates that any of the elements should bleed off of the cover, keep them $1/4$ inch back from all edges.

## Corel*NOTE!*

Graphic representation used on the front cover is often placed on spine to help potential buyers recognize the writer or type of book they are seeking.

*Figure PR6.2.*
*The items that appear on*
*the front panel and spine.*

## Back Panel Elements

Most of these items appear on the back panel; some also appear elsewhere as noted:

- ISBN (International Standard Book Number).
- Bar code with the ISBN.
- Price (back and inside cover).
- Graphic elements (back and spine).
- Description or enticement of what is inside.
- Quotes from peers and reviewers. (See Figure PR6.3.)

Place elements on back panel and spine where required.

## Corel *NOTE!*

The bar code with an ISBN is usually located near the lower section of the back cover. Research the market in which your book will be sold. This information will determine where and how many times the bar code/ISBN should appear. The bar code scanning equipment used by the store that sells the book will determine the type of bar code that you need.

For information concerning ISBN and bar code usage, placement, and colors, contact (212) 337-6971 or check your telephone book for an ISBN Bookland/EAN bar code film master supplier. (For information about creating your own bar code with Corel, see Skill Session 63, "Bar Codes.")

*Figure PR6.3.*
*Elements that appear on*
*the back panel and spine.*

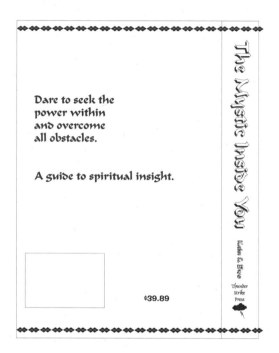

Here is a list of optional items:

- Gate folds
- Pockets
- Perforated book marks
- Outside book covers (dust jacket)

Here is a list of required items on mechanicals:

- Crop or trim marks
- Full or partial bleeds
- Registration marks

The elements used for "The Mystic Inside You" sample book cover are title, author, publisher, wizard, enticement, price, and bar code. The final step is to add marks to guide your printer: crop, fold, and registration marks. It is now ready for film output. (See Figure PR6.4.)

*Figure PR6.4.*
*Final book cover.*

Look at this book's color sections for sample book covers.

# 7

# Video Cassette Box

Because video cassettes have become standardized, their boxes also come in standard sizes. However, there are a variety of video box designs available. Some of them open from the top, side, bottom, or even with a flap like a book would.

Most video boxes are made of cardboard, paper, or plastic or might even have elaborate designs. We will concentrate on a basic video box constructed from cardboard.

Remember to consult the printer you will be working with at the start of your project. The printer might provide you with a specific template for your video box design and assist you with such questions as

- How far should the bleeds extend past the trim size? (They might extend $1/4$ of an inch; confirm this information with your printer.)
- Do you have any limitations when printing with spot colors, 4-color process, or a combination of both?
- Are specific line screen settings are required?
- How should the film for the video box be printed? Emulsion side down? Right reading? (For more information, see Skill Session 51, "Selecting a Printer," and Skill Session 53, "Preparing for Printing.")

Addressing these issues will provide you the necessary information to create a great design, avoid lost time, lost money, missed deadlines, and upset clients. Use a checklist and get verification on agreed-upon design elements before proceeding.

Set your grid to $^1/_8$ inch increments and create all the required panels and flaps with the rectangle tool. The main elements for the basic video box include

- Left panel (A) at 1 inch wide by 7 inches in height.
- Back panel (B) at 4 and $^1/_8$ inches wide by 7 inches in height.
- Right panel (C) at 1 inch wide by 7 inches in height.
- Front panel (D) at 4 and $^1/_8$ inches wide by 7 inches in height.

The flaps include

- Glue flap (E) at 1 inch wide by 7 inches in height.
- Left flap (F) at 1 inch wide by 1 inch in height.
- Top flap (G) at 4 and $^1/_8$ inches wide by 1 inch in height.
- Right flap (H) at 1 inch wide by 1 inch in height.
- Tuck in flap (I) at 4 and $^1/_8$ inches wide by $^3/_4$ inches in height (See Figure PR7.1.)

*Figure PR7.1.*
*The main elements for the*
*basic video box.*

Some of the panels and flaps need to be altered. The left panel (A) and the right panel (C) require a section shaped like a half circle to be removed at the lower center of each panel.

# Corel*NOTE!*

Create a *perfect* circle by pressing the Ctrl key and holding it down while drawing a circle. Select more than one object by pressing the Shift key and choosing the next object.

The next series of instructions as seen in Figure PR7.2 will remove a half circle section on the panels. These half circle sections provide an area for the fingers of the person removing a video cassette from its box.

Create a circle and use it to trim away the unwanted sections of the left and right panels. First draw a $^3/_4$ inch circle and place the center of it at the bottom of the left panel. With the circle still selected, select the left panel and choose the Trim command from the Arrange menu. You will end up with a panel shaped like the one in Figure PR7.2. (See Steps 1 through 2 in Figure PR7.2.) For more information on the Trim command, see Skill Session 24, "Weld, Intersection, and Trim."

*Figure PR7.2.*
*The left and right panels,*
*a circle, and the altered*
*panel.*

Step 1     Step 2

The glue flap (E) will be modified next. The next series of instructions as seen in Figure PR7.3 are used to modify the glue flap.. Use the same $^3/_4$ inch circle as a guide and also place it at the lower-bottom section of the glue flap. Resize the glue flap to a
$^1/_2$-inch width by selecting it and dragging the right side in $^1/_2$ inch toward the left.

Convert the glue flap to curves, and with the Shape tool select the top right node and pull it down by a $^1/_4$ inch. Use the circle as a guide and select the bottom-right node of the glue flap. Raise the node up by $^3/_4$ of an inch from its initial position. Its final position should be up above the circle. (See Steps 1 through 4 in Figure PR7.3.)

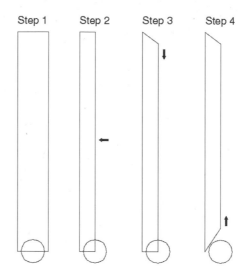

*Figure PR7.3.*
*The modified glue flap*
*panel.*

Step 1    Step 2    Step 3    Step 4

# Corel*NOTE!*

In most cases, your design should not extend onto the glue flap. Ink in that area might make it difficult for the glue to adhere properly.

The next series of instructions, as shown in Figure PR7.4, remove some overlap so the tuck in flap panel will fit. Transform the rectangular shape of the tuck in flap (I) by rounding the corners to $^1/_4$ inch, and then convert it to curves. Delete the two nodes at the bottom.

Select that section with the Shape tool; from the Node edit roll-up, change that section to a line. Pull the left and right bottom nodes down to match the original height of $^3/_4$ inches. See Figure PR7.4.

The next series of instructions, as shown in Figure PR7.5, will modify the left and right flaps so they can close properly. The last change is made to the left and right flaps (F and H). Round the corners $^1/_8$ of an inch. Convert the rectangle to curves. Select the top two left nodes and drag them to the right by $^1/_8$ inch. You can now use the Transform roll-up to flip the panel horizontally 100 percent with the apply to a duplicate button to create the right flap (H). (See Figure PR7.5.)

*Figure PR7.4.*
*The transformed tuck in*
*flap panel.*

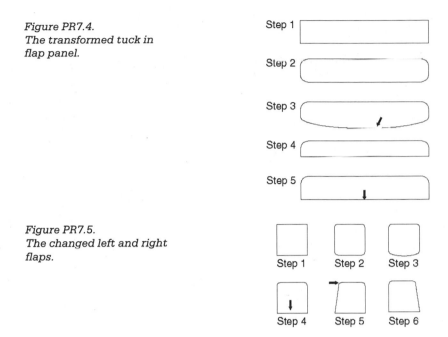

*Figure PR7.5.*
*The changed left and right*
*flaps.*

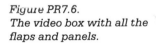

Make sure all of the parts are in their correct positions. Indicate score and fold, crop, registration marks, and cut marks for the trim size. Your printer might use a standard diecut for the trim size. All that is left is to decide where to place your graphics elements and have your finalized design output to film. (See Figure PR7.6.)

*Figure PR7.6.*
*The video box with all the*
*flaps and panels.*

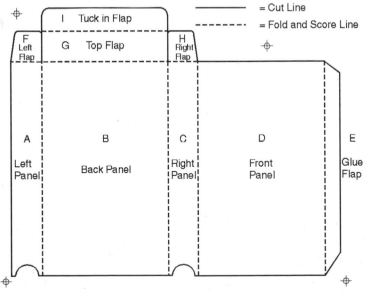

After all of the graphic and text elements are in place, you will get a good idea of what the finished video box will look like. An overhead view of the video box laid flat, with all the graphic and text elements in place, is shown in Figure PR7.7.

*Figure PR7.7.*
*The final video box ready*
*for film output.*

The next figure shows a three dimensional look at the video box once it is assembled. (See Figure PR7.8.)

*Figure PR7.8.*
*The video box in 3D.*

# 8

# Pop-Up Card

Pop-up cards are a great way to promote yourself or company, and they enable you to interactively demonstrate your skills. Pop-up cards, which can be made in many different ways, are inspired by Japanese origami. The example in this project uses a text-based design consisting of a cardstock background and a paper foreground.

In the Grid and Ruler setup dialog box, set your grid to ⅛ inch increments and enable the Show Grid option. Draw the foreground rectangle sized at 5.75 inches in width by 7.0 inches in height. Draw the background rectangle sized at 6.0 inches in width by 7.25 inches in height. Select and center both rectangles to your page. Draw a 6-inch horizontal fold and score line and center it to the rectangles.

The foreground rectangle dictates where your design elements are to be placed. With your nudge settings set to 2.0 inches, use the arrow keys to move the second rectangle out of the drawing area.

Use four guidelines to modify the foreground rectangle an irregular octagon. Place the first guideline 1 ⅜ inch down from the top of the rectangle. Place the second one 1 ⅜ inch up from the bottom. Place the third guideline 1 ⅜ inch in from the left side of the rectangle. Place the fourth one 1 ⅜ inch in from the right. (See Figure PR8.1.)

Figure PR8.1.
On the left are the foreground and background rectangles, and the main horizontal fold and score line. On the right is the foreground rectangle after being modified into an irregular octagon.

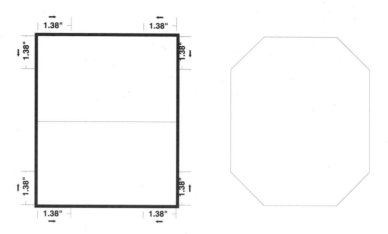

Create and place your graphic design in the center of the octagon, and print it. Use this print-out of the pop-up card as a template.

Place a sheet of paper over the template and place both on a light table. Then score the dashed lines, slice the cut lines, and fold the card in half. The legend indicates which lines will be folded concave, convex, or cut.

Push the characters toward you so that when you fold the card they point away from the middle of it. Make sure the parts of the card that are not part of your design fold the opposite direction from the characters. (See Figure PR8.2.)

Figure PR8.2.
The graphic design is positioned on the octagon. Score, fold, and cut lines are printed out to be used as guidelines.

# Corel *NOTE!*

The lines representing the score and fold (convex and concave), and cut lines should not be printed on your final design unless they are an integral part of the design.

Print the background rectangle on colored card stock. Center and glue your pop-up to it. Be careful not to glue down the parts that pop out! Use the outline of the background rectangle to trim the card down to its finished size and you are done. (See Figure PR8.3.)

*Figure PR8.3.*
*The finished card.*

Here are two more examples of pop-up cards. Get creative and design your own or turn your existing design into one of these great-looking attention getting cards. (See Figure PR8.4.)

*Figure PR8.4.*
*Two other types of pop-up*
*card designs.*

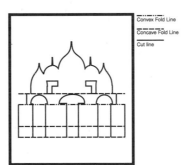
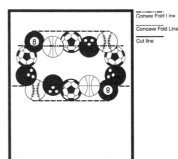

# Creating a Business Card

A business card is the most basic of marketing tools. Everyone has one; and some have several. With the tools that Corel provides, it is not difficult to create some really fantastic results. This project walks you through the creation of a full color business card from its design through the final printing.

## Preparing the Photographs

The first part of creating the business card is merging two photographs together. This is accomplished in Photo-Paint. The first photograph is a stock photo stored in TIFF format. Figure PR9.1 shows the photograph open in Photo-Paint.

We want to add the picture of coauthor Foster Coburn to the card so that he seamlessly is merged into the background. When the photograph was taken, it was shot against a white background so that it would be easy to mask. We scanned the picture into PHOTO-PAINT and masked it using the Magic Wand tool. Using the Add to Mask button (+), it was easy to mask all of the white areas of the image. Next, the mask was inverted using the Mask Invert command so that everything except the white area was selected. Once this was completed, Foster was converted to a floating object using the Object Create from Mask command. You'll see the marching ants around the object in Figure PR9.2 and note that the Objects roll-up shows the two separate images in the file. For more information on the masking techniques used, see Skill Session 78, "An Introduction to Masks and How to Use Them."

*Figure PR9.1.*
*Stock photo for the*
*background of the card.*

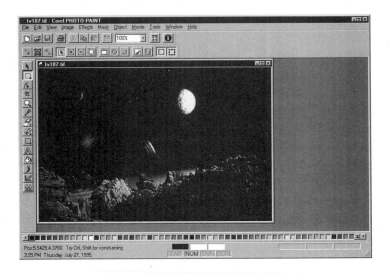

*Figure PR9.2.*
*Floating object to be*
*merged with the back-*
*ground.*

To combine these two images into a single file, drag Foster's picture off of the original image and drag him onto the background of the stock photo. The size of Foster's picture was too large for the background, but with the sizing handles (just as in CorelDRAW), it was very easy to reduce his size until he fit on the background.

A frequent problem when merging images in this manner is that a *ghost* might appear around the image. This can be easily removed by feathering the edges of the smaller image slightly. So, select the photograph of Foster and choose the Object Feather command. You'll get the dialog box shown in Figure PR9.3. We've chosen a width of 2, with soft edges. Clicking on Preview will show the changes to be made. You'll now see that the edges of the picture blend more naturally into the background.

*Figure PR9.3.*
*Feathering the edge of the*
*photograph so that it*
*blends better with the*
*background.*

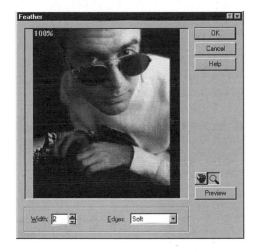

The last step is to convert the image from a 24-bit, RGB image to a 32-bit CMYK image. This step is very important because it is going to be done at some time before the image gets printed. Many times, this step is neglected and the printed image looks nothing like the on-screen image—which can be upsetting. By doing the conversion now, it will allow us to get a much better idea of how the final business card will look. From the Image menu, choose Convert To CMYK Color (32-bit). After the file is converted, save it in the Corel PHOTO-PAINT (CPT) format. This will retain the floating objects should you decide to change the image in the future.

## Adding the Text in Draw

Now we're ready to put all the pieces together in CorelDRAW. We want to finish the file, because adding text in PHOTO-PAINT would cause it to look jaggy. It is also much easier to control placement of objects in CorelDRAW.

The first step is to set the page to the correct size. Choose Page Setup from the Layout menu. In the Page Setup dialog box, choose a Custom page, oriented as Landscape measuring 2.0 high by 3.5 inches wide.

We also want to bring in some guidelines so that we know where the edges of the card will be. So drag a horizontal guideline out at 0 inches and 2 inches. Also drag vertical guidelines to 0 inches and 3.5 inches.

Choose Import from the File menu and bring in the bitmap background created in Photo-Paint. You'll notice in Figure PR9.4 that the bitmap is larger than the card itself. This is done on purpose to provide a bleed area for the card. Cards are printed on larger paper than their final size. They are never cut too accurately, so we are providing extra art to compensate for that inaccuracy.

Next we want to add the text and logo on top of the bitmap background. To help us keep these two parts separate, we are going to create a new layer for the text. Select Layers Manager from the Layout menu, and you will get the Layers roll-up. From the flyout on the upper-right corner, choose New and a new layer will be added named Layer 2. For this simple project, we chose not to name our layers, but you may want to change the name of Layer 1 to Background and Layer 2 to Text.

*Figure PR9.4.*
*The business card*
*background in*
*CorelDRAW.*

Make sure to select Layer 2 (or Text, if you've renamed it) so that any new items will be on that layer. We've added several blocks of text, as well as a company logo. A common problem when adding text over a bitmap is that it can be difficult to distinguish in all places. Therefore, we've added a drop shadow behind the text. The text itself was filled with the Gold color found on the default palette. The drop shadow was filled with Yellow.

There are several steps to follow for creating each of the drop shadow pieces. First, copy the original text and then paste in another copy. Choose Order To Back from the Arrange menu and then immediately choose Order Forward One. We then used the nudge keys (the arrows on the keyboard) to nudge the text .005 inches to the right and down. The amount of nudge can be set in the Tools Options dialog box, which is described in Skill Session 4, "Customizing and Setting Preferences." Finally, we changed the fill color to yellow. This was repeated for each text object. The logo worked the same way, except that the outline color had to be changed to yellow as well. The business card now looked like Figure PR9.5.

*Figure PR9.5.*
*The business card after all elements have been added.*

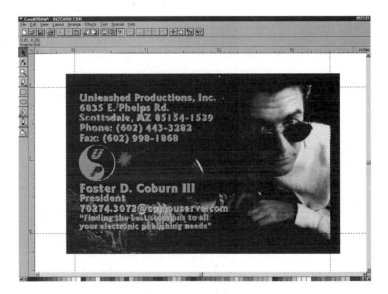

The last thing we did was to draw two rectangles. One of them was outside of all of our artwork and the other was drawn to the exact page size of the card itself. These two rectangles were then combined, filled with white, and given no outline. This allowed us to preview what the final card would look like. You might have noticed that the photograph did not extend to the edge of the artwork, but with the final cut shown in Figure PR9.6 you'll see why this wasn't necessary.

Figure PR9.6.
A final look at the finished
card.

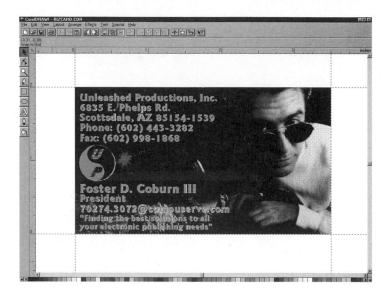

After all the artwork was finished, we sent the CDR file to ColorCard Express of Blackwood, New Jersey. They have created some proprietary equipment just for printing color business cards. The results are incredible and the cost is many times less than getting a two-color card from a local printer. For more information, contact ColorCard Express at (800) 772-4830.

# Text Effects Templates

Using ready-made templates is a technique that was first introduced in *CorelDRAW! 5 Unleashed*. The ready-made templates in this skill session include templates for fitting text to a path, extruding text, and enveloping text. Each template is included on the CD-ROM that come with the book. They are listed as TMPL*xx*.CDR (*xx* is the number for each template shown in Figures P10.3 through P10.5). The template files can be found on disc number one in the Projects\proj10 folder.

The idea behind using templates is to save time by not having to create a certain effect from scratch. There is only one rule you must follow if you want to create your own templates. That rule is to Center Justify the master text before you apply the effect. The concept behind templates is to apply an effect to text and then re-use the effect in other projects by just changing the font and/or the point size.

## Text on a Path

We have created six templates using the techniques you were taught in Skill Session 40, "Fitting Text to a Path." You can use these templates in your projects to save time in re-creating them each time.

The following steps take you through the process of importing, resizing, and ungrouping the templates so you can use them efficiently.

1. Import the template you want from the CD-ROM included in this book, using the Import command in the File menu. The template is displayed on the page in the file on which you are currently working. It will appear as a group of objects.

2. Before you ungroup the template, resize the template to the size you want.

3. Next, ungroup the template using the Ungroup command in the Arrange menu. The template is now ready to edit. Figure PR10.1 uses the TEMPL01.CDR. This is the template used for fitting text to an ellipse.

*Figure PR10.1.*
*Editing text on a path*
*using templates.*

4. Select the text, hold down the Ctrl key, and click the text again. The text is now independently selected and the status line will indicate that you have text selected.

5. You can now edit the text in the normal way—by either using the shortcut method Ctrl+Shift+T or by selecting the Edit Text dialog box from the Text pull-down menu. Notice that when you change fonts or point size the text still remains correctly placed on the path.

All the templates work the same as the others; however, when you have more than one word on a path you must click the word you want to edit more than once while holding down the Ctrl key until the word you want is selected. Anything more than one word on a path is a compound object, thus the need to continue clicking until the correct word is selected.

Figure PR10.2 displaying TEMPL02.CDR, shows the bottom word changed on the right. To make this change you would need to click the mouse twice while you hold down the Ctrl key.

Figure PR10.3 shows all six templates. We hope you find them useful in your projects. You should also try making some ready-made templates of your own because these are only samples.

*Figure PR10.2.*
*Editing a second word on*
*a path.*

*Figure PR10.3.*
*The Fit Text to Path*
*Templates 1 through 6.*

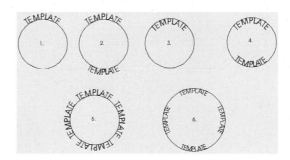

## Extrusion Templates

We have created seven extruded templates using the techniques you were taught in Skill Session 31, "Extruding." You can edit Templates 7 through 13 by clicking the text portion of the extrusion and then using the Edit Text dialog box to change the text as you did in the preceding section. Figure PR10.4 shows the seven extrude templates.

*Figure PR10.4.*
*Templates 7 through 13—*
*Extrusion.*

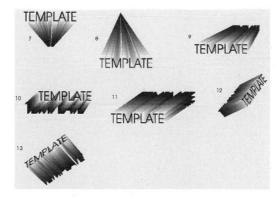

## Envelope Templates

We have created six envelope templates using the techniques you were taught in Skill Session 29, "Enveloping." You can edit templates 14 through 19 by clicking the text and then using the Edit Text dialog box to change the text, as you did previously. Figure PR10.5 shows the six envelope templates.

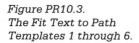

*Figure PR10.5.*
*Templates 14 through 19—*
*Envelope.*

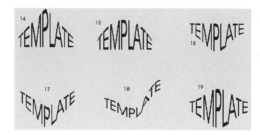

# Corel*NOTE!*

A final reminder: All the templates will come in as a group if you're importing them into your projects. You must ungroup the imported template before doing any editing of the text. If you have merely opened the template as a new file, you do not have to use the Ungroup command. All the templates will come in as read-only because they were stored on the CD-ROM. When you re-save the file under a new name to your hard drive they will be saved correctly.

# 11

# Logo Design

Logos have certain minimum requirements. They must be easily recognizable when reduced to the size of a dime (approximately $1/2$ inch in diameter). When it looks right in black and white, it will always work in color.

Here are some questions you might have when creating a logo:

■ Should the logo have no connection to the product or company?

■ Does the client want qualities of the company or product to be reflected?

■ Should the logo convey a description of product ingredients or qualities of the company?

The answers will depend on the product, service, target market, and client.

Many logos are created for trademark use only. They might be created from combinations of text and numbers, words, and an endless variety of shapes. The characteristics of a logo might be nondescriptive of the company it represents. Keep in mind that most completely made-up logos are considered the most successful types of logos.

## Corel *TIP!*

Descriptive logos may not be desirable for a new company.

The logo in this project is for a locksmith named Cactus Keys. One requirement for their logo is to convey a high quality of service. The following steps describe the creation of the cactus-shaped key logo.

1. Draw a rectangle $3/4$-inch wide by 1-inch tall. Doing this will round the corners $1/8$ of an inch. From the Arrange menu, convert the rectangle to curves and delete the two left side nodes. Marquee-select the left side of the object with the Shape tool; in the Node Edit roll-up, select the to line icon.

2. Draw two rectangles $3/4$ inch wide by $1/4$ inch tall. Draw a third rectangle 1 inch wide by $1/4$ inch tall. Round the corners of the rectangles so they look like capsules.

   Select the modified rectangle and align the two small capsules to the top and bottom of it. Duplicate one of the small capsules to use later. Align the larger capsule with the center of it and weld all four sections to form the head for the key.

3. Add a small circle to the tip of the key head and combine them. Select the duplicate of the small capsule you made earlier, and reduce it by 41.6 percent.

   Make a copy of it and position them between the "arms" of the key head. Use them to trim a section away from the key head. Select the key head and apply an offset of 0.04 inch, 1 step, and an inside contour to it.

4. Separate and ungroup the contour effect. Use the arrow keys to nudge it out of the way for the moment. Draw a rectangle 2 inches wide by $3/8$ of an inch tall. Overlap it near the right side of the key head. Select them both and weld them. (See Figure PR11.1.)

*Figure PR11.1.*
*Steps 1–4 used in the creation of the Cactus Keys logo.*

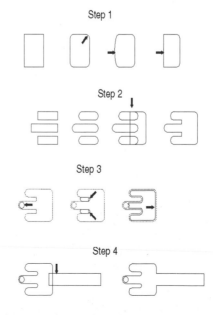

Step 1

Step 2

Step 3

Step 4

5. Nudge the contour shape back into place. Then select, rotate, and use the reduced capsules to trim away sections at the "neck" of the key.

6. Create some small rectangles and use them to trim away sections from the length of the key.

7. Create some small shapes and weld them to the length of the key.

8. Draw two long, thin rectangles. Place them along the length of the key. Convert them to curves and edit their right sides to fit the key. (See Figure PR11.2.)

*Figure PR11.2.*
*Steps 5–8 used in the*
*creation of the Cactus*
*Keys logo.*

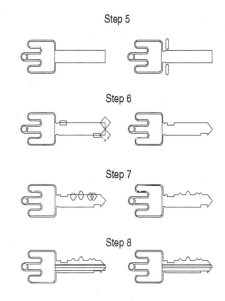

9. Create a large, rounded-corner rectangle and surround the key with it. Add any necessary text and apply your desired fills and effects. (See Figure PR11.3.)

*Figure PR11.3.*
*Step 9 used in the creation*
*of the Cactus Keys logo.*

## Trademark Hatching Patterns

The logo/trademark design is finished, and you have the client's approval. Now you are ready to tackle your next assignment. Is there more? Well, in some cases there is. An ad agency or large design firm might have a specific person or department that handles this next step: getting your trademark filed with the Patent and Trademark Office. If you have no idea how to achieve this, it is to your benefit to consult with a patent and trademark attorney or similar entity.

The Patent and Trademark Office has certain requirements for trademark design and submission. See the last paragraph of this chapter for how to obtain further information.

This section covers the patterns required by the Patent and Trademark Office to indicate color in trademarks. If part of your trademark is colored red, for example, there is a pattern to use that represents that color. (See Figure PR11.4.)

*Figure PR11.4.*
*Trademark patterns and*
*their colors.*

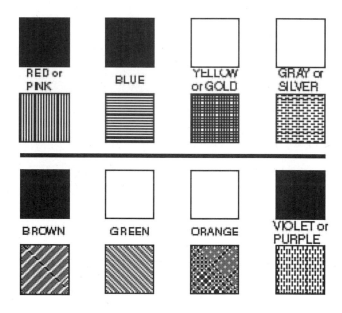

Creating patterns in Corel is easy. Use the following steps to create the patterns seen in Figure PR11.5.

1. Draw two vertical lines an inch long. Place them an inch apart from each other. Blend them with 11 steps.

2. Duplicate and rotate #1 90 degrees.

3. Place a duplicate of #2 on top of a duplicate of #1. Change the number of blend steps to 8 on both.

4. Duplicate #2 and change the lines to the dash setting in the Outline Pen dialog box in the Style section and then offset every other line $1/8$ of an inch horizontally.

5. Duplicate #1 and rotate 45 degrees.

6. Duplicate #5 and flip horizontally.

7. Plate a duplicate of #5 on top of a duplicate of #6. Change the number of blend steps to 8 on both.

8. Duplicate #4 and rotate 90 degrees.

*Figure PR11.5.*
*Patterns 1–8.*

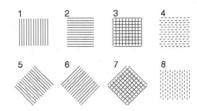

When you have finished the patterns, choose Pattern from the Create submenu under the Tools menu to place them in your Full Color Pattern library (see the Tools menu in the "Command Reference" section for more information).

Duplicate your trademark. Fill the appropriate sections with the patterns that correspond to the colors in your original logo/trademark. (See Figure PR11.6.)

*Figure P11.6.*
*Colored logo/trademark*
*and rectangles filled with*
*logo colors and the*
*corresponding patterns.*

Additional information concerning the requirements for filing a trademark application are available in a booklet titled "Basic Facts about Trademarks," which may be obtained by writing to the U.S. Department of Commerce, Patent and Trademark Office, Washington, D.C. 20231, or by calling (703) 557-INFO.

# 12

# Drawing With PowerLines

Many computer-drawn images have a certain look that tells the viewer right away that the image was created on a computer. In many cases it is undesirable for an image to appear as though it has been created with a computer program. There are many computer programs offering special effects that can give an image a painted or handdrawn, non-computer look to images.

When you enable the Apply When Drawing option, lines will be drawn with the selected PowerLine effect. Using PowerLines will make your file complicated. The design in this project is a logo for a racehorse breeder called EquestiRace Stables. First, let's draw the parts that make up the horse's head.

## The Horse Head

First draw the basic shape of the horse head. Use five lines to make up the front and back of the neck, the chin, the right sight of the head and nose, and the left side of the right ear. (See Figure PR12.1.)

*Figure PR12.1.*
*The placement of the lines*
*that result in the basic*
*shape for the horse head.*

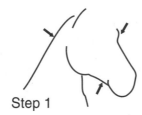

Step 1

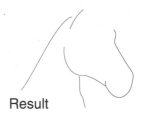

Result

Next draw four shapes for the top of the nose, the nostril, and the mouth opening. Make sure the nostril is a closed path. (See Figure PR12.2.)

*Figure PR12.2.*
*The lines that form the*
*sections for the nose and*
*mouth.*

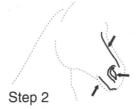

Step 2

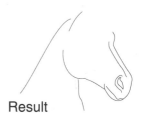

Result

Now create eight shapes for the ears and eyes. Use a circle for the eyeball. Make sure the inner sections of the ear are closed paths. (See Figure PR12.3.)

*Figure PR12.3.*
*The shapes created for the*
*eyes and ears.*

Step 3

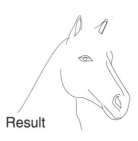

Result

Use seven different lines to create the horse's mane. Place five of them on the back of the neck, and the other two on top of the head. (See Figure PR12.4.)

*Figure PR12.4.*
*The placement of the lines*
*for the mane.*

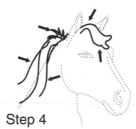

Step 4

Result

All that's left to finish the horse head is to select the eyeball, nostril, and two inner ear sections and fill them with a uniform color. Then position a couple of character lines on the neck and face. (See Figure PR12.5.)

*Figure PR12.5.*
*The ears, eyes, and nose*
*are filled, and character*
*lines are placed on the*
*head and neck.*

Step 5

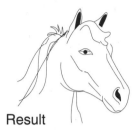

Result

Select all of the lines and objects and bring up the PowerLine roll-up. Select Wedge 3 from the roll-up and set the Max. Width to 0.10 inches. Press the Apply button. (See Figure PR12.6.)

*Figure PR12.6.*
*The outcome of the*
*PowerLine effect.*

Step 6

Result

## The Text and Base

Use Artistic Text to type in the name of the racehorse breeder: EquestiRace Stables. Draw a circle to use as the base for the logo. The circle will also be used to fit the text to path. Fill the circle with a gradient tone set to a radial fill. (For more information on Fills, see Skill Session 16, "The Fill Tool.")

Use the Fit Text To Path roll-up to place the word EquestiRace at the top of the circle. Then use it to place the word Stables at the bottom of the circle. (For more information on Fit Text To A Path, see Skill Session 40, "Fitting Text To A Path.")

Select the circle and text, and choose the separate command from the Arrange menu. Then duplicate the text and position it on top of the original text. This forms a drop shadow effect. (See Figure PR12.7.)

*Figure PR12.7.*
*The finished EquestiRace*
*Stable's logo, by a nose!*

# 13

# Floor Plan

The floor plan designed in this project shows the use of numerous features in CorelDRAW. The most important feature of CorelDRAW 6 used is the increase in page size. This enables the house to be drawn life-size rather than to scale. Layers are also used extensively to separate the floor plan itself from some of the many items located throughout the house. And finally, the Weld and Trim drawing tools make the creation of the plan fairly quick and easy.

## Laying Out the Page

The page size is left at the default value of 8.5×11 inches rather than changing the page size to the full image size created. This just means that the Fit to Page option will have to be activated to print the image. Guidelines are added to indicate where walls are to be added. This makes it easier to make sure that they are located in the right place. The grid is set so that it is located every three inches. Once the guides and grid are set, the Snap to Grid and Snap to Guidelines (found in the Layout menu) are activated.

## Creating the Walls

The edge of objects in most projects is just a single line, but the walls of a floor plan have a thickness that needs to be shown. That means each wall will have double lines; there isn't a tool in CorelDRAW that automatically creates such a shape. However, it is fairly easy to do this by using the Weld tool and a few rectangles. Draw overlapping rectangles where one dimension is the thickness of the wall and the other dimension is the length of the wall. Once you have these rectangles in place, simply select both of them and use the Weld roll-up (or preferably the QuickWeld command) to weld the two rectangles together. Figure P13.1 shows the rectangles before and after welding them together.

*Figure P13.1.*
*Overlapping rectangles*
*before and after welding*
*to create a corner in a*
*wall.*

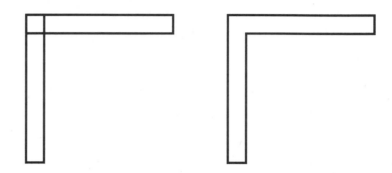

Another problem will come into play when you need to make openings in the walls for windows and doors. You can do this by continuously drawing new rectangles and making sure they are spaced correctly, but it can be done much easier with the Trim roll-up. Draw a square the exact size of the opening. For example, you might need a 30-inch square for interior doors. Place this square over the wall where you want an opening. Select the square and, using the Trim roll-up, click Trim and use the big arrow to select the wall. Similarly, you can select the square, and then Shift-select the wall and use the QuickTrim command. Figure P13.2 shows a wall and "door tool" before and after making the opening in the wall.

*Figure P13.2.*
*The wall and "door tool"*
*before and after cutting an*
*opening in the wall.*

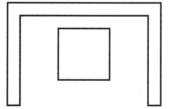 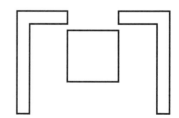

## Layering by Category

Once the floor plan layout is finished, other layers will be added for the details of the house. These details include electrical outlets, switches, fans and smoke detectors, lights and ceiling fans, and more. Layers are not required, but it enables these features to be turned on and off very quickly so that only a certain part of the

plan can be seen at once. Figure P13.3 shows the Layers Manager roll-up after
additional layers have been added.

*Figure P13.3.*
*Layers Manager roll-up*
*after adding layers for*
*other items to be included*
*in the house.*

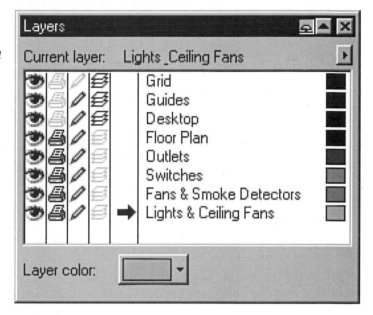

The electrical outlets consist of a rectangle for the outer wall plate, and two
rounded rectangles for the receptacles, with tiny rectangles and ellipses for the
plug holes. These are drawn life-size because the entire plan is life-size. They are
placed along the walls on which they will be installed. The switches are very
similar except that they have only a single smaller rectangle inside of the rectangle
for the wall plate. Switches and wall plates are colored differently to help differentiate between the two.

Ceiling fans were created from a single circle surrounded by four ellipses representing the fan blades. One of the ellipses was placed and then its center of
rotation marker was moved to the middle of the center circle. The ellipse was then
rotated 90 degrees and the Apply to Duplicate was pressed. This was repeated
until all four blades were drawn. Once it was created, it was grouped and then
copied to all other locations where it was necessary. Figure P13.4 shows the
finished ceiling fan symbol.

Lights are simply a circle with no fill; smoke detectors are given a gray fill. Exhaust
fans were given a fill that is half white and half black at a 45 degree angle. This is
done with a linear fountain fill from black to white with two steps at a 45 degree
angle. Figure P13.5 shows the Fountain Fill dialog box with all the correct settings
to create this effect and Figure P13.6 shows the finished symbol.

*Figure P13.4.*
*The finished ceiling fan*
*symbol.*

*Figure P13.5.*
*Fountain Fill dialog box*
*with the necessary*
*settings to create the fill*
*for the exhaust fans.*

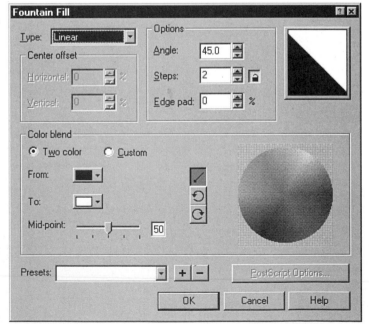

The shapes in this image were created in Corel Draw and then brought into PhotoPaint for colorizing using mainly texture fills. The glasses belong to Peter McCormick, who created this image, and were scanned in. The cookie, crumbs and all, was baked by his wife Sue and Pete only had one bite before he scanned it into this image.

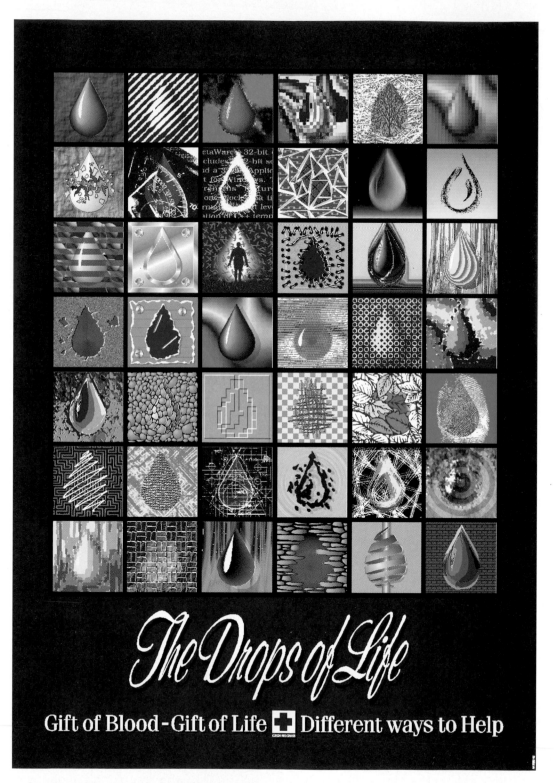

Radim Mojzis' drawing entitled "The Drops of Life" was the winner of the Goodwill Poster Grand Prize and Best of Show in Corel's 1995 World Design Contest.

Michael Koester was the winner of the Product Illustration category of Corel's World Design Contest for December 1994. He also won the Grand Prize of the Product Illustration category with the above image.

"Corel at St. Basil Cathedral" was created by Kelly Murdock. The balloon and cathedral were positioned and rendered out on a blue background using CorelDREAM 3D. They were then brought into PHOTO-PAINT where they were masked and placed on a background created using the Julia Set Explorer effect.

| | | | | |
|---|---|---|---|---|
| Samples 6 Brake Light | Ripples density changed to 10 | Color changed Texture 23340 | Color changed Texture 31183 | Color changed Texture 32181 |
| Samples 6 Elephant Skin | Color changed Texture 25605 | Color change Texture 18013 | Color change Softness 10 | Color change Texture 15885 |
| Styles Cosmic Clouds | Red Softness changed to 10 | Green Softness changed to 10 | Texture number changed to 15272 | Texture number changed to 23158 |
| Samples 6 Ellipse of sun | Color change Texture 7343 | Color Change Texture 20938 | Color Change Texture 4208 | Color Change Texture 2999 |
| Samples Quartz, Polished | Texture number changed to 8447 | Rainbow Grain changed to 50 | Softness changed to 100 | Grain changed to 100 |

*Figure P13.6.*
*The finished exhaust fan*
*symbol.*

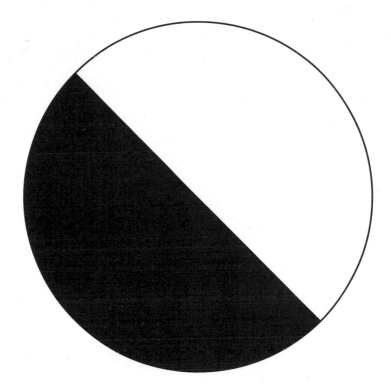

Many more layers could easily be added to this layout such as heating and cooling, plumbing, telephone wiring, cable wiring, and so on.

Figure P13.7 shows a portion of the floor plan with all of the symbols that have been added so far. Notice that the rulers are for the full measurement of the house rather than drawn to a smaller scale.

Figure P13.7.
Section of the floor plan
with all symbols shown.

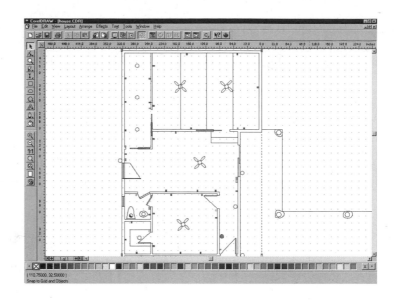

## Finishing the Plan

After the plan was finished in CorelDRAW, it was taken to an architect who drew up blueprints from it. The full plan along with an artist's sketch (which was scanned) are shown in Figure P13.8.

Figure P13.8.
The complete floor plan
with an artist's rendering.

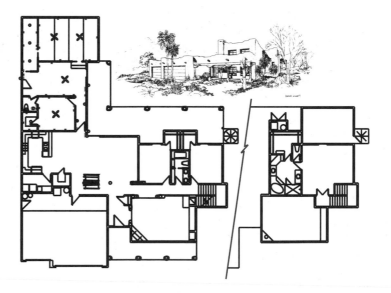

# 14

# Complex Object Map

Imagine you call up some needed artwork for a map project, and you find that it has a missing piece! Quick, what now? If there are two or more complex objects that share a common border, you can use the edge of one object to create the edge of the missing piece.

This is a lot like a jigsaw puzzle. To create a complex object you can use one of two different methods. This project discusses the Node method and illustrates the Trim method.

## Node Method

The Node method is a painstaking way to re-create a missing piece or object, but it does work. Let's say that the missing object you need to re-create is a state on a map that borders another state on the right-hand side. Usually you would create a freeform shaped object. Then you would add, delete, or break and reposition existing nodes to edit the object into the desired shape.

1. Duplicate the first object. If you need to convert the duplicate object to curves, with the Shape tool select the duplicate object's top and bottom nodes on the right side border and use the Break command from the Node Edit roll-up to break the selected nodes.

# Corel*NOTE!*

> Before being able to select and break nodes, the selected object must be converted to curves. If the previous procedure had been applied to a rectangle, the status line would indicate that you now have a curve with six nodes on two subpaths.

2. With the duplicate object selected, choose the Break Apart command from the Arrange menu. The status line should read that you have two objects selected. Delete the object on the left side. Nudge the remaining section from the duplicate object two inches to the right of the first object.

3. Move and align with the remaining section from the duplicate object to the shape that requires the border. Select both of them and then choose Combine from the Arrange menu. The two previously unconnected objects now become one combined object with an open path.

4. With the Shape tool select and join the nodes to turn the combined object open path object into an enclosed object that you can apply a fill to. (For more information on the Shape\Node tool see Skill Session 7, "The Shape Tool.")

# Corel*NOTE!*

> You can apply a fill to an object that has an open path, but until that path is closed you will not be able to see or print the applied fill.

## Trim Method

Figure PR14.1 shows the map and its missing piece. Normally, you would rebuild the piece or redraw it from scratch. That is, of course, if the missing piece can be found elsewhere. Meanwhile there is that deadline you must meet.

Fortunately, you can rather quickly rebuild the missing piece and make your deadline. In this case we have all the other pieces that surround the missing piece. Select the objects that surround the missing piece and make duplicates of them. (See Figure PR14.2.)

*Figure PR14.1.*
*Step 1: The map and its*
*missing piece.*

*Figure PR14.2.*
*Step 2: The pieces that*
*surround the missing*
*object.*

Draw a rectangle that completely engulfs the area that makes up the missing piece. Select the rectangle and one of the surrounding pieces and choose the Trim command from the Arrange menu.

In the Shaping roll-up group press Weld and enable the Other Object option. Use the large black arrow to select the object to trim. See Skill Session 24, "Weld, Intersection, and Trim," for more information on trimming. (See Figure PR14.3.)

*Figure PR14.3.*
*Step 3: The rectangle and*
*the first piece used to trim*
*a section away from it.*

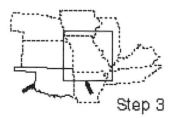

Figure PR14.4 demonstrates the result of using the Trim command on the rectangle. Continue this procedure, select the surrounding pieces, the rectangle, and the Trim command until all the sections are trimmed away from the rectangle.

*Figure PR14.4.*
*Step 4: The modified*
*rectangle after using the*
*Trim command.*

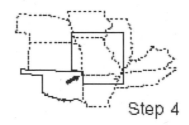

# Corel *TIP!*

> You can select all of the surrounding pieces at once, and then apply the Trim command to the rectangle.

Using the Trim method is quick, but sometimes there are some remnants that are created when you trim another object. (See Figure PR14.5.) These remnants are usually undesirable. Use the Shape tool to remove them. First, marquee select all of the nodes and convert them to cusps. (For more information on the Shape tool, see Skill Session 7.)

After deleting the remnants you will be left with an object that fits the hole in your map. (See Figure PR14.6.)

After you have used the Node method or Trim method to put together the various pieces of your map, you can fill them with color or pattern fills to differentiate the countries and their boundaries.

*Figure PR14.5.*
*Step 5: The newly created*
*object and its remnants.*

*Figure PR14.6.*
*Step 6: The finished*
*trimmed rectangle*
*replaces the missing piece.*

# 15

# Brochure

This brochure for a custom puzzle manufacturer employs a tri-fold design consisting of a custom die-cut rolodex card and a mail-in order form card. This lets the recipient tear the cards out and keep them. The folding sections of the tri-fold and the cards combine to form a functional marketing tool.

## Tri-Fold Panels

1. Bring up the Page Setup dialog box and set the orientation to landscape. In the Size section, select custom and set the size to 9 inches by 13 inches. In the Display section, press the Add Page Frame button. In the Page section, press the OK button.

2. Select the frame and transform it to create the panels. Place the transform roll-up in Scale & Mirror mode. Set the Horizontal section at 33% and the Vertical section to 100%. Press the Apply to Duplicate button. The transformed duplicate frame will center itself to your page.

3. Make two copies of the transformed frame; align one to the left side of the page frame and the other to the right side of the frame.

## Mail-in Order Form

The mail-in form occupies a very standard rectangular shape. Always find out from your local post office what the correct dimensions are for any mail-in form or card.

1. Select the inside right panel. Transform it 66.6% horizontally and press the Apply To Duplicate button.

2. Align it to the top right of the inside-right panel. Use this small panel for the mail-in order form. These panels form the basis for the brochure. (See Figure PR15.1.)

*Figure PR15.1.*
*The steps for the tri-fold*
*basic panel sections and*
*mail-in form.*

| Inside Right Panel | Inside Center Panel | Inside Left Panel |
|---|---|---|
| Steps 1-4 | | |
| | | Order Form |

## Rolodex Card

The rolodex card is a bit more complex. You will need to create several pieces. Besides creating the card, you will need to create sections for the rolodex slots, and a custom-shaped tab.

1. Bring up the Grid & Ruler Setup dialog box. Press the Grid tab. In the Frequency section, set the Horizontal and Vertical settings to 8.0 per inch and press the OK button.

   Draw two rectangles, one for the main section of the card and a smaller one for the tab section. Make the card 4 inches wide by $2\,^1/_4$ inches in height, and the tab 2 inches wide by $^1/_2$ inch in height.

   Set the small rectangle near the top of the large rectangle and align it to the left side. Make sure the small rectangle overlaps the large one by $^1/_8$ inch.

2. Select the Small rectangle and the Add Perspective command from the Effects menu. When the bounding box appears, select the top-left handle. Hold the Shift and Ctrl keys down together, and drag the handle by $^1/_8$ inch to the right.

3. Convert the small rectangle to curves. Use the Shape tool to select and delete the two nodes on the top and bottom horizontal lines of the rectangle.

Marquee-select all of the nodes. In the Node Edit roll-up, select the line Icon to change any curved lines to straight lines. Select the left and right side middle nodes, and align them with the top of the large rectangle. (See Figure PR15.2.)

*Figure PR15.2.*
*Steps 1, 2, and 3 for the*
*main section and tab*
*sections of the rolodex*
*card.*

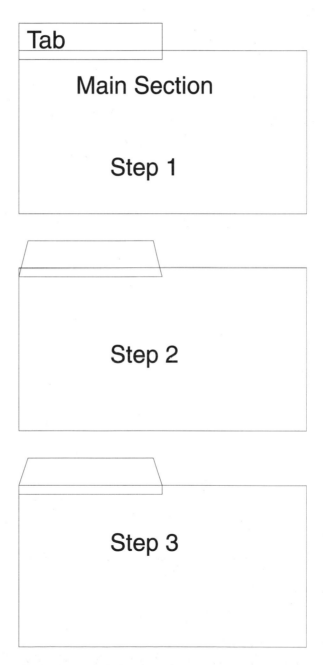

## Puzzle-Shaped Tab

Normally, the tab section would be done. Considering this brochure is for a puzzle manufacturer, utilize the tab to reinforce what the company does. In this case, the shape of the tab is a puzzle-like piece. This feature distinguishes the card and lets the potential customer easily locate it.

4. Draw two rectangles $1/4$ inch by $1/2$ inch. Place the first one at the top center of the tab. Overlap the tab by $1/4$ inch. Use it to trim a section away from the tab.

   Rotate the second one 90 degrees. Place it on the right side center of the tab. Overlap it onto the tab by $1/4$ inch. Select the tab and second rectangle, and choose the Weld command from the Arrange menu. Select the tab and card and weld them to each other. (See Figure PR15.3.)

## Track Slots

Slots are needed to hold the rolodex card on the rolodex's tracks.

5. Reset the grid to 16 per inch. Draw a $1/4$-inch wide by $3/8$-inch tall rectangle. Round the corners of the rectangle with the Shape tool to $1/16$ inch. Draw a second rectangle $1/8$-inch wide by $1/2$-inch tall. Center it to the rounded corner rectangle and overlap it by $1/4$ inch. Select both rectangles and weld them.

6. Place the slots $1\,3/8$ inch in from the left and $1/2$ inch up from the bottom of the card. Duplicate the slot and move it $3/4$ inch to the right.

   Select both slots and the card. Choose the Trim command from the Arrange menu. Delete the slots. (See Figure PR15.4.)

Position the rolodex card on the right panel of the tri-fold brochure near the bottom. Select all and duplicate. Use the Transform roll-up to apply a horizontal flip. Use the flipped duplicate for the reverse side of the brochure. (See Figure PR15.5.)

If required, add your registration marks, crop marks, fold marks, score marks, and any die-cuts. All that is left is to position your graphic elements and have it printed. (See Figure PR15.6.)

*Figure PR15.3.*
*Step 4—altering the tab for*
*the rolodex card.*

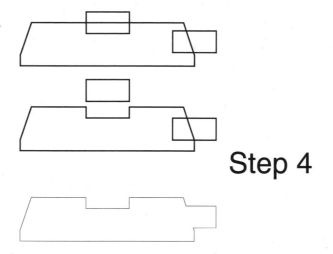

## Step 4

## Step 5

*Figure PR15.4.*
*Steps 5 and 6—creating*
*the slots.*

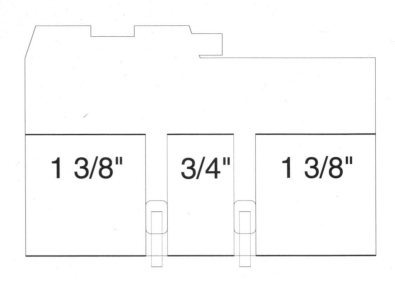

1 3/8"    3/4"    1 3/8"

# Step 6

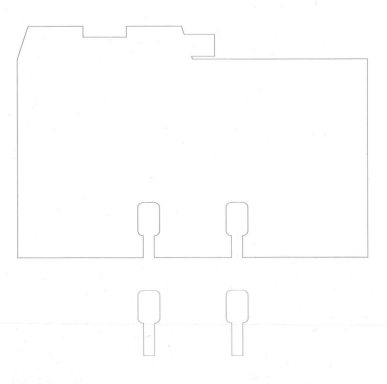

*Figure PR15.5.
The outside
and inside
panels for the
brochure.*

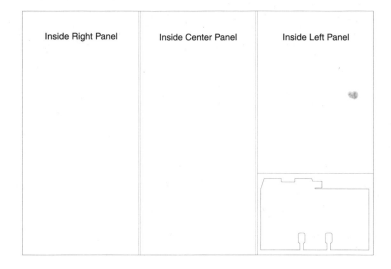

Figure PR15.6.
The final brochure.

# Labels

CorelDRAW provides access to more than 800 different label formats. Many of these are the standard label formats from Great Britain, the United States, and Germany. They include Ace Laser, Avery, Briefumshlag, HERMA, LEITZ, MACO, Nebs, and Tenza, just to name a few.

You can create these labels quickly by picking out a format from the Page Setup dialog box. To view the labels, select Page Setup from the Layout pull-down menu. In the Page Size section, select Labels from the pull-down menu.

The preview window changes to display the currently selected label format. Below the preview window is the list of available label samples. (See Figure PR16.1.)

*Figure PR16.1.*
*The current label style*
*selected from the Page*
*Setup dialog box.*

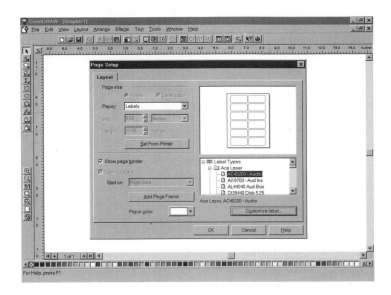

## Custom Labels

If you can't find a label that fits your needs, you can create a custom label by altering existing label styles or creating a brand-new setup. Select Labels in the Page Setup dialog box. Click the Customize Label button below the list of standard labels. This brings up the Customize Label dialog box. (See Figure PR16.2.)

*Figure PR16.2.*
*The Customize Label*
*dialog box.*

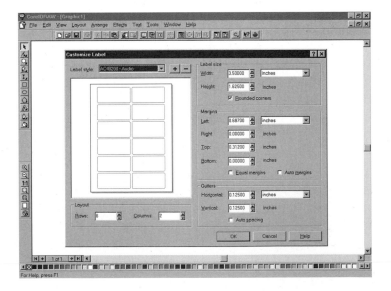

In the Customize Label dialog box, you can choose from such options as Size, Margins, Rows, Columns, and Gutters. You can choose to save your custom labels if you use them often, or adjust an existing label format that doesn't adequately fit your specific settings. Choose the label style closest to the one you want from the label list in the Page Setup dialog box, and then click the Customize label button. In the Customize Label dialog box, establish the layout and size for the label.

## Saving Custom Labels

To save a custom label, select the Layout pull-down menu and then the Page Setup command. In the Page Setup dialog box, choose the Labels option from the Paper list section and press the Customize label button. In the Customize Label dialog box, set the label size and layout. Next choose the Add button to invoke the Save Settings dialog box. Type in the name for the custom label and press OK. A directory called User Defined is added to the label list and your custom label is placed there.

## Deleting Labels

To eliminate custom or standard label styles, select Layout and then Page Setup. Pick the Labels option from the Paper list section. Press the Customize label button. Choose the label you want to remove from the Label Style section. Choose the subtract button. Before removing the label, Corel will ask you if you are sure you want to delete it.

## Multiple Labels

Each label you create is placed on a separate page so that you can print several different labels on a single sheet of letter size (8.5 inches × 11 inches) paper. Each label appears on your screen as a one page document. Most label formats have more than one label per letter size page. Each label takes up a full page by itself, but the size of the "full page" is exactly the same as the size of the label. To create a complete page of identical labels, cut and paste your first image to a series of new pages. For something like identical return address labels, use cut and paste to assemble an entire sheet of labels.

For instance, if the label style you select has two labels across and six labels down, one 8 $^1/_2$-by-11-inch sheet will contain a total of 12 labels. This means your Corel drawing should have 12 pages to create one sheet of this size label.

If your list contains 36 different labels and you are using this label format, you will have a 36-page document. Because the setup has 12 labels per letter-size sheet, you would actually be printing only three pages. This custom label setup has three across and seven labels down. It is placed in the User Defined directory. (See Figure PR16.3.)

*Figure PR16.3.*
*Custom labels are*
*automatically placed in*
*the User Defined folder.*

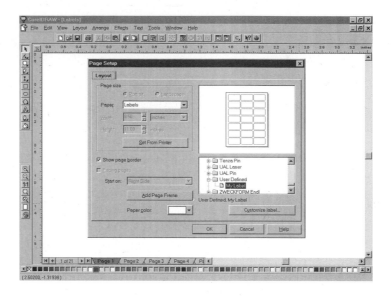

The page setup in your document shows the custom label size. The label information, such as name, address, and so on, is typed in on the page. The status line tells you this is a 21-page document. The return address shown was copied and pasted into the other 20 pages that make up the document for this sheet of labels. (See Figure PR16.4.)

*Figure PR16.4.*
*The label and on-screen*
*page layout.*

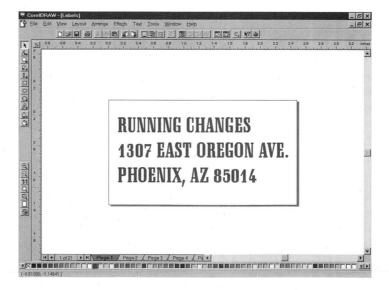

To see what your full sheet of labels looks like, bring up the Print dialog box and click the Options button. The Print Options dialog box displays the full sheet of labels. (See Figure PR16.5.)

*Figure PR16.5.*
*The sheet of labels as it*
*appears in the Print*
*Options dialog box.*

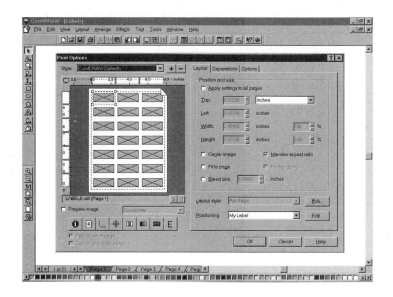

# 17

# Envelope Mailer

This project uses a design consisting of a custom, die-cut mailer/envelope combination. A mail-in order house might send an envelope/mailer combination to their customers. This makes sending in a payment or ordering a product easier for the customer.

## Basic Panels

The next series of steps will take you through the creation of the basic panel sections for the envelope mailer.

1. Create two panels that are 7 inches wide and $4\frac{1}{8}$ inches tall. Stack and center them, one above the other.

2. Create a third panel $7\frac{1}{4}$ inches wide and $4\frac{1}{8}$ inches tall. Place it below the two panels.

3. Draw a small rectangle that is 3 inches wide and $1\frac{1}{4}$ inches tall. Give rounded corners. Place it approximately $\frac{1}{2}$ inch down from the top, and 1 inch in from the right of the third panel. (See Figure PR17.1.)

*Figure PR17.1.*
*The basic panel sections*
*for the envelope mailer.*

## Left and Right Panels

The mailer requires flaps that have an adhesive section. The adhesive is activated when moistened. The next series of steps will take you through the creation of the left and right panels for the envelope mailer.

1. Draw a rectangle that is 1 inch wide and 4 $^1/_8$ inches tall.

2. Select the rectangle and choose the Add Perspective command. Raise the lower-left handle by 1 inch.

3. Make a duplicate and convert it to curves. With the Shape tool, select the duplicate and delete the three nodes on the right side and the center node on the left side.

4. Select all the nodes. In the Node Edit roll-up, press the To Line icon.

5. Fill the small polygon with 10 percent black and give it no outline attribute.

6. Select both polygons, then duplicate and flip them horizontally to create the right side flap. (See Figure PR17.2.)

*Figure PR17.2.*
*Steps 1–6: Creating the*
*left- and right-side flaps.*

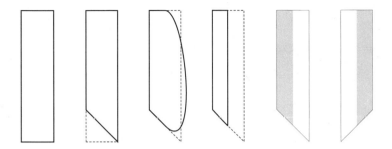

*Figure PR17.2.*
*Steps 1–6: Creating the*
*left- and right-side flaps.*

## Bottom Flap and Glue Section

The next series of steps will take you through the creation of the bottom flap and glue sections for the envelope mailer. Draw a rectangle 7 $\frac{1}{4}$ inches wide by 1 inch tall. Apply the preceding technique to it in order to create the bottom flap and the glue section. Then, place all the flaps in position on the third panel. All these sections make up the inside of the mailer. (See Figure PR17.3.)

*Figure PR17.3.*
*All the flaps and panels for*
*the inside of the envelope*
*mailer.*

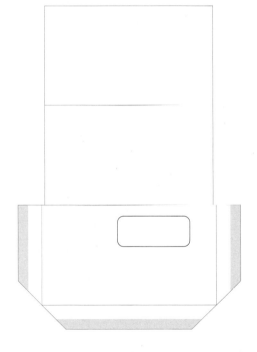

## Outside Panels

The next series of steps will take you through the creation of outside panel sections for the envelope mailer. Select all the sections and make a duplicate. Flip the duplicate horizontally and delete the sections for the glue. The sections that remain make up the outside of the mailer. (See Figure PR17.4.)

*Figure PR17.4.*
*The sections for the*
*outside of the envelope*
*mailer.*

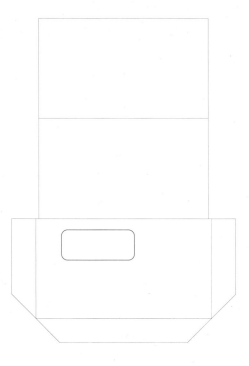

Position and place all of your required graphic elements. This includes (but is not limited to) logos, the return address, and a postage graphic. (See Figures PR17.5 and PR17.6.)

*Figure PR17.5.*
*The outside graphic*
*elements.*

Step 5

Result

*Figure PR17.6.*
*The inside graphic*
*elements.*

**Inside Self Mailer**

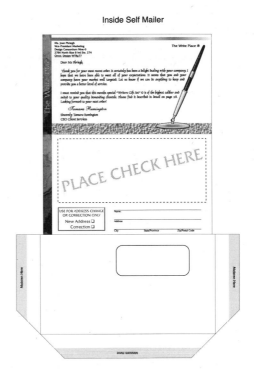

## Part XI

# Command Reference

**1**

# File Menu Commands

The File pull-down menu includes commands for opening new or existing files, and printing or exiting current CorelDRAW files. Other commands include saving, importing, exporting, and sending.

## New | Document

Select this option to create a new drawing using the default settings.

## Selection

Keyboard shortcut: Alt+F, N, D or Ctrl+N (or select the Page icon from the ribbon bar)

Pointing device: File | New | Document

## Usage

Select various commands from this menu:

1. Select New | Document from the File pull-down menu to start a new drawing file. (See Figure CR1.1.)

*Figure CR1.1.*
*The File pull-down menu.*

# New | From Template

Select this command to open an existing Corel template file from the New From Template dialog box. These templates include predesigned files such as brochures, business cards, menus, and so on. (For more information see Skill Session 58, "Styles and Templates.")

## Selection

Keyboard shortcut: Alt+F, N, F

Pointing device: File | New | From Template (or select the Open Folder icon from the ribbon bar)

## Usage

1. Select New | From Template from the File pull-down menu to open a template.

# Open

This command opens an existing document.

## Selection

Keyboard shortcut: Alt+F, O or Ctrl+O (or select the Open File Folder icon from the ribbon bar)

Pointing device: File | Open

## Usage

1. Select Open from the File pull-down menu.
2. Choose the directory and type of file you want to open.
3. Select the file, and in the Open Drawing dialog box press the Open button.

# Close

This command closes the current file.

## Selection

Keyboard shortcut: Alt+F, C

Pointing device: File | Close

## Usage

1. Select Close from the File pull-down menu.
2. The file automatically closes.

# Save

Select this option to save the current drawing to the hard drive or a drive of your choice.

## Selection

Keyboard shortcut: Alt+F, S or Ctrl+S

Pointing device: File | Save

## Usage

1. Open a new CorelDRAW file.
2. Create elements that make up the file.
3. Select Save from the File pull-down menu to save current placement and settings.
4. In the Save Drawing dialog box, name the file and choose a directory.
5. Under the Thumbnail section, select from five choices in the list. If you can't remember what the file consists of by just seeing the name, the Thumbnail provides a visual preview of the file before you open it.
6. Click the Save button.

# Corel *NOTE!*

You can save CorelDRAW 6 files as CorelDRAW 5.0 files.

# Save As

To save an existing file under a new name, choose Save As from the File pull-down menu.

## Selection

Keyboard shortcut: Alt+F, A

Pointing device: File | Save As

## Usage

1. Open an existing file.
2. To create a new version of the same file for editing, select Save As from the File pull-down menu.
3. In the Save Drawing dialog box, give the file a new name and/or directory. Use this command to make minor or major changes to the new file while still retaining the original file intact.
4. Click the Save button.

# Corel *NOTE!*

> Selecting Save As from the File pull-down menu also brings up the Save Drawing dialog box.

# Save All

This command saves all open documents.

## Selection

Keyboard shortcut: Alt+F, L

Pointing device: File | Save All

## Usage

1. Select Save All from the File pull-down menu.
2. All open files are automatically saved.

# Import

Select this option from the File pull-down menu for a selection of files to import. Corel can import over 70 kinds of file formats, including .DXF, .MET, .BMP, .CDR, .WPG, and .TIF.

## Selection

Keyboard shortcut: Alt+F, I or Ctrl+I

Pointing device: File | Import (or select the Import icon from the ribbon bar)

## Usage

1. Select Import from the File pull-down menu.
2. In the Import dialog box, select the type of file you wish to import from the Files of Type pull-down menu.
3. Change directories if necessary and locate the file you wish to import.
4. Click the Import button.

There are many file import filters. These include graphic, text, animation, and so on. (For more information about import filters, see Skill Session 48, "Import Filters.")

# Export

Select this option from the File pull-down menu for a selection of files to export. CorelDRAW can export over 30 kinds of file formats, including .PCX, .EPS, .TTF, and .GEM.

## Selection

Keyboard shortcut: Alt+F, E or Ctrl+H (or select the Export icon from the ribbon bar)

Pointing device: File | Export

## Usage

1. Select Export from the File pull-down menu.
2. In the Export dialog box, select how you want your file or selected object to be exported from the Save As Type pull-down menu.
3. Select a new directory if necessary.
4. Click the Export button.

Different file export filters have various options from which to select. These include color, black and white, grayscale, and so on. (For more information about export filters, see Skill Session 49, "Export Filters.")

## Send

Select this command to transmit your document via fax or e-mail.

## Corel*NOTE!*

This command is available only if you previously installed MS Exchange Module with Windows 95.

### Selection

Keyboard shortcut: Alt+F, D

Pointing device: File | Send

### Usage

1. Select Send from the File pull-down menu.
2. Select format in the Choose Profile dialog box.
3. Press the OK button.

## Print

Select Print to call up the Print dialog box. You can print the present document as well as select which printer to use. Different printers have their own dialog boxes and options for printing your file. (See Skill Session 50, "Printing," for more information.)

### Selection

Keyboard shortcut: Alt+F, P or Ctrl+P

Pointing device: File | Print (or select the Printer icon from the ribbon bar)

### Usage

1. Select Print from the File pull-down menu.
2. In the Print dialog box, select from various options.
3. Once you have selected your options, press the OK button.

# Print Merge

Select the Print Merge command to bring up the Print Merge dialog box. This merges your drawing with a text file and sends it to print.

## Selection

Keyboard shortcut: Alt+F, M

Pointing device: File | Print Merge

## Usage

1. Select Print Merge from the File pull-down menu.
2. In the Print Merge dialog box, select your text file.
3. Press the Merge button.
4. The merged text file and your drawing are sent to the printer.

# Recent File

The Recent File command is available when you first use Corel. After creating a file and closing it, the Recent File command is replaced with the names of the last file you closed. This command keeps track of the last four files you have closed. Select this option to open one those last four files, and then type the number next to the file you want to open, or click its filename.

## Selection

Keyboard shortcut: None

Pointing device: File | Recent File

## Usage

1. Select Recent File from the File pull-down menu.
2. Choose the file from the list.

# 1, 2, 3, or 4

Selecting 1, 2, 3, or 4 opens up previous CorelDRAW documents in the order that you last worked on them. This function lists only four previous files at a time.

## Selection

Keyboard shortcut: Alt+F and then 1, 2, 3, or 4

Pointing device: File | 1, 2, 3, or 4

## Usage

1. In the File pull-down menu, select from any of up to four previously opened documents.
2. Press the number next to the document you want to open.
3. The selected document opens.

This opens previous CorelDRAW files and bypasses the Open command in the File pull-down menu. This only works if any files have been previously opened.

# Exit

This command shuts down your current file and application.

## Selection

Keyboard shortcut: Alt+F, X or Alt+F4

Pointing device: File | Exit

## Usage

Select Exit from the File pull-down menu to exit the current CorelDRAW session.

# 2

# Edit Menu Commands

The Edit menu (see Figure CR2.1) provides selections for undoing, redoing, or repeating the last change you made. You can also cut, copy, paste, delete, duplicate, and clone. The commands Copy Properties From, Select All, Object, and certain others are found in this menu.

Use the Edit | Undo command to cancel your last change. Use the Edit | Redo command to reproduce your last change. The Repeat command reiterates the last command or action (rotating an ellipse) on the selected object.

## Undo

Select this option to undo the last change you made. (See Figure CR2.1.) You can have up to 99 levels of Undo, but setting the levels of Undo to 99 will cause Corel to use more memory. (For more information about Undo, see Skill Session 4, "Customizing and Setting Preferences.")

*Figure CR2.1.*
*The Edit menu.*

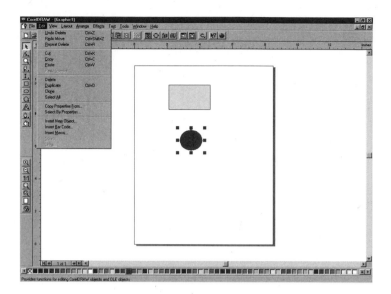

# Corel*NOTE!*

The Undo command does not affect the following operations: change of view (Zoom In, Zoom Out, and so on), file operations (Open, Save, Import), or any selection operation (marquee-select, node select). Edit | Undo works only during the current session. Undo works with all object manipulations such as skew, fill, rotate, as well as others.

## Selection

Keyboard shortcut: Alt+E, U or Ctrl+Z or Alt+Backspace

Pointing device: Edit | Undo

## Usage

1. Select Undo from the Edit pull-down menu. The object returns to its previous form.
2. Undo can be repeated up to 99 times. Levels are set in Options in the Tools menu.

## Redo

The Redo command lets you redo the last changes you have made to your drawing, up to 99 levels. The Redo command changes according to the last effect applied (Redo Delete, Redo Fill, and so on). This command is accessible after selection of the Undo command.

## Selection

Keyboard shortcut: Alt+E, E

Pointing device: Edit | Redo

## Usage

1. Select Redo from the Edit pull-down menu.
2. The objects transform back to their previous attributes.

# Repeat

Select Repeat to reproduce the last modification you have made to your document. This is useful when you want to duplicate a command or action, such as moving an object.

## Selection

Keyboard shortcut: Alt+E, R or Ctrl+R

Pointing device: Edit | Repeat

## Usage

1. Manipulate objects using Clone, Move, and so on.
2. Select the objects to which you want to repeat the attributes.
3. Choose Repeat from the Edit pull-down menu.
4. The selected objects now mirror the most recent command or action.

# Cut

This command allows you to delete an object from your document and place it in the Clipboard. The *Clipboard* is a temporary area used to transfer information between Windows applications.

## Selection

Pointing device: Edit | Cut

Keyboard shortcut: Alt+E, T or Ctrl+X (or select the Cut icon from the ribbon bar)

## Usage

1. Select the objects you want to cut from your document.
2. Select Cut from the Edit pull-down menu.
3. The CorelDRAW is Cutting prompt appears on-screen.
4. The cut object is now placed in the Clipboard.

# Copy

The Copy command differs from the Cut command. It allows you to temporarily copy objects to the Clipboard without removing them from your document.

## Selection

Keyboard shortcut: Alt+E, C or Ctrl+C (or select the Copy icon from the ribbon bar)

Pointing device: Edit | Copy

## Usage

1. Select the objects you want to copy from your document.
2. Select Copy from the Edit pull-down menu.
3. The CorelDRAW is Copying prompt appears on-screen.
4. A copy of the object is now placed in the Windows Clipboard. The original object is left in your file.

# Paste

This command sends the last objects you have cut or copied from the Clipboard back into your drawing.

## Selection

Keyboard shortcut: Alt+E, P or Ctrl+V (or select the Paste icon from the ribbon bar)

Pointing device: Edit | Paste

## Usage

1. Cut or copy the objects you want to paste.
2. Select Paste from the Edit pull-down menu to insert the objects from the Clipboard into your file.

# Corel*NOTE!*

> When you paste, copy, or cut objects, they will position themselves where the original objects were.

# Paste Special

This command lets you paste OLE objects into your document from other applications.

## Selection

Keyboard shortcut: Alt+E, S

Pointing device: Edit | Paste Special

## Usage

1. After you've copied or cut objects from another application, select Paste Special from the Edit pull-down menu.

   This allows you to paste such information as charts or text documents into your Corel file.

2. The Paste Special dialog box appears. Select how you want the information to be pasted in. Next, click the OK button.

# Corel*NOTE!*

> First, open a file in another application (such as Corel Photo-Paint). Next, cut or copy an object and then minimize the application. Return to CorelDRAW, and you can now activate Paste Special. The Paste Special option inserts the copied or cut object from the Clipboard into your CorelDRAW document. It also establishes a link to the original source file.

# Delete

Edit | Delete allows you to eliminate selected objects from your document. When you delete, you can use Undo to bring back what you have deleted.

## Selection

Keyboard shortcut: Alt+E, L or Delete

Pointing device: Edit | Delete

## Usage

1. Select the objects that you want to delete.
2. Select Delete from the Edit pull-down menu.

## Duplicate

The Duplicate command allows you to select an object (or objects) and replicate it directly on-screen.

# Corel*NOTE!*

> The Duplicate command does not erase the contents of the Windows Clipboard.

## Selection

Keyboard shortcut: Alt+E, D or Ctrl+D

Pointing device: Edit | Duplicate

## Usage

1. Select the objects you wish to duplicate.
2. Select Duplicate from the Edit pull-down menu.
3. The duplicate object will be positioned according to the settings in Preferences.

## Clone

This command creates a twin from the selected object. The original object becomes the *master object*. Most attributes you give the master object will be applied to its clones automatically. (For more information, see Skill Session 27, "Cloning," and Skill Session 36, "Copying and Cloning Effects.")

## Selection

Keyboard shortcut: Alt+E, N

Pointing device: Edit | Clone

## Usage

1. Select the objects you want to clone.
2. Select Clone from the Edit pull-down menu.
3. The master object's clone appears automatically.

## Select All

Choose this option to select everything in your document, including objects you cannot see, objects not in your drawing page, and objects that are on top of each other.

## Corel*NOTE!*

> If you can see an object but can't select it, check the layer that it's on. The Locked option might be enabled. (For more information, see Skill Session 21, "Layers.")

## Selection

Keyboard shortcut: Alt+E, A

Pointing device: Edit | Select All

## Usage

1. Create or place various objects in your document.
2. Choose Select All from the Edit pull-down menu. All objects in your document are now selected.

## Copy Properties From

Use this command to copy characteristics such as PowerLines, fills, outlines, pen colors, and text attributes to other objects.

## Selection

Keyboard shortcut: Alt+E, F

Pointing device: Edit | Copy Properties From

## Usage

1. Select the objects you want to change.
2. Select Copy Properties From in the Edit pull-down menu.
3. The Copy Attributes dialog box will appear.
4. Select the desired options and then click the OK button.
5. Use the large black arrow to select the object from which you wish to copy attributes.
6. Your objects will now reflect the options chosen in the Copy Attributes dialog box.

# Select By Properties

Choose this option to bring up the Select By Properties roll-up. Use it to locate an object through its attributes. (For more information about the Select By Properties roll-up, see Skill Session 5, "Roll-Ups.")

## Selection

Keyboard shortcut: Alt+E, I

Pointing device: Edit | Select By Properties

## Usage

1. Choose Select By Properties.
2. The Find By Properties roll-up appears.
3. Choose which properties to use.
4. Press the Select button.

# Insert New Object

Select this function to insert objects from other applications. The Insert Object dialog box displays a list of object types from which you can select the object to insert into your document.

## Selection

Keyboard shortcut: Alt+E, W

Pointing device: Edit | Insert New Object

## Usage

1. Select Insert New Object from the Edit pull-down menu.
2. In the Insert Object dialog box, choose the object type from the list. This inserts the selected object type into your Corel drawing.
3. Click the OK button.

# Insert Bar Code

Pick this function to invoke the Insert New Object dialog box, then choose Bar Code from the Object Type list and press the OK button. The Corel Bar Code Wizard appears, which allows you to create a bar code. (For more information, see Skill Session 63, "Bar Codes.")

## Selection

Keyboard shortcut: Alt+E, B

Pointing device: Edit | Insert Bar Code

## Usage

1. Select Insert Bar Code from the Edit pull-down menu.
2. The Insert Object dialog box opens, choose Bar Code from the Object Type list.
3. Click the OK button.

# Insert Memo

Select this function to run the CorelMEMO program, which allows you to create and insert a memo. (For more information on CorelMEMO, see Skill Session 64, "CorelMEMO.")

## Selection

Keyboard shortcut: Alt+E, M

Pointing device: Edit | Insert Memo

## Usage

1. Select Insert Memo from the Edit pull-down menu.
2. Create your memo in the CorelMEMO application.
3. Click File | Exit to insert the memo into your file.

# Object

The Object command allows you to revise, open, or rebuild OLE objects. The status line indicates what type of object it is.

## Selection

Keyboard shortcut: Alt+E, O

Pointing device: Edit | Object

## Usage

1. Select OLE Object.
2. Choose Object from the Edit pull-down menu; the Edit, Open, Convert flyout is enabled.
3. Select Option from flyout and apply.

# Links

Use this command to open, view, remove, or update linked objects. (For more information about editing links, see Skill Session 73, "OLE.")

## Selection

Keyboard shortcut: Alt+E, K

Pointing device: Edit | Links

## Usage

1. Select the OLE object.
2. Choose Links from the Edit pull-down menu.
3. The Links dialog box will appear, displaying all links in the current file.

## Selection

Keyboard shortcut: Alt+E, M

Pointing device: Edit | Select Across Frames

**3**

# View Menu Commands

The View pull-down menu consists of commands for activating tools that are displayed on-screen. These tools include rulers, the status bar, color palettes, and toolbars. Options in this menu allow you to control the view of objects in various modes, including wireframe, full-screen preview, and preview selected only. (See Figure CR3.1.)

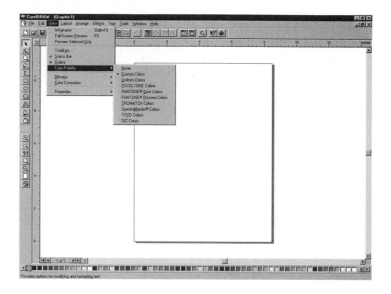

*Figure CR3.1.*
*The View pull-down menu*
*with Color Palette flyout*
*menu.*

# Wireframe

The Wireframe command allows you to turn attributes of the objects in your drawing on or off while displayed.

## Selection

Keyboard shortcut: Alt+V, E or Shift+F9

Pointing device: View | Wireframe

## Usage

1. Select Wireframe from the View pull-down menu. This toggles you between preview mode and wireframe mode.

# Full-Screen Preview

Use the Full-Screen Preview command to view your drawing without the toolbox, status lines, and palettes displayed.

## Selection

Keyboard shortcut: Alt+V, P or F9

Pointing device: View | Full-Screen Preview

## Usage

Select Full-Screen Preview from the View pull-down menu. A color preview of the current file appears on-screen. All attributes including fills, bitmaps, patterns, and so on are displayed.

# Preview Selected Only

If you want to see only specific objects in your drawing, select them and then enable the Preview Selected Only option from the View pull-down menu. Only the selected objects are displayed in your full-screen preview.

## Selection

Keyboard shortcut: Alt+V, O

Pointing device: View | Preview Selected Only

## Usage

1. Select the objects to be previewed.
2. Select Preview Selected Only from the View pull-down menu. The screen now displays selected objects exclusively.

# ToolBars

This command brings up the Toolbars dialog box. Use it to indicate which toolbars are displayed, to change their display size, and to customize them.

## Selection

Keyboard shortcut: Alt+V, A

Pointing device: View | ToolBars

## Usage

1. Select ToolBars from the View pull-down menu.
2. Click the box next to the toolbar that you want to enable. A check mark appears next to the selected tool.
3. Click the OK button and the toolbar is displayed on-screen.

# Corel*NOTE!*

> You can click the toolbox with the right mouse button to display a selection of settings for the various tools.

## Status Bar

The Status Bar command toggles the status bar on or off. The status bar has been activated if a check mark appears next to Status Bar command in the menu. (For more information about Status Bar, see Skill Session 2, "Getting Started In CorelDRAW.")

# Corel*NOTE!*

> The status bar displays information such as the position of your cursor on the screen. You can resize the height of the status bar.

### Selection

Keyboard shortcut: Alt+V, S

Pointing device: View | Status Bar

### Usage

1. Select Status Bar from the View pull-down menu. The status bar appears on-screen.
2. Select Status Bar from the View pull-down menu a second time. The status bar disappears from the screen.

## Rulers

The Rulers command toggles the rulers on or off. The rulers have been activated if a check mark appears next to Rulers in the menu. (For more information about Rulers, see Skill Session 19, "Grid and Ruler Setup," and Skill Session 20, "Guidelines.")

## Selection

Keyboard shortcut: Alt+V, R

Pointing device: View | Rulers

## Usage

1. Select Rulers from the View pull-down menu. The rulers appear on-screen.
2. Select Rulers from the View pull-down menu a second time. The rulers disappear from the screen.

# Color Palette

The Color Palette command allows you to select a palette from the following list and then display the selected palette on-screen. (For more information about palettes, see Skill Session 67, "Color Models and Color Palettes.") Here is the list:

> None
> Custom Colors
> Uniform Colors
> Focoltone Colors
> Pantone Spot Colors
> Pantone Process Colors
> Trumatch Colors
> SpectraMaster Colors
> Toyo Colors
> DIC Colors

## Selection

Keyboard shortcut: Alt+V, L

Pointing device: View | Color Palette

## Usage

1. Select Color Palette from the View pull-down menu.
2. Choose a palette from the flyout menu. The enabled palette is indicated by a black dot.

# Bitmaps

The Bitmaps command brings up the High Resolution/Visible flyout menu. High Resolution increases the clarity of your bitmap and Visible determines whether you can see the bitmap in wireframe mode. (For more information, see the skill sessions in the "Bitmap Workshop" part of this book.)

## Corel*NOTE!*

Bitmaps cannot be made visible and invisible in preview mode.

### Selection

Keyboard shortcut: Alt+V, B

Pointing device: View | Bitmaps

### Usage

1. Select Bitmaps from the View pull-down menu.
2. Choose High Resolution to improve the display of your bitmap or choose Visible to view the bitmap in wireframe mode.

## Color Correction

The Color Correction command has a flyout that contains the following options: None, Fast, Accurate, Simulate Printer, and Gamut Alarm. The None option uses no color correction and allows for the fastest screen redraw. Fast allows color correction, based on your system color profile, and results in improved color display with a fast screen redraw.

The Accurate option displays colors more precisely. Simulate Printer is based on the selected printer's color profile. These options slow down screen refresh of bitmaps. Gamut Alarm reveals colors that are not accessible in the printer's range. Colors that are "out of gamut" are shown as a uniform color. The default setting for them is black.

### Selection

Keyboard shortcut: Alt+V, C

Pointing device: View | Color Correction

# Layou
# Com

The Layout pull-down me
multiple page documents
Page, Delete Page, Go To
Manager, Styles Manager
lines Setup, and the "Snap
from this menu. (See Figu

## Usage

1. Select Color Correction from the View pull-down menu.
2. Choose from the five options in the flyout menu.
3. A black dot will appear next to your selection.

## Properties

The Properties command allows you to view the property sheets and edit the attributes of your objects, tools, and styles through the flyout menu.

### Selection

Keyboard shortcut: Alt+V, I

Pointing device: View | Properties

## Usage

1. Select Properties from the View pull-down menu.
2. Choose Object, Tool, or Styles from the flyout menu.
3. Alter the properties in the Object, Tool, or Styles dialog box.
4. Press the Apply or OK button.

Figure CR4.1.
The Layout pull-down
menu.

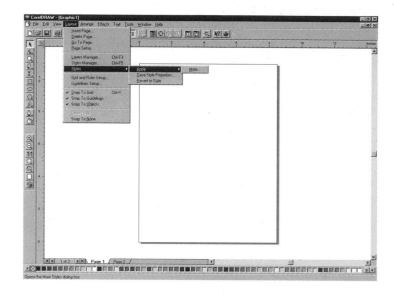

## Insert Page

This command invokes the Insert Page dialog box. You can have up to 999 pages in your Corel drawing. The pages can be inserted before or after the page number specified in the Insert Page dialog box.

## Corel*NOTE!*

When you have more than a one-page document, use the arrows at the lower left of the screen (next to the horizontal scroll bar) for selecting a page.

## Selection

Keyboard shortcut: Alt+L, I

Pointing device: Layout | Insert Page

## Usage

1. Select Insert Page from the Layout pull-down menu.
2. In the Insert Page dialog box, type in a new value or use the arrows to increase or decrease the number of pages to insert.

# Delete Page

The Delete Page option brings up the Delete Page dialog box, where you can delete one or several pages from a multipage document.

## Selection

Keyboard shortcut: Alt+L, D

Pointing device: Layout | Delete Page

## Usage

1. Select Delete Page from the Layout pull-down menu.
2. In the Delete Page dialog box, delete the selected page or type a new page number to delete.
3. Press the OK button.

# Go To Page

The Go To Page command allows you to move from one page to another in a multiple page document.

# Corel *NOTE!*

> At the lower-left area of the screen, next to the horizontal scroll bar, there is a status bar that indicates the current page (for example, "page 2 of 3"). You can click this section to invoke the Go To Page dialog box.

## Selection

Keyboard shortcut: Alt+L, G

Pointing device: Layout | Go To Page

## Usage

1. From the Layout pull-down menu, select Go To Page to bring up the dialog box.
2. Type the page number that you want to go to.
3. Press the OK button.

# Page Setup

Select this command to bring up the Page Setup dialog box. Page setups include page orientation such as landscape or portrait, layout, size, color, and more.

## Selection

Keyboard shortcut: Alt+L, P

Pointing device: Layout | Page Setup

## Usage

1. Select Page Setup to bring up the dialog box.
2. Choose from the available default settings or use your own custom settings.
3. Press the OK button.

## Corel*NOTE!*

> To bring up the Page Settings dialog box, you can also double-click the page border of the printable area of the screen.

# Layers Manager

Selecting this command brings up the Layers roll-up. You can add additional layers as well as rename them and change the attributes of individual layers. For more information about the Layers Manager, see Skill Session 21, "Layers" and Skill Session 5, "Roll-Ups."

## Selection

Keyboard shortcut: Alt+L, L or Ctrl+F3

Pointing device: Layout | Layers Manager

## Usage

1. Select Layers Manager from the Layout pull-down menu.
2. In the Layers roll-up, you can change the settings of each layer as well as the order in which they appear.

# Styles Manager

Selecting this command invokes the Styles Manager. You can save and apply styles to text and graphics. For more information about the Styles roll-up, see Skill Session 58, "Styles and Templates" and Skill Session 5, "Roll-Ups".

## Selection

Keyboard shortcut: Alt+L, Y or Ctrl+F5

Pointing device: Layout | Styles Manager

## Usage

1. Select Styles Manager from the Layout pull-down menu.
2. Select the styles you wish to apply to paragraphs or text, such as bullets or indents. Or you can create your own style by changing attributes such as boldfaced or italicized text.
3. Press Apply Style from the roll-up submenu.

# Styles

In the Styles flyout menu, you may choose from the following selections: Apply, Save Style Properties, and Revert to Style. Selecting Apply | More brings up the Apply Style dialog box, where you can select a style from the list to apply to your object. Choosing Save Style Properties brings up the Save Style As dialog box, where you can select attributes for the style and then give it a name. The Revert to Style option clears the current style from the selected object.

## Selection

Keyboard shortcut: None

Pointing device: Layout | Styles

## Usage

1. Select Styles from the Layout pull-down menu.
2. Select from the options in the flyout menu.

# Grid and Ruler Setup

This command brings up the Grid & Ruler Setup dialog box, where you can change the settings for the following sections: Drawing Scale, Grid Frequency, and Grid Origin. For more information on Grid Setup, see Skill Session 19, "Grid and Ruler Setup."

# Corel *NOTE!*

Double-clicking the rulers invokes the Grid & Ruler Setup dialog box.

## Selection

Keyboard shortcut: Alt+L, R

Pointing device: Layout | Grid Setup

## Usage

1. Select Grid Setup from the Layout pull-down menu.
2. In the dialog box, change the settings to accommodate your requirements.
3. Press the OK button.

# Guidelines Setup

This command opens up the Guidelines Setup dialog box. In this dialog box, you can change the settings of your guidelines and their position. You can have objects snap to the guideline. For more information on the Guidelines Setup dialog box, see Skill Session 20, "Guidelines."

# Corel *NOTE!*

To create guidelines, click once on the rulers with the left button on your pointing device. Then drag the pointing device toward the drawing window. A guideline is created where the pointing device button is released. Double-clicking the guidelines invokes the Guidelines Setup dialog box.

## Selection

Keyboard shortcut: Alt+L, U

Pointing device: Layout | Guidelines Setup

## Usage

1. Select Guidelines Setup from the Layout pull-down menu.

2. In the Guidelines Setup dialog box, you can change the existing guides to accommodate your current drawing requirements.

3. Choose from various options that allow you to place the guides horizontally, vertically, and diagonally. You can also delete, move, and add new guides.

# Snap To Grid

Use Snap To Grid if you want the objects on your screen to adhere to the grid while you are placing them in your drawing.

## Selection

Keyboard shortcut: Alt+L, S or Ctrl+Y

Pointing device: Layout | Snap To Grid

## Usage

1. Select Snap To Grid from the Layout pull-down menu.

2. Turn the grid on or off. A check mark indicates that it is enabled.

# Snap To Guidelines

Enable this option to snap your on-screen objects to the guidelines. You can set guidelines by clicking the rulers with the left mouse button and pulling them onto the screen.

## Selection

Keyboard shortcut: Alt+L, E

Pointing device: Layout | Snap To Guidelines

## Usage

1. Turn your guidelines on by selecting Snap To Guidelines from the Layout pull-down menu.

2. Set your guidelines by pulling them off the rulers onto your screen.

# Snap To Objects

If you want an object on your screen to stick to other objects, select Snap To Object from the Layout pull-down menu.

### Selection

Keyboard shortcut: Alt+L, O

Pointing device: Layout | Snap To Objects

### Usage

1. Select Snap To Objects from the Layout pull-down menu.
2. An object will snap to the nodes of another object when this option enabled.

## Snap To All

Select Snap To All when you want to enable all of the snap options: Snap To Grid, Snap To Guidelines, and Snap To Objects.

### Selection

Keyboard shortcut: Alt+L, A

Pointing device: Layout | Snap To All

### Usage

1. Select Snap To All from the Layout pull-down menu.
2. Your object will now snap to other objects, grids, and guidelines in your drawing.

## Snap To None

Select Snap To None when you want to disable all of the snap options: Snap To Grid, Snap To Guidelines, and Snap To Objects.

### Selection

Keyboard shortcut: Alt+L, N

Pointing device: Layout | Snap To None

### Usage

1. Select Snap To None from the Layout pull-down menu.
2. All snap to options are now turned off.

**5**

# Arrange Menu Commands

The Arrange pull-down menu provides roll-ups for transforming, and aligning and distributing the objects in your drawing. Commands for arranging the objects include Order, Group, and Ungroup. The Combine, Break Apart, Weld, Intersection, and Trim options are also in this menu. Use the Separate command to detach objects that have these effects applied to them: blend, extrude, or fit to path. Convert To Curves, allows you to change Artistic text, ellipses, rectangles, and polygons into an objects called *curves*. (See Figure CR5.1.)

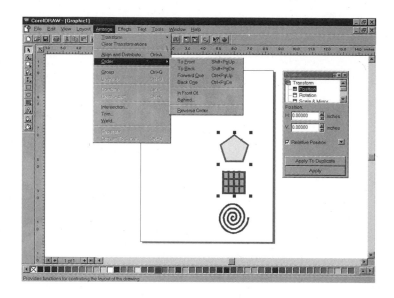

*Figure CR5.1.
The Arrange pull-down
menu with the Order
flyout and Transform roll-
up displayed.*

## Transform

Select this option to invoke the Transform roll-up. Use the flyout menu to select the mode of the roll-up. These modes include position, rotate, scale and mirror, size and skew. For more information, see Skill Session 26, "Transform."

## Corel*NOTE!*

> Apply skew to an object to give it a slant. This allows you to make text appear italic even if you don't have the italic version. Regardless, true italic text is always preferable. See "True Italic Versus Skewing," in Skill Session 44, "Basic Typography."

## Selection

Keyboard shortcut: Alt+A, T

Pointing device: Arrange | Transform (or select the transform roll-up icon from ribbon bar)

## Usage

1. Select Transform.
2. Select one of the various modes in the flyout (for example, position).
3. The Transform roll-up group appears in position mode.

# Clear Transformations

Select an object and choose Clear Transformations. This clears any alterations, such as skewing or resizing, that you have applied to the object.

## Selection

Keyboard shortcut: Alt+A, L

Pointing device: Arrange | Clear Transformations

## Usage

1. Select an object and then select Clear Transformations.
2. Your object is restored to its original configuration.

# Align and Distribute

Use this option to center an object to your page, or select more than one object and align them to each other. Use Distribute to spread objects out evenly across a page, or in relation to each other. (For more information about aligning and distributing objects, see Skill Session 17, "Aligning and Distributing.")

## Selection

Keyboard shortcut: Alt+A, A or Ctrl+A

Pointing device: Arrange | Align (or select the align and distribute icon from ribbon bar)

## Usage

1. Select the objects to be moved.
2. Select Align and Distribute from the Arrange pull-down menu, and the roll-up appears.
3. Press the Apply button.

# Corel*NOTE!*

> The last object you select is what the other objects will align to.

# Order

If you select Order, a flyout menu appears. The selections include To Front, To Back, Forward One, Back One, In Front Of, Behind, and Reverse Order. This allows you to change the position of one or more objects. When you draw an object, it is placed in front of the last object drawn. This is a default setting. (For more information, see Skill Session 18, "Object Ordering.")

## Corel*NOTE!*

The Reverse Order option functions only with two or more objects selected.

## Selection

Keyboard shortcut: Alt+A, O

Pointing device: Arrange | Order

## Usage

1. Select objects that you want to switch the order of.
2. Select Order from the Arrange pull-down menu.
3. From the flyout menu, select the option you want.

To change the position of the stacking order of the objects in your drawing, in relation to each other, select from the following commands in the Order flyout menu.

# Order | To Front

Use this command to move one or more objects to the front of all objects in your document. (For more information, see Skill Session 18.)

## Selection

Keyboard shortcut: Alt+A, O, F or Shift+PgUp

Pointing device: Arrange | Order | To Front

## Usage

1. Select the objects you want to summon to the front.
2. Select Order from the Arrange pull-down menu.
3. From the flyout menu, select To Front. The selected objects will now be transferred to the front.

# Order | To Back

Use this command to move one or more objects to the back of all other objects in your document. (For more information, see Skill Session 18.)

## Selection

Keyboard shortcut: Alt+A, O, B or Shift+PgDn

Pointing device: Arrange | Order | To Back

## Usage

1. Select the objects you want to send to the back.
2. Select Order from the Arrange pull-down menu.
3. From the flyout menu, select To Back. The selected objects are moved to the back.

# Order | Forward One

Use this command to move one or more objects forward by one position in your document. (For more information, see Skill Session 18.)

## Selection

Keyboard shortcut: Alt+A, O, O or Ctrl+PgUp

Pointing device: Arrange | Order | Forward One

# Corel *NOTE!*

When you select Forward One or Back One, the selected objects will move forward or back by one position. For example, if there are three objects and the object that you have selected is the third from the front, selecting Forward One will make it second from the front.

## Usage

1. Select the objects you want to move forward one.
2. Select Order from the Arrange pull-down menu.
3. From the flyout menu, select Forward One. The selected objects will now be moved up by one position.

# Order | Back One

Use this command to move one or more objects back by one position in your document. (For more information, see Skill Session 18.)

## Selection

Keyboard shortcut: Alt+A, O, N or Ctrl+PgDn

Pointing device: Arrange | Order | Back One

## Usage

1. Select the objects you want to send back.
2. Select Order from the Arrange pull-down menu.
3. From the flyout menu, select Back One. The selected objects will be moved back by one position.

# Order | In Front Of

Use this command to move one or more objects in front of another object in your document. (For more information, see Skill Session 18.)

## Selection

Keyboard shortcut: Alt+A, O, I

Pointing device: Arrange | Order | In Front Of

## Usage

1. Select the object you want to place before another object.
2. Select Order from the Arrange pull-down menu.
3. From the flyout menu, select Before Object.
4. With the large black arrow, select the object in front of which you want to place your second object.

# Order | Behind

Use this command to move one or more objects behind another object in your document. (For more information, see Skill Session 18.)

## Selection

Keyboard shortcut: Alt+A, O, I

Pointing device: Arrange | Order | Behind

## Usage

1. Select the object you want to place in back of another object.
2. Select Order from the Arrange pull-down menu.
3. From the flyout menu, select Behind.
4. With the large black arrow, select the object behind which you want to place your second object.

# Order | Reverse Order

Use this command to reverse the order of two or more objects in your document. (For more information, see Skill Session 18.)

## Selection

Keyboard shortcut: Alt+A, O, R

Pointing device: Arrange | Order | Reverse Order

## Usage

1. Select the objects that you want to transpose the order of.
2. Select Order from the Arrange pull-down menu.
3. From the flyout menu, select Reverse Order. The selected objects will now be in reverse order.

# Group

This option allows you to group selected objects, including text. When you have created and placed objects in the order you require, select those objects and group them. This permits you to move the grouped objects as if they were a single unit. (For more information about grouping, see Skill Session 22, "Grouping and Ungrouping.")

## Selection

Keyboard shortcut: Alt+A, G or Ctrl+G

Pointing device: Arrange | Group

## Usage

1. Select the objects that you want to group.
2. Select Group from the Arrange pull-down menu.
3. The grouped objects can be moved as a single item.

# Ungroup

Select this option to unassemble objects that are grouped. (For more information about Arrange | Ungroup, see Skill Session 22.)

## Selection

Keyboard shortcut: Alt+A, U or Ctrl+U

Pointing device: Arrange | Ungroup

## Usage

1. Select a group of objects.
2. Select Ungroup from the Arrange pull-down menu. The objects are now ungrouped and can be moved independently.

# Combine

The Combine command allows you to create a single object from several objects. The combined object will take on the attributes of the last object selected. For example, create a red and blue rectangle, select the blue rectangle last, and then combine the objects. The red one will now be blue. (For more information about combining, see Skill Session 23, "Combining, Breaking Apart, and Separating Objects.")

## Corel *NOTE!*

When you combine text, it has the same effect as converting it to curves. Your text is now a curve and will not be editable. (For more information, see Skill Session 25, "Converting to Curves.")

## Selection

Keyboard shortcut: Alt+A, C or Ctrl+L

Pointing device: Arrange | Combine

## Usage

1. Select the objects you want to combine.
2. Select Combine from the Arrange pull-down menu. The status line now reflects one object, with $x$ number of nodes.

# Break Apart

Select the Break Apart option to split combined objects into separate sections. (For more information about breaking combined objects apart, see Skill Session 23.)

## Selection

Keyboard shortcut: Alt+A, B or Ctrl+K

Pointing device: Arrange | Break Apart

## Usage

1. Select the object that you want to break apart.
2. Select Break Apart from the Arrange pull-down menu. The object is now broken down into individual sections.

# Intersection

Use Intersection to produce a new shape from the overlap of several objects. (For more information, see Skill Session 24, "Weld, Intersection, and Trim.")

## Selection

Keyboard shortcut: Alt+A, I

Pointing device: Arrange | Intersection

## Usage

1. Select the overlapping objects from which you want to produce a new shape.
2. Select Intersect from the Arrange pull-down menu. Your objects will now form a new object from the overlap of the selected objects.

# Trim

Use Trim when you want to cut an object's shape into another object. (For more information about Trim, see Skill Session 24.)

## Selection

Keyboard shortcut: Alt+A, R

Pointing device: Arrange | Trim

## Usage

1. Select the object you want to trim with along with the object you want to cut.
2. Select Trim from the Arrange pull-down menu.

# Weld

This command bonds several objects to create an entirely new shape. A complex shape, such as a key, can be made rather quickly by placing elements such as ellipses together with a few rectangles. You can also create odd shapes by combining and node-editing, but welding is easier and faster. (For more information about Weld, see Skill Session 24.)

## Selection

Keyboard shortcut: Alt+A, W

Pointing device: Arrange | Weld

## Usage

1. Select the objects you want to weld.
2. Select Weld from the Arrange pull-down menu. Your objects will now be connected into one shape.

# Separate

The Separate option is used to detach objects that have such effects as blend, contour, extrude, and so on, applied to them. (For more information about separating, see Skill Session 23.)

## Selection

Keyboard shortcut: Alt+A, S

Pointing device: Arrange | Separate

## Usage

1. Select an object that has an effect applied to it, such as a blend.
2. Select Separate from the Arrange pull-down menu.
3. Your object is now separated into three independent parts.

# Corel*NOTE!*

For blends, the three parts resulting from the Separate command include the starting and ending objects that were blended. The steps between, which created the blend, will be a group of *x* number of objects, where *x* is the number of steps in the blend.

## Convert To Curves

This option converts rectangles, ellipses, polygons and Artistic text to curves. Convert text to curves when your service bureau does not have the fonts you are using. Although this does away with supplying the service bureau with the fonts, it might expand the size of your file. (For more information about converting text and other objects to curves, see Skill Session 25.)

# Corel*NOTE!*

Paragraph text cannot be converted to curves.

## Selection

Keyboard shortcut: Alt+A, V or Ctrl+Q

Pointing device: Arrange | Convert To Curves

## Usage

1. Select an object, such as Artistic text, a rectangle, or a polygon, that you want to convert to curves.
2. Select Convert To Curves from the Arrange pull-down menu.

**6**

# Effects Menu Commands

The Effects pull-down menu provides the Add Perspective command for adding perspective to an object. There are also eight commands that, when executed, bring up the Effects roll-up group. This roll-up displays in its title bar which effect mode is currently active: Envelope, Blend, Extrude, Contour, PowerLine, Lens, Bitmap Color Mask, and PowerClip. You can return objects to their original attributes by selecting Clear Effect. The Copy and Clone options copy and clone effects from one object to another. (See Figure CR6.1). For more information, see Skill Sessions 28–36 in the "Effects Workshop" section of this book as well as Skill Session 5, "Roll-Ups."

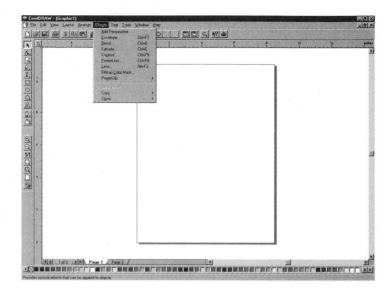

*Figure CR6.1.
The Effects pull-down
menu.*

# Add Perspective

Select an object and choose Add Perspective, and a border with four nodes appears around the object. These nodes allow you to manipulate the perspective of your object, providing the illusion of distance and depth. For more information, see Skill Session 28, "Perspective."

## Selection

Keyboard shortcut: Alt+C, A

Pointing device: Effects | Add Perspective

## Usage

1. Create an object.
2. Select Add Perspective from the Effects pull-down menu.
3. Select the × that appears on-screen and move it to change the perspective of the object.
4. Nodes appear around your object. Select and move the nodes individually to give your object a new appearance.

# Corel*NOTE!*

> If the × does not appear on-screen, the point of origin is too far. Use the Zoom tool to zoom out until the × can be seen.

## Envelope

The Envelope effect can be seen as a container, used to mold text or objects. For example, you can apply the shape of an ellipse to a text object. This causes the text to become shaped like the ellipse. For more information, see Skill Session 29, "Enveloping."

### Selection

Keyboard shortcut: Alt+C, E or Ctrl+F7

Pointing device: Effects | Envelope

### Usage

1. Select Envelope from the Effects pull-down menu.
2. In the Envelope roll-up, you can apply existing settings. You can also edit the object's envelope manually.

## Blend

Select Blend from the Effects pull-down menu to apply a series of steps that link one object to another. For more information, see Skill Session 30, "Blending."

### Selection

Keyboard shortcut: Alt+C, B or Ctrl+B

Pointing device: Effects | Blend

### Usage

1. Select the objects to blend.
2. Select Blend from the Effects pull-down menu.
3. Specify the number of steps in the roll-up.
4. Click the Apply button.

# Extrude

If an object is selected when you invoke the Extrude effect, you'll see a preview of the effect on your object. The on-screen preview uses the current settings displayed in the roll-up. For more information about the Extrude roll-up, see Skill Session 31, "Extruding," and Skill Session 5, "Roll-Ups."

## Selection

Keyboard shortcut: Alt+C, X or Ctrl+E

Pointing device: Effects | Extrude

## Usage

1. Select an object and choose Extrude from the Effects pull-down menu.
2. Change the settings in the Extrude roll-up and preview what the extruded object will look like.
3. Click the Apply button. Your object now appears to be three-dimensional.

# Contour

The Contour effect allows you to add concentric duplicates of an object to the center, the inside, or the outside of the object. You can also change the offset, number of steps, and the outline and fill attributes of the contour. For more information about the Contour roll-up, see Skill Session 32, "Contour."

## Selection

Keyboard shortcut: Alt+C, N or Ctrl+F9

Pointing device: Effects | Contour

## Usage

1. Select an object and select Contour from the Effects pull-down menu.
2. In the Contour roll-up, choose whether to apply your contour to the center, inside, or outside of your object.
3. Change the number in the Offset box.
4. Change the number in the Steps box.
5. Choose an outline color.
6. Select the Color Wheel tab in the Contour roll-up to choose a fill for the contour. The object color will blend toward the color of the contour fill.

7. Click the Apply button to see the contour applied to your object. This gives the illusion of a pyramid or stacking of objects viewed from overhead. A contour may appear to look like a blend.

# Corel*NOTE!*

> The number of steps to the contour is limited to 999.

## PowerLine

You can choose to draw with the Pencil tool in PowerLine or normal mode. Select the object to which you want to apply PowerLine effects (for example, a calligraphy effect or the effect of drawing from thick to thin lines). For more information, see Skill Session 33, "PowerLines."

# Corel*NOTE!*

> You can apply PowerLine effects to objects as well as lines.

### Selection

Keyboard shortcut: Alt+C, P, or Ctrl+F8

Pointing device: Effects | PowerLine

### Usage

1. Select an object and invoke the PowerLine.
2. Change the settings in the roll-up and select the default effect you want your object to look like.
3. Click the Apply button. Your object will reflect the form of the selected effect.

## Lens

The Lens effect consists of the following 12 lenses: Transparency, Magnify, Brighten, Invert, Color Limit, Color Add, Tinted Grayscale, Heat Map, Custom Color Map, Wireframe, Fish Eye, and None. Once you select a lens and apply it to an object, the results will appear in the lens.

You can apply a lens to single objects, closed paths, or groups of objects. When applying a lens to a group of objects, the lens will affect each object in the group. For more information about the Lens roll-up see Skill Session 34, "Lens," or Skill Session 5.

# Corel *NOTE!*

> When a lens is applied to an object filled with a non-uniform color, the lens will reflect the color in the Color box in the Lens roll-up. If you save a drawing that contains a lens affect to a version of CorelDRAW earlier than version 5, the lens effect will appear grayed out.

## Selection

Keyboard shortcut: Alt+C, L or Alt+F3

Pointing device: Effects | Lens

## Usage

1. Select an object and select Lens
2. Choose from the 12 options.
3. Type in the amount you want applied and press the Apply button.
4. Your object now has a lens reflecting whichever option you applied (Magnify, for example).

# Color Bitmap Mask

The Bitmap Color Mask effect has selections for changing and masking existing colors of a bitmap. For more information about the Color Bitmap Mask roll-up see Skill Session 46, "Cropping and Hiding Bitmaps," or Skill Session 5.

## Selection

Keyboard shortcut: Alt+C, C

Pointing device: Effects | Bitmap Color Mask

## Usage

1. Select an object and select Bitmap Color Mask.
2. Choose the eyedropper icon and select a color from the bitmap to mask.
3. Press the Apply button.

# PowerClip

Select PowerClip from the Effects pull-down menu, and a cascading menu with four options appears. These options are Place Inside Container, Extract Contents, Edit Contents, and Finish Editing This Level.

When using PowerClip, the object you paste inside another object is called the *contents*, and the object you are pasting inside of is called the *container*. Once PowerClip has been applied to these objects, they become a unit known as a PowerClip object. A PowerClip object can contain five levels of contents. For more information, see Skill Session 35, "PowerClip," and Skill Session 5.

# Corel*NOTE!*

You can resize, stretch, or rotate the container and contents objects individually, or you can resize, stretch, or rotate the entire PowerClip object. The container keeps layered and grouped images together.

## Selection

Keyboard shortcut: Alt+C, W

Pointing device: Effects | PowerClip

## Usage

1. Select an object and select PowerClip.
2. Select from the four options.
3. Your object now appears with the PowerClip applied.

# Clear Effect

The Clear Effect command clears the last effect applied to an object. For example, if the last effect applied to the object was Extrude, the Effects pull-down menu reads Clear Extrude.

## Selection

Keyboard shortcut: none

Pointing device: Effects | Clear Effect

## Usage

1. Select an object with an effect applied to it.
2. Select Clear Effect from the Effects pull-down menu.
3. The object's last applied effect is removed.

# Copy

Select Copy from the Effects pull-down menu, and a cascading menu with eight choices appears. These choices are Perspective From, Envelope From, Blend From, Extrude From, Contour From, PowerLine From, Lens From, and PowerClip From. Select one of these options, and a large black arrow appears. With this arrow, choose the object from which you are copying the effect.

## Selection

Keyboard shortcut: Alt+C, Y

Pointing device: Effects | Copy

## Usage

1. Select an object and select Copy.
2. From the eight options, choose an effect to copy.
3. Select the object you are copying the effect from with the large black arrow.
4. Your object now has the effect that you copied from the other object.

# Clone

Select Clone from the Effects pull-down menu, and a cascading menu with four choices appears. These choices are Blend From, Extrude From, Contour From, and PowerLine From. Select one of these options, and a large black arrow appears. With this arrow, choose the object from which you are copying the effect.

## Selection

Keyboard shortcut: Alt+C, O

Pointing device: Effects | Clone

## Usage

1. Select an object and select Copy.
2. Now choose from the four options.
3. Select the object you are cloning the effect from with the large black arrow.
4. Your object now has the effect that you cloned from the other object.

**7**

# Text Menu Commands

The Text pull-down menu provides commands for editing text attributes. The commands include Character, Paragraph, Columns, and Text Options. You can also select Fit Text To Path, Align To Baseline, and Straighten Text. Type Assist, Spell Checker, Thesaurus, Find, Replace, Convert, and Change Case are also found on this menu. (See Figure CR7.1.) Many of these text options are also covered in the "Text Workshop" section of this book. (See Skill Sessions 37 through 44.)

## Corel *NOTE!*

Click the toolbox with the right mouse button and select Text from the pop-up list to invoke the Text toolbar.

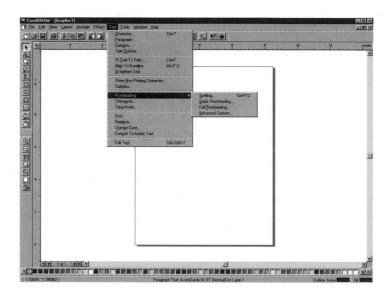

*Figure CR7.1.*
*The Text pull-down menu.*

## Character

Select this command to invoke the Character Attributes dialog box, where you change the attributes of the selected text.

## Corel*NOTE!*

> Double-clicking the nodes of selected text with the Shape tool also invokes the Character Attributes dialog box.

## Selection

Keyboard shortcut: Alt+X, C or Ctrl+T

Pointing device: Text | Character

## Usage

1. Select the text.
2. Select Character from the Text pull-down menu.
3. The Character Attributes dialog box appears on-screen.
4. Change the attributes such as the font, size, and measuring system as well as the style and the placement of your text.

5. Press the OK button.

Added features include Underline, Overline, and Strikeout. For more information, see Skill Session 37, "Changing Text Attributes."

# Corel*NOTE!*

> The Size attribute in the Character Attributes dialog box can be accessed by pressing Alt and the underlined character in the word size. (For example, to access the Size option press Alt+Z from your keyboard.)

## Paragraph

Select Paragraph from the Text pull-down menu to invoke the Paragraph dialog box. In the section called Category, there are four selections: Spacing, Tabs, Indents, and Effects. Each category has its own Paragraph dialog box. For more information, see the "Paragraph Text" section of Skill Session 14, "The Text Tool."

# Corel*NOTE!*

> Resizing Artistic text changes the point size of the text. Resizing Paragraph text changes the size of the frame, not the size of the text.

## Selection

Keyboard shortcut: Alt+X, P

Pointing device: Text | Paragraph

## Usage

1. Select Paragraph text.
2. Select Paragraph in the Text pull-down menu.
3. In the Paragraph dialog box, select the category to which you want to make changes.
4. Make the changes you want by selecting from the options.
5. Click the OK button.

## Columns

The Columns command brings up the Columns dialog box, where you can apply columns and gutters to your Paragraph text. For more information about paragraphs, see Skill Session 14.

### Selection

Keyboard shortcut: Alt+X, M

Pointing device: Text | Columns

### Usage

1. Select Paragraph text.
2. Select Columns in the Text pull-down menu.
3. In the dialog box, make the changes you want by selecting from the options.
4. Click the OK button.

## Text Options

The Text Options command from the Text pull-down menu invokes the Text Options dialog box. From this dialog box you can change how your text is displayed on-screen or alter its formatting. For more information, see Skill Sessions 37 through 44 in the Text Workshop section of this book.

### Selection

Keyboard shortcut: Alt+X, O

Pointing device: Text | Options

### Usage

1. Select text.
2. Select Text Options from the Text pull-down menu to open the Text Options dialog box.
3. Choose attributes from the Text or Formatting categories.
4. Click the OK button.

## Fit Text To Path

The Fit Text To Path command allows you to manipulate your text to conform to odd-shaped paths through the Fit Text To Path Roll-Up. For more information about Fit Text To Path, see Skill Sessions 5, "Roll-Ups," and 40, "Fitting Text to Path."

# Corel *NOTE!*

Fit Text To Path is available only for Artistic text mode.

## Selection

Keyboard shortcut: Alt+X, T or Ctrl+F

Pointing device: Text | Fit Text To Path

## Usage

1. Select Artistic text.
2. Select the object to which you are fitting the text.
3. Select Fit Text To Path from the Text pull-down menu.
4. In the Fit Text To Path roll-up, select your options and click the Apply button.

# Align To Baseline

The Align To Baseline command realigns the nodes of any text that has been altered to an imaginary baseline.

# Corel *NOTE!*

The baseline is an imaginary horizontal line. All the characters in a font rest on this line.

## Selection

Keyboard shortcut: Alt+X, L or Alt+F12

Pointing device: Text | Align To Baseline

## Usage

1. Select altered text.
2. Select Align To Baseline from the Text pull-down menu.
3. The text is aligned to its imaginary baseline.

## Straighten Text

The Straighten Text option from the Text pull-down menu removes transformations, such as rotation or skewing, previously applied to text. The text is returned to original form.

### Selection

Keyboard shortcut: Alt+X, S

Pointing device: Text | Straighten Text

### Usage

1. Select altered text.
2. Select Straighten Text from the Text pull-down menu.

## Show Non-Printing Characters

The Show Non-Printing Characters command allows you to display non-printing characters, such as page breaks, paragraph ends, and tabs, in the Edit Text dialog box. For more information, see Skill Sessions 37 through 44 in the "Text Workshop" section of this book.

### Selection

Keyboard shortcut: Alt+X, N

Pointing device: Text | Show Non-Printing Characters

### Usage

1. Select Show Non-Printing Characters from the Text pull-down menu to display these characters in the Edit Text dialog box.

## Statistics

The Statistics command displays a current description of the text in your document (for example, the number of words, lines, and characters).

### Selection

Keyboard shortcut: Alt+X, I

Pointing device: Text | Statistics

## Usage

1. Select Statistics from the Text pull-down menu.
2. The Text dialog box appears displaying a description of the selected text attributes.

# Proofreading

The Proofreading command brings up a flyout consisting of the following four selections: Spelling, Quick Proofreading, Full Proofreading, and Advanced Options. For more information, see Skill Sessions 37 through 44 in the "Text Workshop" section of this book.

## Selection

Keyboard shortcut: Alt+X, R

Pointing device: Text | Proofreading

## Usage

1. Select Proofreading from the Text pull-down menu.
2. Choose spelling or one of the proofreading options.
3. Select from the options in the dialog box.

# Thesaurus

When you want to use words with similar meanings, you can select Thesaurus from the Text pull-down menu. The Thesaurus dialog box gives you the option of checking for synonyms and definitions of words.

# Corel*NOTE!*

> To look up a word that is not in your document, select Thesaurus and the dialog box will come up; type the word you want to check in the Synonym For box and then click the Look Up button.

## Selection

Keyboard shortcut: Alt+X, U

Pointing device: Text | Thesaurus

## Usage

1. Select the text you want to check or just invoke the Thesaurus without text selected.
2. Select Thesaurus from the Text pull-down menu.
3. Select Look Up to check for synonyms.
4. Choose whether to replace the word or cancel.

# Type Assist

The Type Assist command allows you to predetermine text characteristics such as capitalization of the first letter of a sentence, capitalization of a proper name, typographic quotes, defining shortcuts, and replacing text while typing. Once a word is complete (indicated by punctuation or a space) the corrections will appear.

## Selection

Keyboard shortcut: Alt+X, E

Pointing device: Text | Type Assist

## Usage

1. Select Type Assist from the Text pull-down menu.
2. Select the options you require.
3. Type in replacement text and press the OK button.

# Find

The Find command invokes the Find dialog box, where you can perform word searches.

## Selection

Keyboard shortcut: Alt+X, F

Pointing device: Text | Find

## Usage

1. Select Find from the Text pull-down menu.
2. Type the word you want to find in the Find What box.

3. Decide whether or not you want the Match Case option enabled, and check this option if you do.

4. Click the Find Next button to find your word.

# Replace

Select the Replace command to invoke the Replace dialog box, where you can perform word substitutions.

## Selection

Keyboard shortcut: Alt+X, A

Pointing device: Text | Replace

## Usage

1. Select Replace from the Text pull-down menu.
2. In the Find What section, type the word you want to replace.
3. In the Replace With section, type the new word.
4. Click the Replace button.

# Change Case

The Change Case command brings up the Change Case dialog box where you can alter the selected text. Choose from the following options: Sentence case, lowercase, UPPERCASE, Title Case, or tOGGLE cASE.

## Selection

Keyboard shortcut: Alt+X, H

Pointing device: Text | Change Case

## Usage

1. Select text.
2. Select Change Case from the Text pull-down menu.
3. Choose a case option.
4. Press the OK button.

## Convert To Paragraph/Artistic Text

Use the Convert command to transform selected Paragraph text into Artistic text. By the same token, Artistic text can be transformed into Paragraph text.

### Selection

Keyboard shortcut: Alt+X, V

Pointing device: Text | Convert To Paragraph/Artistic Text

### Usage

1. Select text.
2. Select Convert To from the Text pull-down menu.

## Edit Text

The Edit Text command allows you to revise Artistic or Paragraph text in the Edit dialog box. Options are available for altering character and paragraph attributes through this dialog box. For more information, see Skill Session 14 and Skill Sessions 37 through 44 in the "Text Workshop" section of this book.

### Selection

Keyboard shortcut: Alt+X, X or Ctrl+Shift+T

Pointing device: Text | Edit Text

### Usage

1. Select the text you want to edit.
2. Select Edit Text from the Text pull-down menu.
3. In the dialog box, revise the text.
4. For Artistic text, choose Character. For Paragraph text, choose Character or Paragraph.
5. Change the settings in the dialog box.
4. Click the OK button.

**8**

# Tools Menu Commands

To modify CorelDRAW's defaults, select Options from the Tools pull-down menu. The Symbols and Preset roll-up are also accessed from here. The Tools pull-down menu furnishes commands for creating patterns, arrows, and symbols. You can also select several other commands. (See Figure CR8.1.)

*Figure CR8.1.*
*The Tools pull-down*
*menu.*

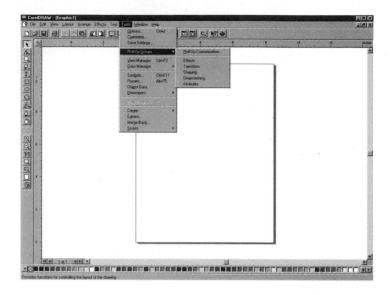

# Options

Select Options to invoke the Options dialog box. The General section is displayed. Next to the General button are the Display and Advanced buttons. Select them to display the settings for each section. For more information about changing default settings, see Skill Session 4, "Customizing and Setting Preferences."

## Selection

Keyboard shortcut: Alt+T, O or Ctrl+J

Pointing device: Tools | Options

## Usage

1. Select Options from the Tools pull-down menu.
2. Change the appropriate settings in the Options dialog box's General, Display, and Advanced sections.
3. Press the OK button.

# Customize

The Customize command brings up the Customize dialog box. There are five sections you can customize. They include Keyboard, Menu, Toolbars, Roll-Ups, and Color Palette. For more information on roll-ups, see Skill Session 5, "Roll-Ups."

## Selection

Keyboard shortcut: Alt+T, U

Pointing device: Tools | Customize

## Usage

1. Select Customize from the Tools pull-down menu.
2. Press the tab for the section you want to customize and then change the settings.
3. Press the OK button.

# Save Settings

Press this command to change the default setting. This command will use the settings of your current drawing as the default setting for any new Corel drawings you open in the future.

## Selection

Keyboard shortcut: Alt+T, I

Pointing device: Tools | Save Settings

## Usage

1. Make any changes you need to the default settings, such as placement of the status bar and so on.
2. Select Save Settings from the Tools pull-down menu.
3. A prompt box appears. Choose from the options in it to reject or accept the current settings as the default.

# Roll-Up Groups

The Roll-Up Groups command brings up a submenu that displays the Roll-Up Customization command and a list of roll-up groups.

## Selection

Keyboard shortcut: Alt+T, G

Pointing device: Tools | Roll-Up Groups

## Usage

1.  Select Roll-Up Groups from the Tools pull-down menu to see a list of the roll-up groups in use.

# Roll-Up Customization

The Roll-Up Customization command brings up the Customize dialog box, with the Roll-Ups section active.

## Selection

Keyboard shortcut: Alt+T, G, R

Pointing device: Tools | Roll-Up Groups | Roll-Up Customization

## Usage

1.  Select Roll-Up Groups | Roll-Up Customization from the Tools pull down menu to change settings for the roll-ups.

# Roll-Up Groups | Effects, Shaping, Dimensioning, Transform, and Attributes

The Roll-Up Groups command brings up a flyout menu that includes the roll-up customization: Effects, Shaping, Dimensioning, Transform, and Attributes. The Transform roll-up can also be accessed from the ribbon bar.

## Selection

Keyboard shortcut: None

Pointing device: Tools | Roll-Up Groups | Effects, Shaping, Dimensioning, Transform, or Attributes

## Usage

1.  Select Roll-Up Groups from the Tools pull-down menu to see a list of the roll-up groups.
2.  Choose a roll-up group from the list.
3.  The selected roll-up appears on-screen.

# View Manager

The View Manager command brings up the View Manager roll-up. From the View Manager roll-up, you can give names to areas of your drawing that have different zoom views, and then access them instantly by double-clicking on the name in the roll-up. This is a handy feature to have when finalizing a complex illustration. For more information about View Manager, see Skill Session 72, "Multiple Document Interface."

## Selection

Keyboard shortcut: Alt+T, V, or Ctrl+F2

Pointing device: Tools | View Manager

## Usage

1. Choose an object in your drawing and pick a view of it that accommodates you, by zooming in on it.
2. Select View Manager from the Tools pull-down menu.
3. Press the button with the Plus sign on it. This action creates a new field with the default name of "View 1."
4. Then if required, change the name of the newly created view field by double-clicking on it in the roll-up and typing in the new name.
5. To create more fields in the View Manger Roll-Up, repeat steps 1 through 4.

# Color Manager

The Color Manager command brings up a submenu with two selections. The first one is Color Wizard. Use the Color Wizard to help you readjust your scanner, monitor, and printer. This allows scans, displays, and printers to more closely match colors from device to device. The second selection is Select Color Profile. Choose this command to bring up the Corel Color Manager dialog box. For more information about Color Manager, see Skill Session 68, "Color Management."

## Color Wizard

## Selection

Keyboard shortcut: Alt+T, C, W

Pointing device: Tools | Color Manager | Color Wizard

## Usage

1. Select Color Manager | Color Wizard from the Tools pull-down menu.
2. Use the Wizard to assist you in producing a method for Color Management.

## Select Color Profile

### Selection

Keyboard shortcut: Alt+T, C, S

Pointing device: Tools | Color Manager | Select Color Profile

### Usage

1. Choose Color Manager and then Select Color Profile from the Tools pull-down menu.
2. The Corel Color Manager dialog box appears.

# Symbols

The Symbols command brings up the roll-up for over 5000 symbols, including text characters and icons. For more information about the Symbols roll-up, see Skill Sessions 5 and 62, "Creating Custom Arrowheads, Patterns, and Symbols."

# Corel *TIP!*

> The Symbols roll-up can be activated from the ribbon bar by pressing the star-shaped symbols icon.

### Selection

Keyboard shortcut: Alt+T, B or Ctrl+F11

Pointing device: Tools | Symbols

### Usage

1. Select Symbols from Tools pull-down menu.
2. Search for a symbol and a desired category.

3. Select the Tiling options if desired.

4. Drag and drop the symbol onto the drawing.

# Presets

This command invokes the Presets roll-up, where you can apply preset effects to your object. Some of these effects include linear fills, outlines, extrusions, and so on. For more information, see Skill Sessions 5, "Roll-Ups," and 61, "Presets."

## Selection

Keyboard shortcut: Alt+T, R or Alt+F5

Pointing device: Tools | Presets Roll-Up

## Usage

1. Select Presets Roll-Up from the Tools pull-down menu.

2. From the pull-down menu found below the thumbnail of the current default preset, select from the list of other available presets. Then, press the Apply button.

# Object Data

The Object Data command brings up the roll-up with a database of field and value options. You can create or edit fields with specific information such as name, costs, comments, and so on. To change or create fields, you must have at least one object selected. For more information on the Object Data roll-up, see Skill Session 5 and 59, "Object Database."

## Selection

Keyboard shortcut: Alt+T, E

Pointing device: Tools | Object Data

## Usage

1. Select the Object Data from the Tools pull-down menu.

2. Select an object on your screen.

3. Either create a new field or edit the existing field information for the selected object.

# Dimensions

The Dimensions command brings up a flyout menu with two options: Linear and Angular. Click either of these options to invoke the Dimensioning roll-up. You can choose from styles of numbers such as decimal, fractional, architectural, and so on from the roll-up. For more information, see Skill Sessions 5 and 10, "The Dimension Tool."

## Selection

Keyboard shortcut: Alt+T, D, L or A respectively

Pointing device: Tools | Dimensions | Linear, Angular

## Usage

1. Select the Dimensions command from the Tools pull-down menu.
2. Select Linear or Angular from the flyout menu.
3. Select the options for the settings you want to adjust from the roll-up.
4. Press Apply to accept the changes.

# Task-Progress

The Task-Progress command lets you govern the way your computer's CPU resources are put to use. Choose the Task-Progress command to open the Task Progress dialog box. You can regulate the way your computer's CPU resources are employed when issuing multiple, parallel operations (multi-tasking) in CorelDRAW from this dialog box.

By using the options in this dialog box, you can appoint more resources to one item than another, this assists in maximizing efficiency. The maximized efficiency is attained by assigning a priority to each item in the list. The higher the priority rating assigned to a procedure, the more CPU resources are applied to the performance of that procedure.

## Selection

Keyboard shortcut: Alt+T, T

Pointing device: Tools | Task-Progress

## Usage

1. Select Task-Progress from the Tools pull-down menu.
2. It oversees the progress of multi-threaded tasks.

# Create

The Create command allows you to create new patterns, arrows, symbols, and outline styles from objects.

## Arrow

Use the Arrow command to create arrows from selected objects. For more information about creating arrows, see Skill Session 62.

# Corel *TIP!*

> When creating arrows, you cannot use objects that are grouped. However, objects that have been combined or welded can be used.

## Selection

Keyboard shortcut: Alt+T, A, A

Pointing device: Tools | Create | Arrow

## Usage

1. Select an object.
2. Select Create from the Tools pull-down menu and Arrow from the Create flyout menu.
3. Click OK in the **Create Arrow** dialog box prompt.

# Pattern

The Pattern command allows you to create your own patterns out of objects. In the Pattern dialog box there are three settings for Resolution for two-color patterns: Low, Medium, and High. Select the Two Color option.

Select the Full Color option to create a pattern that retains the object's current colors. When creating a full-color pattern, you will be asked to name the pattern. For more information about creating patterns, see Skill Session 62.

## Selection

Keyboard shortcut: Alt+T, A, P

Pointing device: Tools | Create | Pattern

## Usage

1. Open a file or draw an object with which to create a pattern.
2. Select Create from the Tools pull-down menu and Pattern from the Create flyout menu. The Create Pattern dialog box appears.
3. Select Two Color or Full Color.
4. Click the OK button. The cursor becomes a large crosshair.
5. Marquee-select the area you want to use for your pattern.
6. Click the OK button in the Create Pattern dialog box.
7. Name your pattern in the Save Full-Color Pattern dialog box.

# Symbol

The Symbol command creates symbols from the selected object and places it in the Symbols Roll-Up under an existing or new category. (For more information on Create Symbol, see Skill Session 62.)

# Corel *TIP!*

When creating symbols, you cannot use objects that are grouped. However, objects that have been combined or welded can be used.

## Selection

Keyboard shortcut: Alt+T, A, S

Pointing device: Tools | Create | Symbol

## Usage

1. Select the object you want to create a symbol with.
2. Select Create from the Tools pull-down menu and then Symbol from the Create flyout menu.
3. Select a category for the symbol in the Create Symbol dialog box or create a new category.
4. Click the OK button.

# Extract

You can take any text created in a CorelDRAW file and edit it in a word processing program. This helps when you have a large text file to revise. For more information about Extract, see Skill Session 41, "Extracting and Merging Back Text."

## Selection

Keyboard shortcut: Alt+T, X

Pointing device: Tools | Extract

## Usage

1. Select the text you want to edit.
2. Select Extract from the Tools pull-down menu.
3. In the Extract dialog box, name the file.
4. Click the OK button.
5. Open the file in a word processing program, make your edits, and then save the file.

# Corel *TIP!*

Before extracting any text, be sure to save your changes in your drawing.

# Merge-Back

Use Merge-Back to insert text edited in a word processing program back into your CorelDRAW file. For more information about Merge-Back, see Skill Session 41.

## Selection

Keyboard shortcut: Alt+T, K

Pointing device: Tools | Merge-Back

## Usage

1. Select Merge-Back from the Tools pull-down menu.
2. In the Merge Back dialog box, select the text.

3. Click the OK button.

4. The text will appear in your document.

# Scripts

The Scripts command runs the Corel SCRIPT module, which enables you to complete a succession of instructions with one command. Use scripts to automate repetitious tasks or simplify complex procedures, but they can also prompt for user input, display messages, and interact with other applications.

## Scripts | Run

### Selection

Keyboard shortcut: Alt+S, R

Pointing device: Tools | Scripts | Run

### Usage

1. Select Scripts | Run from the Tools pull-down menu.

2. This opens the Run Script program. You can choose from existing scripts.

## Scripts Corel SCRIPT Editor

Use the Corel SCRIPT Editor to produce and revise Corel SCRIPT script files. Corel script files are Windows text files, so the Corel SCRIPT Editor operates like a typical text editor. Other features included in the Corel SCRIPT Editor are: debug, run, and test the script files. For more information on Corel SCRIPT Editor see skill session 92, "Corel SCRIPT."

### Selection

Keyboard shortcut: Alt+S, E

Pointing device: Tools | Scripts | Corel SCRIPT Editor

### Usage

1. Select Scripts | Corel SCRIPT Editor from the Tools pull-down menu.

2. This opens the Corel SCRIPT Editor program, which lets you edit an existing script.

**9**

# Window Menu Commands

The Window pull-down menu provides the selections for New Window, Cascade, Tile Horizontally, Tile Vertically, Arrange Icons, and Refresh Window as well as a list of currently open windows (see Figure CR9.1). For more information about windows, see the "Window Elements" section of Skill Session 3, "Using Menus and Dialog Boxes."

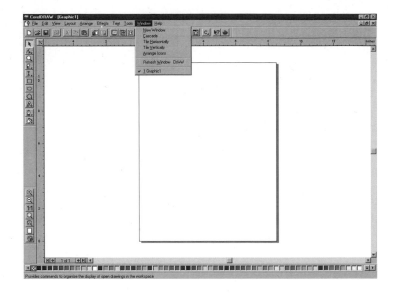

*Figure CR9.1.
The Window pull-down
menu. Use the Window
command to see a list of
options for viewing your
open files.*

# New Window

The New Window command allows you to open additional windows or files without having to close the window with which your are currently working.

## Selection

Keyboard shortcut: Alt+W, N

Pointing device: Window | New Window

## Usage

1. Select New Window from the Window pull-down menu.
2. A new window or file will open.

# Cascade

The Cascade command places all open windows in front of each other in a staggered formation.

# Corel *NOTE!*

> The currently selected window will be automatically moved forward.

## Selection

Keyboard shortcut: Alt+W, C

Pointing device: Window | Cascade

## Usage

1. Select Cascade from the Window pull-down menu.
2. The open files will now appear staggered in front of each other.

## Tile Horizontally

The Tile Horizontally command places all of the currently open windows side by side in a horizontal manner.

## Selection

Keyboard shortcut: Alt+W, H

Pointing device: Window | Tile Horizontally

## Usage

1. Select Tile Horizontally from the Window pull-down menu.
2. Your open files will automatically appear tiled.

## Tile Vertically

The Tile Vertically command places all of the currently open windows stacked on top of each other in a vertical fashion.

### Selection

Keyboard shortcut: Alt+W, V

Pointing device: Window | Tile Vertically

### Usage

1. Select Tile Vertically from the Window pull-down menu.
2. Your open files will automatically appear stacked with the currently selected file on top.

## Arrange Icons

The Arrange Icons command places all minimized windows side by side, starting at the lower-left corner of your screen.

### Selection

Keyboard shortcut: Alt+W, A

Pointing device: Window | Arrange Icons

### Usage

1. Select Arrange Icons from the Window pull-down menu.
2. The minimized windows will arrange themselves at the bottom of your screen.

## Refresh Window

When zooming in and out of your drawing or when working up close with the Shape tool, remnants from your modified objects may appear to remain on-screen. To eliminate these remnants, select Refresh Window from the View menu.

### Selection

Keyboard shortcut: Alt+W, W or Ctrl+W

Pointing device: View | Refresh Window

## Usage

1. Select Refresh Window from the View menu.
2. The screen residue from your altered objects will disappear.

# Opened Windows List

Selecting a number from the list of open windows automatically brings that window to the front.

## Selection

Keyboard shortcut: Alt+W, 1, 2, 3, and so on.

Pointing device: Window | 1, 2, 3, and so on.

## Usage

1. Select the number of the corresponding file you wish to move forward from the Window pull-down menu.

# Help Menu Commands

# 10

The Help pull-down menu provides the following selections: Help Topics, What's This?, Tutorial, and About CorelDRAW. (See Figure CR10.1.) When you select Help from the ribbon bar (the cursor and question mark icon at the far right), your cursor will turn into an arrow with a question mark (?) beside it. For more information about the Help pull-down menu see the "Getting Help" section in Skill Session 3, "Using Menus and Dialog Boxes."

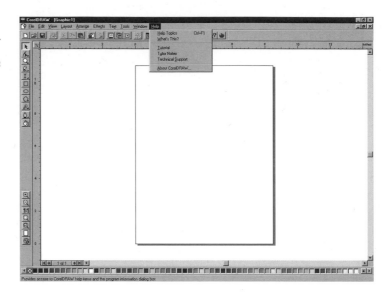

*Figure CR10.1.*
*The Help pull-down menu.*
*Use the Help command to*
*locate general information*
*about CorelDRAW.*

# Help Topics

The Help Topics command brings up the Help Topics dialog box, where you can review the contents or the index, or do a search for help on a specific topic.

## Selection

Keyboard shortcut: F1

Pointing device: Help | Help Topics

## Usage

1. Select Help Topics from the Help pull-down menu.
2. The Help Topics dialog box will appear with several categories. Click the category you want to review.

## Corel*NOTE!*

> When a command is grayed out or unavailable, select the command and press F1 to get Help about it.

# What's This?

Select this command and the cursor changes into the What's This ? cursor. Click a segment of the application to display a help topic concerning the object you have selected.

## Selection

Keyboard shortcut: None

Pointing device: What's This?

## Usage

1. Select What's This? from the Help pull-down menu.
2. With the What's This ? cursor, select a section in the program.
3. Information regarding the section you have selected is displayed.

# Tutorial

The Tutorial command opens a window with lesson selections about CorelDRAW. This command is optional when installing Corel. Some of the lessons are "Filling Objects," "Transforming Objects," "Outlining Objects," and so on.

## Selection

Keyboard shortcut: ALT+H, T

Pointing device: Help | Tutorial

## Usage

1. Select Tutorial from the Help pull-down menu.
2. Choose the lesson you want to review.
3. Choose the Forward button to go through the lessons in sequential order.

# About CorelDRAW

The About CorelDRAW command opens a dialog box that consists of such information as the version of CorelDRAW, who the copy registered is to, the serial number, the amount of free disk space, the number of objects or groups of objects in the current drawing, and so on.

## Selection

Keyboard shortcut: ALT+H, A

Pointing device: Help | About CorelDRAW!

## Usage

1. Select About CorelDRAW from the Help pull-down menu.
2. Check dialog box for information and press OK when you are done.

# Part

# XII

# Appendixes

# Glossary

**A sizes** Paper sizes measured in metric units. You can choose from A3, A4, and A5 sizes through the Page Setup command in the Layout menu.

**.ABK** The filename extension for backup files created by CorelDRAW for drawings while you are working on them. These files are created at regular intervals and deleted when you exit CorelDRAW or choose the New command from the File menu. You can control the time between backups by entering the amount of time in the Advanced section of the Options dialog box. You can also determine the folder in which they are saved. These files are created in the event of a system crash, enabling you to retrieve the file you were working on in the state it was in the last time it was backed up. *See also* Backup.

**Active window** The window in which you are working.

**.AI** The filename extension for Adobe Illustrator files. A vector graphic file format that CorelDRAW can import and export.

**Artistic text** Text that can be fitted to a path and manipulated with commands in the Effects menu. Selecting the Text tool and then clicking in the drawing window enables you to add text up to 32,000 characters long. If you apply a special effect to Paragraph text, you are limited to 4000 characters. *See also* Paragraph text.

**Ascender** The part of a letter that extends above the main body (x-height) in certain lowercase letters—for example, *d* and *h*. *See also* Descender.

**ASCII** American Standard Code for Information Interchange. A standard code for representing characters and nonprintable control codes such as carriage returns and page breaks.

**Aspect ratio** The ratio of the width of an image to its height. You can change the aspect ratio of an object in CorelDRAW by stretching it in one direction. You do this either by selecting it and dragging a middle control handle or by using the Stretch command in the Effects menu.

**Attributes** Characteristics assigned to objects using the Outline and Fill tools. Outline attributes include thickness, color, and line style (solid, dashed, dotted, or arrowheads). An object's Fill attribute can be a solid color, fountain fill, pattern, or texture. Text objects also have attributes, including typeface and character spacing.

**Auto-panning** A feature in CorelDRAW that automatically scrolls the drawing window when you drag beyond its borders. You can turn Auto-panning off or on in the dialog box that is displayed when you select Preferences from the Tools menu.

**Autotrace** A feature in CorelDRAW that automatically generates a vector drawing from an imported bitmap image.

**B size** Paper size measured in metric units. You can choose the B5 size through the Page Setup command in the Layout menu.

**Backup** Files in CorelDRAW with a .BAK or .ABK extension. CorelDRAW creates a backup of the drawing you are working on at preset intervals and whenever you use the Save or Save As command to save it. You can open a backup file by changing the extension to .CDR. You can change the period between backups by entering the time in numbers in the Backup parameters box located in the Advanced section of the Options dialog box, accessed from the Tools pull-down menu.

**.BAK** The filename extension for the backup file CorelDRAW creates for a drawing while it is open. This backup file is created each time you save a drawing using the Save or Save As command. You can eliminate the creation of this backup file by removing the × from the Make Backup When Save box in the Advance section of the Options dialog box. To access the options dialog box, choose Options from the Tools pull-down menu. If you leave the Make Backup When Save box checked, a duplicate of your file will be saved with a .BAK extension. *See also* Backup.

**Baseline** The imaginary line to which characters in a line of type align.

**Bézier curves** A method computer graphics programs use to represent curved surfaces. A Bézier curve has two endpoints and a set of control points that enable you to change the shape of the curve.

**Bézier drawing mode**   One of two ways you can draw lines and curves using the Pencil tool. Bézier mode enables you to draw in a point-to-point style by clicking once and then clicking again on another spot on the page. A line is then drawn between the two points.

**Bitmap**   An image composed of a series of dots (pixels). Scanners and paint programs, such as Corel PHOTO-PAINT, generate this kind of image.

**Bleed**   The potion of a printed image that extends beyond the edge of the page frame. This added area allows for any errors in the trimming process.

**Blend**   The process of mixing one object of one color with another of a different color through a series of intermediate steps. The Blend command in the Effects menu does this automatically.

**.BMP**   The filename extension for Windows bitmap files. CorelDRAW can import and export files in BMP format.

**Calligraphic**   An effect created with the Outline tool, in which objects are given an outline that varies in thickness. This gives curved objects a hand-drawn appearance. *See also* PowerLines.

**Cap height**   The distance from the baseline to the top of an uppercase character.

**.CDR**   The filename extension for files created in CorelDRAW.

**Center of rotation**   A circle with a dot in the center that appears in the middle of a selected object when you double-click it. Moving this marker changes the axis around which the object rotates.

**.CGM**   The filename extension for Computer Graphics Metafile, a vector graphics file format that CorelDRAW can import and export.

**Character attributes**   Characteristics such as typeface, style, and point size that are assigned to characters in a block of text using the Edit Text command in the Text menu.

**Character set**   The letters, punctuation marks, and special characters in a particular font. An underscore (_) symbol or mathematical symbols are examples of special characters.

**Check box**   A square box in a dialog box used to turn options on or off. An option is on when an × appears in the check box and is off when the check box is empty.

**Child object**   An object created when you select an object within a group of objects while holding down the Ctrl key. The child object can then be transformed separately without affecting the other objects in the group. A child object has round handles when selected rather than the usual square handles.

**Click**   The action of quickly pressing and releasing the mouse button.

**Clip art**   Predrawn images that can be brought into CorelDRAW and edited or used as is.

**Clipboard**   A temporary storage area provided by Windows to store information. This information then can be pasted back into the same or a different application.

**Clipping holes**   The process of combining two objects using the Combine or Trim command from the Arrange menu. This creates a transparent hole so that underlying objects are visible. Also known as *masking*.

**Clone**   A duplicate of an object that is created with the Clone command in the Edit menu.

**CMYK**   An acronym for *Cyan*, *Magenta*, *Yellow*, and *Black*—the ink colors used in four-color process printing. CorelDRAW enables you to specify colors using CMYK values.

**CMX**   Corel Presentation Exchange. Presentation Exchange format is a special file format for exchanging information between Corel applications. When it is used, it replaces the native CDR format. Saving files with Presentation Data attached will significantly add to the file size.

# Corel*NOTE!*

> Two versions are available—Version 5 (older Corel products) and Version 6 (32-bit). Version 6 will not work in versions 5 or older but Version 5 will work in 6.

**Color Manager**   A tool that can determine the capabilities of your monitor, printer, and scanner to create a system color profile to help in the display, printer output, and scanning quality of these devices on your system.

**Color palette**   The color bar along the bottom of the CorelDRAW screen that enables you to choose outline and fill colors for selected objects. Choosing Color Palette in the View menu opens a flyout menu with commands for turning the palette on and off or displaying other types of palettes.

**Color proof**   The preliminary step in the color printing process. Sometimes called a prepress proof, it shows how an image will look when it's printed. Proofing provides an opportunity to make corrections and adjustments before final printing.

**Color separation**   The process of separating the colors in an image into the primary printing colors: cyan, magenta, yellow, and black.

**Command**   A word or phrase in a menu that starts an action.

**Command button**   A button in a dialog box used to start an action, such as displaying another dialog box.

**Composite**   A preliminary version of a design combining all image, line art, and text elements. Also known as *comp*.

**Constrain**   The effect that occurs when your movements are limited—for example, when you hold down the Ctrl key while transforming an object with the mouse. Holding down the Ctrl key while rotating an object forces the object to rotate in 15-degree increments. The number of degrees can be changed in the Options dialog box accessed from the Tools menu.

**Continuous tone**   An image represented by graduated tones from black to white, as in a photograph.

**Contour**   A feature in CorelDRAW that enables you to apply contour lines to an object. The Contour roll-up is accessed by clicking Contour in the Effects menu.

**Control object**   A term used in CorelDRAW to differentiate the original object from those created when you apply the Blend or Extrude command.

**Control point**   Points extending from nodes along a curved object that determine the angle at which the curve passes through the node. Control points appear when you select a node or segment with the Shape tool. Nodes associated with straight lines do not have control points.

**CorelMOVE**   A program that came with CorelDRAW 4 and 5 for creating and editing animation. The files can be imported into Corel PRESENTS.

**Corel PHOTO-PAINT**   A program that comes with CorelDRAW for creating and editing bitmap images.

**Corel SHOW**   A program that came with CorelDRAW 3, 4, and 5 for creating slide shows. The files can be imported into Corel PRESENTS.

**Crop**   The process of using the Shape tool to remove part of an area of an imported bitmap. The parts that are not displayed on-screen or printed are still stored in the bitmap file so that your file size will not be reduced.

**Crop marks**   Alignment marks at the corners of a page printed on a PostScript printer. Used as aids for trimming the paper to the proper size, crop marks are turned on in the Options dialog box accessed from the Print dialog box. To view the Options dialog box, click the Options button in the Print dialog box. The Crop Marks will appear only if the page size in CorelDRAW is smaller than the paper size of the printer.

**Crosshairs**   Marks at the corners of a sheet of paper or film used for aligning color separations. CorelDRAW automatically adds crosshairs when printing color separations to a PostScript printer. Also refers to the pair of intersecting lines that can be dragged from the spot where the rulers meet and to the cursor, which can be displayed through the Preferences command in the Tools menu. Also known as *registration marks*.

**Cursor** The on-screen, arrow-shaped pointer controlled by the movement of the mouse or pen. The shape of the cursor changes depending on the tool or command selected. Also called the mouse pointer.

**Curve object** An object with nodes and control points that can be manipulated to change its shape. Curved objects are created when you draw with the Pencil tool. You also can convert text and objects drawn with the Rectangle and Ellipse tools into curved objects using the Convert to Curves command in the Arrange menu.

**Cusp** A type of node that permits a curve to pass through it at a sharp angle. Node types are selected from the Node Edit menu. The menu is revealed when you double-click a node or segment with the Shape tool.

**Default printer** The printer that CorelDRAW automatically uses to print a drawing when you choose the Print command from the File menu. Choose the printer you want as the default printer by clicking the printer's icon in the Windows Control Panel.

**Default settings** Predefined options built into a program.

**Descender** The part of a letter that extends below the main body (x-height) in certain lowercase letters, for example, *j* and *q*. *See also* Ascender.

**Deselect** The process of removing the selection handles from the object you have currently selected. The best way to make sure you do not select another object when deselecting the first object is to click somewhere *off* the page area.

**Destination file** The file into which an embedded or linked object is being inserted. *See also* Embedded object *and* Linked object.

**Dialog box** A window displayed when additional information is needed to perform an action.

**Direction keys** The arrow keys and the Home, End, PgUp, and PgDn keys. The arrow keys nudge objects in small steps. They also move the insertion point when entering or editing text on-screen or in a dialog box. The Home and End keys select the start and end nodes on a curved object. They also move the insertion point in a block of text to the beginning or end of a line.

**Folder** Folders were referred to as directories prior to Windows 95. They are part of a structure used to organize files on a disk. Folders are given names and can be divided into sub-folders. For example, you can create a folder called CDRFILES for storing most of your files created in CorelDRAW and a sub-folder called CDRFILES\SPECIAL for special files you create in CorelDRAW.

**Dithered color** Dots of one or more different colors placed very close together to simulate the desired color. Windows uses dithering to display colors that the graphics adapter is unable to display. *See also* Pure color.

**Double-click** The action of pressing and releasing the mouse button twice in quick succession.

**DPI** An acronym for *dots per inch*. A measure of a printer's resolution. Typical desktop laser printers print at 300 dpi; imagesetters are capable of printing at resolutions of over 5000 dpi. The more dots per inch, the smoother the output appears.

**Drag** The action of moving the mouse while holding down the mouse button. Releasing the button completes the action.

**Drawing window** The portion of the CorelDRAW screen that is available for drawing (usually defined by a rectangular outline with a drop shadow). Although you are free to draw anywhere on the screen, only objects on the drawing window will print. *See also* Printable Page.

**Drop-down list box** A list box that appears in dialog boxes and opens to display a list of choices when you click the arrow. If the list cannot accommodate all available options, scroll bars are provided. *See also* List box.

**.DXF** The filename extension for AutoCAD files. CorelDRAW can import and export files in this format.

**Edit** The process of changing an object using commands in the Edit, Layout, Effects, Text, and Arrange menus or the Pick, Shape, Outline, and Fill tools.

**Editable preview** One of two ways to view objects in the drawing window. In editable preview (the default view), you see the outlines and fills of objects as you create them. In the wireframe view, objects are displayed in skeleton form. Because objects redraw more quickly without outlines and fills, you might find it quicker to edit complex drawings in wireframe view. You can switch freely between views by choosing Wireframe from the View menu.

**Em space** A unit of measurement used primarily in typesetting to specify the space between characters and words. An em space is equal in width to a capital M in the point size being used. For example, in 12-point type, an em space is approximately 12 points wide.

**Embedded object** Information from a file created in one application that's been inserted into a file in another application. For example, you can embed a graphic created in CorelDRAW into a Microsoft Word document. The embedded information can be edited from within the application in which it is embedded. In this case, the graphic can be edited from within Word.

**Emboss**   An effect created in CorelDRAW by using two offset duplicates of the original and coloring one duplicate light and one dark to give the illusion of the original being recessed. Also, an effect automatically created in Corel PHOTO-PAINT, accessed through the Effects menu.

**En space**   A unit of measurement used primarily in typesetting to specify the space between characters and words. An en space is equal to the width of a capital N in the point size being used. This is usually half the width of an M. *See also* Em space.

**End node**   The small square at the end of an open path that appears when you select the path with the Shape tool. The end node is distinguishable from the start node by its smaller size. You can toggle between the start and end nodes with the Home and End Keys.

**Envelope**   A feature in the Effects menu that enables you to distort the shape of an object by manipulating the bounding box that contains the object. You can use predefined shapes or use the freehand method. The Envelope roll-up is accessed from the Effects pull-down menu.

**.EPS**   The filename extension for Encapsulated PostScript files. CorelDRAW can import EPS files created in Adobe Illustrator. The EPS files CorelTRACE creates can be imported by CorelDRAW and other PC programs, such as Ventura Publisher and Adobe PageMaker.

**Export**   A command found in CorelDRAW's File menu that enables you to export all or part of a image on the CorelDRAW screen to formats other than .CDR.

**Extension**   Characters preceded by a period in a filename that identify the type of information in the file. The extension .TIF, for example, indicates the file contains a bitmap.

**Extrude**   A feature in the Effects menu that enables you to give objects a three-dimensional effect.

**File previewer**   In the Open Drawing dialog box, a small bitmap representation that enables you to see what the selected file contains before you open it.

**Film**   Photosensitive sheets on which images are transferred either as positives or negatives. These sheets are then used to create printing plates. An option in the Print Options dialog box enables you to create film negatives for printing on an image setter.

**Film Recorder**   A device that reproduces on film the images from a computer screen. The film can then be developed into slides or prints using conventional photographic processes.

**Filter**   A program that translates information from one format to another. CorelDRAW's import filters, for example, enable you to open graphics created in Corel PHOTO-PAINT and many other applications.

**Flyout menu**   An extra menu that appears to the side of certain selections in drop-down menus and dialog boxes within CorelDRAW.

**FOCOLTONE**   A color system providing a range of colors that includes at least 10 percent of one process color that is common to another FOCOLTONE color. For example, if you have a solid-filled FOCOLTONE blue object butted against a solid-filled FOCOLTONE red object, there will be at least ten percent Cyan in the red object and at least ten percent Magenta in the blue object. Using this color system lessens the need to trap when outputting color separations.

**Font**   A set of characters in a given typeface and point size—for example, 12-point Helvetica. Some fonts are also available in different weights or styles, such as bold and italic.

**Fountain fill**   A fill that fades gradually from one color to another. CorelDRAW now enables you to use as many different colors as you want in a fountain fill. Also called a gradient or graduated fill. CorelDRAW enables you to create linear, radial, conical, and square fountain fills using the Fountain Fill icon in the Fill tool menu or the Fill roll-up window.

**Four-color process**   The process of reproducing color artwork using four separate sheets of film that represent the cyan, magenta, yellow, and black content of the artwork.

**Frame**   The rectangle that encloses a block of Paragraph text created with the Text tool. Also, a command in the Text menu used to format Paragraph text.

**Freehand drawing mode**   One of two ways you can draw lines and curves using the Pencil tool. In Freehand mode, you draw by moving the mouse pointer as you would a pencil on paper. *See also* Bézier mode.

**.GDF**   The filename extension for vector graphics files used by IBM mainframe computers. CorelDRAW imports and exports these graphics as PIF files, which can be translated to GDF format by the mainframe computer.

**GEM**   Acronym for *Graphics Environment Manager*. A menu-driven interface used by programs such as the old Xerox Ventura Publisher. Also a filename extension for files created by programs such as GEM Artline; CorelDRAW can import and export files in this format.

**.GIF**   The filename extension for files in a bitmap format that is commonly used to store digitized color photographs. CorelDRAW imports and exports files in this format.

**Grayscale image**   An image, typically created from a scanner, in which continuous tones are represented as uniform shades of gray. CorelDRAW can import and display grayscale images with up to 256 levels of gray and print them on a PostScript printer.

**Grid**   A series of evenly spaced horizontal and vertical lines used to align objects. The spacing is specified through the Grid Setup command in the Layout menu. You also can force objects to snap to the grid by turning on Snap to Grid in the Layout menu.

**Grid markers**   Points on the screen that help you lay out your drawing. The grid markers are normally turned off. You can turn the grid markers on by choosing Grid and Rulers Setup from the Layout pull-down menu and selecting Show Grid in the Grid tab.

**Group**   The process of making one or more objects into a single selectable object with the Group command in the Arrange menu. Grouping is useful when you want to keep individual elements in a graphic from being accidentally moved or otherwise altered.

**Guidelines**   Nonprinting lines used to align objects. Guidelines can be placed anywhere in the drawing window by clicking and dragging on the rulers or by using the Guidelines Setup command in the Layout menu. By turning on Snap to Guidelines in the Layout menu, you can force objects to a guideline when they are drawn or moved near it.

**Gutter**   The space between columns of Paragraph text.

**Halftone**   The process of reproducing a continuous-tone image, such as a black-and-white photograph, using dots of various sizes. On laser printers that cannot print different-sized dots, the halftone is produced by printing different numbers of dots in a given area.

**Halftone screen**   A method of representing an image made up of gradually changing shades into a series of dots so that when they are printed, they will look like the original. CorelDRAW enables you to set the type and frequency of dots as well as the screen angle to eliminate moiré patterns when printing to PostScript devices. By changing the type, frequency, and angle, you can create different looks to CorelDRAW PostScript fills.

**Handles**   Small squares that appear on the corners and sides of an object's highlighting box when the object is selected. You use these handles to resize and stretch an object. When you click on an already selected object, the handles change to arrows. You use the arrows to rotate and skew the object.

**Hanging indent**   A format applied to Paragraph text in which the first line of text begins farther to the right than do subsequent lines.

**Hints**    Information included with fonts to improve their appearance when printed in small point sizes. TrueType and Adobe Type 1 fonts are hinted.

**Hourglass cursor**    The mouse pointer during an operation such as printing. No other actions can be performed until the pointer reappears.

**HPGL**    An acronym for *Hewlett-Packard Graphics Language*. A file format created by programs such as AutoCAD for printing drawings on plotters. CorelDRAW can import and export HPGL files with the extension .PLT.

**HSB**    An acronym for *Hue*, *Saturation*, and *Brightness*—the components in the HSB color model. HSB is one of three color models CorelDRAW provides for creating process colors.

**Hue**    In the HSB color model, hue is the main attribute in a color that distinguishes it from other colors. Blue, green, and red, for example, are all hues. *See also* Saturation.

**Icon**    A small graphic symbol that represents various elements in Windows and CorelDRAW. For example, the tools in CorelDRAW are represented by icons.

**Image header**    An optional bitmap image created when you save a CorelDRAW file or export it in EPS format.

**Image setter**    A generic term for printers capable of printing text and graphics (line art and photographs) at resolutions of about 1200 dots per inch and more.

**Import**    A command found in CorelDRAW's File menu that enables you to import different file formats into CorelDRAW. It enables you to import file formats such as PCX or TIF, and even CDR, for use in your CorelDRAW images.

**Insertion point**    A flashing vertical bar that indicates where text will be inserted when you type. The insertion point appears when you click a text block with the Text tool and also in dialog boxes that require you to type information.

**Inter-character spacing**    The amount of spacing between characters of text. You can adjust inter-character spacing interactively with the Shape tool or by entering numeric values in the alignment tab section of the Character Attributes dialog box. See Skill Session 14, "The Text Tool."

**Inter-line spacing**    The amount of spacing between the baselines of text. It is also called leading. You can adjust inter-line spacing interactively with the Shape tool or by entering numeric values in the alignment tab section of the Character Attributes dialog box. See Skill Session 14, "The Text Tool."

**Inter-paragraph spacing**    The amount of spacing between blocks of Paragraph text separated by pressing Enter. You can adjust inter-Paragraph text by entering numeric values in the alignment tab section of the Character Attributes dialog box. See Skill Session 14, "The Text Tool."

**Interruptible Display** A feature in CorelDRAW that stops the screen during a redraw whenever the primary mouse button or a key is pressed. If you are working on a complex drawing, Interruptible Display can save time by enabling you to select tools and commands without waiting for the screen to redraw completely. You can turn Interruptible Display on and off with the Preferences dialog box, accessed through the Tools menu.

**Intersection** A feature that enables you to create a new object in the shape of the area that is formed by two overlapping objects.

**Inter-word spacing** The amount of spacing between words of text. You can adjust inter-word spacing interactively with the Shape tool or by entering numeric values in the alignment tab section of the Character Attributes dialog box. See Skill Session 14, "The Text Tool."

**Jaggies** A stair-step effect that often occurs when a bitmap image is enlarged.

**JPEG** A file format that compresses bitmap images into smaller file sizes than the standard formats such as PCX and TIF.

**Justification** Refers to the alignment of text. You can choose from several justification options in CorelDRAW, including left, right, and center.

**Kerning** The process of reducing the spacing between pairs of letters. Moving certain pairs letters, such as AV, closer together improves their appearance when printed. You can kern text interactively with the Shape tool or by entering numeric values in the Alignment tab of the Character Attributes dialog box. See Skill Session 14, "The Text Tool."

**Landscape** A page that is oriented so that it prints from left to right across its longest dimension.

**Layer** A plane on which objects are placed. You can control how objects in your drawing overlay one another by moving the layers and the objects they contain up or down in a stacking order. Moving and editing layers is done in the Layers Manager roll-up. Select Layers Manager from the Layout pull-down menu to open the Layers Manager roll-up. You also can make layers invisible and nonprintable. See Skill Session 21, "Layers."

**Leading** The amount of spacing between baselines of text. Referred to as interline spacing in CorelDRAW. You can adjust the amount of leading interactively with the Shape tool or by entering numeric values in the alignment tab section of the Character Attributes dialog box. See Skill Session 14, "The Text Tool."

**Lens effect** An procedure that enables you to apply special effects on top of objects. The Lens roll-up is accessed from the Effects pull-down menu.

**Limitcheck error**    A PostScript printing error that occurs when a drawing contains too many line segments for the printer to reproduce. CorelDRAW provides a Flatness control in the Print Options dialog box that helps overcome this problem. See Skill Session 50, "Printing," for additional information.

**Line art**    In traditional graphic arts, an illustration containing only black and white.

**Line style**    Solid, dashed, or dotted-line types selected from the Outline Pen dialog box or the Pen roll-up window. See Skill Session 15, "The Outline Tool," for more information.

**Linked object**    A reference or placeholder for information inserted into a file. Changes made to the information from the application that created the linked object are reflected automatically in the destination files.

**Lino**    Short for *Linotronic*, a line of PostScript imagesetters used for high-resolution printing.

**List box**    Boxes that appear in dialog boxes and display a list of options. If the list cannot accommodate all available options, scroll bars are provided. *See also* Drop-down list box.

**LPI**    An acronym for *lines per inch*. Used to measure halftone screen frequencies.

**Marquee box**    The dashed box created by dragging around objects with the Pick tool or around nodes with the Shape tool. Enclosing objects and nodes with a marquee box selects them.

**Marquee-select**    A method of selecting multiple objects with the Pick tool or multiple nodes with the Shape tool by dragging a dotted rectangle around them.

**Masking**    The combining of two objects, using the Combine or Trim command from the Arrange menu, to create a transparent hole through which underlying objects are visible. Also known as *clipping holes*.

**Maximize**    The process of enlarging an application window to full-screen size.

**Menu**    A list of commands that appears when you choose a name in the menu bar. The menu bar appears below the title bar that is at the top of the window.

**Menu bar**    The bar near the top of the window that contains the names of the program menus.

**Mirror**    The process of creating a mirror reflection of an object by using the Scale and Mirror command in the Transform roll-up, accessed from the Arrange menu. You also can mirror an object by dragging on a middle handle of the selected object.

**Moiré pattern** Undesirable patterns in an image printed from color separations with incorrect halftone screen angles.

**Multiple select** A method of selecting multiple objects with the Pick tool or multiple nodes with the Shape tool by holding down the Shift key and clicking on the objects or nodes one at a time.

**Negative** An image in which the values in the original are reversed so that black areas appear white, white appears black, and colors are represented by their complements. CorelDRAW can print color separations as negatives if the Film Negative button is depressed in the Print Options dialog box.

**Nodes** The points at the ends of line and curve segments in a curve object. Also refers to the small, hollow squares along the outlines of objects drawn with the Rectangle and Ellipse tools and those next to characters in a text object.

**Nudge** The action of moving objects in small steps by using the arrow keys. The incremental amount of movement can be set in the Options dialog box, which is accessed in the Tools menu. See Skill Session 4, "Customizing and Setting Preferences."

**Object Properties menu** A menu accessed by right-clicking an object. The Object Properties menu contains most of the commands found in the menu bar and provides a quicker access to them.

**OCR-TRACE** A program that comes with CorelDRAW that automatically traces bitmap images. The result is a vector graphic that you can import into CorelDRAW for editing. OCR-TRACE also supports Optical Character Recognition (OCR), which enables you to scan in text and then import the text into CorelDRAW and other word processing applications.

**One-point perspective** The process of lengthening or shortening one side of an object's perspective bounding box to create the impression that the object is receding from view in a single direction.

**OLE2** Object Linking and Embedding: technology that enables you to embed or link objects, including text, graphics, sound, and others, into another document or applications. The latest version of CorelDRAW enables you to use drag-and-drop to manipulate objects.

**Orthogonal extrusion** Projecting an object using the Extrude feature so that opposite sides are parallel to one another. Contrasts with Perspective extrusion, in which opposite sides recede toward a vanishing point.

**Overprint** The process of printing over an area that has already been printed. Overprinting is used in CorelDRAW to create traps in color-separated artwork. You also can use it to overprint selected spot colors for certain visual effects. *See also* Trap.

**Page border** The page border is the rectangle with the drop shadow in the drawing window that represents the printable area. It is also called the printable page. You can turn the Page border on and off by clicking Page Setup in the Layout pull-down menu and then removing the × from the Show page border check box in the Page Setup dialog box.

**Paint program** A generic term referring to computer illustration programs that create graphics as bitmaps. Corel PHOTO-PAINT is an example of a paint program. *See also* Vector graphics.

**Palette** A collection of colors displayed along the bottom of the CorelDRAW screen and in the Uniform Color and Outline Color dialog boxes.

**PANTONE** A standard color-matching system in which solid (spot) colors are specified using color sample books. You can use this system in CorelDRAW to specify colors.

**Paragraph text** Text in blocks of characters. Selecting the Paragraph Text tool and then dragging it to create a bounding box enables you to add text with the following limitations: Each paragraph is limited to 32,000 characters; there are 32,000 paragraphs in each set of linked frames; and there are 32,000 sets of linked frames in one file. *See also* Artistic text.

**.PAT** The filename extension for files containing full-color patterns used to fill objects in CorelDRAW. You can open these files and edit the patterns just as you can other objects.

**.PCT** The filename extension for vector graphics files used by Macintosh computers. CorelDRAW imports PICT 1 (black-and-white) and PICT 2 (color) files and exports PICT 2 files.

**.PCX** The filename extension for bitmap files created by Corel PHOTO-PAINT and other paint programs. CorelDRAW can import and export files in this format, including those containing color and grayscale information.

**Photo CD** A process developed by the Eastman Kodak company that converts 35mm film negatives or slides into digital format and stores them on a compact disc (CD).

**.PIC** The filename extension used by two different vector graphics file formats. One format is created by Lotus 1-2-3 and can be imported by CorelDRAW. The other format is used by slide-making equipment, such as VideoShow or Slidemaker, and can be exported by CorelDRAW.

**Pica** A unit of measurement used primarily in typesetting. One pica equals approximately $1/6$ of an inch.

**.PIF**   The filename extension for vector graphics files that CorelDRAW can import and export. PIF is an intermediate format that IBM mainframe computers translate to GDF format for use in mainframe applications.

**Pixels**   Dots on a computer or television screen that combine to form an image. Short for picture elements.

**.PLT**   The filename extension for vector graphics files conforming to the HPGL format. These are primarily files created by programs such as AutoCAD for printing drawings on plotters. CorelDRAW can import and export HPGL files with the extension .PLT.

**Point**   A unit of measurement used primarily in typesetting for designating type sizes. There are 72 points to an inch and 12 points to a pica.

**Portrait**   A page size that is less wide than it is tall.

**Positive**   An image in which dark, light, and color values are the same as the original. *See also* Negative.

**PostScript fonts**   PostScript fonts were developed to be used with Adobe's PostScript page-description language, but the language is not necessary to use the fonts. PostScript fonts are the native format to laser printers and imagesetters and are the preferred format to use.

**PostScript**   A page-description language with which a program can describe the text and graphics it wants the printer to output. Several features in CorelDRAW require the use of a PostScript printer.

**PostScript textures**   Variable pattern fills that require the use of a PostScript printer to print. Textures are selected through the PostScript icon in the Fill tool flyout menu.

**PowerClip**   A feature that enables you to place objects inside other objects. The PowerClip feature is accessed by selecting PowerClip in the Effects pull-down menu.

**PowerLines**   A feature in CorelDRAW that enables you to draw predefined shapes with the pencil tool. The PowerLine feature is accessed by selecting PowerLine in the Effects pull-down menu.

**Presets**   A feature that enables you to apply certain predrawn CorelDRAW effects to a single object.

**Preview screen**   A viewing option that uses the entire screen to display your drawings. You can switch to the Preview screen by choosing Show Preview from the View menu or by pressing F9. Pressing any key returns you to the drawing window.

**Primary mouse button**   The button on the mouse that is used for most actions, such as selecting objects or icons. It is usually the left mouse button.

**Printable page**   The rectangle with the drop shadow that appears in the drawing window.

**Process color**   The primary colors used in four-color process printing: cyan, magenta, yellow, and black. *See also* Four-color process.

**Proof**   The trial print of a graphic that shows how it will look when output in its final form.

**Pure color**   Any color that individual pixels on a computer screen can assume. On a monochrome screen, there are only two pure colors, black and white. Color screens typically might display 8, 16, 256, or 16 million pure colors. *See also* Dithered color.

**Radio button**   A rectangular, square, or round button in a dialog box that turns an option on or off. When two or more options are available, only one can be selected. They are also called option buttons.

**Rasterizer**   A program that converts vector graphics into bitmaps for printing on a non-PostScript printer.

**Registration marks**   Marks on paper or film used for aligning color separations. CorelDRAW automatically adds registration marks when printing color separations to a PostScript printer. Also known as *crosshairs*.

**Resident fonts**   Typefaces permanently stored in the printer's memory. PostScript printers typically have 35 resident typefaces, such as Times and Helvetica.

**Resolution**   In printing, a term referring to the number of dots per inch (dpi) the printer is capable of printing. Typical laser printers have resolutions of 300 dpi; imagesetters have resolutions of approximately 1200 or 2400 dpi. The more dots per inch, the smoother the output.

**RGB**   An acronym for *Red*, *Green*, and *Blue*. RGB refers to the colors used in many bitmap drawing applications. RGB colors are also the colors used by your monitor to display images on-screen.

**Roll-up**   A floating dialog box. Roll-ups contain many of the controls found in dialog boxes: command buttons, text boxes, drop-down list boxes, and so on. But, unlike most dialog boxes, the window stays open after you apply the selected options. This enables you to make adjustments and experiment with different options without having to continually reopen a dialog box.

**Rotate**  The process of turning an object around its center axis using the Rotate command in the Transform roll-up. You can access the Transform roll-up by selecting Transform in the Arrange pull-down menu. You can also rotate an object by dragging a corner handle with arrows revealed when you click twice on the outline of an object.

**Ruler crosshairs**  The pair of intersecting lines that can be dragged from the spot where the rulers meet. Used to check the alignment of objects and to reset the 0,0 point on the rulers.

**Rulers**  Measuring tools displayed on the left side and along the top of the drawing window.

**Sans serif**  A typeface, such as Helvetica, that lacks serifs. *See also* Serif.

**Saturation**  In the HSB color model, the component that determines the purity, intensity, and brightness of a color.

**Scale**  The process of resizing an object by equal amounts horizontally and vertically using the Stretch and Scale command in the Transform roll-up, which is accessed from the Effects pull-down menu. You also can scale by dragging a corner handle on the object's highlighting box.

**Scanner**  A device that converts images on a page or transparency into digital form. CorelDRAW can import scanned images in PCX, TIFF, TARGA, and JPEG formats. *See also* Bitmap.

**SCODL**  A file format used by film recorders for making slides.

**Screen angles**  When printing color separations, the angles at which each of the four process colors are printed to avoid undesirable moiré patterns. These angles can be specified in CorelDRAW's Print dialog box. *See also* Halftone screen.

**Scroll**  To shift the view in the drawing window to see portions of a drawing outside the current viewing area. CorelDRAW provides scroll bars along the edges of the drawing window and an Auto-panning feature that scrolls the drawing window automatically whenever you drag beyond its borders. *See also* Auto-panning.

**Secondary mouse button**  Usually the right mouse button. This button has come into use much more regularly since the introduction of Windows 95—primarily for right-clicking objects in order to bring up the Object Properties dialog box.

**Segments**  Lines or curves between nodes in a curve object.

**Select**  The process of choosing an object with the Pick tool or a node or segment with the Shape tool.

**Serif** The short strokes at the ends of individual letters in some typefaces, such as Times Roman. Sans serif typefaces, such as Helvetica, lack these strokes.

**Service bureau** A commercial business that prints customer-provided documents or artwork, usually on high-resolution PostScript devices.

**Size** The process of resizing an object either horizontally or vertically using the Size command in the Transform roll-up, accessed from the Arrange pull-down menu. You also can resize an object by dragging a selection handle on the object's highlighting box.

**Skew** The process of slanting an object using the Skew command in the Transform roll-up accessed from the Arrange pull-down menu. You can also skew by dragging a side handle that is revealed when you double-click on an object.

**Snap** To force an object being drawn or moved to a grid line, guideline, or another object. You can turn Snap on and off by choosing commands in the Layout menu.

**Source file** The file that contains information being embedded or linked. *See also* Embedded object *and* Linked object.

**Spot color** In offset printing, solid colors commonly specified using the PANTONE color-matching system. Spot color is used whenever exact colors are required. CorelDRAW also uses the PANTONE system to specify spot colors.

**Start node** The small square at the beginning of an open path revealed when you select the path with the Shape tool. The start node is distinguishable from the end node by its larger size.

**Status Line** An area on the screen that shows information about the currently selected object or node and the action in progress.

**Subscript** Characters smaller than and positioned below the baseline of other characters in a word or line of text.

**Superscript** Characters smaller than and positioned above the x-height of other characters in a word or text string.

**Symbol** A predrawn graphic located in the Corel symbols roll-up. You access the Symbols roll-up by selecting Symbols in the Tools pull-down menu.

**Texture fills** Fills made of predefined texture patterns that are fully editable. PostScript fills are also included in this category but are not editable. Texture fills can be accessed from the Fill dialog box and the Fill roll-up.

**.TGA** The filename extension for files in Targa format, which is a bitmap format that is commonly used to store digitized color photographs. CorelDRAW imports and exports files in this format.

**.TIF** The filename extension for Tagged Image File Format, which is a bitmap graphic format that CorelDRAW can import and export. You can import and export color and grayscale TIF files.

**Tile** The process of printing a drawing larger than the printer's paper size on multiple pages. You can print drawings in tiles from CorelDRAW by choosing Tile in the Print Options dialog box. You also can tile bitmap, vector, and texture fills into an object created in CorelDRAW.

**Title bar** The bar along the top of a Windows application that contains the name of the application and the maximize, minimize and exit boxes. In CorelDRAW, the title bar also contains the name of an open file.

**Toggle** The action of alternately turning a program function on and off. For example, the Show Rulers, Show Status Line, and Color Palette commands in CorelDRAW's Display menu toggle on and off.

**Toolbar** The toolbar holds a collection of icons that provide quick access to commonly used features.

**Toolbox** The collection of icons on the left side of the CorelDRAW screen used to perform tasks such as drawing objects or choosing outline and fill attributes.

**Trap** The process of adding a slight overlap between adjacent areas of color to avoid gaps caused by registration errors. You can create traps in CorelDRAW if you are printing color separations. Also referred to as *chokes* or *spreads*.

**Trim** A feature that enables you to cut off a portion of an object with another object. The Trim command is accessed from the Arrange pull-down menu.

**TrueType fonts** Fonts that print as vectors or bitmaps, depending on the capabilities of your printer. TrueType fonts print as they appear on-screen and can be resized to any height.

**TRUMATCH** A color-matching system for specifying process colors. This system is available in CorelDRAW.

**Two-color pattern** Fill made of bitmap images. CorelDRAW supplies a collection of bitmap patterns. You can even make your own and save them as new patterns.

**Type Assist** Enables you to build shortcut words when entering repetitive information in Paragraph or Artistic text.

**Type style** Variations within a typeface. Some common styles include roman (regular or normal), bold, italic, and bold italic.

**Typeface** Characters of a single type design, such as Avante Garde or Bookman. Most typefaces are available in different variations or styles. Some common styles include Roman (regular or normal), bold, italic, and bold italic.

**Uniform color** A solid color, black, white, or shade of gray that is used to color the outline or fill objects. You can select uniform fills from the Fill tool menu or the Outline tool menu, their respective roll-up windows, the Outline Color and Uniform Fill dialog boxes, and the on-screen color palette. Isn't it wonderful to have so many places to color an object or outline?

**Vector graphics** Graphics created in programs such as CorelDRAW in which shapes are represented as a series of lines and curves. These contrast with bitmap graphics, which are created pixel-by-pixel in paint programs and by scanners. Also referred to as object-based graphics. *See also* Rasterizer *and* Paint program.

**Weld** A feature that enables you to combine the perimeters of overlapping objects into one single object so that the resulting combined object has a single outline. The Weld roll-up is accessed from the Arrange pull-down menu.

**Weight** The thickness of outlines assigned to objects using the Outline tool. Sometimes used to refer to different type styles (normal, light, bold, and so on).

**Window** A rectangular area on the screen in which applications are displayed. Every application window has a title bar and menu bar along the top and one or two scroll bars along the sides or bottom.

**Wireframe view** One of two ways of viewing objects in the drawing window. In wireframe view, objects display in skeleton form without fills or outlines. Because the screen redraws faster in this view, you might want to use it for editing complex drawings. In the other view, editable preview, you see the outlines and fills of objects as you create them. You can switch freely between views by choosing Wireframe from the View menu.

**.WMF** The filename extension for Windows Metafile, which is a vector graphic format that CorelDRAW can export.

**.WPG** The filename extension for WordPerfect's graphics files, which is a vector graphic format that CorelDRAW can export.

**WYSIWYG** An acronym for *What You See Is What You Get*. A term describing a program's capability to provide an accurate on-screen representation of what an image or document will look like when printed.

**x-height** The part that makes up the main body of a lowercase letter, equal to the height of a lowercase *x*.

# Shortcuts

## Shortcuts to Dialog Boxes

| *ACTION* | *RESULT* |
| --- | --- |
| Double-click page border | Page Setup |
| Double-click guideline | Guidelines Setup |
| Double-click ruler | Grid and Ruler Setup |
| Double-click character node | Character Attributes |
| Select object, press F11 | Fountain Fill |
| No object selected, press F11 | New object Fountain Fill (changes default setting) |
| Select object, press Shift+F11 | Uniform Fill |
| No object selected, press Shift+F11 | New object Uniform Fill (changes default setting) |
| Select object, press F12 | Outline Pen |
| No object selected, press F12 | New object Outline Pen (changes default setting) |
| Select object, press Shift+F12 | Outline Color |
| No object selected, press Shift+F12 | New object Outline Color (changes default setting) |

## Dialog Box Keys

| ACTION | RESULT |
|--------|--------|
| Press Tab | Repositions to the next check box, list box, text box, command button, or group of option buttons |
| Press Shift+Tab | Repositions to the previous check box, text box, list box, command button, or group of option buttons |
| Press arrow keys | Repositions and selects within an active group of option buttons |
| Press spacebar | Selects the active command button or turns on or off the active check box |
| From within an active list box press letter | Repositions to the next item beginning with the letter key used in an active list box keys |
| Press Alt+underlined letter | Picks the item with the underlined letter |
| Press Enter | Selects the active command button |
| Press Esc | Cancels the command and closes the dialog box |

## Toolbox Shortcuts

### Pick Tool

| ACTION | RESULT |
|--------|--------|
| Double-click | Selects all objects in the drawing |
| Hold down Ctrl | Restrains an object when it is moved horizontally or vertically; stretches or scales in increments of 100 percent; rotates and skews in required degrees |
| Hold down Ctrl+Shift | Stretches in two directions in increments of 100 percent; scales in four directions in increments of 100 percent |
| Press Esc | Deselects all selected objects |
| Press Tab | Selects objects consecutively |
| Press Shift+Tab | Selects objects in reverse order |

| ACTION | RESULT |
|--------|--------|
| Press spacebar | Selects the Pick tool |
| Press left arrow | Moves selected object(s) to the left |
| Press right arrow | Moves selected object(s) to the right |
| Press up arrow | Moves selected object(s) up |
| Press down arrow | Moves selected object(s) down |
| With an object selected press the plus sign from the numeric keypad | Makes a copy of the original object (and places it behind the original object) |

## Shape Tool

| ACTION | RESULT |
|--------|--------|
| Double-click | Brings up the Node Edit roll-up |
| Hold down Shift | Chooses more than one node; changes complement of nodes selected when marqueeing nodes; moves conflicting Envelope handles in reverse directions |
| Hold down Ctrl | Restrains the position of a node or control point to multiples of 90 percent; restrains the position of characters to the nearest baseline; moves conflicting envelope handles in reverse directions; restrains the position of perspective handles to horizontal or vertical |
| Hold down Shift+Ctrl | Chooses all nodes on a path or subpath; positions the side or corner envelope handles in reverse directions; positions conflicting perspective handles in reverse directions of equal distance |
| Press Home | Chooses the originating node of a curve |
| Press Shift+Home | Switches the selection of the originating node off and on |
| Press Ctrl+Home | Chooses the initial subpath in the selected curve |
| Press Shift+Ctrl+Home | Switches the selection of the initial subpath off and on |
| Press End | Chooses the last node of a curve |

*continues* 1243

## Shape Tool continued

| ACTION | RESULT |
|---|---|
| Press Shift+End | Switches the selection of the last node off and on |
| Press Ctrl+End | Chooses the final subpath in the selected curve |
| Press Shift+Ctrl+End | Switches the selection of the final subpath off and on |
| Press Delete | Deletes the selected node |
| Press plus key | Inserts additional an node to a chosen point on the path |
| Press minus key | Deletes the chosen nodes |
| Press Tab | Moves the currently chosen node forward along the curve |
| Press Shift+Tab | Moves the currently chosen node backward along the curve |
| Press left arrow | Moves the chosen characters or nodes to the left |
| Press right arrow | Moves the chosen characters or nodes to the right |
| Press up arrow | Moves the chosen characters or nodes up |
| Press down arrow | Moves the chosen characters or nodes down |

## Knife Tool

| ACTION | RESULT |
|---|---|
| Double-click | Brings up the Tool Properties dialog box |

## Eraser Tool

| ACTION | RESULT |
|---|---|
| Double-click | Brings up the Tool Properties dialog box |

## Zoom Tool

| ACTION | RESULT |
| --- | --- |
| Double-click | Brings up the View Manager roll-up |

## Pencil Tool

| ACTION | RESULT |
| --- | --- |
| Double-click | Brings up the Tool Properties dialog box |
| Hold down Shift | Removes lines when retracing steps of a path being drawn |
| Hold down Ctrl | Restrains the position of control points to specific increments when drawing in Bézier mode; restrains Freehand; changes Bézier and Angular dimension lines to required angle |

## Bézier Tool

| ACTION | RESULT |
| --- | --- |
| Double-click | Brings up the Tool Properties dialog box |

## Dimension Tool

| ACTION | RESULT |
| --- | --- |
| Double-click | Brings up the Dimension roll-up |

## Rectangle Tool

| ACTION | RESULT |
| --- | --- |
| Double-click | Adds a page frame to your drawing |
| Hold down Ctrl | Creates squares |
| Hold down Ctrl+Shift | Creates squares from the inside out |
| Hold down Shift | Creates rectangles from the inside out |

## Ellipse Tool

| ACTION | RESULT |
| --- | --- |
| Double-click | Brings up the Tool Properties dialog box |
| Hold down Ctrl | Creates circles |
| Hold down Ctrl+Shift | Creates circles from the inside out |
| Hold down Shift | Creates ellipses from the inside out |

## Polygon Tool

| ACTION | RESULT |
| --- | --- |
| Double-click | Brings up the Tool Properties dialog box |
| Hold down Ctrl | Creates polygons |
| Hold down Ctrl+Shift | Creates constrained polygons from the inside out |
| Hold down Shift | Creates freeform polygons from the inside out |

## Spiral Tool

| ACTION | RESULT |
| --- | --- |
| Double-click | Brings up the Tool Properties dialog box |
| Hold down Ctrl | Creates spirals |
| Hold down Ctrl+Shift | Creates constrained spirals from the inside out |
| Hold down Shift | Creates freeform spirals from the inside out |

## Graph Paper Tool

| ACTION | RESULT |
| --- | --- |
| Double-click | Brings up the Tool Properties dialog box |
| Hold down Ctrl | Creates a graph paper grid |
| Hold down Ctrl+Shift | Creates a constrained graph paper grid from the inside out |
| Hold down Shift | Creates a freeform graph paper grid from the inside out |

## Text Tool

| ACTION | RESULT |
|--------|--------|
| Select text and double-click | Brings up the Edit Text dialog box |
| Press up, down, left, or right arrows | Repositions the insertion point in the desired direction |
| Press Home | Repositions the insertion point at the front of the current line |
| Press Ctrl+Home | Repositions the insertion point at the front of the text |
| Press End | Repositions the insertion point at the end of the current line |
| Press Ctrl+End | Repositions the insertion point at the end of the text |
| Press PgUp/PgDn | Scrolls the text-editing window in the Text dialog box |
| Press Shift+left arrow, right arrow | Chooses one character at a time in the Text dialog box |
| Press Shift+Home | Chooses all text in front of the insertion point to the front of the line |
| Press Shift+End | Chooses all text behind the insertion point to the end of the line |
| Press backspace | Deletes chosen characters or text in front of the insertion point |
| Press Delete | Deletes chosen characters or text behind the insertion point |
| Press Enter | Starts a new line |
| Press Ctrl+X | Cuts chosen text to the Clipboard |
| Press Ctrl+C | Copies chosen text to the Clipboard |
| Press Ctrl+V | Inserts text from the Clipboard |
| Press Ctrl+left arrow | Repositions the insertion point to the beginning of the word in front of the insertion point |
| Press Ctrl+right arrow | Repositions the insertion point to the beginning of the word in back of the insertion point |
| Press Ctrl+up arrow | Repositions the insertion point to the preceding paragraph |

*continues*

## Text Tool continued

| ACTION | RESULT |
|---|---|
| Press Ctrl+down arrow | Repositions the insertion point to the following paragraph |
| Press Ctrl+Home | Repositions the insertion point to the beginning of the frame |
| Press Ctrl+End | Repositions the insertion point to the end of the frame |
| Press Shift+left arrow | Chooses the character to the left of the insertion point |
| Press Shift+right arrow | Chooses the character to the right of the insertion point |
| Press Ctrl+Shift+left arrow | Chooses the word to the left of the insertion point |
| Press Ctrl+Shift+right arrow | Chooses the word to the right of the insertion point |
| Press Shift+up arrow | Chooses one line up from the insertion point |
| Press Shift+down arrow | Chooses one line down from the insertion point |
| Press Ctrl+Shift+up arrow | Chooses text in front of the insertion point to the preceding paragraph |
| Press Ctrl+Shift+down arrow | Chooses text from behind the insertion point to the end of the frame |
| Press Ctrl+Shift+Home | Chooses text in front of the insertion point to the beginning of the frame |
| Press Ctrl+Shift+End | Chooses text behind the insertion point to the end of the frame |
| Press Ctrl+Shift+PgUp | Chooses text in front of the insertion point to the beginning of the text block |
| Press Ctrl+Shift+PgDn | Chooses text behind the insertion point to the end of the text block |
| Press Ctrl+backspace | Deletes the word in front of the insertion point |
| Press Ctrl+Delete | Deletes the word behind the insertion point |
| Press Ctrl+1 | Paragraph style 1 |
| Press Ctrl+2 | Paragraph style 2 |
| Press Ctrl+3 | Paragraph style 3 |

# Corel *NOTE!*

You can select individual letters, numbers, characters, and words with the Shape tool.

## Function Keys

| ACTION | RESULT |
| --- | --- |
| Press F1 | Gets help or more information about the currently selected command or open dialog box |
| Press Shift+F1 | Gets more information about the on-screen item or active command |
| Press F2 | Choose the Zoom In command from the Zoom tool menu |
| Press Ctrl+F2 | Activates the View Manager roll-up |
| Press Alt+F2 | Activates the Dimension roll-up |
| Press Shift+F2 | Zooms in on selected object(s) |
| Press F3 | Chooses the Zoom Out command from the Zoom tool menu |
| Press F4 | Views all objects in the drawing window |
| Progs F5 | Chooses the Pencil tool |
| Press F6 | Chooses the Rectangle tool |
| Press F7 | Chooses the Ellipse tool |
| Press Alt+F7 | Activates the Transform roll-up |
| Press Ctrl+F7 | Activates the Envelope roll-up |
| Press Shift+F7 | Activates the Pen roll-up |
| Press F8 | Chooses the Artistic Text tool |
| Press Shift+F8 | Chooses the Paragraph Text tool |
| Press Ctrl+F8 | Activates the PowerLine roll-up |
| Press F9 | Switches between the normal display and the preview screen mode |
| Press Ctrl+F9 | Activates the Contour roll-up |
| Press Shift+F9 | Switches between wireframe and editable preview views |
| Press F10 | Chooses the Shape tool |
| Press Alt+F10 | Aligns the selected text to the baseline |

*continues* 1249

## Function Keys continued

| ACTION | RESULT |
| --- | --- |
| Select object and press F11 | Activates the Fountain Fill dialog box |
| Select object and press Shift+F11 | Activates the Uniform Fill dialog box |
| Press Ctrl+F11 | Activates the Symbols roll-up |
| Select object and press F12 | Activates the Outline Pen dialog box |
| Select object and press Shift+F12 | Activates the Outline Color dialog box |

## Menu Command Keys

## Corel*NOTE!*

All file menus and their commands can be accessed by pressing Alt+ the underlined letter of the menu or command (for example, Alt+F will pull down the File menu), with the exception of commands under the same menu that have the same letter underlined.

## Corel *TIP!*

The "Command Reference" section of this book displays the menus.

## Document Icon

| ACTION | RESULT |
| --- | --- |
| Press icon, Alt+R | Restore |
| Press icon, Alt+M | Move |
| Press icon, Alt+S | Size |
| Press icon, Alt+N | Minimize |
| Press icon, Alt+X | Maximize |

| ACTION | RESULT |
|--------|--------|
| Press icon, Ctrl+F4 | Close |
| Press icon, Ctrl+F6 | Next |

## File Menu

| ACTION | RESULT |
|--------|--------|
| Press Alt+F | File |
| Press Ctrl+N | New, Document |
| Press Alt+F,F | From Template |
| Press Ctrl+O | Open |
| Press Alt+F,C | Close |
| Press Ctrl+S | Save |
| Press Alt+F,A | Save As |
| Press Alt+F,L | Save All |
| Press Ctrl+I | Import |
| Press Ctrl+H | Export |
| Press Alt+F,D | Send |
| Press Ctrl+P | Print |
| Press Alt+F,M | Print Merge |
| Press Alt+F,X | Exit |
| Press Alt+1,2,3, or 4 | Opens one of the last four previously opened files |

## Edit Menu

| ACTION | RESULT |
|--------|--------|
| Press Alt+E | Edit |
| Press Ctrl+Z | Undo |
| Press Ctrl+Shift+Z | Redo |
| Press Ctrl+R | Repeat |
| Press Ctrl+X | Cut |
| Press Ctrl+C | Copy |

*continues* 1251

## Edit Menu continued

| *ACTION* | *RESULT* |
| --- | --- |
| Press Ctrl+V | Paste |
| Press Alt+E,S | Paste Special |
| Press Delete | Delete |
| Press Ctrl+D | Duplicate |
| Press Alt+E,N | Clone |
| Press Alt+E,A | Select All |
| Press Alt+E,F | Copy Properties From |
| Press Alt+E,F,P | Outline Pen |
| Press Alt+E,F,C | Outline Color |
| Press Alt+E,F,F | Fill |
| Press Alt+E,F,T | Text Attributes |
| Press Alt+E,I | Select By Properties |
| Press Alt+E,W | Insert New Object |
| Press Alt+E,B | Insert Bar Code |
| Press Alt+E,M | Insert Memo |
| Press Alt+E,O | Object |
| Press Alt+E,K | Links |

## View Menu

| *ACTION* | *RESULT* |
| --- | --- |
| Press Alt+V | View |
| Press Shift+F9 | Wireframe |
| Press F9 | Full-Screen Preview |
| Press Alt+V,O | Preview Selected Only |
| Press Alt+V,A | Toolbar |
| Press Alt+V,S | Status Bar |
| Press Alt+V,R | Rulers |
| Press Alt+V,L | Color Palette |
| Press Alt+V,L,N | None |
| Press Alt+V,L,C | Custom Colors |

| ACTION | RESULT |
|--------|--------|
| Press Alt+V,L,U | Uniform Colors |
| Press Alt+V,L,F | FOCOLTONE Colors |
| Press Alt+V,L,S | PANTONE Spot Colors |
| Press Alt+V,L,P | PANTONE Process Colors |
| Press Alt+V,L,T | TRUMATCH Colors |
| Press Alt+V,L,M | SpectraMaster Colors |
| Press Alt+V,L,Y | TOYOColors |
| Press Alt+V,L,I | DIC Colors |
| Press Alt+V,B | Bitmaps |
| Press Alt+V,B,H | High Resolution |
| Press Alt+V,B,V | Visible |
| Press Alt+V,C | Color Correction |
| Press Alt+V,C,N | None |
| Press Alt+V,C,F | Fast |
| Press Alt+V,C,A | Accurate |
| Press Alt+V,C,S | Simulate Printer |
| Press Alt+V,C,G | Gamut Alarm |
| Press Alt+V,I | Properties |
| Press Alt+V,I,O | Object |
| Press Alt+V,I,T | Tools |
| Press Alt+V,I,S | Style |

## Layout Menu

| ACTION | RESULT |
|--------|--------|
| Press Alt+L | Layout |
| Press Alt+L,I | Insert Page |
| Press Alt+L,D | Delete Page |
| Press Alt+L,G | Go to Page |
| Press Alt+L,P | Page Setup (Size section opens as default) |
| Press Ctrl+F3 | Layers Manager |
| Press Ctrl+F5 | Styles Manager |

## Layout Menu continued

| ACTION | RESULT |
| --- | --- |
| Press Alt+L,T | Styles |
| Press Alt+L,T,A,M | Styles \| Apply \| More |
| Press Alt+L,T,S | Styles \| Save Style Properties |
| Press Alt+L,T,R | Styles \| Revert to Style |
| Press Alt+L,R | Grid & Ruler Setup |
| Press Alt+L,U | Guidelines Setup |
| Press Ctrl+Y | Snap To Grid |
| Press Alt+L,E | Snap To Guidelines |
| Press Alt+L,O | Snap To Objects |
| Press Alt+L,A | Snap To All |
| Press Alt+L,N | Snap To None |

## Arrange Menu

| ACTION | RESULT |
| --- | --- |
| Press Alt+A | Arrange |
| Press Alt+A,T | Transform |
| Press Alt+F7 | Position |
| Press Alt+F8 | Rotate |
| Press Alt+F9 | Scale & Mirror |
| Press Alt+F10 | Size |
| Press Alt+F11 | Skew |
| Press Ctrl+A | Align and Distribute |
| Press Alt+A,O | Order |
| Press Shift+PgUp | To Front |
| Press Shift+PgDn | To Back |
| Press Ctrl+PgUp | Forward One |
| Press Ctrl+PgDn | Back One |
| Press Alt+A,O,I | In Front Of |
| Press Alt+A,O,E | Behind |
| Press Alt+A,O,R | Reverse Order (must have at least two objects selected) |

| ACTION | RESULT |
| --- | --- |
| Press Ctrl+G | Group |
| Press Ctrl+U | Ungroup |
| Press Ctrl+L | Combine |
| Press Ctrl+K | Break Apart |
| Press Alt+A,I | Intersection |
| Press Alt+A,R | Trim |
| Press Alt+A,W | Weld |
| Press Alt+A,S | Separate |
| Press Ctrl+Q | Convert to Curves |

## Effects Menu

| ACTION | RESULT |
| --- | --- |
| Press Alt+C | Effects |
| Press Alt+C,A | Add Perspective |
| Press Ctrl+F7 | Envelope |
| Press Ctrl+B | Blend |
| Press Ctrl+E | Extrude |
| Press Ctrl+F9 | Contour |
| Press Ctrl+F8 | PowerLine |
| Press Alt+F3 | Lens |
| Press Alt+C,C | Bitmap Color Mask |
| Press Alt+C,W | PowerClip |
| Press Alt+C,W,P | Place Inside Container |
| Press Alt+C,W,X | Extract Contents |
| Press Alt+C,W,E | Edit Contents |
| Press Alt+C,W,F | Finish Editing This Level |
| Press Effects, Clear Effect | Clear Effect |
| Press Alt+C,Y | Copy |
| Press Alt+C,Y,P | Perspective From |
| Press Alt+C,Y,E | Envelope From |

*continues*

## Effects Menu continued

| *ACTION* | *RESULT* |
| --- | --- |
| Press Alt+C,Y,B | Blend From |
| Press Alt+C,Y,X | Extrude From |
| Press Alt+C,Y,C | Contour From |
| Press Alt+C,Y,O | PowerLine From |
| Press Alt+C,Y,L | Lens From |
| Press Alt+C,Y,W | PowerClip From |
| Press Alt+C,O | Clone |
| Press Alt+C,O,B | Blend From |
| Press Alt+C,O,X | Extrude From |
| Press Alt+C,O,C | Contour From |
| Press Alt+C,O,O | PowerLine From |

## Text Menu

| *ACTION* | *RESULT* |
| --- | --- |
| Press Alt+X | Text |
| Press Ctrl+T | Character |
| Press Alt+X,P | Paragraph |
| Press Alt+X,M | Columns Press |
| Press Alt+X,O | Options |
| Press Ctrl+F | Fit Text To Path |
| Press Alt+F12 | Align To Baseline |
| Press Alt+X,S | Straighten Text |
| Press Alt+X,N | Show Non-Printing Characters |
| Press Alt+X,I | Statistics |
| Press Alt+X,R | Proofreading |
| Press Ctrl+F12 | Spelling |
| Press Alt+X,Q | Quick Proofreading |
| Press Alt+X,P | Full Proofreading |
| Press Alt+X,A | Advanced Options |
| Press Alt+X,U | Thesaurus |

| ACTION | RESULT |
| --- | --- |
| Press Alt+X,E | Type Assist |
| Press Alt+X,F | Find |
| Press Alt+X,A | Replace |
| Press Alt+X,H | Change Case |
| Press Alt+X,V | Convert |
| Press Ctrl+Shift+T | Edit Text |

## Tools Menu

| ACTION | RESULT |
| --- | --- |
| Press Alt+T | Tools |
| Press Ctrl+J | Options |
| Press Alt+T,U | Customize |
| Press Alt+T+I | Save Settings |
| Press Alt+T,G,R | Roll-Up Groups \| Roll-Up Customization |
| Press Alt+T,V | View Manager |
| Press Alt+T,C | Color Manager |
| Press Alt+T,C,W | Run Color Wizard |
| Press Alt+F,C,S | Select Color Profile |
| Press Ctrl+F11 | Symbols |
| Press Alt+F5 | Presets |
| Press Alt+T,E | Object Data |
| Press Alt+T,D | Dimensions |
| Press Alt+F2 | Linear |
| Press Alt+T,D,A | Angular |
| Press Alt+T,T | Task Progress |
| Press Alt+T,A | Create |
| Press Alt+T,C,A | Arrow |
| Press Alt+T,A,P | Pattern |
| Press Alt+T,A,S | Symbol |
| Press Alt+T,X | Extract |
| Press Alt+T,K | Merge-Back |

*continues*

## Tools Menu continued

| ACTION | RESULT |
|--------|--------|
| Press Alt+T,S | Scripts |
| Press Alt+T,S,R | Run |
| Press Alt+T,S,E | Corel SCRIPT Editor |

## Window Menu

| ACTION | RESULT |
|--------|--------|
| Press Alt+W | Window |
| Press Alt+W,N | New Window |
| Press Alt+W,C | Cascade |
| Press Alt+W,H | Tile Horizontally |
| Press Alt+W,V | Tile Vertically |
| Press Alt+W,A | Arrange Icons |
| Press Ctrl+W | Refresh Window |
| Press Alt+W,1,2, and so on | 1 Graphic1, 2 Graphic2, where Graphic1 etc. equals the name of other open Corel documents, and so on |

## Help Menu

| ACTION | RESULT |
|--------|--------|
| Press Alt+H | Help |
| Press Ctrl+F1 | Help Topics |
| Press Alt+H,W | What's This? |
| Press Alt+H,T | Tutorial |
| Press Alt+H,U | Tutor Notes |
| Press Alt+H,S | Technical Support |
| Press Alt+H,A | About CorelDRAW! |

## Right Mouse Button Click

| ACTION | RESULT |
|---|---|
| Press right mouse button on title bar | Title bar flyout |
| Press right mouse button on the tool ribbon bar | Toolbar flyout |
| Press right mouse button on a toolbox | Toolbar flyout |
| Press right mouse button on a tool | Properties flyout |
| Press right mouse button on a palette | Palette bar flyout |
| Press right mouse button on the status line | Status Line flyout |
| Press right mouse button on the page | Combination menu's flyout |
| Press right mouse button on the desktop | Combination menu's flyout |
| Press right mouse button ruler | Grid and Ruler Setup flyout guidelines a Setup flyout |
| Press right mouse button below the menu bar | Document flyout |
| Press right mouse button on an object on-screen | Object flyout |

# Third-Party Resources

The resources found for this book grew quite a bit from the last edition, and therefore we decided to include the information on the CD-ROM in Adobe Acrobat format. This allows you to read the information on your screen or print it out if you desire. There are approximately 100 pages of listings for companies producing products that may be useful to CorelDRAW users.

There are four separate files of information. CLIPART.PDF gives a list of all known clip art vendors, and some of the companies have provided descriptions of the products they carry. FONTS.PDF gives a list of all companies that sell fonts or font-related products and again some of them have provided product descriptions. MISCPROD.PDF lists sources of information, plug-in filters for PHOTO-PAINT, special forms of output, sources of special paper, and other hardware and software that you may find useful. Lastly, PHOTOS.PDF lists all companies that sell stock photos along with descriptions of their collections.

All of these files are located in the \DOCUMENT folder of the CD-ROM included with this book. The Acrobat Reader, which will be required to open the files, is found in the \DOCUMENT\READER folder. To use the files, simply install the Acrobat Reader and then open the file you want to read or print. Documentation for the Acrobat Reader is also provided in online format. You can open these documents by choosing the appropriate icon in the *CorelDRAW! 6 Unleashed* Program group.

# The Enclosed CD-ROM

The CD-ROM included with this book contains a wealth of software for CorelDRAW 6 users, including

- Supporting files for the book's projects and skill sessions
- Award-winning CorelDRAW images
- Hundreds of unique, professional graphics and photos from leading graphics and photo suppliers
- Sample plug-in filters for Corel PHOTO-PAINT
- Listings of Corel-related, third-party resources
- Evaluation versions of commercial software
- Shareware and freeware utilities

The sections that follow describe how to set up and use the CD-ROM.

## Getting Started

The Windows menu program on the disc allows you to easily navigate through and install the included software. Before you run the menu program, you need to run the disc's setup program, which will create a program group.

After you insert the CD-ROM into your drive, the Windows 95 AutoPlay feature will automatically display an introductory screen. This screen gives you a choice of running the setup program or the CD-ROM menu.

If you've turned off the Windows 95 AutoPlay feature for your CD-ROM drive, follow these steps to get started:

1. Click the Start button and choose Run.

2. Type `D:\SETUP.EXE` in the box and click OK. If your CD-ROM drive is not drive D, substitute the correct letter.

3. The opening screen of the setup program will appear. Click the OK button and follow the directions in the program. A program group named *CorelDRAW 6 Unleashed* will be created.

4. Click the CD-ROM Menu icon in this new program group to start the menu program for the disc.

When the setup has completed, click the CD-ROM Menu icon to begin your exploration. If you experience problems with the disc, click the Troubleshooting icon. Click Read Me First to read a brief guide to using the CD-ROM menu program.

## Where Files Are Located

Many of the book's skill sessions and projects have sample files on the CD-ROM, which allow you to follow along with the author. Table D.1 lists where these and other files are located on the CD-ROM.

**Table D.1. Location of files on the CD–ROM.**

| Directory | Description |
| --- | --- |
| COLOR | Original graphics files used for the color inserts in the book. |
| DEMOS | Evaluation versions of commercial software, arranged in directories by product. |
| DOCUMENT | Corel-related resource listings in Adobe Acrobat format. Also includes sample issues of the *CorelDRAW Journal* and *TAGline*, located in subdirectories. |
| GOODIES | Bonus paper textures; patterns and templates from the authors. |
| GRAPHICS | Graphics from the authors in CDR, TIF, and CPT formats, arranged in directories by graphics format. |
| PROGRAMS | Shareware and freeware utilities. |

| Directory | Description |
|-----------|-------------|
| PROJECTS | Files for projects, arranged by project number. |
| SAMPLES | Sample graphics, photos, and fonts from third-party vendors, arranged in directories by category and company. |

# Production Notes

**E**

The production of this book spanned many different software packages, running on both the Macintosh and PC platforms. This may be disconcerting to those who see no reason why a Macintosh should be used to produce a book on the leading PC graphics product. Simply put, it was used due to convenience and not in any way due to its superiority or inferiority.

Most of the writing and editing was done in Microsoft Word for Windows 6.0.

The screen shots throughout the book were captured in Collage (a few were done with Corel Capture). Most of the other figures were drawn in CorelDRAW 5 and 6. The color pages may contain a few images that were partially created in other software products. This is noted in the descriptive text. Scanning was done on a Hewlett-Packard Scan Jet IIc.

The color pages were output on an Agfa Accuset imagesetter direct to film from CorelDRAW 5 and 6, using Microsoft's standard PSCRIPT (PostScript) driver . This combination provided high quality without the limitcheck errors produced by many imagesetters faced with complex images.

The typefaces used for the layout of this book are the Font Company's FC-Serifa family, Corel's WaldoIcons, and Macmillan Publishing's MCPdigital. Layout was done in PageMaker for Macintosh 5.1.

The large amount of files needed for the CD-ROM were transferred using writable CD-ROMs created with Corel's CD-Creator. Because many of the files exceeded the size of floppy disks even when compressed, these CD-ROMs have proved to be lifesavers.

# Index

# Add to Your Sams Library Today with the Best Books for Programming, Operating Systems, and New Technologies

## The easiest way to order is to pick up the phone and call

# 1-800-428-5331

## between 9:00 a.m. and 5:00 p.m. EST.
## For faster service please have your credit card available.

| ISBN | Quantity | Description of Item | Unit Cost | Total Cost |
|---|---|---|---|---|
| 0-672-30570-4 | | PC Graphics Unleashed (Book/CD-ROM) | $49.99 | |
| 0-672-30638-7 | | CD-ROM Madness (Book/CD-ROM) | $39.99 | |
| 0-672-30590-9 | | The Magic of Interactive Entertainment, 2E (Book/CD-ROM) | $44.95 | |
| 0-672-30322-1 | | PC Video Madness! (Book/CD-ROM) | $39.95 | |
| 0-672-30516-X | | Corel Photo-Paint 5 Unleashed (Book/CD-ROM) | $45.00 | |
| 0-672-30612-3 | | The Magic of Computer Graphics (Book/CD-ROM) | $45.00 | |
| 0-672-30717-0 | | Tricks of the Doom Programming Gurus (Book/CD-ROM) | $39.99 | |
| 0-672-30707-3 | | Fractal Design Painter 3.1 Unleashed (Book/CD-ROM) | $49.99 | |
| 0-672-30517-8 | | CorelDRAW! 5 Unleashed (Book/2 CD-ROMs) | $49.99 | |
| 0-672-30308-6 | | Tricks of the Graphic Gurus (Book/2 Disks) | $49.95 | |
| ❏ 3 ½" Disk | | Shipping and Handling: See information below. | | |
| ❏ 5 ¼" Disk | | TOTAL | | |

Shipping and Handling: $4.00 for the first book, and $1.75 for each additional book. Floppy disk: add $1.75 for shipping and handling. If you need to have it NOW, we can ship product to you in 24 hours for an additional charge of approximately $18.00, and you will receive your item overnight or in two days. Overseas shipping and handling adds $2.00 per book and $8.00 for up to three disks. Prices subject to change. Call for availability and pricing information on latest editions.

**201 W. 103rd Street, Indianapolis, Indiana 46290**

**1-800-428-5331 — Orders    1-800-835-3202 — FAX    1-800-858-7674 — Customer Service**

Book ISBN 0-672-30754-5

# Get The Whole Picture

# For Half Price! We'll Meet You 1/2 Way

We want you to get a FULL ANNUAL SUBSCRIPTION TO *COREL MAGAZINE* FOR 1/2 PRICE! That's right, a full year's worth of the most exciting and dynamic computer graphics magazine for the design professional and business graphics user today –all for a mere $19.98*U.S.!

This is no half-hearted offer. No indeed. Written by CorelDraw users for CorelDraw users, each colorful issue of *Corel Magazine* helps you get the very most out of your software and hardware.

Read *Corel Magazine*, and if you like it even half as much as we think you will, we'll meet you half-way—take us up on our offer. Just fill out the attached card and fax it back for faster service. We're certain you'll appreciate getting the whole picture at half the price!

(*First time subscribers only!)

## Fax To: 512-219-3156          P.O. Box 202380 • Austin, Tx 78720

○ **YES! I WANT THE WHOLE PICTURE FOR 1/2 PRICE!** Sign me up for my full annual subscription to *Corel Magazine*. By responding to this special one-time offer, I'll pay only $19.98 U.S. and save 50% off the regular subscription rate of $39.95 U.S. (Offer Expires July 31, 1996)

*Fax: 512-219-3156*

○ **PLEASE BILL ME $19.98 U.S.**

○ **PAYMENT ENCLOSED**
(Offer restricted to U.S. only)

Name: _____

Title: _____

Company _____

Address _____

City _____ State _____

Postal Code/ZIP _____

Country _____

Signature _____ Date _____

**Please Circle The Appropriate Answers:**

1. Do you use CorelDraw?
   A. Yes    B. No
   If yes, which version do you use?
   A. 5.0    B. 4.0    C. 3.0    D. Other    E. 6.0
   On which platform?
   A. Windows  B. OS/2  C. Unix  D. CTOS

   E. Other _____

2. Your primary business:
   A. Advertising, publishing, graphic design, public relations
   B. Computer hardware or software manufacturer/distributor
   C. Engineering–all types    D. Financial services–all types
   E. Educational–all levels    F. Science/research
   G. Public utility, telecommunications, transportation
   H. Government–all levels    I. Retail, restaurant
   J. Medical   K. Video or entertainment production

   L. Other _____ .

3. Do you specify, authorize, or purchase computer graphics products or services?
   A. Yes    B. No
   If yes, circle all that apply:
   A. Workstations    B. PCs    C. Monitors/boards
   D. Input devices/scanners    E. Printers/output devices
   F. Hard disks/CD-ROM/tape drives

   G. Other _____

4. Primary use of CorelDraw–circle all that apply:
   A. Multimedia              B. Publishing
   C. Technical Documentation    D. Advertising
   E. Training  F. Medical Imaging    G. Packaging
   H. Artistic Design      I. Signs/Silkscreening/Stencilling

   J. Other _____

# The
# *CorelDRAW! 6 Unleashed*
# CD-ROM

The CD-ROM included with this book contains a
wealth of software for CorelDRAW! 6 users, including:

- Supporting files for projects in the book
- Hundreds of unique, professional graphics and photos from leading graphics and photo suppliers
- Award-winning CorelDRAW! images
- Sample plug-in filters for Corel PHOTO-PAINT
- Listings of Corel-related third-party resources
- Evaluation versions of commercial software
- Shareware and freeware utilities

## Getting Started

Insert the disc in your CD-ROM drive and follow the steps below to get started. Appendix D
contains more detailed information about using the CD-ROM.

When you insert the CD-ROM into your drive, an introductory screen will automatically
appear that gives you choice of running the setup program or running the CD-ROM menu.
The CD-ROM menu program allows you to navigate through all the software on the disc.
You can easily install software, view graphics, read information about products, and more.

If you turned off the AutoPlay function of your CD-ROM drive, follow these steps:

1. Click the Start button and choose Run.
2. Type D:\SETUP.EXE in the box and click OK. If your CD-ROM drive is not drive D, substitute the correct letter.
3. The opening screen of the setup program will appear. Click the OK button and follow the directions in the program. A Program Manager group named CorelDRAW 6 Unleashed will be created.
4. Click the CD-ROM Menu icon in this group to start the menu program for the disc.

### Minimum System Requirements

Windows 95
CorelDRAW! 6
4MB RAM (8MB recommended)
CD-ROM Drive
SVGA (256 color) display
Windows-compatible mouse or pointing device